CALIFORNIA
Political
Almanac
1 9 9 3 - 1 9 9 4

California Journal Press

C A L I F O R N I A
Political
Almanac
1 9 9 3 - 1 9 9 4

Stephen Green, Editor

With
Amy Chance • James Richardson
Rick Rodriguez • Kathie Smith •

Introduction by Dan Walters

John L. Hughes, Production Editor
Lori Korleski Richardson, Graphics
Mary Elizabeth Buchin, Copy Editor

California Journal Press

ISBN 0-930302-86-9

To our colleague,

Thorne Gray

Preface

In the summer of 1989, a team of writers and editors at The Sacramento Bee was assembled by longtime political columnist Dan Walters. Our goal was to produce a book that would give California what The Almanac of American Politics provides on the national scene — a reliable and comprehensive source book on the issues, the players and the political process. The result was the California Political Almanac, published the following winter.

We all knew there would be demand for such a book. But few of us expected it would instantly gain acceptance as the standard reference on California politics. During the recent campaign year, it was gratifying to see the Almanac cited again and again in news stories originating from California.

This third edition contains all the background and insight of the first two. But we've expanded and updated old chapters, and added new features. The results of the 1992 elections have been incorporated. New officeholders and appointees have been profiled, new data on the economy and social change in the Golden State has been analyzed along with the impacts of reapportionment. Throughout, the reader will find more charts, better maps and an expanded index.

The writing and editing team, meanwhile, has changed slightly, but it still includes some of the most knowledgeable political journalists in the state. They account for more than 150 years of combined experience covering government at all levels, from local cemetery districts to the halls of Congress.

We are indebted to the editors, librarians and managers of The Sacramento Bee and McClatchy News Service, who have given us moral support and generously allowed us to use their computer systems. We received excellent counsel from the staff of California Journal magazine, a subsidiary of our publisher. Many readers also sent us comments and thoughtful suggestions for updating the work. And finally, we wish to thank our spouses, families and significant others, who tolerated the long nights and weekends that were spent away from them while we completed this project.

Stephen Green
Sacramento
February 1993

Contents

Charts

Maps

1

California–a state of change

An overview by Dan Walters

California is the planet's most diverse society. At no time in mankind's history have so many people of so many ethnic and national groups, practicing so many different religions, speaking so many different languages and engaged in so many different kinds of economic activities gathered in one place. It would follow, therefore, that California's politics would be equally complex. And they are, but not exactly in the ways that one might think.

Rather than reflecting the incredible socioeconomic and demographic diversity, the state's politics have been, at least through the 1980s and into the early 1990s, the almost exclusive province of California's relatively affluent and middle-aged Anglo population. And until the dramatic 1992 elections, that meant a steady rightward movement in the state's political climate.

The Democrats won big in California in 1992, reversing, at least in result, what had been more than a decade of Republican domination at the top of the ticket and steady GOP gains in the lower reaches of politics. Just at the moment when the Republicans seemed poised to succeed Democrats as the state's dominant party, a rapidly deteriorating economy, wedge issues such as abortion, newly minted Democratic unity and organization strength and severe fracturing in GOP ranks combined to change the prevailing partisan tone. The lingering question, however, was whether what happened in 1992 represented a semipermanent political shift or was merely an aberration.

The state's political evolution, meanwhile, both reflects and contrasts with its rapid socioeconomic evolution. As it functions as a living social laboratory, so does California test the ability of the traditional American system of government to cope with social and economic change beyond the wildest imagination of the system's creators. A major question for the 1990s and beyond is whether features of government developed in the 18th and 19th centuries — the two-party system, separately elected legislative and executive branches of government, counties and cities formed along traditional lines — can function within such an incredibly wide range of social and cultural values.

There has been renewed interest in academic and some political circles for broader restructuring of the California political system in order to attune it to social reality. A unicameral Legislature, perhaps expanded to several hundred members, the encouragement of multiple parties, experimentation with the parliamentary system and the reformation of counties into regional governments are among the structural changes now being studied by both political scientists and politicians who are convinced that the present system cannot function effectively. California voters have signaled that they want change through the adoption of legislative and congressional term limits and some new legislators, coming into the Capitol under those same limits, are demanding change as well.

To understand the political currents flowing through California in the late 20th century, one must first understand its social and economic currents. And if one accepts the wave theory of social development—each wave consisting of economic change, followed by social change, followed by political change—California is in the third, or political phase, of its third wave.

The first wave lasted for roughly a century, from the early days of white settlement in the 1840s to the onset of World War II. The gold rush aside, that century was one in which California was a relatively unimportant place in the larger scheme of things. Its economy was resource-based—mining, agriculture, timber— and it had a decidedly rural ambience. Los Angeles, with its orange groves, vegetable fields and low buildings, resembled an overgrown Midwestern farm city, the presence of a few movie studios after World War I and the Pacific Ocean notwithstanding. San Francisco had a more cosmopolitan reputation, along with its cable cars and Chinatown, but it was the socioeconomic exception. California was white, Republican and quiet. It was largely ignored by the rest of America, whose population was centered in the East and had, if anything, a European outlook.

WAR BRINGS ECONOMIC AND SOCIAL CHANGE

All of that changed, suddenly and dramatically, on Dec. 7, 1941, when the Japanese bombed Pearl Harbor and plunged the United States into world war. Suddenly, America was forced to consider Asia as a factor in its future, and the window through which the nation viewed the war in the Pacific was California. Overnight, seemingly, the state was transformed into an industrial giant to serve the war effort, sprouting countless dozens of aircraft assembly lines, shipyards, steel mills and all of the other trappings needed to fight a modern war. And it became a staging point for the war, a training ground for soldiers, sailors and airmen.

It was war, but it also was a sudden economic change for the state. California was jerked into the industrial 20th century. And that economic transformation had an equally rapid social impact: hundreds of thousands and then millions of Americans were drawn or sent to the state to participate in the war effort.

While there had always been a steady flow of domestic emigrants to the state (some of whom, like the ill-fated Donner Party, regretted the decision to move), it was nothing compared to what happened during World War II and continued almost unabated after the war. "Gone to California" became a terse explanation for the sudden absence of families in hundreds of Midwestern, Southern and Eastern communities. It was one of history's great migrations, and one that actually began a few years before the war when refugees from the Dust Bowl, as chronicled in John Steinbeck's Grapes of Wrath, came to California in a desperate search for work and formed the nucleus of life and politics in agricultural areas of the state, such as the Central Valley.

As the expanding industrialism of California created jobs, it drew emigrants and they, in turn, formed the nucleus of a new industrial middle class. These young emigrants had vast ambitions for themselves and their families. They wanted schools, highways, parks and homes. And they provided, during the postwar years, the core backing for politicians who promised to fulfill those desires.

California's prewar Republicanism was of a particular variety. Rooted in the abolitionism of the Civil War era and the prairie populism of such men as William Jennings Bryan and Robert LaFollette, California's Republicans were reformist and progressive. The state's great Republican reformer, Hiram Johnson, set the tone for the 20th century when he led efforts to break the stranglehold that Southern Pacific Railroad and other entrenched economic interests had on the Legislature. Small farmers had battled for decades with the railroad over freight rates, the clashes being both political and, in one instance, violent. With Johnson—governor and later a U.S. senator—marshaling public opinion, California enacted a series of pioneering political reforms that included the initiative, referendum and recall, all designed to increase popular control of politicians. Decades later, the initiative was to become a tool of special interests, rather than a barrier, but that was after social and political developments beyond Johnson's ability to foresee.

Johnson set a tone of high-minded Republicanism that survived for decades. Democrats were weak, able to elect only one, one-term governor, Culbert Olsen, in 1938, despite the dramatic rise of the Democratic Party nationally after Franklin Roosevelt became president.

Olsen's Republican successor, Earl Warren, was out of the Johnson mold, and he became the only governor ever elected three times, going on to even greater fame as chief justice of the U.S. Supreme Court from 1953 to 1969. Warren was governor during and immediately after World War II, while the state was undergoing its big economic and social evolution. He responded to the demands of California's growth with far-reaching investments in public infrastructure, schools, highways, parks and other facilities that not only served the state's fast-growing population but laid the foundation for even greater public works in the future.

It was during this period that California began developing a national reputation for political unpredictability as it became a battleground for the ideological wars sweeping through America. Postwar California politics revolved mainly around Cold War issues, typified by the 1950 U.S. Senate contest between a young Republican congressman named Richard Nixon and a liberal political activist named Helen Gahagan Douglas, the wife of actor Melvyn Douglas. Nixon won after a brutal, bigoted campaign in which he implied that Douglas was sympathetic to communism. It was a polarizing political battle that launched Nixon on his way toward political immortality—and some would say, immorality. And it marked a turn away from centrist politics by both parties.

Democrats began veering to the left through such organizations as the California Democratic Council, which was established by Alan Cranston and other liberals to strengthen party identification in a state where "cross-filing" allowed candidates to obtain the nominations of both parties. The CDC also battled the more conservative elements then in control of the party. The Republicans took a turn to the starboard, with conservatives such as U.S. Sen. William Knowland, an Oakland newspaper publisher, assuming a larger role in the party as moderates of the Earl Warren-Goodwin Knight faction fell from grace in the absolutist atmosphere of the day.

At the time, in the mid- and late-1950s, social change favored the Democrats. Emigrants who had come to California to take jobs in the expanding industrial economy, their ranks swollen by returning veterans, put down roots and became politically active. As they did, they expanded the Democratic Party's base—especially since the Republicans were in the process of turning right, alienating voters who had supported Warren and his centrist philosophy.

THE NEW BREED

Jesse Unruh was archetypal of the new breed of lawmakers. Unruh came to California from Texas during the war, remaining to attend the University of Southern California, where he became active in campus politics as leader of a band of liberal veterans. Within a few years after graduating from USC, Unruh was heavily involved in politics on a larger scale and won a seat in the state Assembly. It was the perfect territory for the consummate political animal, and his arrival coincided with the general rise of Democratic fortunes in the 1950s.

The 1958 election was the pivotal event in the postwar rise of the state's Democratic Party, a direct result of the social and economic changes brought about by World War II. Sen. Knowland, who had led the right-wing Republican contingent in the Senate during the early- and mid-1950s, was openly hostile to President Dwight Eisenhower's "modern Republicanism," which included Warren's appointment to the Supreme Court. Knowland saw Eisenhower, Warren, Thomas Dewey and other Republican leaders from the East as leading the party, and the nation, astray, refusing to confront expansionist communism around the globe and temporizing on such domestic issues as labor union rights and welfare spending.

Knowland wanted to take the party back to the right and hoped to do it by running for president in 1960, when Eisenhower's second term would end. But he thought the California governor's office would be a more powerful platform for a presidential campaign than a seat in the U.S. Senate. Knowland's major impediment was the moderate Republican governor of the time, Goodwin Knight, who didn't want to give up the governorship. Knight had been Warren's lieutenant governor, had inherited the top spot when Warren was appointed to the Supreme Court and had then won a term on his own in 1954. He wanted to run for re-election in 1958.

Knowland solved his problem simply by ordering Knight to step aside. With the rightists firmly in control of the party machinery, Knight was forced to obey, agreeing, with obvious reluctance, to run for Knowland's Senate seat. But Knowland, in his preoccupation with Eisenhower, Communist expansionism and other weighty matters, didn't bother to consider whether his forced switch with Knight would sit well with California voters. With an arrogance that bordered on stupidity, he assumed that the voters would do whatever he wanted them to do. He was wrong. Democrat Edmund G. Brown Sr., the liberal attorney general, was elected governor and Democratic Rep. Clair Engle was elected to the Senate. Knight might have been re-elected governor and Knowland given another term in the Senate, but instead both were retired by the voters.

DEMOCRATS TAKE OVER

It was a banner year for the Democrats. In addition to winning the top two spots on the ballot, they also took firm control of the Legislature. Over the next eight years, during this peak of Democratic hegemony, the most ambitious policy agenda in California history became reality. With Unruh at the helm of the Assembly as speaker, the early Brown years saw a torrent of liberal, activist legislation ranging from an ambitious water development scheme to pioneering civil rights and consumer protection measures.

While Unruh sharpened the ideological focus of the Assembly, taking it to the left, the state Senate remained a bastion of rural conservatism. For a century, the Senate's 40 seats had been distributed on the basis of geography, rather than population, in a rough approximation of the U.S. Senate's two-to-a-state system. No senator represented more than two counties and giant Los Angeles County, with a third of the state's population, had just one senator. With most of California's 58 counties being small and rural, it gave the Senate a decidedly rural flavor. Conservative Democrats and Republicans formed a solid majority. Even so, Pat Brown guided much of his progressive agenda through the upper house, using his unmatched skills of personal persuasion on Democratic senators.

In 1966, as Brown was winding up his second term, the U.S. Supreme Court, still under the leadership of Earl Warren, handed down its far-reaching "one-man, one-vote" decision that required legislative seats to be apportioned on the basis of population, even though the U.S. Senate retained its two-to-a-state makeup. And as the state Senate's districts were redrawn in response to the ruling, there was a huge shift of power from rural to urban counties, strengthening not only Democrats generally but liberals within the party. But that didn't take effect until after another man had assumed the governorship, the result of another clash between two big-name politicians.

RISE OF RONALD REAGAN

Brown wanted to run for a third term in 1966 but Jesse Unruh thought—or so he said later—that Brown had promised to step aside in his favor. Whatever the precise truth of the matter, there was a big rupture between the two most powerful California politicians of the day, and in the long run, both would suffer from it. Brown ran for his third term, but his break with Unruh, some public fumbles, a rising level of social unrest and the appearance of an ex-movie actor named Ronald Reagan spelled disaster for those ambitions.

Reagan, a moderately successful B-movie leading man and television actor, was enticed to run against Brown by a consortium of wealthy Southern California businessmen. At the time, television had become a new and powerful factor in political campaigning. Televised debates had doomed Richard Nixon's bid for the presidency in 1960, which was followed by a hopelessly desperate run against Brown for the governorship in 1962. In 1964, Reagan had made a powerful television speech for Barry Goldwater, the Republican presidential candidate.

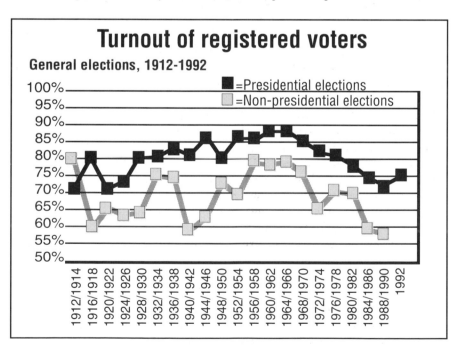

Turnout of registered voters

General elections, 1912-1992

■ =Presidential elections
□ =Non-presidential elections

Reagan was, the businessmen decided, just the man to take on non-telegenic Pat Brown in 1966.

The Republican kingmakers were right. Even though the Democratic phase of the postwar political era was not yet concluded, and even though a large majority of California voters were Democrats, Reagan buried Pat Brown and his bid for a third term by emphasizing Brown's shortcomings and stressing a conservative, get-tough attitude toward civic and campus unrest. The strength of Reagan's win swept several other Republicans into statewide offices.

Two years earlier, Reagan's old chum from Hollywood, song-and-dance-man George Murphy, had defeated Pierre Salinger for a California Senate seat. Salinger, who had been John Kennedy's press secretary, was appointed to the Senate by Pat Brown after Clair Engle died during his first term.

With Murphy in the U.S. Senate (he was defeated in his second-term bid by John Tunney in 1970), Reagan in the governor's office and Republicans holding other statewide offices, the GOP appeared once again to be on the ascendancy. But it all proved to be a short spurt. It would take another socioeconomic cycle for the Republicans to begin a real, long-term rise in influence among voters.

The GOP won control of the Assembly (for two years) in 1968, but for most of Reagan's eight years as governor, he had to deal with a Democratic-controlled Legislature. Unruh was gone after losing his own bid for the governorship in 1970, but another Southern California liberal, Bob Moretti, took his place. There were occasional compromises between the conservative governor and the liberal legislators, most notably on welfare reform, but it was a period remarkable for its dearth of serious policy direction from Sacramento. The Pat Brown-Jesse Unruh legacy was not undone, Reagan's rhetoric notwithstanding. But neither could liberals advance their agenda. It was a time of stalemate.

DE-INDUSTRIALIZING CALIFORNIA

Even as Reagan and Moretti did battle in Sacramento, another economic-social-political cycle, largely unnoticed at the time, was beginning to manifest itself.

The period of intense industrialization in California began to wind down in the 1960s. Asia, principally Japan, had risen from the devastation of the war to become a new industrial power. Californians began buying funny-looking cars stamped "Made in Japan" and domestic automakers began shutting down their plants in California. The steel for those cars was made not in Fontana but Japan or Korea. Even tire production began to shift overseas. One factory at a time, California began to de-industrialize.

California was not the only state to experience damaging foreign competition in basic industrial production in the 1960s and 1970s, but what happened here was unusual. The state underwent a massive economic transformation, from a dependence on basic industry to an economy rooted in trade (much of it with the nations of Asia), services and certain kinds of highly specialized manufacturing, especially

California voting patterns–gubernatorial races

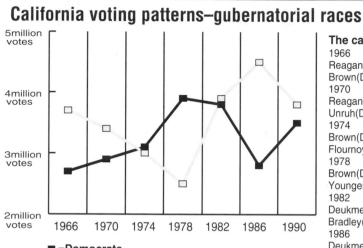

■ =Democrats

☐ =Republicans

The candidates:
1966
Reagan(R)
Brown(D)
1970
Reagan(R)
Unruh(D)
1974
Brown(D)
Flournoy(R)
1978
Brown(D)
Younger(R)
1982
Deukmejian(R)
Bradley(D)
1986
Deukmejian(R)
Bradley(D)
1990
Wilson(R)
Feinstein(D)

California voting patterns–senate races

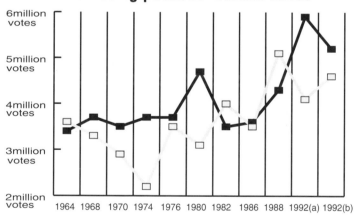

The candidates:

1964	1974	1982	1992 (a)
Salinger(D)	Cranston(D)	Wilson(R)	Feinstein (D)
Murphy(R)	Richardson(R)	Brown(D)	Seymour (R)
1968	1976	1986	1992 (b)
Cranston(D)	Hayakawa(R)	Cranston(D)	Boxer (D)
Rafferty(R)	Tunney(D)	Zschau(R)	Herschensohn(R)
1970	1980	1988	
Tunney(D)	Cranston(D)	Wilson(R)	
Murphy(R)	Gann(R)	McCarthy(D)	

of the high-tech variety centered in the Silicon Valley south of San Francisco. Computers and associated devices and services—including a huge aerospace industry tied to Pentagon contracts—became the new backbone of the California economy, one that exploded with growth until a corrosive recession struck the state in 1990. But before both the boom and the bust, there was a lull.

Rapid population growth that California had experienced during the postwar years, driven by domestic immigration, slowed markedly in the 1970s as industrial job opportunities stagnated. California was still growing, even growing a bit faster than the nation as a whole, but it was much less dramatic than what had occurred earlier. And California began to experience another phenomenon: an outflow of residents to other states.

In retrospect, that lull in growth may have been politically misleading. It persuaded the state's leaders, first Reagan and then his successor, Democrat Jerry Brown, that the infrastructure of services and facilities that had been built after World War II was adequate, that it was time to retrench, to tighten budgets and to cut back on public works, whether they be state buildings in Sacramento or freeways in Los Angeles. It was a collective and indirect policy decision that was to have serious and adverse consequences in later years.

A DIFFERENT KIND OF POLITICIAN

Jerry Brown, son of the man Reagan had defeated for governor in 1966, burst into state politics in 1970 by getting himself elected secretary of state, a mostly ministerial office with few powers or opportunities for publicity. But Brown, a young former seminarian who was the personal antithesis of his back-slapping father, seized the moment.

The Watergate scandal that had erupted in 1972 and destroyed Richard Nixon's presidency two years later focused public attention on political corruption. Brown grabbed the issue by proposing a political reform initiative and shamelessly pandering to the media, especially television. He bested a field of relatively dull Democratic rivals, including Bob Moretti, to win the party's nomination for governor and then took on Houston Flournoy, the Republican state controller, who was a throwback to the earlier era of Republican moderation but who came across in media terms as dull.

Even so, it was a whisker-close race. Ultimately, Brown was elected not so much on his political acumen, but because of his name and because the post-Watergate political climate had raised Democratic voter strength to near-record levels. At the height of Democratic potency in California in 1976, 59 percent of California voters identified themselves as Democrats in an annual party preference poll while just over 30 percent said they were Republicans. Democrats ran up huge majorities in the Legislature; at one point, after the 1976 elections, Republicans fell to just 23 seats in the 80-member Assembly. Even Orange County, the seemingly impregnable bastion of Republicanism, had a Democratic registration plurality.

With the younger Brown sitting in the governor's office and big Democratic majorities in the Legislature, there was a spurt of legislative activity—much of it involving issues, such as farm labor legislation and bread-and-butter labor benefit bills—that had been stalled during the Reagan years.

Brown preached a homegrown political philosophy that defied easy categorization. It was liberal on civil rights, labor rights and environmental protection but conservative on taxes and spending. Brown defined the philosophy in a series of slogan-loaded speeches in which he talked of teachers being content with "psychic income" rather than salary increases and California facing an "era of limits." It contrasted directly with the expansionist policies of his father and most other postwar governors.

THE PROPERTY TAX REVOLT

At first, Brown was a hit. The words and a rather odd personal lifestyle drew attention from national political reporters starved for glamour in the post-John F. Kennedy world of Jerry Ford and Jimmy Carter. Soon, there was a steady stream

Social and political demographics

	1970	1980	1990	1990 voters*
Population	20 million	23.8 million	29.8 million	7.7 million
Anglo	15.6 million 78%	15.8 million 66.4%	17 million 57%	81%
Hispanic	2.4 million 12%	4.6 million 19.3%	7.6 million 26%	5%
Asian	.6 million 3.2 %	1.6 million 6.6%	2.6 million 9%	4%
African American	1.4 million 6.9%	1.8 million 7.5%	2 million 7%	9%

* Exit polls of voters, November 1990 election, by Voter Research and Surveys of pundits to Sacramento and a flurry of effusively praiseful articles in national media. Brown was a star, it seemed, a Democratic Reagan. Brown believed it. And scarcely more than a year after becoming governor, he was running for president. As Brown turned his political attention eastward—or skyward, according to some critics—Brown neglected California politics. And they were changing again.

While the state's economy roared out of a mid-1970s recession, property values soared. As they rose, so did property tax bills. It was an issue too prosaic for Jerry Brown, whose sights by then were firmly fixed on the White House. But it was just the ticket for two aging political gadflies, Howard Jarvis and Paul Gann.

Raising the specter of Californians being driven out of their homes by skyrocketing property tax bills, Jarvis and Gann placed on the ballot a radical measure to slash property taxes and hold them down forever. Republican candidates, seeking an issue to restore their political power, seized upon Proposition 13, as the measure was numbered on the June 1978 ballot. Belatedly, Brown and legislative leaders devised a milder alternative for the same ballot.

Proposition 13 was enacted overwhelmingly and Brown, then running for re-election against the state's terminally dull attorney general, Evelle Younger, did a 180-degree turn. Sensing that the tax revolt could be his political downfall, Brown proclaimed himself to be a "born-again tax cutter" and pushed a state tax cut as a companion to Proposition 13. Younger failed to exploit the opening in the fall campaign and Brown breezed to an easy re-election victory in November. Almost immediately, Brown began plotting another run for the White House in 1980, this time as an advocate of balanced budgets, spending limits and tax cuts. Brown was nothing if not ambitious and opportunistic, qualities that were to be his political undoing.

Brown's re-election aside, the 1978 elections marked the beginning of a long slide for the Democratic Party after it had enjoyed two decades of dominance. Democrats suffered major losses in legislative races that year and a flock of conservative Republicans, dubbing themselves "Proposition 13 babies," came to Sacramento—out of caves, liberals said—prepared to conduct ideological war.

REBIRTH FOR THE REPUBLICANS

In ensuing years, Republicans both gained and lost legislative seats, with a net increase even in the face of a Democratic reapportionment plan in 1982 that was designed specifically to keep the party in power. And Democrats suffered a massive hemorrhage of voter strength. Their lead in party identification eroded year by year until it reached parity at about at about 45 percent each in the late 1980s. There was a corresponding shrinkage in the voter registration gap as well. In the mid-1970s, voter registration favored Democrats by, at most, a 57 percent to 34 percent margin. By the late 1980s, the Democrats had dipped to below 50 percent for the first time in a half-century while Republican registration climbed to nearly 40 percent. Democrats even lost a fraction of a point in 1988 when they committed $4 million to a huge voter registration drive in support of Michael Dukakis' presidential campaign and the slide continued in 1990, contributing to Democrat Dianne Feinstein's narrow loss to Republican Pete Wilson in their duel for the governorship.

The unofficial voter registration numbers were even worse for the Democrats. It's estimated that at least 1 million, and perhaps as many as 2 million, of California's 14 million registered voters don't exist. The official euphemism for those phantom names is "deadwood," and it exists because California's voter registration laws make it relatively difficult to drop people from the rolls when they die or move. Some mobile Californians may be counted two or three times as registered voters in different jurisdictions. And because Democrats are more likely to change addresses than Republicans, an adjustment for the deadwood tends to reduce their ranks more.

It's generally acknowledged among political demographers and statisticians that stripping the voter rolls of duplicate or missing names would reduce official Democratic registration to 47 percent or 48 percent and raise Republican registra-

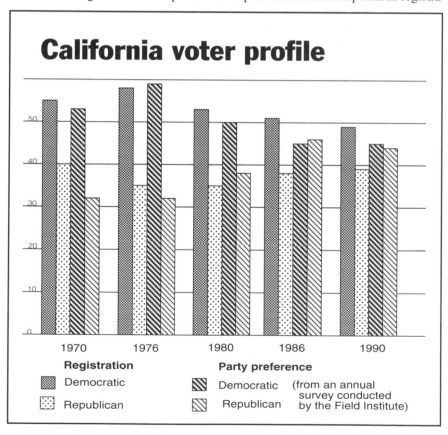

California voter profile

1970 1976 1980 1986 1990

Registration
- ▨ Democratic
- ▱ Republican

Party preference
- ▧ Democratic
- ▨ Republican

(from an annual survey conducted by the Field Institute)

tion above 40 percent. That's why Democratic legislators have resisted efforts to purge the rolls of non-persons. Adjustment to a true figure would bring registration closer to the 45 percent to 45 percent identification margin garnered in recent polls. The state's leading pollster, Mervin Field, adjusts the voter registration split to 48 percent to 42 percent in his polling, saying the number is based on surveys of actual registration.

THE DEMOCRATS' CRISIS

Whatever the real number, the Democratic side was declining and the Republican side gaining. And some Democratic officials, most notably Secretary of State March Fong Eu, were warning that the party was in danger of slipping into minority status.

The roots of the trend may be found in the socioeconomic currents evident in California during the late 1970s and 1980s. As the state's postindustrial economy shifted into high gear in the late 1970s, it created millions of jobs and, like the postwar period of industrialization, began attracting new waves of immigrants to fill them. But these immigrants didn't come from Indiana, Tennessee and Texas with their political consciousness already formed. They came from Mexico, Taiwan, Korea and the Philippines.

By the late 1980s, California's population was growing by some 2,000 people a day and half of them were immigrants, mostly from other nations of the Pacific Rim with whom California was establishing ever-stronger economic ties. California was developing, in short, into the new American melting pot in which dozens of languages and cultures were represented.

As newcomers poured into central cities, especially Los Angeles, San Francisco and San Jose, there was a commensurate outpouring of Anglo families into the suburbs. And as those suburbs filled and home prices soared, there was an even more dramatic movement into the new suburbs, located in former farm towns such as Modesto and Stockton in the north and Riverside and Redlands in the south. These new suburbanites—white and middle-class—shifted their political allegiance to the Republicans and their promises of limited government and taxes. Areas that had once been dependably Democratic, such as Riverside and San Bernardino counties, evolved into Republican registration majorities as they suburbanized and exploded with population. Prosperity encouraged the conversion, as did the popularity of Ronald Reagan in the White House.

A 1988 California Poll revealed Anglo voters favored Republicans by a 50 percent to 41 percent margin. And that was critical because non-Anglos, while identifying with the Democratic Party by substantial margins, were not voting in numbers anywhere close to their proportions of the population. Exit polls in elections during the 1980s revealed that more than 80 percent of California's voters were Anglos, even though they had dipped to under 60 percent of the population.

At the other extreme, Asians doubled their numbers in California between the late 1970s and the late 1980s, surpassing African Americans to become almost 10 percent of the population. Yet Asians accounted for just 2 percent to 4 percent of voters. The fast-growing Latino population was approaching one-fourth of the total by the late 1980s, but were only 6 percent or 7 percent of the voters until the 1992 election, when their numbers spiked upward. Among non-Anglo minorities, only African Americans voted in proportion to their numbers—roughly 8 percent of both population and electorate. But they are also the slowest-growing of the minority populations.

Thus, the 1980s saw a widening gap between the ethnic characteristics of California and those of voters, who not only were white but better educated, more affluent and—perhaps most important—markedly older than the non-Anglo non-voters. By 1986, half of California's voters were over 50 years old, a reflection of the rapid aging of the Anglo population, and the aging process continued as the state entered the 1990s and the baby boomers edged into middle age.

THE CHARACTERISTIC GAP

In brief, while California's population was moving in one direction—toward a multiracial, relatively young profile—the electorate was moving in another. And this characteristic gap was driving California politics to the right, toward a dominant mood of self-protection and reaction. Republicans scored well among older voters with appeals on crime and taxes. Democrats, hammered on these and other hot button issues, scrambled to find some response and were mostly unsuccessful until the atmosphere underwent a sharp change in 1992.

The characteristic gap made itself evident on a wide variety of specific issues and contests, but was most noticeable when it came to issues of taxes and spending. The Proposition 13 property tax revolt in 1978 and the subsequent passage of a public spending limit measure promoted by Paul Gann in 1979 were the first signs that the climate had changed. Republican George Deukmejian's 1982 election to the governorship on a no-new-taxes, tough-on-spending platform (along with tough-on-crime) was another indication. Deukmejian, a dull-as-dishwater former legisla-tor and attorney general, represented a 180-degree change of style from the unpredictable Brown.

The demands for more spending were coming from and for a growing, relatively young non-Anglo population, while the political power was being held by a relatively old, Anglo bloc of voters. By the late 1980s, a majority of California's school children were non-Anglo, but less than a quarter of California's voters had children in school—one example of how the characteristic gap affected political decision-making.

A 1987 poll conducted for the California Teachers Association revealed that older voters would kill any effort to raise state taxes for education. A CTA consultant told the group that even "arguments about grandchildren and overall societal need don't work." And if education was losing its basic political constituency—voters with children in public schools—other major spending programs, such as health and welfare services for the poor, had even smaller levels of support.

Deukmejian resisted new taxes, vetoed Democratic spending bills, trimmed the budget and saw his popularity among voters soar. He was re-elected by a landslide in 1986, defeating for the second time Los Angeles Mayor Tom Bradley. Even Deukmejian, who gloried in the "Iron Duke" image, relented in 1989 as the Gann spending limit enacted by voters 10 years earlier gripped the state budget. He was under pressure from business interests to spend more to relieve traffic congestion, but he refused to raise gasoline taxes. And even if he had agreed to a tax boost, the spending limit would have prevented the money from being spent. Finally, the governor and legislative leaders reached agreement on a complex package that put a measure to loosen the Gann limit and to increase the gasoline tax before voters in 1990. It passed but other tax measures on the 1990 ballot were summarily rejected, indicating that only something as universally used and popular as transportation could overcome the continuing resistance of California voters to higher taxes.

THE ESSENTIAL QUESTION

As California entered the 1990s, therefore, the essential public policy question was whether an aging Anglo population would continue to dominate the political agenda, even in the face of pressure from business executives for more spending on infrastructure to maintain the state's business climate.

One might think the solution to the Democrats' political woes would be to register and organize millions of non-Anglo voters, rather than continue to face an erosion of support among white middle-class Californians. Ex-Gov. Jerry Brown, who went into political exile after losing a U.S. Senate bid in 1982, returned to the stage in 1989 by running for and winning the state Democratic Party chairmanship on a promise to bring minorities and economically displaced whites into the party in record numbers and thereby reverse its decline. The unfaithful, Republican-voting Democrats would, in effect, be banished from the party as it took a couple of steps to the left.

But as simple as that sounds, it's a very complex task. There are barriers of citizenship, of language and of a tendency among refugees from authoritarian regimes not to stick their necks out politically. That's a tendency most evident among Asians, whose cultural traditions discourage direct connections to government and politics.

There are problems for the Democrats, too, in creating a party image that is attractive to minorities who may be social and political conservatives. Republicans regularly garner 40-plus percent of the Hispanic vote, for instance, and some Democratic Party positions, such as being pro-choice on abortion, are hard-sells among Hispanics. GOP candidates do even better among Asian voters, as few as they may be.

There also are internal barriers, such as the traditionally powerful role that

African Americans have played within the Democratic Party. Rhetoric about a "Rainbow Coalition" notwithstanding, minority groups do not automatically cooperate on matters political and there is, in fact, some friction. If these weren't serious enough problems, Brown also faced continued skepticism among more traditional elements of the party who saw him as a loser.

While Brown raised millions of dollars during the first two years of his party chairmanship, he also spent millions on staff and infrastructure and when Democrats narrowly lost the governorship in 1990, many supporters of the Democratic candidate, Dianne Feinstein, blamed Brown. Feinstein had consciously attempted to woo middle-class white voters back from the Republicans and her failure touched off another round in the Democrats' perennial debate over ideological positioning and tactics.

The issue was resolved, more or less by default, when Brown was replaced as state party chairman by Phil Angelides, a one-time legislative staffer who had become a prominent and wealthy land developer in Sacramento. Brown quit to run for the U.S. Senate but then, for reasons that remained unclear, switched courses again and made a run for the presidency that became one of the oddest sidebars to the 1992 presidential campaign.

Angelides, who had played a prominent role in Dukakis' presidential campaign in 1988, clearly favored the strategy of trying to bring back middle-class voters and that coincided, rather neatly, with the ascendancy of Bill Clinton as the party's presidential candidate in 1992. With Angelides' organizational and fund-raising ability on conspicuous display, Democrats got their act together in California in 1992, signing up hundreds of thousands of new voters, especially in middle-class suburbs where reapportionment threatened the party's grip on the Legislature and the congressional delegation. For the first time in more than a decade, Democratic voter strength, both in registration and party identification polls, increased, albeit not dramatically.

The Democrats new-found organizational strength was accompanied by a virtual disintegration of the Republican Party structure in the state because of deep divisions between moderates, led by Gov. Wilson, and a strong religious right coalition. The Republican split, ironically, occurred just as the party won a hard-fought battle over reapportionment.

REAPPORTIONMENT FOLLIES

After the 1980 census, Democrats maintained their hold on the Legislature and expanded their control of the state's congressional delegation with a highly partisan reapportionment plan. In effect, they preserved their power in the face of real-world trends. The plans were approved by then-Gov. Brown and a state Supreme Court dominated by liberal Brown appointees. Conditions for the Democrats were not as favorable for the post-1990 census reapportionment and the stakes were much, much higher.

The relative lull in California population growth during the 1970s meant that the state was awarded only two new congressional seats after the 1980 census, its delegation increasing from 43 to 45. Prior to the 1980s reapportionment, the 43-member delegation had been divided 22-21 in favor of Democrats. It was a fair division of the seats in terms of both overall party identification and total congressional vote in the state, both of which were evenly divided between parties. But after the late Rep. Phil Burton completed what he called "my contribution to modern art," a plan rejected by voters via referendum but ordered into use by the state Supreme Court for the 1982 elections, the delegation was 28-17 in favor of Democrats. That result was stark evidence that gerrymandered reapportionment of district boundaries works. And it was so well done that Republicans were able to gain only two seats in subsequent elections, leaving the delegation at 26-19.

California's population growth was much, much higher in the 1980s. The additional 6 million people who came to California between 1980 and 1990 were roughly a quarter of total U.S. population growth. The state was awarded seven new congressional seats, giving it not only the largest congressional delegation in the nation but the largest of any state in the nation's history.

Republicans wanted redress. They believed they should have roughly half of the California seats, which would mean receiving all of the new ones. And it would have been very, very difficult for the Democrats to pull a repeat of 1982, not only in congressional reapportionment, but in the redrawing of legislative districts.

Initially, Republicans pinned their hopes vis-a-vis reapportionment on Deukmejian's running for a third term in 1990. Thus, he would have been available to veto any gerrymander drawn by majority Democrats in the Legislature. But after dropping hints that he was interested in a third term, Deukmejian announced in early 1989 that he would retire after his second term was completed.

GOP leaders, stretching as high as the White House, then engineered a strategic coup. They persuaded Wilson, the one-time San Diego mayor who had defeated Jerry Brown for a U.S. Senate seat in 1982 and won a second term handily in 1988, to run for governor in 1990, seeing him as the GOP candidate with the best chance of retaining the governorship.

The selection of a Democratic candidate didn't go as easily. Attorney General John Van de Kamp, a liberal with strong environmental and consumer protection credentials, was the early favorite. His only declared rival, ex-San Francisco Mayor Dianne Feinstein, refused to drop out, however, even when her campaign manager quit with a blast at her commitment to the race.

Feinstein fashioned a decidedly more centrist image for herself, arguing that a liberal such as Van de Kamp was headed for certain defeat at Wilson's hands. Among other things, she supported the death penalty, a litmus test issue for many Democrats. Van de Kamp, meanwhile, had made a strategic decision that turned out to be an error. Taking his own nomination for granted, Van de Kamp committed many of his campaign dollars to promoting three initiative measures—one on political reform, one on the environment and one on crime—that he planned to use as the basis of his campaign against Wilson.

That left Van de Kamp strapped for cash when the duel with Feinstein became close, while she tapped her wealthy husband, financier Richard Blum, for critical millions. Feinstein won the nomination and engaged in an expensive shootout with Wilson, her one-time political ally when she was mayor of San Francisco and he was a U.S. senator. Wilson won narrowly and became California's 36th governor, thus putting himself into position to protect Republican interests on reapportionment—as well as to confront the many problems of a fast-growing and diverse state, including a worsening budget crisis. Although Wilson and Feinstein spent more than $40 million in 1990, it was a less-than-overwhelming Republican victory since Wilson won less than 50 percent of the total vote.

A final factor in reapportionment was that minority groups, especially those representing Hispanics, believed they, too, were damaged by the 1982 reapportionment. So they pressured Democrats for new representation in both congressional and legislative seats. Initially, Democrats—led by Assembly Speaker Willie Brown—tried to negotiate their way out of their dilemma, offering Republicans guaranteed gains in both the Legislature and Congress in return for equally strong guarantees that Democrats would retain control. There was a substantial sentiment among Republican politicians toward such a settlement, primarily because the alternative, throwing the issue to the courts, was less certain.

Brown tried to capitalize on the Republican divisions, openly courting conservative Assembly members who were at ideological odds with Wilson, promising them locked-in congressional seats if they would abandon the governor. Ultimately, however, Brown and a few right-wing plotters could not put together a veto-proof deal and Democrats simply passed their plans and allowed Wilson to veto them, thus moving reapportionment debate to the state Supreme Court.

The court, which had drawn reapportionment maps after a similar stalemate between the Legislature and then-Gov. Ronald Reagan 20 years earlier, used the same consultants and within weeks had created 172 legislative and congressional districts that closely followed demographic trends—shifting more power from the cities to the suburbs, which enhanced Republican prospects, and creating more minority seats, especially Latino seats, within urban areas. The federal Voting Rights Act largely dictated the latter result.

SNATCHING DEFEAT FROM JAWS OF VICTORY

Wilson and Republican leaders were jubilant. They saw an unprecedented opportunity to seize control of the Capitol for the first time in decades—a prospect that was enhanced by the passage of the term limits initiative in 1990, which would eventually force many entrenched Democratic incumbents to surrender their seats.

What looked good for Republicans on paper, however, turned out to be not so good in practice because of their own divisiveness.

The postwar history of the California Republican Party has been one of recurrent conflict between moderates and conservatives. In 1982, with the election of Deukmejian to the governorship (after he had defeated the right-wing candidate, Mike Curb, in the primary) and Pete Wilson to the U.S. Senate, the centrists regained the influence they had lost during the Ronald Reagan and early post-Proposition 13 years.

With patronage from the governor's office and the Senate, Republican moderates enjoyed a rebirth of influence within the party and right-wingers complained privately and publicly about being ignored. Their only bastion was the Assembly Republican caucus, which continued to be dominated by the "Proposition 13 babies" or "cavemen," as some dubbed them.

Conservatives stopped short of open revolt. They didn't balk, for instance, about having Wilson as their candidate for governor in 1990 because they wanted a winner who would protect the party on reapportionment. But issues such as abortion divide the party bitterly as it seeks some new common theme in the post-Cold War, post-Reagan era.

Wilson had scarcely been inaugurated when the sniping began. Conservatives were irritated by Wilson's selection of moderate state Sen. John Seymour—a former conservative who had flip-flopped on abortion—as his successor in the Senate and were put off by Wilson's advocacy of new taxes to balance the state budget. The moderate-conservative split flared sharply late in the 1991 session of the Legislature, when moderates, encouraged if not abetted by Wilson, seized control of the Assembly GOP caucus. And it raged throughout 1992.

The right captured much of the party apparatus and fielded numerous candidates for legislative and congressional seats while Wilson and the moderates belatedly challenged them in the June primaries. Conservatives won most of the head-to-head battles but several found themselves unelectable in swing districts that more moderate Republican candidates could have won.

After more than a dozen years of electoral gains, Republicans were hurt in 1992, too, by the state's rapidly deteriorating economy; by the unpopularity of Republican President George Bush, who virtually abandoned a state that the GOP had won in the previous five presidential elections; by the resurgent political activism of women over abortion; and, finally, by the fact that the California Democrats finally had gotten their act together under Angelides.

Thus, what had appeared to be a golden opportunity for Republicans to make gains turned into a virtual wash while Democrats swept the major races for president and two U.S. Senate seats. It was, in brief, a Republican debacle that left open the question of whether Wilson could win re-election in 1994.

Democrats emerged from the 1992 elections with high hopes for ousting Wilson. Early oddsmaking favored state Treasurer Kathleen Brown, daughter of one former governor and sister of another, as the most likely Democratic candidate to challenge Wilson, who also could face a conservative opponent in the Republican primary.

Democrats elected two women to the U.S. Senate in 1992 and women comprise a strong majority of Democratic voters, so Brown's possible candidacy is enhanced immeasurably by her gender. She spent much of the 1992 campaign season criss-crossing the state on behalf of Democratic candidates for the Legislature, thereby earning chits that could be cashed in later. Other potential Democratic candidates are Insurance Commissioner John Garamendi, who was Clinton's California chairman in 1992, and Controller Gray Davis, Jerry Brown's one-time chief of staff who ran unsuccessfully for the Senate in 1992.

LEGISLATURE FALLS DOWN ON THE JOB

The 1993 legislative session began with Democrats in firm control, but with dozens of seats being held by newcomers who were elected under term limits and who were impatient for both parties to set aside their ceaseless infighting and to do something for a state besieged by economic woes (unemployment reached 10 percent in late 1992) and social friction (dramatically underscored by racial rioting in Los Angeles) and facing a third year of fiscal crisis, with multibillion-dollar budget deficits forecast.

In the last decade, reapportionment, as partisanly slanted as it may have been, was one of the Legislature's few decisive actions. Increasingly, the Legislature drew within itself, preoccupied with such games of inside baseball as campaign strategy, fund-raising and partisan and factional power struggles. It seemed unable, or unwilling, to cope with the huge policy issues raised by the dynamics of the real world outside the Capitol: population growth, ethnic diversification, transportation congestion, educational stagnation, environmental pollution.

The Legislature, which Jesse Unruh recast as a full-time professional body in the 1960s, had once been rated as the finest in the nation. The 1980s saw not only policy gridlock but a rising level of popular disgust with antics in the Legislature, fueled by several official investigations into corruption and a more critical attitude by the Capitol press corps.

California's political demography is at least partially responsible for the Legislature's lethargy. Legislators are torn between the demands and aspirations of California's new immigrant-dominated population and the limits set by white, middle-class voters. But the very professionalism that was Unruh's proudest achievement also has contributed to the malaise. Full-time legislators, many of them graduates of the Legislature's own staff, are naturally preoccupied with their personal political careers. Thus legislative duties that conflict with those careers are shunted aside.

Throughout the decade, reformers proposed institutional changes to restore the Legislature's luster, such as imposing limits on campaign spending and fund raising (which have increased geometrically) and providing public funds to campaigns. Voters endorsed a comprehensive reform initiative in 1988, but they also approved a more limited version placed on the ballot by some legislators and special-interest groups. The first provided public funds for campaigns while the second specifically barred such spending, and the second gained more votes. The result was that most of the first initiative was negated, but nearly all of the second was invalidated by the courts.

As a years-long federal investigation of Capitol corruption erupted in indictments in 1989, the Legislature itself began drafting reforms designed to raise its standing with an increasingly cynical public. These reforms—a tightening of conflict-of-interest rules, including a ban on receiving speaking fees from outside groups—were approved by voters in 1990. But voters also approved an initiative that would, if it clears the courts, impose tough term limits on lawmakers, eliminate their pensions and sharply reduce the Legislature's spending on its own operations.

Mostly, however, the impotence of the Legislature manifested itself in an explosion of initiative campaigns that took issues directly to voters, bypassing the Capitol altogether. Initiatives became so popular that lawmakers and even candidates for governor began sponsoring them as vehicles to make policy or gain favorable publicity. Gubernatorial hopeful John Van de Kamp proposed, for instance, a political reform initiative that he had hoped would take advantage of the popular disdain for the Legislature, and another to deal with environmental matters. The Republican candidate for governor in 1990, Pete Wilson, trumpeted his own initiative to deal with crime. In addition to their publicity-generating value, initiatives sponsored by candidates allow them to slide around voter-imposed limits on direct campaign fund raising.

A few more women and a few more younger voters turned out in 1992, but the overall profile of the state's voters remains white, middle-to-upper-middle-class and middle-aged—characteristics that are unlikely to change dramatically in the near future. While half of California's current voters are over 50, it could reach 60 percent by the turn of the century.

The state, meanwhile, is heading toward a non-Anglo majority by middecade and the largest unsettled question about California politics is not whether Republicans or Democrats control, but whether the surging Latino and Asian populations will claim political power commensurate with their numbers. There are some signs of that occurring, mostly at the local level, but neither community has developed charismatic leaders who could move their latent political power in one direction or another, much as Martin Luther King and Jesse Jackson mobilized the political potential of African Americans.

Thus, the real story of California's 21st century political development will be the extent to which today's newcomers become tomorrow's voters and how their cultural values change the political landscape.

2

The unending budget mess

It was on a Wednesday, at 1:45 a.m., that Gov. Pete Wilson picked up his pen and signed the record $57.4 billion budget for the 1992-93 fiscal year. With that simple act, the longest budget stalemate in California history came to an end on Sept. 2, 1992.

California had been without a budget for a record 64 days while Wilson and legislators carped at each other over the best way to resolve a projected $10.7 million revenue shortfall. Wilson prolonged the budget debate for weeks, even refusing to allow the Legislature to see his revised spending plans. But the impasse was finally broken when the governor called a press conference to declare, "Enough is enough!" He agreed to repackage his school finance proposal in a form acceptable to the Legislature. And within two weeks, he had a budget on his desk that he could sign.

Republican Wilson claimed victory in the budget battle, a stunning comeback from the drubbing handed him by legislative Democrats the previous year. But his view was in the minority. Most others described the protracted stalemate as a disgraceful display of political gamesmanship at the expense of the public. That conclusion was further buttressed by opinion polls that showed public disgust with the performance of both the governor and the legislators at an all-time high.

In the midst of the budget debate, California was forced to pay its bills and employees with rubber checks that many banks eventually stopped accepting. Local governments teetered on the verge of bankruptcy and hardships were inflicted on hundreds of thousands who depend upon government services at all levels. Wall Street financial houses downgraded the state's bond ratings — again — guaranteeing higher costs in the future to repay state debt. And as if to rub salt in the wound, commentators nationwide sneered at further evidence of the decline of the Golden State.

Worst yet, the budget Wilson signed wasn't balanced and everyone involved with the process knew it. The only question was how much it was out of whack. That question would be answered the following spring, when it was determined that the recession-battered economy had caused revenue collections to fall $3.27 billion below projections. By December 1992, preliminary estimates were that California would face an $8 billion to $10 billion budget gap when the new fiscal year budget was put together the following June. And that was only a preliminary guess.

But if there were no winners in the 1992-93 budget battle, there were losers aplenty. Cuts fell hardest on those least able to defend themselves: sick, blind, disabled and elderly people; welfare recipients and their children; students at all levels; and civil servants. The $1.3 billion in cuts for local governments, from cities and counties to park districts, would have a boomerang effect. Local governments had no choice but to slash their services as well and impose new taxes where possible.

At the same time, steps were in motion to make it even more difficult for political leaders to write the next budget. In November, voters narrowly approved Proposition 162, which put public pension funds off limits for future budget-balancing raids. And the state courts ruled that the state could no longer pay state workers with IOUs when a budget hasn't been enacted by the July 1 deadline. Payments must be in cash.

Many taxpayers expressed bewilderment at California's fiscal morass. After all, Gov. George Deukmejian left office in 1991 claiming he'd taken the state from "IOU to A-OK." But the source of the problem was simple enough: As the economy weakened, state revenues dropped and gobbled up the outgoing governor's reserve funds — and then some.

State finances suffer quickly in a recession; fewer paychecks and less spending prompt a slump in sales and income taxes, and state costs increase as more people call upon welfare, unemployment and other safety-net programs. In 1991, California's big economic engine could still be counted on to generate more revenue than had been available in the previous year, but nowhere near enough to keep pace with the state's rising Medi-Cal, welfare, school and prison populations.

Early evidence suggested Deukmejian's administration would leave the state foundering in more than $800 million of red ink by the end of the 1990-91 fiscal year — and that was before the Persian Gulf War began. Nothing in the state's 140-year history compared to the financial disarray incoming Gov. Pete Wilson confronted as he took the podium in the state Assembly on Jan. 9, 1991, to deliver his State of the State message as California's 36th governor.

"Now more than ever, to lead is to choose," Wilson said. "And our choice must be to give increasing attention and resources to the conditions that shape children's lives. The emphasis must be more preventative than remedial — a vision of government that is truly as uncomplicated as the old adage that an ounce of prevention is worth a pound of cure."

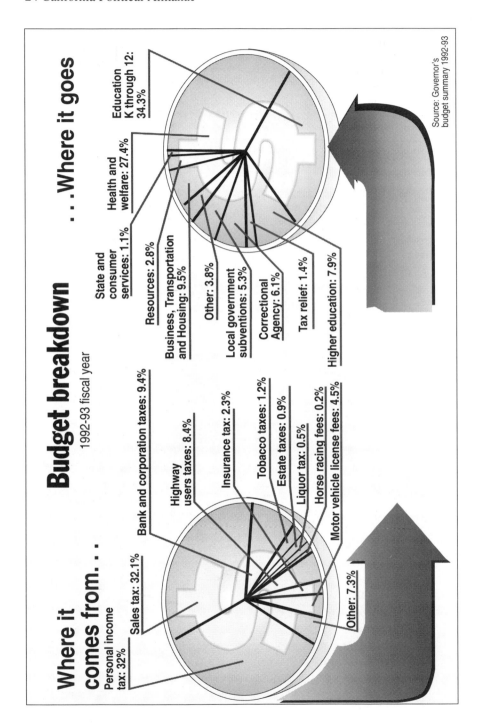

Budget breakdown
1992-93 fiscal year

Where it comes from. . .
Personal income tax: 32%
Sales tax: 32.1%
Bank and corporation taxes: 9.4%
Highway users taxes: 8.4%
Insurance tax: 2.3%
Tobacco taxes: 1.2%
Estate taxes: 0.9%
Liquor tax: 0.5%
Horse racing fees: 0.2%
Motor vehicle license fees: 4.5%
Other: 7.3%

. . .Where it goes
Education K through 12: 34.3%
Health and welfare: 27.4%
State and consumer services: 1.1%
Resources: 2.8%
Business, Transportation and Housing: 9.5%
Other: 3.8%
Local government subventions: 5.3%
Correctional Agency: 6.1%
Tax relief: 1.4%
Higher education: 7.9%

Source: Governor's budget summary 1992-93

Wilson's message represented a sharp shift from Deukmejian's approach to California's problems, but where Deukmejian had fought to close a $3.6 billion gap between anticipated revenues and spending demands for the 1990-91 budget, Wilson would face a recession-driven shortfall of monster proportions. By the end of March 1991, Wilson was declaring a "budget emergency," projecting a $12.6 billion shortfall.

Wilson faced most of the same problems Deukmejian had faced in shaping a state budget to fit his priorities. State finances have been in a turmoil ever since 1978, when Proposition 13, the famous property tax limitation initiative, gutted local government finances and prompted a redistribution of state revenues. More tax measures followed, among them one indexing the income tax to inflation to protect Californians against "bracket creep," the automatic tax hikes that occurred as inflation pushed taxpayers into higher tax brackets. Inheritance and gift taxes were repealed, the business inventory tax was wiped out and new tax credits were invented and spread around. The loss to state government between 1978 and the 1988-89 fiscal year exceeded $190 billion, according to a study by Legislative Analyst Elizabeth Hill. Most notably, voters approved Proposition 4 in 1979, writing a state and local spending limit into the Constitution. The cap became known as the Gann limit after its main sponsor, the late tax critic Paul Gann. Spending was tied to population growth and inflation. Excess revenue was to be returned to taxpayers.

The Gann limit meant little until the 1986-87 fiscal year, when California's once powerful economy produced an unexpected surge in revenue. After nearly a decade of Proposition 13 austerity, the state's public schools and universities needed the money, but the spending cap dictated otherwise. Just over $1 billion was returned to the state's taxpayers during the Christmas season of 1987-88.

Those were the years of federal tax reform, state tax conformity, deficit spending on the federal level and unpredictable peaks and troughs for California's revenues. Shortage followed surplus. Teachers, school administrators, parents and other educators, with the exception of those representing the state's two university systems, launched an initiative campaign designed to protect themselves from gubernatorial vetoes and the state's wavering finances.

In June 1988, they failed at the polls. But in November, 50.7 percent of the voters — the barest of majorities — approved Proposition 98, under which public schools and community colleges were henceforth guaranteed some 40 percent of the state's general fund budget and, in the event of a Gann limit surplus, half of the money that would have gone back to taxpayers.

To Wilson in his first days in office the state's finances must have resembled a windshield just after an encounter with a good-sized bug — some cleaning up would be necessary before he could even see where he wanted to go. On all sides, Wilson could see the problems he would confront and he mentioned many — overstuffed schools, more and more homeless people, workers without health insurance, growing welfare and Medi-Cal caseloads, swollen prisons, overwhelming crime, child abuse and neglect and failing county governments.

Where were the solutions? By 1991, there were some answers, and they helped a little. A trigger was in place to automatically trim welfare grants and other cost-of-living increases when state revenues lagged. The trigger was a victory for Deukmejian and the Assembly Republicans, who won it as part of the settlement that ended what was then the longest budget stalemate in state history the previous year. The savings for Wilson's budget amounted to $800 million, of which less than $150 million would come from the Aid to Families with Dependent Children program.

Proposition 98 also was amended under provisions of Proposition 111, the omnibus budget reform and transit tax measure approved in June 1990, which requires a cut in school spending in proportion with other budget cuts when state revenues lag. The savings here totaled $500 million in the 1990-91 fiscal year, giving a boost to Wilson's upcoming spending proposals. In addition, the voters, by approving Proposition 111, had agreed to double state motor vehicle fuel taxes, part of an $18.5 billion, 10-year transportation plan that would at least keep the Caltrans budget from contributing to the fiscal mess. The Caltrans budget sprang to life, and so did the state's highway and mass transit programs.

In his first budget as governor, Wilson eventually agreed to some $7 billion in new taxes and fees along with a series of internal reforms. Not only did this fail to stave off a deficit at the end of Wilson's first full fiscal budget year in office, but conservative Republicans, never warm to moderate Wilson, erupted in outrage. Wilson had signed the biggest tax increases in California history, they screamed. He'd out-taxed and out-spent even the most liberal of Democratic governors!

No doubt that strengthened Wilson's resolve to come out of the next round of budget talks in better political shape. He vowed to hold the line on taxes and spurn "smoke and mirrors" fixes offered by Democratic leaders. They'd do it his way, or not at all. In the end, Wilson didn't give much. The question remained whether his stonewalling forced him to pay an even greater political price by alienating practically every constituency in the state. The verdict will be rendered in the 1994 gubernatorial election.

THE BUDGET PROCESS

Politicians love to declare that government should be "run like a business." They are fond of insisting the state should "live within its means." They insist state finances can be managed like a frugal "family bank account." Statements like those may pave the high road in fiscal debates for elective office, but against the reality of California's annual budget bill they are about as valid as assertions that groundhogs can predict the weather.

The California economy is the sixth or seventh largest in the world. The state's budget is by far the largest in the nation. The business of collecting and spending more than $57 billion a year on schools, welfare, health, prisons, parks, highways and a myriad of other governmental functions is complex, tedious, politically intricate and a task that requires the expertise of hundreds of people. The money flows in from taxes, fees, tideland oil royalties, multinational corporations and even the poor, who make co-payments for Medi-Cal and other services. Much of it goes exclusively into one or another of nearly 1,000 special funds, earmarked for specific needs. Sales taxes, personal income taxes and bank and corporation taxes flow to the biggest pot of all, the $43.3 billion general fund.

All of that complexity is compressed into a single legislative vehicle, the annual budget bill, which is introduced by the governor within the first 10 days of each calendar year.

By January, of course, the budget has been months in the making. Department heads, agency heads and the governor's Department of Finance have been shaping it since the previous April to balance it with anticipated revenue. Reams of calculations have been completed. Programs are trimmed or expanded to conform to the governor's priorities. There will be winners and losers. If there is any fight left in the losers, and there always is, they will take their case to the Legislature.

In practice, the budget is introduced separately in both the Senate and the Assembly. The governor may be a Republican, Democrat, independent or a Martian, but his budget bills are always authored by the chairmen of the Senate and Assembly fiscal committees, both of whom are members of the majority party. In 1993, as for the past decade, they were Assemblyman John Vasconcellos, D-Santa Clara, chairman of the Assembly Ways and Means Committee, and Sen. Alfred Alquist, D-San Jose, chairman of the Senate Budget and Fiscal Review Committee. They reshape the governor's proposals, following guidance from their colleagues. They are in effective command of the most important bill of any legislative session, a two-volume document that lists appropriations for virtually every function of state government.

Much has to be done, of course, before the budget bills even begin to take shape for consideration by the full Legislature. In late February, the non-partisan legislative analyst reports on the governor's budget proposal. The study commonly exceeds 1,400 pages of detail distilled from the work of dozens of specialists drawing upon the expertise throughout the government and the state as a whole. The budget subcommittees start on the smaller budgets first, particularly those that depend on special funds and have the money they need to confront the problems they manage. Programs that rely on the general fund come later. The final revenue estimates arrive in May, once the April tax bills are opened and the money is counted.

Eventually, the Assembly and Senate bills must pass by a two-thirds majority in each house (a constitutional requirement that gives the minority party, or minority coalitions, the power to block the budget). Differences are worked out in a six-member conference committee. In the end, a unified product must be approved, again by a two-thirds majority.

The Constitutional deadline for final legislative action is supposed to be June 15. The governor is supposed to sign the bill by the beginning of the new fiscal year, July 1. He can use his line-item veto authority to reduce appropriations set by the Legislature, but he cannot restore any spending the lawmakers cut. Usually the governor is able to sign the budget on time, but major budget delays occurred in 1978, 1979, 1980, 1983, 1990 and 1992. No one was betting that 1993 would be an exception to the recent history of stalemates.

3

The constitutional officers: marking time until '94

To be governor of California in recent decades is to stand in the wings of the national political stage. Ronald Reagan proved most adept at moving into the spotlight, and George Deukmejian did his best to avoid it. But the state's chief executive automatically commands attention, owing largely to the 54 electoral votes that make California enormously important in any presidential election.

Earl Warren, elected three times as governor, sought the Republican presidential nomination twice before going on to preside for 16 years as chief justice of the U.S. Supreme Court. Edmund G. "Jerry" Brown Jr. shone in a string of 1976 primaries as he made a characteristically tardy bid to seize the Democratic presidential nomination from Jimmy Carter, then tried to unseat Carter in 1980.

Brown's father, Edmund G. "Pat" Brown Sr., had been governor for two years when he first flirted with the possibility of a vice-presidential nomination. The former state attorney general, who defeated Republican William Knowland for the governor's job in 1958, was eventually frustrated in his hopes for higher office. He turned his attention instead to the less glamorous business of building the staples of government known collectively as the "infrastructure." Three decades later, the elder Brown's accomplishments – a bond issue to increase water supplies to Southern California, more investment in the university system, faster freeway construction for a rapidly growing state – are remembered fondly by elected officials facing a new crush of growth.

Brown's terms as governor also are memorable for their contribution to capital punishment history in a state where voters have demanded that political leaders be willing to put violent criminals to death. An opponent of capital punishment who nevertheless believed it was his job as governor to carry out state law, Brown described the agony of his clemency decisions in death penalty cases in a book published in 1989. "It was an awesome, ultimate power over the lives of others that no person or government should have, or crave," he wrote. "Each decision took something out of me that nothing – not family or work or hope for the future – has ever been able to replace."

Brown, whose defeat of Republican gubernatorial candidate Richard Nixon in 1962 prompted Nixon's infamous "You won't have Nixon to kick around anymore" press conference, was looking forward in 1966 to running against a political neophyte named Ronald Reagan. But the mediagenic actor, railing against disorder on college campuses and appealing to an electorate unnerved by the Watts riots, denied Brown a chance to join Warren as a three-term governor. Reagan continued while governor to fine-tune the conservative message that would propel him to the presidency, but he was largely unsuccessful in matching his fiscal actions with his anti-government rhetoric. In 1967, the former Democrat, who bashed the bureaucracy and welfare state in his public appearances, signed what was then the largest tax increase in state history in order to shore up the sagging budget he inherited from Pat Brown.

Reagan was replaced by Jerry Brown, a self-proclaimed spokesman for a younger generation demanding change and imagination in government. If Jerry Brown followed his father's footsteps to the governor's office, he seemed determined to carve out his own path once he got there. The father was a consummate political mingler; the son standoffish. Pat was a spender; Jerry a relative tightwad. Pat laid pavement; Jerry discouraged freeway construction in favor of car pooling and mass transit. Similarly, the younger Brown's contributions as governor were less concrete. More than anything else, he is remembered for his personal idiosyncrasies: his refusal to live in the governor's mansion, the mattress on the floor of his austere apartment, his 1979 trip to Africa with singer Linda Ronstadt.

Brown used his appointment power to fill state jobs with a more diverse group of people, but some of those appointments became enormous liabilities with voters. Transportation Director Adriana Gianturco defended the much-hated "diamond lanes" imposed on drivers, who resented state attempts to force them to share rides. Supreme Court Chief Justice Rose Bird, ultimately ousted by voters in 1986, came to symbolize a criminal justice system seen as too sympathetic to criminals. Deukmejian used both to score points in his gubernatorial campaigns. Yet even Deukmejian eventually had to acknowledge that the state could not simply build its way out of its traffic congestion problem and came to emphasize car pooling as necessary. Brown also takes credit for influencing his Republican successor on other fronts, including energy and technology. Brown says his emphasis on minority hiring helped push the Deukmejian administration in that direction.

But it was Brown's slapdash style and nearly perpetual campaign for president – a quest he continued unsuccessfully in 1992 – that voters turned away from in 1982, when they elected Courken George Deukmejian Jr. Deukmejian decided from the beginning to stick to the basics. He didn't bombard Californians with many new ideas. He said he was convinced voters wanted a competent manager, and he did little to deviate from that mission. He did his best to avoid revenue-raising measures that might be labeled tax increases, built prisons and appointed judges who he said took a "common-sense" approach to fighting crime.

Deukmejian's first election was the closest race for California governor since 1902. He beat Los Angeles Mayor Tom Bradley by just 1.2 percent of the votes cast, actually losing to Bradley in Election Day votes and winning on absentee ballots. Four years later, Deukmejian trounced Bradley in a rematch, winning by more votes than any governor since Warren locked up both the Republican and Democratic nominations before his re-election victory in 1946.

By the time Deukmejian finished his two terms, he believed he had accomplished much of what he had set out to do. He had said "no" to billions of dollars in state

SALARIES

Governor	$120,000
Lt. Governor	$90,000
Attorney General	$102,000
Secretary of State	$90,000
Controller	$90,000
Treasurer	$90,000
Supt. of Public Instruction	$102,000
Insurance Commissioner	$95,052
Member, Board of Equalization	$95,052
Speaker of the Assembly	$63,000
Senate President Pro Tem	$63,000
Assembly/Senate Floor Leaders	$57,750
Legislator	$52,500
Chief Justice, Supreme Court	$127,104
Associate Justice	$121,207
Appellate Court	$113,632
Superior Court Judge	$99,297
Municipal Court Judge	$90,680
President, University of California	$243,500
UC chancellors	$165,000-243,300
Chancellor, California State University system	$175,000
CSU presidents	$115,956-134,800

Many elected officials opted to take a 5 percent pay cut beginning in 1991 as California struggled through a recession. Legislators receive other direct compensation, including per diem pay of $100 a day for attending legislative sessions ($18,584 a year tax free) and their $4,800 car allowance. They also receive health, dental and vision benefits.

spending proposals, racking up one-year records for vetoing both bills and budget items. He could point to a state unemployment rate half of that facing the state when he took office, thanks to job development he attributed to his no-new-taxes posture.

At the close of his two terms, nearly two-thirds of California's judges were Deukmejian appointees, including five of the seven members of the state Supreme Court. His appointments had reconstructed the Supreme Court with justices willing to impose a voter-approved death penalty, leaving the stage set for California's first execution since 1967 to take place on April 21, 1992. He also had pushed a massive construction program to more than double the number of state prison beds.

But California was beginning to want more in a governor than a warrior against taxes and crime. Deukmejian had worn out his welcome with business leaders, who liked lower tax bills as long the state provided the services they needed. At a time when businesses were increasingly finding they couldn't move their products and services freely on California's congested highways, the governor had to be coaxed into supporting a hike in the state's road-building tax on gasoline.

In addition, a population explosion and the accompanying demand for state services were blowing the lid off a voter-imposed spending cap that Deukmejian defended. Rather than raise the state's gas tax, Deukmejian initially shifted more responsibility for road-building to local government, signing a 1987 bill that gave counties

ELECTIONS 1902-1990

Year	Candidate	Vote
1902	George C. Pardee (R)	48.06%
	Franklin K. Lane (D)	47.22%
1906	James Gillett (R)	40.4%
	Theodore Bell (D)	37.7%
1910	Hiram Johnson (R)	45.9%
	Theodore Bell (D)	40.1%
1914	Hiram Johnson (Pg)	49.7%
	John Fredericks (R)	29.3%
	J.B. Curtin (D)	12.5%
1918	William Stephens (R)	56.3%
	Theodore Bell (I)	36.5%
1922	Friend Wm. Richardson (R)	59.7%
	Thomas Lee Woolwine (D)	36%
1926	C.C. Young (R)	71.2%
	Justus Wardell (D)	24.7%
1930	James Rolph Jr. (R)	72.1%
	Milton Young (D)	24.1%
1934	Frank Merriam (R)	48.9%
	Upton Sinclair (D)	37.7%
1938	Culbert Olson (D)	52.5%
	Frank Merriam (R)	44.2%
1942	Earl Warren (R)	57%
	Culbert Olson (D)	41.7%
1946	Earl Warren (R &D)	91.6%
	Henry Schmidt (Prohibition)	7.1%
1950	Earl Warren (R)	64.8%
	James Roosevelt (D)	35.2%
1954	Goodwin Knight (R)	56.8%
	Richard Graves (D)	43.2%
1958	Pat Brown (D)	59.8%
	William Knowland (R)	40.2%
1962	Pat Brown (D)	51.9%
	Richard Nixon (R)	46.8%
1966	Ronald Reagan (R)	56.6%
	Pat Brown (D)	41.6%
1970	Ronald Reagan (R)	52.8%
	Jesse Unruh (D)	45.1%
1974	Jerry Brown (D)	50.2%
	Houston Flournoy (R)	47.3%
1978	Jerry Brown (D)	56%
	Evelle Younger (R)	36.5%
1982	George Deukmejian (R)	49.3%
	Tom Bradley (D)	48.1%
1986	George Deukmejian (R)	60.54%
	Tom Bradley (D)	37.37%
1990	Pete Wilson (R)	49.25%
	Dianne Feinstein (D)	45.79%

I: Independent; Pg: Progressive.

CALIFORNIA GOVERNORS

Governor	Party	Inauguration
Peter H. Burnett	Independent	December 1849
John McDougal	Independent	January 1851
John Bigler	Democrat	January 1852
John Bigler	Democrat	January 1854
J. Neeley Johnson	American	January 1856
John B. Weller	Democrat	January 1858
Milton S. Latham	Lecompton Democrat	January 1860
John G. Downey	Lecompton Democrat	January 1860
Leland Stanford	Republican	January 1862
Frederick F. Low	Union	December 1863
Henry H. Haight	Democrat	December 1867
Newton Booth	Republican	December 1871
Romualdo Pacheco	Republican	February 1875
William Irwin	Democrat	December 1875
George C. Perkins	Republican	January 1880
George Stoneman	Democrat	January 1883
Washington Bartlett	Democrat	January 1887
Robert W. Waterman	Republican	September 1887
Henry H. Markham	Republican	January 1891
James H. Budd	Democrat	January 1895
Henry T. Gage	Republican	January 1899
George C. Pardee	Republican	January 1903
James N. Gillett	Republican	January 1907
Hiram W. Johnson	Republican	January 1911
Hiram W. Johnson	Progressive	January 1915
William D. Stephens	Republican	March 1917
William D. Stephens	Republican	January 1919
Friend Wm. Richardson	Republican	January 1923
C. C. Young	Republican	January 1927
James Rolph Jr.	Republican	January 1931
Frank F. Merriam	Republican	June 1934
Frank F. Merriam	Republican	January 1935
Culbert L. Olson	Democrat	January 1939
Earl Warren	Republican	January 1943
Earl Warren	Rep.-Dem.	January 1947
Earl Warren	Republican	January 1951
Goodwin J. Knight	Republican	October 1953
Goodwin J. Knight	Republican	January 1955
Edmund G. "Pat" Brown	Democrat	January 1959
Edmund G. "Pat" Brown	Democrat	January 1963
Ronald Reagan	Republican	January 1967
Ronald Reagan	Republican	January 1971
Edmund G. "Jerry" Brown Jr.	Democrat	January 1975
Edmund G. "Jerry" Brown Jr.	Democrat	January 1979
George Deukmejian	Republican	January 1983
George Deukmejian	Republican	January 1987
Pete Wilson	Republican	January 1991

the power to ask voters for sales tax increases to pay for transportation. But by 1989, even Republicans who shared Deukmejian's determination to hold the line on state spending chafed at what they saw as a lack of gubernatorial activism, and Deukmejian successfully campaigned for a measure to raise the state's gas tax and adjust the spending limit.

As the country entered a recession in 1990, Deukmejian also watched his carefully cultivated fiscal legacy unravel. He left behind a state budget shortfall of unprecedented proportions, saddling his successor, Pete Wilson, with a far larger financial crisis than the one inherited from Jerry Brown. That shortfall was one of the many legacies left by anti-tax crusaders Howard Jarvis and Paul Gann, who in 1978 tapped into an underlying anger about government spending with Proposition 13. The initiative and its follow-up, a voter-imposed limit on government spending promoted by Gann, still shape California politics, forcing any aspiring officeholder who wants to be taken seriously to tiptoe around the subject of taxes.

The anti-tax movement marked the beginning of the end for Jerry Brown, who irreparably damaged his credibility by campaigning against the initiative, then embracing it with enthusiasm once it passed. Brown was defeated by Republican Pete Wilson in his 1982 bid for the U.S. Senate and left the political scene for a six-year sabbatical. Brown returned to campaign for and win the chairmanship of the state Democratic Party in February 1989. "The time," he told party members, "is ripe for resurgence." But it became clear that he was most interested in reviving his own political career. He resigned from the state party job two years early to plan a run for the U.S. Senate that eventually became a run for president in 1992.

Whether the Democratic Party would continue its decadelong, post-Proposition 13 fade in voter registration was one of the unspoken themes of the 1990 campaign for governor, one intertwined with growing concern among Californians about a widely perceived deterioration in the quality of their lives.

Republicans – Deukmejian being the chief example – prospered during the 1980s by aligning themselves with the Proposition 13-inspired mood of limited taxation and government spending; Democrats, who ordinarily favor a more activist government, were left befuddled by the onset of tax-cut fever. Republican Pete Wilson won election as governor by finding a middle ground, denouncing his opponent, Democrat Dianne Feinstein, as a "tax-and-spend liberal" while refusing to rule out tax increases himself – shunning the "read my lips" school of campaigning that had helped put George Bush in the White House in 1988. Within weeks of Wilson's inauguration, it was clear that he had been wise to avoid an anti-tax pledge.

PETE WILSON BOGS DOWN

More than 20 years ago, as Pete Wilson contemplated leaving his state Assembly seat to run for mayor of San Diego, his administrative assistant sketched out the pros and cons on a yellow legal pad. There were big problems in San Diego, a city racked by government scandal and rampant growth. The Navy town, tucked away near the

Mexican border, was hardly noticed by most Californians. The job was probably a political cul-de-sac. On the other hand, managing a city might demonstrate executive ability, experience that Wilson could point to if he someday ran for governor. "I knew he wanted to be governor, and I wanted him to be governor," said Bob White, who has been Wilson's top aide ever since.

So Wilson pulled up his Sacramento stakes and went south to take charge of San Diego.

As Wilson debated in 1989 whether to run for governor, political consultant Stu Spencer warned him that California might very well be ungovernable. The view, like the warnings about San Diego, did not dissuade Wilson from entering the race. But two years into

Pete Wilson

Wilson's term, there were increasing signs that Spencer may have been right.

A string of man-made, natural, economic and political disasters seemed to follow Wilson like a cloud. He faced fires, floods, earthquakes, drought and California's first execution in 25 years. He raised taxes to cope with the state's worst financial mess since the Great Depression, and presided for 64 long days in 1992 over a budget deadlock that forced state government to issue IOUs for the first time since the 1930s. His longtime political aide and press liaison, Otto Bos, died in June 1991 of a heart attack at age 47 while playing soccer in a weekend league.

As the bad news multiplied, a view of Wilson as the victim of unprecedented bad luck began to give way to a perception that he bore some personal responsibility for the depth of his unpopularity, the worst of any California governor in three decades.

In his first year in office, Wilson had proposed and enacted the largest tax increase in California history, threatening Republicans privately that they would make themselves "fucking irrelevant" if they refused to compromise with Democrats on a budget-balancing deal. But he spent much of the next year sounding like a reincarnation of anti-tax crusader Howard Jarvis, refusing to consider any tax increases to balance the budget. When pressed about the inconsistency, he offered a revisionist view of his willingness to raise taxes the year before, saying he had argued at the time that raising taxes was "a mistake."

Wilson also sent mixed signals on gay rights. One year after vetoing a 1991 bill banning job discrimination against homosexuals, Wilson signed a narrower measure that he said would protect gay rights without exposing California employers to the threat of costly lawsuits.

Democrats, who gave Wilson an extended honeymoon in his first year, were confused by his new-found anti-tax zeal and his wavering position on gay rights. Was he the compassionate conservative who proposed preventive programs to keep children healthy, in school and out of prison? Or was he the heartless budget-cutter who would sacrifice his moderate social positions in an instant to mollify the religious right?

The cooperative spirit in the Capitol was severely squeezed by the political pressures that came with the once-a-decade redistricting of legislative and congressional districts and the budget constraints brought on by a severe recession. In the 1992 budget fight, Wilson vowed to allow "chaos" to reign for as long as it took to convince Democratic legislators to do things his way. But he underestimated the degree of pain and pressure it would take to force their capitulation. The stalemate damaged both California's national reputation and its bond rating without finding a long-term solution to the state's budget mess. In the end, Wilson and lawmakers faced another multibillion dollar shortfall in 1993.

Wilson also irritated Democrats by proposing a 1992 ballot initiative (Proposition 165) to expand the governor's budgetary powers. Legislators began to charge that the governor had abandoned democracy in favor of one-man rule. By the time a budget was signed in 1992, critics had variously called him a pipsqueak, a terrorist and a petulant child. In November, voters defeated Proposition 165 after a campaign that featured heavy spending by Democrats and state employees, whom Wilson also had thoroughly antagonized. That raised speculation that voters might also be in no mood to grant Wilson a second term in 1994.

Peter Barton Wilson, however, is nothing if not persistent. He failed the bar exam twice before passing on his third try. He practiced law only briefly, however, devoting much of his time after law school to a series of political jobs. He was an advance man for Richard Nixon's gubernatorial campaign in 1962, a paid staff member for a local Republican club and executive director of the San Diego Republican Party Central Committee in 1964. He finally grabbed a seat in the Assembly in 1966. Wilson's plan to catapult from San Diego into statewide office failed in 1978, when he finished fourth in a bid for the GOP gubernatorial nomination. Four years later he considered another try, but settled instead for a successful U.S. Senate race against outgoing Gov. Jerry Brown.

A former Marine who completed his undergraduate studies at Yale University, Wilson continues to come across as someone who wears starched shirts on

Saturdays. When he does relax, he smokes a cigar, puts some Broadway show tunes on the stereo and knocks back a couple of scotches.

Wilson's father, James, a hard-charging advertising executive whom Wilson describes as one of his heroes, never wanted his son to go into politics. But ironically it was at the dinner table, when his dad would deliver "minilectures" on obligation to society, that Wilson said his interest in public service began.

In public-speaking settings, Wilson's self-confident attitude can border on smug. A long line of aides has tried to convince him to shorten his speeches, criticism he listens to but rejects.

Through most of Wilson's career, he's been more centrist than conservative. He has courted the environmental vote with consistent stands on coastal protection, limits on offshore oil drilling, expansion of transit systems and planned growth. On other matters, Wilson, as a U.S. senator, generally supported Reagan administration policies and was an early backer of George Bush's candidacy. In the U.S. Senate, he worked for California industry, particularly agriculture, aerospace and computer electronics.

Probably the most memorable moment of Wilson's Senate years came in May 1985, when he was recovering from an emergency appendectomy. The Senate was considering a complex budget measure, which included a freeze on cost-of-living increases for Social Security recipients, and it appeared that Vice President Bush would be needed to break a tie. At the critical moment, a pajama-clad Wilson was wheeled onto the Senate floor to cast the deciding vote in favor. The episode surfaced again in the closing days of the gubernatorial campaign, when Democratic opponent Dianne Feinstein ran a television ad in which Senate Republican leader Bob Dole joked about Wilson's post-surgery appearance, saying he "does better under sedation."

Wilson has never been a favorite of many state Republicans; he endorsed Gerald Ford over Ronald Reagan in the 1976 presidential campaign. At the 1985 Republican state convention, conservatives almost booed him off the stage. In November 1988, however, Wilson did something that none of his predecessors had been able to do for 36 years: He held onto his U.S. Senate seat for a second term. His re-election opponent, Lt. Gov. Leo McCarthy, had gotten nowhere with his campaign charge that Wilson "left no footprints" in Washington, and it appeared that the "jinxed seat" from California finally had an occupant who would make a career of the Senate.

Then came Deukmejian's announcement that he wouldn't seek a third term. GOP leaders, desperate to have a Republican in the governor's chair when the state was reapportioned after the 1990 census, cast about for someone electable. With no other Republicans holding statewide office, most agreed that only Wilson fit the bill. He was quick to hit the campaign trail again. "I see it very likely as a career capper – and a damn good one," he said in the midst of the campaign.

Wilson hit a low point in the 1992 elections, as Republican candidates he backed took a beating and his budget and welfare initiative, Proposition 165, was soundly defeated. The state campaign for President Bush that he led never got off the ground, and the national campaign eventually opted to write off California. His appointee to the U.S. Senate, John Seymour, lost his seat to Democrat Dianne Feinstein.

Earlier in the year, Wilson had sought to increase pressure on Democrats by calling legislators back to Sacramento for a pre-election October special session on the workers' compensation system, but the complex subject of workers' comp ultimately proved to be a feeble political weapon. Wilson, who had hoped to capture a majority in the 80-seat Assembly and oust Democratic Assembly Speaker Willie Brown, settled for an embarrassing 32 Republican seats.

The election also opened wide rifts within the state Republican Party, divisions expressed early in primary fights in legislative races between Wilson and conservative Christians. The difficulty of the balancing act facing Wilson was evident. He angered conservatives by backing challengers against them in primary fights. Yet he disappointed moderates by wholeheartedly supporting Christian-right candidates who won their primaries, and by making it clear after the election that he would not lead an intra-party effort to oust the religious right.

With the 1994 election already looming large on the horizon, a weakened Wilson sought to cope with a third recessionary budget year and a state unemployment rate topping 10 percent. He faced an uphill battle to restore California's fiscal strength and his own reputation with voters.

PERSONAL: elected 1990; born Aug. 23, 1933, in Lake Forest, Ill.; home, San Diego; education, B.A. Yale University 1955, J.D. UC Berkeley 1962; wife, Gayle; Protestant.

CAREER: U.S. Marine Corps, 1955-58; attorney, 1963-66; Assembly, 1966-71; San Diego mayor, 1971-83; U.S. Senator, 1983-91.

OFFICES: Sacramento (916) 445-2841; Los Angeles (213) 897-0322; San Diego (619) 525-4641; San Francisco (415) 703-2218; Fresno (209) 445-5295.

LEO McCARTHY MOVES ON

The 1992 elections left three-term Lt. Gov. Leo McCarthy a two-time loser in his bid for a U.S. Senate seat and once again unable to escape his relatively powerless post. McCarthy, who had hoped his years in state Democratic politics and high name recognition would finally catapult him into a more substantive statewide office, failed to win his party's nomination in a three-way race against Reps. Mel Levine of Santa Monica and Barbara Boxer of Greenbrae.

Despite the fact that early surveys showed him well ahead of his opponents, the well-worn McCarthy ultimately held little appeal for Democratic voters, who rallied around the idea of electing more women to the U.S. Senate. Boxer went on to win the seat held by a retiring Sen. Alan Cranston, leaving McCarthy's future options limited to a federal appointment or a private-sector job. McCarthy ruled out seeking a fourth term as lieutenant governor, and candidates to replace him began lining up for 1994.

McCarthy had tried for the U.S. Senate in 1988, but found that his squeaky-clean reputation and proven performance on a list of liberal issues were not enough to defeat incumbent Republican Sen. Pete Wilson in a lackluster race. A workaholic and conscientious to a fault, McCarthy can also be sanctimonious and stubborn, qualities that rose to the surface during the prolonged strain of his Senate campaign against Wilson.

McCarthy has endured defeat before, most notably in an agonizing power struggle in 1980 with then-Assemblyman Howard Berman, which ended McCarthy's six years as Assembly speaker. The fight ultimately handed the speakership to fellow San Franciscan Willie Brown after McCarthy and Berman battled to a draw.

Leo McCarthy

McCarthy went on to become lieutenant governor in 1982 and won re-election in 1986 at a time when he was one of the few candidates willing to openly support state Supreme Court Chief Justice Rose Bird during her losing bid to retain her post. By then he had changed his position on the death penalty – the issue that led to Bird's defeat – after years of opposition to capital punishment. Kidnapped as a college student by a man who had just murdered a police officer, McCarthy said his views on violent crime began to change years later when he met the officer's widow.

McCarthy has used his position as lieutenant governor to pursue such issues as environmental protection and nursing-home reform. But his most visible moment in office came on Oct. 17, 1989, when a 7.1-magnitude earthquake struck Northern California. Gov. George Deukmejian was out of the country at the time, leaving McCarthy capably in charge of the early stages of the disaster.

Born in New Zealand, McCarthy grew up in San Francisco as the son of a tavern owner and attended Catholic seminary as a teenager. He served on the San Francisco Board of Supervisors from 1963 to 1968. From there, he moved to the

Assembly, where he soon earned a reputation as a family man who commuted home to San Francisco nearly every night rather than pursue Sacramento's political night life.

PERSONAL: elected 1982; re-elected 1986 and 1990; born Aug. 15, 1930, in Auckland, New Zealand; home, San Francisco; education, B.S. University of San Francisco, J.D. San Francisco Law School; wife, Jacqueline Burke; children, Sharon, Conna, Adam and Niall.

CAREER: legislative aide to Sen. Eugene McAteer, 1959-1963; San Francisco Board of Supervisors, 1963-1968; Assembly 1969-1982; Assembly speaker 1974-1980.

OFFICES: Capitol (916) 445-8994; San Francisco (415) 557-2662; Los Angeles (310) 412-6118.

LIEUTENANT GOVERNORS SINCE 1950		
Goodwin J. Knight	Republican	elected 1950
Harold J. Powers	Republican	appointed 1953
Harold J. Powers	Republican	elected 1954
Glenn M. Anderson	Democrat	elected 1958, '62
Robert Finch	Republican	elected 1966
Ed Reinecke	Republican	appointed 1969
Ed Reinecke	Republican	elected 1970
Mervyn Dymally	Democrat	elected 1974
Mike Curb	Republican	elected 1978
Leo T. McCarthy	Democrat	elected 1982, '86, '90

DANIEL LUNGREN BUILDS BRIDGES

Few familiar with Dan Lungren's tough brand of conservatism would feel comfortable classifying him as a political centrist. But the split between Gov. Pete Wilson and the social conservatives who have captured the state Republican Party machinery leaves a gaping hole in the middle that Lungren began moving to fill in the wake of a disastrous 1992 election cycle.

Lungren made it clear that he would not challenge Wilson in the 1994 Republican primary, as many members of the party's right wing had hoped. Instead, he sought to cast himself as a bridge-builder who could return the party to the successful anti-crime and anti-tax themes it had drifted away from in a year that highlighted the party's internal dispute over abortion.

Lungren, who dubiously distinguished himself by resurrecting the ghost of Willie Horton in a speech to the 1992 Republican National Convention in Houston, spent his first two years as state attorney general remaking the office in his own conservative image.

He insisted that lawyers hired for the office's criminal division handle death penalty appeals regardless of their personal views on the issue and vigorously pursued California's first execution in 25 years, that of double murderer Robert Alton Harris. He generated controversy as he demoted civil rights lawyer Marian Johnston and folded prosecution units specializing in fraud and white-collar crime into the department's criminal division. He also quit handling lawsuits involving most state personnel matters, which had been a major responsibility of the office. Lungren blamed the cuts on budget troubles, as a national recession coincided with a flood of federal death penalty appeals.

Lungren also tangled publicly with state schools chief Bill Honig, who was charged in March 1992 with illegally using state funds in connection

Dan Lungren

with a consulting firm run by his wife. Although the investigation was technically initiated under former state Attorney General John Van de Kamp, it was under Lungren that state investigators searched Honig's San Francisco home and a grand jury indicted the schools chief. Honig charged that Lungren had joined an effort by conservative Christians to drive him from office; Lungren maintained that he had a responsibility to investigate Honig's questionable activity regardless of the source of the accusations.

Democrats had hoped to block Lungren's political ascension in 1988, when the state Senate refused to confirm his nomination as state treasurer by then-Gov. George Deukmejian. But Republicans may have had the last laugh in 1990, when Lungren was elected in his own right to be attorney general, an even more prominent constitutional office. Aided by a massive voter-turnout program conducted that year by Republican gubernatorial candidate Pete Wilson, Lungren narrowly defeated San Francisco District Attorney Arlo Smith to become the state's chief law enforcement official.

Lungren, who spent 10 years in Congress as a law-and-order conservative, had abandoned an exploratory candidacy for the U.S. Senate in 1986 because he was unable to raise enough money. When his hopes of becoming state treasurer following the death of longtime Democratic Treasurer Jesse Unruh in 1987 were dashed, he returned to private practice in a Sacramento law firm and began to plan his campaign for attorney general instead.

Lungren, who at 6 years old began walking precincts for a GOP congressional candidate, isn't the only member of his family with political ties. His father was Richard Nixon's personal physician, and his younger brother, Brian, is a political consultant who managed his campaign for attorney general. Lungren served as an assistant to Republican U.S. Sens. George Murphy of California and Bill Brock of Tennessee, and was a special assistant to the Republican National Committee. He was practicing law in Long Beach when he was elected to Congress. Watchdog groups consistently classified his congressional votes as conservative, and he earned the wrath of Japanese-American groups for voting against reparations to Japanese-Americans who were interned during World War II.

Lungren is an entertaining and dynamic public speaker, and his competitive nature and intense personality make him a candidate to be reckoned with should he seek higher office. The attorney general's office has long been a trampoline for those aspiring to be governor. While John Van de Kamp's 1990 loss proved the route is not infallible, Earl Warren, Pat Brown and, most recently, George Deukmejian bounced into the chief executive's chair by that route. In a state where voters are solidly pro-choice, however, Lungren's political Achilles' heel is abortion.

PERSONAL: elected 1990; born Sept. 22, 1946; home, Roseville; education, B.A. University of Notre Dame, J.D. Georgetown University Law School; wife, Barbara "Bobbi" Lungren; children, Jeffrey, Kelly and Kathleen.

CAREER: U.S. Senate aide, 1969-70; Republican National Committee staff, 1971-72; private law practice in Long Beach, 1973-78, and in Sacramento 1989-1991; U.S. House of Representatives 1979-1989.

OFFICES: Sacramento (916) 322-3360; San Francisco (415) 703-1985; Los Angeles (213) 897-2000; San Diego (619) 237-7351.

ATTORNEYS GENERAL SINCE 1950

Edmund G. "Pat" Brown	Democrat	elected 1950, '54
Stanley Mosk	Democrat	elected 1958, '62
Thomas C. Lynch	Democrat	appointed 1964
Thomas C. Lynch	Democrat	elected 1966
Evelle J. Younger	Republican	elected 1970, '74
George Deukmejian	Republican	elected 1978
John Van de Kamp	Democrat	elected 1982, '86
Dan Lungren	Republican	elected 1990

GRAY DAVIS: SELF-INFLICTED WOUNDS

In a state known for no shortage of negative political advertising, Gray Davis' 1992 primary campaign for the U.S. Senate managed to set a new standard for sleaze.

His campaign ran a television ad likening Democratic opponent Dianne Feinstein to Leona Helmsley, the New York hotelier convicted of tax evasion. "Helmsley is in jail; Feinstein wants to be a senator," the ad said, attempting to equate Helmsley's legal problems with a civil suit filed against Feinstein by the Fair Political Practices Commission. The ad was soundly denounced by Democrats and Republicans alike as one of the worst in California politics.

Davis' attack had little effect on Feinstein, who went on to win the U.S. Senate seat held by Pete Wilson appointee John

Gray Davis

Seymour. But Davis did succeed in sabotaging his own standing in political circles with a campaign destined to be remembered as sexist and unfair.

Born Joseph Graham Davis Jr. in New York, Davis moved to California with his family at age 11. A graduate of Stanford University and Columbia University law school, he served two years in the U.S. Army in Vietnam.

In 1974, with a stint as finance director for Tom Bradley's successful mayoral race under his belt, the slim and soft-spoken Davis made his first run at statewide office. He filed for the Democratic nomination for state treasurer, then learned to his dismay that former Assembly Speaker Jesse Unruh had decided to enter the race. It was no contest. "I was the doormat Jess stepped on in his road back to political prominence," Davis later recalled.

Davis then went to work as the chief of staff for Jerry Brown, who became governor that year. Putting aside his own ambitions for the moment, he helped forge Brown's thrifty image and ran interference with the Legislature, surviving a continual power struggle among the young governor's top aides. By 1981, however, Davis was restless and ready to run for the state Assembly. Elected to the 43rd District representing West Los Angeles in 1982, he won re-election two years later.

Those years laid the groundwork for Davis' second statewide run. When veteran state Controller Kenneth Cory announced his retirement just days before the filing deadline in 1986, Davis was already sitting on a $1 million campaign fund that enabled him to dash in and win the seat. He was also helped politically by the statewide publicity he had generated for himself with his 1985 effort to encourage companies to picture missing children on milk cartons, grocery bags and billboards. The program featured prominently in his campaign ads.

Although controversial Supreme Court Chief Justice Rose Bird presided at Davis' 1983 wedding, he sidestepped the issue in his race for controller, saying he did not want to prejudice cases involving the controller's office that someday could come before the court. He emerged largely unscathed by the Bird-bashing and Brown-battering leveled at Democratic candidates that year. He later narrowly escaped prosecution for using state staff and equipment in his 1986 campaign for controller. Attorney General John Van de Kamp, another Democrat, concluded that taxpayer funds had been used in the campaign, but found insufficient evidence to accuse Davis of any criminal intent.

The controller's office gives Davis a seat on 52 boards and commissions, including the State Lands Commission, where he has been able to express his strong environmental views. He also sits on the state Board of Equalization, signs the state's checks and has a voice in managing some $86 billion in state employee and teacher pension funds. Since his 1986 election, Davis has used the office as a platform to fight offshore oil drilling, defend the state's family planning program, hunt for people to whom the state owes money and, on two occasions, press corporations to donate wetlands to the public.

There is no indication that his ambition for higher office has subsided, despite the wounds he inflicted on himself in his primary campaign against Feinstein. Term limits dictate that Davis can serve only one more term as the state's fiscal watchdog.

PERSONAL: elected 1986; born Dec. 26, 1942, in New York; home, Los Angeles; education, B.A. Stanford University, J.D. Columbia University Law

CONTROLLERS SINCE 1950

Thomas H. Kuchel	Republican	elected 1950
Robert C. Kirkwood	Republican	appointed 1952
Robert C. Kirkwood	Republican	elected 1954
Alan Cranston	Democrat	elected 1958, '62
Houston I. Flournoy	Republican	elected 1966, '70
Kenneth Cory	Democrat	elected 1974, '78, '82
Gray Davis	Democrat	elected 1986, '90

School; wife, Sharon Ryer Davis.

CAREER: chief of staff to Gov. Jerry Brown 1974-1981; Assembly 1983-1986.
OFFICES: Sacramento (916) 445-3028; Los Angeles (310) 446-8846.

A DIFFERENT SHADE OF BROWN

It was fitting, perhaps, that Kathleen Brown's prime-time speech to the 1992 Democratic National Convention was pre-empted on CNN by an interview with her brother. As the daughter of former Gov. Pat Brown and sister of former Gov. Jerry Brown – and as the spouse of television executive Van Gordon Sauter – Kathleen Brown has spent plenty of time in the shadow of the significant men in her life. But as she began to lay the groundwork for an expected run for governor herself in 1994, California's state treasurer moved to make it clear that she believes it is her turn in the spotlight.

Kathleen Brown

"For generations, women have put others first: our parents and kids. Our husbands – and brothers," she said pointedly in the convention address. "But that's just fine, because America now wants leaders who put other people first for a change."

Kathleen Brown's election as state treasurer gave rise to great expectations in Democratic political circles. There was talk that she ultimately would be the first Brown to win a place on the national party ticket. At the very least, most insiders believed she eventually would follow the Brown family tradition of using a lesser constitutional office as a launching pad for a gubernatorial campaign.

In 1990, a year in which voters sent one of their strongest anti-politician signals yet by imposing term limits on legislators, most candidates for statewide office did their best to portray their opponent as the politician in the race. In that context, Brown's bid to become treasurer might have been expected to be an uphill battle at best. Sitting Treasurer Thomas Hayes, a career civil servant, had never run for office before. Appointed by Gov. George Deukmejian to fill out the unexpired term of Jesse Unruh, who had died in office in 1987, Hayes prided himself on his money-management skills. He said he was asking voters to elect a financial manager – not a politician.

Enter Brown, a member of one of the state's most colorful and controversial political families. Her political ties were impossible to hide, and she didn't try. Arguing that the elected office called for a candidate who was more than a pencil-pusher, she said she would be a treasurer who didn't stay in the vault.

Brown, who had been a lawyer at O'Melveny and Myers, a powerhouse in government bond law, capitalized on her family's formidable political connections and her own network as an attorney to beat Hayes at the fund-raising game. In her talking-head TV ads, she came across as steady and sincere. The result was the election of a third Brown to statewide office, bringing the list of constitutional posts the family has held to four – governor, attorney general, treasurer and secretary of state.

Brown was quick to acknowledge that the assets she brought to the campaign – her gender, her political party and her family ties – also were liabilities. Hayes' television strategist, Republican image-maker Roger Ailes, called her "Sister Moonbeam," a reference to the "Gov. Moonbeam" label that captured her brother's image at the close of his two terms as governor. Kathleen Brown preferred to discuss her father's record as governor, recalling his push to build highways, universities and water systems. She charged that Hayes had moved too slowly to sell voter-approved bonds for schools and other facilities.

Brown was elected to the Los Angeles Board of Education in 1975 and re-elected in 1979, the year her marriage to George Rice ended in divorce. The following year, she married Sauter and resigned from the board to join her new husband in New York – a fact that her future opponents almost certainly will use in an attempt to portray her as a political quitter. The couple returned to California in 1987, where Brown can expect her ties to Jerry (she shares his opposition to the death penalty) to follow her throughout an expected 1994 race for governor. Her allies made it clear they wished Jerry would cease his perpetual and increasingly childish quest for political attention. Barring that, Kathleen will have to work overtime to distance herself from her brother's idiosyncrasies, continuing to cast herself as what she calls "a different shade of Brown."

PERSONAL: elected 1990; born Sept. 25, 1945, in San Francisco; home, Los Angeles; education, B.A. Stanford University, J.D. Fordham University School of Law; husband, Van Gordon Sauter; children, Hilary Rice, Sascha Rice, Zebediah Rice, Mark Sauter and Jeremy Sauter.
  CAREER: Los Angeles Board of Education 1975-1980; attorney, 1985-87; Los Angeles Board of Public Works 1987-1989.
  OFFICE: Sacramento (916) 653-2995; Los Angeles (213) 620-4467.

TREASURERS SINCE 1950

Charles G. Johnson	Progressive	elected 1950, '54
Ronald Button	Republican	appointed 1956
Bert A. Betts	Democrat	elected 1958, '62
Ivy Baker Priest	Republican	elected 1966, '70
Jesse M. Unruh	Democrat	elected 1974, '78, '82, '86*
Thomas Hayes	Republican	appointed 1987
Kathleen Brown	Democrat	elected 1990

*Elizabeth Whitney served as acting treasurer following Unruh's death, August 1987-January 1989.

MARCH FONG EU STANDS PAT

March Fong Eu's press releases bill her as the winningest woman in California politics. The first and only Asian-American to be elected to state constitutional office, Eu has served as California's chief elections officer since 1975. She was a four-term assembly-woman when she won the secretary of state's post in 1974. She was re-elected in 1978, 1982, 1986 and 1990. If she tries again in 1994 it would be her sixth and, under voter-approved term limits, final term.

In her last race, however, Eu withstood an unexpectedly strong challenge from Los Angeles City Councilwoman Joan Milke Flores, who campaigned with the slogan "Where was Eu?" Flores complained that Eu has been a chronic violator of the very campaign laws she is supposed to enforce and has

March Fong Eu

done nothing to stem the decline in California voter participation. In particular, she noted that Eu reduced fines against her own campaign in 1986 and 1987 from $26,200 to just $650. Eu agreed in early 1990 to pay the Fair Political Practices

Commission $8,000 to settle a complaint involving 95 reporting violations that could have resulted in penalties for her campaign totaling $190,000. Eu, who readily concedes waiving penalties for late campaign reporting on a bipartisan basis unless a pattern of willful violations is found, called the failures "inadvertent, but not excusable."

Eu cites a long list of accomplishments in office, including a record of fraud-free elections, efficient election reporting and an attack on the national media projections used to forecast election results long before California polls close.

She has failed, however, to use her job as a launching pad for higher office. Jerry Brown, who served one term as secretary of state on his way to becoming governor, made the post a bully pulpit to push for political reform in the post-Watergate era. Eu largely sticks to more mundane tasks, including a thankless effort to boost voter registration and turnout in a state where campaigns dominated by money and media are driving voters away from the polls.

Eu tried to move up in 1987, when she declared herself a Democratic candidate for the U.S. Senate seat held by Republican Pete Wilson. But she demonstrated sketchy knowledge of federal issues in her early meetings with reporters and struggled in her efforts to mount a fund-raising operation. Eu, who had been beaten by a robber in her Los Angeles-area home one week after winning election to her fourth term as secretary of state, put her U.S. Senate campaign on hold to launch a signature-gathering drive for a proposed initiative she called Dimes Against Crimes. The crime initiative was one way to keep her name in the news, a technique she had used to great advantage as an assemblywoman campaigning to ban pay toilets in public buildings. But she failed to raise enough money to qualify her measure.

Ultimately, Eu's biggest political liability proved to be her wealthy husband. Henry Eu, one of 13 sons of one of the wealthiest men in the Far East, refused to reveal details of his business interests, making it impossible for Eu to comply with the disclosure requirements of federal campaign law. She abandoned her Senate campaign in 1987 before it truly began, saying she was forced to choose between her candidacy and her marriage.

A third-generation Californian of Chinese descent, Eu was born in Oakdale in Stanislaus County, the daughter of a laundry owner. Eu began her own career as a dental hygienist and eventually earned a doctor of education degree at Stanford University. Using the Alameda County Board of Education as a springboard, she became the state's first Asian assemblywoman in 1966.

PERSONAL: elected 1974; re-elected 1978, 1982, 1986 and 1990; born March 29, 1922, in Oakdale, Calif.; home, Los Angeles; education, B.S. University of California, Berkeley, M.Ed. Mills College, Ed. D. Stanford University; husband, Henry Eu; children, Matthew Fong Jr., Suyin Fong.

CAREER: Dental hygienist for Oakland public schools 1945-48; chairwoman, division of dental hygiene, University of California Medical Center in San Francisco 1948-51; supervisor of dental health education for Alameda County Board of Education 1956-66; Assembly 1967-74.

OFFICES: Sacramento (916) 445-6371; San Francisco (415) 703-2601; Los Angeles (213) 897-3131; San Diego (619) 525-4113.

SECRETARIES OF STATE SINCE 1950		
Frank M. Jordan	Republican	elected 1950, '54, '58, '62, '66
Pat Sullivan	Republican	appointed 1970
Edmund G. "Jerry" Brown Jr.	Democrat	elected 1970
March Fong Eu	Democrat	elected 1974, '78, '82, '86, '90

HONIG: EDUCATION WARRIOR TO CONVICTED FELON

With reform as his battle cry, state schools chief Bill Honig marched into the 1980s waging political war on behalf of California school children. He campaigned relentlessly for the new money and new attitudes that he said were needed to bring about wholesale changes in the state's classrooms, and he spent much of the decade alternately feuding and making peace with Republicans over spending for education.

But Honig's education crusade began to collapse around him on March 24, 1992, when he was indicted by a Sacramento County grand jury on felony conflict-of-interest charges that left him facing five years in prison. The indictment charged that he had improperly used his office to steer government business to the Quality Education Project, a non-profit foundation established by his wife, Nancy. Less than a year later, a jury took just three hours of deliberations to convict him on all four felony counts.

Bill Honig

Nancy Honig's previous business, a service that managed doctors' offices, had been so successful that she was once featured in a "60 Minutes" segment about women who earn more money than their husbands. She had given up that multimillion dollar enterprise to focus her energies on her husband's first campaign for schools chief. After his election, she began operating the foundation out of their home, organizing training sessions for parents and teachers on how they can work together to help children succeed.

Critics, however, began to question the propriety of school districts purchasing services from the wife of the superintendent of public instruction. Newly elected Attorney General Dan Lungren pursued an investigation that culminated in a search of Honig's San Francisco home and the indictment.

There was ample evidence to support Honig's claims that a state Board of Education dominated by appointees of Honig's nemesis, Gov. George Deukmejian, had long been out to get him. But even Honig allies acknowledged that he had offered his enemies a broad target with his efforts on behalf of his wife's foundation. He was, they concluded, as guilty of political naivete and poor judgment as he was of financial malfeasance.

Born Louis William Honig Jr. in San Francisco, Honig had abandoned a career as a lawyer to become a teacher and was named to the state Board of Education by Gov. Jerry Brown in 1975. By 1982, he said he was angry enough about the lack of education leadership in California to challenge three-term incumbent Wilson Riles for state superintendent of public instruction. Upon his election, Honig plunged into a massive legislative dispute over education funding, emerging with Deukmejian's commitment to a plan that provided hundreds of millions in extra dollars for schools. The landmark package also enacted a series of reforms: a longer school day and year, stricter school discipline, higher pay for entry-level teachers and more stringent high school curriculum requirements for English, social science, science and math.

But maintaining the progress proved difficult as enrollments grew and California experienced an influx of young immigrants requiring extra classroom attention. The demands coincided with new state spending constraints as California began to experience the effects of a budget-capping formula approved by voters in 1979. Honig again marshaled his political forces to demand a "fair share" of the state budget for schools. He lost a major round with Deukmejian in 1987, when legislators decided to return a $1.1 billion surplus to taxpayers rather than find a way to divert the money to education. He returned in 1988 to win voter approval of Proposition 98, an initiative that guarantees a minimum state funding level for schools. Passage of the measure, however, ignited a storm of counterlobbying from doctors, university officials, state employees and others who said it paid for education at the expense of other vital state services.

Honig's star continued to rise quickly enough that he was rumored to be in line for a federal post if the Democrats had won the White House in 1988, and most

Capitol observers expected Honig to run for governor in 1990. But he bowed out of the 1990 race before it began, announcing that he would concentrate on winning a third term and implementing Proposition 98.

Honig's conviction gave Gov. Pete Wilson the chance to appoint his successor, a development that promised to put the Republican governor in a difficult political spot. While conservatives demanded a schools chief who would adhere to an agenda that included school vouchers, Democrats warned that a candidate too far to the right or too politically viable would never win legislative confirmation.

PERSONAL: elected 1982; re-elected 1986 and 1990; born April 23, 1937, in San Francisco; home, San Francisco; education, B.A. and J.D. University of California, Berkeley, M.Ed. San Francisco State University; wife, Nancy Catlin Honig; children, Michael, Carolyn, Steven and Jonathan.

CAREER: clerk for Chief Justice Matthew Tobriner 1963-1964; associate counsel in state Department of Finance 1964-1966; San Francisco corporate and individual lawyer beginning in 1967; elementary school teacher 1972-1976; superintendent of the Reed Union Elementary School District 1979-1982; state Board of Education 1975-1982.

OFFICES: Sacramento (916) 657-2451.

SUPERINTENDENTS OF PUBLIC INSTRUCTION SINCE 1950	
Roy Simpson	elected 1950, '54, '58
Max Rafferty	elected 1962, '66
Wilson Riles	elected 1970, '74, '78
Bill Honig	elected 1982, '86, '90

JOHN GARAMENDI'S OPPORTUNITY

For years, John Garamendi has been one of the Capitol's most ambitious figures. And why not? Garamendi would appear to be the dream candidate: handsome, ex-college football star with degrees from Harvard and the University of California; Peace Corps volunteer with his wife in Ethiopia; son of Basque-Italian parents who carved out a living on ranches in Nevada and the Sierra foothills; bank officer; and devoted father of a handsome family. But until 1990, when he became California's first elected insurance commissioner, Garamendi's career seemed a collection of promising roads that had all lead to dead-ends.

The post of insurance commissioner held great potential for Garamendi. His predecessor's performance had been roundly criticized. Arguably, a frog could have done a better job of regulating California's insurance industry than Roxani Gillespie, who had been appointed to the post by Gov. George Deukmejian. Her cheerleading for the industry provided incentive for the voters to pass Proposition 103 in 1988, which converted the position to an elective one in 1990.

As insurance commissioner, Garamendi has taken a strong pro-consumer posture. With the help of a very busy public relations office, Garamendi's efforts have produced a steady stream of headlines about attempts to wrest rebates from insurance companies, reorganize health care and generally stand in front of the insurance industry with a whip and a chair. This has turned Garamendi into a top Democratic contender in the 1994 race for the governor. But as has often been the case with Garamendi, he has thrown some obstacles in his own path with unpolitic moves that make him a constant butt of jokes among political insiders. Nor was he helped by a tiff with the campaign staff of President Clinton (Garamendi was Clinton's California chairman).

Garamendi first won election to the Assembly in 1974 and moved up to the Senate

John Garamendi

two years later. In 1980, he became majority leader, the No. 2 spot, in a leadership shake-up that made David Roberti president pro tem. But from that quick start, his career tripped and stumbled along, often because he tried to move it too fast.

Garamendi's first fall was in 1982, when he got his ears boxed in a quixotic bid for the Democratic nomination for governor. He could have made a strong run at a lesser statewide office but insisted on going for the top. He also passed up a chance to run for Congress. As Garamendi's reputation for ambition grew in the Senate, he was accused by colleagues of neglecting his duties as majority floor leader. In 1985, he was replaced by Barry Keene. Then in early 1986, Garamendi made himself look foolish to many in the Capitol when he tried to dump Roberti as pro tem and found himself standing alone. His run for state controller in 1986 was another failure.

In 1990 came the insurance commissioner job—a high-profile, statewide job attracting only low-profile candidates. He alone had any name identification. He outspent his opponents, said very little during the campaign and sailed into office.

In a way, Garamendi's efforts to separate himself from common politics have led to his reputation for unreliability. He has been so afraid of being tainted that he refuses to admit to making the sort of deals that any politician, especially one brimming with ambition, must make to survive. That has made his explanations to everyone – lobbyists, legislators, Capitol staffers or reporters – sound like a 10-year-old trying to lie to his parents.

There was no better example than when he resigned his Senate seat two months before winning the insurance commissioner race in 1990 to give his wife, Patti, a boost in her efforts to win his seat. By quitting early, it forced the primary to be consolidated with the November general election, meaning Patti Garamendi's opponent (and the eventual winner), Patrick Johnston, had to run for his Assembly seat and the Senate seat simultaneously. Garamendi said to anyone who would listen that he only wanted to save voters money by resigning early.

Garamendi was handed another golden PR opening in 1992 when he was named the state chairman for Clinton's campaign. But both Garamendi's methods and events outside his control made it a lost opportunity. Garamendi was counting on a hard-fought presidential campaign in California, with him at Clinton's side all the while. Rumors were circulating that Garamendi could end up with a Washington appointment, possibly as the administration health-care czar. At the same time, Patti, after her loss in the state senate race and another defeat in a run for the Assembly, was taking a shot at Congress.

But things went sour for the would-be power couple. Clinton's strong lead in California was never threatened and he had no need to campaign. There went Garamendi's tag-along publicity. In campaigning against Proposition 166, a health-care initiative sponsored by the California Medical Association, Garamendi, without authorization, invoked Clinton's name a few times too many. Plus, Garamendi hit more turbulence with the Clinton people who threw in their lot with Democratic leaders backing another Democratic contender for governor, state Treasurer Kathleen Brown. There went the appointment. To top it off, Patti lost again.

Since taking the commissioner's post, Garamendi has waged a battle against the insurance industry in an effort to enforce Proposition 103. He has issued some tough regulations, stopped an insolvent state earthquake insurance program and tried to badger the Legislature into passing no-fault auto insurance and health-care reform.

As a consumer advocate, he has received good reviews. Yet his fortunes may be tied to his ability to do something, anything, about the festering problem of high auto insurance rates. Unfortunately, most of his initiatives have been tied up in the courts for months and months, and it could be years before some of the issues are resolved.

PERSONAL: elected 1990; born Jan. 24, 1945, in Camp Blanding, Fla.; home, Walnut Grove; Peace Corps; education, B.S. business UC Berkeley, M.B.A. Harvard University; wife, Patricia Wilkinson; children, Genet, John, Christina, Autumn, Merle and Ashley; Presbyterian.

CAREER: Banker and rancher; Assembly 1974-76; Senate 1976-1990.

OFFICES: San Francisco (415) 557-1126; Los Angeles (213) 736-2572; Sacramento (916) 322-3555.

Board of Equalization districts

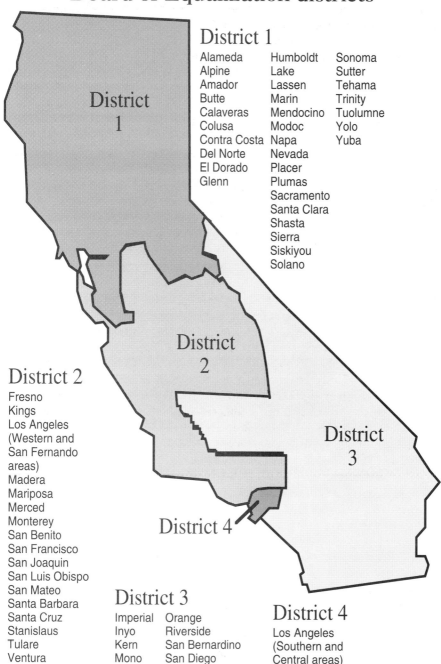

District 1

Alameda	Humboldt	Sonoma
Alpine	Lake	Sutter
Amador	Lassen	Tehama
Butte	Marin	Trinity
Calaveras	Mendocino	Tuolumne
Colusa	Modoc	Yolo
Contra Costa	Napa	Yuba
Del Norte	Nevada	
El Dorado	Placer	
Glenn	Plumas	
	Sacramento	
	Santa Clara	
	Shasta	
	Sierra	
	Siskiyou	
	Solano	

District 2

Fresno
Kings
Los Angeles
(Western and
San Fernando
areas)
Madera
Mariposa
Merced
Monterey
San Benito
San Francisco
San Joaquin
San Luis Obispo
San Mateo
Santa Barbara
Santa Cruz
Stanislaus
Tulare
Ventura

District 3

Imperial	Orange
Inyo	Riverside
Kern	San Bernardino
Mono	San Diego

District 4

Los Angeles
(Southern and
Central areas)

BOARD OF EQUALIZATION

The 1849 California Constitution advanced the notion that "taxation shall be equal and uniform throughout the state, and by 1879 the people made the Board of Equalization a constitutional agency to see to it. Today, the board boasts of its powers to affect virtually every aspect of commerce and government in California, including the taxes paid by more than 900,000 businesses, 300 private utilities and some 4.5 million homeowners.

Operating quasi-judicially, the board hears tax appeals and sets assessments on pipelines, flumes, canals, ditches, aqueducts, telephone lines and electrical systems – in a word, utilities. It acts in a quasi-legislative fashion to adopt rules, regulations and guidance for county tax assessors, and as an administrative body that determines capitalization rates, classifies properties, sets the electrical energy surcharge rate and administers taxes on sales, fuel, alcoholic beverages, cigarettes, insurance, timber, hazardous waste, telephone services and city, county and transit district sales and use taxes. The board collects more than $32 billion in taxes each year: some $25 billion for the state treasury and more than $7 billion in sales, use and property taxes for local government.

But the board frequently is called an anachronism, outmoded, outdated and outpaced by the events it governs. Proposals have been advanced to consolidate it with the Franchise Tax Board and create a tax commission with appointed members. None of the proposals, however, have gotten very far.

The board consists of state Controller Gray Davis and four members elected to four-year terms from districts so extensive that few of the electorate can be expected to know who their representative is. Each member represents one quarter of the state, or roughly 7.5 million people.

In the past, it has been a backwater, albeit a well-paid one, where members could expect to win re-election and serve comfortably until retirement. But in the 1980s, some board members began to demonstrate a bent toward using the job as a rung on the ladder to higher office. Some accepted political contributions from public utilities and other donors who later won favorable board consideration on tax appeals. The board also saw a serious and often publicly acrimonious split, usually pitting William Bennett, its senior member, against the other four. Bennett argued that the others were making tax decisions based on political considerations, often overruling staff recommendations. The board's reputation deteriorated further in 1990, when Bennett was indicted on 23 felony counts involving misuse of state expense accounts and credit cards. Bennett was able to plea-bargain the charges down to one misdemeanor count, and, citing his continuing recovery from emergency heart surgery, he resigned at the end of 1992.

Bennett was not the only board member with legal troubles. Member Paul Carpenter was convicted in September 1990 on political corruption charges stemming from previous service in the state Senate. He was sentenced to 12 years in prison, but an appeals court threw the conviction out and Carpenter was awaiting retrial in 1993. Voters, meanwhile, re-elected him despite his conviction, and he argued that he was entitled to remain on the board. He had himself sworn into office and offered to serve without pay while he appealed his case. State officials maintained, however, that the conviction made him ineligible to hold office, and Wilson appointed Los Angeles lawyer Matt Fong to the post.

Turmoil on the board, coupled with the political scandals involving Carpenter and other lawmakers, did have one productive result. The state Legislature passed a law prohibiting board members from voting on any issue involving someone who has given a campaign contribution of $250 or more in the last 12 months. That's a standard, needless to say, that legislators don't hold themselves to.

Vacant
1st District

William Bennett, the board's senior member, re-signed at the end of 1992, two years before his sixth term was to expire. Gov. Pete Wilson was expected to replace Democrat Bennett with a Republican, shifting the board's majority to the GOP.

Since the previous June, Bennett had been convalescing from heart surgery and hadn't attended hearings. But he'd been under a constant cloud since 1990, when he was accused of filing false expense claims with the state. In April 1991, he was charged with 23 felony counts, but eventually plea-bargained that down to one misdemeanor count to which he pled

William Bennett

no contest. He also paid $5,500 in restitution, a $1,500 fine, and agreed to perform 200 hours of community service. The two-member GOP minority on the board did its best to get him removed from office, but Bennett prevailed in court on a technicality – the misdemeanor was committed during a previous term.

Bennett began his sixth term on the board in 1991. First elected in 1970, he served his first term as chairman in 1972 and again from 1975 through 1983.

The board's first district consists of the following counties: Alameda, Alpine, Amador, Butte, Calaveras, Colusa, Contra Costa, Del Norte, El Dorado, Glenn, Humboldt, Lake, Lassen, Marin, Mendocino, Modoc, Napa, Nevada, Placer, Plumas, Sacramento, Santa Clara, Shasta, Sierra, Siskiyou, Solano, Sonoma, Sutter, Tehama, Trinity, Tuolumne, Yolo and Yuba.

Gray Davis
Member-at-Large

State Controller Gray Davis is a member-at-large of the board and declines to vote on tax matters relating to his campaign contributors. His biographical information appears earlier in this chapter.

Ernest J. Dronenburg Jr.
3rd District

Ernest Dronenburg Jr.

Ernest J. Dronenburg Jr. is a staunch defender of the board and the system it represents, arguing that citizens prefer elected rather than appointed tax officials. He was the chief architect of the Taxpayers' Bill of Rights, which the Legislature enacted in 1989 to give taxpayers better standing when appealing assessments to the board. It has been called the most significant reform in board operations in this century.

When he was elected in 1978, Dronenburg became the first Republican to sit on the board in 24 years. Previously, he had worked as an auditor and field audit supervisor in the board's business taxes department. In off-hours, he and two friends began and operated a racquetball equipment manufacturing and distribution firm in San Diego. He served as president of the manufacturing company and vice president of the distribution company until he resigned after his election to the board.

In the mid-1980s, Dronenburg became a director of Seapointe Savings & Loan, which became one of the nation's fastest and most spectacular S&L failures. When state and federal regulators seized it in May 1986, the S&L had been in business for only 13 months. It had never hired a loan officer and had lost $24 million gambling investors' money on bond futures. Dronenburg, nonetheless, has never suffered politically for the failure.

Active in Republican politics, Dronenburg also has been president of the Federation of Tax Administrators and an executive board member of the National Tax Association. He has been active in issues involving women, disabled people and his Christian faith. His wife, Kathy, is an appointed member of the state Board of Education. His district includes the counties of Imperial, Inyo, Kern, Mono, Orange, Riverside, San Bernardino and San Diego.

PERSONAL: elected 1978; born Aug. 9, 1943, in Washington, D.C.; home, East San Diego County; B.S. San Diego State University; wife, Kathy; three daughters.

CAREER: auditor and field audit supervisor, state Board of Equalization, 1971-1978, small businessman.

OFFICES: 110 West C St., Suite 1709, San Diego 92101 (619) 237-7844; 1020 N St., Sacramento 95814, (916) 445-5713.

Matthew K. Fong
4th District

Matthew K. Fong waged an unsuccessful campaign in 1990 for state controller, but soon thereafter was appointed by Gov. Pete Wilson to the Board of Equalization.

He was named to replace Paul Carpenter following the latter's conviction on corruption charges and subsequent removal from office.

Wilson, seeking to build bridges with the state's Asian-American community, had encouraged Fong to run for state controller in 1990 against incumbent Gray Davis. Fong's decision to do so created an unusual mother-son combination on the state ballot. Fong, a Republican, is the son of longtime Democratic Secretary of State March Fong Eu. His grandfather, who had a pharmacy in San Francisco's Chinatown, also was the first Chinese-American to work for the board. Fong says his grandfather was recruited by the board to explain its laws to the Chinese community and to collect their sales taxes.

Matthew Fong

Despite a negligible background in tax issues, Fong immediately became an activist on the board and quickly earned respect for working hard to master complex issues. His district includes the southern and central sections of Los Angeles County, including most of the city of Los Angeles and 74 other incorporated cities. Reapportionment, however, put both Fong and Democrat Brad Sherman in the same district. Since Fong's current district is heavily Democratic, he is expected to move into a largely inland district with no incumbent prior to the 1994 election.

Fate, however, may intervene. Rumors in early 1993 said that his mother was seeking a job with the new Clinton administration, perhaps as ambassador to a Far Eastern country. If she were to leave office, it's likely Gov. Wilson would appoint Matthew Fong to replace his mother. If not, Fong has expressed interest in running for treasurer in 1994 if Kathleen Brown leaves the job to challenge Gov. Pete Wilson.

PERSONAL: appointed 1990; born Nov. 20, 1953, in Oakland; home, Hacienda Heights; education, B.S. U.S. Air Force Academy, M.B.A. Pepperdine University, J.D. Southwestern University School of Law; wife, Paula; children, Matthew and Jade.

CAREER: attorney, 1985-present; U.S. Air Force (currently a major in the reserves).

OFFICES: 13200 Crossroads Parkway North, City of Industry, (310) 908-0524; 1020 N St., Sacramento 95814, (916) 445-4664.

Brad Sherman
2nd District

Brad Sherman is a tax lawyer and certified public accountant with a Harvard law degree who refers to himself as "a bit on the nerdish side." He won the Democratic nomination for the job in 1990 with an upset win over former Assemblyman Lou

Papan. Two months after Sherman was sworn in, the board's Democratic majority promoted him to chairman, replacing Ernest J. Dronenburg Jr., the first Republican chairman in decades.

Sherman ran as a political reformer, saying he wanted to "give people more confidence in the board and in the property-tax process." But one of his first actions as a board member was to put three of his campaign workers and a campaign aide to Democratic gubernatorial candidate Dianne Feinstein on the state payroll as his "transition" team.

Sherman, who served as a board member of California Common Cause during 1986-1989, is a party activist who estimates he has walked precincts, registered voters, stuffed envelopes and worked in other capacities in more than 40 campaigns in the last 20 years. He also worked as an intern for Secretary of State Jerry Brown in 1973.

Brad Sherman

He has proven to be the most activist board chairman in years, working hard on all the board's arcane tax issues and establishing a record for fairness.

Sherman's district includes the counties of Fresno, Kings, Madera, Mariposa, Merced, Monterey, San Benito, San Francisco, San Joaquin, San Luis Obispo, San Mateo, Santa Barbara, Santa Cruz, Stanislaus, Tulare, Ventura and the northern and western portions of Los Angeles County.

Reapportionment put both Sherman and GOP member Matthew Fong in the same Los Angeles district, which is heavily Democratic. If Fong stays on the board, it seems likely that before the 1994 election he'll move into a mostly inland district with no incumbent.

PERSONAL: elected 1990; born Oct. 24, 1954; education, B.A. University of California at Los Angeles, J.D. Harvard Law School; single.

CAREER: private practice in tax, business and estate law; certified public accountant.

OFFICES: 901 Wilshire Blvd, Suite 210, Santa Monica 90401; (310) 451-5777; 1020 N. St., Room 107, Sacramento 95814; (916) 445-4154.

4

The California judiciary

California voters' confirmation of the five state Supreme Court justices on the ballot in 1990 was notable for its complete lack of controversy. Just four years earlier, an electorate enraged by the court's failure to affirm death sentences had ousted three sitting justices – Chief Justice Rose Elizabeth Bird and Associate Justices Cruz Reynoso and Joseph Grodin. All had been appointed by former Democratic Gov. Jerry Brown and all were targets of demands by crime victims groups for swift executions.

"We need the death penalty. We don't need Rose Bird," Gov. George Deukmejian told audiences as he campaigned for re-election in 1986. Voters agreed, handing him the opportunity to replace the three liberal jurists with conservatives.

By the time Deukmejian left office in 1991, he had secured the sweeping impact on the state's judiciary that he had sought to exert when he became governor. As a state senator in 1978, Deukmejian had authored the law reinstating the death penalty. Later, as attorney general, he cited the governor's ability to appoint judges as his principal reason for wanting the job. Deukmejian had appointed a majority of the Supreme Court justices and about two-thirds of the roughly 1,500 sitting judges in lower courts by the end of his second four-year term in office. Most of his appointees were white males from prosecutorial backgrounds.

To fill the Supreme Court vacancies created by the 1986 election, Deukmejian selected three Court of Appeal justices – John Arguelles, David Eagleson and Marcus Kaufman. The governor elevated Associate Justice Malcolm Lucas, his former Long Beach law partner, to the chief justice's seat. All three of Deukmejian's new associate justices stayed scarcely long enough to fatten their pensions with the salary base provided by the state's top judicial post. They were replaced by Associate Justices Joyce Kennard, Marvin Baxter and Armand Arabian.

The ousted justices, meanwhile, did not go quietly. In the emotional campaign to remove Bird and the others, crime victims groups had argued that the justices were allowing their personal views against capital punishment to influence their interpretations of the law. Bird, who had been the subject of controversy since her 1977 appointment as the first woman on the court, herself aired television campaign ads, something previously unheard of in a Supreme Court election. She attacked Deukmejian for using the "politics of death" to advance his career.

In Grodin's first speech after removal from office, he argued that the political nature of the campaign had undermined the court's independence. Lucas, however, described the circumstances that led to Bird's departure and his elevation as "some very unusual times" and said the court would not preside over a "rush to death."

The court did enter a less controversial period. The Bird court had reversed all but a handful of the death penalty judgments it had reviewed, and the new justices moved quickly to begin affirming death sentences. The Lucas court has given more latitude to trial courts and has been less likely to reverse cases for what prosecutors had argued for years were inconsequential errors. During 1992, the court that Deukmejian reshaped affirmed 33 death penalties and reversed just two.

Although the death penalty was reinstated in 1978, legal challenges prevented anyone from being executed until convicted double murderer Robert Alton Harris died in San Quentin's gas chamber on April 21, 1992. Sentenced to death for the 1978 murders of two San Diego teenagers, Harris was the first person executed by the state in 25 years. The last had been police killer Aaron Mitchell in 1967.

While the justices demonstrated considerable independence on other matters – even to the point of reversing or refusing to hear cases favored by Deukmejian – gubernatorial candidates continued in 1990 to debate just how far they would go to determine the views of the judges they would appoint. Interpreting the 1986 elections as evidence that Californians wanted judges who agree with them on major political questions, Democrat Dianne Feinstein had promised to appoint a "pro-choice" Supreme Court. Republican Pete Wilson had argued that he would appoint judges who would apply the law as written, and that justices' personal views on abortion shouldn't matter.

The court in January 1992 sided with Wilson in the state's redistricting fight, as a six-member majority led by Lucas established legislative and congressional district lines that at the time seemed certain to level the political playing field for Republicans and undercut the Democrats' decadelong dominance. The new lines, however, provided little immediate benefit for the GOP as Democrats capitalized on Republican divisiveness and Bill Clinton's coattails to make an unexpectedly good showing in state races.

The chief justice earns $127,104 a year. The salary for associate justices is $121,207.

State Supreme Court Justices

303 Second Street, South Tower, San Francisco 94107; 415-396-9400.

Malcolm Millar Lucas

Lucas, the 26th chief justice of the court, was Gov. George Deukmejian's first appointee to the state Supreme Court in 1984. A longtime resident of Long Beach, Lucas practiced law there with Deukmejian from 1962 to 1967. He was then appointed by Gov. Ronald Reagan to the Los Angeles County Superior Court and was named by President Richard Nixon to the U.S. District Court in Los Angeles in 1971.

A native of Berkeley, Lucas earned both his undergraduate and law degrees from the University of Southern California. His great-grandfather was a two-term governor of Ohio and later the first territorial governor of Iowa.

Malcolm M. Lucas

PERSONAL: born April 19, 1927, in Berkeley; wife Joan Fisher; children, Gregory and Lisa.

CAREER: appointed by Gov. Deukmejian 1987; associate justice, state Supreme Court 1984-1987; U.S. District Court, Central District of California 1971-1984; Superior Court judge, Los Angeles County 1967-1971; private law practice 1954-1967.

Stanley Mosk

Mosk, who was state attorney general when Gov. Edmund G. "Pat" Brown named him to the court in 1964, was widely considered the front-runner to move up when Chief Justice Donald Wright retired in 1977. But Pat Brown's son, Gov. Jerry Brown, instead chose Rose Bird, a close friend and political ally with no prior judicial experience. The philosophically liberal Mosk had been one of four state Supreme Court justices originally targeted for defeat by conservative organizations. But crime victims groups ultimately opted not to pursue Mosk, and he is now the court's senior member and the only Democratic appointee. Mosk earned his bachelor's and doctorate

Stanley Mosk

of law degrees at the University of Chicago. Before his election as state attorney general, he served as a Los Angeles County Superior Court judge.

PERSONAL: born Sept. 4, 1912, in San Antonio, Texas; wife Edna Mitchell; son, Richard Mitchell.

CAREER: appointed by Gov. Pat Brown 1964; state attorney general 1959-1964; Superior Court judge, Los Angeles County 1943-1959; executive secretary to Gov. Culbert Olson 1939-1943; private law practice 1935-1939.

Ronald George

George, a conservative law-and-order judge who played a pivotal role in the celebrated "Hillside Strangler" case, was Gov. Pete Wilson's first appointee to the court. The seat became vacant when Justice Allen Broussard announced in early 1991 that he intended to retire, leaving court observers to speculate that he had grown lonely as the court's only African American and the only remaining appointee of Gov. Jerry Brown. Wilson's choice left the court without either an African American or Hispanic for the first time since 1977. Citing George's top rating from the State Bar commission that evaluates judicial nominees, Wilson said it would have been "dishonest

Ronald George

and unfair" to ignore that evidence and appoint a minority to the post.

Educated at Princeton University and Stanford University Law School, George was seen in Los Angeles legal circles as a brilliant and ambitious judge who had long coveted a seat on the state's highest court. As a Superior Court judge in 1981, he rejected a motion by then-Los Angeles County District Attorney John Van de Kamp to drop murder charges against "Hillside Strangler" suspect Angelo Buono. Van de Kamp later conceded his decision not to prosecute Buono for the murders of 10 women was a mistake; Buono ultimately was convicted on nine of 10 murder counts with George presiding at the trial.

PERSONAL: born March 11, 1940, in Los Angeles; wife Barbara George; sons Eric, Andrew and Christopher.

CAREER: appointed by Gov. Pete Wilson 1991; associate justice, 2nd District Court of Appeal 1987-1991; Los Angeles County Superior Court judge, 1977-1987; Los Angeles Municipal Court judge, 1972-1977; deputy state attorney general, 1965-1972.

Edward A. Panelli

A judicial moderate, Panelli was nominated by Gov. George Deukmejian to replace retired Supreme Court Justice Otto Kaus and won confirmation by the state's voters in the 1986 general election. Panelli was a Santa Clara County Superior Court judge for 11 years before joining the Court of Appeal in 1983. Before that, he practiced civil and criminal law in San Jose.

His bachelor's and law degrees are from the University of Santa Clara.

PERSONAL: born Nov. 23, 1931, in Santa Clara;

Edward A. Panelli

wife Lorna Mondora; children, Tom, Jeff and Michael.

CAREER: appointed by Gov. Deukmejian 1985; presiding justice, Court of Appeal, 6th Appellate District, 1984-1985; associate justice, Court of Appeal, 1st Appellate District, Division Four 1983-1984; Superior Court judge, Santa Clara County 1972-1983; general counsel, University of Santa Clara 1963-1972; private law practice 1955-1972.

Joyce Luther Kennard

Kennard is the first Asian-born nominee and second female justice in the court's history. She grew up in the Japanese-occupied Dutch East Indies, where she spent three years of her childhood in a Japanese internment camp. She has said she never "used a telephone or saw a television set" until she was 14. As a teenager she lost a leg to an infection. She attended high school in Holland, and at age 20 immigrated alone to the United States in 1961.

She became a naturalized citizen in 1967 in Los Angeles, where she eventually became a trial judge with a reputation as a tough sentencer. Appointed by Gov. George Deukmejian, she succeeded Associate Justice John A. Arguelles, who retired.

Joyce L. Kennard

She earned bachelor's and master's degrees in public administration and her law degree from the University of Southern California.

PERSONAL: born May 6, 1941, in West Java, Indonesia; husband Robert Kennard.

CAREER: appointed by Gov. Deukmejian 1989; Superior Court judge, Los Angeles County 1987-1989; Municipal Court judge, Los Angeles Judicial District 1986-1987; senior attorney for former Associate Justice Edwin F. Beach, Court of Appeal, 2nd Appellate District 1979-1986; deputy attorney general, California Department of Justice, Los Angeles 1975-1979.

Armand Arabian

Arabian, a longtime friend of Gov. George Deukmejian, was the first Armenian-American to be named to the court. Appointed to replace Associate Justice Marcus M. Kaufman, a Deukmejian appointee who served just three years, Arabian has pledged to remain in his job for at least eight years. An outspoken and conservative jurist who is a recreational parachutist in his leisure time, Arabian has won a reputation as a judicial maverick.

As a trial judge in a rape case, he once refused to give the jury the instruction, required at the time, that testimony of rape victims should be viewed skeptically. When the case reached the state Supreme Court, the justices chided Arabian for failing to comply with precedent. But they then ordered that the instruction be barred in all future cases. His action in that case, coupled with his extensive writings on rape law reform, won Arabian the strong backing of women attorneys at his confirmation hearing for the state's highest court.

He has law degrees from both the Southern California Law School and Boston University in addition to a bachelor's degree from BU.

PERSONAL: born December 12, 1934, in New York City; wife Nancy Megurian; children, Allison and Robert.

CAREER: appointed by Gov. Deukmejian 1990; associate justice, Court of Appeal, 2nd Appellate District, Division Three 1983-1990; Superior Court judge, Los Angeles County 1973-1983; Municipal Court judge, Los Angeles Judicial District 1972-1973; private law practice 1963-1972; deputy district attorney, Los Angeles County 1962-1963.

Armand Arabian

Marvin Ray Baxter

As appointments secretary to Gov. George Deukmejian, one of Baxter's chief responsibilities was recommending judges. As Deukmejian's second term drew to a close, Baxter became a nominee himself, accepting an appointment to the 5th District Court of Appeal in Fresno. In 1990, he became the second Armenian-American appointed to the state Supreme Court, replacing retiring Justice David Eagleson.

Baxter, who was co-chairman of Deukmejian's 1982 campaign for governor, grew up in a farming community outside Fresno. He has a bachelor's degree from Fresno State College and a law degree from Hastings College of Law.

Marvin Ray Baxter

PERSONAL: born January 9, 1940, in Fowler, Calif.; wife Jane Pippert; children, Laura and Brent.

CAREER: appointed by Gov. Deukmejian 1990; 5th District Court of Appeal 1988-1990, governor's appointments secretary 1983-1988; private law practice 1969-1983; deputy district attorney, Fresno County 1967-1969.

California Appellate Court Justices

Court of Appeal, 1st Appellate District, Division One, 303 Second Street, South Tower, San Francisco 94107; (415) 396-9666.

Presiding Justice Gary E. Strankman; Associate Justices Robert L. Dossee, William A. Newsom and William D. Stein.

Court of Appeal, 1st Appellate District, Division Two, 303 Second Street, South Tower, San Francisco 94107; (415) 396-9666.

Presiding Justice J. Anthony Kline; Associate Justices John E. Benson, Michael J. Phelan and Jerome A. Smith.

Court of Appeal, 1st Appellate District, Division Three, 303 Second Street, South Tower, San Francisco 94107 (415) 396-9666.

Presiding Justice Clinton W. White; Associate Justices Ming W. Chin, Robert W. Merrill and Kathryn Mickle Werdegar.

Court of Appeal, 1st Appellate District, Division Four, 303 Second Street, South Tower, San Francisco 94107; (415) 396-9666.

Presiding Justice Carl West Anderson; Associate Justices James F. Perley, Marcel Poche and Timothy A. Reardon.

Court of Appeal, 1st Appellate District, Division Five, 303 Second Street, South Tower, San Francisco 94107; (415) 396-9666.

Presiding Justice J. Clinton Peterson; Associate Justices Zerne P. Haning III and Donald B. King.

Court of Appeal, 2nd Appellate District, Division One, 300 South Spring Street, Los Angeles 90013; (213) 897-2307.

Presiding Justice Vaino H. Spencer; Associate Justices Rueben A. Ortega and Miriam A. Vogel.

Court of Appeal, 2nd Appellate District, Division Two, 300 South Spring Street, Los Angeles 90013; (213) 897-2307.

Presiding Justice Donald N. Gates; Associate Justices Morio L. Fukuto and Michael G. Nott.

Court of Appeal, 2nd Appellate District, Division Three, 300 South Spring Street, Los Angeles 90013; (213) 897-2307.

Presiding Justice Joan Dempsey Klein; Associate Justices H. Walter Croskey and Edward A. Hinz Jr.

Court of Appeal, 2nd Appellate District, Division Four, 300 South Spring

Street, Los Angeles 90013; (213) 897-2307.

Presiding Justice Arleigh Woods; Associate Justice Norman L. Epstein.

Court of Appeal, 2nd Appellate District, Division Five, 300 South Spring Street, Los Angeles 90013; (213) 897-2307.

Presiding Justice Paul A. Turner; Associate Justices Herbert L. Ashby, Roger W. Boren and Margaret M. Grignon.

Court of Appeal, 2nd Appellate District, Division Six, 1280 South Victoria, Room 201, Ventura 93003; (805) 654-4502.

Presiding Justice Steven J. Stone; Associate Justices Arthur Gilbert and Kenneth R. Yegan.

Court of Appeal, 2nd Appellate District, Division Seven, 300 South Spring Street, Los Angeles 90013; (213) 897-2307.

Presiding Justice Mildred L. Lillie; Associate Justices Earl Johnson Jr. and Fred Woods.

Court of Appeal, 3rd Appellate District, 914 Capitol Mall, Sacramento 95814; (916) 653-0310.

Presiding Justice Robert K. Puglia; Associate Justices Coleman A. Blease, Rodney Davis, George Nicholson, Vance W. Raye, Arthur G. Scotland, Richard M. Sims III and Keith F. Sparks.

Court of Appeal, 4th Appellate District, Division One, 750 B Street, Suite 500, San Diego 92101; (619) 237-6558.

Presiding Justice Daniel J. Kremer; Associate Justices Patricia D. Benke, Charles W. Froehlich Jr., Richard D. Huffman, Gilbert Nares, William L. Todd Jr., Howard B. Wiener and Don R. Work.

Court of Appeal, 4th Appellate District, Division Two, 303 West Fifth Street, San Bernardino 92401; (714) 383-4442.

Presiding Justice Manuel A. Ramirez; Associate Justices Howard M. Dabney, Thomas E. Hollenhorst, Art W. McKinster and Robert J. Timlin.

Court of Appeal, 4th Appellate District, Division Three, P.O. Box 1378, Santa Ana 92701; (714) 558-6779.

Presiding Justice David G. Sills; Associate Justices Thomas F. Crosby Jr., Henry T. Moore Jr., Sheila Prell Sonenshine and Edward J. Wallin.

Court of Appeal, 5th Appellate District, P.O. Box 45013, Fresno 93718; (209) 445-5491.

Presiding Justice Hollis G. Best; Associate Justices James A. Ardaiz, Tim S. Buckley, Nicholas J. Dibiaso, Thomas A. Harris, Robert L. Martin, William A. Stone, James F. Thaxter and Steven M. Vartabedian.

Court of Appeal, 6th Appellate District, 333 West Santa Clara Street, San Jose 95113; (408) 277-1004.

Presiding Justice Christopher C. Cottle; Associate Justices P. Bamattre-Manoukian, Walter P. Capaccioli, Franklin D. Elia and Eugene M. Premo.

5

The big bad bureaucracy

At 268,419 employees, the state bureaucracy that carries out the decrees of the governor and the Legislature still represents less than 1 percent of the state's population. There are, of course, another 250,000 county employees, hefty school district and special district payrolls and a substantial sprinkling of federal workers toiling at the countless chores that keep the state's people educated and healthy, its streets and workplaces safe and its commerce bustling. And behind all of them stands a virtual army of non-profit and profit-making entrepreneurs hired to undertake the state's pursuits — clinics, emergency rooms, hospitals, janitorial services, security specialists, mental health programs, drug treatment centers and a host of councils, commissions, think tanks and task forces.

Yet taken together, they hardly represent the threat to freedom or the drain on resources that some politicians like to portray. While bureaucrats may be wrapped in red tape and devoted to the evenhanded distribution of blame for their failings, their numbers are not overwhelming.

Nevertheless, the first task of any governor is to tame the previous administration's bureaucracy and to put those countless workers to his or her own use. The civil service system is designed to protect taxpayers against political exploitation of the work force, but a carefully tailored system of civil service exemptions and gubernatorial appointments gives the chief executive the authority he needs to take the reins of government in hand.

When Gov. Pete Wilson took office in 1991, for instance, he had approximately 550 exempt positions to fill in his executive offices and another 100 or so on state boards and commissions, roughly the same as his predecessor, George Deukmejian. In addition, governors can generally reshape the state's judiciary according to their views as appointments become available — in all a significant pool of patronage that becomes theirs to dispense.

Wilson, like almost all governors before him, has used his patronage power to find jobs for political supporters and former Republican officeholders who lost elections or decided not to seek re-election. Within days of his Nov. 6, 1991, victory, for example, Wilson named defeated Republican state Treasurer Thomas Hayes, a respected Capitol veteran, his director of finance. The Hayes appointment didn't raise many eyebrows but others have.

After Wilson's hand-picked successor in the U.S. Senate, Republican John Seymour, lost to former San Francisco Mayor Dianne Feinstein in November, 1992, Wilson appointed Seymour, a former state senator and a Realtor by trade, to a $98,076-a-year job as executive director of the state Housing Finance Agency, a small state office that provides loans to low- and moderate-income home buyers. About the same time, Wilson appointed former Republican state Sen. Ed Davis, who did not seek re-election to his Valencia-area Senate seat, to a part-time $25,500-a-year job on the Alcoholic Beverage Control Appeals Board. And he named former GOP Rep. John Rousselot, who lost his attempt in November to return to Congress, to a $76,872-a-year job on the state board of prison terms.

Wilson also came under fire for hiring two political consultants onto his gubernatorial staff despite the state's weakened fiscal condition. First, he hired veteran Republican political consultant Joe Shumate, who was given the title of deputy chief of staff and a $95,052-a-year salary. His job was primarily to figure out ways to elect more Republicans to the Legislature in 1992. Wilson's efforts were not successful. Even so, a little more than a month after Election Day, Wilson hired Joe Rodota, a 32-year-old Sacramento political consultant whose specialty is researching dirt on Democrats. Rodota was given the title of Cabinet secretary and a $94,813-a-year salary.

Wilson took office surrounded by an inner circle of loyalists as key advisers. He still leans heavily on his longtime chief of staff, Bob White, who served the governor during Wilson's eight years in the U.S. Senate and his 12 years as mayor of San Diego. But Wilson suffered a major loss both personally and professionally when his longtime communications director, Otto Bos, died unexpectedly in 1991.

WHITTLING AT THE BUREAUCRACY

The actual size of the state government work force is measured in "personnel-years," which represent the number of full-time positions or their equivalent. For example, a position that was filled only half of the year would represent 0.5 personnel-years, while three half-time jobs that were filled would represent 1.5 personnel-years. The concept sounds simple enough, but the politicians have been able to find ingenious ways to manipulate the numbers to their advantage.

In 1983, for example, the state work force stood at 228,489 personnel-years — a slight reduction from the year before. Although growth in the work force had been lagging behind the state's population growth for years — a product of the post-Proposition 13 budget crunch — and even behind the growth in state operational expenses, incoming Gov. George Deukmejian was determined to pare back the bureaucracy even more. His budget called for a reduction of 1,016 personnel-years, a half-percent cut. He wanted to achieve the cut while increasing the state's prison and juvenile corrections work force by 1,078 personnel-years. Critics would argue that the staff cutbacks represented reductions in service to the state's neediest people, the poor and unemployed. The administration insisted it was trimming fat, not muscle, and that services remained intact or even improved. In the succeeding years, Deukmejian proposed cutback after cutback in state personnel, all the while balancing the reductions with increases for the growing correctional system. As the state's population continued to balloon, the work force as measured as a ratio of employees per 1,000 residents declined.

Wilson has continued efforts to cut the ratio of employees per 1,000 residents. While total state employment in 1992-93 is up by 40,000 from 10 years ago, the ratio of employees per 1,000 residents declined from 9.2 to 8.6 over the same time. In his budget proposal for the 1993-94 fiscal year, Wilson proposed chopping the ratio to 8.4 employees per 1,000 residents. In fact, Wilson has proposed eliminating several agencies — the Franchise Tax Board, State Allocation Board, the Department of Savings and Loan, the California Energy Commission, the State Lands Commission, the Agricultural Labor Relations Board, the Commission on State Finance and district agricultural associations. While some may ultimately feel the

THE STATE WORK FORCE

Year	Governor	Employees	Employees per 1,000 population
1976-77	Brown	213,795	9.7
1977-78	Brown	221,251	9.9
1978-79	Brown	218,530	9.6
1979-80	Brown	220,193	9.5
1980-81	Brown	225,567	9.5
1981-82	Brown	228,813	9.4
1982-83	Transition	228,489	9.2
1983-84	Deukmejian	226,695	9.0
1984-85	Deukmejian	229,845	8.9
1985-86	Deukmejian	229,641	8.7
1986-87	Deukmejian	232,927	8.6
1987-88	Deukmejian	237,761	8.6
1988-89	Deukmejian	248,173	8.8
1989-90	Deukmejian	254,589	8.8
1990-91	Transition	260,622	8.7
1991-92	Wilson	261,713	8.5
1992-93	Wilson	268,419	8.6
1993-94	Wilson	269,221 (est.)	8.4 (est.)

budget ax, it is likely that the Legislature and Wilson will agree to spare many of the agencies before the budget battle is over in 1993.

It is his appointment power that allowed Wilson to strongly suggest to his top appointees that they voluntarily take a 5 percent pay cut in the midst of the state's budget woes in 1991. Wilson himself took the voluntary cut. But the days have long since passed when state employees depended upon the largess of the governor and the Legislature to increase their pay or improve their benefits. Under the Ralph C. Dills Act of 1977, the administration now negotiates memorandums of understanding on working conditions and wages with 21 recognized bargaining units, represented by 12 employee associations. The MOUs are legal contracts that may remain

BARGAINING AGENTS AND BARGAINING UNITS

Union	Number of employees represented
California State Employees' Association	
Administrative, financial and staff services	27,037
Education and library	1,836
Office and allied	30,231
Professional scientific	2,061
Printing trades	619
Custodial and services	4,286
Registered nurses	2,308
Medical and social services support	1,294
Misc. educational, maritime, library, consultants	493
Association of California State Attorneys	
(attorneys and hearing officers)	2,206
California Association of Highway Patrolmen	5,191
California Correctional Peace Officers Assn.	16,365
California Union of Safety Employees	5,340
California Department of Forestry Employees	
Association (firefighters)	3,186
Professional Engineers in California Government	6,796
California Association of Professional Scientists	1,575
International Union of Operating Engineers	
(stationary engineers)	637
(craft and maintenance)	9,521
Union of American Physicians and Dentists	1,009
California Association of Psychiatric Technicians	6,796
American Federation of State, County and Municipal Employees	
(health and social services, professional)	3,049

in force for as long as three years.

In 1993, Wilson was still asking his appointees voluntarily to continue their 5 percent salary reduction. But unlike previous years, Wilson did not propose any salary or benefit reductions for state workers in his 1993-94 budget. All but one of the state's 21 unions, which represent 136,122 workers, have signed contracts running through 1994, and the proposed Wilson budget contained a 5 percent pay increase for state workers as of Jan. 1, 1994. For most, that will be their first pay raise in three years.

AFFIRMATIVE ACTION IN STATE SERVICE

Deukmejian made progress toward hiring minorities and females in numbers approaching their proportions in society at large. By the end of 1988, the State Personnel Board reported that the labor force overall either met or exceeded the 1980 parity standards for African Americans, Asians, Filipinos and Pacific Islanders. Other minorities had not achieved occupational parity. The board also found women significantly underrepresented in all occupations except clerical work. A 1992 study by the Senate Office of Research indicated that Latinos in particular continued to lag behind in state employment. Not only have they not reached parity in numbers, but as a group Latinos continue to receive the lowest level of pay.

California's bureaucracy includes everything from the Abrasive Blasting Advisory Committee to the Yuba-Sutter Fair Board, although some of the more obscure boards may soon disappear, casualties of the 1993 version of the budget battle. There are commissions on the status of women, government efficiency, water and heritage preservation, councils on the arts and job training, and offices for small business, tourism and community relations. The most significant offices, however, fall under the nine umbrella agencies and departments whose leaders comprise the governor's Cabinet.

BUSINESS, TRANSPORTATION, HOUSING AGENCY

This superagency oversees 13 departments dealing with housing, business and regulatory functions and transportation, including the California Highway Patrol, the state Department of Transportation (Caltrans) and the Department of Motor Vehicles. The agency employs more than 40,000 workers and has a total budget of nearly $6 billion.

For most of Gov. Pete Wilson's first years in office, the agency's secretary was an old friend, Carl D. Covitz. A Republican, Covitz was the founder, owner and president of Landmark Communities Inc. of Beverly Hills, a national real estate investment company. His contact with Wilson extends back to the governor's days as San Diego mayor, when Covitz belonged to the Young Presidents Organization.

From 1987 to 1989, Covitz was undersecretary for the U.S. Department of Housing and Urban Development, a period during which HUD officials were accused of offering grants to former HUD officials or their clients or to projects endorsed by prominent Republicans. Covitz himself was never implicated.

But while in state service, Covitz came under a cloud that he could not escape. He resigned in December 1992 while under investigation for misusing his office. He was accused of lavish spending, treating state employees like servants and of using California Highway Patrol officers and pilots as personal chauffeurs. He also allegedly ran up huge phone and Federal Express bills for personal business.

In early January 1993, Wilson named Covitz's successor, Thomas Sayles, a low-profile member of the administration who had served as commissioner

Thomas Sayles

of the state Department of Corporations since 1991. He has also headed the state's revitalization task force in Los Angeles since June 1992.

Before joining the administration, Sayles was the senior counsel for TRW's Space and Technology Group, a supplier of military and commercial space systems. He also is a former assistant attorney in the U.S. attorney's office and served as a deputy attorney general. Salary: $106,410; Office: 801 K St., Room 1918, Sacramento 95814; (916) 323-5400; Employees: 40,959; Fiscal '91-'92 budget: $5.7 billion (including federal funds mostly for transportation).

Department of Alcoholic Beverage Control

Licenses and regulates the manufacture, sale, purchase, possession and transportation of alcoholic beverages within the state. Director: Jay R. Stroh, Deukmejian holdover; Salary: $99,805; Office: 1901 Broadway, Sacramento 95818; (916) 445-3221; Employees: 342; '92-'93 budget: $24,065,000.

State Banking Department

Protects the public against financial loss from the failure of state-chartered banks and trust companies, including foreign banking corporations, money order or traveler's check issuers and business and industrial development corporations. Superintendent: James Gilleran; Salary: $99,805; Office: 111 Pine St., Suite 1100, San Francisco 94111; (415) 557-3535; Employees: 206; '92-'93 budget: $16,053,000.

Department of Corporations

Regulates the sale of securities, licenses brokers and agents, and oversees franchises, various financial institutions and health plans. Also controls the solicitation, marketing and sale of securities, oversees companies that lend money or receive funds from the public, and deters unscrupulous or unfair promotional schemes. Commissioner: vacant; Salary: $99,805; Office: 1107 Ninth St., 8th Floor, Sacramento 95814; (916) 324-9011; Employees: 408; '92-'93 budget: $26,488,000.

Department of Housing and Community Development

Guides and supports public and private sector efforts to provide decent homes for every Californian, administers low-income housing programs, administers standards for manufactured homes and manages the state's Proposition 77 and Proposition 84 bonded earthquake safety and homeless housing programs. Director: Tim Coyle; Salary: $99,805; Office: 1800 Third St., Suite 450, Sacramento 95814; (916) 445-4775; Employees: 721; '92-'93 budget: $192,839,000.

Department of Real Estate

Licenses real estate agents and developers, protects the public in offerings of subdivided property and investigates complaints. Commissioner: Clark Wallace; Salary: $99,805; Office: 2201 Broadway, P.O. Box 187000, Sacramento 95818; (916) 739-3600; Employees: 387; '92-'93 budget: $26,798,000.

Office of Savings and Loan

Protects the $96 billion in funds deposited in savings accounts held in state associations to ensure the saving and borrowing public is properly and legally served and to prevent conditions or practices that would threaten the safety or solvency of the institutions or be detrimental to the public. Commissioner: Wallace Sumimoto, interim commissioner; Salary: $99,805; Office: 3460 Wilshire Blvd., 300, Los Angeles 90010-2200; (213) 736-2791; Employees: 43; '92-'93 budget: $4,263,000.

California Department of Transportation (Caltrans)

Builds, maintains and rehabilitates roads and bridges in accord with the State Transportation Improvement Program, manages airport and heliport safety and access, helps small- and medium-sized communities obtain and maintain air service, regulates airport noise, helps local governments provide public transportation and analyzes transportation questions. Director: James W. van Loben Sels; Salary: $99,805; Office: 1120 N St., Sacramento 95814; (916) 654-5267; Employees: 19,550; '92-'93 budget: $5.8 billion.

California Highway Patrol

Patrols state highways to ensure the safe, convenient and efficient transportation of people and goods, monitors school bus and farm labor transportation safety and oversees the transportation of hazardous wastes. Commissioner: M.J. Hannigan; Salary: $106,410; Office: 2555 First Ave., P.O. Box 942898, Sacramento 94298-0001; (916) 657-7152; Employees: 8,586; '92-'93 budget: $593,760,000.

Department of Motor Vehicles

Registers vehicles and vessels, issues and regulates driver's licenses and oversees the manufacture, delivery and disposal of vehicles. Director: Frank Zolin; Salary: $99,805; Office: 2415 First Ave., Sacramento 95818; (916) 657-7677; Employees: 8,551; '92-'93 budget: $486,376,000.

Housing Finance Agency

Provides assistance to low- and moderate-income home buyers through the sale of tax-exempt bonds. Director: John Seymour; Salary: $98,706; Office: 1121 L St., 7th floor, Sacramento 95814; (916) 324-4638; Employees: 134; '92-'93 budget: $10,308,000.

TRADE AND COMMERCE AGENCY

This agency, whose director is a Cabinet-level appointee, was created in 1992 through legislation authored by retired state Sen. Rose Ann Vuich, D-Dinuba, and signed by Gov. Wilson.

The new agency basically took over and expanded the duties of the former Department of Commerce. It is the primary agency that promotes business development and job creation and retention to improve the state's business climate. The department also serves as the lead for developing and overseeing the state's international trade efforts. The World Trade Commission and international trade offices fall under the jurisdiction of this agency.

Julie Meier Wright

Agency Secretary Julie Meier Wright served in Wilson's 1990 gubernatorial campaign as statewide chairwoman of "Pro-Wilson '90," a women's coalition supporting his candidacy against now U.S. Sen. Dianne Feinstein. Prior to being appointed director of commerce in 1991, Wright worked for TRW Inc. in Redondo Beach as director of public relations for the company's space and defense sector.

In early 1993, Wright and Environmental Protection Agency Secretary James Strock announced a joint effort to help companies develop markets for products aimed at making businesses more efficient and cleaner. It's that kind of approach the administration hopes to capitalize on despite complaints by businesses that the state's regulations are driving them elsewhere. In an effort to help businesses, Wright has promoted what she calls a "Red Team" approach to bring the government and private sectors together to try to encourage business expansion.

Salary: $106,410 ; Office: 1121 L St., Suite 600, Sacramento 95814; (916) 322-1394; Employees: 184; '92-'93 budget: $41,424,000.

DEPARTMENT OF FOOD AND AGRICULTURE

This is one of three superdepartments whose directors (food, finance and industrial relations) are in the governor's Cabinet. This department is responsible for regulating — some would say protecting — California's food industry, governing everything from pesticide registration and enforcement to raw milk inspections. Other duties include weights and measures enforcement, protecting farm workers, keeping foreign insects and weeds out of the state or eradicating them, maintaining plant inspection stations, checking the safety of meat and poultry, predatory animal control, animal health programs and livestock drug controls, and marketing, statistical and laboratory services for agriculture.

Director Henry Voss was appointed by Gov. George Deukmejian on May 1, 1989, after serving seven years as the chairman of the California Farm Bureau Federation. By the following March, the department was bogged down in an aerial spraying attack against a stubborn Mediterranean fruit fly infestation in the Los Angeles area. With an angry Los Angeles delegation of state senators opposing

Henry Voss

him, Voss barely won confirmation on a 22-7 vote, just one vote more than needed in the 40-member Senate. In spite of the Medfly controversy, Gov. Wilson extended Voss' appointment on Dec. 3, 1990. To appease critics Wilson gave responsibility for monitoring and regulating pesticides to a new California Environmental Protection Agency. With that, the conflict of interest, in which the Department of Food and Agriculture was responsible both for promoting agribusiness and regulating key elements of its safety, was ended.

A farmer's son born in San Jose in 1932, Voss was forced by urbanization to move to Stanislaus County, where the Voss family currently owns 500 acres of peaches, prunes, walnuts and almonds near Ceres. Voss is a specialist in agricultural marketing and has led trade missions on behalf of California agriculture to Europe, Japan, Southeast Asia and Israel. In 1986, he was appointed by President Reagan to the national Commission on Agriculture and Rural Development, a blue-ribbon panel set up to assess the 1985 farm bill. Upon Gov. Deukmejian's recommendation, he was named by U.S. Senate Republican leader Bob Dole to the Commission on Agricultural Workers. He is a member of Sunsweet Growers, Blue Diamond Almond Growers and Tri-Valley Growers, three of the state's leading agricultural cooperatives, and is a past president of the Apricot Producers of California and past chairman of the California Apricot Advisory Board. Salary: $106,410; Office: 1220 N St., Sacramento 95814; (916) 654-0433; Employees: 1,665; '92-'93 budget: $179,449,000.

DEPARTMENT OF FINANCE

The Department of Finance serves as the governor's chief fiscal policy agency, prepares the governor's January budget proposal and his annual May budget revision, reviews all state spending practices and proposals, administers the state budget after it has been adopted and signed, monitors all legislation that has fiscal implications for the state and recommends which bills and budget provisions should be adopted or vetoed. The department also conducts research, produces revenue estimates, analyzes tax policy and tracks population changes.

The director, Thomas Hayes, was appointed Nov. 20, 1990, after his narrow defeat by Kathleen Brown in the election for the office of state treasurer. Born in New York, Hayes moved to California with his Air Force father. Hayes is a Marine veteran who holds the Navy commendation medal for Vietnam service. He earned a master's degree in business from San Jose State University after leaving the military. He worked in the U.S. General Accounting Office before joining the California Legislative Analyst's Office in 1977. He moved to the Auditor General's staff as an assis-

Thomas Hayes

tant auditor general in 1977 and became the auditor general in 1979. In all that time, Hayes remained politically neutral, but he re-registered as a Republican in 1988 when Gov. George Deukmejian tapped him to replace Treasurer Jesse Unruh, who died in August 1987.

As finance director, Hayes develops and manages the state's $51 billion budget and serves on more than 60 authorities, boards and commissions. Salary: $106,410; Office: State Capitol, Room 1145, Sacramento 95814; (916) 445-4141; Employees: 326; '92-'93 budget: $27,210,000.

DEPARTMENT OF INDUSTRIAL RELATIONS

The Department of Industrial Relations is responsible for enforcing California's occupational safety and health laws, administering the compulsory workers' compensation insurance law, adjudicating workers' compensation claims, negotiating in threatened strikes, enforcing laws and promulgating rules on wages, hours and conditions of employment, and analyzing and disseminating statistics on labor conditions. Director: Lloyd Aubry; Salary: $106,410; Office: 1121 L St., Suite 307, Sacramento 95814; (916) 324-4163 or San Francisco office (415) 703-4590; Employees: 2,345; '92-'93 budget: $173,968,000.

HEALTH AND WELFARE AGENCY

This superagency, which covers 11 state departments, administers the state's health, welfare, employment and rehabilitation programs serving people who are poor, mentally ill, developmentally disabled, elderly, unemployed or who have alcohol and drug addiction problems. The agency also administers Proposition 65, the Safe Drinking Water and Toxics Enforcement Act of 1986; is the state's lead agency in administering the Immigration Reform and Control Act of 1986; and manages the state's emergency medical services program. Five departments within the agency oversee long-term care services in residential and institutional settings for the aging, disabled, mentally ill and other needy citizens. Director: Russell Gould; Salary: $106,410; Office: 1600 Ninth St. Room 460, Sacramento 95814; (916) 654-3454; Employees: 37,694; '92-'93 budget: $29.2 billion (including both state and federal funds and local assistance).

Office of Statewide Health Planning and Development

Responsible for developing a statewide plan for health facilities, ensuring construction plans for health facilities conform to state building codes, maintaining a uniform system of accounting and disclosure for health facility costs and ensuring available federal and state assistance is provided to develop needed facilities. Director: Dr. David Werdegar; Salary: $99,805; Office: 1600 Ninth St., 433, Sacramento 95814; (916) 654-1606; Employees: 360; '92-'93 budget: $36,037,000.

Department of Aging

State focal point for federal, state and local agencies that serve more than 4 million elderly Californians, working through 33 Area Agencies on Aging. The agencies manage programs that provide meals, social services and health-insurance counseling and act as advocates for senior citizen issues. The department also manages the state's adult day health care centers, the Alzheimer's Day Care Resource Centers and the multipurpose senior services program, an experimental effort to keep the frail elderly from being unnecessarily admitted to skilled nursing homes or intermediate care facilities. Director: Robert P. Martinez; Salary: $88,062; Office: 1600 K St., 4th floor, Sacramento 95814; (916) 322-5290; Employees: 144; '92-'93 budget: $137,562,000.

Department of Alcohol and Drug Programs

Coordinates planning and development of a statewide alcohol and drug abuse prevention, intervention, detoxification, recovery and treatment system, serving 300,000 Californians largely through programs operated by counties. The department is responsible for licensing the state's methadone treatment programs, multiple-offender drinking driver programs and alcoholism recovery facilities. In addition, the department manages programs aimed at alcohol and drug abuse prevention, particularly among youth, women, the disabled, ethnic minorities and the elderly. The department expects to receive an increase of $22.5 million from the federal Alcohol, Drug Abuse and Mental Health Administration. Director: Andrew Mecca; Salary: $99,805; Office: 1700 K St., 5th floor, Sacramento 95814; (916) 445-1943; Employees: 303; '92-'93 budget: $334,512,000.

Department of Health Services

Manages 11 health programs including the state's $11.4 billion Medi-Cal program (serving an average of 4.3 million people monthly), the Office of AIDS and the Family Planning program. The department is in charge of preventive medical services, public water supplies, toxic substance control, environmental health, epidemiologic studies, rural and community health, radiologic health, maternal and child health and the early detection of genetic disease and birth defects in newborns. The Food and Drug Program seeks to protect consumers from adulterated, mis-branded or falsely advertised foods, drugs, medical devices, hazardous household products and cosmetics and to control botulism in canned products. A licensing office regulates care in some 6,000 public and private health facilities, clinics and agencies. Director: Dr. Molly Joel Coye; Salary: $99,805; Office: 744 P St., 1253, Sacramento 95814; (916) 445-1248; Employees: 4,601; '92-'93 budget: $15.3 billion.

Department of Developmental Services

Coordinates services under the Lanterman Developmental Disabilities Services Act of 1977 for people with developmental disabilities, such as mental retardation, autism or cerebral palsy, to meet their needs at each stage of their lives through individual plans for treatment within their home communities where possible. The department provides 24-hour care for more than 6,000 severely disabled clients through seven state developmental hospitals (Agnews, Camarillo, Fairview, Lanterman, Porterville, Sonoma and Stockton) and indirect care for clients through a statewide network of private, nonprofit regional centers. Director: Dennis Amundson; Salary: $99,805; Office: 1600 Ninth St., 240, Sacramento 95814; (916) 654-1897; Employees: 11,044; '92-'93 budget: $1.275 billion.

Department of Mental Health

Administers the Lanterman-Petris-Short Act, the Bronzan-McCorquodale Act and other federal and state statutes governing services to the mentally ill through county and community nonprofit agencies and through the direct operation of the Atascadero, Metropolitan, Napa and Patton state hospitals and treatment programs for 600 clients at the Department of Developmental Services' Camarillo State Hospital. Services to the mentally ill include community education and consulta-tion, crisis evaluation and emergency care, 24-hour acute care, 24-hour residential treatment, day-care treatment, outpatient care, case management and socialization. The department also manages special programs for the homeless mentally ill, for mental illness associated with AIDS and other special categories. Gov. Wilson shifted responsibility for community mental health treatment to the counties (with a new revenue source) in 1991-92 for a state savings of $432 million. Director: vacant; Salary: $99,805; Office: 1600 Ninth St., 151, Sacramento 95814; (916) 654-2309; Employees: 7,064; '92-'93 budget: $716,119,000.

Employment Development Department

Assists employers in finding workers and workers in finding jobs through a statewide database, manages the unemployment insurance program, collects pay-roll taxes that support worker benefit programs, provides economic and labor market data and administers the Job Training Partnership Act. Under federal guidance, the department manages field offices that provide job placement, employment counseling, vocational testing, workshops and referral services, targeted at groups such as veterans, older workers, the disabled, youth, minorities, welfare families and migrant and seasonal farm workers. Director: Thomas Nagle; Salary: $99,805; Office: 800 Capitol Mall, 5000, Sacramento 95814; (916) 654-8210; Employees: 13,491; '92-'93 budget: $9.2 billion.

Department of Rehabilitation

Helps rehabilitate and find employment for people with mental and physical handicaps. Director: Bill Tainter; Salary: $99,805; Office: 830 K St., 322, Sacramento 95814; (916) 445-3971; Employees: 1,893; '92-'93 budget: $291,403,000.

Department of Social Services

Administers the state's $7.7 billion welfare program for poor children, disabled and elderly residents; provides or manages social services, community care licensing and inspections, disability evaluations, refugee assistance and adoption services; manages the federal food stamp program; regulates group homes, nurseries, preschools, foster homes, halfway houses and day-care centers; administers programs designed to protect children, the disabled and the elderly from abuse or neglect, and manages the state's Greater Avenues for Independence (GAIN) workfare program. Director: Eloise Anderson; Salary: $99,805; Office: 744 P St., 1740, Sacramento 95814; (916) 657-3661; Employees: 4,049; '92-'93 budget: $11.45 billion.

CALIFORNIA ENVIRONMENTAL PROTECTION AGENCY

Gov. Pete Wilson has said he plans to "take charge of California's environment in the 1990s." To that end, Wilson called James Strock, a veteran from the U.S. Environmental Protection Agency, to his side in California. Strock, an environmental lawyer and award-winning author, is California's third secretary for the environment.

Strock has received mixed reviews from competing interests. He has overseen the transfer of the regulation of pesticides from the Department of Food and Agriculture as Wilson pledged, but farm worker and environmental advocates say he has been slow to force chemical manufacturers to comply with disclosure laws. He faced opposition from those groups during his Senate confirmation hearings.

James Strock

As secretary, Strock oversees the operations of the Air Resources Board, California Integrated Waste Management Board, Department of Pesticide Regulation, State Water Resources Control Board, Department of Toxic Substances Control and the Office of Environmental Health Hazard Assessment. Salary:

$106,410. Office: 555 Capitol Mall, Suite 235, Sacramento 95814; (916) 445-3846; Employees: 27; '92-'93 budget: $3,486,000.

Air Resources Board

Holds the primary responsibility for California air quality, including the establishment of clean air standards, research into air pollution, emissions enforcement and smog limitations on automobiles and industries. Chairwoman: Jananne Sharpless (who had been Gov. George Deukmejian's Cabinet secretary for environmental affairs); Salary: $106,410; Members: San Diego County Supervisor Brian Bilbray; Petaluma Mayor Patricia Hilligoss; Orange County Supervisor Harriett Wieder; Eugene Boston, M.D.; Betty Ichikawa; San Bernardino County Supervisor Barbara Riordan; Dr. Andrew Wortman; Robert Lagarias of San Francisco. Members' compensation: $29,354; Office: 2020 L St., Sacramento 95814; (916) 322-2990; Employees: 880; '92-'93 budget: $100,166,000.

State Water Resources Control Board

Regulatory agency with responsibility for administering and granting water rights, maintaining state water quality through monitoring and waste discharge permits, managing toxic cleanups and administering grants for waste treatment facilities. Chairman: vacant; Salary: $95,403; Members: Eliseo Samaniego, John Caffrey, James Stubchaer and Marc Del Piero. Salaries: $92,465; Office 901 P St. 4th floor, Sacramento 95814; (916) 657-0941; Employees: 1,387; budget '92-'93: $414,358,000.

California Integrated Waste Management Board

Responsible for promoting waste reduction, recycling and composting, including environmentally safe transformation of wastes into harmless or useful products or land disposal. Manages landfills through local agencies and administers the California Tire Recycling Act of 1989 to reduce the number of used tires in landfills. Chairman: Michael Frost; Members: Wesley Chesbro of Sacramento, Sam Egigian of La Habra, Jesse Huff of Fair Oaks, Kathy Neal of Oakland and Paul Relis of Santa Barbara; Salaries: $95,403; Office: 8800 Cal Center Dr., Sacramento 95826; (916) 255-2200; Employees: 409; '92-'93 budget: $69,717,000.

Department of Pesticide Regulation

The duties of this relatively new department had previously been in the state Department of Food and Agriculture. For years, the old arrangement had prompted charges that the agriculture department was too cozy with agribusiness to monitor the use of pesticides. All pesticide regulation, from registration and use, to enforcement of pesticide laws, falls under the jurisdiction of this department. Director: James Wells; Salary: $99,805; Office: 1220 N St., A-414, Sacramento 95814; (916) 654-0551; Employees: 362; '92-'93 budget: $44,063,000.

YOUTH AND ADULT CORRECTIONAL AGENCY

This superagency oversees the Department of Corrections and the Youth Authority, which are responsible for the control, care and treatment of convicted felons and civilly committed addicts, and the confinement and rehabilitation of juvenile delinquents. The agency employs some 37,000 workers and has an annual budget of $3 billion.

The agency managed the biggest prison and prison camp construction program in the world during Gov. George Deukmejian's years, although the inmate population continues to grow more quickly than prisons can be built. By February 1991, the state prison system housed 98,137 inmates and the Youth Authority had more than 8,000 wards.

Joe Sandoval

The agency also manages state parole programs, which are being severely cut back, and oversees the state Board of Corrections, the Youthful Offender Parole Board and the Board of Prison Terms. The agency considers itself the largest law enforcement organization in the United States.

Secretary Joe Sandoval was appointed on Oct. 12, 1988, having been Gov. Deukmejian's chief of the California State Police, and was reappointed Feb. 25, 1991, by Gov. Pete Wilson. Sandoval is a veteran of 26 years with the Los Angeles Police Department. He was the primary law enforcement officer at the University of Southern California athletes village for the 1984 Olympics. His last assignment in Los Angeles was commander of some 235 officers in the Hollenbeck area, a community of 300,000. Salary: $106,410; Office: 1100 11th St., 400, Sacramento 95814; (916) 323-6001.

Department of Corrections

Manages 21 correctional facilities including eight reception centers. The department also manages parole programs, prison camps and a community correctional program designed to reintegrate released offenders to society. Director: James H. Gomez; Salary: $99,805; Office: 1515 S St., 351, Sacramento 95814; (916) 445-7682; Employees: 31,578; '92-'93 budget: $2.567 billion.

Youth Authority

Provides programs in institutions and the community to reduce delinquent behavior, help local agencies fight juvenile crime and encourage delinquency prevention programs. The department operates reception centers and clinics as well as 18 conservation camps and institutions for males and females throughout the state. Director: William Kolender; Salary: $99,805; Office: 4241 Williamsbourgh Dr., Sacramento 95823; (916) 262-1468; Employees: 5,036; '92-'93 budget: $362,716,000.

RESOURCES AGENCY

This superagency is responsible for departments and programs that manage the state's air, water and land resources and wildlife. The main departments are Forestry and Fire Protection, Parks and Recreation, Conservation, Fish and Game, Boating and Waterways, the Conservation Corps and the Department of Water Resources, which among its many duties includes the state's Drought Center (and, on occasion, its Flood Center). The agency also oversees or provides backup for the Tahoe Regional Planning Agency, the Wildlife Conservation Board, the Santa Monica Mountains Conservancy, the state Coastal Conservancy, the San Francisco Bay Conservation and Development Commission, the Colorado River

Douglas Wheeler

Board of California and the environmental license plate fund. It has some 16,000 employees and an annual budget of nearly $2.5 billion.

Keeping his pledge to bring "an environmental ethic" to state government, Gov. Pete Wilson chose Douglas P. Wheeler, 48, vice-president of the World Wildlife Fund and Conservation Foundation, to be his secretary for resources. Wheeler was appointed on Dec, 26, 1990, to replace outgoing Secretary Gordon Van Vleck, the cattleman who managed state resources throughout former Gov. George Deukmejian's two terms.

Wheeler has held positions in the U.S. Department of Interior, the American Farmland Trust, the National Trust for Historic Preservation and the Sierra Club, where he was executive director in 1985-86. (He left the position amicably, deciding he was not the activist that the Sierra Club seemed to want.)

Wheeler inherited a troubled agency. The departments of Fish and Game, and Parks and Recreation had suffered some of the most intense budget difficulties of any state agency. Fish and Game was beset by management scandals. The Coastal Commission, after years of Deukmejian budget cuts, was under attack for not protecting the coastline. Environmentalists were turning to the initiative, with varying success, to protect state forests and wildlife and to launch aggressive mass transit programs. Salary: $106,410; Office: 1416 Ninth St., Room 1311, Sacramento 95814; (916) 653-5656.

California Conservation Corps

A work force of some 2,000 young men and women that performs nearly 3 million hours of conservation work each year, including flood patrol, fire restoration, tree planting, stream clearance, trail building, park maintenance, landscaping, home weatherization and wildlife habitat restoration. Director: Al Aramburu;

Salary: $88,062; Office: 1530 Capitol Ave., Sacramento 95814; (916) 445-0307; Employees: 398; '92-'93 budget: $50,276,000.

Department of Conservation

Promotes the development and management of the state's land, energy, mineral and farmland resources, and disseminates information on geology, seismology, mineral, geothermal and petroleum resources, agricultural and open-space land, and container recycling and litter reduction. Director: Ed Heidig; Salary: $88,062; Office: 801 K St., 24th floor, Sacramento 95814; (916) 322-1080; Employees: 560; '92-'93 budget: $404,481,000.

Department of Forestry and Fire Protection

Provides fire protection and watershed management services for private and state-owned watershed lands. Responsibilities include fire prevention, controlling wildlife damage and improving the land and vegetative cover for economic and social benefits. Director: Richard A. Wilson; Salary: $99,805; Office: 1416 Ninth St., 1505, Sacramento 95814; (916) 653-5121; Employees: 4,446; '92-'93 budget: $411,892,000.

Department of Fish and Game

Responsible for maintaining all species of wildlife; providing varied recreational use of wild species, including hunting and fishing, providing for the scientific and educational use of wildlife; and protecting the economic benefits of natural species, including commercial harvesting of wildlife resources. The department also has charge of the newly enacted oil-spill prevention and cleanup program. Director: Boyd H. Gibbons; Salary: $99,805; Office: 1416 Ninth St., 12th Floor, Sacramento 95814; (916) 653-7667; Employees: 2,065; '92-'93 budget: $150,005,000.

Department of Boating and Waterways

Responsible for public boating facilities, water safety, water hyacinth control, beach erosion, small-craft harbor development (through loans and grants) and yacht and ship brokers licensing. Director: John R. Banuelos; Salary: $80,726; Office: 1629 S St., Sacramento 95814; (916) 445-6281; Employees: 64; '92-'93 budget: $11,797,000.

Department of Parks and Recreation

Acquires, designs, develops, operates, maintains and protects the state park system; helps local park agencies through loans and grants; and interprets the natural, archaeological and historical resources of the state. State parks, recreation areas and historic monuments are designed to provide recreation, improve the environment and preserve the state's history and natural landscapes. The department is involved in underwater parks, a statewide trail network, state beaches and piers, coastal and Sierra redwood parks, an off-highway vehicle system and management of the Hearst San Simeon Castle and the Anza-Borrego Desert State Park. Director: Donald W. Murphy; Salary: $99,805; Office: 1416 Ninth St., 1405,

Sacramento 95814; (916) 445-6477; Employees: 2,881; '92-'93 budget: $206,531,000.

Department of Water Resources

Responsible for managing, developing and conserving the state's water, from flood control to drought responses and drinking water safety, under the provisions of the California Water Plan. The department operates Oroville Reservoir, the California Aqueduct and related facilities, and manages the key Delta water supply in conjunction with the U.S. Bureau of Reclamation. Director David Kennedy has undertaken a massive effort to resolve the state's long-standing water supply conflicts through private negotiation and has achieved some success. Salary: $99,805; Office: 1416 Ninth St., 1115-1, Sacramento 95814; (916) 653-7007; Employees: 2,796; '92-'93 budget: $949,218,000.

STATE AND CONSUMER SERVICES AGENCY

This superagency covers an array of departments and programs that include the departments of Consumer Affairs, Fair Employment and Housing, General Services and Veterans Affairs and the Fair Employment and Housing Commission, Building Standards Commission, State Personnel Board, State Fire Marshal, Franchise Tax Board, Museum of Science and Industry, the Public Employees Retirement System and the State Teachers' Retirement System.

In November 1992, Wilson named Sacramento County Supervisor Sandra Smoley to the Cabinet-level job, a post she assumed when her term on the Sacramento board ended on Jan. 4, 1993. Smoley was an unsuccessful candidate for Congress in 1992,

Sandra Smoley

losing in the Republican primary. She had been a county supervisor for 20 years.

Smoley oversees an agency with 11 departments, nearly 15,000 employees and an annual budget of nearly $700 million. Wilson predicted that Smoley would work hard to protect consumer and civil rights but also would not "smother" businesses under state regulations. Smoley succeeded Bonnie Guiton, who resigned in June 1992 to accept an academic post at the University of Virginia. Salary: $106,410; Office: 915 Capitol Mall, Suite 200, Sacramento 95814; (916) 653-3817.

Department of Consumer Affairs

Oversees the Bureau of Automotive Repair, the Contractors' State License Board and the California Medical Board, the Division of Consumer Services and two dozen more small boards, bureaus and commissions that for the most part license and regulate "professional" services. A number of the semiautonomous boards have had severe staff reductions and have been accused of protecting people in professions they regulate. One of the chief antagonists is the department director, James Conran, who has attempted to gain more control over operations. The boards are Accountancy, Architectural Examiners, Barber Examiners, Barbering and Cosmetology, Behavioral Science Examiners, Dental Examiners, Funeral Directors and Embalmers, Geologists and Geophysicists, Guide Dogs for the Blind, Landscape Architects, Examiners of Nursing Home Administrators, Optometry, Pharmacy, Polygraph Examiners, Professional Engineers, Registered Nursing, Certified Shorthand Reporters, Structural Pest Control, Examiners in Veterinary Medicine, Vocational Nurse and Psychiatric Technician Examiners and the Cemetery Board; the bureaus of Collection and Investigative Services, Electronic and Appliance Repair, Personnel Services and Home Furnishings; the Tax Preparers Program; and the Athletic Commission. Salary: $99,805; Office: 400 R St., 3000, Sacramento 95814; (916) 445-1254; Employees: 2,300; '92-'93 budget: $209,456,000.

Department of Fair Employment and Housing

Enforces the state civil rights laws that prohibit discrimination in employment, housing and public services and endeavors to eliminate discrimination based on race, religion, creed, national origin, sex, marital status, physical handicap, medical condition or age (over 40). Complaints are pursued before the Fair Employment and Housing Commission. Director: Nancy Gutierrez; Salary: $88,062; Office: 2016 T St., Suite 210, Sacramento 95814; (916) 739-4616; Employees: 198; '92-'93 budget: $11,469,000.

Office of the State Fire Marshal

Coordinates state fire services, adopts and enforces minimum statewide fire and panic safety regulations, controls hazardous materials and helps the film industry with special effects. State fire marshal: Ronny J. Coleman; Salary: $88,062; Office: 7171 Bowling Drive, Suite 600, Sacramento 95823; (916) 262-1870; Employees: 151; '92-'93 budget: $11,616,000.

Franchise Tax Board

Administers the personal income tax, the bank and corporation tax laws, the homeowners and renters assistance program, and performs field assessments and audits of campaign expenditure reports and lobbyist reports under the Political Reform Act of 1974. The members are state Controller Gray Davis; the chairman of the state Board of Equalization, Brad Sherman; and state Director of Finance Thomas Hayes. Executive officer: Gerald Goldberg; Salary: $99,805; Office: P.O. Box 1468, Sacramento 95812; (916) 369-4543; Employees: 4,449; '92-'93 budget: $212,810,000.

Department of General Services

Manages and maintains state property, allocates office space, monitors contracts, insurance and risks, administers the state school building law and helps small and minority businesses obtain state contracts. It also has jurisdiction over the state architect, the offices of telecommunications, local assistance, procurement, energy assessments, buildings and grounds, and the state police. Director: John Lockwood; Salary: $99,805; Office: 1325 J St., 1910, Sacramento 95814; (916) 445-3441; Employees: 4,233; '92-'93 budget: $480,510,000.

State Personnel Board

Manages the state civil service system including the Career Opportunities Development Program. Members: President Richard Carpenter, Alice Stoner, Lorrie Ward, Florence Bos and one vacancy. Members' compensation: $29,354; Executive officer: Gloria Harmon; Salary: $86,640; Office: 801 Capitol Mall, Sacramento 95814; (916) 653-1028; Employees: 164; '91-'92 budget: $13,174,000.

Public Employees' Retirement System

Administers pension, disability, health, Social Security and death benefits for more than 1 million past and present public employees, and is the nation's largest pension plan. Participants include state constitutional officers, legislators, judges, state employees, most volunteer fire fighters, school employees (except teachers) and others. Executive officer: Dale Hanson; Salary: $99,805; Office: 400 P St., Sacramento 95814; (916) 326-3829; Employees: 843; '92-'93 budget: $128,866,000.

State Teachers' Retirement System

Administers the largest teacher retirement system in the United States with 340,700 members and 123,900 receiving benefits. Chief executive officer: James Mosman; Salary: $99,805; Office: 7667 Folsom Blvd., Sacramento 95826; (916) 387-3700. Employees: 427; '92-'93 budget: $2.248 billion.

Department of Veterans Affairs

Administers the Cal-Vet farm and home loan program, helps veterans obtain benefits and rights to which they are entitled and supports the Veterans Home of California, a retirement home with nursing care and hospitalization. The program is expected to expand rapidly in response to a 1992 court ruling that all California residents who are veterans are eligible for loan programs, not just those who entered the service from California. Director: B.T. Hacker; Salary: $99,805; Office: 1227 O St., Sacramento 94295; (916) 653-2573; Employees: 1,094; '92-'93 budget: $1.005 billion.

SECRETARY OF CHILD DEVELOPMENT, EDUCATION

Declaring children to be the state's most precious resource, Gov. Pete Wilson pledged to give them a healthy start in life and in school. His Cabinet would include a new position, secretary for child development and education, a post for which he chose Maureen DiMarco, a Democrat who had endorsed his campaign.

Wilson gave DiMarco the task of restructuring the state's delivery of social, health and mental health services to children in a period of severe budget constraints. She also chairs a new Inter-Agency Council for Child Development. Wilson said his approach would be preventive rather than corrective for the state's educational and children's needs. He considered such expenses to be investments in the future rather than costs.

DiMarco, of Cyprus, was immediate past president of the California School Boards Association and outgoing president of the board of the Garden Grove Unified School District in Orange County. In 1983, she worked as a consultant for former state schools **Maureen DiMarco** chief Bill Honig, and she was frequently critical of former Gov. George Deukmejian's education policies. Salary: $106,410. Office: Building, 1121 L St., 600, Sacramento 95814; (916) 323-0611; Employees: 20; '92-'93 budget: $1,739,000.

BOARD OF EDUCATION

Establishes policy and adopts rules and regulations for kindergarten through 12th grade, where authorized by the Education Code. Major duties include selecting textbooks for grades kindergarten through eight, developing curriculum frameworks, approving district waivers from regulations and regulating the state testing program, teacher credentialing and school district reorganizations. In practice, the board is subsidiary to the state superintendent of public instruction, who is a constitutional officer elected by the voters. But the board frequently clashed over the budget and educational reforms with former Superintendent Bill Honig, who was forced to resign in 1993 after being convicted of felony conflict of interest charges involving a school program run by his wife, Nancy.

Members: President Joseph Stein, Dorothy Lee, William Malkasian, Irene Cheng (student member), Gerti Thomas, Marion McDowell, Yvonne Larsen, Frank Light, Benjamin Montoya and Kathryn Dronenburg. Office: 721 Capitol Mall, Room 532, Sacramento, 95814; (916) 657-5478.

DEPARTMENT OF EDUCATION

Administers the state's kindergarten through high school education system for 5.1 million pupils by coordinating and directing the state's local elementary and high school districts. The primary goal is to provide education policy to local districts, approve instructional materials and offer curriculum leadership. Superintendent: vacant. Salary: $102,000; Office: 721 Capitol Mall, Sacramento 95814; (916) 657-2451; Employees: 2,285; '92-'93 budget: $24.5 billion.

UC BOARD OF REGENTS

Governs the nine campuses of the University of California, five teaching hospitals and three major laboratories operated under contracts with the U.S. Department of Energy. The 18 members have been appointed to 12-year terms since 1974, when terms were reduced from 16 years. The same amendment reduced the number of ex-officio members from eight to seven. The long-term appointment of a regent is considered to be among the most prestigious civic positions in California, much prized by the wealthy and politically well-connected. And because of their long terms, regents often survive the terms of the governors who appointed them. As the UC system has struggled with budget cuts, regents have been forced to give up a number of lavish perks.

The regents (and the end of their terms) are Gov. Pete Wilson, president;Lt. Gov. Leo McCarthy; Assembly Speaker Willie Brown; state superintendent of schools (currently vacant); Jack Peltason, president of the university; Meredith Khachigian, chairwoman (2001); William Bagley (2002); Roy Brophy (1998); Clair Burgener (2000); Yvonne Brathwaite Burke (1993); Frank Clark Jr. (2000); W. Glenn Campbell (1996); John G. Davies (2004); Tirso del Junco (1997); Alice Gonzales (1998); Jeremiah Hallisey (1993); S. Sue Johnson (2002); Leo Kolligian (1997); Howard Leach (2001); Stephen Nakashima (2004); Dean Watkins (1996); Harold Williams (1994); Alex Wong (student regent, 1993); Jacques Yeager (1994); Carl J. Stoney Jr. (alumni); Paul J. Hall (alumni). President's salary: $243,500 plus $36,500 in deferred compensation; Office of the secretary of the regents: 650 University Hall, Berkeley 94720; (510) 642-0502. The university system's overall budget, including federal funds and research labs, is about $9 billion. The system has an enrollment of 166,000 students.

University of California Chancellors

Jack Peltason, University System President; Chang-Linn Tian, Berkeley; Theodore Hullar, Davis; L. Dennis Smith, (acting chancellor) Irvine; Charles Young, Los Angeles; Raymond L. Orbach, Riverside; Richard Atkinson, San Diego; Julius Krevans, M.D., San Francisco; Barbara Uehling, Santa Barbara; Karl S. Pister, Santa Cruz; Charles Shank, director, Lawrence Berkeley Laboratory; John Nuckolls, director, Lawrence Livermore National Laboratory; and Siegfried Hecker, director, Los Alamos National Laboratory.

TRUSTEES OF THE STATE UNIVERSITIES

Sets policy and governs collective bargaining; personnel matters, including appointment of the system president and university chancellors, budget decisions and capital outlays. Members are appointed by the governor for eight-year terms. The trustees (and the end of their terms) are Gov. Pete Wilson; Lt. Gov. Leo McCarthy; Assembly Speaker Willie Brown; state superintendent of schools (currently vacant); Barry Munitz, chancellor; Anthony Vitti, chairman, (1997); Claudia Hampton (1994); Marianthi Lansdale (1993); Dr. John Kashiwabara

(1994); Roland Arnall (1998); Martha Falgatter (1995); William Campbell (1995); Marian Bagdasarian (1996); R. James Considine Jr. (alumni, 1994); Terrance Flanigan (1999); James Gray (1998); Ralph Pesqueira (1996); Ted Saenger (1997); Ronald Cedillos (1999); Bernard Goldstein (faculty, 1993); Ameze Washington (student, 1993); Chancellor's salary: $149,040; Office: 400 Golden Shore, Long Beach, 90802; (310) 985-250 Enrollment: 372,000. System budget '91-'92: $2.1 billion.

California State University Presidents

Barry Munitz, University System Chancellor; Tomas Arciniega, Bakersfield; Robin Wilson, Chico; Robert Detweiler, Dominguez Hills; John Welty, Fresno; Milton Gordon, Fullerton; Norma Rees, Hayward; Alistair McCrone, Humboldt; Curtis McCray, Long Beach; James Rosser, Los Angeles; Blenda Wilson, Northridge; Bob Suzuki, California State Polytechnic University, Pomona; Donald Gerth, Sacramento; Anthony Evans, San Bernardino; Thomas Day, San Diego; Robert Corrigan, San Francisco; J. Handel Evans, San Jose; Warren Baker, California Polytechnic State University, San Luis Obispo; Bill Stacy, San Marcos; Ruben Armina, Sonoma; Lee R. Kerschner, Stanislaus.

GOVERNORS, CALIFORNIA COMMUNITY COLLEGES

California's 71 community college districts comprise the largest postsecondary education system in the nation, with 107 campuses statewide serving approximately 1.4 million students. Each district is managed by a locally elected governing board, but a statewide Board of Governors and chancellor provide leadership, a presence before the Legislature and policy guidance.

Board members are President Robert Rivinius of Sacramento, Phillip Bardos of Los Angeles, Philip del Campo of San Diego, Yvonne Gallegos Bodle of Ventura, Timothey Haidinger of San Diego, Paul Kim of North Hollywood, David Lee of Milpitas, Michael Madrid (student member from Moorpark), John Parhurst of Folsom, Alice Petrossian of Glendale, Shirley Ralston of Orange, John Ricc of Palo Alto, Larry Toy of Hayward, David Willmon of Riverside and Julia Li Wu of Los Angeles. Chancellor: David Mertes; Salary: $106,404; Office: 1107 Ninth St., Sacramento 95814; (916) 445-8752; '92-'93 budget (all campuses): $2.64 billion.

FAIR POLITICAL PRACTICES COMMISSION

Established by the voter-approved Political Reform Act of 1974, the commission enforces campaign expenditure reporting, conflict-of-interest statements, other disclosure rules and campaign restrictions. Propositions 73 and 68, rival initiatives that were both approved in 1988, fell largely under the commission's jurisdiction but were gutted by court decisions in 1990. Proposition 68 was sponsored by Common Cause and Proposition 73 was sponsored by the unlikely alliance of Assembly Republican leader Ross Johnson of La Habra, Independent Sen. Quentin Kopp of San Francisco and Democratic Sen. Joseph Montoya of Whittier. (Montoya later was sentenced to prison on political corruption charges.)

In the first of the court decisions, U.S. District Court Judge Lawrence Karlton ruled in September 1990 that Proposition 73's contribution limits and its ban on fund transfers among candidates unfairly limited political speech. Two months later, the state Supreme Court ruled that no provisions of Proposition 68 could take effect because Proposition 73 had won more votes and provided a "comprehensive regulatory scheme related to the same subject."

The decisions meant that California no longer had any restrictions on how much money individuals or organizational political action committees could contribute to political candidates, and fund transfers between candidates for the Legislature, once banned, were permissible, according to one analysis. The decisions also meant Proposition 73's restrictions against public campaign financing were thrown out, too, but so far no one has stepped up to enact such a provision.

In the meantime, the Legislature passed an ethics package that included restrictions on travel, health-related expenses, vehicle, gift and other purchases with campaign proceeds and reimbursements of unused campaign funds. A significant part of the package became Proposition 112, approved in the June 1990 primary election, further restricting gifts and honorariums for lawmakers and personal use of campaign funds while establishing an independent Citizens Compensation Commission to set the pay for legislators and constitutional officers.

Within this framework, the FPPC adopts regulations governing disclosure of conflicts of interest, campaign finances and lobbyist activities and is empowered to fine public officials and candidates. Other elements of campaign enforcement are the responsibility of the secretary of state and the attorney general. Chairman: Ben Davidian; Salary: $95,403; Members: Rick Brandsma, James Rushford, Deborah Seiler and one vacancy; Office: 428 J St., Suite 800, Sacramento 95814; (916) 322-5901; Employees: 60; '92-'93 budget: $6,039,000.

TRANSPORTATION COMMISSION

Administers state highway planning and construction and other state transportation programs, including mass transit and rail transportation services. Chairman: Jerome Lipp; Members: Dean Dunphy, vice chairman; Joseph Duffel, Octavia Diener, Jerry Epstein, Daniel Fessler, Assemblyman Richard Katz, Kenneth Kevorkian, William Leonard Sr., Sen. Quentin Kopp and Robert Shelton. Executive director: Robert I. Remen; Commissioners receive $100 a day, but they have taken a voluntary 5 percent ($5) pay cut. Office: 1120 N St., Room 2233., Sacramento 95814; (916) 654-4245; Employees: 16; '92-'93 budget: $1,437,000.

CALIFORNIA ENERGY RESOURCES CONSERVATION AND DEVELOPMENT COMMISSION

Responsible for siting major power plants, forecasting energy supplies and demands, developing energy conservation measures and conducting research into questions of energy supply, consumption, conservation and power plant technology. Chairman: Charles Imbrecht (term ends 1998); Salary: $95,403; Members: Barbara Crowley (1994), Richard A. Bilas (1997), Art S. Kevorkian (1995), Sally Rakow (1996); Salaries: $92,465; Office: 1516 Ninth St., Sacramento 95814; (916) 324-3000; Employees: 476; '92-'93 budget: $84,743,000.

PUBLIC UTILITIES COMMISSION

Responsible for providing the public with the lowest reasonable rates for utilities and transportation services, and assures that utilities and transportation companies render adequate and safe services. President: Daniel Fessler; Salary $95,403; Commissioners: Patricia Eckert, Norman Shumway, two vacancies; Salaries: $92,465; Office: 505 Van Ness Ave., San Francisco 94102-3298; (415) 703-1282; Employees: 1,091; '92-'93 budget: $80,539,000.

SEISMIC SAFETY COMMISSION

Responsible for improving earthquake safety in California; inventories hazardous buildings, sponsors legislation, pursues programs to strengthen state-owned buildings. Executive director: L. Thomas Tobin; Salary: $78,276; Office: 1900 K St., Suite 100, Sacramento, 95814; (916) 322-4917; Employees: 13; '92-'93 budget: $2,024,000.

STATE LANDS COMMISSION

Administers state interest in more than 4 million acres of navigable waterways, swamp and overflow lands, vacant school sites and granted lands and tidelands within 3 miles of the mean high-tide line (one of the few state agencies not controlled by the governor). Members: State finance director Thomas Hayes, Republican; Lt. Gov. Leo McCarthy, Democrat; and Controller Gray Davis, Democrat. Executive Officer: Charles Warren; Salary: $88,056; Office: 1807 13th St., Sacramento 95814; (916) 322-7777; Employees: 220; '92-'93 budget: $16,069,000.

CALIFORNIA COASTAL COMMISSION

Charged with the state management of coastal resources, an area extending generally about 1,000 yards inland (but as much as 5 miles inland in some areas) and 3 miles seaward for the 1,100-mile length of the California coast, excluding San Francisco Bay. The commission was established in 1976 to succeed the California Coastal Zone Commission, a temporary agency created by the voters in 1972. The 15-member commission certifies local governments to manage the coastal zone in accordance with state-approved plans. Gov. Deukmejian attempted to abolish the agency in the early years of his administration and when that failed he cut the commission's budgets sharply. Executive director: Peter Douglas; Salary: $83,364; Office: 45 Fremont St., Suite 2000, San Francisco 94105; (415) 904-5200; Employees: 113; '92-'93 budget: $9,607,000.

MAJOR RISK MEDICAL INSURANCE

A program designed to provide health insurance for residents who are unable to find insurance in the open market by supplementing the cost of premiums with $30 million from tobacco taxes. Chairman: Cliff Allenby; Members: Soap Dowell, Rita Gordon, Ralph Schaffarzick, M.D.; Office: 744 P St., Room 1077, Sacramento 95814; (916) 324-4695; Employees: 13; '92-'93 budget: $106,567,000.

6

California Legislature:
Unrepresentative and unrespected

"Last year here was the most dreadful year of my entire life. We fought and we fought and we fought – and we produced little."
–Veteran Democratic Assemblyman John Vasconcellos, nominating Willie Brown for his seventh term as speaker, Dec. 7, 1992.

"I kind of wondered what everybody was doing. You see all these people, but not much is getting done."
–Republican Jan Goldsmith, reflecting on his first day in the state Capitol as a new assemblyman, Dec. 7, 1992.

"The voters will not continue to be patient forever."
–Democrat Willie Brown, after taking the oath as speaker, Dec. 7, 1992.

Even measured by the legislators' notoriously low standards, the 1991-92 legislative session was remarkably awful. The forces of divided government, mediocrity, partisanship and procrastination that had been building up for two decades finally brought the institution to complete meltdown in 1992. In what evolved into the worst fiscal crisis of any state in American history, California's Legislature could not pass a budget until 64 days past the July 1 constitutional deadline (the new budget was signed Sept. 2, 1992). The state ran out of money, issued paper scrip and drove many of its vendors into bankruptcy and its creditors into apoplexy. And when a budget was finally approved, it was so fatally flawed that within weeks analysts were predicting it was $7.5 billion in the red.

As veteran legislators took their seats for a new session in 1993, they had all the enthusiasm of shell-shocked troops forced back to the front. The prospect of renewed trench warfare was all that awaited them. Relations between the Legislature and the governor were at an all-time low.

The platter of issues for the new Legislature was, in truth, filled with leftovers grown rancid by inaction and economic recession. Solutions were still needed for modernizing the state's water system, fixing a declining education system and making the streets safe from crime. Health care, insurance rates and the workers' compensation system were all still in need of major revision.

The combination of frustration, reapportionment, ambition, old-age, term limits, indictments and – in a few cases, voter wrath – drove 30 incumbent legislators from office in 1992 (not counting Democratic Sen. Herschel Rosenthal, who lost in a Democratic Senate primary but can keep his seat for another two years because of a quirk in reapportionment). A few lost in primaries, a rare occurrence. Others decided to pack it in and not run for re-election. With more lucrative offers on the outside, Assemblyman Bruce Bronzan quit right before the election and Senate Majority Leader Barry Keene resigned a few days after the votes were counted. As the new session unfolded, the freshman class was the largest in 26 years.

The turnover in the Assembly was uncommonly large, with 27 new members in the 80-member house (and more still to come as special elections unfold). Democrats held 47 seats and Republicans 32 as the 1993 session opened. All of the new faces in the Senate – two Democrats and two Republicans – moved up from the Assembly. The split was 23 Democrats, 14 Republicans and two independents – again handing Senate President Pro Tem David Roberti a workable majority. There were also three vacancies.

REAPPORTIONMENT RESULTS

The Legislature's membership again did not reflect the state's demographics, although the 1992 reapportionment made strides in that direction. Still largely on the mark was Mark Russell's joke at a 1991 dinner for California legislators: "I've been on a tour of state legislatures – mostly they are a bunch of fat, white guys pretending to hurt each other."

That said, the new Legislature showed gains for minorities and, especially, for women. The 1990 federal census – upon which the apportionment of legislative seats was based – showed that women comprised more than half of the population in California. In the Legislature, women in 1992 won 28 seats out of 120, or 23 percent, an increase of six. (Women went from 17 in the 1991-92 Assembly to 22 in the new Assembly and from five in the old Senate to six in the new one.)

The 1990 census also showed that the state was 43 percent non-white. Yet whites held 80 percent of the seats (64 in the Assembly and 32 in the Senate). Latinos comprised more than a quarter of all state residents, but there were just 10 in the Legislature, or 8.3 percent (7 in the Assembly, 3 in the Senate). Asian Americans boosted their percentage of the state population to 9 percent, but the Legislature had only one Asian American, the first in 12 years. There were nine African Americans,

7.5 percent of the Legislature, compared to a 7 percent African American population statewide. Of the Legislature's top four leaders, only one – Assembly Speaker Willie Brown – is not white.

"This house does not yet reflect the diversity of the people of the state of California, but it comes closer than any other elected body of being appropriately representative of what California is and what California will become," said Brown, after taking the oath for his seventh term as speaker.

To those not completely sunk by cynicism, there was a sliver of hope: the big crop of new faces. Members of the freshman class were different. More important, they considered themselves different.

"We tend to be older; we come from business backgrounds, not government," said Assemblywoman Valerie Brown of Sonoma on her first day in office. And she is a Democrat.

"I think there is going to be a reluctance to buy into the rituals and expectations," she said. "There isn't the time to do the dancing. That doesn't mean I don't respect the system, but it will be my charge to make the system work for me and the people I represent."

LEADERS

Willie Brown emerged from the 1992 Assembly elections more powerful than ever – and bent on wreaking revenge on Gov. Pete Wilson. Despite a supposedly unfriendly reapportionment of legislative districts by the Republican-dominated state Supreme Court and a prediction by Gov. Wilson that Republicans would gain a majority of seats in the Assembly, Democrats actually gained seats in November 1992. (The 47 Democrat, 32 Republican split was expected to change because a number of Assembly members were preparing to run in special elections for vacant congressional and state Senate seats.)

Over in the state Senate, President Pro Tem David Roberti easily held onto his position. But colleagues were beginning to grow weary of his 12-year rule and were talking openly about the "post-Roberti" era. (Assembly Democrats would not dare speak of any such "post-Brown" era.)

Senate Republicans again chose as their leader the rich and natty Ken Maddy of Fresno and, for his second-in-command, the ideologically pure Bill Leonard of Big Bear. Maddy's relations with both his Democratic colleagues and Wilson remained good. But Maddy showed signs of boredom in the job and frustration with never-ending budget battles. His stable of thoroughbred race horses was beginning to hold more interest for him than politics.

For Assembly Speaker Brown, the new class presented a knotty challenge as he attempted to size it up, learn each member's quirks (translated: price) and keep it from rebelling. To his advantage, he had helped to elect many of the new members, again proving his mastery at directing an election machine. But compounding the speaker's challenge was that the new class would soon be in control anyway because

Speakers of the Assembly

Name	P*	Year(s)	Name	P*	Year(s)
Thomas J. White	–	1849	John C. Lynch	R	1895
John Bigler	D	1849,51	Frank L. Coombs	R	1897
Richard P. Hammond	D	1852	Howard E. Wright	R	1899
Isaac B. Wall	D	1853	Alden Anderson	R	1899
Charles S. Fairfax	D	1854	Cornelius W. Pendleton	R	1901
William W. Stow	W	1855	Arthur G. Fisk	R	1903
James T. Farley	A	1856	Frank C. Prescott	R	1905
Elwood T. Beatty	D	1857	R.L. Beardslee	R	1907
N.E. Whiteside	D	1858	P.S. Stanton	R	1909
William C. Stratton	D	1859	A.H. Hewitt	R	1911
Phillip Moore	D	1860	C.C. Young	R-P	1913-17
R.N. Burnell	DD	1861	Henry W. Wright	R	1919,21
George Barstow	R	1862	Frank Merriam	R	1923,25
Tim Machin	U	1863	Edgar C. Levey	R	1927-31
William H. Sears	U	1864	Walter J. Little	R	1933
John Yule	U	1866	F.C. Clowdsley	R	1934
Caisas T. Ryland	D	1868	Edward Craig	R	1935
George H. Rogers	D	1870	William Moseley Jones	D	1937
Thomas B. Shannon	R	1872	Paul Peek	D	1939
Morris M. Estee	I	1874	Gordon H. Garland	D	1940,41
G.J. Carpenter	D	1876	Charles W. Lyon	R	1943,45
Campbell P. Berry	D	1878	Sam L. Collins	R	1947-52
Jabez F. Cowdery	R	1880	James W. Silliman	R	1953-54
William H. Parks	R	1881	Luther H. Lincoln	R	1955-58
Hugh M. Larue	D	1883	Ralph M. Brown	D	1959-61
William H. Parks	R	1885	Jesse M. Unruh	D	1961-68
William H. Jordan	R	1887	Robert T. Monagan	R	1969-70
Robert Howe	D	1889	Bob Moretti	D	1971-74
Frank L. Coombs	R	1891	Leo T. McCarthy	D	1974-80
F.H. Gould	D	1893	Willie Brown Jr.	D	1980-

Key to parties: A=American, D=Democrat, DD=Douglas Democrat, I=Independent, P=Progressive, R=Republican, U=Union; – denotes no party.

of term limits. Brown must leave office by 1996 (unless, as some expect, he is successful in his challenge of Proposition 140 in court). The speaker and his legislative lieutenants talked of grooming the new class, but they kept the Assembly's myriad rules tightly within their grasp.

The Assembly Republicans were yet again victims of leadership fratricide. Term limits were very much at work, with less experienced members rising to leadership positions. The newest Republican Assembly leader (the sixth since Brown became speaker) was Jim Brulte of Ontario, beginning only his second term. Considered a protege of former leader Patrick Nolan (the third GOP leader during Brown's speakership), Brulte was barely ensconced in his new offices as GOP leader before Brown was kicking him around. Relishing his authority, the speaker refused each of Brulte's requests to pick the Republican members of committees.

Brown also broke the tradition of giving the minority party vice-chairs, instead appointing a number of new members, including Democrats, to help train them for taking over the house once term limits forces the retirement of veteran chairmen. And, adding insult, Brown decided to mix up the seating in the Assembly. No longer do Republicans sit on the north side and Democrats on the south side of the chambers. Instead, Democrats and Republicans are seated as one big dysfunctional family.

"This is a place where you get labeled right away with terms I'm not sure I even understand," said a bewildered new Assemblyman Jan Goldsmith, R-Poway, on his first day. "It's not just the media, it's everybody. Every time I see my name, it's next to the word 'moderate' or 'Wilsonite.' They don't know what I've done in Poway. They haven't the faintest idea how I'm going to react here."

Whether Goldsmith realized it or not, legislative leaders were working overtime to figure out how Goldsmith would react – and how to win his votes.

THE CONSTANT CAMPAIGN

While in office, legislators live their lives on a constant campaign, much like their congressional counterparts in Washington. "It is the nearest thing to Congress outside Washington, D.C.," says political scientist Alan Rosenthal of Rutgers University in New Jersey, an authority on state legislatures. "California is way out there beyond where any other legislatures are in terms of political partisanship, full-time campaigning and the cost of campaigns. California is almost another nation."

When the Legislature is in session – generally eight-to-nine months each year minus vacation recesses – lawmakers usually arrive Monday morning and are gone by midafternoon Thursday. By day, legislators juggle committee assignments, floor sessions and their own bills. By night, many partake of the fund-raiser circuit at Sacramento watering holes frequented by lobbyists and staffers. On weekends, lawmakers spend their time toiling in their districts doing "constituent work," which is not very different from campaigning. Those from Southern California spend much of their life getting to and from airports.

In the 1990s, it cost an average of $700,000 to win a seat in the state Senate – more than twice as much as it did to win a seat in Congress. That fact alone means legislators spend considerable time and energy courting those who can write checks to fill campaign coffers.

Presidents pro tempore of the Senate

Name	P*	Year(s)	Name	P*	Year(s)
E. Kirby Chamberlain	–	1849	R.F. Del Valle	D	1883
Elcan Haydenfeldt	W	1851	Benjamin Knight Jr.	D	1885
Benjamin F. Keene	D	1852-1854	Stephen M. White	D	1887, 1889
Royal T. Sprague	D	1855	Thomas Fraser	R	1891
Delos R. Ashley	A	1856	R.B. Carpenter	R	1893
Samuel H. Dosh	D	1857	Thomas Flint Jr.	R	1895-1903
Samuel A. Merritt	D	1858	Edward I. Wolfe	R	1905-1909
W.B. Dickenson	D	1859	A.E. Boyton	R	1911,1913
Isaac N. Quinn	D	1860	N.W. Thompson	R	1915
Richard Irwin	DD	1861	Arthur H. Breed	R	1917-1933
James Safter	R	1862	William P. Rich	R	1935, 1937
A.M. Crane	U	1863	Jerrold L. Seawell	R	1939
R. Burnell	U	1864	William P. Rich	R	1941
S.P. Wright	U	1866	Jerrold L. Seawell	R	1943, 1945
Lansing B. Misner	U	1868	Harold J. Powers	R	1947-1953
Edward J. Lewis	D	1870	Clarence C. Ward	R	1954-1955
James T. Farley	D	1872	Ben Hulse	R	1955-1956
William Irwin	D	1874	Hugh M. Burns	D	1957-1969
Benjamin F. Tuttle	D	1876	Howard Way	R	1969-1970
Edward J. Lewis	D	1878	Jack Schrade	R	1970
George F. Baker	R	1880	James R. Mills	D	1971-1980
William Johnston	R	1881	David Roberti	D	1980-

Key to parties: A=American, D=Democrat, DD=Douglas Democrat, I=Independent, P=Progressive, R=Republican, U=Union; – denotes no party.

Federal probes, term limits and budget stalemates have done nothing to change that fact of Capitol life. Campaign spending studies, however, consistently show that legislators spend comparatively little money on actual electioneering. Mostly, they spend money being a politician – junkets, meals to schmooze donors and power-brokers, tickets to sports events, gifts for supporters, charitable contributions to make a favorable impression in the community and donations to other politicians. A computer analysis by The Sacramento Bee showed legislative incumbents with safe seats spent an average of 40 percent of their campaign funds on such activities.

For a brief time it appeared voters might have done something to stem the campaign fund-raising binge by approving Proposition 73 in 1988. Although the measure had serious flaws, it put limits on campaign contributions. But in a lawsuit engineered by then-state Democratic Party Chairman Jerry Brown, the contribution limits were thrown out by a federal judge in 1990. The free-for-all campaign spending resumed in California for the 1992 election just in time for Jerry Brown to run for president as a born-again believer in contribution limits.

In comparison with other high-achievers in society, legislators are not particularly well paid. They got a raise for the 1991-92 session from the Citizens Compensation Commission created by Proposition 112. Legislative pay went from $40,816 to $52,500 a year coupled with an additional $18,584 in living allowances ($100 a day for each day the Legislature is in session and the member attends, an amount set by the state Board of Control). Legislative leaders were given a pay differential: The speaker of the Assembly and Senate president pro tempore were given $63,000 a year while the majority and minority leaders of each house got $57,750. Many lawmakers, however, still earn lower salaries than some aides.

FBI AGENTS LURKING UNDER THE DOME

Federal agents have been investigating members of the California Legislature almost continually since the early 1980s. Those efforts bore fruit in the 1990s. Three senators – Democrats Paul Carpenter, Joseph Montoya and Alan Robbins – were convicted of a slew of federal corruption charges for taking bribes while in office.

The first of the investigations began in the early 1980s after the Legislature passed a bill that would have overturned local ordinances banning fireworks (it was vetoed by then-Gov. Jerry Brown). The probe of the activities of former fireworks mogul W. Patrick Moriarty yielded convictions of several Southern California officials, but only one legislator – Democratic Assemblyman Bruce Young of Norwalk. His conviction was later overturned.

Legislators had no sooner caught their breath from the Moriarty affair when the FBI lifted the lid in August 1988 on an even bigger investigation, officially code-named Brispec for "Bribery Special Interest." Beginning in 1985, undercover agents had posed as Southern businessmen in search of a bill to benefit their sham companies in return for campaign contributions. They spread more than $50,000 among Capitol figures.

Agents gathered enough evidence in their "sting" to obtain search warrants for the offices of Patrick Nolan, the Assembly's Republican leader at the time; his close associate, Assemblyman Frank Hill, R-Whittier; Assemblywoman Gwen Moore, D-Los Angeles; and Sen. Joseph Montoya, D-Whittier. Montoya eventually was convicted and sentenced to federal prison on bribery and money-laundering charges. Former Sen. Paul Carpenter, by then a member of the state Board of Equalization, was convicted on similar charges soon thereafter. Moore eventually was cleared, but others are still waiting to learn their fate.

Robbins, D-Encino, also was convicted, under a plea bargain, with evidence that flowed in after the sting. Prosecutors discovered an unexpected benefit of their sting when witnesses were emboldened to come forward with new tales of corruption under the dome. Sending chills through the lobbying corps, it was soon revealed that Robbins had been wearing a hidden microphone for the FBI. Not long after, the biggest of the big-time lobbyists, Clayton Jackson – whose lobbying firm has been consistently the most lucrative in Sacramento – was raided by federal authorities with search warrants.

In connection with that probe came yet another. A Sacramento-based federal grand jury indicted Mark Nathanson, a Beverly Hills real estate tycoon whom Speaker Brown had appointed to the Coastal Commission. Federal prosecutors threw the book at Nathanson for allegedly taking a bribe. Nathanson's trial was scheduled to begin in April 1993 and federal prosecutors said they would seek a maximum 15 year prison sentence if they won. But they made little secret of their bigger ambition: They wanted Nathanson to make a deal and provide evidence of more corruption.

Shaken by all this federal activity, the Legislature tightened its ethical standards by placing Proposition 112 on the June 1990 ballot. Once approved, the measure subjected legislators for the first time to enforceable conflict-of-interest laws, banned honorariums and restricted gifts to $250 a year in value from any single source.

LEGISLATION

The Legislature has had a modicum of success making laws in some areas. The 1991-92 session produced legislation granting family leave to care for dependents and a modest gay-rights bill, all legislation that had been vetoed in earlier sessions by George Deukmejian.

Since 1985, the Legislature has approved sweeping measures to reduce smog and garbage, passed a modest revision in workers' disability compensation and taken a step toward modernizing the state's transportation system by placing a successful measure on the June 1990 ballot to raise gasoline taxes. Legislators also passed a mandatory seat-belt law, lowered the blood-alcohol standard for drunken driving and summoned the political courage to approve restrictions on the sale of semiautomatic weapons.

In the wake of the Exxon Valdez oil spill in Alaska, the Legislature approved a landmark oil spill cleanup law with a $500 million emergency fund. State lawmakers also garnered enough votes to enact the first far-reaching welfare reform since Ronald Reagan was governor, approving in 1985 a "workfare" plan called GAIN. And lawmakers and the governor stiffened numerous criminal laws and appropriated hundreds of millions of dollars throughout the decade to pay for a massive prison building program.

The fact remained, however, that of the 5,000 or so bills before the Legislature each session, most dealt with mundane district issues or tinkered with business regulations. Indeed, the Legislature had become largely a regulatory body, spending considerable time refereeing "scope of practice" disputes between various medical professions (podiatrists and orthopedic surgeons waged one memorable battle over the right to perform surgery on the ankle) and dealing with licensure matters ranging from building contractors to interior decorators. Gouging out tax exemptions for a favored few – art collectors, ostrich farmers, solar energy producers – remained a favorite pastime.

INITIATIVES ABOUND

The Legislature's biggest achievements were usually accomplished under the threat of a more Draconian initiative from the outside. A number of organizations found it easier – and cheaper than lobbying the Legislature – to draft their own law, gather enough signatures and take their measure directly to the voters. The result was a bewildering array of ballot proposals, some by outsiders, many by individual lawmakers and others by the Legislature itself.

However, voters administered a dose of tonic in November 1990, when they rejected all but six of 28 ballot measures. That election may have signaled that the high-water mark for initiatives has passed. On the June 1992 primary ballot, there were no initiatives; the November general election ballot had a manageable 13 propositions and eight were rejected, including the governor's welfare-cutting proposal.

Historically, California became the 10th state in the nation to enact the initiative and referendum by special election on Oct. 10, 1911, during the term of reformist Gov. Hiram Johnson. Petitions designed to enact or reform statutes can be placed on the ballot with the valid signatures of 5 percent of the total number of votes cast for governor in the most recent gubernatorial election. Constitutional amendments can be placed before the voters with the backing of 8 percent of the total vote. In theory, initiatives are restricted to making one change at a time in the Constitution, not wholesale revisions. There were signs that the courts were beginning to enforce that single-subject rule. An appellate court struck down Proposition 105, the consumer's right-to-know act, on grounds that it was too broad. However, the state Supreme Court dashed the hopes of legislators by refusing to strike down term limits based on the single-subject rule.

The voters approved term limits in 1990 with the passage of Proposition 140, but they picked an initiative that may prove more problematic than the situation it was meant to correct. Proposition 140, the brainchild of retiring Los Angeles County Supervisor Pete Schabarum and pushed by the remnants of the organization founded by anti-tax crusaders Howard Jarvis and Paul Gann, passed by 53 percent – not exactly a resounding mandate.

The initiative imposed the following limits:

• Constitutional officers, like the governor, are limited to two terms of four years each, or eight years. The initiative did not mention the newest constitutional officer, the insurance commissioner, thus that position has no term limit.

• State senators elected in 1990 – the even-numbered districts – are limited to two terms of four years each, or eight years. State senators who were not up for election in 1990 get one more term if they are re-elected in 1992. That anomaly in the initiative creates a paradox: state Sen. William Leonard, R-Big Bear, first elected to the Senate in 1988, must leave by 1996. However, Sen. Ralph Dills, R-Garden Grove, first elected to the Legislature in 1938 and re-elected to the Senate in 1990, is not required to leave until 1998.

• Assembly members, who face election every two years, are limited to three terms in office, or six years.

• All limits were imposed for life, thus legislators and constitutional officers cannot sit out a term before running for their old offices. But they can seek a new office.

LIVING UNDER TERM LIMITS

Legislators wasted no time in seeking new career opportunities after the 1990 and 1992 elections. Among the first to go was Assembly Speaker Pro Tem Michael Roos of Los Angeles, who took a job heading an educational foundation. In 1992, four Assembly members – Democrats Tom Hayden and Teresa Hughes; Republicans Cathie Wright and David Kelley – moved up to the state Senate, giving themselves a new lease on legislative life. And, in the case of Fresno Democratic Assemblyman Bruce Bronzan, he announced he was leaving even before the Nov. 3, 1992 election. Facing no opponent, Bronzan was re-elected. He stuck around long enough to vote for Willie Brown for another term as speaker and then split to take a lucrative job with the University of California, an institution that was increasingly shameless in its pandering to legislators (the university sponsored a "retreat" in San Diego for the entire state Senate in December and paid for it by dipping into the trough of special interests that regularly lobby in Sacramento such as the California Cable Television Association). Senate Majority Leader Barry Keene of Benicia also bailed out to take a job running a business-oriented tort reform association.

Proposition 140 also shut down the Legislature's retirement system and cut its operating budget by 38 percent. Meeting the new budget restrictions required a massive reduction in personnel and to accomplish that lawmakers offered staffers severance pay equivalent of five months salary in what became known as the "golden kiss-off." Many of the most talented people took the offer, creating critical vacancies on key committee staffs. Their departure in the early months of 1991 also contributed to one of the rockiest – and most unproductive – starts for a legislative session in modern times.

Critics maintained that legislators made a difficult situation worse by failing to eliminate unnecessary jobs in order to save essential staff. In February 1991, legislative leaders sued to overturn Proposition 140, arguing, in part, that the Legislature had been rendered a less-than-equal branch of government with the executive branch because of the required budget cuts. They lost.

An unintended consequence of Proposition 140 was the demise of two small but important offices: the Legislative Analyst and the Auditor General. The analyst's staff provided legislators with impartial reviews of the state's budget and fiscal condition, reviewed bills for conflicts and unintended consequences, and also wrote the nonpartisan analyses of ballot measures for ballot pamphlets. The auditor reviewed state programs for waste and fraud, and also received anonymous tips on misconduct by state workers through a special 800-number. In its 35-year history, the auditor returned $6 to the taxpayers for every $1 spent on audits.

Legislative leaders, who refused to cut any more people from personal staffs or such dubious functions as the Senate's protocol office and the Speaker's Office of Majority Services, decided the analyst and auditor were expendable. Propositions 158 and 159 were put on the November 1992 ballot to establish the two offices as independent entities and thus free them from the budget restrictions in Proposition 140. But there was no visible campaign on their behalf and both failed by lopsided margins. The auditor went out of business in December 1992 and the analyst was to disappear on June 30, 1993, unless an alternative source of money was found.

BIOGRAPHICAL SKETCHES

Biographical sketches for each legislator follow this introduction. Legislators are listed in alphabetical order. Following the sketches are election results for the previous two campaigns, where applicable, and the amount of money raised for the campaign, where available. Campaign contribution data for 1992 were compiled by Kim Alexander of California Common Cause using California Secretary of State records and several data bases. Figures include contributions raised in 1991 for June 1992 primaries where applicable.

Voter registration figures listed are those as of the Nov. 3, 1992, general election. Party registration figures are listed if the party had attained at least 2 percent of total registration in a district; candidate results are listed if a candidate attained at least 5 percent of the vote in the election for that district. Primary votes are not listed.

RATINGS

Ratings are listed from a spectrum of six ideological and trade groups. The score represents the percentage of time the officeholder voted in agreement on bills of interest to that organization. Where "NR" is listed, the legislator was not rated by that organization, usually because the legislator did not cast enough votes for a fair rating or because the legislator was elected too late in the session.

Rating methodologies used by organizations sometimes vary. The California Political Almanac only uses ratings for votes on actual legislation, and not those based on campaign rhetoric. Floor-vote ratings only are given here; some organizations also offer ratings for committee votes. For a complete list and analysis of how each organization compiled its ratings, the reader should contact the organization. Previous editions of the California Political Almanac contained rating scorecards from the National Rifle Association and Free Market Political Action Committee. Both organizations have discontinued legislative ratings. The California Teachers' Association ratings, included in previous editions, were not completed in time for publication.

AFL-CIO — The California American Federation of Labor-Congress of Industrial Organizations, the largest labor federation in the nation, based its ratings on a career average for each legislator. The latest ratings available included votes through 1991; 27 bills for senators, 31 bills for Assembly members. The issues included workplace safety, support of gay rights and parental leave, civil rights, health care and child care. (916) 444-3676; (415) 986-3585.

CalPIRG — California Public Interest Research Group, a non-profit consumer and environmental organization founded in 1972, based its 1992 ratings on 22 bills for senators and Assembly members. Issues included expanded environmental protections, consumer labeling standards, pesticide reduction, child support collection programs, campaign finance reform and a support for a state constitutional revision commission. (916) 448-4516; (213) 278-9244.

CLCV — The California League of Conservation Voters, the largest and oldest state political action committee, is a political arm for more than 100 environmental organizations. Ratings are based on 1991 votes on 39 bills. Issues included park bonds, stream protection, lead testing, pesticide regulation and timber protection. The ratings reflect support by the League for the Sierra Accord reached with Wilson; however, a number of environmental organizations, including the Sierra Club, opposed the compromise. The actual vote of each legislator on the Sierra Accord is given in the Key Votes section. (415) 896-5550; (213) 826-8812.

NOW — California National Organization for Women, Inc., a prominent women's rights group affiliated with the national organization, based its ratings for members of both houses on 10 bills in 1992. The issues included abortion, poverty, family leave, sexual assault, gay rights, domestic violence, sexual harassment and women's health. (916) 442-3414.

CofC — The California Chamber of Commerce, a statewide business group, based its ratings on 19 bills for senators, 18 bills for Assembly members in the 1991-92 session. Bills included opposition to a Democratic plan for workers' compensation reform, opposition to new penalties for workplace safety violations, support of economic development tax credits and opposition to new wetlands protection. (916) 444-6670.

CalFarm — California Farm Bureau, representing agricultural interests, based its ratings on 10 bills for senators, 20 bills for Assembly members in the 1991-92 session. Issues included support of farmland protection, opposition to school districts imposing taxes, opposition to a Democratic workers' compensation reform plan, opposition to the Sierra Accord timber protection compromise and swifter pest eradication. (916) 446-4647.

KEY VOTES

Votes cast by each legislator on 18 bills from the previous three sessions are listed following biographical sketches. The bills, reflecting a diversity of issues, were selected by the editors of the California Political Almanac. If a legislator was not yet serving in the Legislature at the time of the vote, the bill has been deleted from the list for that legislator. If a legislator was absent or abstained, but serving in office, it is noted with "nv" for "not voting."

A majority vote bill requires 21 votes for passage in the 40-member Senate, and 41 votes in the 80-member Assembly. A two-thirds majority measure — also called an urgency bill — requires 27 votes in the Senate and 54 votes in the Assembly. Constitutional amendments, tax levies, appropriations bills and laws that take effect immediately require a two-thirds vote.

Except on procedural votes, the majority voting requirements do not change regardless of vacancies or absences from the floor. For instance, 54 votes are always required in the Assembly to pass the budget even if there are vacant seats. The strict vote requirement means that an absence or abstention has the same effect as a "no" vote. A common strategy for killing legislation is to organize abstentions, as occurred in 1992 with AB 2405, a death penalty measure listed below.

Bill numbers are recycled during each two-year legislative session. Readers looking for more detailed information about a bill need to find the bill listed in the appropriate legislative digest or history for the particular session.

Bills listed here are arranged chronologically based on the final vote in the last house.

1987-88 session:

Parent consent abortion: AB 2274 — by Assemblyman Robert Frazee, R-Carlsbad; signed by Gov. Deukmejian — The bill required minor girls to have parental permission to get an abortion. The state has been under a court restraining order preventing enforcement. That order was upheld by the state Court of Appeal in October 1989. The majority-vote bill passed the Assembly on June 25, 1987, by

46-28 and the Senate on Sept. 10, 1987, by 25-11. YES was in favor of parental consent to get an abortion; NO was against.

Limit product tort: SB 241 — by Sen. William Lockyer, D-Hayward; signed by Gov. Deukmejian — The bill contained a series of procedural and substantive changes in liability laws reached as part of a "peace accord" between doctors, lawyers and insurance companies. The final compromises were worked out on a napkin at a bar. The bill was seen by legislators on the final night of the year's session, and a number of lawmakers complained — to no avail — that they wanted more time for review. The bill displayed Speaker Brown's mastery at muscling a bill through the Legislature. The majority-vote bill passed in both houses on Sept. 11, 1987, approved by the Senate by 25-1 and the Assembly by 63-10. YES favored limiting liability laws; NO was against.

Clean Air Act: AB 2595 — by Assemblyman Byron Sher, D-Stanford; signed by Gov. Deukmejian — The landmark bill expanded the powers of local air quality districts and required a phased reduction of smog-causing emissions into the 21st century. Those in favor contended that it marked a major step toward clean air; opponents argued that it allowed too much intervention by unelected officials into business and local land-use. The majority-vote bill passed the Senate on Aug. 29, 1988, by 25-4 and the Assembly on Aug. 31, 1988, by 47-27. YES was in favor of the new smog restrictions; NO was against.

1989-90 session:

Assault gun ban: SB 292 — by Sen. David Roberti, D-Los Angeles, and AB 357 by Assemblyman Michael Roos, D-Los Angeles; signed by Gov. Deukmejian — The two interlocking bills (double-joined) restricting the sales of semiautomatic, military-style assault weapons were bitterly opposed by the National Rifle Association, and their passage marked a major setback to its political clout. The bills gained momentum after the massacre of children in a Stockton schoolyard. Since the bills were part of a package, the vote given here is a combination of the votes on both bills (no member voted in favor of one and against the other). The vote is shown in a member's biography if the member voted on at least one bill. Absences or abstentions are only noted if a member missed voting on both bills. The Roberti-authored majority-vote bill (SB 292) passed the Assembly on April 17, 1989, by 41-34 and the Senate on May 4, 1989, by 29-8. The Roos-authored majority-vote bill (AB 357) passed the Assembly on May 18, 1989, by 41-35 and the Senate on the same day, 27-11. YES favored the restrictions; NO was against.

Ban AIDS discrimination: AB 65 — by Assemblyman John Vasconcellos, D-San Jose; vetoed by Gov. Deukmejian — The bill would have banned discrimination in employment against anyone stricken with acquired immune deficiency syndrome. Proponents argued that those with AIDS are sometimes fired from their jobs by fearful employers even though the disease is not easily transmitted. Opponents said the bill went too far in restricting businesses, such as restaurants that have lost business when patrons learned a cook had AIDS. The majority-vote bill passed the Assembly on June 29, 1989, by 46-32, and the Senate on Sept. 11, 1989, by 25-6. YES favored banning discrimination against AIDS victims; NO was against.

Restrict abortion funds: amendments to 1990-91 fiscal year budget bill — by Sen. John Doolittle, R-Rocklin, and Assemblyman Phillip Wyman, R-Tehachapi; failed passage — Doolittle and Wyman, in their respective houses, proposed amendments to the 1990-91 state budget that would have restricted state-funded Medi-Cal abortions to cases of rape, incest, fetal abnormality or danger to the mother's life. The amendment, in the wake of U.S. Supreme Court rulings tightening restrictions on abortion, was seen as a test on where each California legislator stood on the issue. Amendments require a majority of those present and voting for passage. Doolittle's amendment failed in the Senate on June 11, 1990, by 12-24; Wyman's Assembly amendment failed on July 19, 1990, by 23-42. YES was in favor of restricting Medi-Cal abortions; NO was in favor of maintaining Medi-Cal abortions.

1991-92 session:

Sales tax hike: AB 2181 — by Assemblyman John Vasconcellos, D-San Jose; signed by Gov. Wilson — raised the state sales tax by 1 $1/4$ cents as part of the 1991-92 fiscal year budget-balancing package. The new tax was supposed to generate $4 billion of the $7.2 billion in new revenue proposed by Wilson to balance the $56.4 billion state spending plan, but revenues fell short of projections. A half cent of the increased tax was set to expire, or "sunset," in July 1993. The two-thirds majority bill passed the Senate June 16, 1991, by 28-10, and the Assembly June 28, 1991, by 54-22; YES was for raising sales taxes; NO was against.

Wealth tax hike: SB 169 — by Sen. Alfred Alquist, D-San Jose; signed by Gov. Wilson — The measure raised the top income tax rate from 9.3 percent to 10 percent for Californians who make $100,000 a year and couples who make $200,000 a year; and to 11 percent for those who make $200,000 a year and couples who make $400,000 a year. The bill was part of the budget-balancing package for the 1991-92 fiscal year and was projected to bring in $2.3 billion in new revenues, a projection that fell short because of the recession. Wilson initially said he was against the tax proposal but caved in 16 days into the new fiscal year under Democratic pressure. The two-thirds majority bill passed the Assembly on July 16, 1991, by 54-23, and the Senate on July 16, 1991, by 27-11. YES was for raising upper-income tax rates; NO was against.

Strong gay rights: AB 101 — by Assemblyman Terry Friedman, D-Los Angeles; vetoed by Gov. Wilson — Few bills in decades have sparked such widespread, emotional public reaction on all sides. The measure would have given gays new legal protections against discrimination in housing and employment. It was bitterly opposed by many conservative Republicans, the religious right and the business community. Wilson, who had indicated he would sign a proposal when he ran for governor, vetoed the measure. His veto sparked riots in several cities. In his unusually lengthy veto message, Wilson said he feared AB 101 would have hurt California's job climate by exposing "innocent employers" to unfair and costly lawsuits. He said his action was not meant to satisfy what he called a "tiny minority of mean-spirited, gay-bashing bigots." The majority-vote bill passed the Senate on July 11, 1991, by 25-10, and the Assembly on Sept. 13, 1991, by 43-31. YES was for anti-discrimination protection for gays; NO was against.

Parental leave: AB 77 — by Assemblywoman Gwen Moore, D-Los Angeles; signed by Gov. Wilson — The bill required large employers to provide up to 16 weeks of unpaid leave within a two-year period to employees to care for sick family members or newborn children. The new law covered an estimated 68 percent of California's workers — more than 9 million people — and 5.6 percent of the state's employers, according to the California Labor Federation. Deukmejian had vetoed an earlier version. The majority-vote bill passed the Senate on Sept. 12, 1991, by 24-13, and the Assembly on Sept. 13, 1991, by 48-29. YES was for parental leave; NO was against.

Timber compromise: SB 300 — by Sen. Tim Leslie, R-Auburn; defeated — would have protected trees growing beside rivers and streams, added two representatives from environmental organizations to a nine-member state Board of Forestry. Although a number of environmental organizations endorsed the measure, along with others related to the so-called "Sierra Accord," it was opposed by the Sierra Club. Legislative opposition ran the gamut from conservatives, who called it a "jobs destruction act," to liberals, who claimed it did not go far enough. The defeat marked a major setback for Wilson's effort at showcasing a compromise between timber companies and environmentalists. Other double-joined bills on the issue that were sent to Wilson could not go into effect because of the defeat of SB 300. The majority-vote bill passed the Senate on June 10, 1991, by 21-13, and was defeated in the Assembly on Feb. 6, 1992, by 34 to 34. YES was in favor of the timber-cutting compromise; NO was against.

Execution by injection: AB 2405 — by Assemblyman Tom McClintock, R-Thousand Oaks; signed by Gov. Wilson — Measure made the injection of lethal drugs an alternative to the gas chamber, which had been the only method of execution allowed under state law for decades. The bill was drafted after the April 1992 execution of Robert Alton Harris in the San Quentin gas chamber. In that case, American Civil Liberties Union lawyers fought to save Harris' life by arguing that death by gas is cruel and unusual punishment. McClintock's bill allows the condemned to choose either gas or injection, but if they do not choose in 10 days the execution will be carried out in the gas chamber. It should be noted that a number of longtime death penalty opponents abstained from voting, thus accounting for the relatively high number of absentees, particularly in the Assembly. The majority-vote bill passed the Senate on Aug. 9, 1992, by 22-5, and the Assembly on August 11, 1992, by 56-1. YES was for allowing condemned prisoners the option of death by lethal injection; NO was against the proposal.

Limited gay rights: AB 2601 — by Assemblyman Terry Friedman, D-Los Angeles; signed by Gov. Wilson — the measure wrote into law the Wilson administration's approach to handling job discrimination complaints by gays and lesbians. It lets a worker seek protection from the state labor commissioner, who investigates complaints and has the power to restore jobs and order employers to pay back wages. A number of gay rights activists said it did not go far enough (it was not as encompassing as AB 101 of a year earlier), while it was opposed by the religious right and a number of conservatives. The majority-vote bill passed the Senate on Aug. 24, 1992, by 24-11, and the Assembly on Aug. 26, 1992, by 44-32. YES was for Wilson's approach to gay rights; NO was against.

Universal health insurance: SB 6 — by Sen. Art Torres, D-Los Angeles; vetoed by Gov. Wilson — Providing a legislative test on proposals for universal health care, the relatively mild measure would have created a commission to design a universal health care plan and report recommendations to the Legislature. The measure was showcased by state Insurance Commissioner John Garamendi and Wilson's veto was at least partly aimed at forestalling a potential gubernatorial opponent in 1994. The majority-vote bill passed the Assembly on July 9, 1992, by 43-31, and the Senate on Aug. 27, 1992, by 21-12. YES was for a universal health care commission; NO was against.

1992-93 Budget act: AB 979 — (no author); signed by Wilson — The $57.4 billion budget act for 1992-93 fiscal year was produced during the longest budget stalemate of any state in American history. The budget contained cuts in welfare for families, aid to people with disabilities and the elderly, health care for the poor and schools. For liberals, the budget cut too deeply and, in the end, many voted against it. The budget contained major fee increases for college students but, unlike the 1991-92 budget, no major tax increases. The budget was signed Sept. 2, 1992 — a record 64 days into the new fiscal year — after enabling legislation was sent to Wilson. The two-thirds majority budget bill was passed by the Senate on Aug. 28, 1992, by 33-5, and the Assembly on Aug. 29, 1992, by 54-24. YES was for the budget; NO was against.

Campaign reform: SCA 4 — by Sen. Barry Keene, D-Ukiah; defeated in the Assembly — The measure would have placed on the November 1992 ballot a state constitutional amendment that would have required campaign contribution limits, voluntary taxpayer donations to a financing system for legislative candidates, spending limits for candidates who accept public financing and restrictions on transfering campaign funds between candidates. The bill incorporated proposals put forward for years by California Common Cause. Had the amendment passed in both houses, it would have needed final approval by a majority of the voters to go into effect. However, it did not reach the ballot because it did not receive a two-thirds majority in each house. The two-thirds majority bill passed the Senate on June 4, 1992, by 28-6, and was defeated in the Assembly on Aug. 31, 1992, by 35-37. YES favored putting the campaign finance proposal on the ballot for voter approval; NO was for keeping the proposal off the ballot.

Offshore oil ban: AB 10 — by Assemblyman Dan Hauser, D-Arcata; signed by Wilson — The measure banned offshore oil drilling within the state's three-mile coastal limit for the Mendocino and Humboldt counties coasts. It wrote into law a ban that was adopted by the state Lands Commission in 1988. Similar legislation was vetoed by Gov. Deukmejian. A companion measure, AB 854, by Assemblyman Ted Lempert, D-San Mateo, extending the coastal sanctuary south to San Simeon, was also approved and signed by Gov. Wilson. The vote here is for AB 10. The majority vote bill passed the Senate Aug. 26, 1992, by 25-9, and the Assembly on Aug. 31, 1992, by 51-26. YES favored banning offshore oil drilling in northern state waters; NO was against such restrictions.

Charter schools: AB 2585 — by Assemblywoman Delaine Eastin; vetoed by Gov. Wilson — The cornerstone measure for a number of leading education thinkers in the Legislature, the measure would have let teams of educators and parents win charters to try out innovative education programs, either in separate schools or in classrooms within existing schools. Wilson vetoed the bill, but signed a weaker measure, SB 1448, by Sen. Gary Hart, D-Santa Barbara, to let 100 schools run charter schools as an experiment. AB 2585, the Eastin bill featured here, would have given more power to individual teachers, principals and parents in the management of individual schools and was viewed warily by both school boards and teachers' unions, thus making the bill difficult for both liberals and conservatives. The majority-vote bill passed both houses Aug. 31, 1992, by 21-16 in the Senate; and by 69-3 in the Assembly. YES was for setting up a program for "charter schools" statewide; NO was against.

IDEOLOGICAL SCORECARD

The ideological spectrum can be used as a measure of each member's vote on the above issues. Note that liberal and conservative members sometimes vote the same for diametrically opposite reasons. Three bills listed below are marked as "tossups" for moderates because members generally acknowledged as moderates broke on both sides of those particular issues. The charter school bill drew support and opposition across ideological lines (reflecting its novelty as an idea), thus it was a "tossup" for everyone.

	LIBERAL	MODERATE	CONSERVATIVE
Parent consent abortion:	NO	TOSSUP	YES
Limit product tort:	NO	YES	YES
Clean air act:	YES	YES	NO
Assault gun ban:	YES	YES	NO
Ban AIDS discrimination:	YES	YES	NO
Restrict abortion funds:	NO	TOSSUP	YES
Sales tax hike:	YES	YES	NO

	LIBERAL	MODERATE	CONSERVATIVE
Wealth tax hike:	YES	YES	NO
Strong gay rights:	YES	TOSSUP	NO
Parental leave:	YES	YES	NO
Timber compromise:	NO	YES	NO
Execution by injection:	NO	YES	YES
Limited gay rights:	YES	YES	NO
Universal health insurance:	YES	YES	NO
1992-93 budget act:	NO	YES	YES
Campaign reform:	YES	YES	NO
Off shore oil ban:	YES	YES	NO
Charter schools:	TOSSUP	TOSSUP	TOSSUP

HOW THE LEADERS VOTED

The Assembly Republicans had three leaders during the time period of the bills listed. The resignations of Assembly Republican leaders were as follows: Patrick Nolan on Nov. 10, 1988; Ross Johnson on July 17, 1991; and Bill Jones on Nov. 4, 1992. The votes listed below are during the time each was leader.

	DEMOCRATS		REPUBLICANS	
	Senate	Assembly	Senate	Assembly
	Roberti	Brown	Maddy	Nolan/Johnson/Jones
Parent consent abortion:	YES	NO	YES	YES
Limit product tort:	YES	YES	YES	YES
Clean Air Act:	YES	YES	nv	NO
Assault gun ban:	YES	YES	NO	NO
Ban AIDS discrim:	YES	YES	nv	NO
Restrict abortion funds:	YES	NO	NO	YES
Sales tax hike:	YES	YES	YES	NO
Wealth tax hike:	YES	YES	YES	NO
Strong gay rights:	YES	YES	YES	NO
Parental leave:	YES	YES	NO	NO
Timber compromise:	YES	NO	NO	YES
Execution by injection:	YES	nv	YES	YES
Limited gay rights:	YES	YES	YES	NO
Universal health insur:	YES	YES	nv	NO
1992-93 Budget Act:	YES	YES	YES	YES
Campaign Reform:	YES	nv	YES	NO
Off shore oil ban:	YES	YES	NO	NO
Charter schools:	YES	YES	NO	nv

COMMON ABBREVIATIONS

AB — Assembly Bill
ACA — Assembly Constitutional Amendment
AI — American Independent Party
Assn. — Association
CSU — California State University
J.D. — Juris doctor (modern law degree)
L — Libertarian party
M.P.A. — Masters, Public Administration
NR — Not Rated
nv — not voting
P&F — Peace and Freedom party
SB — Senate Bill
SCA — Senate Constitutional Amendment
UC — University of California
USC — University of Southern California
USMC — U.S. Marine Corps

Senators and district numbers

1 LESLIE, Tim, R-Carnelian Bay
2 VACANT (Keene)
3 MARKS, Milton, D-San Francisco
4 THOMPSON, Mike, D-St. Helena
5 JOHNSTON, Patrick, D-Stockton
6 GREENE, Leroy, D-Carmichael
7 BOATWRIGHT, Daniel, D-Concord
8 KOPP, Quentin, ind.-San Francisco
9 PETRIS, Nicholas, D-Oakland
10 LOCKYER, Bill, D-Hayward
11 MORGAN, Rebecca, R-Los Altos
12 McCORQUODALE, Dan, D-Modesto
13 ALQUIST, Alfred, D-San Jose
14 MADDY, Ken, R-Fresno
15 MELLO, Henry, D-Santa Cruz
16 VACANT (Rogers)
17 ROGERS, Don, R-Tehachapi
18 HART, Gary, D-Santa Barbara
19 WRIGHT, Cathie, R-Simi Valley
20 ROBERTI, David, D-Van Nuys
21 RUSSELL, Newton, R-Glendale
22 ROSENTHAL, Herschel,
       D-Los Angeles
23 HAYDEN, Tom, D-Santa Monica
24 TORRES, Art, D-Los Angeles
25 HUGHES, Teresa, D-Inglewood
26 CALDERON, Charles, D-Whittier
27 BEVERLY, Robert, R-Long Beach
28 WATSON, Diane, D-Los Angeles
29 HILL, Frank, R-Whittier
30 DILLS, Ralph, D-Gardena
31 LEONARD, William, R-Redlands
32 VACANT (Royce)
33 LEWIS, John, R-Orange
34 AYALA, Ruben, D-Chino
35 BERGESON, Marian,
       R-Newport Beach
36 PRESLEY, Robert, D-Riverside
37 KELLEY, David, R-Hemet
38 CRAVEN, William, R-Oceanside
39 KILLEA, Lucy, ind.—San Diego
40 DEDDEH, Wadie, D-Chula Vista

California Senate districts

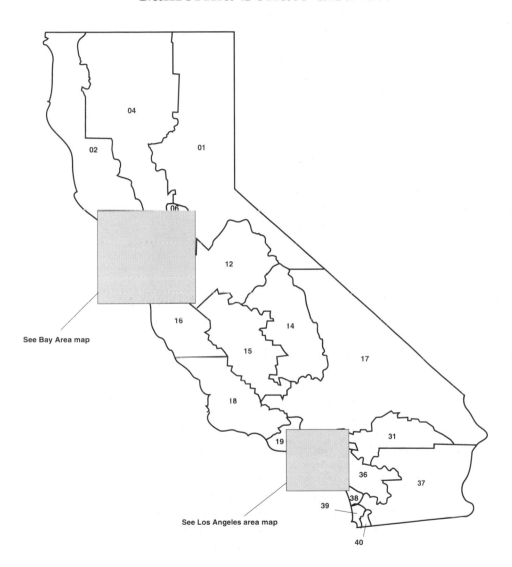

See Bay Area map

See Los Angeles area map

Bay Area Senate districts

Los Angeles Senate districts

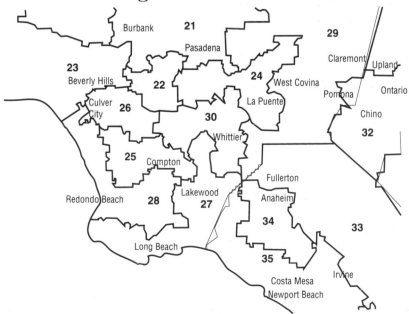

SENATE
Vacancies
2nd Senate District

The craggy North Coast with its dwindling stands of old-growth forest remains outside the economic mainstream of the state. Quaint bed-and-breakfast inns dot the Mendocino and Humboldt County coastlines. The district has a national park — Redwoods — although residents nearby have always resented it as a symbol of a lost timber industry. The new Pelican Bay state prison in Crescent City has brought a new economic base for some, but the unlikely spot for a prison is awkward for transporting prisoners, and it has brought urban problems with it. Reconfigured in the 1992 reapportionment, the district now takes in the premier wine-growing regions of Lake, Napa and Sonoma counties. Grapes have now supplanted marijuana as the district's chief cash crop.

A generation ago, California's scantly populated north coast voted Republican most of the time, even though it had a majority of nominally Democratic voters. But the area's politics began to change in the late 1960s, when the decline of the timber industry was accompanied by an influx of counterculture urban refugees. As loggers became fewer and the newcomers more numerous, the political pendulum made a slow but steady swing to the left, with environmental and lifestyle issues becoming dominant in local politics. By the late 1980s, the region was voting solidly Democratic. The harbinger of that change occurred in 1972, when a young Democratic attorney from Santa Rosa, Barry Keene, was elected to a vacant state Assembly seat. Keene spent six years in the Assembly before moving into the region's state Senate district. Keene, however, quit before the 1993-94 session got under way to become a lobbyist for a business-oriented tort reform organization.

The vacancy opened opportunities for Democrats in search of safer terrain. State Sen. Mike Thompson, D-St. Helena, planned to run in a March 1993 special election for the seat. Thompson's home in St. Helena was reapportioned into the 2nd Senate District in 1992, although he continued to represent the Central Valley 4th Senate District, which is far more Republican.

Thompson's impending shift to a new Senate district rankled Assemblyman Dan Hauser, D-Arcata, who really wanted a shot at the seat but decided not to run against Thompson. "It is disappointing and unfortunate for all of us that Senator Thompson has decided to leave the constituents he was elected to serve, move into the district I have represented for 10 years and run for this seat in order to protect himself from a possible loss in two years. Such is ambition and politics," Hauser grumped.

REGISTRATION: 55.4% D, 31.05% R

16th Senate District

Most of the valley floor of the southern San Joaquin Valley lies in this district, an area where agriculture and oil coexist with relative harmony. Severe overdrafting of groundwater and the buildup of salts and wastes from irrigation threaten the agricultural future of this area, as does the steady erosion of air quality caused by the oil industry. But this is not an area where environmental awareness has much of a following. The political leadership springs from business interests with 19th Century attitudes. And no one ever got far here taking on agribusiness or big oil.

The reapportionment lines were carefully drawn to create a mostly Hispanic district (51 percent). It begins south of Chowchilla, skirts around Madera and follows a contorted path south to include poorer areas of Fresno and the Highway 99 cities stretching to Bakersfield. If Latinos would vote, this would be a safe place for one of their own to win a Senate seat. But the power structure remains in the hands of white growers and small-town business people. There also are a number of new prisons in the district whose employees tend to be conservative.

Republican Sen. Don Rogers of Bakersfield had represented large portions of this district. But the new Democratic numbers gave him incentive to move south to Tehachapi in 1992 and to run in an area more suited to Republicans. Once elected, he resigned the 16th District, necessitating a special election in March 1993.

REGISTRATION: 59.9% D, 29.4% R

32nd Senate District

This largely Latino district contains territory formerly represented by Democratic Sen. Ruben Ayala, who was redistricted into a new 34th Senate District in Orange County. The 32nd was left vacant when Republican Sen. Ed Royce won a seat in Congress representing parts of Orange County. Essentially, the Supreme Court's map-makers swapped numbers with the 34th and the 32nd districts.

The 32nd district includes the communities of Pomona, the dairy farms and prisons of Chino and the boom towns along the Interstate 10 corridor: Fontana, Upland, Ontario and part of western San Bernardino with concentrations of minorities. Fontana, in particular, has undergone a remarkable turnabout. Facing economic collapse when Kaiser Steel closed its World War II-vintage mill, the working-class town has come back from the dead with housing tracts and new businesses.

Ayala may choose to run in a March 1993 special election for this seat since it contains his home and territory he has represented for two decades.

REGISTRATION: 52.9% D, 37.8% R

Alfred E. Alquist (D)
13th Senate District

Lying in the core of Santa Clara County, the 13th Senate District takes in the heart of San Jose and portions of Santa Clara, Sunnyvale and Mountain View. The area has mirrored the transformation and growth of California in the last 30 years. Where once there were orchards and canneries, now there are housing tracts, high-tech industries, traffic and smog. Following the 1992 reapportionment, the district is almost one-third Latino and 18 percent Asian.

Democrat Alfred Alquist, the oldest member of the Legislature, has served long enough to see all those changes. Elected to the part-time Assembly in 1962, Alquist was among the first class of "full-time" legislators elected to the Senate in 1966.

Alquist has had a generally successful career, though one with plenty of ups and downs. His landmark legislation created the Energy Commission and the Seismic Safety Commission and established earthquake construction standards for hospitals. Alquist has had his stamp on every major piece of earthquake

Alfred Alquist

preparedness legislation of the last three decades. He could take grim satisfaction in knowing that many of the laws he authored doubtlessly saved thousands of lives in the Oct. 17, 1989, Bay Area earthquake.

Alquist, however, has become the Andrei Gromyko of the Legislature — iron-faced, publicly devoid of humor (although wryly funny in private), well past his prime, but still a force not to be crossed lightly. At his peak, Alquist was chairman of the all-powerful Appropriations Committee. But in 1986, he agreed to relinquish his post to mollify critics of Senate President Pro Tem David Roberti within his own party. Roberti split Alquist's committee in two. Alquist kept his imprint on the immensely complicated state spending plan as chairman of a new Budget and Fiscal Review Committee, a panel chiefly responsible for the Senate version of the state budget each year, but lost power over the daily workings of legislation, which go before the reduced Appropriations Committee now chaired by Sen. Robert Presley, D-Riverside. Each year, Alquist and Assembly Ways and Means Chairman John Vasconcellos take turns chairing the budget conference committee, where the final budget legislation is shaped. In 1992, during the longest budget stalemate for any state in American history, it was Alquist's turn to chair the budget conference committee. But it was clear that Alquist was tired and Vasconcellos, for all intents and purposes, ran the meetings.

Alquist is known for a stormy temper, much in evidence in 1985, when he had a fabled shouting match with enfant terrible Assemblyman Steve Peace over an Alquist bill to establish a nuclear waste disposal compact with other states. Exactly what was said is still disputed; some witnesses (including Sen. Ken Maddy) claim Peace called Alquist a "senile old pedophile" while thrusting his right index finger toward him. Peace claims that he (only) called the elder senator a "pitiful little creature." Whoever was right was unimportant; an outraged Senate responded by killing all of Peace's remaining bills for the year.

Although Alquist has authored his share of major legislation, he also has had his share of petty, narrow-interest bills. In 1985, Alquist, an ex-railroad employee, won passage of a bill that would have required freight trains longer than 1,500 feet to have a caboose. Deukmejian vetoed the bill.

Alquist's wife, Mai, died in 1989. Outspoken, and a character in her own right in the Legislature, she was her husband's political confidant for years. Many thought that he would retire at the end of 1992, but he chose to seek one more term and won easily.

PERSONAL: elected 1966; born Aug. 2, 1908, in Memphis, Tenn.; home, Santa Clara; Army WWII; education, attended Southwestern University; widower, one child; Protestant.

CAREER: railroad yardmaster; transportation supervisor; Assembly 1962-1966.

COMMITTEES: Budget & Fiscal Review (chair); Constitutional Amendments (vice chair); Appropriations; Energy and Public Utilities; Governmental Organization.

OFFICES: Capitol, (916) 445-9740, FAX (916) 323-8386; district, 100 Paseo de San Antonio, 209, San Jose 95113, (408) 286-8318, FAX (408) 286-2338.

TERM LIMIT: 1996

REGISTRATION: 53.5% D, 30.1% R

1992 CAMPAIGN:

Alquist – D		60.5%	$732,237
Michael Iddings – R		31.2%	
John Webster – L		8.3%	

1988 CAMPAIGN:

Alquist – D		64.8%	$592,405
Daniel Bertolet – R		31.4%	$66,314

RATINGS:

AFL-CIO	CalPIRG	CLCV	NOW	CofC	CalFarm
88	55	84	86	21	10

KEY VOTES:

Parent consent abort:	NO	Limit product tort:	nv	Clean Air Act:	YES
Assault gun ban:	YES	Ban AIDS discrim:	YES	Restrict abortion funds:	NO
Sales tax hike:	YES	Wealth tax hike:	YES	Strong gay rights:	YES
Parental leave:	YES	Timber compromise:	YES	Execution by injection:	YES
Limited gay rights:	YES	Universal health insure:	YES	1992-93 Budget Act:	nv
Campaign Reform:	nv	Offshore oil ban:	YES	Charter schools:	YES

Ruben S. Ayala (D)
34th Senate District

Tucked into the eastern end of the Los Angeles basin, this jig-saw piece of a district was once centered in San Bernardino County. After the 1992 reapportionment, it has become an Orange County district with some serious implications for longtime incumbent Ruben Ayala. The 34th District contains parts of Garden Grove, nearly all of Buena Park, Santa Ana and western Anaheim. It has a high minority population, which should be good for Ayala, but voter registration is only slightly more Democrat than Republican and that could make it tough for Ayala to be re-elected here in 1994.

More than anything else, Ayala is and remains a San Bernardino County politician. He lives in Chino and has represented the western San Bernardino Valley for two decades in the Legislature. He may very well bailout of the 34th District and run in a March 1993 special election to the new 32nd District, which is vacant and contains the San Bernardino County territory of the old 34th.

Even in his old territory, Ayala had a tough time getting re-elected his last time out. In 1990, Ayala faced a strong challenge from Republican Assembly-

Ruben Ayala

man Charles Bader of Pomona. The race was the best chance Republicans had of wresting a seat away from the Democrats that year. Ayala and Bader spent monumental amounts of cash and fought a bare-knuckled race. In the end, Ayala raised more money and was able to pull out a narrow victory with the help of Larry Sheingold, the Senate staffer most responsible for Democratic wins in recent years.

Ayala is an energetic legislator, jealously guarding the parochial interests of San Bernardino County. He has kept a state building in San Bernardino by warding off the encroachments of Riverside's legislators to the south, and sought new escape-proofing measures for the cluster of prisons in Chino at the behest of middle-class homeowners terrified by the bloody massacre of a family by an escapee in 1984.

Ayala is the former chairman of the principal committee on water issues and has labored to expand and modernize the state's water system with little success. To be sure, the task might defy even the most diplomatic and clever of lawmakers, but the bullheaded Ayala's efforts took on the trappings of a personal war.

In 1987-88, backed by Gov. George Deukmejian, Ayala worked out a limited proposal to upgrade levees in the Sacramento River Delta. The plan also included rehabilitation projects at the Salton Sea and elsewhere in the southern end of the water system. But the proposal met unexpected opposition from Northern California Republican Sen. Jim Nielsen, and that was just too much for Ayala. Giving up in a burst of fury on the Senate floor, Ayala lashed out at all who had differences with him on the details, and the state entered its worst drought in decades with few significant improvements to its water system.

Ayala has also been at loggerheads with Sacramento Valley legislators over building an Auburn Dam. Ayala has proposed selling a statewide general obligation bond to pay for the dam, but he has been blocked by Auburn area legislators, who maintain that their area should have first rights to the water. Ayala counters that if the entire state is paying for the dam, the entire state should get the benefit of the water. The seeds of compromise are probably there somewhere.

At the start of the 1993-94 session, Ayala won a coveted seat on the five-member Senate Rules Committee, which runs the Senate, replacing Democrat Henry Mello. But Ayala had to give up his chairmanship of the agriculture and water committee. In one of those strangely choreographed legislative dances, Ayala ended up being named vice chairman of the committee, allowing him to keep a heavy hand in water issues. The new chairman, Democrat Dan McCorquodale, will feel Ayala's presence in big ways and small.

PERSONAL: elected 1974 (special election); born March 6, 1922, in Chino; home, Chino; USMC 1942-1946 WWII (South Pacific theater); education, attended junior college and UCLA Extension, graduated electronics school; wife, Irene; three children; Roman Catholic.

CAREER: Insurance; Chino School Board 1955-1962; Chino City Council 1962-1964; Chino mayor 1964-1965; San Bernardino County Board of Supervisors 1965-1973.

COMMITTEES: Agriculture & Water Resources (vice chair); Local Government (vice chair); Business & Professions; Rules; Transportation; Veterans Affairs.

OFFICES: Capitol, (916) 445-6868, FAX (916) 445-0128; district, 9620 Center Ave., 100, Rancho Cucamonga 91730, (909) 466-6882, FAX (909) 941-7219.

TERM LIMIT: 1998

REGISTRATION: 46.3% D, 42.1% R

1990 CAMPAIGN:	Ayala – D	51.8%	$1,032,997
	Charles Bader – R	48.2%	$761,778
1986 CAMPAIGN:	Ayala – D	66%	$307,332
	Steve Turner – R	34%	$12,250

RATINGS:	AFL-CIO	CalPIRG	CLCV	NOW	CofC	CalFarm
	83	81	NR	29	37	30

KEY VOTES:

Parent consent abort:	YES	Limit product tort:	YES	Clean Air Act:	YES
Assault gun ban:	YES	Ban AIDS discrim:	NO	Restrict abortion funds:	YES
Sales tax hike:	nv	Wealth tax hike:	YES	Strong gay rights:	NO
Parental leave:	YES	Timber compromise:	nv	Execution by injection:	YES
Limited gay rights:	NO	Universal health insure:	YES	1992-93 Budget Act:	YES
Campaign Reform:	YES	Offshore oil ban:	NO	Charter schools:	YES

Marian C. Bergeson (R)
35th Senate District

Reapportionment made life easier for Marian Bergeson, coastal Orange County's representative in the state Senate since 1984. Bergeson's old 37th District was a geographic monster that stretched over portions of four counties. It had been created by the Legislature in 1981 from bits and pieces left over after other districts had been drawn. Its constituents ranged from the very wealthy residents of Newport Beach to the poorest Latino farm workers in the Imperial Valley. High levels of population growth throughout the district, however, guaranteed that reapportionment would shrink its boundaries and that is exactly what happened when the state Supreme Court drew new maps following the 1990 census.

The new 35th District retained the northern Orange County coast, including three cities with "beach" in their names — Huntington, Newport and Laguna — and it was perfect for Bergeson, whose home is in Newport Beach. With the chore of representing so many diverse cities, counties and constituencies lifted from her shoulders, Bergeson easily won re-election to a third term in 1992. Given the overwhelming Republican registration of the district, approaching 60 percent, the Democrats never even considered a challenge.

Marian Bergeson

Bergeson was the Republican Party's unsuccessful nominee for lieutenant governor in 1990 and she has never been close to the party's right wing. That prevented her from achieving much clout during her eight years in the Assembly, but in the less ideological Senate she has flourished, becoming chair of the Senate Local Government Committee and playing a major role in shaping budget and growth-management legislation.

Bergeson also presided over difficult hearings to reorganize the South Coast Air Quality Management District and has attempted for years to streamline state contracting policies for highway construction. She also has been on the two-house budget conference committee that irons out differences between the Senate and Assembly versions of the state's spending plan.

As the campaign for lieutenant governor indicated, Bergeson would like to move on to other political pastures. She tried to persuade then-Gov. George Deukmejian to appoint her treasurer after Democrat Jesse Unruh died in 1987 but was passed over twice. Because her odd-numbered district gives her a "free ride" to run for statewide office, Bergeson may try again in 1994 when several second-tier constitutional offices are expected to open up.

She is also considered to be a potential appointee to replace Bill Honig, who was forced to give up his superintendent of schools post after being convicted of felony conflict of interest in 1993. Bergeson is one of the few Republicans who could possibly be confirmed by both houses of the Legislature.

PERSONAL: elected 1984; born Aug. 31, 1925, in Salt Lake City; home, Newport Beach; education, B.A. elementary education Brigham Young University; graduate studies UCLA; husband Garth Bergeson, three children; Mormon.

CAREER: Newport Mesa school board 1965-1977; president of California School Boards Association; Assembly 1978-1984.

COMMITTEES: Local Government, (chair); Housing & Urban Affairs (vice chair); Appropriations; Health & Human Services; Industrial Relations; Transportation.

OFFICES: Capitol, (916) 445-4961, FAX (916) 445-9263; district, 140 Newport Center Dr., 120, Newport Beach 92660, (714) 640-1137, FAX (714) 640-1523.

TERM LIMIT: 1996

REGISTRATION: 32.6% D, 53.2% R

1992 CAMPAIGN:

Bergeson – R	62.2%	$481,320
Dorianne Garcia – D	32.7%	$755
Eric Sprik – L	5.0%	

1988 CAMPAIGN:

Bergeson – R	71.1%	$374,806
Pat McCabe – D	26.6%	$16,358

RATINGS:

AFL-CIO	CalPIRG	CLCV	NOW	CofC	CalFarm
30	64	50	36	58	50

KEY VOTES:

Parent consent abort:	YES	Limit product tort:	YES	Clean Air Act:	NO
Assault gun ban:	YES	Ban AIDS discrim:	nv	Restrict abortion funds:	YES
Sales tax hike:	YES	Wealth tax hike:	NO	Strong gay rights:	nv
Parental leave:	NO	Timber compromise:	NO	Execution by injection:	NO
Limited gay rights:	NO	Universal health insure:	NO	1992-93 Budget Act:	YES
Campaign Reform:	YES	Offshore oil ban:	YES	Charter schools:	NO

Robert G. Beverly (R)

27th Senate District

Bob Beverly is the visual embodiment of a distinguished politician with his snow-white hair and courtly manners. And he never had much trouble getting himself elected to the Legislature from districts along Los Angeles County's southern coast, first as an assemblyman for 10 years and, since 1976, as a member of the state Senate. But the reapportionment maps drawn up by the state Supreme Court did Republican Beverly no favors. His old 29th District was split and his home in Manhattan Beach (where he had been city attorney, city councilman and mayor before his election to the Legislature) was placed in a district with a distinctly Democratic tilt. To run for re-election in 1992, Beverly had to move his residence to

Robert Beverly

Redondo Beach, part of the reconfigured and renumbered 27th District, which had a much-better GOP registration profile.

It also meant that Beverly had to campaign in some communities, such as Bellflower, Lakewood and Hawaiian Gardens, that were not only new to him but had strong Democratic leanings, while retaining more familiar and more Republican territory in Long Beach (the district includes two-thirds of that city). The district also has an overseas component: Catalina Island and its 3,000 strongly Republican residents 26 miles off the coast.

The upshot was that Beverly found himself in a surprisingly desperate battle against Democrat Brian Finander and only the infusion of help from his friends in the Legislature and in the lobbying corps in Sacramento saved Beverly from an ignominious end to his long legislative career. He wound up winning re-election by just over 5,000 votes — and may have been saved by the strong showing (9,000 votes) of a Peace and Freedom Party candidate. Beverly thus has one last term in the Senate before term limits end his 30-year legislative career in the Capitol.

The book on Beverly is that he isn't the most productive person to serve in the Legislature, but by no means is he the worst. He's an insider who never participates in the Capitol's ideological wars and only rarely in the power struggles; a close personal friend of the Senate's Republican leader, Ken Maddy; and someone who takes care of the minimal legislative needs of his district while voting as a loyal Republican. The badge of his insider status is his seat on the Senate Rules Committee, the panel that exercises bipartisan control over the business of the house.

He also gets along well with Democrats in the Senate, including Senate President Pro Tem David Roberti, and was a key swing vote for Roberti's bill banning semiautomatic assault weapons. Labeling Beverly, however, does not do justice to the role he plays in the Senate. He shows himself motivated to a great extent not by ideology but by personal relationships. Beverly often presides over the Senate; his quick rulings and even temper at the rostrum are richly valued by Roberti and his colleagues. Beverly may be in the minority, but he is certainly in the club that runs the Legislature. When Sen. Bill Lockyer crashed a meeting in David Roberti's office in the spring of 1989 to complain about secret budget deals, he found Beverly among those inside. When Assembly Speaker Willie Brown went to Lloyd's of London in 1986, among those he took with him was Beverly.

The jovial Beverly carries water for a lot of people. He authored the bill for Gov. George Deukmejian that rebated $1.1 billion to taxpayers. A 1987 Beverly bill restored $86.6 million in aid to the state's urban school districts previously cut by Deukmejian. Other, lesser bills by Beverly are worthy of note. In the waning days of the 1989 session, he pushed a measure allowing members of the Signal Hill City Council to circumvent conflict-of-interest laws so they could vote on a proposed development that could boost their property values. He has pushed hard on a measure to exempt certain over-the-counter stock transactions from state regulation. One of the most hotly contested measures behind the scenes was a Beverly bill to exempt employees of mortgage banking firms from having to hold a real estate license.

At the start of 1991, Beverly reportedly sought appointment to the Board of Equalization seat held by Paul Carpenter, who was convicted on federal corruption charges. But Beverly was passed over by Gov. Pete Wilson in favor of political neophyte Matt Fong, the GOP son of Democratic Secretary of State March Fong Eu.

PERSONAL: elected 1976; born July 1, 1925, in Belmont, Mass.; home, Redondo Beach; USMC 1943-1946; education, attended UCLA 1946-1948, J.D. Loyola University; wife Bettelu, three children; Protestant.

CAREER: city attorney; Manhattan Beach City Council, mayor 1958-1967; Assembly 1967-1976 (Assembly Republican Leader).

COMMITTEES: Appropriations (vice chair); Banking, Commerce & International Trade; Elections & Reapportionment; Governmental Organization; Rules.

OFFICES: Capitol, (916) 445-6447; district, 1611 S. Pacific Coast Highway, 102, Redondo Beach 90277, (310) 540-1611, FAX (310) 540-2192.

TERM LIMIT: 1996

REGISTRATION: 46.8% D, 40.7% R

1992 CAMPAIGN:	Beverly – R	47.3%	$481,381
	Brian Finander – D	45.4%	$123,483
1988 CAMPAIGN:	Beverly – R	67.2%	$248,232
	Jack Hachmeister – D	29.5%	$0

RATINGS:	AFL-CIO	CalPIRG	CLCV	NOW	CofC	CalFarm
	52	60	50	36	58	20

KEY VOTES:

Parent consent abort: YES	Limit product tort: YES	Clean Air Act:	YES
Assault gun ban: YES	Ban AIDS discrim: YES	Restrict abortion funds:	NO
Sales tax hike: YES	Wealth tax hike: YES	Strong gay rights:	YES
Parental leave: NO	Timber compromise: NO	Execution by injection:	YES
Limited gay rights: YES	Universal health insur: NO	1992-93 Budget Act:	YES
Campaign Reform: YES	Offshore oil ban: YES	Charter schools:	NO

Daniel E. Boatwright (D)
7th Senate District

As the San Francisco Bay Area has grown into the fourth-largest metropolitan region in the United States, development has oozed out "through the tunnel" in the Berkeley Hills into Contra Costa County. The Diablo Valley, once a sleepy string of towns connected by two-lane roads, is now crisscrossed with freeways and covered with concrete-and-glass towers. Walnut Creek even has a skyline.

In the 1930s, it was a long train ride to Oakland for basic services like doctors for the oil refinery workers in Avon, and not much in-between. Now the massive Bishop Ranch industrial park houses high-tech industry and housing tracts cover the hillsides and valleys. The headquarters of Chevron is here, and its executives live nearby in places like the exclusive walled community of Blackhawk with its nearby classic car museum and a supermarket with brass carts and a pianist.

The region has a conservative bent more akin to Orange County than the rest of

Northern California, reflected in the editorial pages of the newspapers belonging to aging right-wing publisher Dean Lesher.

Combative Democrat Dan Boatwright has been a central figure in Contra Costa politics for three decades, first in local offices, then eight years in the Assembly and since 1980 in the Senate. He has survived tough elections, a 1980s Internal Revenue Service investigation that sought $112,000 in back taxes for 1976 and a 1984 civil trial in which he was acquitted of taking money for official favors. Newspapers have written about the $10,000 Boatwright received from a law firm, one of whose clients was seeking an $8.7 million tax break through a Boatwright

Dan Boatwright

bill. His girlfriend was a featured witness in his civil trial.

Along the way, Boatwright has been called the "Teflon senator" in honor of his ability to slough off negative media coverage without it damaging his political career, an ability much on display in 1988, when he easily turned back a Democratic primary challenge from popular Contra Costa County Supervisor Sunne McPeak.

In the arena of the state Capitol, Boatwright has been one of the Legislature's biggest bullies. He and his longtime and now-departed chief aide, Barry Brokaw, were known as two of the savviest operators inside the building. When Boatwright was chairman of the Appropriations Committee, he arbitrarily killed without a hearing dozens of Assembly bills in a single day in 1986, setting off howls of protests from offended lawmakers. David Roberti stuck up for his demagogic chairman, but was repaid a year later when Boatwright tried to line up enough votes to depose Roberti as the leader of the Senate. Roberti swiftly sacked Boatwright as chairman of Appropriations, setting off a vintage Boatwright outburst: "If he wants to sit up in his little ivory tower and be besieged every day for the rest of his term, he's come to the right guy," Boatwright said of Roberti. "I was a combat infantryman in Korea, had my ass shot off, and I know how to fight a war. If he wants war, he's got war ... I'll throw hand grenades, go get a big bazooka. I mean, I know how to fight a war."

But no amount of public invective got Boatwright his job back (and he was not, by the way, wounded in Korea). Roberti, who eventually brings those he punishes back inside the tent, reached a detente with Boatwright in 1988 when he poured in thousands of dollars and drafted innumerable Senate staffers to help Boatwright meet McPeak's challenge. Roberti bolstered Boatwright's status by giving him a new job, chairmanship of the new Bonded Indebtedness Committee. After the conviction of Sen. Joseph Montoya on federal corruption charges, Boatwright moved into one of the Senate's best assignments, chairman of the Business and Professions Committee, with authority over regulatory legislation.

Since his acceptance back into the fold, Boatwright appears to be a changed man. Unlike Montoya, Boatwright does not appear to be shaking down campaign contributions from those with business before the committee. At the start of the 1991-92 session, Boatwright authored a sweeping bill to close tax loopholes.

And even some of the old bluster has departed. At least some of his new and mellower demeanor may reflect the fact that his Senate district also has changed, from one that solidly favored Democrats to one that most likely will elect a Republican whenever Boatwright departs. The district kept its number seven — but lost loyal Democratic voters in the largely African American city of Richmond and was pushed further into wealthier, Republican-voting communities of southern Contra Costa County and eastern Alameda County, including much of the Livermore Valley. Those changes dropped Democratic registration some 7 percentage points. It had little effect on Boatwright's 1992 re-election over Republican Gil Marguth, a former state assemblyman who made only a token and ill-financed effort.

PERSONAL: elected 1980; born, Jan. 29, 1930, in Harrison, Ark.; home, Concord; Army 1948-1952 (Korea); education, B.A. political science and J.D. UC Berkeley; divorced, three children; Protestant.

CAREER: lawyer; Contra Costa deputy district attorney 1960-1963; Concord City Council 1966-1972, mayor 1966-1968; Assembly 1972-1980.

COMMITTEES: Business & Professions (chair); Banking, Commerce & International Trade; Budget & Fiscal Review; Elections & Reapportionment; Revenue & Taxation; Transportation.

OFFICES: Capitol, (916) 445-6083, FAX (916) 456-7367; district, 1001 Galaxy Way, 210, Concord 94520 (510) 689-1973, (510) 830-2871, FAX (510) 825-3321.

TERM LIMIT: 1996

REGISTRATION: 45.5% D, 40.3% R

1992 CAMPAIGN:	Boatwright – D	58.0%	$1,023,657
	Gilbert Marguth Jr. – R	41.9 %	$183,193
1988 CAMPAIGN:	Boatwright – D	63%	$1,215,545
	William Pollacek – R	37%	$243,386

RATINGS:	AFL-CIO	CalPIRG	CLCV	NOW	CofC	CalFarm
	85	73	77	72	26	30

KEY VOTES:

Parent consent abort:	YES	Limit product tort:	nv	Clean Air Act:	YES
Assault gun ban:	YES	Ban AIDS discrim:	YES	Restrict abortion funds:	NO
Sales tax hike:	YES	Wealth tax hike:	NO	Strong gay rights:	nv
Parental leave:	YES	Timber compromise:	YES	Execution by injection:	YES
Limited gay rights:	nv	Universal health insure:	nv	1992-93 Budget Act:	YES
Campaign Reform:	YES	Offshore oil ban:	YES	Charter schools:	YES

Charles M. Calderon (D)

30th Senate District

The reapportionment plan that the state Supreme Court adopted after a partisan stalemate in the Capitol contained an ethnic bias — one dictated largely by federal law. The federal Voting Rights Act requires that maximum effort be made to enhance the political opportunities for underrepresented minorities and in California that meant the creation of legislative and congressional districts specifically for Latinos. The San Gabriel Valley east of downtown Los Angeles met the criteria for special treatment and thus the area's one Latino state senator, Charles Calderon, found his district divided into two, each with a very large Latino population base. He could have chosen either of the two — the 24th and the 30th — for representational purposes for the final half of his term and he chose the latter with its 75 percent Latino population and extremely strong Democratic registration.

Charles Calderon

Presumably, Calderon, having established his district office in the 30th, will be running for re-election in 1994. The 30th District runs from Huntington Park on the west to Whittier on the east and from Montebello on the north to Norwalk — the largest city in the district — on the south. In addition to Latinos, the district is the home to a significant concentration of Asians, although the largest Asian communities of the San Gabriel Valley were concentrated in the 24th District. The district also contains one city, Industry, that has no population and a second, Paramount, with just three residents. These cities were created specifically as sites for industrial facilities.

Calderon's predecessor, Joe Montoya, held this Senate seat for 12 years and probably would have been re-elected indefinitely. But Montoya, one of the Capitol's biggest "juice players," was convicted on federal bribery and racketeering charges in 1990, the first legislator imprisoned in the FBI's on-going "Brispec" undercover investigation. During Montoya's travails, Calderon moved from Monterey Park to Whittier and in so doing perfectly positioned himself to grab off Montoya's seat. Calderon had little trouble winning the seat in an April 1990 special election. His only formidable potential opponent, then-Assemblywoman Sally Tanner, decided not to run.

Calderon, a former prosecutor, couldn't have left the Assembly at a better time. He had fallen in with four other youngish Assembly members who hung out at Paragary's restaurant in midtown Sacramento. The group eventually plotted the overthrow of Speaker Willie Brown and became known as the "Gang of Five." At the start of the 1989 session, the rebels formed a brief alliance with Republican

Assembly leader Ross Johnson that had Republicans voting for Calderon for speaker. The effort failed. Calderon had no trouble winning a full Senate term in November 1990. But less than a year into his new job, he ran for the Los Angeles County Board of Supervisors in January 1991. His theory was that the San Gabriel Valley held the balance of votes in the new, court-ordered Hispanic seat. While his theory may have been right, he did not make the run-off.

Aside from his involvement in the endless petty intrigues of the Capitol, Calderon is generally a competent legislator. His chief legislative accomplishment has been in shepherding interstate banking legislation through to Gov. George Deukmejian's signature, dodging obstacles thrown in his way by Sen. Alan Robbins, D-Encino, and the savings and loan industry, then riding on the peak of its clout. Calderon's bill opened California to out-of-state banks over a phased-in period. Robbins, meanwhile, joined Montoya in federal prison as he, too, fell victim to the federal investigation. Calderon did not inherit the chairmanship of the Senate Business and Professions Committee from Montoya, but the Senate leadership did make him chairman of the Toxics and Public Safety Management Committee — a significant position for a politician from the heavily polluted San Gabriel Valley.

PERSONAL: elected 1990 (special election); born March 12, 1950, in Montebello; home, Whittier; education, B.A. CSU Los Angeles, J.D. UC Davis; divorced, two children; unaffiliated Christian.

CAREER: lawyer; city attorney's prosecutor; school board member 1979-1982; legislative aide to Assembly members Richard Alatorre and Jack Fenton; special consultant to Secretary of State March Fong Eu; Assembly 1982-1990.

COMMITTEES: Toxics & Public Safety Management (chair); Agriculture & Water Resources; Banking, Commerce & International Trade; Budget & Fiscal Review; Health & Human Services; Judiciary; Local Government; Veterans Affairs.

OFFICES: Capitol, (916) 327-8315; district, 617 W. Beverly Blvd., Montebello 90640, (213) 724-6175, FAX (213) 724-6566.

TERM LIMIT: 1998

REGISTRATION: 79.8% D, 10.5% R

1990 CAMPAIGN: Calderon – D   62.8% $106,931

Joe Urquidi – R   32% $1,190

APRIL 10, 1990 SPECIAL ELECTION:

Calderon – D   68.1% $166,039

Joe Urquidi – R   27.1% $6,104

RATINGS:	AFL-CIO	CalPIRG	CLCV	NOW	CofC	CalFarm
	91	68	87	50	11	30

KEY VOTES: (includes votes from Assembly service 1982-90)

Parent consent abort:	YES	Limit product tort:	YES	Clean Air Act:	YES
Assault gun ban:	YES	Ban AIDS discrim:	YES	Restrict abortion funds:	NO
Sales tax hike:	YES	Wealth tax hike:	YES	Strong gay rights:	YES
Parental leave:	YES	Timber compromise:	nv	Execution by injection:	nv
Limited gay rights:	nv	Universal health insur:	YES	1992-93 Budget Act:	YES
Campaign Reform:	YES	Offshore oil ban:	nv	Charter schools:	YES

William A. Craven (R)

38th Senate District

Sliced out of the upscale beach communities of "North County" (the northern part of San Diego County), the safely Republican 38th District stretches along Interstate 5 from the horse track of Del Mar to the Marine Corps base at Camp Pendleton. Much of San Diego County's growth over the last decade has been here and North County politics tend to focus on growth control. It is a land of checkerboard develop-ment, strawberry farms and quick-buck artists. It is one of the most livable corners of the state, where life is easy and a home is expensive. The Supreme Court's reapportionment gave the district a chunk of Southern Orange County, including San Juan Capistrano and San Clemente, where Richard Nixon once had his

William Craven

"Western White House." If anything, it is a safer district than ever for Republicans.

Republican Bill Craven has long been a figure in North County's civic and political life. An ex-Marine major, he epitomizes the Californians who have found their paradise in northern San Diego County. Craven came from Philadelphia, settled in North County and served on the Oceanside Planning Commission. He won a seat on the San Diego County Board of Supervisors in 1970. Five years later, he was in the Assembly, and three years after that he was in the Senate.

Craven is often called David Roberti's favorite Republican. Democrat Roberti often looks to Craven for advice. The two have built a cordial, trusting friendship verging on a cross-party alliance. Craven is one of the barons of the five-member Rules Committee that runs the Senate. The chain-smoking Craven often presides over the committee in Roberti's absence.

Craven has served as a bridge between the ideological poles of an increasingly fractured Senate. He helps the house function. And the Republicans can't take Craven's vote for granted; more than once Roberti has won a swing vote from Craven. In 1992, poor health caused him to be absent for much of the session and many thought his absence made it harder to end the 64-day budget stalemate. His absence certainly made it no easier.

Craven's legislative accomplishments are solid though not flashy. In 1990, he successfully authored SB 2475, which restricts advertisements for adult videos to sections of stores reserved for adults only. After years of labor, he also won approval of a state university campus for his district, which is being established in San Marcos. The administration building will be named for Craven. As chairman of the Select Committee on Mobile Homes, Craven is considered the Legislature's expert on such legislation, an area of major interest to many of his older constituents.

Craven was publicly outraged at the behavior of fellow Republican John Lewis, who was charged with forgery as an Assemblyman for faking Ronald Reagan's name on campaign literature in 1986. Although the charges were thrown out, Craven moved to close loopholes in the law that helped Lewis.

Although Craven was back at his desk at the start of the 1993-94 session, his friends and colleagues continued to worry about his health.

PERSONAL: elected 1973; born June 30, 1921, in Philadelphia; home, Oceanside; USMC 1942-1946, 1950-1953; education, B.S. economics Villanova University; wife Mimi, three children; Roman Catholic.

CAREER: actor, salesman, county information officer and analyst; San Marcos city manager; San Diego County supervisor; Assembly 1973-78.

COMMITTEES: Rules (vice chair); Elections & Reapportionment (vice chair); Agriculture & Water Resources; Business & Professions; Local Government.

OFFICES: Capitol, (916) 445-3731; district, 2121 Palomar Airport Road, 100, Carlsbad 92009, (619) 438-3814, FAX (619) 931-5745.

TERM LIMIT: 1998

REGISTRATION: 31.1% D, 51.9% R, 2.2% AIP

1990 CAMPAIGN:	Craven – R	66.7%	$442,621
	Jane Evans – P&F	18.2%	$0
	Scott Olmsted – L	15.1%	
1986 CAMPAIGN:	Craven – R	85%	$272,425
	Betsy Mill – L	15%	$0

RATINGS:

AFL-CIO	CalPIRG	CLCV	NOW	CofC	CalFarm
52	44	NR	14	26	10

KEY VOTES:

Parent consent abort:	YES	Limit product tort:	nv	lean Air Act:	YES
Assault gun ban:	YES	Ban AIDS discrim:	YES	Restrict abortion funds:	nv
Sales tax hike:	NO	Wealth tax hike:	nv	Strong gay rights:	NO
Parental leave:	NO	Timber compromise:	NO	Execution by injection:	nv
Limited gay rights:	NO	Universal health insure:	YES	1992-93 Budget Act:	YES
Campaign Reform:	nv	Offshore oil ban:	nv	Charter schools:	nv

Wadie P. Deddeh (D)

40th Senate District

South from San Diego and arrayed along Interstate 5 are the South Bay communities of Chula Vista, National City, Imperial Beach, Bonita and San Ysidro (part of the city of San Diego). Much of the South Bay has undergone monumental change in the last decade, but pockets remain untouched. National City is still an expanse of shipyards and the "Mile of Cars." Chula Vista, just to the south, is breaking out of its mold with ambitious plans for waterfront hotels and housing tracts. Imperial Beach is what California beach towns used to be — laid-back and a bit seedy — but it is also going broke as a municipality. And all of these communities have one overriding denominator: their proximity to Mexico, with its steady flood of illegal aliens, drugs and Tijuana's sewage system polluting beaches and farms.

Wadie Deddeh

Wadie Deddeh was elected to the Assembly in 1966, the year the Legislature went full-time. Deddeh won a seat in the Senate after the last reapportionment in 1981. His attention to legislating, however, has waxed and waned over the years.

In 1992, Deddeh tried to get out of the Legislature by running for a congressional seat. But he could not secure the Democratic nomination of his South Bay voters. Soon after he lost the primary, he had a change of heart about not accepting an $8 a day hike in living expenses from the state. "I've already fulfilled my commitment," he huffed. He also changed his mind about taking a 5 percent cut in legislative pay that he had requested in March 1992.

Born and educated in Iraq, Deddeh spent much of the 1980s entreating President Ronald Reagan to appoint him ambassador to his native land. When war began with Iraq in 1991, Deddeh found himself in the uncomfortable position of being the most prominent Iraqi-American in California. Despite keeping a studiously low profile, he has been the subject of threats. With relatives in Baghdad, the Iraqi war was a particularly painful period for Deddeh. But he made it clear that his loyalties were not divided. A week after Operation Desert Storm began, Deddeh gave an emotional floor speech in the Senate.

"There is no doubt," he said, "that our troops with God's help shall prevail — will prevail. As I stand before you at this moment, there's a great pain because on both sides of this armed camp in the Middle East, personally I'm touched because I have relatives, cousins, aunts, uncles, from whom we haven't heard, and probably when this is all over, who knows that some of them will perish." He evoked tremendous sympathy from his colleagues, who stood for a minute of silent prayer following his speech.

Deddeh has had a rather up-and-down time with internal Senate politics. When longtime Transportation Committee Chairman John Foran decided to retire at the end 1986, Deddeh ascended to the chairmanship of the committee — one of supreme importance to his district with its creaky infrastructure. Less than two years later, Deddeh squandered his chairmanship by supporting Deukmejian's ill-fated nominee for state treasurer, Republican Dan Lungren. Senate President David Roberti sacked Deddeh as Transportation chairman and appointed in his place independent Sen. Quentin Kopp of San Francisco, who in the last hours before the Lungren vote switched from support to opposition.

Roberti later resurrected Deddeh by creating a new committee on veterans affairs for him to chair. In 1990, Roberti further elevated Deddeh to the chairmanship of the powerful Senate Revenue and Taxation Committee, a post used historically as a "juice committee" to squeeze campaign contributions from special interests. But to the delight of public-interest organizations, Deddeh has been attempting to use his chairmanship to block new loopholes in the tax code with limited success.

At the start of the 1993-94 session, Deddeh was named chairman of a newly formulated Banking, Commerce and International Trade Committee. That assignment should allow him to indulge his interest in international issues. Throughout the 1980s, Deddeh was one of the Senate's biggest junketeers. He considers himself something of a foreign policy buff and has accepted free trips to the Middle East, Europe and throughout the Pacific.

Deddeh's Senate seat is up in 1994. If he doesn't retire, he may get a strong challenge from Republicans.

PERSONAL: elected 1982; born Sept. 6, 1920, in Baghdad, Iraq; home, Chula Vista; education, B.A. English University of Baghdad 1946, M.A. University of Detroit 1956, graduate work economics, government and political science San Diego State University; wife Mary-Lynn Drake, one child; Roman Catholic.

CAREER: political science teacher, Southwestern Community College, Chula Vista; Assembly 1966-1982.

COMMITTEES: Banking, Commerce & International Trade (chair); Education; Health & Human Services; Insurance, Claims & Corporations; Veterans Affairs.

OFFICES: Capitol, (916) 445-6767, FAX (916) 327-3522; district, 430 Davidson St., C, Chula Vista, 91910, (619) 427-7080, (619) 426-7369.

TERM LIMIT: 1998

REGISTRATION: 45.6% D, 38.9% R

1990 CAMPAIGN:	Deddeh – D	56.6%	$603,086
	Muriel Watson – R	36.6%	$2,871
	Roger Batchelder – P&F	3.6%	
1986 CAMPAIGN:	Deddeh – D	69%	$450,384
	William Hoover – R	29%	$7403

RATINGS:	AFL-CIO	CalPIRG	CLCV	NOW	CofC	CalFarm
	88	86	72	43	42	40

KEY VOTES:

Parent consent abort:	YES	Limit product tort:	YES	Clean Air Act:	YES
Assault gun ban:	YES	Ban AIDS discrim:	YES	Restrict abortion funds:	YES
Sales tax hike:	NO	Wealth tax hike:	YES	Strong gay rights:	YES
Parental leave:	YES	Timber compromise:	YES	Execution by injection:	YES
Limited gay rights:	YES	Universal health insure:	YES	1992-93 Budget Act:	YES
Campaign Reform:	YES	Offshore oil ban:	YES	Charter schools:	NO

Ralph C. Dills (D)

30th Senate District

This horseshoe shaped Los Angeles County district has a large minority and immigrant population. It includes the Latino neighborhoods of Montebello and the blur of used-car lots and tacky shopping centers that comprises Gardena, Norwalk, Bell Gardens, South Gate, Maywood, Huntington Park and Pico Rivera. It is an overwhelmingly Democratic district, one designed for a minority legislator. However, that will have to wait until Gardena's Ralph Dills shuffles on.

It is hard to think of the Legislature without Dills, who arrived in the Assembly during the second term of Franklin D. Roosevelt. In those days, the Legislature was controlled by corrupt lobbyist Artie Samish

Ralph Dills

and Dills was known mostly as one of the Dills Brothers. His brother, Clayton, was an assemblyman until his death. Another brother was a Capitol elevator operator. Although Dills has been there a very long time, he is not the oldest legislator; that distinction goes to Al Alquist of San Jose.

Dills has had several careers, nearly all of them lengthy. In the 1930s, he was a saxophone player working jazz clubs, then a teacher. An organizer in Democratic New Deal worker leagues, he won an Assembly seat in 1938. In his first 10 years in the Assembly, Dills authored the legislation creating California State University, Long Beach. He quit to accept a judicial appointment in 1949, then returned to Sacramento as a senator in 1967 in the first class of "full-time" legislators. "He's quite a guy!" his campaign literature proclaims.

Dills became chairman of the powerful Governmental Organization Committee in 1970, a panel with an ironclad grip on liquor, horse racing, labor unions, oil leases and gambling legislation. Dills has long been known as the liquor industry's best friend in Sacramento. He has pushed legislation to give beer and wine distributors regional monopolies — bills vetoed with a vengeance by Gov. George Deukmejian as reeking with special-interest odor.

Dills has not fared much better with Gov. Pete Wilson. In 1992, the governor vetoed Dills' SB 1978, which would have required the state to grant any employee a paid leave of absence for the employee to serve as a union official. The governor said operational needs of the state should not be subordinated to union needs. Dills also has helped bury anti-smog bills, incurring the wrath of environmentalists, who are left wondering why the bills went to his committee in the first place.

At the start of the 1991-92 session, Dills was given a seat on the Revenue and Taxation Committee, where he became a proponent of tax loopholes for various interests, including the snack food, newspaper and candy industries. He retained those committee assignments, including his powerful chairmanship, at the start of the 1993-94 session.

As the most senior senator, Dills is entitled by protocol to preside over the floor sessions of the Senate, a largely ceremonial post but with power to gum up the works. His parliamentary calls and flowery mannerisms have irritated some of his younger colleagues, who have persuaded him to preside less often. He has also toned down his garish clothing style.

Dills does not visit his district as often as most of his colleagues visit theirs, preferring to make his real home in the Sacramento suburbs. His voters do not seem to mind, for Dills has had no problem getting re-elected.

PERSONAL: elected 1966; born Feb. 10, 1910, Rosston, Tex.; home, Gardena; education, graduate of Compton College and UCLA, M.A. from USC, J.D. Loyola University; wife Elizabeth "Bette" Lee, three children.

CAREER: saxophone player; teacher; lawyer; Assembly 1938-1949; municipal judge 1949-1966.

COMMITTEES: Governmental Organization (chair); Appropriations; Education; Revenue & Taxation; Veterans Affairs.

OFFICES: Capitol, (916) 445-5953, FAX (916) 323-6056; district, 16921 S. Western Ave., 201, Gardena 90247, (310) 324-4969, FAX (310) 329-5244.

TERM LIMIT: 1998

REGISTRATION: 65.1% D, 24.7% R

1990 CAMPAIGN:	Dills – D	68.3%	$615,454
	Timothy Poling – R	31.7%	$0
1986 CAMPAIGN:	Dills – D	72%	$432,111
	Anthony Gray – R	25%	$2,325

RATINGS:	AFL-CIO	CalPIRG	CLCV	NOW	CofC	CalFarm
	92	77	73	86	16	30

KEY VOTES:

Parent consent abort:	NO	Limit product tort:	YES	Clean Air Act:	YES
Assault gun ban:	YES	Ban AIDS discrim:	YES	Restrict abortion funds:	NO
Sales tax hike:	YES	Wealth tax hike:	YES	Strong gay rights:	YES
Parental leave:	YES	Timber compromise:	YES	Execution by injection:	NO
Limited gay rights:	YES	Universal health insure:	YES	1992-93 Budget Act:	NO
Campaign Reform:	YES	Offshore oil ban:	NO	Charter schools:	YES

Leroy F. Greene (D)
6th Senate District

The Capitol is not only where Leroy Greene spends most of his working hours, it is also the middle of his district, which encompasses nearly all of the city of Sacramento and much of the unincorporated urban area surrounding the city. Boundaries changed a bit during reapportionment, but the district's economic and political ambience remains virtually the same.

The district was originally tailored to Greene's political specifications by Democratic leaders following the stunning 1980 defeat of the Democratic dean of the Senate, Al Rodda, by conservative Republican upstart John Doolittle. During the post-census reapportionment Democrats reconfigured Rodda's old district to lop off the most Republican suburbs and to concentrate strength in Democratic city precincts. And a clever change of district numbers forced Doolittle to stand for re-election in 1982, just two years into his first term. Doolittle faced Greene, who had spent 20 years in the Assembly representing a mid Sacramento district. Greene defeated Doolittle, but another change of district lines after the election created another new district in which Doolittle successfully ran in 1984.

Leroy Greene

The district Democrats crafted for Greene was more Democratic than the one Rodda had represented, but it was not a perverse gerrymander, and the Supreme Court, which undertook reapportionment after the 1990 census, went along with the logic of having one Senate district cover the capital city and nearby suburbs.

Greene represents a city that is one of the state's fastest-growing and fastest changing. Sacramento teeters on the verge — local boosters think it is there already — of big-city status. The area's traditional dependence on government payrolls lessened in the 1980s as financial and high-tech industries moved into the area, many of them relocating or expanding from the Bay Area. With that change came a decided shift to the right in Sacramento politics, which had been solidly Democratic. The central city and its closest suburbs, however, remain Democratic and thus the 6th District, with a Democratic registration comfortably over 50 percent, is safe for the party for the foreseeable future.

As an assemblyman, Greene was an often acerbic, highly active legislator with an interest in education. A civil engineer who practiced in Sacramento for years, Greene was chairman of the Assembly Education Committee and carried numerous bills to finance construction, reconstruction and operation of public schools.

After moving to the Senate, Greene moved into the background, no longer playing a leading role in shaping major legislation, seemingly content to support the

Democratic Party line on issues and to carry local-interest bills, although a later appointment as chairman of the Senate Revenue and Taxation Committee raises his profile somewhat. In the wake of the passage of Proposition 112, a sweeping ethics ballot measure approved in 1990, Greene was appointed chairman of a new Senate Ethics Committee.

Greene survived a stiff challenge from Republican Sandra Smoley, then a Sacramento County supervisor, in 1986. But he had only token opposition in 1990. He can seek a fourth term in the Senate in 1994 before term limits end his legislative career, but due to his age and bouts of ill health, there is a widespread belief in the Capitol that he may retire rather than run again. His wife, Denny, died in 1991 after a long illness.

PERSONAL: elected 1982; born Jan. 31, 1918, in Newark, N.J.; home, Carmichael; Army WWII; education, B.S. civil engineering Purdue University; widower, one child; no religious affiliation.

CAREER: civil engineer 1951-1978, owned firm; Assembly 1962-1982; newspaper columnist; radio talk show host.

COMMITTEES: Revenue & Taxation (chair); Senate Ethics (chair); Appropriations; Banking, Commerce & International Trade; Business & Professions; Education; Energy & Public Utilities; Governmental Organization; Industrial Relations.

OFFICES: Capitol, (916) 445-7807, FAX (916) 327-6341; district, P.O. Box 254646, Carmichael 95825, (916) 324-4937.

TERM LIMIT: 1998

REGISTRATION: 54.9% D, 33.6% R

1990 CAMPAIGN:	Greene – D	53.7%	$507,849
	Joe Sullivan – R	40.4%	$8,745
1986 CAMPAIGN:	Greene – D	61%	$1,023,365
	Sandra Smoley – R	40%	$1,108,081

RATINGS:	AFL-CIO	CalPIRG	CLCV	NOW	CofC	CalFarm
	89	82	74	72	21	20

KEY VOTES:

Parent consent abort:	NO	Limit product tort:	YES	Clean Air Act:	nv
Assault gun ban:	YES	Ban AIDS discrim:	YES	Restrict abortion funds:	NO
Sales tax hike:	YES	Wealth tax hike:	YES	Strong gay rights:	YES
Parental leave:	YES	Timber compromise:	YES	Execution by injection:	nv
Limited gay rights:	YES	Universal health insur:	YES	1992-93 Budget Act:	YES
Campaign Reform:	YES	Offshore oil ban:	YES	Charter schools:	YES

Gary K. Hart (D)

18th Senate District

On a coastal corridor from San Luis Obisbo to Ventura, the 18th Senate District includes growth-controlled Santa Barbara, Oxnard and the laid-back communities surrounding UC Santa Barbara. The district, which also runs along the spine of the low but rugged Santa Ynez Mountains, has an environmentalist tilt but is decidedly upscale with a low Democratic registration, making it an increasingly volatile battleground.

Democrat Gary K. Hart — he took up using his middle initial to distinguish himself from that other Gary Hart — has managed to balance the sometimes conflicting political tendencies of this district. A former teacher, Hart is popular among growth-controllers and environmentalists. He gets high marks from his colleagues for intellect and integrity.

Gary K. Hart

As chairman of the Senate Education Committee, he has become the Senate Democrats' chief expert and increasingly visible spokesman on education issues. Hart has strenuously opposed college and university fee increases proposed by Gov. Pete Wilson and voted against the final 1992-93 budget despite a record 64 day stalemate. Hart was prepared to keep fighting to protect education.

He also did something else unusual. During the fall of 1992, while other legislators were running their re-election campaigns or taking long vacations, Hart taught a high school social studies class in Sacramento. He said it gave him a reality check like nothing else could in the Capitol.

Hart has had some notable successes legislating during the Wilson years. Wilson signed Hart's version of a "charter schools" pilot project that would give parents, teachers and principals new independence in running individual schools. Wilson vetoed a more sweeping measure by Hart's counterpart in the Assembly, Democrat Delaine Eastin.

While many child-care proposals died or were vetoed in recent years, Republican Gov. George Deukmejian signed a Hart bill offering tax credits to employers who establish savings programs for the use of their employees' children. Many employers are beginning to take advantage of the Hart bill.

When the political infighting gets rough, however, Hart often bows out — a trait that has contributed to his inability to move into a leadership role. Perhaps that is one of the reasons he seems bored with the Legislature. He ran for Congress in 1988 in one of the hardest-fought congressional contests in the nation, falling less than 1 percentage point short of beating longtime Republican Rep. Robert Lagomarsino. Both national parties threw everything they could muster into the race. Ronald Reagan came down from his ranch (in a neighboring Senate district) to stump for Lagomarsino. In the end, Lagomarsino won but was wounded.

Hart then gave up on the idea of moving to Congress. He ran for re-election in 1990 instead of giving it another try and passed up the chance to run in 1992, when his Senate seat would not be in jeopardy if he lost.

Hart has given every indication he will run for state superintendent of public instruction to replace Bill Honig in 1994. But it remains to be seen whether Hart has the stamina to withstand what promises to be an elbow-to-elbow Democratic primary with the likes of Eastin.

PERSONAL: elected 1982; born Aug. 13, 1943, in San Diego, Calif.; home, Santa Barbara; education, B.A. history Stanford University., M.A. education Harvard University; wife Cary Smith, three children; Protestant.

CAREER: teacher; Assembly 1974-1982.

COMMITTEES: Education (chair); Natural Resources & Wildlife (vice chair); Budget & Fiscal Review; Business & Professions; Constitutional Amendments; Energy & Public Utilities.

OFFICES: Capitol, (916) 445-5405, FAX (916) 322-3304; district, 1216 State St., 507, Santa Barbara 93101, (805) 966-1766, FAX (805) 965-1161.

TERM LIMIT: 1998

REGISTRATION: 42.6% D, 41.0% R, 2.1% AIP

1990 CAMPAIGN:	Hart – D	60.4%	$506,361
	Carey Rogers – R	35.4%	$16,252
1986 CAMPAIGN:	Hart – D	65%	$583,271
	DeWayne Holmdahl – R	33%	$166,150

RATINGS:	AFL-CIO	CalPIRG	CLCV	NOW	CofC	CalFarm
	93	82	95	86	16	20

KEY VOTES:

Parent consent abort:	NO	Limit product tort:	nv	Clean Air Act:	YES
Assault gun ban:	YES	Ban AIDS discrim:	YES	Restrict abortion funds:	NO
Sales tax hike:	YES	Wealth tax hike:	YES	Strong gay rights:	YES
Parental leave:	YES	Timber compromise:	nv	Execution by injection:	nv
Limited gay rights:	YES	Universal health insure:	nv	1992-93 Budget Act:	NO
Campaign Reform:	YES	Offshore oil ban:	YES	Charter schools:	YES

Thomas E. Hayden (D)

23rd Senate District

This Los Angeles County coastal district includes comfortable Pacific Palisades, the beach houses and canyons of Malibu, portions of liberal West Los Angeles and the left-of-center environs of Santa Monica. The district extends into Beverly Hills and over the ridges into the San Fernando Valley to include Woodland Hills.

The Democrat who occupies its seat happens to be one of the nation's most controversial figures, Tom Hayden. How he got there in 1992 proved to be one of the most expensive high-profile shoot-outs among Democrats in years.

Hayden was first reapportioned out of his Assembly district by Willie Brown, who was anxious to be rid of Hayden, and then by the state Supreme Court.

Hayden's legislative career appeared at last to be at an end. But Hayden instead challenged longtime Senate Democrat Herschel Rosenthal for the 23rd District seat. Rosenthal, who wasn't facing re-election for another two years in the 22nd District, decided to try for the seat because it looked safer than his own.

What followed was a blitz of mailers in a three-way Democratic primary between Hayden, Rosenthal and Democratic activist Catherine O'Neill of Pacific Palisades. Hayden, who spent more than $750,000 on the primary — mostly his own money — ended up winning the Democratic nomination by less than 600 votes. Winning in November was largely pro forma given the heavy Democratic registration.

Tom Hayden

To the public, Hayden is probably the best known member of the California Legislature, with the possible exception of Brown. Hayden is a subject in scores of books, magazine and newspaper articles spanning three decades. He is certainly the only legislator whose comings and goings are charted by People magazine. Hayden has a life that transcends the narrow world of the Legislature. Whatever he does in Sacramento is almost beside the point.

As a founder of Students for a Democratic Society, and as one of the authors of the New Left's manifesto, The Port Huron Statement, Hayden's place in postwar American history is assured. He was put on trial as one of the Chicago Eight, accused of fomenting the riot at the 1968 Democratic convention and sentenced to five years in prison. Back then, Hayden was urged to go underground because friends feared he would be murdered in prison. Those were the days when Hayden vented speeches calling for "revolutionizing youth" through "a series of sharp and dangerous conflicts, life and death conflicts."

But Hayden drew back from the revolutionary life. His Chicago conviction was overturned in 1972. His marriage to Jane Fonda won him star status and something the New Left had lacked: a sizable bank account. With Fonda's money, Hayden rejoined the mainstream by running for the U.S. Senate in 1976 against Democratic incumbent John Tunney. Hayden lost and incurred the wrath of many Democratic leaders, who accused him of weakening Tunney, leaving him vulnerable to defeat by Republican S.I. Hayakawa.

In the wake of his U.S. Senate campaign, Hayden created the Campaign for Economic Democracy (which became Campaign California.) Hayden's groups have won success at the ballot box, most notably the Proposition 65 water purity measure, and in helping to close Sacramento's troubled Rancho Seco nuclear power plant. The organization has pockets of strength in the Bay Area, Chico, Sacramento and, of course, in Hayden's home base of Santa Monica.

But his organizations also have suffered notable setbacks. Hayden was one of the major backers of the "Big Green" environmental initiative in 1990 that would have created a new elected statewide position of "environmental advocate." Some thought the position tailor-made for Hayden. He and his organizations poured money into the initiative. But it went down in flames after multimillion spending by industrial and agribusiness opponents.

Hayden's fame and success have come with a heavy price. There are those who will always consider him a traitor for having supported the Communist side during the Vietnam War and believe he should have been put on trial for treason. Some of Hayden's colleagues when he was in the Assembly, particularly Gil Ferguson, routinely refused to vote for a Hayden bill regardless of its merits because his name was on it. And legislative life appears to have contributed to the breakup of his marriage with Fonda.

Hayden is the Legislature's loner. He counts only a handful of his colleagues as his friends, chief among them his former Assembly seatmate, Tom Bates, who represents Berkeley. Hayden was an indirect beneficiary of the 1987-1988 "Gang of Five" rebellion against Willie Brown. In sacking rebel Democrat Gary Condit as chairman of the Governmental Organization Committee, the speaker had to reshuffle other chairmanships. To Hayden went the chairmanship of the Assembly Labor Committee. But he showed too much independence to suit Brown's labor constituency, and the speaker shunted him aside at the start of the 1991-92 session. Hayden's relations with Brown went steadily downward.

Hayden's interests are wider than the Legislature. He is a die-hard baseball fan and goes to baseball fantasy camps for middle-aged men. He has lately taught college-level classes — not on politics, but on environmental values as expressed through religious traditions. In recent interviews, he said he has become more of an environmentalist than he was in his earlier anti-war years.

Although Hayden at times seems bored in a sea of legislative mediocrity, he remains one of the Legislature's more astute observers and original thinkers. He occasionally votes with Republicans on crime issues and favors the death penalty. Hayden has concentrated on toxic waste and higher education issues, particularly strengthening the state's community colleges. He also has focused on oversight of the University of California's Lawrence Livermore nuclear weapons lab, much to its discomfort.

He came full circle in 1992, re-emerging as something of a hero to college students as a vocal opponent of Pete Wilson's plans for raising college and university fees. For that and other reasons, he ended up voting against the state budget in the Assembly despite 64 days of stalemate. Hayden also has become something of a self-styled expert on energy issues and his committee assignments in the Senate should allow him to continue that interest.

At the start of the 1993-94 session, Hayden tried to shake things up in the staid Senate by asking that its dress code be waived so that he wouldn't have to wear a coat and tie. He was given a firm no.

PERSONAL: elected 1992; born Dec. 11, 1939, in Detroit; home, Santa Monica; education, B.A. history University of Michigan; divorced, one child and one stepchild; Roman Catholic.

CAREER: founder, Students for a Democratic Society; founder, Campaign for Economic Democracy, Campaign California; author; teacher; Assembly 1982-1992.

COMMITTEES: Energy & Public Utilities; Housing & Urban Affairs; Natural Resources & Wildlife; Toxics & Public Safety Management; Transportation.

OFFICES: Capitol, (916) 445-1353; district, 10951 W. Pico Blvd., 202, Los Angeles 90064, (310) 451-5733.

TERM LIMIT: 2000

REGISTRATION: 54.6% D, 31.0% R

1992 CAMPAIGN: Hayden – D   55.9% $1,018,084
                 Leonard McRoskey – R   33.1% $35,495

RATINGS: (Ratings and Key Votes from Assembly service 1982-92)

AFL-CIO	CalPIRG	CLCV	NOW	CofC	CalFarm
97	85	100	86	17	30

KEY VOTES:

Parent consent abort:	NO	Limit product tort:	NO	Clean Air Act:	YES
Assault gun ban:	YES	Ban AIDS discrim:	YES	Restrict abortion funds:	nv
Sales tax hike:	YES	Wealth tax hike:	YES	Strong gay rights:	YES
Parental leave:	YES	Timber compromise:	NO	Execution by injection:	NO
Limited gay rights:	YES	Universal health insure:	nv	1992-93 Budget Act:	NO
Campaign Reform:	YES	Offshore oil ban:	YES	Charter schools:	YES

Frank Hill (R)
29th Senate District

Bobbing and weaving through the San Gabriel Valley, this Senate district covers the eastern-most part of Los Angeles County. It takes in the old neighborhoods of Claremont and Pomona and the conservative think tanks nearby, and the instant housing developments of Diamond Bar and West Covina. The district also crosses the Whittier Hills and includes a piece of Whittier. It is carved around pockets of Latinos and is therefore safe for Republicans. Incumbent Frank Hill had little trouble getting re-elected in his new district in 1992, facing the same Democratic opponent, Sandy Hestor, he had faced in a 1990 special election in his old 31st District.

Frank Hill

In the Senate, Hill has turned out to be something of a maverick, much in evidence during the protracted 1992 budget stalemate. Day after day, Hill and Democratic Assemblyman Phil Isenberg kept concocting new proposals to get the state out of its budget mess. In so doing, Hill irked Gov. Pete Wilson and the Senate Republican leader, Ken Maddy. Wilson felt undercut and Maddy felt upstaged by a young protege.

While the Hill-Isenberg proposals appeared to have the effect of getting the governor and legislative leaders at least talking, Hill paid a price in his own party for his independence. At the start of the 1993-94 session, Maddy had Hill stripped of his position as the lead Republican representative on the budget committees. But that probably will not muzzle Hill if the state again faces budget gridlock. He is now one of the first people reporters talk to for an analysis of budget proposals.

Hill's prospects for a bright political future are clouded by an ongoing federal probe. Hill's office was one of four searched in 1988 by federal agents as part of its undercover "sting" investigation into influence peddling in the state Capitol. Hill reportedly remains a subject of the probe. Although his election opponents have attempted to capitalize on the investigation, voters were evidently unimpressed.

Hill has been in the Legislature since he was 28, and he is generally well-liked on both sides of the aisle. He has been in politics even longer, having served as the Whittier office manager for former Rep. Wayne Grisham and as an aide in Washington, D.C., to U.S. Sen. S.I. Hayakawa. In Sacramento, Hill used his political skills to move quickly into a leadership post among Assembly Republicans, eventually serving as their liaison with Gov. George Deukmejian.

Hill gained some statewide exposure as a leader in the successful 1986 initiative drive to declare English the state's official language. While he supports more education funding in general, he also has become known for his opposition to mandatory bilingual education, arguing for local control over those decisions.

Hill is considered a strong voice for the liquor industry. In the closing days of the 1989 session, he made an impassioned floor speech in the Assembly against fellow Republican Bill Leonard's bill lowering the blood-alcohol standard to 0.08 for drunken driving. The bill is now law.

PERSONAL: elected 1990 (special election); born Feb. 19, 1954, in Whittier; home, Whittier; education, A.A. political science Mt. San Antonio College in Walnut; B.A. political science UCLA; M.A. public administration Pepperdine University; wife Faye, two children; Episcopalian.

CAREER: Washington office manager U.S. Sen. S.I. Hayakawa 1976-1978; field director Rep. Wayne Grisham 1978-1982; Assembly 1982-1990.

COMMITTEES: Insurance, Claims & Corporations (vice chair); Budget & Fiscal Review; Governmental Organization; Health & Human Services.

OFFICES: Capitol, (916) 445-2848, FAX (916) 327-8817; district, 15820 E. Whittier Blvd., H, Whittier 90603, (310) 947-3021, FAX (310) 943-2690.

TERM LIMIT: 1996

REGISTRATION: 41.5% D, 46.3% R

1992 CAMPAIGN: Hill – R   56.2% $879,112
     Sandy Hester – D   43.8% $22,234
APRIL 10, 1990 SPECIAL ELECTION:
     Hill – R   60.8% $701,053
     Janice Graham – D   35.6% $39,270

RATINGS:

AFL-CIO	CalPIRG	CLCV	NOW	CofC	CalFarm
15	45	25	14	68	90

KEY VOTES: (includes some votes from Assembly service 1982-90)

Parent consent abort:	YES	Limit product tort:	YES	Clean Air Act:	YES
Assault gun ban:	NO	Ban AIDS discrim:	NO	Restrict abortion funds:	YES
Sales tax hike:	NO	Wealth tax hike:	NO	Strong gay rights:	NO
Parental leave:	NO	Timber compromise:	NO	Execution by injection:	YES
Limited gay rights:	NO	Universal health insur:	nv	1992-93 Budget Act:	YES
Campaign Reform:	NO	Offshore oil ban:	nv	Charter schools:	NO

Teresa P. Hughes (D)

25th Senate District

When Teresa Hughes moved from the Assembly to the Senate in 1992, she continued a linear political succession dating back three decades. Mervyn Dymally began the sequence in 1962 when he was elected to the state Assembly. He moved up to the Senate in 1966 and his aide, Bill Greene, succeeded him in the Assembly. When Dymally was elected as California's first African American lieutenant governor in 1974, Greene followed him into the Senate via special election and another Dymally aide — Hughes — took Greene's place in the Assembly. Dymally, meanwhile, was defeated for re-election in 1978 and shifted to Congress two years later. He retired from politics in 1992 as did Greene, who had been plagued

Teresa Hughes

by ill health, including a heart attack, and alcoholism. That opened the door for Hughes to capture the Senate seat that Dymally and Greene had held and she did so with no serious challenge.

As reconstituted and renumbered by the state Supreme Court's reapportionment plan, the 25th District is a compact chunk of impoverished South-Central Los Angeles that exemplifies the social and political trends on the poorer side of the Santa Monica Freeway. Inglewood, home of the Los Angeles Lakers and the Hollywood Park horse racing track, anchors the northwestern corner of the district.

While the district is more than 40 percent Latino, fewer than 10 percent of its registered voters are Latino, and African American politicians remain dominant, despite a shrinking African American population that's already less than 40 percent.

And that's not likely to change until sometime in the 21st Century. There's also a growing Asian population in the district, including the heavily Asian city of Gardena.

Hughes, a former social worker, teacher, school administrator and college professor, was most visible in the Legislature as chairwoman of the Assembly Education Committee. But at the start of the 1991-92 session, she was summarily booted out by Speaker Willie Brown and replaced with Delaine Eastin of Union City, a suburb south of Oakland. The move marked a major power shift on the education panel away from the gorilla-sized Los Angeles Unified School District and toward suburban schools. The speaker never publicly explained why he canned Hughes, but privately those close to Brown said he thought Hughes was plodding and ineffective. Brown also was under pressure from more aggressive and intellectually supple liberals in the Democratic caucus, who wanted a crack at forging education policy. And Hughes was already planning to leave the Assembly to run for the Senate.

Hughes was never as successful in the fractious Assembly as the Senate education leaders were in shaping consensus on controversial issues and innovative programs. Brown threw Hughes a bone by appointing her to chair a Ways and Means subcommittee on state administration, a not-insignificant post but one with considerably less clout and visibility. The grumpy Hughes made it clear she did not like the demotion and she hesitated before accepting the subcommittee chair.

Hughes has pushed several AIDS-related bills, including a 1987 measure signed into law that allows doctors to disclose AIDS test results to spouses of people who have been tested. She also has backed legislation to require condom standards to make sure that the prophylactics block the AIDS virus. If Hughes was alienated from Speaker Brown in the Assembly, the Senate's Democratic leaders gave her a warm welcome by appointing her to chair the Public Employment and Retirement Committee, a semi-important position that solidifies her close connections to public employee unions.

PERSONAL: elected 1992; born Oct. 3, 1932, in New York City; home, Los Angeles; education, B.A. Hunter College; M.A. New York University; Ph.D. Claremont College; husband Frank Staggers, two children; Roman Catholic.

CAREER: teacher, school administrator; professor of education, CSU Los Angeles; aide to Sen. Mervyn Dymally 1973; Assembly 1975-1992.

COMMITTEES: Public Employment & Retirement (chair); Energy & Public Utilities; Governmental Organization; Health & Human Services; Local Government.

OFFICES: Capitol, (916) 445-2104, FAX (916) 327-5703; district, 1 Manchester Blvd., 401, Inglewood 90301, (310) 410-0393.

TERM LIMIT: 2000
REGISTRATION: 75.2%, 15.0 R

1992 CAMPAIGN: Hughes – D   76.8% $513,681
              Cliff McClain – R   18.8% $0

RATINGS: (all Ratings and Key Votes from Assembly service 1975-92)

AFL-CIO	CalPIRG	CLCV	NOW	CofC	CalFarm
95	95	88	100	17	25

KEY VOTES:

Parent consent abort:	NO	Limit product tort:	nv	Clean Air Act:	YES
Assault gun ban:	YES	Ban AIDS discrim:	YES	Restrict abortion funds:	NO
Sales tax hike:	YES	Wealth tax hike:	YES	Strong gay rights:	YES
Parental leave:	YES	Timber compromise:	YES	Execution by injection:	YES
Limited gay rights:	YES	Universal health insur:	YES	1992-93 Budget Act:	NO
Campaign Reform:	nv	Offshore oil ban:	YES	Charter schools:	NO

Patrick W. Johnston (D)

5th Senate District

The 5th Senate District includes all but the rural southwest corner of San Joaquin County and the southern portion of Sacramento County, including portions of east Sacramento, Campus Commons, Arden-Arcade, Rancho Cordova, part of Carmichael, Laguna, Elk Grove, Galt and others. San Joaquin County cities in his district include Stockton, Lodi, Manteca, Lathrop and Tracy.

In the mid-1970s, some newcomers burst onto the political scene in Stockton and surrounding areas. A young rancher named John Garamendi won an Assembly seat and then quickly moved into the state Senate. He hired another young man, Patrick Johnston, as his aide. Johnston won election to the Assembly in

Patrick Johnston

his own right in 1980 and by 1990 he found himself face-to-face not only with John Garamendi, who was on his way to becoming the first elected state insurance commissioner, but John's wife, Patti, who was eager to replace her husband in the Senate.

In fact, Garamendi quit his seat early — more than two months before the November election for insurance commissioner — in an attempt to give his wife an edge over Johnston. The plan was to have the special election for his seat consolidated with the general election. Since Johnston could not have his name removed as a candidate for re-election to the Assembly, it was hoped that he would look overly ambitious as he technically ran for two offices. But the maneuver backfired. The Garamendis were accused of trying to manipulate the process to create a family dynasty. Johnston beat Patti Garamendi and nine others in the first round, then easily won the run-off from the top Republican vote-getter, Philip

Wallace. Patti Garamendi spent $621,122 on her effort, which included more than $500,000 she loaned her campaign from personal funds.

It wasn't Johnston's first tough election. In 1980, he challenged a Democratic incumbent, Assemblyman Carmen Perino, in the June primary. It was a nasty battle that was made nastier by a power struggle for the speakership of the Assembly that year and by the personal nature of local politics. Johnston defeated Perino but his struggle was just beginning. His November tussle with Republican Adrian Fondse was one of the sleaziest in California history, complete with anti-Johnston mailings appealing to racial prejudices and other dirty tricks. The initial vote count showed Fondse winning, but a recount, certified by Johnston's fellow Democrats in the Assembly, unseated Fondse and declared Johnston the victor by 35 votes out of some 84,000 cast.

Johnston, a former journalist who once aspired to the Roman Catholic priesthood, has achieved a reputation as a liberal reformer and as one of the state's brighter legislators. He proved his adaptability while chairing the Assembly's Finance and Insurance Committee, a major "juice committee" with jurisdiction over banks and insurance companies and whose members are showered with attention from industry lobbyists. Johnston has not been shy about accepting campaign contributions, trips and other goodies from special interests, but he has earned kudos from affected industries and consumers alike for his honesty and evenhanded operation of the committee.

Johnston put himself in the thick of the battles over auto insurance and was a critic of both the industry and its self-appointed reformers in what seemed to be a politically dangerous move during California's wild, five-way insurance initiative war in 1988. Since then, he has continued to avoid the populist road paved by Proposition 103, the winner of that initiative war, and instead has joined with consumer groups in pushing a no-fault system that he has said holds out the best chance to control insurance rates and service.

Johnston took a front seat in the controversial battle over workers' compensation system reform when he accepted the chairmanship of the Senate Industrial Relations Committee for the 1993-94 legislative session. Any reform measures dealing with the ailing system will go through Johnston's committee.

In 1992, Johnston crafted the Delta Protection Act, which was signed into law by Gov. Wilson. The Act established a 19-member commission with the task of developing a resource management plan for the Delta to protect it from overdevelopment. The bill met with resistance from developers and some local officials, who feared the loss of local autonomy, but Johnston persevered, conducting local hearings and inviting input from citizens. Ultimately, the plan received the blessings of the California Farm Bureau, the Audubon Society, the boating and fishing industries and a number of local governments. Johnston has said he feels more pride over that bill than anything else he has accomplished for his district.

No one will accuse Johnston of ignoring popular feelings. He was one of the first in the Capitol to react to the savings and loan industry scandals, but he was also one of the few who pushed investigations and reforms that were actually substantive.

PERSONAL: elected 1991 (special election); born Sept. 3, 1946, in San Francisco; home, Stockton; education, B.A. philosophy St. Patrick's College, Menlo Park; wife Margaret Mary Johnston, two children; Roman Catholic.

CAREER: Reporter for a Catholic newspaper; probation officer, Calaveras County; chief of staff to Sen. John Garamendi 1975-1980; Assembly 1980-1991.

COMMITTEES: Industrial Relations (chair); Appropriations; Bank, Commerce & International Trade; Education; Insurance, Claims & Corporations; Natural Resources & Wildlife; Public Employment & Retirement; Transportation.

OFFICES: Capitol, (916) 445-2407; district, 31 E. Channel St., 440, Stockton 95202, (209) 948-7930, FAX (209) 948-7993.

TERM LIMIT: 1996

REGISTRATION: 50.6% D, 38.7% R

1992 CAMPAIGN:

	Johnston – D	57.5%	$585,609
	Ron Stauffer – R	37.3%	$30,144
	Eric Roberts – L	5.2%	

JAN. 8, 1991, SPECIAL ELECTION:

	Johnston – D	56.8%	$565,424
	Philip Wallace – R	38.2%	$58,234
	Thomas Tryon – L	5.1%	

RATINGS:

AFL-CIO	CalPIRG	CLCV	NOW	CofC	CalFarm
90	86	78	79	21	20

KEY VOTES: (includes votes from Assembly service 1980-91)

Parent consent abort:	NO	Limit product tort:	YES	Clean Air Act:	YES
Assault gun ban:	YES	Ban AIDS discrim:	YES	Restrict abortion funds:	NO
Sales tax hike:	YES	Wealth tax hike.	YES	Strong gay rights:	YES
Parental leave:	YES	Timber compromise:	YES	Execution by injection:	nv
Limited gay rights:	YES	Universal health insure:	YES	1992-93 Budget Act:	YES
Campaign Reform:	YES	Offshore oil ban:	YES	Charter schools:	YES

David G. Kelley (R)
37th Senate District

Whether the state Supreme Court intended it or not, its creation of this district in the 1992 reapportionment was tailor-made for Republican David Kelley. It takes in the rural and desert portions of Riverside County, the agriculturally rich Imperial County and rural eastern San Diego County along the U.S.-Mexico border. Upscale communities including Palm Springs and Rancho Mirage are within the district. So too are intensely poor communities, including Calexico and El Centro. The district has a large Latino population — 28 percent — which is politically muted (only 12 percent of the registered voters are Latino). The seat was carved from pieces represented by Democrat Robert Presley and Republican Marian Bergeson, both of whom had oversized districts going into reapportionment.

David Kelley

Republican citrus farmer David Kelley did not have to work hard to get elected in this district in 1992. He fit the power structure to a T. Kelley is one of the four new faces in the state Senate, but there is really nothing new about him to his fellow state senators. In the Assembly, Kelley coasted through legislative life, heard from occasionally with outbursts against farm-worker unions and the leaders of the Republican Assembly caucus, whom he can now safely ignore. He carried little legislation beyond his pet gold-coin collector bills. He did not even do much in the way of district bills, leaving that to Riverside County Democrats.

Kelley's intrigue against various Republican leaders in the Assembly won him a number of enemies. Finally, Kelley backed a winner for Assembly Republican leader — fellow farmer Bill Jones of Fresno. But Jones did not put Kelley on his leadership team. Jones turned out to be a dud anyway, but by then Kelley had turned his sights on winning the new Senate seat.

Kelley came to the Legislature relatively late in life after becoming wealthy from his acres of productive trees in the Hemet-San Jacinto Valley. He was instrumental in helping George Deukmejian gain the trust of agricultural interests in the 1982 GOP gubernatorial primary, but Kelley got little in return.

In 1990, Kelley persuaded the state Department of Fish and Game to propose a 2,800-acre "wildlife area" next to his ranch in an unsuccessful attempt to protect his irrigation supply. Although the agency staff drew up a proposal to buy the $4.1 million property, the Kelley-backed proposal died when a review board found nothing environmentally sensitive about the land — and a huge housing development went there instead. The developer accused Kelley of a conflict of interest because he was the ranking Republican on the Assembly Water, Parks and Wildlife Committee, which oversees the Fish and Game Department. "Well, it wasn't necessarily in my interest," Kelley responded to an interviewer. "It's an interest of a lot of growers out there, too, because they don't want to lose the water that they have for their farming operations."

PERSONAL: elected 1992; born Oct. 11, 1928, in Riverside; home, Hemet; education, B.S. agriculture, Calif. State Polytechnic University, Pomona; USAF 1949-1953; wife Brigitte, four children; Lutheran.

CAREER: citrus farmer; Assembly 1978-1992.

COMMITTEES: Agriculture & Water Resources; Appropriations; Banking, Commerce & International Trade; Business & Professions; Transportation.

OFFICES: Capitol, (916) 445-5581, FAX (916) 327-2187; district, 6840 Indiana Ave., 150, Riverside 92506, (909) 369-6644, FAX (909) 369-0366.
TERM LIMIT: 2000
REGISTRATION: 38.3% D, 46.6% R

1992 CAMPAIGN:			
Kelley – R	52.5%	$480,375
Jim Rickard – D	37.7%	$14,837
Renate Kline – P&F	6.2%	

RATINGS: (all Ratings and Key votes are from Assembly service 1978-92)

AFL-CIO	CalPIRG	CLCV	NOW	CofC	CalFarm
12	36	7	29	100	85

KEY VOTES:

Parent consent abort:	YES	Limit product tort:	YES	Clean Air Act:	YES
Assault gun ban:	NO	Ban AIDS discrim:	NO	Restrict abortion funds:	YES
Sales tax hike:	YES	Wealth tax hike:	YES	Strong gay rights:	NO
Parental leave:	NO	Timber compromise:	NO	Execution by injection:	YES
Limited gay rights:	NO	Universal health insure:	NO	1992-93 Budget Act:	YES
Campaign Reform:	NO	Offshore oil ban:	NO	Charter schools:	YES

Lucy L. Killea (independent)

39th Senate District

Starting on Coronado Island, the 39th District heads east, taking in the heart of San Diego's featureless bedroom neighborhoods on the bluffs overlooking San Diego's sports stadium. The district includes Democratic pockets in Hillcrest and Mission Hills, but is otherwise strongly Republican and has the smallest minority population of any San Diego County district.

Upon the retirement of Republican Jim Ellis, another Republican, Larry Stirling, had little trouble getting elected to this seat in 1988. But to the total surprise of Capitol insiders, he quit after less than a year to take a judgeship in the San Diego Municipal Court. Stirling's 1989 resignation set off one of the

Lucy Killea

strangest political events in modern state history: a special election that became a national referendum on abortion rights and the bounds of the Catholic Church's involvement in politics.

At first glance, it looked as if Democratic Assemblywoman Lucy Killea stood no chance of winning. Killea, a Catholic, was solidly pro-choice on abortion and her rival, Assemblywoman Carol Bentley — then in her first term — was anti-abortion. Polls showed that while the San Diego region was conservative, more than two-thirds of adults were pro-choice. And polls also showed Killea was better known.

The special election snoozed along as a local affair until Roman Catholic Bishop Leo T. Maher, now deceased, sent Killea a letter (by fax machine) informing her that she could no longer receive communion at her parish. He leaked the letter to a television station — and everything backfired on him.

Killea's campaign became an overnight national media event. She took a quick trip to New York to appear on the Phil Donahue show with Geraldine Ferraro (Bentley declined Donahue's invitation). Killea was the subject of stories in USA Today, the Washington Post and the New York Times. Her election night headquarters in an El Cajon union hall was covered not just by local media but by national networks and live on CNN. It was more than Bentley could overcome and Killea was elected.

With her new-won notoriety, Killea was not long in the Senate before she signaled she was not content to slip back into legislative obscurity. She soon complained that while every other Democrat chaired a committee, she had none. Senate President Pro Tem David Roberti reshuffled committee assignments and gave her the chair of the Senate Bonded Indebtedness Committee. That, however, was not good enough.

In truth, Killea, the improbable winner of a special election, looked at the numbers for the district in 1992 and did not like what she saw. No matter how reapportionment shook-out (and she had reason to believe Roberti would do nothing to give her a safer district) Killea would have a tough time holding the seat. Compounding the equation, Republican Ellis said he would come out of retirement to take it back for the Republicans.

So Killea took a big gamble. She dropped out of the Democratic Party and ran as an independent. Her move cost her friends and admirers — including many who had worked in her special election. But in November 1992, she not only held the seat, she demolished the conservative Ellis. Democrats can still grumble about her traitorous behavior, but Killea still votes like a Democrat and is still pro-choice on abortion.

Killea's route to the Legislature was a bit unusual. She was an Army intelligence officer in World War II and was then detailed to the State Department as an aide to Eleanor Roosevelt during the first general assembly of the United Nations. She went on to serve nine years in the CIA in the 1950s. Killea later lectured in history, and is an expert on Mexican border affairs, having served as executive director of Fronteras de las Californias. Although a Democrat at the time, she was appointed by Republican Mayor Pete Wilson to the San Diego City Council to fill a vacancy in 1978. She has remained cordial with Wilson and his chief of staff, Bob White.

As a legislator, Killea has authored numerous bills on hazardous waste and was among the many parents in the 1985 legislative effort that brought forth the state's "workfare" program. She has also concentrated on international trade incentives and Mexican border issues, both of major interest to the San Diego area.

Killea has been pushing for a state constitutional convention to reform the

California Legislature into a unicameral body — an idea that does not win her many friends among her colleagues.

PERSONAL: elected 1989 (special election); born July 31, 1922, in San Antonio, Tex.; home, San Diego; Army 1943-1948 WWII; education, B.A. history Incarnate World College, Tex.; M.A. history University of San Diego; Ph.D. Latin American history UC San Diego; husband John, two children; Roman Catholic.

CAREER: State Department personal secretary and administrative assistant to Eleanor Roosevelt (delegate to United Nations 1946); Central Intelligence Agency 1948-1957; U.S. Information Agency 1957-1960; vice president Fronteras de las Californias; university lecturer; research and teaching assistant; San Diego City Council 1978-1982; Assembly 1982-1989.

COMMITTEES: Appropriations; Business & Professions; Education; Insurance, Claims & Corporations; Transportation.

OFFICES: Capitol, (916) 445-3952, FAX (916) 327-2188; district, 2550 5th Ave., 152, San Diego 92103-6691, (619) 696-6955, FAX (619) 696-8930.

TERM LIMIT: 1996

REGISTRATION: 39.1% D, 42.9% R, 2.2% AIP

1992 CAMPAIGN: Killea – independent   60.4% $587,412
                  Jim Ellis – R   33.0% $395,234

DEC. 5, 1989 SPECIAL ELECTION:
                  Killea –D   51% $474,703
                  Carol Bentley –R   48.9% $195,689

RATINGS:

	AFL-CIO	CalPIRG	CLCV	NOW	CofC	CalFarm
	90	82	92	86	42	10

KEY VOTES: (includes some votes during Assembly service 1982-89)

Parent consent abort:	NO	Limit product tort:	YES	Clean Air Act:	YES
Assault gun ban:	YES	Ban AIDS discrim:	YES	Restrict abortion funds:	nv
Sales tax hike:	NO	Wealth tax hike:	YES	Strong gay rights:	YES
Parental leave:	YES	Timber compromise:	YES	Execution by injection:	nv
Limited gay rights:	YES	Universal health insure:	YES	1992-93 Budget Act:	YES
Campaign Reform:	YES	Offshore oil ban:	YES	Charter schools:	YES

Quentin L. Kopp (independent)
8th Senate District

Starting on the western tip of San Francisco, this district takes in many of the city's older neighborhoods, including the Sunset district, and then stretches to the fog-shrouded suburb of Pacifica. Moving south, the district includes upscale Burlingame and Hillsborough and the middle-class communities of South San Francisco, Milbrae, Daly City and part of San Mateo. Heavily Democratic, this district has remained as sure a bet for Democrats as there can be in politics — which is to say strange things can happen.

The Assembly's "lead-foot" Lou Papan (so named for his speeding tickets while commuting between the Bay Area and Sacramento) thought he was a shoo-in to replace retiring Sen. John Foran in 1986. But Republicans, mortified at the prospect of having the highly partisan Papan in the Senate, deserted their own candidate and threw their money behind San Francisco Supervisor Quentin Kopp, who ran as an independent. Kopp was elected as the Legislature's first independent in decades. The district, which after the 1992 reapportionment is half white and 28 percent Asian, remains safe for Kopp.

Kopp remains more interesting in San Francisco politics than in the Capitol. His scraps with Dianne

Quentin Kopp

Feinstein when she was mayor are legendary (Kopp actually had a date with Feinstein in their younger days). In fact, his scraps with nearly every San Francisco political figure from Willie Brown on down are legendary. In March 1987, Kopp hinted that he might (again) run for mayor with typical Kopp elocution: "Many people are importuning me to make the race." Instead, one of his aides managed the mayoral campaign of San Francisco Examiner columnist Warren Hinkel. Kopp toyed with running in 1991 but again bowed out — probably to his regret.

In the Capitol, Kopp has shown plenty of shrewdness. Registered as an independent, he votes with Democrats on leadership issues, although he has increasingly gone his own way on budget and tax matters.

His sharp elbows earned him a powerful post — and the wrath of Gov. George Deukmejian. A day before the 1988 confirmation vote on Deukmejian's hand-picked nominee for state treasurer, Dan Lungren, Kopp said he was behind Lungren all the way. On the day of the vote, Kopp switched, earning the gratitude of Senate President Pro Tem David Roberti. Democrat Wadie Deddeh, who voted for Lungren, found himself stripped of the powerful chairmanship of the Transportation Committee. Kopp got Deddeh's job. Kopp has become well-schooled in transportation issues and should become the dominant legislator on the issue if Assembly Transportation Committee Chairman Richard Katz can get himself elected mayor of Los Angeles.

As a senator, Kopp has continually pushed for an early presidential primary date. Kopp has also pushed bills to strengthen public records and open meetings laws. He successfully authored a bill that tightened the conflict-of-interest rules for members of the state Board of Equalization. In recent sessions, Kopp has pushed consolidation of the Board of Equalization with the state Franchise Tax Board — an idea Gov. Pete Wilson swiped to use in his January 1993 budget proposal.

Kopp also should be remembered for joining forces with Republican Assemblyman Ross Johnson and Democratic Sen. Joe Montoya to write Proposition 73, a measure that limited the size of campaign contributions and banned public financing for election campaigns. That initiative was approved by the voters in June 1988 but was ruled unconstitutional by a federal judge in 1990. Montoya eventually went to federal prison on corruption convictions, but Kopp has remained his friend, even helping him draft appeals.

Kopp's committee assignments at the start of the 1993-94 session are a bit, well, strange. He retained his chairmanship of Transportation, but was bounced from Housing and Urban Affairs and given an assignment on the Agriculture and Water Resources Committee. The only other urbanite on the agriculture panel is Democrat Charles Calderon, not exactly a favorite of David Roberti. Although the agriculture committee is hardly the ideal assignment for a San Francisco legislator, doubtless Kopp will have plenty of opinions on the subject and won't be shy in voicing them.

PERSONAL: elected 1986; born Aug. 11, 1928, in Syracuse, N.Y.; home, San Francisco; USAF 1952-1954; education, B.A. government & business Dartmouth College, J.D. Harvard University; wife Mara, three children; Jewish.

CAREER: lawyer; San Francisco Board of Supervisors 1972-1986.

COMMITTEES: Transportation (chair); Agriculture & Water Resources; Budget & Fiscal Review; Education; Local Government; Revenue & Taxation.

OFFICES: Capitol, (916) 445-0503, FAX (916) 327-2186; district, 363 El Camino Real, 205, South San Francisco 94080, (415) 952-5666. FAX (415) 589-5953.

TERM LIMIT: 1998

REGISTRATION: 58.2% D, 24.4% R

1990 CAMPAIGN:	Kopp – independent	72.7%	$1,227,499
	Patrick Fitzgerald – D	18%	$0
	Robert Silvestri – R	9.3%	$0
1986 CAMPAIGN:	Kopp – independent	47%	$749,203
	Louis Papan – D	46%	$1,731,002
	Russell Gray – R	8%	

RATINGS:	AFL-CIO	CalPIRG	CLCV	NOW	CofC	CalFarm
	61	68	71	57	53	60

KEY VOTES:

Parent consent abort:	YES	Limit product tort:	NO	Clean Air Act:	YES
Assault gun ban:	YES	Ban AIDS discrim:	YES	Restrict abortion funds:	NO
Sales tax hike:	NO	Wealth tax hike:	YES	Strong gay rights:	YES
Parental leave:	NO	Timber compromise:	NO	Execution by injection:	YES
Limited gay rights:	YES	Universal health insure:	NO	1992-93 Budget Act:	NO
Campaign Reform:	NO	Offshore oil ban:	YES	Charter schools:	NO

William R. Leonard Jr. (R)
31st Senate District

The heir to archconservative, gun-toting Bill Richardson's Senate district was Assemblyman Bill Leonard. And the district he got was mostly desert and rock,

spanning a territory from San Bernardino north hundreds of miles across the Mojave Desert to Bishop,
deep in the Owens Valley. The district was so immense that it abutted a district represented by a
senator from Stockton. Leonard said he did not mind
the district — but he wore out a lot of tires covering it
and, in truth, he was a bit more urbane than the rough-
and-ready Richardson.

So when the 1992 reapportionment maps were
approved, Leonard was delighted with his new district. Still unbeatable for a Republican, Leonard got
suburban portions of Riverside and San Bernardino
counties, including upscale Redlands, Upland, Yucaipa

William Leonard

and the boomtown bedroom communities of Moreno
Valley. He got additional friendly territory with the retirement communities of
Hemet and San Jacinto. He still has southern San Bernardino County desert land,
including the Twenty-Nine Palms Marine base. Ninety percent of the registered
voters in this district are white.

Leonard, who is both smoother and more intellectual than Richardson, has a
conservatism that is just as rigid — with some innovations. The San Bernardino
native son won the seat after serving 10 years in the Assembly. He had originally
come to Sacramento as one of the "Proposition 13 babies," elected the same year the
property tax limitation initiative passed. His father, William Sr., has been a longtime
figure in area politics and serves on the state Transportation Commission. After his
Senate election, Leonard successfully passed off his Assembly seat to former aide
Paul Woodruff.

Leonard has moved swiftly through the ranks of Senate Republicans. He was
elevated to the second ranking position as Republican Caucus Chairman soon after
John Doolittle vacated the post to run for Congress in 1990. As such, Leonard is
responsible for the Senate GOP election machinery.

In 1992, Leonard took the lead for Senate Republicans on workers' compensation issues. A cornerstone of Gov. Pete Wilson's agenda, Leonard proved himself
a tenacious fighter for the governor's program. He is poised to play an even more
visible role on the issue in the 1993-94 session, having had himself appointed as vice
chairman of the Industrial Relations Committee, the committee primarily responsible for workers' comp in the Senate. The post will at least give him some additional
symbolic leverage.

On other issues, Leonard is unwavering in his opposition to gun control and is
intensely anti-abortion. He has opposed anything that looks like a tax increase. But
he is not anti-government. While in the Assembly, Leonard annually introduced
legislation to ban the internal combustion engine. He honed the idea into a serious
bill that won Assembly approval in 1987. That measure would have phased in clean-

burning methanol vehicles in the 1990s. The bill was supported by major auto manufacturers. But after opposition from oil companies, the bill was buried in the Senate by Democratic Sen. Ralph Dills of Gardena, chairman of the Governmental Organization Committee.

In 1990, Leonard succeeded in moving through the Senate SCA 1, which would have allowed local school districts to approve bonds with a majority vote instead of two-thirds. The constitutional amendment was defeated largely by Republicans in the Assembly, who pulled the measure down on a 43-28 vote. Some months later, Leonard's idea was enthusiastically embraced by Wilson, who prominently mentioned it in his first State of the State address.

Leonard considered running for one of the new congressional seats that opened up in 1992, but decided instead to remain in the state Senate — for the time being.

PERSONAL: elected 1988; born Oct. 29, 1947, in San Bernardino; home, Big Bear; education, B.A. history UC Irvine, graduate work CSU Sacramento; wife Sherry Boldizsar, three children; Presbyterian.

CAREER: Real estate management; director San Bernardino Valley Municipal Water District 1974-1978; Assembly 1978-1988; Republican Caucus Chairman 1990-present.

COMMITTEES: Industrial Relations (vice chair); Appropriations; Housing & Urban Affairs; Toxics and Public Safety Management.

OFFICES: Capitol, (916) 445-3688, FAX (916) 327-2272; district, 400 N. Mountain Ave., 109, Upland 91786, (909) 946-4889, FAX (909) 982-1197.

TERM LIMIT: 1996

REGISTRATION: 41.1% D, 47.1% R

1992 CAMPAIGN: Leonard – R 99.9% $498,399

1988 CAMPAIGN: Leonard – R 66% $402,887

Sandra Hester – D 34% $70,153

RATINGS:

AFL-CIO	CalPIRG	CLCV	NOW	CofC	CalFarm
19	23	23	7	84	80

KEY VOTES: (includes some votes from Assembly service 1978-88)

Parent consent abort:	YES	Limit product tort:	YES	Clean Air Act:	NO
Assault gun ban:	NO	Ban AIDS discrim:	NO	Restrict abortion funds:	YES
Sales tax hike:	NO	Wealth tax hike:	NO	Strong gay rights:	NO
Parental leave:	NO	Timber compromise:	NO	Execution by injection:	YES
Limited gay rights:	NO	Universal health insur:	NO	1992-93 Budget Act:	YES
Campaign Reform:	NO	Offshore oil ban:	NO	Charter schools:	NO

Robert Timothy Leslie (R)

1st Senate District

This district takes in the northeastern corner of the state and runs south through mountains, Lake Tahoe and into the Sierra foothills. It ends in the desert of Mono County on the eastern side of the Sierra and Calaveras County on the western side.

At one point, the district protrudes onto the Sacramento Valley floor, taking in Butte and Yuba Counties. It is a heavily forested and lightly populated
district throughout most of its expanse. Pockets of
population include Susanville, with its prison, the
overbuilt Tahoe basin and the valley cities of Chico,
Oroville and Marysville. Western Placer County,
which is rapidly filling up with Sacramento suburbanites, is one of the fastest-growing areas of the state.
The 1992 reapportionment strengthened the 1st District as a Republican stronghold.

Tim Leslie

The district's state senator, Tim Leslie, a former
lobbyist and legislative aide of minimal distinction,
has been in the right places at the right times. In 1986,
Republican Leslie was elected to the Assembly, the improbable winner over a
Democratic candidate hand-picked by Assembly Speaker Willie Brown. Leslie's
opponent, Jack Dugan, went down in flames after it was discovered he had never
voted in a statewide election.

In the Assembly, Leslie did little of note. His district was decidedly suburban,
upscale and conservative. He got in a minor flap with the press over sponsoring a
tax-break bill for a local company in Loomis, one of the more affluent communities
near Sacramento. Mostly, Leslie did the bidding of Republican governors and
legislative leaders, voting their way and keeping his mouth more or less shut. Leslie
was the consummate backbencher.

When the enormously controversial John Doolittle won a seat in Congress in
1990, the politically reliable Leslie became the pick of Gov. Pete Wilson to succeed
Doolittle in the state Senate. The only problem was that Leslie did not live in the
district. So he rented a home in Auburn in the foothills in order to run in the special
election. Despite a spirited challenge from Republican Bob Dorr, an El Dorado
County supervisor, Leslie got 43 percent of the vote in the March 1991 primary. In
the May run-off, Leslie beat Democrat Patti Mattingly of Yreka, a moderate
Siskiyou County supervisor.

In the sedate Senate, Leslie has shown moderate signs of life. He carried the
governor's Sierra Accord timber bill that would have preserved some old-growth
stands and protected trees along rivers and streams. But the bill ran into heavy flak
from environmentalists, who believed it was a sell-out, and business interests, who
thought it went too far. Leslie was not a skilled enough legislative technician to get
the bill approved by his former Assembly colleagues.

Behind the scenes, Leslie has squared off — quietly, of course — with Sen.
Ruben Ayala, the chairman of the Senate Agriculture and Water Resources
Committee, over the issue of building an Auburn Dam. Protecting his parochial
interests, Leslie wants the water from such a dam to serve his district first. Ayala,

who has pushed for a general obligation bond proposal to build such a dam (bringing jobs to the Auburn area as a side benefit), maintains that if the entire state is paying for a dam the entire state should get the water. There the issue remains stuck.

At the start of the 1993-94 session, Leslie got first-rate committee assignments. He was named to not just one, but two, vice chairs: Budget and Fiscal Review and Judiciary. The assignments give him the opportunity to be the lead Senate Republican on two high-profile issues — the state budget and crime. Sen. Frank Hill of Whittier had been the lead budget negotiator for Senate Republicans, but he showed too much independence to suit Minority Leader Ken Maddy, R-Fresno. So Maddy replaced Hill on Budget and Fiscal Review with the more pliable Leslie. It's a place where one tends to make enemies. But it also gives Leslie a better platform to push a bill close to his heart - one to abolish the California Lottery.

PERSONAL: elected 1991; born Feb. 4, 1942, in Ashland, Ore.; home, Carnelian Bay; education, B.S. political science CSU Long Beach; M.A. public administration USC; wife Clydene, two children; Presbyterian.

CAREER: real estate; Assembly Ways & Means Committee consultant 1969-1971; lobbyist for County Supervisors' Association of California 1971-1980; Assembly 1986-1991.

COMMITTEES: Budget & Fiscal Review (vice chair); Judiciary (vice chair); Health & Human Services; Natural Resources & Wildlife.

OFFICES: Capitol, (916) 445-5788; district, 1200 Melody Lane, Suite 110, Roseville 95678, (916) 969-8232.

TERM LIMIT: 1996

REGISTRATION: 42.5% D, 43.6% R

1992 CAMPAIGN:

Leslie – R		54.7%	$404,667
Thomas Romero – D		35.8%	$10,379
Kent Smith – Green		9.5%	

MAY 14, 1991 SPECIAL ELECTION:

Leslie – R		54.6%	$729,227
Patti Mattingly – D		43.1%	$450,368

RATINGS:

	AFL-CIO	CalPIRG	CLCV	NOW	CofC	CalFarm
	10	23	19	14	84	60

KEY VOTES: (includes votes from Assembly service 1986-91)

Parent consent abort:	YES	Limit product tort:	YES	Clean Air Act:	NO
Assault gun ban:	NO	Ban AIDS discrim:	NO	Restrict abortion funds:	YES
Sales tax hike:	NO	Wealth tax hike:	NO	Strong gay rights:	NO
Parental leave:	NO	Timber compromise:	YES	Execution by injection:	YES
Limited gay rights:	NO	Universal health insure:	NO	1992-93 Budget Act:	YES
Campaign Reform:	NO	Offshore oil ban:	NO	Charter schools:	NO

John Lewis (R)

33rd Senate District

Senatorial representation for mid-Orange County underwent two traumatic changes in 1991. First, Sen. John Seymour resigned to accept an appointment to the U.S. Senate from his old friend, newly elected Gov. Pete Wilson (he was defeated by Democrat Dianne Feinstein in 1992). Second, the state Supreme Court sharply altered legislative districts after taking over reapportionment from a deadlocked Capitol.

John Lewis

Seymour's departure touched off a battle among Republicans — Democrats weren't a factor because of the district's overwhelming GOP registration — and no fewer than three Republican members of the Assembly, plus four others, ran in the March, 1991, special election. The winner was the most conservative and controversial of the three, John Lewis, and he easily won re-election in 1992 in the reconfigured district.

Seymour's old 35th District underwent slenderization and a change of numbers, to 33, during reapportionment as Orange County was awarded a new Senate district, the 34th. As reconstituted, the 33rd stretches from Fullerton in the northern end of the county to Mission Viejo on the south and includes pieces of the county's two largest cities, Santa Ana (the county seat) and Anaheim, the home of the county's most famous feature, Disneyland.

Lewis, an heir to a dog food fortune, had represented much of the district as an assemblyman for 11 years before the 1991 special election. It was anything but a high-profile legislative career since Lewis, perhaps the most conservative member of the Legislature, almost never made a floor speech and only rarely even carried a bill. He devoted himself, instead, to behind-the-scenes plotting on behalf of other conservatives running for legislative office. In the Assembly, he was considered to be the tactical brains behind the so-called "cavemen," a conservative faction that dominated Assembly GOP politics for much of the 1980s. That led to Lewis' role in a bizarre incident stemming from the 1986 campaigns, when Republican leader Pat Nolan, head of the caveman faction, made a strenuous effort to expand GOP ranks in the Assembly.

In 1989, Lewis was indicted by a Sacramento County grand jury and accused of forgery for sending out letters bearing the faked signature of President Ronald Reagan during the '86 campaign. Going to households in several hotly contested races, the letters accused Democratic incumbents of favoring drug dealers. Lewis contended that the indictment was political, arguing that Democratic state Attorney General John Van de Kamp ignored campaign dirty tricks committed by Democratic legislative candidates in seeking charges against him.

The state Court of Appeal in Sacramento threw out the indictment on the grounds that a faked signature on campaign literature did not constitute legal forgery. Although Lewis beat the rap, fellow Republican Bill Craven from the Senate said Lewis' behavior was reprehensible and pushed legislation to fill the loophole.

As a senator, Lewis has pretty much followed his pattern as an assemblyman: saying and doing little publicly while confining his political efforts to the back rooms of the Capitol. He votes against many bills, especially those that cost money, but seems to pursue no overall legislative goals.

PERSONAL: elected 1991; born Nov. 2, 1954, in Los Angeles; home, Orange; education, B.A. political science USC; wife Suzanne Henry; Protestant.

CAREER: aide to Assemblyman Dennis Brown; investment manager; Assembly 1980-1991.

COMMITTEES: Constitutional Amendments (chair); Business & Professions (vice chair); Agriculture & Water Resources; Insurance, Claims & Corporations; Natural Resources & Wildlife.

OFFICES: Capitol, (916) 445-4264, FAX (916) 324-2896; district, 1940 W. Orangewood Ave., 106, Orange 92668, (714) 939-0604, FAX (714) 939-0730.

TERM LIMIT: 1996

REGISTRATION: 31.0% D, 56.3% R

1992 CAMPAIGN:

Lewis – R	64.1%	$417,086
Samuel Eidt – D	29.0%	$0
Doyle Guhy – L	6.9%	

MAY 14, 1991, SPECIAL ELECTION:

Lewis – R	67.7%	$222,789
Frank Hoffman – D	26.7%	
Erik Sprik – L	5.6%	

RATINGS:

AFL-CIO	CalPIRG	CLCV	NOW	CofC	CalFarm
3	11	14	7	84	70

KEY VOTES: (includes votes from Assembly service 1980-91)

Parent consent abort:	YES	Limit product tort:	YES	Clean Air Act:	NO
Assault gun ban:	NO	Ban AIDS discrim:	NO	Restrict abortion funds:	YES
Sales tax hike:	NO	Wealth tax hike:	NO	Strong gay rights:	NO
Parental leave:	NO	Timber compromise:	NO	Execution by injection:	YES
Limited gay rights:	NO	Universal health insure:	NO	1992-93 Budget Act:	YES
Campaign Reform:	nv	Offshore oil ban:	NO	Charter schools:	NO

William Lockyer (D)
10th Senate District

Taking in San Francisco Bay's eastern shoreline south of Oakland, this Alameda County district includes the middle-class cities of San Leandro, Fremont and

Hayward before extending over the hills into a portion
of the Livermore Valley. Although it is a Democratic
district, it has a conservative bent and was changed
little in either economic or political orientation by the
court-ordered reapportionment that followed the 1990
census.

Democrat William Lockyer, one of the Capitol's
most enigmatic figures and the district's officeholder
since 1982, is the archetypal former legislative staffer
turned legislator. He spent a decade in the Assembly
after working as an aide to one of the Legislature's
most powerful figures of the 1960s, Assemblyman
Robert Crown. Although he can be charming and no
one questions his intelligence or penchant for hard

William Lockyer

work, his personal — and often public — behavior is erratic, marked by bouts of bad
temper that provide Bay Area headline writers with plenty of fodder. During a
particularly tedious committee hearing in 1985, Lockyer cut short fellow Democrat
Diane Watson of Los Angeles, leaving her sputtering, "Can I finish my thought?"
Lockyer retorted, "Well, if you had a thought it would be great," and added that he
was fed up with her "mindless blather." Lockyer later apologized, but Watson has
barely spoken to him since.

His temper also got the best of him during the last week of the 1990 legislative
session. In a hallway outside the Senate chambers, Lockyer began baiting trial
lawyer lobbyist Bob Wilson, a former senator who was one of Lockyer's predecessors as chairman of the Judiciary Committee. Wilson lost his cool and the two got
into a shoving match (Lockyer later said Wilson threw a "girlie punch" at him). And
Lockyer also threw a temper tantrum during the Senate's 1990 ethics workshop. It
wasn't anything about ethics that bothered him; it was the bright lights being used
to videotape the session.

Although Lockyer has been an insider on more major legislation than most of his
colleagues, he still behaves as though he is being slighted as an outsider. In June
1989, Lockyer barged into a private meeting between Senate President David
Roberti and a handful of other senators working out which big-ticket bills would
move out of the Appropriations Committee. To their wonderment, Lockyer pro-
tested that he wanted a chance to make a pitch for his bills. Lockyer has blamed his
erratic tendencies on a fondness for junk food and once told the Oakland Tribune,
"I would like people to know that I am a lovable eccentric and not a dysfunctional,
strange one."

Temperament aside, Lockyer as Judiciary Committee chairman has been a major
force in the big issues of the last few sessions, including repeal of the business
inventory tax, abortion, the death penalty, auto insurance, workers' compensation,
tort reform and gun control. In 1990, he authored — or, more precisely, spearheaded

— SB 25, the first major legislative overhaul of sentencing laws in years. But Gov. George Deukmejian vetoed the comprehensive bill.

Interestingly, Lockyer had served as chairman of the Judiciary Committee for several years before he got around to taking the State Bar exam, passing it in 1988 after attending night law school while serving in the Legislature.

Lockyer was among lawmakers and lobbyists who drafted a peace pact between major economic forces on a napkin at Frank Fat's restaurant two days before the end of the legislative session in September 1987 — a fabled meeting that culminated months of negotiations between doctors, lawyers and insurance companies over the state's liability laws. Lockyer got the related bill bearing his name through the Senate with little difficulty. Speaker Willie Brown ramrodded it through the Assembly over the strenuous objections of several liberal Democrats. Lockyer proudly displayed the napkin on the Senate floor. Now that the napkin deal has expired, Lockyer will be in the middle of efforts by lawyers to change medical malpractice and other liability laws.

Lockyer wears his ambition on his sleeve, making little secret of his desire to succeed Roberti in the Senate's top political position when term limits end Roberti's career in 1994. That has placed him and another relatively young senator, Art Torres, in a rivalry. There were hot rumors that some sort of deal would be worked out under which Roberti would step down in 1993, but finally there was a peace pact of sorts negotiated under which Roberti continued to serve while the two aspirants gave themselves two more years to line up support to become his successor.

PERSONAL: elected 1982; born May 8, 1941, in Oakland; home, Hayward; education, B.A. political science UC Berkeley, teaching credential CSU Hayward, J.D. McGeorge; divorced, one child; Episcopalian.

CAREER: teacher; school board member; legislative assistant to Assemblyman Bob Crown 1968-1973; Assembly 1973-1982.

COMMITTEES: Judiciary (chair); Appropriations; Elections & Reapportionment; Governmental Organization; Industrial Relations; Revenue & Taxation; Toxics & Public Safety Management.

OFFICES: Capitol, (916) 445-6671; district, 22634 Second Street, 104, Hayward 94541, (510) 582-8800, FAX (510) 582-0822.

TERM LIMIT: 1998

REGISTRATION: 55.5% D, 29.6% R

1990 CAMPAIGN:

Lockyer – D		60.6%	$1,037,242
Howard Hertz – R		39.4%	$528

1986 CAMPAIGN:

Lockyer – D		71%	$445,583
Bruce Bergondy – R		29%	$0

RATINGS:

AFL-CIO	CalPIRG	CLCV	NOW	CofC	CalFarm
94	95	86	86	21	40

KEY VOTES:

Parent consent abort:	nv	Limit product tort:	YES	Clean Air Act:	YES
Assault gun ban:	YES	Ban AIDS discrim:	YES	Restrict abortion funds:	NO
Sales tax hike:	YES	Wealth tax hike:	NO	Strong gay rights:	YES
Parental leave:	YES	Timber compromise:	YES	Execution by injection:	YES
Limited gay rights:	YES	Universal health insur:	YES	1992-93 Budget Act:	YES
Campaign Reform:	YES	Offshore oil ban:	YES	Charter schools:	YES

Kenneth L. Maddy (R)

14th Senate District

This sprawling district takes in a big chunk of the farm-dominated San Joaquin Valley as well as some of the most scenic areas in the Sierra Nevada. The district is far more compact than the previous one that spanned Yosemite to the outskirts of Santa Barbara. The district is now focused in Fresno. The population is three-fourths white and safely Republican.

Whatever the district makeup, Republican Ken Maddy has had no trouble getting re-elected. A political moderate who is popular with colleagues on both sides of the aisle, Maddy has parlayed his agricultural roots, concerns about health care and lifelong love for horses and horse racing into legislative successes.

Ken Maddy

As Republican leader, Maddy enjoys a good working relationship with Senate President Pro Tem David Roberti, the leader of the Democrats. In fact, Maddy and Roberti protect each other in the house to mutual advantage. The arrangement gives Maddy more power in the Senate than Republican strength (a mere 13 seats) would otherwise dictate. Unlike his Republican counterpart in the Assembly, Maddy for all intents and purposes names the Republican members of committees and vice chairs. In return, Roberti can count on Maddy's cooperation in running the Senate and does not have to endure the disruptive and counterproductive antics that are the rule in the Assembly.

In Maddy's early career, he endured tough campaigns and a couple of political and personal setbacks. In 1978, while still an assemblyman, he made a bid for governor with a campaign that got him nearly a half-million votes despite being an unknown entity outside Fresno. Having given up his Assembly seat to run for governor, Maddy was out of politics for a few months. But the resignation of Sen. George Zenovich quickly brought him back, and he won a hard-fought special election to fill the seat.

Maddy's first marriage foundered after he won his Senate seat, and he later married the wealthy heiress to the Foster Farms chicken fortune, Norma Foster. That gave him resources to pursue his intense passion for thoroughbred horse racing. The

Maddys have become A-list socialites, not only in Sacramento and the San Joaquin Valley, but in the playgrounds of the wealthy along Orange County's gold coast, where they maintain a weekend residence.

Handsome and articulate, Maddy saw his star rise quickly in the Senate, especially since his longtime pal, Bill Campbell, was the minority leader. Maddy became caucus chairman, the No. 2 party position, but he and Campbell lost a power struggle several years later to a conservative faction. In 1987, Maddy returned in a countercoup and became minority leader.

Maddy has been on everyone's list of rising Republican stars since his better-than-expected shot at the governorship in 1978. While he has toyed with seeking statewide office again, he has never taken the plunge, except to apply for a gubernatorial appointment as state treasurer.

Maddy was among the leaders attempting to solve a record-long budget deadlock in 1992. He felt undercut, however, by onetime protege Frank Hill, who was the Senate Republican representative to the Joint Budget Conference Committee. Hill and Democratic Assemblyman Phil Isenberg free-lanced their own budget proposals throughout the long budget stalemate. Outsiders credited the Hill-Isenberg initiatives with helping to bring an end to the impasse. But Maddy was definitely irked at Hill and had him bounced as the lead Republican on the budget committee at the start of the 1993-94 session.

Maddy has tried to find common ground with Democrats in order to hold the state's presidential primary earlier in the year, so far without success. In addition, Maddy, unlike some of his Republican colleagues, has pushed to guarantee basic health care for 3.2 million working Californians and their families, although he has differed with Democrats on how such a program should be financed.

Maddy was under some pressure from supporters to run for governor in 1990 after George Deukmejian announced he would retire, but decided against it and now seems content to end his active political career in the Senate. He has said he intends to retire when he is 60 — or when there is a Maddy-supported highway bypass through Livingston, site of the only traffic light on Highway 99 in California and headquarters of the Foster Farms chicken empire Maddy now shares. Given that he will be 60 in 1994, Capitol insiders speculate that Maddy will retire after his current term is completed.

PERSONAL: elected 1979 (special election); born May 22, 1934, in Santa Monica; home, Fresno and ranch east of Modesto; USAF 1957-60; education, B.S. agriculture CSU Fresno, J.D. UCLA; wife Norma Foster; three children and six stepchildren; Protestant.

CAREER: lawyer; horse breeder; Assembly 1970-1979; Senate Minority Leader 1987- present.

COMMITTEES: Governmental Organization (vice chair); Constitutional Amendments; Revenue & Taxation.

OFFICES: Capitol, (916) 445-9600; district, 2503 W. Shaw Ave., 101, Fresno

93711, (209) 445-5567, FAX (209) 445-6009.

TERM LIMIT: 1998

REGISTRATION: 43.5% D, 45.7% R

1990 CAMPAIGN:	Maddy – R	100%	$815,745
1986 CAMPAIGN:	Maddy – R	69%	$423,828
	Michael LeSage – D	31%	$15,955

RATINGS:	AFL-CIO	CalPIRG	CLCV	NOW	CofC	CalFarm
	38	32	17	57	79	50

KEY VOTES:

Parent consent abort:	YES	Limit product tort:	YES	Clean Air Act:	nv
Assault gun ban:	NO	Ban AIDS discrim:	nv	Restrict abortion funds:	NO
Sales tax hike:	YES	Wealth tax hike:	YES	Strong gay rights:	YES
Parental leave:	NO	Timber compromise:	NO	Execution by injection:	YES
Limited gay rights:	YES	Universal health insure:	nv	1992-93 Budget Act:	YES
Campaign Reform:	YES	Offshore oil ban:	NO	Charter schools:	NO

Milton Marks (D)

3rd Senate District

Milton Marks

This district, which includes Marin County, part of Sonoma County and northeastern San Francisco, is tailor-made for a Democrat — or a Milton Marks.

Marks has represented the district for more than three decades, including the first 19 years as a moderate-to-liberal Republican. Throughout his career, which began in the Assembly in 1958, Marks has been a maverick. He is a tireless campaigner who has built support through personal contact at myriad district events.

Marks took a brief respite from the Legislature in 1966, when Democratic Gov. Pat Brown appointed him to a San Francisco Municipal Court judgeship. But he returned to politics the following year, when California's new Republican governor, Ronald Reagan, supported Marks' successful effort to fill a vacant state Senate seat in a special election. In the subsequent years, Marks steered an independent course in the Senate, often voting with Democrats on environmental, civil liberties and social issues, much to the consternation of Republican colleagues. His credentials as a Republican got a brief boost in 1982, when, at the coaxing of the Reagan White House, he unsuccessfully ran against powerful Democratic Rep. Phil Burton, who died shortly after his re-election victory. Democrats, infuriated at Marks' challenge of Burton, targeted him in 1984, supporting Lia Belli, the wife of a prominent San Francisco attorney, but Marks won easily.

Marks' switch to the Democratic Party came in January 1986, when he cut a deal with Senate President Pro Tem David Roberti. In exchange for his change in affiliations, Marks, who had possessed negligible clout inside the Republican caucus, was immediately made caucus chairman, the No. 3 position among Senate Democrats. Some Republicans weren't bothered by Marks' defection. "We'll miss him like a case of hemorrhoids," quipped ultraconservative Sen. H.L. Richardson, who once punched Marks when both were Republicans in the Senate. Yet Marks' defection was significant. It marked the beginning of a numerical downhill slide for Republicans in the Senate.

Marks was chairman of the Elections and Reapportionment Committee during the 1992 reapportionment. He and his able staff worked hard to draft a plan, but in the end, they had no real impact on redistricting since it was done by the state Supreme Court.

Marks' legislation is decidedly liberal. His bills have included measures to purge voter rolls of non-voters in combination with programs aimed at increasing registration. He also has proposed making it a crime to raise veal calves in enclosures that do not meet minimum requirements and to give tax advantages to artists, a measure vetoed by Gov. George Deukmejian. Marks was one of the few state legislators to vote in July 1989 against a resolution urging that flag burning be made a crime.

Many thought he would retire at the end of his 1992 term. But Marks, who is known far and wide in San Francisco for attending every bar mitzvah, birthday and funeral, had no intention of going anywhere except back to Sacramento. He was re-elected with no trouble at all.

PERSONAL: elected 1967 (special election); born July 22, 1920, in San Francisco; home, San Francisco; Army WWII (Philippines); education, B.A. Stanford University, J.D. San Francisco Law School; wife Carolene Wachenheimer, three children; Jewish.

    CAREER: lawyer; Assembly 1958-1966; municipal court judge 1966.

    COMMITTEES: Elections & Reapportionment (chair); Business & Professions; Housing & Urban Affairs; Judiciary; Natural Resources & Wildlife.

    OFFICES: Capitol, (916) 445-1412, FAX (916) 327-7229; district, 30 N. San Pedro Road, 160, San Rafael 94903, (415) 479-6612.

    TERM LIMIT: 1996

    REGISTRATION: 59.5% D, 22.3% R, 2.4% Green

1992 CAMPAIGN:	Marks – D	66.4%	$742,627
	Bill Boerum – R	25.1%	$13,117
1988 CAMPAIGN:	Marks – D	66.4%	$578,897
	Carol Marshall – R	30%	$155,500

RATINGS:	AFL-CIO	CalPIRG	CLCV	NOW	CofC	CalFarm
	90	95	95	100	21	20

KEY VOTES:

Parent consent abort:	NO	Limit product tort:	YES	Clean Air Act:	YES
Assault gun ban:	YES	Ban AIDS discrim:	YES	Restrict abortion funds:	NO
Sales tax hike:	YES	Wealth tax hike:	YES	Strong gay rights:	YES
Parental leave:	YES	Timber compromise:	NO	Execution by injection:	NO
Limited gay rights:	YES	Universal health insure:	YES	1992-93 Budget Act:	YES
Campaign Reform:	YES	Offshore oil ban:	YES	Charter schools:	YES

Daniel A. McCorquodale (D)

12th Senate District

Dan McCorquodale

The 12th Senate District, represented by Democrat Dan McCorquodale, includes the San Joaquin Valley and foothill counties of Stanislaus, Tuolumne, Merced and Mariposa and all but the southeast corner of Madera county. It ends at the northwest suburbs of the city of Fresno.

In the 1992 reapportionment McCorquodale lost urban Santa Clara County, where he was once a county supervisor, and with it a big chunk of his urban constituency. He kept Stanislaus County, a mostly flat, agriculture-dominated region that includes the cities of Modesto, Turlock and Ceres. Although the San Joaquin Valley is rapidly becoming urbanized, it retains its strong rural and conservative roots. In anticipation of redistricting, McCorquodale bought a small house on the outskirts of Modesto a few years earlier. Following reapportionment, he and his wife, Jean, a Santa Clara County real estate agent, moved to Stanislaus County.

In 1993, McCorquodale won a choice assignment as chair of the Senate Agriculture and Water Resources Committee, which oversees key legislation on water issues facing the state. In so doing, McCorquodale relinquished chairmanship of the Senate Natural Resources Committee, which went to Sen. Mike Thompson, D-St. Helena. The assignment was a sort of consolation prize for Thompson, who lobbied hard for the agriculture job.

McCorquodale replaced Sen. Ruben Ayala on the water committee when the later was named to the powerful Rules Committee. But McCorquodale will still have the gruff Ayala breathing down his neck. Ayala, in a move that protects his committee staff, was named as vice chair of the panel. This is an unusual move in the Senate, where minority Republicans generally are given vice chair assignments.

The plodding McCorquodale's new post as chair of the Agriculture and Water Resources Committee should give him a leg up in establishing himself as an expert on issues of importance to the economic welfare of his agriculture-based district. Some of his earlier crusades, such as his legislative battle for humane treatment of zoo elephants, tended to puzzle, if not alienate, some of his valley constituents.

When McCorquodale chaired the Natural Resources and Wildlife Committee he took an active role in trying to settle major disputes between environmentalists, hunters and business interests. An ardent fisherman, he has pushed environmental causes in the area of fisheries, parks, offshore oil drilling, timber harvesting and clean air.

McCorquodale had an earlier political career in the San Diego area, once serving as the mayor of Chula Vista, but changed direction after his first wife committed suicide. He abandoned politics to champion programs for the disabled, something he continues to do as chairman of the Senate Special Developmental Disabilities and Mental Health Committee. McCorquodale returned to political life after relocating in the San Jose area. While running successfully for the board of supervisors, he developed the practice of personally walking every precinct during every campaign. It's a good technique for the naturally friendly McCorquodale.

In 1982, McCorquodale narrowly defeated incumbent Republican Sen. Dan O'Keefe. In 1986, Republicans tried bouncing back by waging a $1.3 million campaign to defeat McCorquodale, who was generally more liberal than his district. But McCorquodale worked hard and handily won a bruising re-election battle over his GOP challenger, Santa Clara County Supervisor Tom Legan. And in 1990, he buried his Republican opponent, Lori Kennedy, by 18 percentage points.

After years of battling Republican administrations, McCorquodale successfully authored legislation that established the San Joaquin Valley Unified Air Pollution Control District, an eight-county valley regional air quality district with expanded enforcement authority. He was considering pushing similar legislation in the 1993-94 session for a regional transportation authority.

PERSONAL: elected 1982; born Dec. 17, 1934, in Longville, La.; home, Modesto; USMC 1953-1956; education, B.A. education San Diego State University; wife Jean, two children; Protestant.

CAREER: special-education teacher; Chula Vista city councilman and mayor; Santa Clara County Board of Supervisors.

COMMITTEES: Agriculture & Water Resources (chair); Transportation (vice chair); Budget & Fiscal Review; Business & Professions; Constitutional Amendments; Insurance, Claims & Corporations; Natural Resources & Wildlife; Public Employment and Retirement.

OFFICES: Capitol, (916) 445-3104, FAX (916) 327-8801; district, 1020 15th St., B, Modesto 95354, (209) 576-6231, FAX (209) 576-6092.

TERM LIMIT: 1998

REGISTRATION: 51.1% D, 37.9% R

1990 CAMPAIGN:	McCorquodale – D	59%	$802,650
	Lori Kennedy – R	41%	$2,224
1986 CAMPAIGN:	McCorquodale – D	56%	$1,480,626
	Tom Legan – R	44%	$1,384,357

RATINGS:

AFL-CIO	CalPIRG	CLCV	NOW	CofC	CalFarm
95	73	85	79	16	20

KEY VOTES:

Parent consent abort:	NO	Limit product tort:	YES	Clean Air Act:	YES
Assault gun ban:	YES	Ban AIDS discrim:	YES	Restrict abortion funds:	NO
Sales tax hike:	YES	Wealth tax hike:	YES	Strong gay rights:	YES
Parental leave:	YES	Timber compromise:	YES	Execution by injection:	YES
Limited gay rights:	YES	Universal health insure:	NO	1992-93 Budget Act:	YES
Campaign Reform:	YES	Offshore oil ban:	YES	Charter schools:	nv

Henry J. Mello (D)
15th Senate District

This is one of the most diverse Senate districts, not only geographically but politically and demographically. It contains some of the state's most beautiful beach communities – Carmel, Monterey, Pacific Grove, Santa Cruz – and some of the state's most productive farmland, including the Salinas Valley, the setting for John Steinbeck's novels. The political spectrum ranges from the liberal Santa Cruz to the conservative farm-area politics of Hollister. Residents include the wealthy and movie stars — Clint Eastwood was briefly mayor of Carmel — as well as burgeoning Latino populations in cities like Salinas, Soledad and Watsonville. While court-ordered reapportionment changed the district's number (from 17) and its boundaries somewhat, it remains largely what it has been for decades.

Henry Mello

Henry Mello, a farmer, businessman and hulking Capitol presence, has attempted to walk a political tightrope in response to his diverse constituency. He is a moderate Democrat and a nervous one. On some controversial issues, he tries to give a little to each side. In 1989, for example, he voted in favor of a virtual ban of semiautomatic military-style assault weapons despite heavy pressure in his district from members of the National Rifle Association. Later in the year, when a key vote came up to require purchasers of rifles to wait 15 days between the time they buy rifles and the time they can be picked up, Mello, again under pressure from the NRA, called the waiting period "outrageous" and voted against it.

The switcheroo on gun control is typical of Mello's situational approach to politics, which eschews consistency of any kind. For years, that made him the swing vote on the powerful five-member Rules Committee, which routes legislation to committees and can block confirmation of gubernatorial appointees. The other four members of Rules were two liberal Democrats and two Republicans, and Mello held the balance of power, which made him a frequent target of lobbyists for and against bills and nominees. Most of the time, there was no telling how Mello would vote. Often, his position seemed to depend on who talked to him last or whether he had taken a personal interest in the outcome.

Mello gave up his seat on Rules as the 1993 legislative session began and became the Senate's majority floor leader, the No. 2 Democrat, succeeding Barry Keene, who resigned his seat in the Senate. Mello was tapped for the position by Senate President David Roberti to head off a political fight between two other senators, Bill Lockyer and Art Torres, who wanted the majority leader's position as a stepping stone to Roberti's job after he is forced to leave the Senate by term limits in 1994.

By bringing Mello into the leadership position, however, Roberti elevated a politician who is, by common consent, one of the least popular in the Capitol for his inconsistent, tit-for-tat approach to politics and his often-bullying demeanor. On occasion, Mello has generated controversy in his district by carrying bills to help local developers and other businesses in ways that some believe might have adverse environmental effects or benefit big contributors.

In 1990, for example, a timber company controlled by Orange County developer Donald Koll, a large contributor to legislative and statewide campaigns, couldn't get a harvesting permit and subsequently couldn't find a buyer for some land. Mello carried a bill to have the state purchase the 1,500 acres of forest in the Santa Cruz mountains for $6 million, claiming the move would save a grove of redwoods. But the purchase, inserted in a statewide park bond, was voted down in November 1990.

In 1991, when the state was facing an unprecedented budget deficit requiring cuts in many vital programs, Mello was criticized for proposing a $3.5 million allocation for the state to participate in the 1992 World's Fair in Spain.

He also played hardball with the Walt Disney Co. in 1991 and its bill to waive some environmental regulations so that it could build a new theme park in Long Beach Harbor. After months of trying to meet the ever-increasing price of Mello's support, Disney gave up under the thin cover that it was turning its attention to expansion of Disneyland.

When he isn't involved in heavy-handed politics, Mello seems to have a genuine interest in services to senior citizens. He carried a bill to create the Senior Legislature, an annual gathering of senior citizens from throughout the state at which they set their legislative priorities. Mello has frequently carried Senior Legislature proposals, measures ranging from housing and day care to lunch programs and nursing homes. He has also taken a special interest in victims of Alzheimer's.

Given the relatively weak Democratic registration in his district and the enmity he generates among environmentalists and others on the Democratic left, Mello should be vulnerable to a serious Republican challenge. But none has been forthcoming through four elections, although local Republicans have fantasized about recruiting actor Clint Eastwood as their candidate. Mello faced a semiserious Democratic primary challenge in 1992 from a candidate who made much of his cozy relations with developers and other special interests, but Mello breezed to an easy re-election in November.

PERSONAL: elected 1980; born March 27, 1924, in Watsonville; home, Watsonville; education, attended Hartnell Junior College; wife Helen, four children.

CAREER: farmer; Santa Cruz Board of Supervisors 1967-1974; Assembly 1976-1980; Senate Majority Leader 1992-present.

COMMITTEES: Appropriations; Governmental Organization; Health & Human Services; Natural Resources & Wildlife.

OFFICES: Capitol, (916) 445-5843, FAX (916) 448-0175; district, 92 Fifth St., Gilroy, 95020, (408) 848-1437, FAX (408) 848-6311.

TERM LIMIT: 1996
REGISTRATION: 51.2% D, 31.9% R

1992 CAMPAIGN:	Mello – D	58.4%	$961,060
	Edward Laverone – R	34.1%	$31,773
	Susanne Espinoza – P&F	7.5%	
1988 CAMPAIGN:	Mello – D	71%	$603,760
	Harry Damkar – R	29%	$115,863

RATINGS:	AFL-CIO	CalPIRG	CLCV	NOW	CofC	CalFarm
	87	82	80	86	21	40

KEY VOTES:

Parent consent abort:	YES	Limit product tort:	nv	Clean Air Act:	nv
Assault gun ban:	YES	Ban AIDS discrim:	YES	Restrict abortion funds:	NO
Sales tax hike:	YES	Wealth tax hike:	YES	Strong gay rights:	YES
Parental leave:	YES	Timber compromise:	YES	Execution by injection:	YES
Limited gay rights:	YES	Universal health insur:	YES	1992-93 Budget Act:	YES
Campaign Reform:	YES	Offshore oil ban:	YES	Charter schools:	NO

Rebecca Q. Morgan (R)
11th Senate District

On its western shore, the 11th Senate District includes Half Moon Bay, then loops over the San Andreas fault to the wealthy bedroom communities of the mid-San Francisco peninsula, including Redwood City, Palo Alto and Menlo Park. Then it curves around to the equally affluent western suburbs of San Jose, Campbell and Los Gatos. That makes the 11th District's senator — and it has been Becky Morgan since 1984 — Silicon Valley's representative in the upper house of the Legislature. And that also means it is a Republican district, but one whose pro-business outlook is tempered with a liberal approach to social issues and the environment. The area has produced a long string of maverick Republican politicians, such as former Reps. Pete McCloskey, Ed Zschau and Tom Campbell, who were all labeled "closet Democrats" by conservative elements of their party.

The success of the Silicon Valley has come with a price. Once thought of as clean industry, high-tech manufacturing has proven to be a big polluter. The valley holds a number of toxic waste sites on the federal Superfund cleanup list. Fairchild Camera, among the first polluters discovered, used highly toxic solvents in its processing that leaked into the groundwater supplies.

Republican Morgan is very much a product of her district. Her husband, James C. Morgan, is the millionaire president of Applied Materials Inc., one of the Silicon Valley firms on the toxic cleanup list. The San Jose-based environmental organization Silicon Valley Toxics Coalition once accused Sen. Morgan of having a conflict of interest by chairing an important toxics subcommittee in the Senate. Nonsense, she replied.

Rebecca Morgan

Soon after Pete Wilson was elected governor, Morgan seemed to be under consideration to fill his U.S. Senate seat. She looked a good bet — a moderate woman, pro-choice on abortion and a solid fund-raiser. Her husband, however, did her no favors when he told an interviewer from Forbes Magazine in October 1990 about why he was building a $100 million expansion in Austin, Tex., and not in California. "The cost of land in Northern California is excessive and the attitude of state and local government toward industry is pathetic," James Morgan said. After much press speculation, state Sen. Morgan asked Wilson to take her name off the list for U.S. senator — if there really was a list (Wilson eventually said he picked his first choice: John Seymour).

Morgan has steered an independent course, sometimes going against the Republican grain in the Senate by voting to restrict semiautomatic weapons and to uphold abortion rights. Morgan made her own quiet protest against the U.S. Supreme Court's 1989 abortion rulings by removing from her office wall an autographed portrait of Associate Justice Anthony Kennedy.

She is popular among her colleagues, although she is inconsistent on her feet and is noted for missing some of the nuances in legislation. She has a reputation for vote-switching during roll calls — not through any scheming but because of a lack of understanding or a genuine quandary over its merits. That often reflects her moderate politics when faced with ideologically divisive legislation.

Morgan has maintained strong ties to the business community. At the start of the 1991-92 session, she began pushing SB 103 to give a property tax break to Luz International Corp., the operator of a huge solar electricity plant in the Mojave Desert. The Wilson administration, however, said the bill would cost San Bernardino County millions, one-third of which would have to be replaced by the fiscally strapped state general fund to support schools.

Morgan, a former teacher, has focused on education issues. She won passage of a bill to tighten restrictions on "diploma mills" in 1989 and has pushed for a $207 million pilot project in the schools. She had been considering a run for state school superintendent in 1994. With the conviction of school chief Bill Honig on charges of steering state contracts to his wife's firm, Morgan became a top candidate for appointment to the job.

Among those cheering Morgan on to greater heights is the area's Republican assemblyman, Charles Quackenbush, who makes little secret of his ambition to move into her Senate seat.

PERSONAL: elected 1984; born Dec. 4, 1938, in Hanover, N.H.; home, Los Altos Hills; education, B.S. Cornell University, M.A. business administration Stanford University; husband James, two children; Protestant.

CAREER: teacher; banker; school board member; Santa Clara County Board of Supervisors 1981-1984.

COMMITTEES: Education (vice chair); Revenue & Taxation (vice chair); Budget & Fiscal Review; Energy & Public Utilities.

OFFICES: Capitol, (916) 445-6747, FAX (916) 323-4529; district, 750 Menlo Ave., 100, Menlo Park 94025, (415) 688-6330, FAX (415) 688-6334.

TERM LIMIT: 1996

REGISTRATION: 45.9% D, 38.4% R

1992 CAMPAIGN:	Morgan – R	64.5%	$733,226
	Frank Trinkle – D	30.7%	$5,621
1988 CAMPAIGN:	Morgan – R	60.7%	$640,868
	Tom Nolan – D	36.1%	$90,629

RATINGS:	AFL-CIO	CalPIRG	CLCV	NOW	CofC	CalFarm
	38	45	NR	57	68	60

KEY VOTES:

Parent consent abort:	NO	Limit product tort:	nv	Clean Air Act:	YES
Assault gun ban:	YES	Ban AIDS discrim:	YES	Restrict abortion funds:	NO
Sales tax hike:	YES	Wealth tax hike:	YES	Strong gay rights:	YES
Parental leave:	YES	Timber compromise:	nv	Execution by injection:	YES
Limited gay rights:	YES	Universal health insur:	NO	1992-93 Budget Act:	YES
Campaign Reform:	YES	Offshore oil ban:	YES	Charter schools:	NO

Nicholas C. Petris (D)
9th Senate District

Lining San Francisco Bay's eastern shoreline, the 9th Senate District takes in a polyglot that includes the affluent, white Piedmont hills, the intensely poor African American neighborhoods of Oakland and the leftist environs of Berkeley and its University of California campus. Reapportionment removed a piece of conservative Contra Costa County and added Richmond, which made it more safely Democratic. The district is 32 percent African American, 13 percent Latino and 14 percent Asian.

Democrat Nicholas Petris, one of the last unbend-
ing liberals in the Capitol, is the only senator this
district — in all its incarnations — has known since
the inception of the full-time Legislature in 1966. For
years, the silver-haired, courtly Petris has railed against
growers for their treatment of farm workers; pushed,
with limited success, bills requiring warning signs in
fields where pesticides have been sprayed; and cham-
pioned the rights of criminal defendants, mental patients, the poor and the elderly. And he is a vocal
champion of the state's influential trial lawyers, standing against all efforts to tighten the state's "deep
pockets" tort liability laws, efforts he sees as victim-
izing consumers.

Nicholas Petris

But the last decade of Republican rule in the governor's office has not been kind
to Petris. It has been two decades since he authored landmark legislation like the
Lanterman-Petris-Short Act, which brought major changes to the mental-health
system, and the post-Proposition 13 world has not been receptive to his pleas for
more funding for health care and education.

The cantankerous, right-wing Sen. H.L. Richardson, now retired, once claimed
that Petris pulled the strings of Senate President Pro Tem David Roberti. Although
that's a vast overstatement, Petris' influence in keeping the Senate Democrats left
of center should not be underestimated. He still uses his position on the Judiciary
Committee as a bully pulpit and he also sits on the all-powerful Rules Committee.
But, clearly, he is slowing down.

Beyond policy matters, one of Petris' major interests is Greece. He quotes from
the Greek classics during his floor speeches and serves as the unofficial leader of
the equally unofficial caucus of Greek-American legislators, often authoring
resolutions that support that nation in its squabbles with Turkey. The high-point for
that group came in 1988, when Michael Dukakis ran for president.

Petris' home in the Oakland Hills burned down during the tragic fire in October
1991. Lost in the inferno was his collection of more than 10,000 books, painstak-
ingly collected over a lifetime, including an extensive collection of Greek works and
a volume written by Harry Truman that the president had signed along with a framed
picture of Petris and Truman while Truman was signing the book. At a ceremony
on the Senate floor, fellow senators presented Petris with volumes from their
collections. Some gave him one or two; others, such as Ruben Ayala, gave him a box
of books. "It was a very moving thing. It reduced me to tears," Petris said.

PERSONAL: elected 1966; born Feb. 25, 1923, in Oakland; home, Oakland;
Army 1943-1946 WWII; education, B.A. UC Berkeley, J.D. Stanford University;
wife Anna S. Vlahos; no children; Greek Orthodox.

CAREER: lawyer, Assembly 1958-1966.

COMMITTEES: Budget & Fiscal Review; Industrial Relations; Judiciary; Rules.

OFFICES: Capitol, (916) 445-6577, FAX (916) 327-1997; district, 1970 Broadway, 1030, Oakland 94612, (510) 286-1333, FAX (510) 286-3885.

TERM LIMIT: 1996

REGISTRATION: 69.8% D, 14.1% R, 2.9% Green

1992 CAMPAIGN:	Petris – D	84.6%	$376,727
	David Campbell – P&F	15.4%	
1988 CAMPAIGN:	Petris – D	74.7%	$342,680
	Greg Henson – R	21.4%	$0

RATINGS:	AFL-CIO	CalPIRG	CLCV	NOW	CofC	CalFarm
	94	91	91	100	16	30

KEY VOTES:

Parent consent abort:	NO	Limit product tort:	nv	Clean Air Act:	YES
Assault gun ban:	YES	Ban AIDS discrim:	nv	Restrict abortion funds:	NO
Sales tax hike:	YES	Wealth tax hike:	YES	Strong gay rights:	YES
Parental leave:	YES	Timber compromise:	YES	Execution by injection:	NO
Limited gay rights:	YES	Universal health insure:	YES	1992-93 Budget Act:	YES
Campaign Reform:	YES	Offshore oil ban:	YES	Charter schools:	YES

Robert B. Presley (D)
36th Senate District

The heart of the populated west end of Riverside County is in this district with a slice of mountainous northern San Diego County, including Palomar and Fallbrook. This district is much compacted in size from when it stretched out through ritzy desert communities and pockets of rural poverty to the Colorado River in Blythe. The center of gravity is Riverside, the earth-toned stucco housing tracts of Moreno Valley and the horse country of Norco and the chicken ranches near Corona.

Robert Presley

When Robert Presley won this seat in 1974, there were considerably fewer people living in that vast expanse. In the years since, it has become the fastest-growing region of the state, and that creates no end of political problems for the Democratic incumbent. But Presley has managed to win handily every four years in Riverside County despite its increasingly Republican tilt.

A former Riverside County sheriff's deputy who rose through the ranks to become second in command, Presley's law-and-order credentials are impeccable — and his exploits as a detective are still the stuff of local lore. He won a Bronze

Star in Italy in World War II for staying behind enemy lines with the wounded until an American counteroffensive came to the rescue.

As a senator, Presley is the area's preeminent politician — practically Riverside County's unofficial "mayor," resolving disputes between competing local power interests. He has cultivated the old power structure, personified by the "Monday Morning Group" of Riverside businessmen, and it has shown him unmatched loyalty. Presley's power on the local scene has long eclipsed Riverside County's other legislators and all of the area's mayors and county supervisors.

Politically, Presley calls himself a conservative and hints periodically that he will become a Republican. In 1982, he ran a write-in campaign for the Republican nomination and won, thus enabling himself to run as the nominee of both major parties. He can be expected to play a similar game leading up to his 1994 re-election.

One of Presley's district bills has gotten caught up in the federal probe of Capitol corruption, although it appears he had nothing to do with the machinations of interest to prosecutors. In January 1993, the FBI subpoenaed his files on a heavily lobbied bill he carried that would have given special treatment to a luxury hotel near Palm Springs in an area he used to represent. The bill became a magnet for lobbyists and deal-makers in the Capitol before it was vetoed by Gov. George Deukmejian.

"It became the damnedest thing," Presley told the Los Angeles Times after federal authorities took his records. "First thing you know, there are 900 lobbyists lined up on both sides."

Over the years, Presley has cemented his relationship with Democratic President Pro Tem David Roberti, and reaped considerable benefits, not the least being the chairmanship of Appropriations, the Senate's second most powerful committee next to Rules. As chairman he has won plaudits for fairness, but he is not as fast with the gavel — or as ruthless — as his predecessor, Democratic Sen. Dan Boatwright of Concord.

Presley's legislative achievements are considerable and wide-ranging. His legislation has included the state's vehicle smog-check program, reorganizing and strengthening the South Coast Air Quality Management District, bringing reason to chaotic child welfare laws, stiffening numerous criminal laws and establishing new parklands. Another bill toughened ethical standards for lawyers and forced the State Bar Association to begin addressing its lengthy backlog of complaints against member lawyers. Presley also has embarked on an effort to strengthen the discipline system of the medical profession.

As chairman of the joint prison committee, Presley has carried the legislation authorizing the construction of every new prison of the last decade. And he has become a potent critic of wasteful spending, inadequate health care, poor management and outdated practices in the prison system.

PERSONAL: elected 1974; born Dec. 4, 1924, in Tahlequah, Okla.; home, Riverside; Army 1943-1946 WWII (Italy); education, A.A. Riverside City College, FBI National Academy; wife Ahni Ratliff, three children; Baptist.

CAREER: Riverside County Sheriff's department 24 years, undersheriff.

COMMITTEES: Appropriations (chair); Agriculture & Water Resources; Judiciary.

OFFICES: Capitol, (916) 445-9781; district, 3600 Lime Street, 111, Riverside 92501, (909) 782-4111, FAX (909) 276-4483.

TERM LIMIT: 1998

REGISTRATION: 39.6% D, 48.2% R

1990 CAMPAIGN:	Presley – D	53.6%	$964,484
	Raymond Haynes – R	46.4%	$70,527
1986 CAMPAIGN:	Presley – D	61%	$401,632
	Anne Richardson – R	39%	$22,969

RATINGS:	AFL-CIO	CalPIRG	CLCV	NOW	CofC	CalFarm
	66	68	80	29	53	50

KEY VOTES:

Parent consent abort:	YES	Limit product tort:	YES	Clean Air Act:	YES
Assault gun ban:	YES	Ban AIDS discrim:	YES	Restrict abortion funds:	YES
Sales tax hike:	YES	Wealth tax hike:	YES	Strong gay rights:	NO
Parental leave:	NO	Timber compromise:	YES	Execution by injection:	YES
Limited gay rights:	NO	Universal health insure:	YES	1992-93 Budget Act:	YES
Campaign Reform:	YES	Offshore oil ban:	YES	Charter schools:	YES

David A. Roberti (D)

23rd Senate District

On a rain-soaked Monday in January 1991, David Roberti stood in the rotunda of the state Capitol and greeted his third governor as president pro tempore of the Senate, the top post in the state's upper house. On the day of Pete Wilson's inaugural, Roberti's hold on power was probably at its height.

It has been a very rough ride for Roberti since then. The institution led by Roberti and Assembly Speaker Willie Brown was soon wrenched by term limits, budget deficits and reapportionment. In fact, the biggest loser of the 1992 reapportionment was Roberti. The state Supreme Court redistricting plan sliced up Roberti's old 23rd Senate District, forcing him into a thicket of bad choices just to stay in office, let alone maintain his leadership post.

David Roberti

Roberti ended up running in a special election in the old 20th Senate District to replace Sen. Alan Robbins, who was forced from office in a plea bargain on federal corruption charges. When Roberti would not pay the stiff fee demanded by Marlene Bane (the wife of then-Assemblyman Tom Bane, D-Tarzana), Roberti suddenly found himself facing on the ballot a former Bane aide, Carol Rowen, who was running as a Republican, no less. The special election cost Roberti more than $1 million — money that could have been spent helping other Democrats win legislative seats.

Running in the 20th District allowed Roberti to avoid opposing one of his Senate Democratic allies in a 1992 primary in a newly configured Senate district. But the move also meant that Roberti had to win a new political base in the San Fernando Valley, a more conservative area than the Hollywood Hills he had represented for decades. Roberti, the son of Italian immigrants, had represented central Los Angeles in the Legislature since he was elected to the Assembly in 1966, then the youngest legislator at age 27. He moved up to the Senate in a 1971 special election.

The move to the new district meant one other thing for Roberti — he would be the first legislator tossed from office under term limits in 1994. Under the convoluted provisions of Proposition 140, a legislator who serves more than half of a term has a full term counted against him or her. Thus, because he had been re-elected in 1988, Roberti will have served two terms under Proposition 140 and must therefore leave in 1994.

The old 20th Senate District included the smog-shrouded eastern San Fernando Valley, holding the middle-class communities of Van Nuys, Reseda, Panorama City, Mission Hills, Pacoima and other towns that blend one into the other. With pockets of Jewish, working-class and upscale voters, the district voted generally Democratic with a conservative tinge.

The new 20th District has the largest minority population of any district in the San Fernando Valley, standing at 46 percent Latino, and is strongly Democratic. It likely will go to a minority candidate in 1994 unless Roberti can find a way to have term limits declared unconstitutional.

In the meantime, Roberti's Democratic colleagues have begun talking openly of the "post-Roberti era" — a subject they would never have dared speak of a few years ago. A number of Democrats were resentful of Roberti's costly special election race, apparently believing he should have committed political hara-kiri and given them the money instead. Life is not easy in Roberti's southwestern corner office of the Capitol.

Roberti and Brown were sworn-in as the leaders of their respective houses on the same December 1980 day, triumphant following their coups. Forces that brought both to power were the same — the advent of the full-time Legislature in 1966 and the highly partisan atmosphere it engendered over the years. But their styles and personalities could not be more different.

Brown had noisily grabbed power by forming a coalition with Republicans (who thought he would be a weak speaker), while Roberti had quietly arranged the overthrow of President Pro Tem Jim Mills, who was planning to step aside anyway. Roberti had taken advantage of Senate Democratic fears following the 1980 election loss of Senate dean Al Rodda of Sacramento in a highly partisan, and decidedly ungentlemanly, contest with John Doolittle. While Mills, a milquetoast Democrat, had entertained notions of handing off his mantle to the genteel Robert Presley, Senate liberals had other designs and elevated Roberti to pro tem on his promise to protect their seats in the upcoming 1981 reapportionment. There would be no more Rodda incidents if Roberti could help it. Holding power in the Senate became dependent not on legislative prowess but on keeping incumbents re-elected, something Roberti first demonstrated in 1982, when he defended then-Sen. Alex Garcia, who was known mostly for his prolonged absences from the Capitol, against a Democratic primary challenge from then-Assemblyman Art Torres. Garcia lost, but Roberti had demonstrated his fidelity to incumbents.

Roberti's anti-abortion rights view is the one issue that puts him at odds with his caucus. His tirades against Planned Parenthood are legendary. Even so, he enthusiastically supported the winning candidacy of Lucy Killea (who was then a Democrat) in a 1989 special election dominated by her pro-choice stance and conflict with her Catholic bishop.

Like Willie Brown, Roberti has had his hands full keeping his caucus together during successively worse state budget crises. Roberti, however, has shown more willingness to work with Pete Wilson than has Brown (to Brown's great displeasure). Roberti made the first substantive moves with the Republican governor to break impasses in both the 1991 and 1992 budget fiascoes. Roberti's relatively good working relationship with Wilson is all the more remarkable given his stormy relationship with Republican George Deukmejian (who got along much better with the speaker).

Although Roberti gained power on a partisan wave, he has proven a more complex politician. He enjoys cordial relations with many of his Republican colleagues, particularly with Republican leader Ken Maddy — a relationship in marked contrast to the poisoned blood among Democratic and Republican leaders in the Assembly. Some Republicans are even Roberti confidants, particularly Oceanside's Bill Craven, who sits with Roberti on the Rules Committee that governs Senate operations.

Roberti and the Rules Committee seem to have chosen a different path than Speaker Brown in the wake of Proposition 140. Roberti moved quickly, without complaining, to trim the Senate staff while Brown whined to the bitter end in making cuts. Roberti hired an outside ethics expert, Michael Josephson, to conduct an all-day ethics workshop for senators (who hated every second of it). Brown, on the other hand, hunkered down in his bunker and blamed the press for his troubles.

In contrast to Brown's flashy clothes and fast cars, Roberti is a pet-loving homebody who wears dark suits and is devoutly Catholic. Roberti's weaknesses are for hearty food and travel, particularly to Italy. His wife, June, his closest political adviser, is seldom seen in the Capitol.

The introverted Roberti has never been as prominent in politics outside the Capitol as Willie Brown. The San Francisco Chronicle once headlined a story about

Roberti: "The Unknown Man Running the Senate." He disdains dabbling at presidential king-making, unlike Brown, and has been openly skeptical of advancing California's June presidential primary to March. He seems to believe presidential politics are a distraction from policy-making in California.

Roberti has steadily racked up a solid legislative record. His bills have run the gamut from consumer protection to child welfare, hazardous waste, energy and crime. By using his full weight as leader of the Senate, Roberti won passage in 1989 of a law restricting semiautomatic assault weapons and, later that year, convinced his nervous colleagues to embrace ethics reforms limiting outside income. Those reforms were embodied in Proposition 112, approved by voters in June 1990. Roberti, often accompanied by Maddy, stumped for the measure. By contrast, the speaker kept his distance, showing no enthusiasm for the reforms and disdainfully declaring he would do nothing to help it pass. Roberti also authored the implementing legislation for Proposition 112, without which the ethics reforms would have had no teeth.

Wilson has appeared more cognizant of Roberti's power than Deukmejian and has gone out of his way to soothe senatorial egos. Even as he has condemned the Assembly for inaction, Wilson has often praised the Senate for being "the responsible house."

On another level, Roberti is the head of a huge organization that keeps the Senate lurching along. As pro tem, Roberti has built a highly skilled staff, ruled initially with an iron-fist by Jerry Zanelli, who was executive officer of the Senate Rules Committee. But Roberti fell out with Zanelli, who became a lobbyist, and replaced him with Clifford Berg, an icy bureaucrat who has become the most powerful staffer in the Legislature, administering Roberti's huge staff, doling out office space and committee assignments to senators and overseeing Roberti's policy analysts.

Roberti has faced three senatorial challenges to his leadership post, but emerged from each struggle stronger than before. In those struggles, Roberti did not hesitate to strip his opponents of committee chairmanships and other perks. But Roberti, not wanting to surround himself with malcontents, also brought the chastened rebels back into his fold after a measured time of exile. His challengers at various times — Paul Carpenter, John Garamendi and Dan Boatwright — were all later given committee chairmanships.

Despite Roberti's lack of media appeal, he has sometimes entertained ambitions of moving into statewide office such as attorney general. Roberti is an able fundraiser and should not be discounted. During the 1990 election cycle, although he was not up for re-election, Roberti raised $4,935,217, doling most of it out for initiatives and causes.

PERSONAL: elected 1971; born May 4, 1939, in Los Angeles; home, Los Angeles; education, B.A. political science Loyola University, J.D. USC; wife June; Roman Catholic.

CAREER: lawyer; law clerk; deputy attorney general 1965-1966; Assembly 1966-1971; Senate president pro tempore 1980-present.

COMMITTEES: ex officio member of all standing and joint committees; Rules (chair); Judiciary.

OFFICES: Capitol, (916) 445-8390, FAX (916) 323-7224; district, 6150 Van Nuys Blvd., 400, Van Nuys 91401, (818) 901-5588, FAX (818) 901-5562.

TERM LIMIT: 1994

REGISTRATION: 58.4% D, 28.9% R

JUNE 2, 1992, SPECIAL ELECTION:

Roberti – D	42.9%	$1,461,196
Carol Rowen – R	38.4%	$141,524
Glenn Trujillo Bailey – Green	8.1%	
John Vernon – L	6.9%	

1988 CAMPAIGN (in 23rd Senate District):

Roberti – D	67.8%	$3,920,485
Tom Larkin – R	26.3%	$0

RATINGS:

AFL-CIO	CalPIRG	CLCV	NOW	CofC	CalFarm
95	100	91	79	26	20

KEY VOTES:

Parent consent abort:	YES	Limit product tort:	YES	Clean Air Act:	YES
Assault gun ban:	YES	Ban AIDS discrim:	YES	Restrict abortion funds:	YES
Sales tax hike:	YES	Wealth tax hike:	YES	Strong gay rights:	YES
Parental leave:	YES	Timber compromise:	YES	Execution by injection:	YES
Limited gay rights:	YES	Universal health insure:	YES	1992-93 Budget Act:	YES
Campaign Reform:	YES	Offshore oil ban:	YES	Charter schools:	YES

Donald A. Rogers (R)
17th Senate District

This cactus-and-sagebrush district takes in most of the Mojave Desert, the San Gabriel Mountains and the southern end of the San Joaquin Valley in oil-rich Kern County. The northern two-thirds of San Bernardino County, including the gas-stop towns of Barstow and Victorville, are also included as well as all of sparsely populated Inyo County. Geographically, the district is centered in Death Valley. But 70 percent of its people live in a chunk of northern Los Angeles County. The district is heavily Republican.

When Republican Sen. Don Rogers, who had represented the Bakersfield area in the Legislature since 1978, was reapportioned into a heavily Democratic district, he decided to set up political shop in the

Donald Rogers

16th District. The move, however, meant he had to run for election in 1992 even though he had won re-election to the Senate only two years earlier in the old 16th District. After winning in the 17th, Rogers resigned from the 16th District, forcing a special election for that seat.

Rogers has always had an appeal in the southern San Joaquin Valley. Bakersfield voters, many of them conservative descendants of the Dust Bowl migration, seem to identify with the Louisiana-born man who built his first career as an oil geologist. It didn't seem to bother them when Rogers filed Chapter 13 bankruptcy protection in 1992 to keep the Internal Revenue Service from selling his assets to pay back taxes, interest and penalties. The IRS succeeding in seizing Rogers private plane, at one point, but most of his other assets were safely squirreled away in trusts.

As a legislator, Rogers has marked himself as perhaps the Senate's strongest opponent of environmental legislation, particularly anything affecting the oil industry. His knee-jerk opposition is so strong it is taken for granted by colleagues, thus diluting whatever persuasive powers he might have. In 1990, he was the lone "no" vote in the Senate against a bill to set up a $100 million fund for oil-spill cleanups (in the Assembly, the single "no" vote was cast by fellow Bakersfield legislator Trice Harvey). Rogers' floor speech against the bill on Aug. 31, 1990, left many in the chamber gasping.

"Sure, we're probably going to have more oil spills," he began. "But let's state fact. The ones that have occurred — the one that occurred in Santa Barbara, it was too bad. That was a blow out. However, the effect did not last very long. It wasn't but a few months until all effects, all evidence of the spill, had disappeared due to the work of mother nature and the work of the response people. ... Even up in Alaska, you go there now and you have to look pretty hard to find any evidence of the spill up in Prince William Sound."

Rogers was a vocal opponent of a ban on semiautomatic assault weapons. He didn't endear himself to his Democratic colleagues when he mailed a fund-raising appeal billing himself as the "commanding officer and founder of the Republican Air Force." The plea went on: "The RAF has remained high above the quagmire of socialism and has effectively stayed the evils constantly trying to invade the California Legislature."

At the start of the 1993-94 session, Rogers got one of the few chairmanships handed to a Republican, albeit a minor one — chair of the Senate Veterans Affairs Committee. The move allowed Senate leaders to finesse Rogers off the more important Budget and Fiscal Review Committee — a panel that has enough trouble passing a budget without having ideologues running amok.

PERSONAL: elected 1986; born April 22, 1928, in Natchitoches, La.; home, Tehachapi; USMC 1946-1948; education, B.S. geology Louisiana State University; wife Marilyn L. Miller, three children; Mormon.

CAREER: oil geologist; owner of a geological consulting firm and partner in a petroleum firm; Bakersfield City Council 1973-1978; Assembly 1978-1986.

COMMITTEES: Veterans Affairs (chair); Agriculture & Water Resources; Insurance, Claims & Corporations; Natural Resources & Wildlife; Public Employment & Retirement.

OFFICES: Capitol, (916) 445-6637, FAX (916) 443-4015; district, 1326 H St., Bakersfield 93301, (805) 395-2927, FAX (805) 861-9413.

TERM LIMIT: 1996

REGISTRATION: 36.9% D, 49.2% R, 2.3% AIP

1992 CAMPAIGN:

Rogers – R		52.2%	$296,985
William Olenick – D		38.9%	$9,872

1990 CAMPAIGN (in 16th District):

Rogers – R		52%	$492,674
Ray Gonzales – D		44%	$120,072

RATINGS: (includes votes from Assembly service 1978-86)

AFL-CIO	CalPIRG	CLCV	NOW	CofC	CalFarm
9	14	5	21	74	8

KEY VOTES:

Parent consent abort:	YES	Limit product tort:	YES	Clean Air Act:	NO
Assault gun ban:	NO	Ban AIDS discrim:	nv	Restrict abortion funds:	YES
Sales tax hike:	NO	Wealth tax hike:	NO	Strong gay rights:	NO
Parental leave:	NO	Timber compromise:	NO	Execution by injection:	nv
Limited gay rights:	NO	Universal health insure:	NO	1992-93 Budget Act:	YES
Campaign Reform:	NO	Offshore oil ban:	NO	Charter schools:	NO

Herschel Rosenthal (D)

22nd Senate District

This compact district was drawn to hold the heavily Latino population of East Los Angeles. Two-thirds of the population is Spanish-speaking and Asian Americans comprise 16 percent. Democratic registration is overwhelming; Republican candidates need not apply. It is a cinch that a non-white Democrat will win this seat — eventually.

Herschel Rosenthal

At the moment, however, the 22nd District is represented by Herschel Rosenthal, an old-fashioned liberal who is a product of the political organization led by Reps. Henry Waxman and Howard Berman. Before the Supreme Court started carving up the district, Rosenthal's 22nd Senate District was the heart of the liberal westside of Los Angeles. Reapportionment stuck that territory into the new 23rd Senate District, so Rosenthal decided to move with his turf and sought the new 23rd District seat in 1992 even though he had been re-elected to the old 22nd two years earlier.

The election for the new 23rd District should have been a cinch for Rosenthal, except that he was up against none other than Tom Hayden, who was fighting for his political life. After a bruising and expensive Democratic primary in June 1992 between Hayden, Rosenthal and Catherine O'Neill, Hayden emerged the winner by less than 600 votes. It marked a major loss for the Berman-Waxman machine and left Rosenthal's political future up in the air.

Rosenthal still represents the 22nd District for another two years. He could ask East Los Angeles voters, with whom he does not have much affinity, to re-elect him in 1994. In the meantime, Rosenthal will have to spend the next two years sitting in the Senate with Hayden and sharing some committee assignments.

Rosenthal has made his legislative mark primarily in utilities law. He was the Senate Democrats' negotiator in breaking a tricky two-year stalemate over how to spend $154 million that California received from a national $2.1 billion judgment against several oil companies for overcharging during the 1974 oil crisis. The agreement reached in the spring of 1989 earmarked $60 million to start replacing about one-third of the state's unsafe school buses, and the rest was used to help poor people meet their utility bills and other energy and traffic projects.

Rosenthal's yearly financial disclosure statements have been among the more entertaining for their restaurant and travel listings. He is among the more traveled lawmakers, enjoying a steady stream of junkets courtesy of corporations, most of which have business pending before the public utilities committee he chairs. On the side, Rosenthal is a horse racing fanatic who owns all or part of several horses. He even dresses like a race-track tout in mismatched slacks and plaid jackets that look as though a horse once wore them.

Rosenthal, who was among the Democrats underwhelmed with his party's crop of candidates for governor in 1990, won notoriety in an otherwise boring summer of 1989 by trying to get actor James Garner to run for governor. Garner declined, reportedly telling Rosenthal it would mean giving up his $6 million a year income.

PERSONAL: elected 1982; born March 13, 1918, in St. Louis, Mo.; home, Los Angeles; Navy; education, attended UCLA; wife Patricia Staman, two children; Jewish.

CAREER: partner ADTYPE Service Co. Inc.; Assembly 1974-1982.

COMMITTEES: Energy & Public Utilities (chair); Business & Professions; Elections & Reapportionment; Governmental Organization; Health & Human Services; Housing & Urban Affairs; Industrial Relations; Insurance, Claims & Corporations.

OFFICES: Capitol, (916) 445-7928; district, 1950 Sawtelle Blvd., 210, Los Angeles, 90025, (310) 479-5588, FAX (310) 477-8172.

TERM LIMIT: 1998

REGISTRATION: 63.3% D, 21.2% R

1990 CAMPAIGN: Rosenthal – D   64.6% $875,866
Michael Schrager – R   30.9% $4,671

1986 CAMPAIGN: Rosenthal – D   68% $488,292
                         Daniel Sias – R   29% $0
RATINGS: AFL-CIO   CalPIRG   CLCV   NOW   CofC   CalFarm
                    97   95   91   100   21   40

KEY VOTES:

Parent consent abort:	NO	Limit product tort:	YES	Clean Air Act:	nv
Assault gun ban:	YES	Ban AIDS discrim:	YES	Restrict abortion funds:	NO
Sales tax hike:	YES	Wealth tax hike:	YES	Strong gay rights:	YES
Parental leave:	YES	Timber compromise:	YES	Execution by injection:	nv
Limited gay rights:	YES	Universal health insure:	YES	1992-93 Budget Act:	NO
Campaign Reform:	YES	Offshore oil ban:	YES	Charter schools:	YES

Newton R. Russell (R)

21st Senate District

Democrats needn't apply in this Los Angeles County district that includes territory north of downtown Los Angeles, picking up pieces of wealthy suburbs in the San Fernando and San Garbriel Valleys. The district includes the posh — and very white — suburbs of San Marino and Pasadena, La Canada, Sunland-Tujunga and Burbank. Latinos compromise 22 percent of the population but a considerably smaller proportion of the registered voters.

Newton Russell has been in the Legislature for a quarter of a century, beginning his career in the Assembly in 1964 and moving to the Senate 10 years later. The senator is a hard-working, consummate conservative, rarely breaking from the Republican

Newton Russell

caucus line. In fact, it was something of a mild surprise when Russell reversed himself in 1989 and supported a bill that would have heavily fined insurers who illegally canceled automobile policies following the passage of Proposition 103.

In recent years, Russell has been most visible for his involvement in bills dealing with sex education at schools. In 1988, he successfully pushed a bill, signed into law by Gov. George Deukmejian, that requires schools to encourage students to abstain from intercourse until they are ready for marriage and to teach respect for monogamous, heterosexual marriage. Russell said that measure was "not intended to preach morals. It is intended to give teens useful, factual tips." The following year, he introduced a bill that would require written parental consent for children to receive sex education, and another to prohibit schools from providing counseling to students other than career, academic or vocational without the same written consent.

His legislation for the 1993-94 session have a decidedly law-and-order tilt, perhaps reflecting the post-Los Angeles riot fear of his constituents. His bills include SB 20, which would increase penalties for suspects fleeing police.

Russell also is one of the Senate's resident parliamentarians, frequently rising to object to breaches of rules. And those protests about parliamentary games led to a series of procedural reforms in the Senate, designed to prevent legislation from slipping into law without notice and full airing. Russell has been mentioned in Republican legislative circles as a replacement for Ken Maddy as minority leader should he step aside or falter politically.

PERSONAL: elected 1974 (special election); born June 25, 1927, in Los Angeles; home, Glendale; Navy WWII; education, B.S. business administration USC, attended UCLA and Georgetown University; wife Diane Henderson; three children; Protestant.

CAREER: insurance agent; Assembly 1964-1974.

COMMITTEES: Banking & Commerce (vice chair); Energy & Public Utilities (vice chair); Insurance, Claims & Corporations; Local Government; Transportation.

OFFICES: Capitol, (916) 445-5976, FAX 324-7543; district, 401 N. Brand Blvd., 424, Glendale 91203-2364, (818) 247-7021, FAX (818) 240-5672.

TERM LIMIT: 1996

REGISTRATION: 43.8% D, 42.7% R

1992 CAMPAIGN:	Russell – R	50%	$460,284
	Rachel Dewcy – D	43.7%	$14,241
1988 CAMPAIGN:	Russell – R	68.4%	$284,413
	Louise Gelber – D	28.3%	$121,146

RATINGS:	AFL-CIO	CalPIRG	CLCV	NOW	CofC	CalFarm
	20	18	33	14	74	50

KEY VOTES:

Parent consent abort:	YES	Limit product tort:	nv	Clean Air Act:	nv
Assault gun ban:	NO	Ban AIDS discrim:	NO	Restrict abortion funds:	YES
Sales tax hike:	YES	Wealth tax hike:	NO	Strong gay rights:	NO
Parental leave:	NO	Timber compromise:	YES	Execution by injection:	YES
Limited gay rights:	NO	Universal health insure:	NO	1992-93 Budget Act:	YES
Campaign Reform:	YES	Offshore oil ban:	NO	Charter schools:	NO

Michael Thompson (D)
4th Senate District

Following Interstate 5 north to the Oregon border, this sprawling district takes in the college town of Davis and the flat farmlands of the northern Central Valley. It includes Redding, the largest city north of Sacramento, and spectacular river country, including the wild McCloud. Also in the district are Mount Shasta and the headwaters of the Sacramento River, poisoned when a train overturned into the river in 1991.

The region is friendly to Republicans and elected Jim Nielsen in 1978. Nielsen served a stint as Senate Republican leader before he was ousted following GOP election losses. In the process, he underwent some unusual personal changes. Twice-divorced and thrice-married, Nielsen became a fundamentalist Christian. He created a stir in 1989 by declaring during a radio show that AIDS "may be God's way" of punishing "mankind (for) what kind of promiscuous society we've become." All of that contributed heavily to his narrow loss in 1990 to Democrat Mike Thompson of St. Helena.

Michael Thompson

The ice-cool Thompson worked for seven years as an aide to Assemblywoman Jacqueline Speier, D-South San Francisco, and Assemblyman Lou Papan, D-Millbrae, both liberals. He also has been a political science lecturer at state universities. Thompson, a Vietnam veteran who won a purple heart for his wounds as a platoon leader in the 173rd Airborne Brigade, has avoided the liberal label in order to hold the seat in what remains a marginal region for Democrats. He pledged to serve no more than two terms if elected, but if Proposition 140's term limits are upheld by the courts, that will not be an issue.

In the campaign against Nielsen, Thompson won farm votes by opposing the "Big Green" environmental initiative and by charging that Nielsen sided with interests wanting to ship more water from the north to the south. Nielsen, who was the only Senate incumbent to lose in 1990, outspent Thompson by almost 3 to 1.

In his first year in the Senate, Thompson was clearly the low Democrat on the totem pole. Time and again Democratic leader David Roberti shambled over to his desk to ask for a hard vote — and got it. At the start of the 1993 session, he was rewarded with chairmanship of the Natural Resources and Wildlife Committee.

Thompson is actively looking for safer territory. He planned to run in a special election for the 2nd Senate District seat vacated by Democrat Barry Keene. Portions of Thompson's prereapportionment district — including the senator's St. Helena home — will become part of the 2nd District in 1994. To ingratiate himself with voters in Vallejo, however, Thompson established a temporary residence in that heavily Democratic town, and began referring to himself in news releases as "D-Vallejo," even though that city is not in the 4th Senate District to which he was elected in 1990.

PERSONAL: elected 1990; born Jan. 24, 1951, in St. Helena; home, St. Helena; Army, Vietnam; education, B.A. public administration CSU Chico, course work for M.S. public administration CSU Chico; wife Jan, two children.

CAREER: chief of staff, Assemblyman Louis Papan 1984-1987; chief of staff, Assemblywoman Jacqueline Speier 1987-1990.

COMMITTEES: Natural Resources & Wildlife (chair); Housing & Urban Affairs (acting chair); Agriculture & Water Resources; Banking, Commerce & International Trade; Budget & Fiscal Review; Health & Human Services; Veterans Affairs.

OFFICES: Capitol, (916) 445-3353, FAX (916) 323-6958; district, 1040 Main St., 101, Napa 94559, (707) 224-1990; 50 D St., FAX (707) 224-4133.

TERM LIMIT: 1998

REGISTRATION: 48.3% D, 37.9% R, 2% AIP

1990 CAMPAIGN: Thompson – D   48% $598,322
Jim Nielsen (incumbent) – R   46.4% $1,516,132

RATINGS:

AFL-CIO	CalPIRG	CLCV	NOW	CofC	CalFarm
82	95	74	86	16	20

KEY VOTES:

Sales tax hike:	YES	Wealth tax hike:	YES	Strong gay rights:	YES
Parental leave:	YES	Timber compromise:	YES	Execution by injection:	YES
Limited gay rights:	YES	Universal health insure:	YES	1992-93 Budget Act:	YES
Campaign Reform:	YES	Offshore oil ban:	YES	Charter schools:	YES

Art Torres (D)
24th Senate District

In this district, one is more likely to hear people speaking a language other than English. More than 60 percent of the residents are Latino living in one of the cities of the San Gabriel Valley. Also in the district is Monterey Park with its huge Chinese immigrant population. Other cities include Alhambra, San Gabriel, Rosemead, El Monte, Baldwin Park, La Puente and Azusa. It is a haven for new immigrants, both legal and illegal, from every corner of the globe.

In Art Torres, these residents have a bright, articulate and passionate representative. He is mediagenic, one of the best speakers in the Legislature, a devoted father and an affable-but-shrewd political operator. It is those qualities that for years have prompted political insiders to anoint Torres as the Hispanic with the best chance of being elected to statewide office.

Art Torres

Yet Torres' political future has been clouded by personal problems, including a divorce and two arrests within 14 months for drunken driving. At the time of his first arrest in 1988, Torres was carrying a bill to take away the licenses of minors convicted of alcohol and drug-related offenses. Torres, who publicly confessed to being an alcoholic and went through treatment, had no problem being re-elected in 1990, gaining 69 percent of the vote.

Torres is ambitious, and when a court-created seat on the Los Angeles County Board of Supervisors came up for election in early 1991, he entered a crowded field in the hopes of becoming the first Hispanic in this century to sit on that powerful board. For Torres, it was more than an attempt to win the vaunted seat. It was a test of his personal appeal in light of his problems. He met with mixed results. Although Torres was one of the top two vote-getters in the primary election, he lost the run-off by 10 percentage points to Los Angeles City Councilwoman Gloria Molina, who had once worked for him.

Torres remains an active and effective legislator. He has fought for causes of importance to Latino voters, such as bilingual education and to block the siting of a prison in his district. He has seized on statewide issues and has pressed for a crackdown on the disposal of toxic wastes, to improve child nutrition, to ban the importation of foreign produce tainted with pesticide residues, to raise the minimum wage and to set up a system to destroy vicious dogs and fine their owners.

He also has become the Legislature's expert on immigration policy, possibly the top expert in all of state government. He has traveled extensively in Latin America and Southeast Asia, where the newest Californians are coming from, and he has shown a holistic understanding of immigrant issues ranging from education to health. Torres has assembled a talented staff on the subject that has proven to be a resource throughout state government. He is one of the few legislators who seems to have grasp on where the state is headed.

Lately, Torres seems to have a number of irons in the fire. He has put out feelers among his Senate colleagues about becoming president pro tem, hoping to succeed David Roberti in 1994 when term limits will cut Roberti's career short. He has apparently been approached about leaving the Senate to become a highly paid lobbyist. And, through a long friendship with Interior Secretary Bruce Babbitt, whose 1988 campaign for president he headed in California, Torres may leave for an appointment in the Clinton administration.

PERSONAL: elected 1982; born Sept. 24, 1946, in Los Angeles; home, Los Angeles; education, B.A. government UC Santa Cruz, J.D. UC Davis; John F. Kennedy teaching fellow Harvard University; divorced, two children.

CAREER: lawyer; Assembly 1974-1982.

COMMITTEES: Insurance, Claims & Corporations (chair); Appropriations; Education; Elections & Reapportionment; Energy & Public Utilities; Governmental Organization; Judiciary; Natural Resources & Wildlife; Toxics & Public Safety Management; Transportation.

OFFICES: Capitol, (916) 445-3456, FAX (916) 444-0581; district, 107 S. Broadway, 2105, Los Angeles 90012, (213) 620-2529, FAX (213) 617-0077.

TERM LIMIT: 1998

REGISTRATION: 58.5% D, 28.6% R

1990 CAMPAIGN:

Torres – D	69%	$753,582
Keith F. Marsh – R	25%	$0

1986 CAMPAIGN: Torres – D   72% $378,993
Lee Prentiss – R   24% $0

RATINGS: AFL-CIO CalPIRG   CLCV   NOW   CofC   CalFarm
96   77   90   93   21   20

KEY VOTES:

Parent consent abort:	YES	Limit product tort:	YES	Clean Air Act:	YES
Assault gun ban:	YES	Ban AIDS discrim:	YES	Restrict abortion funds:	NO
Sales tax hike:	NO	Wealth tax hike:	YES	Strong gay rights:	YES
Parental leave:	YES	Timber compromise:	YES	Execution by injection:	nv
Limited gay rights:	YES	Universal health insure:	YES	1992-93 Budget Act:	YES
Campaign Reform:	YES	Offshore oil ban:	YES	Charter schools:	YES

Diane E. Watson (D)

26th Senate District

When the 1993-94 session of the Legislature con-
vened, Diane Watson returned to Sacramento with an
attitude — maybe more of an attitude would be a more
accurate description. Watson has long been considered one of the Legislature's more contentious and
demanding members, someone who appeared to be in
a perpetual state of anger. But her dudgeon reached
new heights in 1992 when she lost a very close
election for a powerful seat on the Los Angeles
County Board of Supervisors to former Rep. Yvonne
Braithwaite Burke amid charges and countercharges
of election dirty tricks.

Diane Watson

Back in the senate, she'll be representing — and
presumably running for re-election from — a district
whose boundaries were much altered by the state Supreme Court's reapportionment
plan but whose despair never seems to change. The Supreme Court dropped the
more upscale oceanside portions of Watson's 26th District (Watson's old district
was the 28th) and it's now concentrated in the poorest portions of South-Central Los
Angeles, plus Culver City. It's the area that was most directly and disastrously
affected by the May 1992 riots that erupted after a jury acquitted white policemen
of beating African American motorist Rodney King — the worst riots in American
history.

Fewer than half of the 26th District's residents are African American, thanks to
fast-growing populations of poor immigrants from Latin America and Asia, but the
district's voters are overwhelmingly African American and Democratic. Their
majority among voters will likely remain unchallenged into the 21st Century.

Watson spent three short years on the Los Angeles school board as one of its most
vocal (and most televised) members in the 1970s, during a period of high racial

tensions involving the district's forced busing plan. She made a splash when she first came to Sacramento in 1975. She was the first African American woman elected to the Senate, a club heretofore comprised primarily of old white men set in their ways (symbolized by the high leather chairs in the back of their chambers). In those years, she seemed to specialize in crashing the party and opening the windows.

But Sacramento has gotten used to her. Most of the old boys have retired or died, and many of the more recent newcomers are better at grandstanding than Watson. Though she can cause havoc, Watson doesn't generate much warmth from her colleagues and has increasingly found herself isolated. She has crossed swords with her colleagues on numerous issues, ranging from welfare revision to setting ethical standards — and lost. Her snits with Democratic Sen. Bill Lockyer are legendary, with the two trading insults across the dais in the Judiciary Committee. She is also known as one of the most difficult bosses in the Capitol, treating legislative staffers with disdain.

Watson has, however, shown her loyalty to David Roberti during leadership tussles, and he has returned the loyalty, even to the point of paying off her delinquent credit cards. As chairwoman of the Health and Human Services Committee, Watson oversees the welfare system in the state, enabling her to position herself as one of the chief critics of Republican social program slashing. In 1985, she filibustered a bipartisan legislative package for major welfare reforms (dubbed GAIN) that set up a "workfare" program for 190,000 recipients, most of them single mothers. Watson called it a "forced labor program," and held a lengthy committee hearing in the waning hours of that year's session, but the bill passed over her objections.

When Republican Pete Wilson became governor and proposed cuts in welfare grants to balance the state budget, Watson quickly emerged as a leading opponent — although summitry did eventually produce welfare reductions. "We had a wonderful two or three days with him. The honeymoon is over," she huffed not long after his inaugural.

Her dogma notwithstanding, Watson has looked for new solutions to some of the more vexing problems of her urban district. At the start of the 1991-92 session she introduced SB 224, which would enact procedures for the establishment of graffiti abatement districts with taxing powers to attack vandalism. And she has fought hard to protect Family Planning funds.

Watson's career has been marked by brushes with scandal. The circumstances surrounding her Ph.D. in education administration were called into question in 1989, when the Sacramento district attorney's office investigated allegations that she had used state staff and equipment to prepare her dissertation. District Attorney Steve White concluded that legislative record-keeping was so shoddy that the allegations could not be proved or disproved and the matter was dropped.

She has not escaped scrutiny from the Fair Political Practices Commission. In December 1989, Watson agreed to pay a penalty of $21,075 for using campaign funds to pay for such expenses as a family reunion, credit-card charges, airline tickets and a party. Watson takes numerous junkets worldwide from trade associations and others with business in the Legislature. She routinely uses her campaign fund for a wide range of expenses not traditionally associated with campaigning, like buying flowers for friends. She voted against the 1989 ethics reform package that ultimately tightened the rules for such spending, telling her colleagues that it "went too far." During an ethics workshop for senators in January 1991, Watson made clear her standards. "We're not ordinary people," she said.

PERSONAL: elected 1978; born Nov. 12, 1933, in Los Angeles; home, Los Angeles; education, A.A. Los Angeles City College, B.A. UCLA, M.S. CSU Los Angeles, Ph.D. Claremont Graduate School; single; Roman Catholic.

CAREER: teacher; school administrator; textbook author; Los Angeles Unified School District board 1975-1978.

COMMITTEES: Health & Human Services (chair); Budget & Fiscal Review; Education; Insurance, Claims & Corporations; Judiciary.

OFFICES: Capitol, (916) 445-5215, FAX (916) 327-2599; district, 4401 Crenshaw Blvd., 300, Los Angeles 90043, (213) 295-6655, FAX (213) 295-0910.

TERM LIMIT: 1998

REGISTRATION: 52.1% D, 33.5% R

1990 CAMPAIGN:	Watson – D		85.2%		$291,369
1986 CAMPAIGN:	Watson – D		72%		$304,886
	Armand Vaquer – R		21%		$1.925

RATINGS:	AFL-CIO	CalPIRG	CLCV	NOW	CofC	CalFarm
	96	81	89	100	16	50

KEY VOTES:

Parent consent abort:	NO	Limit product tort:	nv	Clean Air Act:	YES
Assault gun ban:	YES	Ban AIDS discrim:	YES	Restrict abortion funds:	NO
Sales tax hike:	YES	Wealth tax hike:	NO	Strong gay rights:	YES
Parental leave:	YES	Timber compromise:	YES	Execution by injection:	NO
Limited gay rights:	YES	Universal health insur:	YES	1992-93 Budget Act:	NO
Campaign Reform:	YES	Offshore oil ban:	YES	Charter schools:	YES

Cathie Wright (R)
19th Senate District

The canyons and badlands of the northwestern San Fernando Valley hold amusement parks, old citrus groves and Highway 101. The 19th Senate District sprawls over pieces of two counties, Los Angeles and Ventura, and its new suburbs and old money translate into solidly Republican territory, one with a GOP registration that approaches 50 percent and far outweighs the Democratic strength.

Ed Davis, the colorful former Los Angeles police chief, represented the 19th District for 12 years. When he decided to retire from the Legislature, it touched off a battle royal between two factions of Republicans who had been feuding for years, one headed by Davis and the other by Assemblywoman Cathie Wright.

Their squabbling dated back to 1982, when Davis ran for the U.S. Senate and charged that another Republican candidate, Rep. Bobbi Fiedler, had tried to bribe him to quit the race. The resulting investigation and prosecution of Fiedler fatally injured both of their senatorial campaigns. Wright plunged into the primary race to replace Davis while the Davis faction backed a former assemblywoman, Marion LaFollette, who had been an integral part of the factional feud. The depth of the enmity was displayed when a reporter asked Davis whether he could ever support Wright as his successor. "Maybe," he replied, "if she was running against a mass murderer. But it would depend on how many people he had killed."

Cathie Wright

Wright emerged as the winner from the primary fight with LaFollette, which, given the overwhelming Republican registration of the district, made her election to the Senate a certainty. But as she took her seat in the Legislature's upper house, joining a handful of other women, the controversy that has dogged Wright's political career seemed likely to re-emerge.

Wright hasn't played a big role in shaping legislation since her first election to the Assembly in 1980. But her extracurricular activities have made headlines at home and in Sacramento. In 1989, there were a series of published reports that Wright had interceded with state motor vehicle and judicial authorities in early 1988 to prevent her daughter, Victoria, from losing her driver's license for a string of traffic tickets. Wright denied doing any wrong, but a report from the Ventura County District Attorney's Office concluded that she had tried to fix Victoria's tickets on several occasions and had even solicited help in contacting judicial officials from the Assembly's top Democrat, Speaker Willie Brown.

That incident led to another. In December 1988, Wright refused to go along with Republican efforts to deny Brown re-election as speaker, and for that, there were demands among Republicans that Wright be stripped of her seat on the Assembly Rules Committee. The GOP caucus voted to drop Wright from the committee, but Brown, invoking another rule, protected her from being dumped. In 1991, Wright was appointed by Brown as vice chair of the Assembly Ways and Means Committee, the single most powerful committee slot for a minority party member. That made her the lead Republican during the protracted budget battle of 1992, one in which she often infuriated colleagues of both parties with obtuse positions. Republicans were more furious than Democrats because she undercut their efforts to eliminate boards and commissions. Some obscure commission would no sooner be on the chopping block, with Republicans and Democrats in agreement, when Wright would ride to its rescue.

Ideologically, Wright has ranged from alliances with the far right to more moderate positions and even a working relationship with Brown. She was one of four Republicans to vote in August 1990 for a resolution by Gil Ferguson that sought to justify internment of Japanese Americans during World War II as a military necessity.

PERSONAL: elected 1992; born May 18, 1929, in Old Forge, Pa.; home, Simi Valley; education, A.A. accounting Scranton Community College, Penn.; widow; one child; Roman Catholic.

CAREER: insurance underwriter; school board; City Council and mayor Simi Valley 1978-1980; Assembly 1980-1992.

COMMITTEES: Public Employment & Retirement (vice chair); Budget & Fiscal Review; Education; Health & Human Services; Judiciary; Toxics & Public Safety Management.

OFFICES: Capitol, (916) 445-8873, FAX (916) 327-7544; district, 2345 Erringer Rd., 212, Simi Valley 93065, (805) 522-2920, FAX (805) 522-1194.

TERM LIMIT: 2000

REGISTRATION: 40.6% D, 45.2% R

1992 CAMPAIGN:

	Wright – R	53.2%	$593,975
	Henry Starr – D	38.8%	$83,605

RATINGS: (all Ratings and Key Votes from Assembly service 1980-92)

AFL-CIO	CalPIRG	CLCV	NOW	CofC	CalFarm
12	18	15	21	100	85

KEY VOTES:

Parent consent abort:	YES	Limit product tort:	YES	Clean Air Act:	NO
Assault gun ban:	NO	Ban AIDS discrim:	NO	Restrict abortion funds:	YES
Sales tax hike:	NO	Wealth tax hike:	NO	Strong gay rights:	NO
Parental leave:	NO	Timber compromise:	NO	Execution by injection:	YES
Limited gay rights:	NO	Universal health insure:	NO	1992-93 Budget Act:	YES
Campaign Reform:	NO	Offshore oil ban:	NO	Charter schools:	YES

Assembly districts

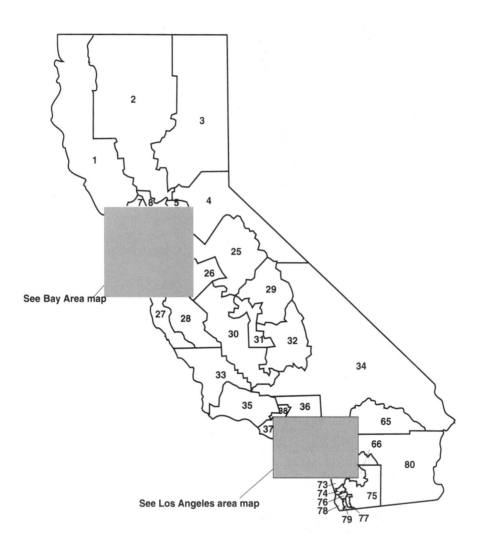

See Bay Area map

See Los Angeles area map

Bay Area districts

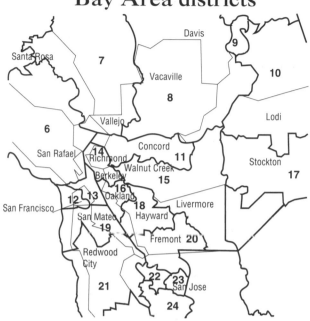

Los Angeles districts

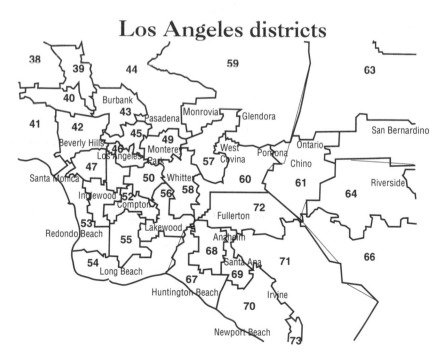

Assembly members and district numbers

1	HAUSER, Dan, D-Arcata	42	MARGOLIN, Burt, D-Los Angeles
2	STATHAM, Stan, R-Oak Run	43	NOLAN, Patrick, R-Glendale
3	RICHTER, Bernie, R-Chico	44	HOGE, Bill, R-Pasadena
4	KNOWLES, David, R-Cameron Park	45	POLANCO, Richard, D-Los Angeles
5	COLLINS, B.T., R-Carmichael	46	CALDERA, Louis, D-Los Angeles
6	BRONSHVAG, Vivien, D-Kentfield	47	MOORE, Gwen, D-Los Angeles
7	BROWN, Valerie, D-Sonoma	48	ARCHIE-HUDSON, Marguerite,
8	HANNIGAN, Tom, D-Fairfield		D-Los Angeles
9	ISENBERG, Phillip, D-Sacramento	49	MARTINEZ, Diane, D-Rosemead
10	BOWLER, Larry, R-Elk Grove	50	ESCUTIA, Martha, D-Huntington Park
11	CAMPBELL, Robert, D-Martinez	51	TUCKER, Curtis Jr., D-Inglewood
12	BURTON, John, D-San Francisco	52	MURRAY, Willard, D-Paramount
13	BROWN, Willie, D-San Francisco	53	BOWEN, Debra, D-Marina Del Rey
14	BATES, Tom, D-Berkeley	54	KARNETTE, Betty, D-Long Beach
15	RAINEY, Richard, R-Walnut Creek	55	MCDONALD, Juanita, D-Carson
16	LEE, Barbara, D-Oakland	56	EPPLE, Robert, D-Cerritos
17	ANDAL, Dean, R-Stockton	57	SOLIS, Hilda, D-El Monte
18	KLEHS, Johan, D-San Leandro	58	NAPOLITANO, Grace, D-Norwalk
19	SPEIER, Jackie, D-Burlingame	59	MOUNTJOY, Richard, R-Arcadia
20	EASTIN, Delaine, D-Fremont	60	HORCHER, Paul, R-Whittier
21	SHER, Byron, D-Palo Alto	61	AGUIAR, Fred, R-Ontario
22	VASCONCELLOS, John,	62	BACA, Joe, D-San Bernardino
	D-Santa Clara	63	BRULTE, Jim, R-Rancho Cucamonga
23	CORTESE, Dominic, D-San Jose	64	WEGGELAND, Ted, R-Riverside
24	QUACKENBUSH, Charles, R-San Jose	65	WOODRUFF, Paul, R-Moreno Valley
25	SNYDER, Margaret, D-Modesto	66	HAYNES, Ray, R-Murrieta
26	CANNELLA, Sal, D-Ceres	67	ALLEN, Doris, R-Cypress
27	FARR, Sam, D-Carmel	68	PRINGLE, Curt, R-Garden Grove
28	AREIAS, Rusty, D-San Jose	69	UMBERG, Tom, D-Garden Grove
29	JONES, Bill, R-Fresno	70	FERGUSON, Gil, R-Newport Beach
30	COSTA, Jim, D-Hanford	71	CONROY, Mickey, R-Orange
31	VACANT (Bronzan)	72	JOHNSON, Ross, R-Fullerton
32	HARVEY, Trice, R-Bakersfield	73	MORROW, Bill, R-Oceanside
33	SEASTRAND, Andrea,	74	FRAZEE, Robert, R-Carlsbad
	R-San Luis Obispo	75	GOLDSMITH, Jan, R-Poway
34	HONEYCUTT, Kathleen, R-Hesperia	76	GOTCH, Mike, D-San Diego
35	O'CONNELL, Jack, D-Carpinteria	77	CONNOLLY, Tom, D-Lemon Grove
36	KNIGHT, William 'Pete,' R-Palmdale	78	ALPERT, Deirdre, D-Coronado
37	TAKASUGI, Nao, R-Oxnard	79	PEACE, Steve, D-Chula Vista
38	BOLAND, Paula, R-Granada Hills	80	BORNSTEIN, Julie, D-Palm Desert
39	KATZ, Richard, D-Panorama City		
40	FRIEDMAN, Barbara,		
	D-North Hollywood		
41	FRIEDMAN, Terry B., D-Encino		

ASSEMBLY
Vacant
31st Assembly District

Just days before the Nov. 3, 1992, election in which incumbent Democrat Bruce Bronzan was running unopposed, Bronzan announced that he would quit the legislature in January to accept a job as associate dean of the University of California, San Francisco medical school.

Bronzan's untimely departure set the stage for a special election on March 2 with a runoff date of April 27 in the event no candidate received a majority vote. It is unlikely that Bronzan's departure will change the political balance in the Legislature because Democrats hold a strong registration edge in the district.

The 31st Assembly District includes parts of two counties: Fresno, including the southern part of the city of Fresno, and western Tulare County. The district divides the cities of Fresno, Visalia and Tulare in order to maximize the Hispanic presence, which is now 52.2 percent. The overall minority population is almost 69 percent.

REGISTRATION: 63.0% D, 26.7% R

Fred Aguiar (R)
61st Assembly District

The 61st Assembly District includes Chino, Chino Hills, Ontario, Rancho Cucamonga and Pomona's Latino neighborhoods. In the 1992 redistricting, the Supreme Court designed the 61st as a minority district. As a result it is 55 percent minority, including 41.7 percent Latino. But Latinos account for only 20 percent of the registered voters.

Fred Aguiar

The district is almost evenly divided between Republicans and Democrats, with Democrats accounting for 45 percent of the electorate and Republicans 44 percent. In the general election, Democratic candidate Larry Simcoe, a fireman, won in the Los Angeles precincts, but his Republican opponent, Fred Aguiar, easily swept the larger Republican portions of San Bernardino County. Aguiar is a veteran of local politics. He was first elected to the Chino City Council in 1978 and was re-elected in 1982. In 1986, he was elected mayor and was re-elected to that post in 1992.

A Democrat until 1989, Aguiar was endorsed by several influential Democrats during the election. He benefited in the general election from both high name recognition and a healthy war chest and easily defeated his less well-known opponent.

PERSONAL: elected 1992; born Dec. 3, 1948, in Artesia; home, Chino; attended Mt. Sac Junior College and Cal Poly Pomona; Army (Vietnam); wife Patti, one child; Roman Catholic.

CAREER: businessman/developer; city councilman, 1978-1986; mayor of Chino, 1986-1992.

COMMITTEES: Agriculture; Housing & Community Development; Local Government.

OFFICES: Capitol, (916) 445-1670, FAX (916) 445-0385; district, 304 West F St., Ontario 91762.

TERM LIMIT: 1998

REGISTRATION: 65.5% D, 43.9% R

1992 CAMPAIGN:

Aguiar – R	58.4%	$375,163
Larry Simcoe – D	36.3%	$135,920
Cynthia Allaire – Green	5.3%	

RATINGS and **KEY VOTES**: Newly elected

Doris J. Allen (R)
67th Assembly District

Democrats enjoyed a brief period of dominance in Orange County politics during the 1970s, but one by one, Democratic legislators fell to Republican challenges beginning in 1978. The 71st Assembly District, in the central portion of the county, was one of the last Democratic bastions left. In 1982, incumbent Chester Wray was beaten by Doris Allen, who had gained local prominence as a school district trustee and leader of an anti-busing campaign.

Allen, as a woman and a Republican, has not been part of the Assembly's ruling circles. She feuded publicly with one of the more influential Republican leaders, Gerald Felando, who was defeated in his 1992 re-election bid. The issue that divided Allen and

Doris Allen

Felando is the one that became her legislative preoccupation: mismanagement of the state Fish and Game Department (another male-dominated bastion) and, in particular, its regulation of commercial fishing. She saw Felando, who represented San Pedro, as pushing the interests of commercial fishermen over those of sport fishermen. Allen embarrassed Gov. George Deukmejian's administration by exposing several management scandals in the Fish and Game Department. But few in her caucus have shown any interest in supporting her attempts to make the agency more accountable.

On a shoestring budget, Allen successfully promoted Proposition 132 on the

November 1990 ballot, which banned use of gill nets in coastal waters. Commercial fisherman opposed the measure. Her proposition was the only one of six environmental measures to pass.

Early in 1991, Allen was one of three Assembly members who ran for a state Senate seat vacated by John Seymour, who had been appointed to Gov. Pete Wilson's former post in the U.S. Senate. But she lost in the primary to John Lewis.

In 1992, Allen successfully opposed a legislative proposal that would have raised cigarette taxes by 2 cents a pack to fund breast cancer research and prevention programs. Allen argued that the lawmakers were looking in the wrong place for research funds. Both she and her sister have suffered from breast cancer, Allen told her hushed colleagues as she spoke on the floor of the Assembly, but neither of the women smoked. A better source of funding, she said, would be to tax birth control pills and fertility drugs. The measure failed.

Reapportionment put Allen in the same district with two other Republican incumbents, Tom Mays of Huntington Beach and Nolan Frizelle of Fountain Valley. Assembly colleagues made no secret of their support of either of the men over Allen. But she squeaked by the primary and easily won the runoff against an underfunded Democrat.

PERSONAL: elected 1982; born May 26, 1936, in Kansas City, Mo.; home, Cypress; education, attended University of Wyoming, Golden West College, IBM School in Kansas City, Long Beach Community College and Hallmark Business School; divorced, two children; Protestant.

CAREER: co-owner lighting business, Lampco; trustee, Huntington Beach Union School District.

COMMITTEES: Ways & Means; Health; Natural Resources.

OFFICES: Capitol, (916) 445-6233, FAX (916) 445-2751; district, 5252 Orange Ave., 100, Cypress 90630, (714) 821-1500, FAX (714) 821-8524.

TERM LIMIT: 1996

REGISTRATION: 35.3% D, 51.0% R

1992 CAMPAIGN: Allen – R — 59.2% — $335,951
Ken LeBlanc – D — 33% — $54,413
Brian Schar – L — 7.8%

1990 CAMPAIGN: Allen – R — 60.5% — $98,098
Peter Mathews – D — 39.5% — $54,621

RATINGS:

AFL-CIO	CalPIRG	CLCV	NOW	CofC	CalFarm
15	27	9	29	100	80

KEY VOTES:

Parent consent abort:	YES	Limit product tort:	YES	Clean Air Act:	YES
Assault gun ban:	NO	Ban AIDS discrim:	NO	Restrict abortion funds:	YES
Sales tax hike:	NO	Wealth tax hike:	YES	Strong gay rights:	NO
Parental leave:	NO	Timber compromise:	NO	Execution by injection:	YES
Limited gay rights:	NO	Universal health insur:	NO	1992-93 Budget Act:	YES
Campaign Reform:	NO	Offshore oil ban:	YES	Charter schools:	YES

Deirdre W. Alpert (D)

78th Assembly District

This elongated district runs down the south San Diego County coast from La Jolla to Imperial Beach. It includes Coronado, Mission Bay and Balboa Park. Voters here tend to be moderate and independent – almost half of them voted for Dianne Feinstein in the 1990 gubernatorial race despite a strong Republican registration edge.

Deirdre Alpert

In 1988, Republican Sunny Mojonnier breezed to an easy, third-term re-election as the district's Assembly member. But in the succeeding two years, Mojonnier ran into a world of trouble. She was fined $13,000 by the state Fair Political Practices Commission for double billing the state and her campaign fund for personal expenses. She used campaign funds to send staffers to a fashion consultant. She used Assembly sergeants-at-arms to do personal chores like pick up her son at school. And she skipped out of Sacramento in July 1990 to take a vacation in Hawaii during the bitter summer budget impasse.

There should have been no way Deirdre "Dede" Alpert could win this seat under the old district configurations. Voter registration favored Republicans by 20 percentage points. But Mojonnier's well-publicized gaffs caught up to her and she barely won her GOP primary. The weakened Mojonnier could not hang on in the general election.

Alpert, a travel agent and a member of the Solana Beach School District Board, skillfully capitalized on Mojonnier's flakiness. Alpert's patrician manners also helped in this middle- to upper-middle class district. Soon after the election, Alpert's husband, Michael, half-joked that he hoped his wife would become a Republican because he figured that was the only way she could hold the seat.

But hold on to it she did, against a well-known moderate Republican, former Assemblyman Jeff Marston. Marston had lost his re-election bid in 1990 to Democrat Mike Gotch in the old 78th District, but he seemed ready and able to take on Alpert. Instead, Marston's campaign faltered from the beginning and Alpert defeated him easily with 54 percent of the vote.

In 1992, Gov. Wilson signed AB 2841 by Alpert, which enacted new standards for breast cancer screening. In 1993, Alpert was elected chair of the Women's Caucus. And early in 1993, she introduced legislation to permit casino gambling on cruise ships traveling in international waters between two ports in the state. Alpert contended that California ports and cities would lose millions of dollars in revenue without the legislation because Attorney General Dan Lungren was interpreting previous legislation as prohibiting most gambling on cruise ships. As a result, cruise lines have begun dropping cities such as San Diego and Catalina from their itineraries to keep their casinos operating.

PERSONAL: elected 1990; born Oct. 6, 1945, in New York City; home, Del Mar; education, Pomona College; husband Michael, three children.

CAREER: Pacific Bell 1966-1969; travel agent 1985-1989; Solana Beach School Board 1983-1990, president 1990.

COMMITTEES: Education; Rules; Utilities & Commerce; Ways & Means.

OFFICES: Capitol, (916) 445-2112, FAX (916) 445-4001; district, 3262 Holiday Court, 209, La Jolla 92037, (619) 457-5775, FAX (619) 452-8173.

TERM LIMIT: 1996

REGISTRATION: 37.8% D, 43.8% R, 2.2% AIP

1992 CAMPAIGN:	Alpert – D	53.4%	$726,083
	Jeff Marston – R	41.3%	$649,400
	Sally Sherry O'Brien – P&F	5.1%	
1990 CAMPAIGN:	Alpert – D	45.7%	$57,403
	Sunny Mojonnier (incumbent) – R	41%	$304,100
	John Murphy – L	10.9%	

RATINGS:

	AFL-CIO	CalPIRG	CLCV	NOW	CofC	CalFarm
	87	91	100	86	28	20

KEY VOTES:

Sales tax hike:	YES	Wealth tax hike:	YES	Strong gay rights:	YES
Parental leave:	YES	Timber compromise:	YES	Execution by injection:	YES
Limited gay rights:	YES	Universal health insur:	YES	1992-93 Budget Act:	YES
Campaign Reform:	YES	Offshore oil ban:	YES	Charter schools:	YES

Dean Andal (R)
17th Assembly District

This district takes in most of San Joaquin County, including Escalon, Linden, Manteca, Tracy, Ripon and Stockton. The main population center is Stockton, one of the most ethnically diverse and politically complex cities in California and one that's in the middle of a growth boom born of the outward push of the Bay Area. For years, Stockton's politics were tightly controlled by a tiny, semisecretive oligarchy. That changed in 1974, when John Garamendi, then an outsider, broke through to win the 26th District seat.

Two years later, Garamendi hopped to the Senate, and was replaced by another Democrat, Carmen Perino. In 1980, Perino was challenged in the primary by Garamendi's aide, Patrick Johnston, and a vicious fight ensued. Johnston won the primary, but nearly lost the general election in November. Johnston held the seat until 1991, when he followed Garamendi into the Senate.

In order to get to the Senate Johnston had to fight a bitter battle with Patti Garamendi, who wanted to succeed her husband.

After her loss in the Senate race, Patti Garamendi, a Democrat, moved from Walnut Grove to Stockton and campaigned for Johnston's Assembly seat. She won 26 percent of the vote in a March 19, 1991, primary, making it into a May 14 runoff with Stockton businessman Dean Andal, who had won the GOP nomination with 28 percent of the vote. Andal, who once worked as an aide to former Rep. Norman Shumway of Stockton, defeated Garamendi.

In 1992, Democrats, believing that Andal's landslide election was a fluke born of Patti Garamendi's unpopularity, made Andal one of their top targets after court-ordered reapportionment failed to improve Republican registration in the district. The

Dean Andal

Democrats reasoned that a moderate Democrat with an agricultural background would be the perfect candidate, and they found their man in Michael Machado. Andal, however, refused to roll over, even after embarrassing revelations that he had hired an investigator to look into Machado's background and the snooper was caught trying to examine the school records of Machado's children. Both parties poured big money into the district and Andal, bucking a Democratic tide elsewhere in the state, won re-election by 1,500 votes.

No sooner had Andal been sworn in for his first full term, however, than he found himself embroiled in new controversy. Although fellow Republicans tabbed him to become their chief spokesman and negotiator on budget issues as vice chairman of the Ways and Means Committee, Speaker Willie Brown snubbed him and named another Republican to the coveted position – a breach of the house's unwritten rules of protocol.

Andal, conservative and smart, seems destined to be one of the GOP's main players. As term limits whittle down the ranks of higher-seniority members, he could become the Assembly's GOP leader.

PERSONAL: Elected 1991; born Oct. 3, 1959, in Salem, Ore.; home, Stockton; education, A.A. Delta College, B.A. UC San Diego; wife Kari, one child.

CAREER: owner of a communications company; San Joaquin County Board of Education.

COMMITTEES: Environmental Safety & Toxic Materials; Labor & Employment; Public Employees & Retirement; Transportation.

OFFICES: Capitol, (916) 445-7931, FAX (916) 327-3519; district, Suite 306, 31 East Channel St., Stockton 95202, (209) 948-7479, FAX (209) 465-5058.

TERM LIMIT: 1996

REGISTRATION: 55.9% D, 34.2% R

1992 CAMPAIGN:			
Andal – R		50.6%	$852,936
Michael Machado – D		49.4%	$374,510

MAY 14, 1991 SPECIAL ELECTION:

Andal – R		56.0%	$163,666
Patti Garamendi – D		41.6%	$452,598

RATINGS:

AFL-CIO	CalPIRG	CLCV	NOW	CofC	CalFarm
13	20	9	29	83	75

KEY VOTES:

Sales tax hike:	NO	Wealth tax hike:	NO	Strong gay rights:	NO
Parental leave:	NO	Timber compromise:	nv	Execution by injection:	YES
Limited gay rights:	NO	Universal health insur:	NO	1992-93 Budget Act:	NO
Campaign Reform:	NO	Offshore oil ban:	YES	Charter schools:	YES

Marguerite Archie-Hudson (D)

48th Assembly District

Marguerite Archie-Hudson

In relative terms, the African American population of Los Angeles is shrinking as Latinos and Asians become more numerous. But politically, the city's African American community remains strong because of its high tendency to vote – as illustrated by the 48th Assembly District. When the state Supreme Court created this district in the heart of South-Central Los Angeles, African Americans were outnumbered by Latinos. But despite the fact that the 48th is more than 50 percent Hispanic, only 6 percent of its voters have that ethic designation so it remains a bastion of African American and Democratic political power. It is, in fact, the most Democratic Assembly district in the state at nearly 90 percent, leaving Republicans (there are only about 6,000 of them registered in the district) an endangered species.

For 14 years, the district was represented by Maxine Waters, an aggressive protege of Assembly Speaker Willie Brown. But she was elected to Congress in 1990. The race to replace Waters ended in the June primary when Marguerite Archie-Hudson, a former administrator at the University of California, Los Angeles, defeated Los Angeles City Councilman Robert Farrell. The Republican candidate in the November general election got only 15 percent of the vote. In 1992 Archie-Hudson cruised to an easy re-election as the district shrank, becoming even more Democratic as it lost its coastal arms. Archie-Hudson and legislative neighbor Gwen Moore, another Democrat, had the distinction of defeating a father-son team of Republicans, Jonathan Leonard II and III.

Archie-Hudson's 1990 campaign wasn't an easy one. The onetime aide to Assembly Speaker Willie Brown had to battle charges that she didn't live in the district and was illegally allowed to use the offices of Waters, who endorsed her. At the start of the Democratic primary campaign, Archie-Hudson downplayed the importance of endorsements. Endorsements had already haunted her once. After spending nine years on the Los Angeles Community College District board of trustees, she lost re-election in 1987 largely on the strength of teachers' union opposition. But in her race for the Assembly, she eventually got strong support from labor and other key officials.

Archie-Hudson pledged to end busing of students, opting to keep them close to neighborhood schools. She promised to offer tax incentives to attract business to South-Central Los Angeles and proposed to establish a community plan that would integrate services from government agencies, schools and churches–all promises that rang hollow when the area was wracked by riots in 1992. In 1993, Speaker Brown elevated Archie-Hudson into the chair of the Higher Education Committee.

PERSONAL: elected 1990; born Nov. 18, 1937, on Younges Island, S.C.; home, Los Angeles; education, B.A. psychology Talladega College, Ala., Ph.D. education UCLA; husband, G. Bud Hudson.

CAREER: program director, UCLA; program director, Occidental College; associate dean and director for educational opportunity for CSUS; district chief of staff Rep. Yvonne Brathwaite Burke; Southern California chief of staff for Assembly Speaker Willie Brown; Board of Trustees, Los Angeles Community College District.

COMMITTEES: Higher Education (chair); Finance and Insurance; Judiciary; Labor & Employment.

OFFICES: Capitol, (916) 445-2363, FAX (916) 323-9640; district, 700 State Dr., 103, Los Angeles 90037, (213) 745-6636, FAX (213) 745-6722.

TERM LIMIT: 1996

REGISTRATION: 87.6% D, 4.8% R

1992 CAMPAIGN:

Archie-Hudson – D	93.1%	$162,376
Jonathan Leonard – R	6.9%	$1,240

1990 CAMPAIGN:

Archie-Hudson – D	79.5%	$273,747
Gloria Salazar – R	15.1%	$0

RATINGS:

AFL-CIO	CalPIRG	CLCV	NOW	CofC	CalFarm
97	95	96	100	17	20

KEY VOTES:

Sales tax hike:	YES	Wealth tax hike:	YES	Strong gay rights:	YES
Parental leave:	YES	Timber compromise:	YES	Execution by injection:	nv
Limited gay rights:	YES	Universal health insur:	YES	1992-93 Budget Act:	NO
Campaign Reform:	nv	Offshore oil ban:	YES	Charter schools:	YES

John Rusty Areias (D)

28th Assembly District

When framers of the post-1980 census reapportionment created the 25th Assembly District, they dubbed it the "Steinbeck seat" because it encompassed the agricultural areas featured in John Steinbeck novels. The district straddled both sides of the coastal range, encompassing San Benito County, Gilroy and Morgan Hill in Santa Clara County, the Salinas area in Monterey County and western Merced County, including Los Banos. The 1992 reapportionment changed the boundaries of the district, renumbered 28, dropping its Merced County portion and thus the Los Banos hometown of its incumbent, Rusty Areias. The district also moved northward into the San Jose suburbs in Santa Clara County.

Rusty Arcias

But Areias had little difficulty winning re-election, despite a slight drop in Democratic registration – once he overcame an embarrassing problem. Areias nearly blew it when he and his staff didn't turn in the required number of signatures on nominating petitions in 1992. Democratic Secretary of State March Fong Eu had to issue a waiver to Areias to place his name on the ballot. He defeated Republican Peter Frusetta, a rancher who used equine excrement to suggest that incumbent politicians should be dumped from office. During the campaign, Frusetta repeatedly charged that Areias was a drug-user, although he couldn't offer a shred of evidence that such was the case. At one forum, he challenged Areias to produce a urine sample. Areias replied that he would if Frusetta would hold the bottle.

Areias, a wealthy dairy farmer, fits the district well. Without him, however, the seat might be vulnerable to Republican penetration due to conservative voting patterns.

Areias gained notoriety in 1988 as a member of the so-called "Gang of Five," a group of Democrats who challenged Assembly Speaker Willie Brown's authority despite having been favored by Brown with choice committee assignments. The challenge was turned back after months of bickering and Areias, who toyed briefly with running for the congressional seat vacated by Rep. Tony Coelho of Merced, returned to Brown's fold as a player on the Democratic team.

Evidence of Areias' return to Brown's good graces was his appointment to chair the Assembly Agriculture Committee in 1991, replacing longtime chairman Norman Waters, who lost his re-election bid. The committee chairmanship has the potential to solidify Areias' already strong ties to agriculture and to make him a more influential political player as Democrats continue in their efforts to court moderate Central Valley residents.

Beyond balancing the sometimes diverse interests of his district, Areias has tried to carve out a role for himself as an advocate of consumer interests, being one of the few legislators to oppose hikes in consumer loan rate ceilings. Two new laws he authored that took effect in 1991 were aimed at curbing credit-card crimes. One prohibits merchants from writing credit card numbers on the backs of checks. The second bans businesses from asking customers to write their telephone numbers and addresses on credit card receipts.

Areias unsuccessfully sought to have landlords pay interest to renters on security deposits. He also proposed a bill to require handgun buyers to go through a brief safety course – a proposal not well-received by the National Rifle Association, of which he is a member. The bill was vetoed.

With his personal wealth, good looks, sharp suits and fast cars, Areias challenges Speaker Brown's position as the Legislature's party animal. Cosmopolitan magazine once named him one of the nation's leading bachelors. But Areias has come under some criticism as a legislator who has misused the services of the Assembly's sergeants-at-arms. He has reportedly had them act as chauffeurs from the early morning hours to well past midnight – some say to squire him and his dates.

Areias is also ambitious, and during a special session in the wake of the 1989 Bay Area earthquake, he served as chairman of a high-profile select committee on earthquake preparedness, reflecting his district's tendency toward such events. He is actively tinkering with a shot at statewide office in 1994 – one of the lesser constitutional offices that will be vacated that year, such as secretary of state, controller or treasurer – because term limits would end his Assembly career in 1996.

PERSONAL: elected 1982; born Sept. 12, 1949, in Los Banos; home, San Jose; education, B.S. CSU Chico; single; Roman Catholic.

CAREER: managing partner family business, Areias Dairy Farms, Los Banos.

COMMITTEES: Agriculture (chair); Finance & Insurance; Higher Education; Refugee Resettlement & International Migration (joint).

OFFICES: Capitol, (916) 445-7380, FAX (916) 327-7105; district, 365 Victor St., L, Salinas 93907-2044, (408) 422-4344, FAX (408) 422-1571.

TERM LIMIT: 1996

REGISTRATION: 51.7% D, 33.9% R

1992 CAMPAIGN:

Areias – D		59.1%	$486,819
Peter Frusetta – R		40.9%	$52,276

1990 CAMPAIGN:

Areias – D		63%	$306,478
Ben Gilmore – R		32%	$22,676

RATINGS:

AFL-CIO	CalPIRG	CLCV	NOW	CofC	CalFarm
91	91	74	86	33	65

KEY VOTES:

Parent consent abort:	YES	Limit product tort:	nv	Clean Air Act:	nv
Assault gun ban:	YES	Ban AIDS discrim:	YES	Restrict abortion funds:	NO
Sales tax hike:	YES	Wealth tax hike:	YES	Strong gay rights:	YES
Parental leave:	YES	Timber compromise:	NO	Execution by injection:	YES
Limited gay rights:	YES	Universal health insur:	YES	1992-93 Budget Act:	YES
Campaign Reform:	nv	Offshore oil ban:	YES	Charter schools:	YES

Joe Baca (D)
62nd Assembly District

The Supreme Court carved out the 62nd Assembly District in San Bernardino County as a minority district. The district was crafted to draw in the minority neighborhoods of San Bernardino plus the cities of Rialto, Colton and Fontana. The population of Latinos, African Americans and Asians in the district tops 56 percent. Latino registration is 22 percent.

Joe Baca

In his first month on the job, Joe Baca became embroiled in a battle of legislative egos when he insisted on a piece of the legislative action to attract a Defense Department accounting center to Norton Air Force Base in San Bernardino County. The base is scheduled for closure in March 1994. The accounting center could provide 4,000 jobs to the region, which was hit hard by the state's economic downturn. Baca authored a bill to appropriate $10 million from special state funds for job training and to establish the base as an enterprise zone, which would help avoid zoning delays. The bill passed the Assembly 73-0 and was sent to the Senate. But veteran Sens. Ruben Ayala, D-Chino, and William Leonard, R-Redlands, had already worked out an agreement with the Wilson administration to carry Norton legislation and Ayala reportedly wasn't too pleased with upstart Baca's interference. "I'm very angry with you," Ayala reportedly shot at Baca during one of many off-the-floor meetings on the issue. "I'll just give you both bills. You'll be the big shot."

Ayala's Republican colleague, Leonard, characterized it as a "dispute over authorship," and worried aloud that it could jeopardize the state's bid for the accounting center. Eventually, Baca carried a bill that would appropriate $1.5 million to upgrade facilities at Norton and provide economic incentives to attract the center to the base. And Ayala carried legislation that would appropriate $10 million for worker training.

Baca, a community college trustee, won his Assembly seat following two earlier failed primary bids against Democratic incumbent Gerry Eaves. When Eaves decided to leave the Legislature and run for San Bernardino County supervisor, Baca saw his opportunity. He defeated Rialto Mayor John Longville and Lois Carson, another community college trustee, in the primary. In the general election Baca easily defeated Republican firefighter Steve Hall.

PERSONAL: elected 1992; born Jan. 23, 1947, in Belin, New Mexico; home, Rialto; education, A.A. Barstow Community College, B.A. CSU Los Angeles; wife Barbara, four children; Roman Catholic.

CAREER: owner of a travel agency; community college trustee.

COMMITTEES: Education (vice chair); Governmental Organization; Public Employees, Retirement & Social Security; Utilities & Commerce.

OFFICES: Capitol, (916) 445-8292, FAX (916) 324-6980; district, 201 North E Street, San Bernardino 92401, (909) 885-2222, FAX (909) 888-5959.

TERM LIMIT: 1998

REGISTRATION: 59.4% D, 31.3% R

1992 CAMPAIGN:

Baca – D	58.6%	$281,318
Steve Hall – R	35.1%	$46,824
Ethel Haas – L	6.3%	

RATINGS and **KEY VOTES**: Newly elected

Tom H. Bates (D)
14th Assembly District

It took the Republicans and the state Supreme Court to give Tom Bates what he could never get from his fellow Democrats: a compact district that didn't include tracts of disgruntled Republicans. Bates' old 12th District was composed of pieces of Alameda and Contra Costa counties left over after Democratic leaders of the Assembly had drawn districts to the specifications of others. The 14th, however, is a solidly Democratic chunk of the East Bay shoreline, including Richmond, Berkeley and Oakland and the court-ordered reapportionment actually improved Bates' registration margin by a few points, giving him a district in which Democrats outnumber Republicans by 5-1.

Tom Bates

After his re-election to a ninth term in 1992, Bates was boasting to colleagues that he will be the Legislature's all-time vote-getter – in part because Republicans don't even try to run someone against him. Bates is perhaps the Assembly's most consistently liberal member and his credentials were solidified when he married Loni Hancock, mayor of Berkeley, the spiritual home of the American political left.

Although Bates wins re-election consistently and is among the highest in seniority, he has never wielded front-rank power, a reflection of his own rather quiet personality and the extremity of his politics. Bates, an Alameda County supervisor for four years, has concentrated on liberal issues such as health care and only in recent years has he achieved a modicum of authority by becoming chairman of the Human Services Committee, which deals with welfare-related legislation.

Bates is a member of the "Grizzly Bears," an ad hoc coalition of liberals who congregate in the rear of the Democratic section of the house. His membership in the group has boosted his career of late because the Grizzlies have gained influence.

The 14th District's strong Democratic bent means that Bates can probably expect to be elected once more before term limits end his Assembly career in 1996. He then may move up the state Senate, if veteran incumbent Nicholas Petris finally retires, or he can hope that a congressional seat becomes available.

PERSONAL: elected 1976; born Feb. 9, 1938, in San Diego; home, Berkeley; education, B.A. UC Berkeley; wife Loni Hancock, two children; no religious affiliation.

CAREER: real estate; Alameda County Board of Supervisors 1972-1976.

COMMITTEES: Human Services (chair); Environmental Safety & Toxic Materials; Natural Resources; Public Safety.

OFFICES: Capitol, (916) 445-7554, FAX (916) 445-6434; district, 3923 Grand Ave., Oakland 94610-1005; (510) 428-1423, FAX (510) 428-1599.

TERM LIMIT: 1996

REGISTRATION: 70.0% D, 12.4% R, 4.1% Green

1992 CAMPAIGN:	Bates – D	82.1%	$158,796
	Marsha Feinland – P&F	17.9%	
1990 CAMPAIGN:	Bates – D	67.7%	$149,527
	Jonathan Gear – R	26.1%	$1,700

RATINGS:	AFL-CIO	CalPIRG	CLCV	NOW	CofC	CalFarm
	96	91	100	72	6	30

KEY VOTES:

Parent consent abort:	NO	Limit product tort:	NO	Clean Air Act:	YES
Assault gun ban:	YES	Ban AIDS discrim:	YES	Restrict abortion funds:	NO
Sales tax hike:	YES	Wealth tax hike:	YES	Strong gay rights:	YES
Parental leave:	YES	Timber compromise:	NO	Execution by injection:	nv
Limited gay rights:	YES	Universal health insur:	YES	1992-93 Budget Act:	NO
Campaign Reform:	YES	Offshore oil ban:	YES	Charter schools:	YES

Paula L. Boland (R)
38th Assembly District

The further north and west one goes in the San Fernando Valley, the more Republican the territory becomes. The 38th Assembly District lies at the western extremity of the valley and laps over the hills into Simi Valley. Among the other communities of note are Fillmore, Chatsworth and Northridge. Simi Valley, home of the Ronald Reagan presidential library, was the focus of nationwide attention in 1992 when an all-white jury in that community acquitted four police officers in the beating of African American motorist Rodney King. The acquittal sparked several days of riots in Los Angeles. African Americans make up less than 3 percent of the population in the district. Latinos account for 16 percent of the population, but only 6 percent of the registered voters.

When Marian La Follette, who had represented the district since 1980, decided not to seek re-election in 1990, there was a scramble on the Republican side to fill the seat. And the winner was Paula Boland, a real estate broker and former Granada Hills Chamber of Commerce president, who was backed by, among others, La Follette's longtime rival in the lower house, Assemblywoman Cathie Wright, R-Simi Valley. Boland got a tougher-than-expected challenge in the general election, however, from Democrat Irene Allert, who hammered away at Boland's anti-abortion views. Despite her incumbency and the favorable registration numbers, Boland found herself in another tough battle in 1992 against Democrat Howard Cohen. She ultimately beat Cohen 54 percent to 41 percent.

Paula Boland

In 1992 Gov. Pete Wilson signed a bill by Boland that provides an exemption to the statute of limitations for adults who want to file criminal charges against people who sexually abused them as children.

A staunch conservative, Boland has worked in the trenches for Republican Party causes for 25 years. Her 1990 race was her first try for elective office, but she has experience in government, having served on the Los Angeles County Local Agency Formation Commission, an influential agency that oversees city incorporations and annexations.

PERSONAL: elected 1990; born Jan. 17, 1940, in Oyster Bay, N.Y.; home, Granada Hills; education, San Fernando Valley High School; husband Lloyd, three children; Roman Catholic.

CAREER: owner real estate brokerage firm, husband continues to manage.

COMMITTEES: Public Safety (vice chair); Environmental Safety & Toxic Materials; Housing & Community Development; Utilities & Commerce.

OFFICES: Capitol, (916) 445-8366, FAX (916) 322-2005; district, 10727 White Oak, 124, Granada Hills, 91344, (818) 368-3838.

TERM LIMIT: 1996

REGISTRATION: 40.7% D, 46.0% R

1992 CAMPAIGN:	Boland – R	53.7%	$384,751
	Howard Cohen – D	40.7%	$15,745
	Devin Cutler – L	5.6%	
1990 CAMPAIGN:	Boland – R	52.5%	$353,601
	Irene F. Allert – D	44%	$112,511

RATINGS:	AFL-CIO	CalPIRG	CLCV	NOW	CofC	CalFarm
	6	18	11	43	94	80

KEY VOTES:

Sales tax hike:	NO	Wealth tax hike:	NO	Strong gay rights:	NO
Parental leave:	NO	Timber compromise:	NO	Execution by injection:	YES
Limited gay rights:	NO	Universal health insur:	NO	1992-93 Budget Act:	YES
Campaign Reform:	NO	Offshore oil ban:	NO	Charter schools:	YES

Julie Bornstein (D)

80th Assembly District

Incumbent Republican Assemblywoman Tricia Hunter moved from her home in Bonita to Riverside County to run in the newly constructed 80th Assembly District, which includes all of Imperial County and a chunk of Riverside County.

Julie Bornstein

In the meantime, Julie Bornstein, an attorney from Palm Desert who was a Bill Clinton delegate at the 1992 Democratic National Convention, was gearing up for a primary fight against incumbent Assemblyman Steve Clute, who had decided to move to Palm Desert rather than run in the 64th District, which included part of his former 68th District. But Clute decided to bow out of the race, although his name remained on the ballot. Clute's decision spared Bornstein from a divisive primary battle.

Hunter, on the other hand, took a beating during the Republican primary when she was accused of being a carpetbagger from San Diego by her opponent David Dhillon, an El Centro city councilman. Hunter was backed by Gov. Pete Wilson and other Sacramento Republicans, bringing a hefty $650,000 war chest to the general election campaign. But Bornstein came into the fray with no incumbency baggage and with a legitimate claim of residency in the district. She defeated Hunter by just 2,198 votes.

Democratic registration in the district was 48 percent just before the general election compared with 40 percent for the Republicans. The gap was due in part to a Democratic registration blitz throughout the state that seemed to catch the Republicans off guard. Many Republicans, including Hunter, doubted whether the newly registered voters would actually cast their ballots. "They paid massive numbers of dollars to get people registered. But what has been the experience is that these people don't vote," Hunter said just before the general election. Oops!

PERSONAL: elected 1992; born, July 7, 1948; home, Palm Desert; education, B.A. and M.A. from UCLA, J.D. USC; husband Steve Gordon, two children; Jewish.

CAREER: attorney, real estate broker, holds teaching credential, Desert Community College District board.

COMMITTEES: Agriculture (vice chair); Finance & Insurance; Higher Education; Housing & Community Development.

OFFICES: Capitol, (916) 445-5416, FAX (916)323-5190; district, 72880 Fred Waring Dr., A-4, Palm Desert 92260, (619) 568-0408.

TERM LIMIT: 1998

REGISTRATION: 48.1% D, 39.8% R
1992 CAMPAIGN: Bornstein – D   49.7% $429,891
               Tricia Hunter (incumbent) – R   49% $1,168,762
RATINGS and **KEY VOTES**: Newly elected

Debra Bowen (D)

53rd Assembly District

The 53rd Assembly District is one of the reasons why Republicans think they should control the state Assembly – and one of the reasons why they don't. As created by the state Supreme Court in its reshuffling of the state's 80 Assembly districts, the 53rd embraces overwhelmingly white, upscale coastal residential areas that have been voting Republican for decades. Included are Redondo Beach, Torrance, Manhattan Beach and Marina Del Rey. The 53rd even has a Republican voter registration plurality.

But if the 1992 elections demonstrated anything, it was that a terrible economy, dissension within the GOP and uncharacteristically sharp organizational work by Democrats can upset conventional wisdom.

Debra Bowen

All of those elements were at work in the 53rd. The district's residents are closely tied to the aerospace industry, which has suffered huge layoffs in the post-Cold War era. Republicans compounded their problem by nominating the most conservative of the GOP candidates who ran. The Democrats, for their part, sensed that the 53rd could be taken, and they hustled.

As it turned out, Democrat Debra Bowen, who was well known in the area as an environmental activist and attorney, won fairly easily with more than 54 percent of the vote, defeating Republican Brad Parton, the mayor of Redondo Beach. For the Democrats, it was one-half of a double win since Republican incumbent Gerald Felando was defeated by another Democratic woman in the adjacent 54th District despite a GOP registration edge. In going two-for-two in the south coastal region of Los Angeles County, the Democrats may have demonstrated that the area's longtime Republican orientation is threatened, at least when they field attractive candidates who campaign on themes that are relevant to the concerns of the region such as jobs and environmental protection.

PERSONAL: elected 1992; born Oct. 27, 1955, in Rockford, Ill.; home, Venice; education, B.A. Michigan State University, J.D. University of Virginia, studied at International Christian University in Tokyo; husband, Brian Gindoff; no stated religion.

CAREER: lawyer specializing in environmental issues.

COMMITTEES: Consumer Protection, Governmental Efficiency & New Technologies (vice chair); Environmental Safety & Toxic Materials; Housing & Community Development; Natural Resources.

OFFICES: Capitol, (916) 445-8528, FAX (916) 327-2201; district, 14411 Crenshaw Blvd., 280, Torrance 90504, (310) 523-4831, FAX (310) 523-4972.

TERM LIMIT: 1998

REGISTRATION: 43.2% D, 41.1% R

1992 CAMPAIGN:		
Bowen – D	54.1%	$488,315
W. Brad Parton – R	41.2%	$799,822

RATINGS and **KEY VOTES**: Newly elected

Larry Bowler (R)
10th Assembly District

Larry Bowler, who won election in the 10th Assembly District with a campaign that focused heavily on his distaste for Assembly Speaker Willie Brown, learned quickly that he would have to pay a price for his strategy. Bowler, who had sworn never to cast a vote for Brown as speaker, was immediately assigned the Capitol's smallest office, a room without windows that is often used for storage and is affectionately known as the "closet." Brown followed up by refusing to grant a request by Bowler, a retired sheriff's lieutenant with 30 years' law enforcement experience, for an assignment to the Assembly's Public Safety Committee. In fact, Bowler, who also asked for nine other committees in which he had an

Larry Bowler

interest, got absolutely nothing he wanted. Instead, he drew committees on education, public employees and utilities.

Elected to a district that includes south Sacramento County, Stockton and northern San Joaquin County, Bowler defeated Democrat Kay Albiani, who ran with a risky strategy by backing Ross Perot's independent candidacy for president. Bowler characterized Albiani as a puppet to Brown and survived disclosures that he was heavily financed by the religious right and had been accused of sexual harassment in 1990 for telling a woman subordinate that she looked as though she had been "rode hard and put away wet."

Bowler began his year as a legislative freshman by vowing to help reform the state's workers' compensation system and streamline education financing. But he acknowledged that one of his first lessons in Capitol politics was that Brown was "more involved in minutiae" than he had believed.

PERSONAL: elected 1992; born July 30, 1939, in Sacramento; home, Elk

Grove; B.A. University of San Francisco 1977; wife Melva, three children; Nazarene.

CAREER: retired sheriff's lieutenant, Sacramento County Sheriffs' Department; U.S. Navy.

COMMITTEES: Education; Public Employees, Retirement and Social Security; Utilities and Commerce.

OFFICES: Capitol, (916) 445-7402; FAX (916) 324-0013; district, 10381 Old Placerville, 120, Sacramento 95827, (916) 362-4161, FAX 362-4164.

TERM LIMIT: 1998

REGISTRATION: 46.7% D, 42.1% R

1992 CAMPAIGN:			
	Bowler – R	53.1%	$613,827
	Kay Albiani – D	42.0%	$307,332

RATINGS and **KEY VOTES**: Newly elected

Vivien Bronshvag (D)
6th Assembly District

Vivien Bronshvag's defeat of Republican Al Aramburu in this North Bay district in part told the story of the 1992 legislative elections for Gov. Pete Wilson. Aramburu, a son of Mexican immigrants and a political moderate who had been a Marin County supervisor for 11 years, was a Wilson loyalist in a Democratic-leaning district.

Vivien Bronshvag

As in other races across the state, Wilson and his allies hoped to portray Bronshvag as a roadblock to workers' compensation reform, claiming that her neurologist husband was among those profiting from the waste in the system. Wilson strategists also had thought Democrats' opposition to cutting welfare benefits with Proposition 165 would work against them. But Aramburu abandoned his support of the initiative in the middle of the campaign, saying the tough times facing county budgets had forced him to break with the governor. And Bronshvag, who together with her husband contributed more than half of the money that financed her campaign, easily won the election.

It was less clear that she would easily settle into her role as a representative of the people. Rumors circulated that she was enjoying the perks of her new-found power just a little too much, and she rapidly was dubbed "The Duchess" by Assembly sergeants-at-arms, who suspected her of imperial tendencies.

As vice chair of the water committee, Bronshvag herself said she planned to focus on environmental issues, saying she represented "not only one of the most pristine districts in the state but the whole nation."

PERSONAL: elected 1992; born July 28, 1942, in Chicago, Illinois; home, Kentfield; B.A. University of Wisconsin; husband Dr. Michael Bronshvag, three children; Jewish.

CAREER: vice president and pension plan administrator for Michael Bronshvag M.D. Inc., formerly art coordinator for Quaker Oats Corporation, designer for Home Place Company.

COMMITTEES: Water, Parks and Wildlife (vice chair); Consumer Protection, Governmental Efficiency and New Technologies; Education; Utilities and Commerce.

OFFICES: Capitol, (916) 445-7783; district, 100 Smith Ranch Rd., 308, San Rafael 94903, (415) 479-4920, FAX (415) 479-2123.

TERM LIMIT: 1998
REGISTRATION: 53.9% D, 30.2% R
1992 CAMPAIGN: Bronshvag – D   53.3% $761,091
                     Al Aramburu – R   39.5% $289,337
RATINGS and **KEY VOTES**: Newly elected

Valerie Brown (D)

7th Assembly District

The 7th Assembly District was one of the few in the state altered in the redistricting process to make it less hospitable for Republican candidates and is now decidedly more Democratic than it used to be. It embraces all of Napa County, and the most heavily populated parts of Sonoma and Solano Counties, including Santa Rosa and Vallejo. Within that area is the heart of the wine country, Mare Island Naval Shipyard, the California Maritime Academy and a growing high-tech industry.

When former Republican Bev Hansen decided to quit the Assembly in 1992, the race for the open seat pitted Sonoma Vice Mayor Valerie Brown against Janet Nicholas, a former Sonoma County supervisor

Valerie Brown

who was appointed to the state Board of Prison Terms by Gov. Pete Wilson. Brown, a former marriage and family counselor who owns and operates an education center designed to give students "an opportunity to boost self-esteem through better academic performance," won the seat with a campaign that capitalized on Wilson's record-setting unpopularity. She also was the beneficiary of a significant Democratic voter registration drive, one that was repeated in many districts across the state as a fractured Republican Party was unable to unify its moderate and conservative forces to perform the nuts-and-bolts work of the election.

PERSONAL: elected 1992; born October 30, 1945, in Kansas City, Missouri; home, Sonoma; education, B.S. University of Missouri 1972, M.A. in counseling psychology; divorced, one child.

CAREER: former mayor and vice mayor of Sonoma; owner and operator of the Sonoma Valley Education Center, former marriage, family and child counselor.

COMMITTEES: Local Government (vice chair), Agriculture; Education; Human Services.

OFFICES: Capitol, (916) 445-8492, FAX (916) 322-0674; district, 50 D St., 301, Santa Rosa 95404, (707) 546-4500, FAX (707) 546-9031.

TERM LIMIT: 1998

REGISTRATION: 56.8% D, 31.3% R

1992 CAMPAIGN: Brown – D   60.2% $524,935

Janet Nicholas – R   35.9% $422,065

RATINGS and **KEY VOTES**: Newly elected

Willie L. Brown Jr. (D)

13th Assembly District

Willie Brown

Willie Lewis Brown Jr. is the ranking state legislator in seniority, the most powerful and certainly the most interesting, someone who engenders strong loyalty, fear and loathing in equal proportions. Rising from the humblest of origins, Brown has held center court in California's ornate Capitol for most of his career and for more than a dozen years has been the Assembly's speaker, breaking all records for longevity and functioning as one of the nation's most influential African American political figures. A fiery orator and a brilliant strategist, Brown has an explosive temper and an equally sharp, urbane wit.

But he leaves many, even those who admire him, wondering if he has any core beliefs other than holding power and enjoying to the hilt all that comes with it. Brown often behaves as if all that counts is Willie Brown. His district is almost an afterthought in his political career, although the Supreme Court's reapportionment of his district changed his personal constituency dramatically for the 1992 elections.

Brown once represented the more affluent western and northern sections of San Francisco, but reapportionment divided the city into western and eastern districts and Brown opted for the eastern one, a much poorer area that also includes much of the city's African American and Latino residents. It made no difference in terms of Brown's own re-election to a 15th term. The entire city is so overwhelmingly Democratic that all Brown needs to do is file his re-election papers every two years.

Brown is a star, and not just in San Francisco and the tight little world of Sacramento politics. He was the Rev. Jesse Jackson's national campaign chairman in 1988.

Brown's roots are modest. An African American youth who had shined shoes in Mineola, Texas, he left the Lone Star State to follow a colorful uncle to San Francisco and never looked back. He went to college at San Francisco State and earned a law degree at Hastings. Brown was a man who seemed destined for big things from the moment he walked onto the Assembly floor as a freshman legislator in 1965. He was a flamboyant, left-leaning, angry-talking young street lawyer who had formed a homegrown liberal political organization with the Burton brothers (Philip and John) and George Moscone, the son of a local fisherman. Brown had an opinion on everything and would voice it to anyone who would listen.

One of his first votes was against the re-election of the legendary Jesse Unruh as speaker of the house. But Unruh tolerated Brown, perhaps because both were raised dirt poor in Texas, both emigrated to California after World War II and both began their political careers as rabble-rousers. "It's a good thing you aren't white," Unruh remarked to Brown one day after the latter had made an especially effective floor speech early in his career. "Why's that?" Brown asked. "Because if you were, you'd own the place," Unruh replied.

Civil rights was the early focus of Brown's legislative career and no matter what the event, he was ready with a quote. When African American athletes Tommy Smith and John Carlos raised their fists in a "black power" salute at the 1968 Olympics, Brown said, "They will be known forever as two niggers who upset the Olympic Games. I'd rather have them known for that than as two niggers who won two medals." Despite statements of that sort, Brown was developing a reputation among Capitol insiders for smart political work. In 1970, he took his first big step up the ladder when friend Bob Moretti became speaker and elevated Brown to chairmanship of the powerful Ways and Means Committee. Brown became a master of arcane matters of state finance and recruited a staff of young advisers who today form the nucleus of his Assembly senior staff.

California's political establishment was beginning to respect, if not like, the young politician. He led the George McGovern faction from California to the Democratic National Convention in 1972 and during a complex and bitter credentials fight delivered a famous "Give me back my delegation" speech that thrust him into the national spotlight.

Moretti was planning to step down in 1974 to run for governor and wanted to lateral the speakership to Brown, but Brown made the worst tactical error of his career in taking for granted the support of Latino and African American members. Secretly, San Francisco's other assemblyman, Leo McCarthy, had courted the minority lawmakers, promising them committee chairmanships and other goodies. When the vote came, they stood with McCarthy, who snatched the speakership from under Brown's nose.

That was the beginning of an in-house exile for Brown, one that became even more intense when he and some supporters plotted an unsuccessfull coup against McCarthy. At one point, Brown was given an office so small that he had to place his filing cabinets outside in the hall. The exile lasted for two years, during which, Brown said later, he underwent intense self-examination and concluded that he had been too arrogant in dealings with colleagues–like calling one member a "500-pound tub of Jello" in public.

McCarthy resurrected Brown's legislative career in 1976 by naming him chairman of the Revenue and Taxation Committee, a fairly substantial job. That gesture paid off in 1979, when another bloc of Democratic Assembly members, led by Howard Berman of Los Angeles, tried to oust McCarthy from the speakership. Brown declared loyalty to his old rival and maintained it during a year of bitter infighting.

At the conclusion of the 1980 elections, Berman had seemingly won enough contested seats to claim the speakership, but the desperate McCarthy backers cut a deal with Republicans to name Willie Brown as speaker. Republicans, who openly feared a Berman speakership, were promised some extra consideration by the new regime. Although they later were to claim that Brown reneged, he has always maintained that he stuck to the letter of the agreement.

Brown's speakership has been controversial. His Democratic flock has both expanded and contracted during his tenure. But until the Supreme Court decreed a reapportionment plan in 1992 after Brown and Republican Gov. Pete Wilson reached a stalemate, Democratic control of the house was never in doubt. The court maps gave Republicans a theoretical opportunity to turn out Brown and the Democrats. But internal GOP strife, coupled with strong organizational work by the Democrats, staved off what could have been a major embarrassment for Brown. Although he had privately conceded that Republicans would pick up at least three or four seats in 1992, the GOP actually lost one and Brown quickly claimed a major victory.

Brown's political brilliance, however, has not muted critics, who say that he has rarely exercised his talents on behalf of substantive policy issues and has, instead, presided over a decline both in the performance and the moral atmosphere of the Legislature. He has been accused of shaking down special interests for millions of dollars in campaign funds, of presiding over a blatantly partisan reapportionment of legislative districts in 1981 and of being too consumed with the inside game.

Brown lists making life easier for legislators as his chief accomplishment as speaker. His principal legislative triumph as speaker, some think, was his authorship of the state's mandatory seat-belt law.

Brown has not remade the speakership, as Unruh did. Rather, he took the vast inherent powers of the office and shaped them into a personal tool. He is less innovator than manipulator. He says that he appoints competent people to staff and committee positions and gives them the tools to work.

Despite aging, Brown is still controversial among the larger public. But as speaker, he's answerable to only two constituencies: voters of his Assembly district and the 79 other members of the Assembly. Brown could not be elected to statewide office, but he doesn't aspire to it. Republicans use Brown as a tool to stir up supporters and raise money, portraying him as the political devil incarnate. He says–with some validity–that such tactics are thinly veiled racism. Likewise, he pins the racist label on his other critics, in and out of the media. So it was not surprising that Brown took it very personally when the voters in November 1990 passed Proposition 140, imposing term limits on legislators and forcing them to cut their staffs. Voter antipathy toward the Legislature was aimed, in part, at Speaker Brown–and he knew it.

In the wake of Proposition 140, Brown bitterly lashed out at the press, calling reporters "despicable" and moving their desks from the side of Assembly chambers to the rear. Brown viewed passage of term limits as an image problem and not as the result of a more deeply seated institutional malaise. One of his most nettlesome and frequent critics, Sherry Bebitch Jeffe, a political scientist with the Claremont Graduate School and a former Unruh staffer, maintains that Brown has become increasingly worried about how history will view his speakership.

"My guess is that he has decided there is some truth to the charges about what has happened to the image of the institution," Jeffe said. "That indicates to me a shred of decency, a shred of understanding that he has had a role in its decline. ... If his legacy is that he helped destroy the legislative institution, I don't believe that is something he can live with."

At least some of the controversy stems from Brown's high-style personal life. The $1,500 Italian-cut suits, the low-slung sports cars and the flashy parties that he throws for personal and political reasons all contribute to the image, as do his liaisons with a string of attractive women (he's long separated from his wife, Blanche, a reclusive dance teacher).

But it is what Brown does to support that lifestyle that raises the most eyebrows. He represents, as an attorney and quasi-lobbyist, a number of well-heeled corporations. His blue-chip client list includes one of the largest landowners in California, the Santa Fe-Southern Pacific Realty (renamed Catellus Inc.). Developers such as the East Bay's Ron Cowan and bond adviser Calvin Grigsby also have put the speaker on retainer.

Occasionally, some clients also do business in Sacramento. Brown's activities on behalf of one of his law clients, Norcal Solid Waste Systems Inc., attracted the attention of the FBI in 1990. The company has increasingly come to dominate the garbage business in Northern California. The FBI, it became known, began looking into allegations that Brown attempted to help the company override local opposition to placing a garbage transfer station in Solano County. In December 1990, federal agents served a new round of subpoenas in the state Capitol for legislation involving the garbage business. Among the bills subpoenaed was a measure that became law allowing a Norcal subsidiary to relocate a dump near Marysville over the objections of local residents.

Regardless of what he does in Sacramento, Brown is a power in and around San Francisco. Former San Francisco Supervisor Terry Francois put it this way a few years ago: "He (Brown) engenders fear like you wouldn't believe. I have just become enthralled at the way he wields power. I don't know a politician in San Francisco that dares take him on."

Until the post-1990 census reapportionment, the greatest threat to Brown's hold on the speakership had come in 1987, when five Democratic members, all of whom had enjoyed close relations with the speaker, declared their independence. The "Gang of Five," as the group was immediately dubbed, demanded procedural changes they said were reforms to lessen the power of the speaker. Before long, they were demanding that Brown step down as speaker. They could have formed a new majority with Republicans, but the GOP leader at the time, Pat Nolan, also had established a close relationship with Brown and protected the speaker's right flank.

Brown stripped the five of their best committee assignments and the war of nerves went on for a year. Eventually, Republicans agreed to form a coalition with the gang. But Brown bolstered his loyalists with enough victories at the polls in 1988 to eke out a paper-thin re-election as speaker. When the Democrats increased their majority in the Assembly in 1990 and added an extra seat in 1992, Brown's grip on the speakership was assured.

Reapportionment was only one in a series of specific matters on which Brown and Wilson clashed in 1991 and 1992. The Brown-Wilson feud, in fact, took on the ambience of a personal duel for dominance of the Capitol, one that grew even more intense after Brown expanded his Democratic ranks in 1992. Brown quickly made it clear that he considered himself to be the Capitol's most important figure and implied that if Wilson wanted anything substantial, he would have to come, hat in hand, to the speaker's office. Thus, the likelihood of legislative creativity from this most enigmatic of figures remained scant.

How long Brown will remain as speaker has become one of the most often asked questions in the Capitol. No one has an answer. Sometimes it seems as if the only reason Brown is still speaker is that his colleagues cannot agree on a replacement. The bitterness of the Berman-McCarthy fight of 1980 – and the "Gang of Five" – are experiences many Assembly members do not wish to repeat. For his part, Brown says he wants to be speaker for the indefinite future–even though the 1990 term limit initiative says he can serve in the Assembly only until 1996.

PERSONAL: elected 1964; born March 20, 1934, in Mineola, Tex.; home, San Francisco; National Guard Reserves 1955-1958; education, B.A. San Francisco State University, J.D. Hastings College of Law; wife Blanche Vitero, three children; Methodist.

CAREER: lawyer, maintains a law practice while in office; Assembly speaker 1980 to present.

COMMITTEES: the speaker of the Assembly is a member of all Assembly committees; (joint) Courthouse Financing & Construction; Fire, Police, Emergency & Disaster Services; Rules.

OFFICES: Capitol, (916) 445-8077, FAX (916) 445-4189; district, 1388 Sutter St., 1002, San Francisco 94109, (415) 557-0784, FAX (415) 557-8936; Southern California, 107 S. Broadway, 8009, Los Angeles 90012, (213) 620-4356.

TERM LIMIT: 1996

REGISTRATION: 64.6% D, 15.1% R, 3.3% Green

1992 CAMPAIGN:	Brown – D	69.5%	$4,826,842
	John Sidline – R	18.9%	$4,739
	Walter Medina – P&F	8.1%	
1990 CAMPAIGN:	Brown – D	64.2%	$6,770,364
	Terrence Faulkner – R	27.1%	

RATINGS:	AFL-CIO	CalPIRG	CLCV	NOW	CofC	CalFarm
	94	95	92	100	28	35

KEY VOTES:

Parent consent abort:	NO	Limit product tort:	YES	Clean Air Act:	YES
Assault gun ban:	YES	Ban AIDS discrim:	YES	Restrict abortion funds:	NO
Sales tax hike:	YES	Wealth tax hike:	YES	Strong gay rights:	YES
Parental leave:	YES	Timber compromise:	NO	Execution by injection:	nv
Limited gay rights:	YES	Universal health insur:	YES	1992-93 Budget Act:	YES
Campaign Reform:	nv	Offshore oil ban:	YES	Charter schools:	YES

James L. Brulte (R)
63rd Assembly District

Republicans have a safe haven in this district, where GOP registration is 50 percent to 40 percent for the Democrats. The district lies south of the San Gabriel Mountains in San Bernardino County, including Loma Linda, Upland and the white enclaves of San Bernardino.

The seat was held for a time by Republican Charles Bader, who vacated it to run for the Senate against incumbent Ruben Ayala in 1990. After a megabuck race, Ayala kept his seat and Bader was sent into political oblivion. Meanwhile, Bader passed his Assembly seat to his chief of staff, Jim Brulte, an imposing man at 6-foot-4 and 260 pounds.

Jim Brulte

Brulte is the quintessential politician of the era. He worked his way into the Legislature, not through service to the community but by service to other politicians. Brulte's resume is stuffed with political jobs, having been active in political campaigns since he was 10. He was an aide to S.I. Hayakawa and an advance man for George Bush.

In his first Assembly campaign, Brulte ran a typically modern operation with direct mail, computerized fund-raising lists and humming fax machines. He overwhelmed an underfunded opponent in the GOP primary, and the general election was a cinch. His Democratic opponent, Robert Erwin, a counselor with the San Bernardino Probation Department and a Vietnam veteran, was no match for Brulte's heavy backing from the area's building industry and all of its Republican legislators and congressmen.

Brulte performed equally well in his 1992 re-election bid, crushing his Democratic opponent, A.L. "Larry" Westwood.

With the start of the 1993 session, Brulte won the top job in the Assembly Republican caucus – minority leader. He replaced Fresno's Bill Jones, who stepped down after the Republicans failed to live up to expectations at the polls. They lost one seat in the Assembly instead of gaining eight as they had hoped.

Brulte approached the minority leader's job ecumenically, naming three assistant minority leaders: conservatives David Knowles of Cameron Park and Andrea Seastrand of San Luis Obispo and moderate Stan Statham of Redding. All the same, Brulte will have his hands full trying to keep the rancorous Republican caucus in line, and maintaining open communication with Gov. Wilson, who tends to be more moderate than Brulte on many issues.

Perhaps even more significantly, Brulte, who is the new kid on the block despite his political background, will have to deal day in and day out with the consummate politician – Assembly Speaker Willie Brown. Almost immediately after Brulte assumed his new post, he crashed head-on into the considerable political force of the speaker. First Brown announced seating assignments on the Assembly floor that created a logistical nightmare for Republican whips by separating GOP freshmen from the rest of the caucus. Then Brown refused to name Republican Assemblyman Dean Andal of Stockton to the Assembly Ways and Means Committee, even though Andal was the Republicans' pick for the job. The speaker instead named Republican Paul Horcher of Whittier as vice chair of Ways and Means. To add insult to injury, Brown named only three Republicans to committee vice chairmanships, reversing a tradition of giving minority party members those posts.

Brulte, for his own political reasons, chose not to clash openly with Brown, at least not so early in the legislative year. Instead, he ignored Horcher's Ways and Means assignment and announced that Assemblyman Pat Nolan of Glendale, would be the Republicans' lead person on the committee and that Andal would be the caucus' budget watchdog.

PERSONAL: elected 1990; born April 13, 1956, in Glen Cove, N.Y.; home, Ontario; Air National Guard Reserve 1974-present; education, B.A. Cal Poly Pomona; single.

CAREER: Staff, U.S. Sen. S.I. Hayakawa in Washington D.C; staff, Republican National Committee; staff, Assistant Secretary of Defense for Reserve Affairs; advance staff, Vice President George Bush; executive director, San Bernardino

County Republican Party; chief of staff, Assemblyman Charles Bader 1987-1990; owns a management consulting firm.

COMMITTEES: As Assembly Republican Leader, Brulte does not serve on any standing committees. He is a member of the Joint Rules Committee.

OFFICES: Capitol, (916) 445-8490, FAX (916) 323-8544; district, 10681 Foothill Blvd., 325, Rancho Cucamonga 91730, (714) 466-9096, FAX (909) 466-9892.

TERM LIMIT: 1996

REGISTRATION: 40.5% D, 48.2% R

1992 CAMPAIGN:	Brulte – R	56.1%	$506,548
	Larry Westwood – D	31.3%	
	Joseph Desist – Green	12.7%	
1990 CAMPAIGN:	Brulte – R	59.9%	$275,634
	Robert Erwin – D	40.1%	$34,208

RATINGS:	AFL-CIO	CalPIRG	CLCV	NOW	CofC	CalFarm
	3	29	12	21	83	65

KEY VOTES:

Sales tax hike:	NO	Wealth tax hike:	NO	Strong gay rights:	NO
Parental leave:	NO	Timber compromise:	YES	Execution by injection:	YES
Limited gay rights:	NO	Universal health insur:	NO	1992-93 Budget Act:	YES
Campaign Reform:	NO	Offshore oil ban:	NO	Charter schools:	YES

John L. Burton (D)
12th Assembly District

Traditionally, San Francisco has been divided into two Assembly districts, one encompassing the eastern section of the city and the other the western. When John Burton returned to the Assembly in 1988, he inherited the eastern district from Art Agnos, who had been elected the city's mayor. Assembly Speaker Willie Brown represented the western half.

Court-ordered reapportionment in 1992 continued the division of the city, but Burton and Brown, two old friends and political allies, decided to switch districts. Burton wound up with the more affluent western half, renumbered as the 12th District. Politically, the switch counts for little since both districts are overwhelmingly Democratic, although the swap

John Burton

did create a little furor when Republican challenger Storm Jenkins tried–unsuccessfully–to persuade a judge that Burton wasn't a resident of the district and therefore should be left off the ballot.

That aside, Burton breezed to a ridiculously easy re-election in 1992 and Brown promptly named him chairman of the Assembly Rules Committee, the obscure but powerful body that acts as the Assembly's internal housekeeper–with power over staff, office perks and the like–and traffic manager for legislation. He chaired the committee years earlier during his first stint in the Assembly.

Burton is one of the Capitol's genuine characters, loud, profane, combative and the building's only self-acknowledged former drug abuser. Burton, his late brother Philip, Willie Brown and George Moscone, who became mayor of San Francisco and was assassinated in 1978, were the founders of a political organization that has dominated San Francisco's major-league politics for more than a generation. John Burton and Willie Brown began in politics together as idealistic young men and close friends. They went to the Assembly, where Brown flourished. Burton moved on to Congress.

The organization's greatest triumph came in the 1981 reapportionment in which brother Philip made his self-named "contribution to modern art" by carving up congressional districts in such a manner that lopsided majorities for the Democrats were preserved throughout the 1980s. One of the more bizarrely shaped districts was for John Burton. But then the Burton machine faltered.

John Burton suddenly quit his seat in Congress, admitting publicly that he had a cocaine and alcohol problem. In 1983, Philip Burton died. His wife, Sala, took over his congressional seat but she died in 1987. The organization was brought back to life in 1987 to move then-Assemblyman Art Agnos into the mayor's office, which in turn opened the door for John Burton to run for the Assembly again. The 1988 special election for Agnos' seat pitted Burton, who had undergone extensive and, he says, successful therapy for his substance abuse, against Roberta Achtenberg, an activist for lesbian and gay rights who was bidding to become the state's first openly lesbian legislator. She spent $333,383 in a sometimes bitter campaign. In the end, Burton's name and the organization's professional-class efforts (and heavier spending) won out and he returned to Sacramento.

Burton may have been the least fresh freshman ever to enter the Assembly. Brown has given him a series of important committee assignments, including chairmanship of the Public Safety Committee, where Burton gleefully has killed Republican lock-'em-up anti-crime bills while crafting Democratic measures that have given his party the edge on crime legislation.

Burton's impact on the Assembly is more often theatrical than legislative. But he functions as a member of Brown's inner circle and the two represent a potent political force on behalf of San Francisco's parochial issues.

PERSONAL: elected 1988 (special election); born Dec. 15, 1932, in Cincinnati; home, San Francisco; Army 1954-1956; education, B.A. social science San Francisco State University, J.D. University of San Francisco Law School; divorced; one child.

CAREER: lawyer; Assembly 1964-1974; U.S. House of Representatives 1974-1982.

COMMITTEES: Rules (chair); Health; Public Safety; Ways & Means; (joint) Legislative Budget.

OFFICES: Capitol, (916) 445-8253, FAX (916) 324-4899; district, 455 Golden Gate Ave., 2202, San Francisco 94102, (415) 557-2253, FAX (415) 557-2592.

TERM LIMIT: 1996

REGISTRATION: 61.1% D, 19.6 R

1992 CAMPAIGN:			
	Burton – D	65.1%	$534,129
	Storm Jenkins – R	26.1%	$40,741
	Kitty Reese – P&F	6.3%	
1990 CAMPAIGN:	Burton – D	100%	$381,864

RATINGS:

AFL-CIO	CalPIRG	CLCV	NOW	CofC	CalFarm
97	95	100	93	22	35

KEY VOTES:

Assault gun ban:	YES	Ban AIDS discrim:	YES	Restrict abortion funds:	NO
Sales tax hike:	YES	Wealth tax hike:	NO	Strong gay rights:	YES
Parental leave:	YES	Timber compromise:	nv	Execution by injection:	nv
Limited gay rights:	YES	Universal health insur:	YES	1992-93 Budget Act:	NO
Campaign Reform:	YES	Offshore oil ban:	YES	Charter schools:	YES

Louis Caldera (D)
46th Assembly District

When Assemblywoman Lucille Roybal-Allard decided to follow her father to Congress, it left a hole in the 46th Assembly District and set up another battle between two Latino political factions who are struggling for control of politics on the heavily Hispanic east side of Los Angeles. Roybal-Allard and Los Angeles County Supervisor Gloria Molina backed Berta Saavedra, who was Roybal-Allard's assistant. The other faction, headed by City Councilman Richard Alatorre, state Sen. Art Torres and Assemblyman Richard Polanco, chose Louis Caldera, a deputy county counsel who had been educated at West Point and Harvard and was a military police officer. Caldera won the primary with 52 percent of the vote and coasted to election in this heavily Democratic district.

Louis Caldera

Among Capitol insiders, Caldera is being hailed as a comer because of his attractive attributes; someone who can carry Latino politics into a new dimension as term limits bring him and other newcomers into relatively high seniority later in the decade.

PERSONAL: elected 1992; born April 1, 1956, in El Paso, Tex.; home, Los Angeles; education, B.S. U.S. Military Academy; law degree and MBA, Harvard University; wife Eva; Catholic.

CAREER: lawyer, Los Angeles deputy county counsel, 1991-92.

COMMITTEES: Finance & Insurance (vice chair); Consumer Protection, Governmental Efficiency & New Technologies; Judiciary; Revenue & Taxation.

OFFICES: Capitol, (916) 445-4843; district, 304 S. Broadway, 580, Los Angeles 90013, (213) 680-4646.

TERM LIMIT: 1998

REGISTRATION: 65.4% D, 19.9% R

1992 CAMPAIGN: Caldera – D   71.8% $175,610
                    David Osborne – R   21.3% $0

RATINGS and **KEY VOTES**: Newly elected

Robert J. Campbell (D)
11th Assembly District

Robert Campbell is one of the most consistently liberal members of the Assembly. And with the high percentage of blue-collar workers and minority residents of a Bay Area district that stretches along the upper reaches of San Francisco Bay from Hercules to Pittsburg, he can afford to be. Reapportionment moved Campbell's district out of his home base in Richmond and further into the Contra Costa County suburbs, halving his once-immense Democractic registration margin. But he was still left with a more than 20-point edge that discouraged Republicans and left him as one of a handful of incumbent legislators who had no re-election challenger.

Robert Campbell

Campbell, a former insurance broker and Richmond city councilman, has only drawn token opposition–when he has any–since his election in 1980. One of Campbell's key interests is education funding. As chairman of the Assembly budget subcommittee that deals with education, he has significant influence on where education dollars are spent. He has fought to restore funding cuts for community colleges and state universities as well as to limit increases in tuition. His efforts have made him popular with the University of California Student Association.

Campbell's liberal leanings also have been evident on environmental legislation, civil liberties issues and measures to help minorities and recently arrived immigrants. And he was one of only a few legislators who had an announced policy of refusing to take fees for speeches before the practice was outlawed.

But the mild-mannered Campbell has not been adept at playing the inside game. Several legislators with less seniority have more clout, and with term limits bringing his Assembly career to an end by 1996, Campbell seems destined never to be more than a marginal player.

PERSONAL: elected 1980; born Dec. 20, 1937, in Los Angeles; home, Richmond; Army, National Guard Reserves 1961-1972; education, B.A. social science and history San Francisco State University, postgraduate studies UC Berkeley; divorced, two children; Roman Catholic.

CAREER: insurance broker; Richmond City Council 1975-1982.

COMMITTEES: Higher Education; Utilities & Commerce; Water, Parks & Wildlife; Ways & Means and subcommittee 2–school finance (chair); Legislative Audit (joint); Legislative Budget; School Facilities.

OFFICES: Capitol, (916) 445-7890, FAX (916) 327-2999; district, 815 Estudillo St., Martinez 94553, (510) 372-7990, FAX (510) 372-0934.

TERM LIMIT: 1996

REGISTRATION: 54.3% D , 31.2% R

1992 CAMPAIGN: Campbell – D   98.1% $153,927
                  (two write-in candidates won a total of 1.9%)

1990 CAMPAIGN: Campbell – D   100% $133,972

RATINGS: AFL-CIO CalPIRG   CLCV   NOW   CofC   CalFarm
              97   100   96   100   22   30

KEY VOTES:

Parent consent abort:	NO	Limit product tort:	NO	Clean Air Act:	YES
Assault gun ban:	YES	Ban AIDS discrim:	YES	Restrict abortion funds:	NO
Sales tax hike:	YES	Wealth tax hike:	YES	Strong gay rights:	YES
Parental leave:	YES	Timber compromise:	NO	Execution by injection:	nv
Limited gay rights:	YES	Universal health insur:	YES	1992-93 Budget Act:	NO
Campaign Reform:	YES	Offshore oil ban:	YES	Charter schools:	NO

Salvatorre Cannella (D)

26th Assembly District

When the state Supreme Court's reapportionment experts decided that the fast-growing Modesto area should have an additional state Assembly seat, it meant a substantial change for one-term Assemblyman Sal Cannella, but one for the better, since Cannella is a Democrat.

Cannella was first elected in 1990 after a fierce partisan battle in the old 27th District, which included all of Stanislaus County and the Atwater-Snelling region of the northern tip of Merced County. Once a solidly Democratic district, albeit one with a conservative tone, the 27th was undergoing rapid change as the Modesto area became a suburban extension of the San Francisco Bay Area. Suburbanizing areas traditionally move toward the Republican Party and the GOP saw the district as a future growth possibility.

Cannella won the seat twice in 1990, once in a special election after Gary Condit was elected to Congress and the second time in the regular election. For Cannella, onetime tool-and-die maker, it was deja vu because he had succeeded Condit as mayor of Ceres and later as a Stanislaus County supervisor.

Sal Cannella

The 1990 special election victory was a sweet one for both Cannella and his party because Republican Richard Lang, a well-known high school principal and Modesto city councilman, was the clear favorite. An overconfident Assembly Republican leader Ross Johnson hailed Lang as being in a "solid position" to defeat Cannella, saying a poll showed him with a 17-point lead. But the election proved to be one place where then-state Democratic Party Chairman Jerry Brown made good on his pledge to mount aggressive voter registration and vote-by-mail drives. Cannella's campaign was also aided by his close ties to organized labor.

In the November rematch, the results were nearly the same. Nevertheless, Republican voter strength continued to grow and Cannella had to worry that he would remain a GOP target for years to come. The Supreme Court changed the situation dramatically, however, when it created a new Modesto-area district. Most of the Republicans were placed in the adjacent 25th District and Cannella wound up with a strong Democratric registration margin. Cannella had an easy re-election win in the new district in 1992.

In his short time in the Legislature, Cannella has been low-key and removed from the power structure – a go-along, get-along regular for Assembly Speaker Willie Brown. He got points for dedication when he left a hospital bed in 1990 to cast a crucial vote in favor of a compromise ending a 28-day stalemate between Gov. George Deukmejian and the Legislature on the budget. His most visible statewide legislation – to increase civil penalties and criminal fines assessed for work place safety and health violations – was vetoed in 1990. But in early 1993, Cannella was given an opportunity to expand his political horizons when Brown elevated him to the chairmanship of the Public Employees, Retirement and Social Security Committee – a plum for someone with strong union connections.

PERSONAL: elected 1990 (special election); born Sept. 23, 1942, in Newark, N.J.; home, Ceres; National Guard 1960-1966; education, Modesto Community College; wife Donna, three children; Roman Catholic.

CAREER: tool-and-die maker.

COMMITTEES: Public Employees, Retirement & Social Security (chair); Agriculture; Local Government; Water, Parks & Wildlife.

OFFICES: Capitol, (916) 445-8570, FAX (916) 445-8849; district, 384 E. Olive, 2, Turlock, 95380, (209) 576-6211, FAX (209) 576-6105.

TERM LIMIT: 1996
REGISTRATION: 54.4% D, 34.2% R

1992 CAMPAIGN:	Canella – D	56.8%	$304,957
	Scott Weimer – R	35.2%	$10,695
	Rob Parks – L	8.0%	
1990 CAMPAIGN:	Canella – D	51.4%	$293,367
	Richard Lang – R	45.2%	$103,040

| RATINGS: | AFL-CIO | CalPIRG | CLCV | NOW | CofC | CalFarm |
| | 93 | 95 | 70 | 57 | 44 | 50 |

KEY VOTES:

Sales tax hike:	YES	Restrict abortion funds:	NO	Strong gay rights:	NO
Parental leave:	YES	Timber compromise:	YES	Execution by injection:	YES
Limited gay rights:	NO	Universal health insur:	YES	1992-93 Budget Act:	YES
Campaign Reform:	YES	Offshore oil ban:	YES	Charter schools:	YES
Wealth tax hike:	YES				

B.T. Collins (R)

5th Assembly District

Suburban Sacramento in 1991 found itself represented by one of the Capitol's most notorious political figures – the outspoken and cantankerous B.T. Collins.

Outrageous, sometimes lovable and loyal to a fault, Collins had built a record of political service to former Democratic Gov. Jerry Brown and former Republican Treasurer Thomas Hayes when Gov. Pete Wilson tapped him to become California Youth Authority director in 1991. Wilson, however, quickly decided he needed Collins elsewhere – in the 5th District Assembly seat vacated when Tim Leslie was elected to the state Senate.

B.T. Collins

Wilson, battling with conservatives in the Assembly Republican Caucus over his proposals to raise taxes, secured Collins as one of his soldiers after a primary campaign that pitted Collins against anti-abortion activist Barbara Alby. As local religious leaders promoted Alby as the "Christian candidate" in the race, Collins – who didn't even live in the district when he decided to run – bridled publicly at what he said were attacks on his atheism. He ultimately won comfortably, the beneficiary of Wilson's fund-raising and political machine. He won re-election in 1992 in a newly configured district encompassing Sacramento's north and northeastern suburbs.

A double amputee, Collins was injured by a grenade during his second tour of duty in Vietnam, undergoing 19 surgeries in seven military hospitals over the course of 22 months. Collins now wears prostheses on his right arm and leg. He's a tireless advocate for veterans' causes and can be very unforgiving when anyone questions American foreign policy. During the early days of the Persian Gulf War, he proclaimed that anyone questioning the U.S. presence is "a whining, sniveling dirt bag."

Yet Collins finds it easy to poke fun at himself. In 1992, he held a fund-raiser advertised as "the Happy Hook Hour" for "one-armed Irish assemblymen." He's become a memorable Sacramento fixture with a series of shocking remarks and out-of-the-ordinary behavior. His short stint as director of the youth authority was marked by his policy decision to return wards' letters if they contained grammatical or spelling errors. As director of the California Conservation Corps in the midst of Gov. Jerry Brown's Medfly crisis, Collins drank Malathion in an effort to prove that the insecticide was harmless. He was less supportive of Brown's re-entry into national politics. "People do not want a screaming, red-faced temper tantrum to be conducting the foreign relations of this country," he told a reporter as Brown campaigned for president in 1992. The news media always loves a clown, so Collins has enjoyed fawning press coverage. Particularly during his years with Jerry Brown, reporters were willing to ignore his public drinking bouts, which were excessive on occasion.

Collins tells anyone willing to listen that he hates his own job as a legislator. That contempt is reflected in his legislative accomplishments, which were almost nil in his first term. But he also has told supporters that he intends to continue his service to Wilson, whom he calls "the toughest S.O.B. I ever met," and run for re-election in 1994.

PERSONAL: elected 1991; born Oct. 17, 1940, Mount Vernon, New York; home, Carmichael; Army, 1964-68 (Vietnam); education, B.S. Santa Clara University, J.D. Santa Clara University School of Law; single; atheist.

CAREER: attorney; Santa Clara University placement director, 1974-1975; deputy legislative secretary, executive secretary and chief of staff to Gov. Edmund G. "Jerry" Brown Jr., 1976-79 and 1981-83; director, California Conservation Corps 1979-1981; investment banker, Kidder, Peabody & Co. 1983-1989; chief deputy state treasurer February 1989-January 1991; director, California Youth Authority March, 1991-July 1991.

COMMITTEES: Human Services (vice chair); Education; Judiciary; Water, Parks & Wildlife.

OFFICES: Capitol, (916) 445-4445, FAX (916) 323-9411; district, 4811 Chippendale, 304-B Sacramento 95841, (916) 349-1995, FAX (916) 349-1999.

TERM LIMIT: 1996

REGISTRATION: 45.3% D, 42.6% R

1992 CAMPAIGN:			
Collins – R	58.8%	$638,484
Joan Barry – D	41.2%	$22,493

SEPT. 17, 1991 SPECIAL ELECTION:

Collins – R	62.1%	$388,659
David McCann – L	37.9%	

RATINGS:

AFL-CIO	CalPIRG	CLCV	NOW	CofC	CalFarm
NR	30	NR	43	100	80

KEY VOTES:

Timber compromise:	NO	Execution by injection:	NO	
Limited gay rights:	NO	Universal health insur:	NO	1992-93 Budget Act: YES
Campaign Reform:	NO	Offshore oil ban:	NO	Charter schools: YES

Tom Connolly (D)

77th Assembly District

This San Diego County district includes the communities of Chula Vista, La Mesa, El Cajon and Lemon Grove as well as a portion of the city of San Diego east of National City. Registration is 39 percent Democratic and 44 percent Republican, but Tom Connolly won the Assembly seat with 44 percent of the vote in a surprise upset that was aided by last-minute Democratic money.

Tom Connolly

Democrats poured about $200,000 into Connolly's campaign in the last few weeks and quickly snipped away Republican Steve Baldwin's lead. The money was used to buy mailers portraying Baldwin as a right-wing Christian fanatic, an image that was further enhanced by a 1991 speech in which Baldwin claimed that the U.S. Air Force had an "official witch."

Democratic strategists recognized that the bitter GOP primary fight between Baldwin and a more moderate former Chula Vista mayor, Gregory Cox, had created an unusual opportunity for the last-minute ambush.

That primary was the real battleground in the 77th District. Baldwin had snagged the nomination with strong backing from the Christian right, which has been especially active in San Diego County. He also had the backing of anti-abortion and gun-control groups. Cox, who had joined the Governor's Office of Planning and Research in April 1991 as a liaison to local government, quit his job with the administration to run for the seat with the blessings of Gov. Wilson and other moderate Republican leaders. After the bitter battle, some of Cox's Republican supporters undoubtedly cast their November votes for Democrat Connolly.

During a practice floor session for new Assembly members shortly after Connolly arrived, he noted that, since motions and bills need an absolute number of votes to pass, either 41 or 54, members could abstain and have the effect of voting no without actually doing so. Democratic floor leader Tom Hannigan cut him off.

"That," Hannigan said, "is a discussion we will have in (closed) caucus." Connolly showed he learns fast. "Oh, captain, my captain, yes sir," he said.

PERSONAL: elected 1992; born May 12, 1946, in Toledo, Ohio; home, Lemon Grove; Army, 1968-70 and USMC 1974-1977; education, B.A. CSU Northridge, J.D. Pepperdine; wife Janet; Roman Catholic.

CAREER: judge advocate USMC; trial lawyer; deputy public attorney; child advocate attorney; vice chair California Conservation Corps board.

COMMITTEES: Government Organization, Judiciary, Public Employees Retirement & Social Security; Revenue & Taxation.

OFFICES: Capitol, (916) 445-3266, FAX (916) 323-8470; district, 323 Olive St., Lemon Grove 91945 (619) 465-7723, FAX (619) 279-9515.

TERM LIMIT: 1998

REGISTRATION: 39.2% D, 44.8% R, 2.1% AIP

1992 CAMPAIGN:	Connelly – D	47.8%	$132,719
	Steve Baldwin – R	44.6%	$337,694
	Jeff Bishop – L	6.1%	

RATINGS and **KEY VOTES**: Newly elected

Mickey Conroy (R)
71st Assembly District

Republicans have this Orange County district wrapped up so tightly that Democrats represent little more than a blip on the registration rolls. The district includes Orange, Villa Park, Mission Viejo and a slice of San Clemente.

Conservative Republican Mickey Conroy won a 1991 special election following a game of musical chairs that saw the former assemblyman for the district, John Lewis, elected to the state Senate to replace John Seymour, who had been appointed to the U.S. Senate by Gov. Pete Wilson. Conroy, a retired Marine Corps pilot, defeated Orange City Councilman William Stener, a moderate backed by the governor, to take the GOP nomination in the

Mickey Conroy

special election. Conroy easily won the runoff election against Democrat Greg Ramsay of Orange. In his re-election bid, Conroy outdistanced Democrat Bea Foster 62 percent to 39 percent.

One of Conroy's first actions upon arriving in Sacramento was to revive old arguments that former anti-Vietnam War activist Tom Hayden should be thrown out of the Legislature. Conroy, a Vietnam veteran, asked the Senate to refuse Hayden the 23rd Senate District seat he won in the 1992 election because Hayden's anti-war activities allegedly violated the state constitution.

Hayden, a Santa Monica Democrat who has served in the Assembly since 1982, countered in a letter to lawmakers that Conroy was recycling "false and slanderous charges" and was attempting to have the Senate override the will of the voters. Hayden survived similar moves to oust him from the Assembly and weathered the Conroy attack as well.

Conroy was one of 23 Assembly Republicans who sent a letter to Gov. Wilson in July 1992 asking him to slash state family planning funds. Wilson had backed bigger budgets for the state Office of Family Planning as part of his preventive-government strategy. But the letter argued that "this controversial, failed program" should not receive preferential treatment when many other state programs are taking major cuts. The letter also called for restrictions on state-funded abortions. The governor's office replied that Wilson was and would continue to be supportive of family planning efforts throughout the state.

PERSONAL: elected 1991 special election; born Nov. 1, 1927, in Footedale, Pa.; home, Orange; USMC retired; education, attended University of Maryland and University of Virginia; wife Ann, two children; Roman Catholic.

CAREER: 21 years in the USMC; businessman.

COMMITTEES: Finance & Insurance; Health; Utilities & Commerce.

OFFICES: Capitol, (916) 445-2778, FAX (916) 324-6872; district, 1940 N. Tustin St, 102, Orange, 92665, (714) 998-0980, FAX (714) 998-7102.

  TERM LIMIT: 1996

  REGISTRATION: 29.4% D, 57.4% R

1992 CAMPAIGN:	Conroy – R	61.8%	$195,735
	Bea Foster – D	38.2%	$2,450

SEPT. 17, 1991 SPECIAL ELECTION:

	Conroy – R	70.8%	$108,484
	Gregory Ramsey – D	29.2%	

RATINGS:	AFL-CIO	CalPIRG	CLCV	NOW	CofC	CalFarm
	NR	25	NR	29	100	85

  KEY VOTES:

Timber compromise:	NO	Execution by injection:	YES	
Limited gay rights:	NO	Universal health insur:	NO	1992-93 Budget Act:	YES
Campaign Reform:	NO	Offshore oil ban:	NO	Charter schools:	YES

Dominic L. Cortese (D)

23rd Assembly District

Dominic Cortese spent 12 years on the Santa Clara County Board of Supervisors before he was elected to the Assembly in 1980. It prepared him well for what has become his primary role in the lower house: an advocate for local government.

For years, Cortese was chairman of the Assembly Committee on Local Government, figuring out ways for local governments to operate in the wake of the property tax-cutting Proposition 13. One of his proposals was to permit – with voter approval – creation of county "service areas" that would have allowed assessments on residents for increased police protection. It was vetoed. Cortese successfully authored several major – though obscure – laws regulating land development.

Dominic Cortese

In 1990, Cortese moved on to a more daunting challenge: He became chairman of the Water, Parks and Wildlife Committee. As such, he is emerging as a major player on water issues. In 1990, he introduced a bill that sent shivers up the backs of developers. It would have required them to identify "a long-term, reliable supply of water" before permits could be issued for a project. And at the behest of the wine industry, he proposed a modest increase in the liquor tax in a constitutional amendment (Proposition 126) designed to head off a steeper tax (Proposition 134) also on the November 1990 ballot. Both of his efforts failed.

Cortese comes from a third-generation San Jose area farm family and is independently wealthy through his family grocery. (He also owns the San Jose Jammers, an expansion team in the minor league Continental Basketball Association.) He is a political moderate who fits his district well. Still, Cortese faced a stiff challenge in 1988 from Republican Buck Norred, who attempted to tie Cortese to liberal Assembly Speaker Willie Brown.

In August 1990, Cortese was charged by the Sacramento County district attorney Steve White with receiving a gift exceeding $10 "that was made and arranged by a lobbyist" between Jan. 1, 1987, and June 1, 1988. Cortese allegedly contacted Carl Burg, a lobbyist for the Painting and Decorating Contractors of California, about bids for a house-painting job when Cortese was sponsoring a bill of interest to painters and decorators. Burg contacted a contractor who bid $3,740 and painted the house. Prosecutors said the contractor wasn't paid, and Cortese later listed it as a gift. He denied any wrongdoing but eventually pleaded no contest in April 1991 and was fined $7,050 and ordered to do 100 hours of community service.

Republicans, curiously, did not attempt to exploit Cortese's legal troubles during the 1990 election and there were reports that Speaker Brown had made a clandestine deal with GOP leaders. They would lay off Cortese and in return, so it was said, the Democrats would not attempt to unseat Glendale Assemblyman Pat Nolan, who was under investigation by federal authorities as part of the probe of influence-peddling in the Capitol. Whatever the case, Cortese faced more substantial trouble in 1992, when reapportionment radically altered districts in the San Jose area. But colleague John Vasconcellos gave Cortese the most Democratic of the new districts, which allowed him to win election to a seventh term.

PERSONAL: elected 1980; born Sept. 27, 1932, in San Jose; home, San Jose; Army 1954-1956; education, B.S. University of Santa Clara; wife Suzanne, five children; Roman Catholic.

CAREER: businessman and farmer, part-owner of Cortese Bros. grocery chain; Santa Clara County Board of Supervisors 1968-1980.

COMMITTEES: Water, Parks & Wildlife (chair); Governmental Organization; Revenue & Taxation; (joint) Legislative Audit; Refugee Resettlement, International Migration & Cooperative Development.

OFFICES: Capitol, (916) 445-8243, FAX (916) 323-8898; district, 100 Paseo de San Antonio, 300, San Jose 95113, (408) 269-6500, FAX (418) 277-1036.

TERM LIMIT: 1996

REGISTRATION: 60.5% D, 24.3% R

1992 CAMPAIGN:	Cortese – D	65.9%	$177,654
	Monica Valladares – R	34.1%	$1,065
1990 CAMPAIGN:	Cortese – D	56.2%	$302,671
	Ron Granada – R	38.1%	$27,934

RATINGS:	AFL-CIO	CalPIRG	CLCV	NOW	CofC	CalFarm
	95	100	85	79	33	35

KEY VOTES:

Parent consent abort:	YES	Limit product tort:	YES	Clean Air Act:	YES
Assault gun ban:	YES	Ban AIDS discrim:	YES	Restrict abortion funds:	nv
Sales tax hike:	YES	Wealth tax hike:	YES	Strong gay rights:	YES
Parental leave:	YES	Timber compromise:	nv	Execution by injection:	YES
Limited gay rights:	YES	Universal health insur:	YES	1992-93 Budget Act:	YES
Campaign Reform:	YES	Offshore oil ban:	YES	Charter schools:	YES

James M. Costa (D)
30th Assembly District

Jim Costa is one of the few members of the Assembly to retain his old number – 30 – even though the district boundaries in the agricultural southern part of the San Joaquin Valley were changed markedly by reapportionment. Once encompassing all or portions of four counties, the new district retained just one section of the old 30th, Kings County, and gained the western half of Kern County, including a small piece of Bakersfield. The 30th Assembly District is almost entirely rural and agricultural, but any resemblance to small family farming is purely coincidental. The game is agribusiness – agriculture on a large and scientific scale – dominated by a relative handful of huge corporate farmers such as the immense J.G. Boswell Co.

Costa, who was once referred to as congressional timber, is a tenacious and skillful politician who works hard for his district. But he is also weighed down by political baggage that could hold him back.

Costa began his career working for Rep. B.F. Sisk, then was an assistant to Rep. John Krebs and, finally, was administrative assistant to Assemblyman (now Rep.) Richard Lehman before winning a seat in the Assembly.

During his more than 10 years in the Assembly, Costa has become an ace legislative technician and one of Assembly Speaker Willie Brown's lieutenants. In 1990, he was chosen by his fellow Assembly Democrats as caucus leader, the No. 4 party position in the lower house. To accept the job, however, Costa gave up chairmanship of the Assembly Water, Parks and Wildlife Committee, where he had protected his district's water interests since 1983.

Jim Costa

On the upside of Costa's career, he's carried several major bond issues, including one that voters approved in 1990 that will result in the expenditure of $1 billion on upgrading rail transportation. He also has doggedly pushed – so far unsuccessfully – to move the state's presidential primary to March in an effort to give California more clout in the selection of candidates.

On the downside, Costa has become one of the Capitol's big juice players, carrying legislation for special-interest groups and accepting large campaign contributions, gifts and speaking fees. He unsuccessfully pushed several anti-rent-control bills for landlords, as well as a measure for beer wholesalers that would have guaranteed them territorial monopolies, which eventually was vetoed by Gov. George Deukmejian.

But it was Costa's arrest on the last night of the 1986 legislative session that brought him his greatest notoriety. Just weeks before he was to face voters for re-election, and while traveling in a state-leased car with a known prostitute at his side, Costa offered $50 to an undercover woman police officer to join them in a three-way sex act, Sacramento police said. Nearly a week later, with his mother nearby, Costa admitted during a press conference in his home district that he had made an error in judgment. Later that month, he was fined $1 and given three years' probation. The episode would have spelled the end of a political career for anyone from a district with a different makeup of voters. But Republicans failed to capitalize on the incident and Costa easily won re-election.

Facing the end of his Assembly career in 1996 under term limits, Costa is now eyeing a seat in the state Senate. He'll run in a special election in 1993 to fill an old, Kern County-centered seat that Republican Don Rogers gave up after he won election in a neighboring district. And if Costa wins the special election, it would give him an incumbency from which to run for re-election in 1994 from a newly created district covering much of the same territory.

PERSONAL: elected 1978; born April 13, 1952, in Fresno; home, Fresno; education, B.S. CSU Fresno; single; Roman Catholic.

CAREER: aide to Rep. B.F. Sisk 1974-1975 and Rep. John Krebs 1975-1976; assistant to Assemblyman Richard Lehman 1976-1978; Assembly Democratic Caucus chair 1991-1992.

COMMITTEES: Transportation; Water, Parks & Wildlife; Ways & Means; (joint) Energy Regulation & the Environment; Fisheries & Aquaculture.

OFFICES: Capitol, (916) 445-7558, FAX (916) 323-1097; district, 1111 Fulton Mall, 914, Fresno 93721, (209) 264-3078, FAX (209) 445-6506; 512 N. Irwin, Hanford 92320, (209) 582-2869.

TERM LIMIT: 1996

REGISTRATION: 56.9% D, 32.2% R, 2.1% AIP

1992 CAMPAIGN:	Costa – D	65.2%	$541,124
	Gerald Hurt – R	34.8%	$17,040
1990 CAMPAIGN:	Costa – D	62.4%	$407,911
	Gerald Hurt – R	37.6%	$8,070

RATINGS:	AFL-CIO	CalPIRG	CLCV	NOW	CofC	CalFarm
	83	86	74	72	33	65

KEY VOTES:

Parent consent abort:	YES	Limit product tort:	YES	Clean Air Act:	YES
Assault gun ban:	YES	Ban AIDS discrim:	YES	Restrict abortion funds:	NO
Sales tax hike:	YES	Wealth tax hike:	YES	Strong gay rights:	YES
Parental leave:	YES	Timber compromise:	YES	Execution by injection:	YES
Limited gay rights:	YES	Universal health insur:	YES	1992-93 Budget Act:	YES
Campaign Reform:	YES	Offshore oil ban:	NO	Charter schools:	YES

Delaine Eastin (D)
20th Assembly District

When Democrat Alister McAlister retired from the Assembly in 1986, Republicans theorized that they might have a chance to pick up his seat, despite its nominally Democratic voter registration. McAlister was one of the most conservative Democrats in the Capitol and his 18th District, the eastern portions of San Jose and nearby suburbs, had a conservative bent to its voting patterns. Both parties made heavy commitments of time, money and people to the contest to succeed McAlister, but a Union City councilwoman named Delaine Eastin saved the seat for the Democrats and has had little trouble keeping it. The 1992 reapportionment pushed the district's boundaries further into the bedroom towns of Alameda and Santa Clara counties, and changed its number to 20.

Eastin, meanwhile, has emerged as one of the Assembly's smartest, hardest working and most pugnacious members. She may be the most riveting woman orator ever to serve in the Legislature. She would even have a chance of becoming the Assembly's first female speaker – if term limits didn't decree that she must leave the house by 1996. Eastin's principal concern is public education and as the chair of the Assembly Education Committee she has been one of the most passionate defenders of school financing during several years of budgetary austerity. It's a role that has not endeared her to Gov. Pete Wilson, whom she often portrays as the bad guy. In defending education's money she has become the darling of the California Teachers Association and other school unions.

Delaine Eastin

Eastin became a tiger on school finance after Assembly Speaker Willie Brown – who is very close to CTA's leaders – inexplicably dumped the Education Committee's longtime chair, Teresa Hughes, and replaced her with Eastin in early 1991. The difference between Hughes and Eastin was subtle but important. Hughes had opposed a compromise in 1989 that shifted some school funding from urban to suburban schools. Eastin supported it. In fact, by selecting Eastin to chair the Education Committee, Speaker Willie Brown appeared to be trying to shore up a weakness in the suburbs on the politically vital issue of education. In picking Eastin, the speaker signaled that the balance of power on education issues was shifting away from Los Angeles. Ray Edmand, president of the Small Schools Association, welcomed Eastin's appointment, saying she "is out of that Los Angeles aura, that Los Angeles sphere of influence."

As Eastin's legislative career has expanded, she has moved politically to the left, away from the moderate politics she adopted as a candidate in 1986. But since she faces no real opposition at the polls, deviation from the politics of her suburban constituents has not hurt her. For example, she declined until late in the 1986 campaign to say whether she supported retention of Chief Justice Rose Bird, a litmus test to many conservatives. She ultimately announced her opposition to Bird, causing the National Organization for Women to drop its endorsement of her. By 1990, however, Eastin had earned a 100 percent rating from NOW.

Eastin kept her distance from Dianne Feinstein's gubernatorial bid in 1990. She publicly stated that Feinstein had snubbed her initial bid for office so she was returning the favor. Eastin instead endorsed John Van de Kamp in the Democratic gubernatorial primary to the displeasure of a number of her women colleagues.

In the Legislature, Eastin has carried a solid list of bills, including those aimed at helping consumers, such as pushing for a pilot project to see if it is feasible and economical to keep the Department of Motor Vehicles open Saturdays to better serve drivers. She is a favorite of environmentalists and has become an advocate for senior citizens. She has also pushed hard for streamlining the San Francisco Bay Area's tangled web of transit districts. Eastin's AB 4 was part of the waste management package signed into law by Gov. George Deukmejian in 1989, setting up market incentives for recycled products. At the start of the 1991-92 session, Eastin reintroduced measures to provide $10,000 grants to cash-strapped school libraries and to reorganize the state's approval process for designing and constructing public buildings – measures vetoed by Deukmejian.

Eastin's intensity, however, can be annoying. Her speaking style often crosses the line into loud lectures rather than gentle persuasion – and her colleagues grumble about it. Her brusk manner could be a hindrance if she decides to run for state school superintendent in 1994, as many expect her to do.

PERSONAL: elected 1986; born Aug. 20, 1947, in San Diego; home, Union City; education, B.A. UC Davis, M.A. UC Santa Barbara; husband Jack Saunders; non-denominational Christian.

CAREER: corporate planner; political science professor De Anza Community College; City Council Union City.

COMMITTEES: Education (chair); Consumer Protection, Governmental Efficiency & New Technologies; Governmental Organization; Transportation.

OFFICES: Capitol, (916) 445-7874, FAX (916) 324-2936; district, 39650 Liberty St., 160, Fremont 94538, (510) 791-2151, FAX (510) 794-3841.

TERM LIMIT: 1996

REGISTRATION: 50.5% D, 33.0% R

1992 CAMPAIGN:	Eastin – D		64.1%		$471,214
	Lindy Batara – R		35.9%		$13,309
1990 CAMPAIGN:	Eastin – D		100%		$410,523

RATINGS:	AFL-CIO	CalPIRG	CLCV	NOW	CofC	CalFarm
	96	100	96	100	22	20

KEY VOTES:

Parent consent abort:	NO	Limit product tort:	YES	Clean Air Act:	YES
Assault gun ban:	YES	Ban AIDS discrim:	YES	Restrict abortion funds:	NO
Sales tax hike:	YES	Wealth tax hike:	YES	Strong gay rights:	YES
Parental leave:	YES	Timber compromise:	YES	Execution by injection:	YES
Limited gay rights:	YES	Universal health insur:	YES	1992-93 Budget Act:	NO
Campaign Reform:	YES	Offshore oil ban:	YES	Charter schools:	YES

Robert D. Epple (D)
56th Assembly District

Reapportionment, when done by an impartial party such as the state Supreme Court, is supposed to create more truly competitive districts than would be drawn by partisan lawmakers. But that didn't prove to be the case in 1992. The court's remap of districts eliminated all but a handful of the districts where no party has a distinct advantage. The 56th is one of the few competitive districts that remain.

In 1988, Norwalk attorney Robert Epple was the surprise winner. Democrat

Epple didn't win by much – 220 votes – but his defeat of incumbent Wayne Grisham helped solidify the Democrats' majority in the Assembly. The court-ordered reapportionment fiddled with the boundaries of the district a bit and changed its number (from 63 to 56), but it was left without a clear partisan edge – a fact demonstrated in the 1992 elections when once again Epple won by the scantiest of margins, fewer than 500 votes over Republican Phillip Hawkins out of more than 130,000 ballots cast.

Robert Epple

The Democratic hierarchy in Sacramento, sensing that Epple was one of its vulnerable incumbents, poured money and people into the district while Hawkins' support from the Republicans was less impressive. Epple represents the kind of district that would appear Democratic. It is comprised mainly of blue-collar communities such as Downey sprawled along Los Angeles County's southern border–communities that were built to house workers in nearby aerospace plants. In recent years, the area has developed large middle-class Asian and Latino populations, nearly 40 perent in the 56th District. But Democrats here are conservative to moderate and they often vote for Republicans.

Grisham, a former congressman, seized the seat in 1984, after Democrat Bruce Young, under investigation for his financial dealings with a campaign contributor, decided not to seek re-election. Grisham, however, had proven to be a lackadaisical campaigner in a 1987 special election to fill a vacant Senate seat. Assembly Speaker Willie Brown and other Democratic leaders smelled blood. They poured money and staff into the district and came out winners.

At the start of his first term, the rotund and affable Epple went to great lengths to walk the moderate line and not give his opponents ammunition to tag him as a Brown puppet. He bucked the Democratic leadership by voting against restricting semiautomatic military-style assault weapons, one of six Democrats to do so. In time, however, Epple has taken a decidedly more liberal line as evidenced by his 100 percent rating scores by three generally liberal organizations. Among his bills, Epple carried a measure to increase the maximum home loans for Cal-Vet loans, a popular issue in his district. But he has remained a low-profile member.

PERSONAL: elected 1988; born Sept. 18, 1947, in Hollywood; home, Norwalk; Army 1966-1970; education, Cerritos Community College and CSU Dominguez Hills, J.D. American College of Law; wife Cheryl, one child; Protestant.

CAREER: lawyer; tax consultant; Cerritos Community College board of trustees 1981-1988.

COMMITTEES: Agriculture; Judiciary; Ways & Means.

OFFICES: Capitol, (916) 445-6047, FAX (916) 327-1784; district, 12009 E. Firestone Blvd., Norwalk 90650, (310) 868-1485, FAX (310) 863-9136.
TERM LIMIT: 1996
REGISTRATION: 49.8% D, 39.0% R

1992 CAMPAIGN:	Epple – D	47.8%	$772,571
	Phillip Hawkins – R	47.4%	$575,164
1990 CAMPAIGN:	Epple – D	59.6%	$502,411
	Diane Boggs – R	40.4%	$77,811

| **RATINGS**: | AFL-CIO | CalPIRG | CLCV | NOW | CofC | CalFarm |
| | 95 | 82 | 87 | 50 | 28 | 20 |

KEY VOTES:

Assault gun ban:	NO	Ban AIDS discrim:	YES	Restrict abortion funds:	NO
Sales tax hike:	YES	Wealth tax hike:	YES	Strong gay rights:	nv
Parental leave:	YES	Timber compromise:	YES	Execution by injection:	YES
Limited gay rights:	YES	Universal health insur:	YES	1992-93 Budget Act:	YES
Campaign Reform:	NO	Offshore oil ban:	YES	Charter schools:	YES

Martha M. Escutia (D)
50th Assembly District

This is one of several districts created by the state Supreme Court specifically to comply with the federal Voting Rights Act, which requires maximization of political opportunities for minority groups. The district embraces a chunk of southeastern Los Angeles plus the cities of Huntington Park and South Gate, and has the largest Latino population of any Assembly district, nearly 90 percent, as well as a comfortable 3-1 Democratic registration majority.

Obviously, the 1992 Democratic primary was the only election that counted and it featured one of several contests between rival Latino groups. One faction is headed by state Sen. Art Torres and Los Angeles City Councilman Richard Alatorre, and the

Martha Escutia

other by Los Angeles County Supervisor Gloria Molina. The Torres-Alatorre candidate was Martha Escutia, an attorney and executive of a non-profit organization. The Molina group picked businesswoman Pat Acosta. After a spirited duel, Escutia won. Her November runoff with Republican Gladys Miller was an afterthought.

PERSONAL: elected 1992; born Jan. 16, 1958, in Los Angeles; home, Huntington Park; education, B.A. University of Southern California, law degree Georgetown University; single; Catholic.

CAREER: attorney, vice president of government affairs and public policy, United Way.

COMMITTEES: Transportation (vice chair); Health; Labor & Employment; Public Employees, Retirement & Social Security; Water, Parks & Wildlife.

OFFICES: Capitol, (916) 445-8188 FAX (916) 324-0012; district, 3512 E. Florence Ave., 201, Huntington Park 90255, (213) 582-7774.

TERM LIMIT: 1998

REGISTRATION: 67.9% D, 20.6% R

1992 CAMPAIGN:	Escutia – D	75.0%	$180,246
	Gladys Miller – R	25.0%	$5,362

RATINGS and **KEY VOTES**: Newly elected

Samuel S. Farr (D)
27th Assembly District

There are those who believe the Central Coast of California is the most beautiful spot on earth. The political custodian of that stretch of California, and its many contradictory forces, is Sam Farr, whose 27th Assembly District – renumbered but little changed in political or social ambience by reapportionment – runs along the coast from Santa Cruz through the Big Sur region south of Monterey to the San Luis Obispo County line. It's an area in which the forces favoring development and those favoring environmental preservation are locked in mortal combat. Farr tries to sidestep as much of the controversy as possible, although he defines himself as an environmental protectionist.

Sam Farr

The son of a state legislator and a onetime legislative staffer himself, Farr was a Monterey County supervisor before winning the Assembly seat in 1980. Given the high rate of turnover in the Assembly, that gives him a fairly high level of seniority, but he has seen the plums of power passed to other hands. To observers of the Assembly, Farr is known mostly as a talented amateur photographer who snaps pictures of his colleagues during floor sessions. He seems to lack the fire to engage in the sometimes brutal politics that lead to power and is seemingly content to practice micro, rather than macro, politics.

Farr took over the chairmanship of the Local Government Committee after the 1990 elections. The Local Government Committee shapes legislation defining the relationship between the state and local governments. Growth-related issues in the 1990s likely will be fought out on Farr's committee, including increasingly voguish proposals to set up regional growth-management agencies.

Farr doesn't have any trouble getting re-elected in a district with a fairly strong Democratic voter registration. (It dropped slightly when reapportionment extended the district southward along the coast.) But he probably will leave the Assembly in 1993 and take his camera to Congress. As of this writing, he was the leading candidate to replace longtime Rep. Leon Panetta, who was appointed budget director in the Clinton-Gore administration.

PERSONAL: elected 1980; born July 4, 1941, in San Francisco; home, Carmel; Peace Corps; education, B.S. Willamette University, attended Monterey Institute of Foreign Studies and Santa Clara School of Law; wife Sharon Baldwin, one child; Episcopalian.

CAREER: assistant administrative analyst for the legislative analyst's office 1969-1971; chief consultant to Assembly Constitutional Amendments Committee 1972-1975; Monterey County Board of Supervisors 1975-1980.

COMMITTEES: Local Government (chair); Education; Finance & Insurance; Natural Resources; Televising the Assembly; (joint) Arts (vice chair); Fisheries & Aquaculture; Refugee Resettlement, International Migration & Cooperative Development; Science & Technology.

OFFICES: Capitol, (916) 445-8496, FAX (916) 327-5914; district, 1200 Aguajito Road, 203, Monterey 93940, (408) 646-1980; 701 Ocean St., 318B, Santa Cruz 95060, (408) 646-1980, FAX (408) 649-2867.

TERM LIMIT: 1996

REGISTRATION: 50.9% D, 30.5% R, 2.8% Green

1992 CAMPAIGN:	Farr – D	60.7%	$335,698
	Susan Whitman – R	35.1%	$22,234
1990 CAMPAIGN:	Farr – D	71.5%	$296,236
	West Walker – R	28.5%	$99

RATINGS:	AFL-CIO	CalPIRG	CLCV	NOW	CofC	CalFarm
	93	100	88	100	17	30

KEY VOTES:

Parent consent abort:	NO	Limit product tort:	YES	Clean Air Act:	YES
Assault gun ban:	YES	Ban AIDS discrim:	YES	Restrict abortion funds:	nv
Sales tax hike:	YES	Wealth tax hike:	YES	Strong gay rights:	YES
Parental leave:	YES	Timber compromise:	YES	Execution by injection:	YES
Limited gay rights:	YES	Universal health insur:	YES	1992-93 Budget Act:	YES
Campaign Reform:	YES	Offshore oil ban:	YES	Charter schools:	YES

Gilbert W. Ferguson (R)

70th Assembly District

Imbedded on the tony beachfront of Orange County, this district includes Newport Beach, Costa Mesa and Laguna Beach. Towns that are the epitome of upscale California suburbanization. Condos, hotels and estates are jammed along the bluffs above the beach. Development here is one of the major reasons voters statewide approved the Coastal Protection Act in 1972, setting up the Coastal Commission and a system for growth control along the shoreline.

Not surprisingly, this stronghold of BMWs and cellular phones had been the most Republican district in the state during the 1980s. But there are pockets of Democratic voters, particularly in Laguna Beach, which has a politically active gay community and turned out by the thousands when Michael Dukakis made a campaign stop in 1988.

The district is so safe for Republicans that it appears incumbent Gil Ferguson can do all sorts of

Gil Ferguson

outlandish things and still not be in trouble with voters. He can vote against the interests of Orange County on transportation issues. He can attempt to rewrite school books to reflect an ultraconservative view of history. And he can even say outrageous things about every ethnic minority and his gay constituents.

Ferguson was elected to the Assembly in 1984 and became a core member of the conservative "cavemen" who made Pat Nolan the Republican Assembly leader. He tends to shoot from the hip. The retired Marine railed against resolutions to make amends for interning Japanese Americans in World War II. "The veterans of Pearl Harbor have read this, and they are outraged!" he said in August 1989, bringing Assemblyman Phil Isenberg, whose wife was among those interned during the war, to his feet. "You should be ashamed!" huffed Isenberg.

Toward the end of the 1990 session, Ferguson fought back with his own resolution, ACR 181, calling on state schools to teach "an honest, objective and balanced" version of history that excuses America for requiring 120,000 Japanese Americans and Japanese immigrants to live behind barbed-wire fences during World War II. It was obvious Ferguson was directing his resolution toward an audience somewhere other than in the Assembly, when, in his floor speech, he told cable TV viewers: "I'd advise you to tape this." He got four votes in the Assembly: his own, Cathie Wright, Phil Wyman, who ran for Congress in 1992 and lost in the primary, and Marian LaFollette, who has since retired.

Ferguson is best known for his effort to oust Tom Hayden from the Legislature. Ferguson has called Hayden a traitor for supporting the North Vietnamese during the war, and he refuses to vote for any bill with Hayden's name on it. Ferguson came close to winning enough votes to have Hayden bounced in 1986.

Aside from his pyrotechnics in the Assembly, Ferguson is a lackluster legislator, authoring little legislation of any note and showing scant interest in learning much about the bills before him in committees. Instead, he spins off elaborate theories about the forces of evil, which usually means Democrats and Communists. He insists that Republican U.S. Attorney David Levi was manipulated by Democrats into investigating the Republican honchos in the Assembly. Never mind that, so far, only Democrats have been prosecuted.

That's why it came as a shock to many people when Ferguson, shortly after the 1992 election, warned in a newspaper interview that the Republican Party is in jeopardy of becoming a minority party if its members don't stop bickering over controversial social issues such as abortion and gay rights. A longtime abortion opponent, Ferguson maintained that abortion rights is no longer an issue, and advocated removing the anti-abortion rights plank from the Republican platform. To do otherwise, he argued, will cause serious harm to the Republican Party. In addition, and equally surprising given his track record on such issues, Ferguson called on his party to increase its base by reaching out to minorities.

PERSONAL: elected 1984; born April 22, 1923, in St. Louis, Mo.; home, Balboa Island; USMC 1942-1968 WWII, Korea and Vietnam; education, attended USC, University of Maryland, B.A. Akron University; wife Anita Wollert, four children; Protestant.

CAREER: officer USMC; president of Corporate Communication, a Newport Beach advertising and public relations firm; corporate vice president of The Gilita Co., a housing development firm; newspaper publisher; columnist for Freedom Newspapers, including the Orange County Register; artist.

COMMITTEES: Finance & Insurance; Housing & Community Development; Revenue & Taxation.

OFFICES: Capitol, (916) 445-7222, FAX (916) 324-3657; district, 4299 MacArthur Blvd., 204, Newport Beach 92660, (714) 756-0665, FAX (714) 756-1935.

TERM LIMIT: 1996

REGISTRATION: 30.0% D, 55.3% R

1992 CAMPAIGN: Ferguson – R 56.7% $327,998
Jim Toledano – D 36.2% $62,845
Scott Bieser – L 7.1%
1990 CAMPAIGN: Ferguson – R 64.7% $406,651
Howard Adler – D 35.3% $1,448

RATINGS:	AFL-CIO	CalPIRG	CLCV	NOW	CofC	CalFarm
	6	19	52	9	94	75

KEY VOTES:

Parent consent abort:	YES	Limit product tort:	YES	Clean Air Act:		NO
Assault gun ban:	NO	Ban AIDS discrim:	NO	Restrict abortion funds:		nv
Sales tax hike:	NO	Wealth tax hike:	NO	Strong gay rights:		NO
Parental leave:	NO	Timber compromise:	NO	Execution by injection:		YES
Limited gay rights:	NO	Universal health insur:	NO	1992-93 Budget Act:		YES
Campaign Reform:	NO	Offshore oil ban:	NO	Charter schools:		YES

Robert C. Frazee (R)

74th Assembly District

This San Diego County district includes the very Republican communities of Vista, San Marcos, Escondido, Del Mar and Solana Beach. Retirees are the fastest-growing segment of the population. Those who work tend to receive their paychecks from one of the sprawling military installations in the area or from businesses in the service sector.

Robert Frazee is another conservative legislator who mirrors his district. Frazee was president of a family-owned flower-growing business when he was elected to the Assembly in 1978. Prior to that, he had been on the Carlsbad City Council for six years, including a stint as mayor.

Robert Frazee

Quiet and courtly, Frazee is generally a pro-business, pro-development vote in the traditional Republican mold. But on a few occasions he has broken away to try and find solutions for social problems. He backed state funding for farm-worker housing, in large part because he has been made aware of the problem in his hometown of Carlsbad. Frazee also has worked to try to rescue financially troubled trauma centers and emergency medical centers, problems that plague big cities.

The issue on which Frazee has been most visible, however, was his 1987 bill to require minors to get parental consent before getting abortions. His bill was signed into law, but was then hung up in the courts. In May 1992, a San Francisco Superior Court judge ruled that the law was unconstitutional. Attorney General Dan Lungren filed an appeal, which was still pending in early 1993.

PERSONAL: elected 1978; born Sept. 1, 1928, in San Luis Rey, Calif.; home, Carlsbad; USMC 1950-1952; wife Delores Hedrick, two children; Congregational.

CAREER: construction; horticulturist; Carlsbad City Council, mayor 1972-1978; chairman, Assembly Republican Caucus.

COMMITTEES: Higher Education; Local Government; Transportation; Water, Parks & Wildlife.

OFFICES: Capitol, (916) 445-2390, FAX (916) 324-9991; district, 2121 Palomar Airport, 105, Carlsbad 92009, (619) 438-5665.

TERM LIMIT: 1996

REGISTRATION: 31.3% D, 50.7% R, 2.3% AIP

1992 CAMPAIGN:

Frazee – R	55.9%	$105,712
Ken Lanzer – D	32.0%	$3,275
Mark Hunt – L	6.6%	
Shirley Marcoux – P&F	5.6%	

1990 CAMPAIGN: Frazee – R   56.9% $220,253
                 Gerald Franklin – D   31.3% $2,208

RATINGS:	AFL-CIO	CalPIRG	CLCV	NOW	CofC	CalFarm
	17	32	15	36	94	80

KEY VOTES:

Parent consent abort:	YES	Limit product tort:	YES	Clean Air Act:	YES
Assault gun ban:	NO	Ban AIDS discrim:	NO	Restrict abortion funds:	YES
Sales tax hike:	YES	Wealth tax hike:	YES	Strong gay rights:	NO
Parental leave:	NO	Timber compromise:	NO	Execution by injection:	YES
Limited gay rights:	NO	Universal health insur:	NO	1992-93 Budget Act:	YES
Campaign Reform:	NO	Offshore oil ban:	YES	Charter schools:	YES

Barbara Friedman (D)
40th Assembly District

Los Angeles Democrat Barbara Friedman won a special election in 1991 only to find herself homeless eight months later in the wake of reapportionment. A liberal Democrat with roots in the labor movement, Friedman came to the Assembly after defeating a conservative Republican, Geoffrey Church, in a special election for Mike Roos' seat in the old 46th District. Roos resigned from the Legislature to head a non-profit group working for Los Angeles school system reforms.

Barbara Friedman

In 1992, new district lines put Friedman in a strong Republican district with veteran conservative GOP lawmaker Patrick Nolan of Glendale. The neighboring districts with strong Democratic numbers were staked out by incumbents Terry Friedman and Burt Margolin, for whom Friedman had once worked as chief of staff. So, with no place else to go, Friedman was gearing up for a run against Nolan. Then, unexpectedly, veteran Assemblyman Tom Bane of Tarzana decided to quit after 24 years in the Legislature to help his wife, Marlene, run her political fund-raising and consulting business. The 78-year-old lawmaker's decision to step down probably saved a lot of grief for both Nolan and Friedman.

Nolan kept his seat, defeating his Democratic opponent by a wide margin despite an increased Democratic registration, and Friedman moved back to her childhood home in the San Fernando Valley, where she easily outdistanced her Republican opponent, band leader Horace Heidt Jr.

Assembly Speaker Willie Brown Jr. gave Friedman some political help early on when he named her to the Assembly Insurance Committee, a "juice committee" so named because its members regularly receive big campaign contributions from industry lobbyists.

Friedman, who was a deputy Los Angeles city controller before running for the Assembly, has proven to be a strong supporter of women's issues. She authored AB 3436, which provided that inmates who show evidence of battered women's syndrome have that taken into account when their sentences are reviewed. Gov. Wilson signed the legislation. Another Friedman bill, which would have placed an additional 2-cent tax on cigarettes to go toward breast cancer research, was defeated on the Assembly floor.

The 40th District includes the communities of Canoga Park and Woodland Hills, Van Nuys and North Hollywood. Minority population in the district is about 42 percent, including a 29 percent Latino population.

PERSONAL: elected 1991; born, Sept. 1, 1949, in Los Angeles; home, North Hollywood; education, B.A. U.C. Berkeley; single; Jewish.

CAREER: chief of staff to Assemblyman Burt Margolin, 1983-1985; assistant to district vice president, Communications Workers of America; assistant city controller, city of Los Angeles.

COMMITTEES: Revenue & Taxation; Ways & Means.

OFFICES: Capitol, (916) 445-7644, FAX (916) 323-8459; district 3400 West 6th St., 401, Los Angeles 90020, (213) 386-8042, FAX (213) 386-7098.

TERM LIMIT: 1996

REGISTRATION: 56.1% D, 30.4% R

1992 CAMPAIGN:

Friedman – D		57.8%	$407,855
Horace Heidt – R		30.5%	$74,337
Jean Glasser – P&F		5.0%	

JULY 30, 1991 SPECIAL ELECTION:

Friedman – D	72.5%	$312,263
Geoffrey Church – R	21%	

RATINGS:

AFL-CIO	CalPIRG	CLCV	NOW	CofC	CalFarm
100	100	100	100	17	15

KEY VOTES:

Strong gay rights:	YES			
Parental leave:	YES	Timber compromise:	YES	Execution by injection:	nv
Limited gay rights:	YES	Universal health insur:	YES	1992-93 Budget Act:	YES
Campaign Reform:	YES	Offshore oil ban:	YES	Charter schools:	YES

Terry B. Friedman (D)
41st Assembly District

When Terry Friedman was first elected to the Legislature in 1986, his district, then numbered 43, was a rock-solid liberal enclave encompassing the upscale neighborhoods of Beverly Hills, West Los Angeles, Brentwood, Westwood and the "student ghetto" surrounding UCLA. Friedman, inheriting the seat from Gray Davis as the latter was elected state controller, enjoyed a 20-point Democratic registration edge. Court-ordered reapportionment, however, hammered the "westside" because its population grew only slightly during the 1980s while the rest of the state was exploding with growth. Three Assembly districts became pieces of two districts, one of them the 41st, and Democratic margins dropped sharply as the new districts took in more conservative neighborhoods north of the Santa Monica Mountains in the San Fernando Valley.

Friedman, therefore, had to hustle in 1992 to gain re-election from a district with a Democratic registration under-50 percent. He did it, defeating Santa Monica City Councilwoman Christine Reed in a district that now includes Santa Monica as well as a

Terry Friedman

long stretch of the San Fernando Valley, including Woodland Hills. Friedman's victory was one of the few happy events in 1992 for the westside political organization controlled by Reps. Henry Waxman and Howard Berman. Friedman was hand-picked by the organization in 1986, won the seat by defeating a rival chosen by Assembly Speaker Willie Brown and has been a loyal Berman-Waxman soldier ever since.

As a law student in 1972, Friedman was one of the organizers in West Los Angeles for George McGovern's presidential campaign and later became a poverty housing lawyer. As an Assembly member, Friedman has kept a close alliance with other "Grizzly Bear" liberals and is personally close to Burt Margolin, another Berman-Waxman politician who holds the other westside Assembly seat. He showed early legislative ability, including winning passage of a bill to force employers to give sick time to employees to care for ailing family members. The bill was vetoed, but it marked Friedman's emergence as a serious legislator.

Friedman carried a successful measure for Los Angeles District Attorney Ira Reiner during the latter's unsuccessful bid for attorney general in 1990. The Friedman-authored law imposes criminal charges on employers and their managers if they fail to notify employees of dangerous working conditions or don't disclose concealed product hazards to consumers.

At the start of the 1991 session, Friedman was appointed chairman of the Assembly Labor and Employment Committee, supplanting Tom Hayden. Friedman carried the long-pending bill that would prohibit employment and housing discrimination against gay men, bisexuals and lesbians by granting them the same status as minorities and other groups under the state's Fair Employment and Housing Act. He won passage of the bill in 1991 only to see it vetoed by Gov. Pete Wilson. But a another version of the bill, making changes that Wilson had sought, was passed and signed in 1992 – a measure many legislative observers rate as the Legislature's most important policy action of the year.

PERSONAL: elected 1986; born Sept. 14, 1949, in Pasadena; home, Los Angeles; education, B.A. UCLA, J.D. UC Berkeley; wife Elise Karl; Jewish.

CAREER: staff lawyer Western Center on Law & Poverty 1976-1978; executive director Bet Tzedek Legal Services 1978-1986.

COMMITTEES: Labor & Employment (chair); Judiciary; Natural Resources.

OFFICES: Capitol, (916) 445-4956, FAX (916) 323-7600; district, 14144 Ventura Blvd., 100, Sherman Oaks 91423, (818) 501-8991, FAX (818) 885-4595.

TERM LIMIT: 1996

REGISTRATION: 50.4% D, 36.6% R

1992 CAMPAIGN:	Friedman – D	55.4%	$806,070
	Christine Reed – R	39.6%	$576,745
	Roy Sykes Jr. – L	5.1%	
1990 CAMPAIGN:	Friedman – D	60.5%	$155,378
	Gary Passi – R	32.7%	$9,359

RATINGS:	AFL-CIO	CalPIRG	CLCV	NOW	CofC	CalFarm
	98	95	100	100	17	15

KEY VOTES:

Parent consent abort:	NO	Limit product tort:	NO	Clean Air Act:	YES
Assault gun ban:	YES	Ban AIDS discrim:	YES	Restrict abortion funds:	nv
Sales tax hike:	YES	Wealth tax hike:	YES	Strong gay rights:	YES
Parental leave:	YES	Timber compromise:	YES	Execution by injection:	nv
Limited gay rights:	YES	Universal health insur:	YES	1992-93 Budget Act:	YES
Campaign Reform:	YES	Offshore oil ban:	YES	Charter schools:	YES

Jan Goldsmith (R)
75th Assembly District

The 75th District is another in the string of Republican-dominated districts in San Diego and Orange counties. This San Diego district borders Imperial County on the east. It includes the northern portion of the city of San Diego and also takes in Santee, Poway, Ramona and the desert around Borrego Springs. More than 80 percent of the residents are white.

Jan Goldsmith, the former mayor of Poway, was Gov. Pete Wilson's pick for the Assembly seat, and Goldsmith turned out to be one of the few winners among Wilson-backed candidates around the state. He defeated anti-abortion activist Connie Youngkin in a tough primary battle, then easily defeated Democrat Dante Cosentino in the general election.

Jan Goldsmith

Shortly after his election, Goldsmith's first name resulted in a couple of cases of mistaken gender. The California National Organization for Women and Assembly

Democratic floor leader Tom Hannigan of Fairfield both counted Goldsmith among the new women legislators. Then, when Goldsmith received his official stationery he discovered that his letterhead said: "Jan Goldsmith. Assemblywoman – 75th District." "I'm cheap," he told a reporter. "I'll just cross out the 'wo.'"

Goldsmith was less amused by the ritual political labeling that is part of Capitol politics. He complained that every time he saw his name it was next to the word "moderate" or "Wilsonite." "They don't know what I've done in Poway. They haven't the faintest idea how I'm going to react here," Goldsmith complained. Goldsmith practiced law for 15 years and teaches at the University of San Diego.

PERSONAL: elected 1992; born Jan. 26, 1951, in New Rochelle, N.Y.; home, Poway; education, B.A. American University in Washington D.C., J.D. University of San Diego; wife Christine, three children; Presbyterian.

CAREER: congressional intern, 1970-72; lawyer/businessman 1976-1988; Poway City Council, 1988-90; professional arbitrator and mediator, 1981-1992; adjunct instructor, negotiation and mediation, University of San Diego School of Law, 1987-1989; judge pro-tem San Diego courts; mayor city of Poway, 1990-92.

COMMITTEES: Consumer Protection & Government Efficiency; Judiciary; Labor & Employment; Transportation.

OFFICES: Capitol, (916) 445-2484, FAX (916) 327-2782; district 12307 Oak Knoll, A, Poway 92064, (619) 486-5191.

TERM LIMIT: 1998

REGISTRATION: 30.9% D, 51.6% R, 2.2% AIP

1992 CAMPAIGN:	Goldsmith – R	64.5%	$469,192
	Dante Consentino – D	27.1%	$8,640

RATINGS and **KEY VOTES**: Newly elected

Michael J. Gotch (D)
76th Assembly District

This compact district lies completely within the city boundaries of San Diego from Rancho Bernardo in the north to Mission Valley in the south. It touches the beach at only one spot, north of LaJolla near Del Mar. With 227,839 registered voters, it is one of the most vote-rich districts in the state.

The Assembly seat was held by Democrat Lucy Killea for seven years until she won a seat in the state Senate in a special election. After Killea left, a special election to fill her seat was held on the same day as the June 1990 primary. Republican Jeff Marston won the seat, nosing out former San Diego City Councilman Mike Gotch, a personable Democrat with movie-star looks and a political ally of Killea's. In the same June election, however, Marston and Gotch won their respective party primaries, so they again faced off in November. This time, Gotch won. Thus the hapless Marston was an assemblyman for all of six months.

A number of Assembly Republicans grumbled afterward that floor leader Ross

Johnson did not do enough to help Marston hold the seat.

Gotch entered the Assembly as anything but a political novice. He is a veteran of numerous ups and downs in San Diego politics and at one time seemed on his way to becoming mayor. As a city councilman, he was strongly identified with environmentalists as a vocal opponent of offshore oil drilling, having served an eight-year stint on the state Coastal Commission.

Then the ride got rough for Gotch. He plunged badly on an issue of intense importance in his beachy council district: a roller coaster. At first, Gotch backed building a park at the site of the former

Mike Gotch

Belmont Park amusement park and preserving its rickety old roller coaster. Then Gotch flip-flopped to support building a shopping center planned by developer friends on the site. He badly miscalculated. Gotch so infuriated Mission Beach residents that his City Council re-election was cast in doubt. Gotch, once the darling of San Diego Democrats, decided to bag it and did not seek re-election to his council seat in 1987. But he did not stray far. He backed in a big way the 1988 presidential candidacy of Gary Hart. But that, too, soured.

Out of office, Gotch worked for developer Doug Manchester and then got a well-paying job as an executive director of a park project. But when Killea unexpectedly moved up to the Senate, Gotch caught the political bug. Had it not been for the baggage he carried into the election from the Belmont Park fiasco, Gotch probably could have coasted easily into the seat against the little-known Marston. As it was, Gotch had a major fight to ultimately win the seat and roll back into politics. While he campaigned, the California Teachers Association put Gotch on its payroll.

The 1992 reapportionment gave Gotch a much more competitive district, and the Republicans targeted the seat as winnable for the GOP. But the conservative candidate, Dick Daleke, pulled a primary victory out from beneath the Wilson administration's pick, moderate Ronnie Delaney.

Democrat Gotch had a much easier time winning against the conservative because he was able to draw votes from moderate Republicans as well as from Democrats. He was also helped by the fact that redistricting removed two neighborhoods from the district that had gone against Gotch in 1990. The Democrats poured money into Gotch's campaign and resources into a successful voter registration drive that added 9,000 Democrats to the voter rolls.

PERSONAL: elected 1990; born Oct. 4, 1947, in San Francisco; home, San Diego; education, B.A. CSU San Diego; wife Janet; Roman Catholic.

CAREER: Local Agency Formation Commission official 1974-1979; San Diego City Council 1979-1987; state Coastal Commission 1980-1988.

COMMITTEES: Natural Resources (vice chair); Health; Local Government; Ways & Means.

OFFICES: Capitol, (916) 445-7210, FAX (916) 324-7895; district, 1080 University Ave., H-201, San Diego 92103, (619) 294-7600, FAX (619) 294-22348.

TERM LIMIT: 1996

REGISTRATION: 40.5% D, 42% R, 2.1% AIP

1992 CAMPAIGN:	Gotch – D	57.3%	$730,515
	Dick Daleke – R	37.0%	$577,937
1990 CAMPAIGN:	Gotch – D	44.7%	$244,067
	Jeff Marston (incumbent) – R	44%	$297,039
	Ed McWilliams – L	6.1%	

RATINGS:	AFL-CIO	CalPIRG	CLCV	NOW	CofC	CalFarm
	97	95	100	86	33	30

KEY VOTES:

Sales tax hike:	YES	Wealth tax hike:	YES	Strong gay rights:	YES
Parental leave:	YES	Timber compromise:	nv	Execution by injection:	YES
Limited gay rights:	YES	Universal health insur:	YES	1992-93 Budget Act:	YES
Campaign Reform:	YES	Offshore oil ban:	YES	Charter schools:	YES

Thomas M. Hannigan (D)
8th Assembly District

The new 8th Assembly District contains most of Solano County and portions of Yolo and Sacramento counties, where former Realtor Tom Hannigan has developed a reputation as a thoughtful, honest and hard-working legislator since he was elected to the Assembly in 1978.

Hannigan began his political career in local government, serving as mayor of Fairfield and later as chairman of the Solano County Board of Supervisors. Accordingly, Hannigan has shown interest in trying to help solve local government funding problems. He was among the early legislators who suggested that Proposition 13 and the state's spending limits needed adjusting. He has proposed giving

Tom Hannigan

counties more money to encourage preservation of agricultural lands under the Williamson Act. He also has been acutely aware of his district's changing nature. He backed proposals to get rail service between Auburn and San Jose, and he pushed to help fund construction of the Vietnam Memorial in Capitol Park through a checkoff on the state income-tax form.

For most of his Assembly career, Hannigan has been recognized as an expert in tax and financial matters, serving a stint as chairman of the Assembly Revenue and

Taxation Committee. In 1986, Hannigan set in motion a move to reform the state income tax. The following year, however, Hannigan relinquished control over the committee when Assembly Speaker Willie Brown named him to replace Mike Roos of Los Angeles as the Democrats' majority leader, one of the top leadership posts. At the time, Democrats were suffering from charges that they were putting politics over policy. Hannigan had a reputation for being more interested in issues than backroom maneuvering and campaign strategy. Since then, there has been some indication that part of Brown's naming of Hannigan to the post was aimed more at image polishing than substantive reform. In fact, much of the overtly political work of raising money and getting candidates elected has simply been shifted to others.

Still, Hannigan's reputation has remained intact. He is considered among the straight-arrows in the Capitol. He told the speaker to back off from his effort to help a law client, Norcal Solid Waste Systems Inc., to site a garbage transfer station in Solano County. Brown's role in the episode became the subject of an FBI probe.

Voter-approved term limits put a damper on Hannigan's future prospects for becoming speaker and left him one of the legislators thinking seriously about bailing out of politics altogether.

PERSONAL: elected 1978; born May 30, 1940, in Vallejo; home, Fairfield; USMC 1963-1966 (Vietnam); education, B.S. University of Santa Clara; wife Jan Mape, three children; Roman Catholic.

CAREER: Fairfield City Council, 1970-1972; mayor, 1972-1974; Solano County Board of Supervisors, 1974-1978; owner and broker of Hannigan & O'Neill Realtors; Assembly majority floor leader.

COMMITTEES: Local Government; Revenue & Taxation; Ways & Means.

OFFICES: Capitol, (916) 445-8368, FAX (916) 327-9667; district, 844 Union Ave., A, Fairfield 94533, (707) 429-2383, FAX (707) 429-1502.

TERM LIMIT: 1996

REGISTRATION: 52.3% D, 32.9% R

1992 CAMPAIGN:	Hannigan – D	57.5%	$663,910
	John Ford – R	36.7%	$7,375
	Richard Fields – L	5.7%	
1990 CAMPAIGN:	Hannigan – D	57.9%	$300,291
	John Ford – R	32.7%	$2,495

RATINGS:	AFL-CIO	CalPIRG	CLCV	NOW	CofC	CalFarm
	95	100	88	86	22	35

KEY VOTES:

Parent consent abort:	NO	Limit product tort:	YES	Clean Air Act:	YES
Assault gun ban:	YES	Ban AIDS discrim:	YES	Restrict abortion funds:	NO
Sales tax hike:	YES	Wealth tax hike:	YES	Strong gay rights:	YES
Parental leave:	YES	Timber compromise:	nv	Execution by injection:	YES
Limited gay rights:	YES	Universal health insur:	YES	1992-93 Budget Act:	YES
Campaign Reform:	YES	Offshore oil ban:	YES	Charter schools:	YES

Trice J. Harvey (R)

32nd Assembly District

The 32nd Assembly District is shaped by the rules of the federal Voting Rights Act, which required changes to protect the voting potential of minorities. The new district includes southeastern Tulare County and a chunk of northern Kern County. The district encompasses all of Porterville, and includes a piece of Visalia and most of Bakersfield and Tulare. The chief industries are agriculture and oil, and the district's politics are steadfastly conservative. Hispanics, who comprise 20 percent of the population, often vote Republican when they bother to vote.

Trice Harvey

Trice Harvey, who was first elected to the Assembly in 1986, easily won re-election in 1992 over his Democratic opponent, Irma Carson, a member of the Bakersfield school board. Harvey is a reliable vote for the conservative Republican minority in the Assembly, but he has not always been on good terms with his own caucus. In 1986, Harvey, then a Kern County supervisor, was the anointed GOP candidate for the Assembly to replace Don Rogers, who had been elected to the Senate. Harvey had been endorsed by virtually all local GOP leaders when then-Assembly Republican leader Pat Nolan abruptly turned against Harvey and backed his rival in the primary, apparently because of Harvey's friendship with Rep. Bill Thomas, a bitter rival of Nolan. But Harvey was able to beat Nolan's candidate, Anna Allen.

Harvey has concentrated on district issues. He sits on the Central Valley Project Transfer Advisory Committee, a 17-member panel appointed by Gov. Wilson to represent agricultural, urban and environmental interests in the negotiations for transfer of the massive water project from the federal government to the state.

Harvey and Rogers are the two staunchest defenders of the oil industry in the Legislature, voting against all environmental regulation affecting the industry – sometimes long after the oil industry has agreed to a compromise. On one occasion Harvey and Rogers stood alone against the 1990 oil spill prevention bill.

Harvey is not doctrinairily against all environmental legislation. He has pushed efforts to limit importation of hazardous wastes into his district, a sensitive local issue. His bill to expand state efforts to learn the cause of high cancer rates among children in the city of McFarland was vetoed by Gov. George Deukmejian, who said it duplicated existing efforts. Harvey also has remained sensitive to the concerns – and burdens of local governments.

He has been among those who advocate special-tax treatment for pet projects. He floated an unsuccessful bill in 1990 to give ostrich breeders a sales tax exemption and vowed to push the bill again in 1991 despite a record state budget deficit. He won passage of a bill giving the artist Cristo a sales tax break for purchasing art materials to construct sculptured yellow umbrellas along Interstate 5. Deukmejian vetoed it.

Harvey also had a role in helping write a happier ending to the "Onion Field" saga. Karl Hettinger was one of two Los Angeles police officers kidnapped in 1963. Hettinger's partner was killed by the kidnappers in an onion field outside Bakersfield while Hettinger escaped, only to suffer years of emotional turmoil. Harvey befriended Hettinger, made him his aide for 10 years and persuaded Deukmejian to appoint Hettinger to complete the remaining 21 months of Harvey's term on the Kern County Board of Supervisors. Hettinger later won election on his own.

A native of Arkansas, Harvey still speaks with a southern twang. During part of his youth his family depended on welfare, an episode that apparently did nothing to soften his attitude toward the downtrodden. Harvey is known as one of the gabbiest members of the Legislature. He delays hearings with seemingly endless banter, much of which has nothing to do with the subject at hand.

PERSONAL: elected 1986; born July 15, 1936, in Paragould, Ark.; home, Bakersfield; B.A. CSU Fresno; wife Jacqueline Stussy, two children; Mormon.

CAREER: County health sanitarian; pharmaceutical salesman; school board member; Kern County Board of Supervisors 1976-1986.

COMMITTEES: Agriculture; Water, Parks & Wildlife; Health; Rules.

OFFICES: Capitol, (916) 445-8498, FAX (916) 324-4696; district, 1800-30th St., 101, Bakersfield 93301, (805) 324-3300.

TERM LIMIT: 1996

REGISTRATION: 42.1% D, 46.9% R, 2.0% AIP

1992 CAMPAIGN:	Harvey – R	65.5%	$447,233
	Irma Carson – D	31.7%	$18,434
1990 CAMPAIGN:	Harvey – R	100%	$296,383

RATINGS:

AFL-CIO	CalPIRG	CLCV	NOW	CofC	CalFarm
10	23	8	21	100	80

KEY VOTES:

Parent consent abort:	YES	Limit product tort:	YES	Clean Air Act:	YES
Assault gun ban:	NO	Ban AIDS discrim:	NO	Restrict abortion funds:	YES
Sales tax hike:	NO	Wealth tax hike:	NO	Strong gay rights:	NO
Parental leave:	NO	Timber compromise:	NO	Execution by injection:	YES
Limited gay rights:	NO	Universal health insur:	NO	1992-93 Budget Act:	YES
Campaign Reform:	NO	Offshore oil ban:	NO	Charter schools:	YES

Daniel E. Hauser (D)

1st Assembly District

California's northwestern coast is so thinly populated that one state Assembly district stretches nearly 300 miles southward from the Oregon border. The area once voted Republican with some regularity, but as the traditional industries of lumber and fishing have faded, and as flower children of the 1960s moved in and established roots, the politics of the area have crept leftward.

As reconfigured under redistricting, the new 1st Assembly District includes much of what used to be the 2nd District, covering all or parts of Del Norte, Humboldt, Mendocino, Lake and Sonoma counties. Since 1982, the region's assemblyman has been Dan Hauser, a onetime insurance adjuster and mayor of Arcata. Hauser chairs the Assembly Housing Committee. He has labored to produce a stream of housing bills, but occupies much of his time trying to avoid being chewed up by the ceaseless environmental controversies that buffet his scenic and resource-rich

Dan Hauser

district. Environmentalists and logging and mining companies battle endlessly over regulations and laws in the region.

Hauser came into office as a Sierra Club candidate. He routinely offers bills and resolutions to ban offshore oil drilling. But in more recent years, Hauser has gravitated more toward the timber industry. Matters came to a head in 1989 when an environmentalist-sponsored bill to put a three-year moratorium on logging old-growth forests came to the Assembly floor. Hauser successfully offered industry-supported amendments that gutted the bill. The bill then died. That and other instances have driven a wedge between Hauser and the increasingly militant environmentalists. But he won re-election handily in 1992 over Humboldt County Supervisor Anna Sparks, known locally as "Chainsaw Annie" for her connections with the timber industry

Just two days after the 1992 election, Hauser announced he would mount a special-election campaign for the 2nd Senate District seat being vacated by Barry Keene of Ukiah. But he later backed away from that fight, anticipating a run for the seat by Sen. Mike Thompson, D-St. Helena, that he said would have made the battle "divisive, costly and unnecessary."

PERSONAL: elected 1982; born June 18, 1942, in Riverside; home, Arcata; education, B.A. Humboldt State University; wife Donna Dumont, two children; Lutheran.

CAREER: insurance claims representative; Arcata City Council, 1974-1978, mayor, 1978-1982.

COMMITTEES: Housing and Community Development (chair); Governmental Organization; Transportation; Water, Parks & Wildlife.

OFFICES: Capitol, (916) 445-8360, FAX (916) 322-5214; district, 510 O St., G, Eureka 95501, (707) 445-7014.

TERM LIMIT: 1996

REGISTRATION: 54% D, 30.8% R, 1.8% AIP, 2.1% Green

1992 CAMPAIGN: Hauser – D   57.2% $663,822
        Anna Sparks – R   34.5% $440,310
        Margene McGee – Green 5.7%
1990 CAMPAIGN: Hauser – D   55.2% $233,187
        Tim Willis – R   31.4% $1,080
        Bruce Anderson – P&F 13.4%

RATINGS:

AFL-CIO	CalPIRG	CLCV	NOW	CofC	CalFarm
95	100	78	100	28	40

KEY VOTES:

Parent consent abort:	NO	Limit product tort:	YES	Clean Air Act:	YES
Assault gun ban:	NO	Ban AIDS discrim:	YES	Restrict abortion funds:	NO
Sales tax hike:	YES	Wealth tax hike:	YES	Strong gay rights:	YES
Parental leave:	YES	Timber compromise:	YES	Execution by injection:	YES
Limited gay rights:	YES	Universal health insur:	YES	1992-93 Budget Act:	YES
Campaign Reform:	YES	Offshore oil ban:	YES	Charter schools:	nv

Ray Haynes (R)

66th Assembly District

The 66th Assembly District is a Republican candidate's paradise. Registration is 53 percent Republican and 35 percent Democrat. Part of the city of Corona and all of Lake Elsinore and Temecula lie within the boundaries. The district includes western Riverside County and a slice of northwest San Diego county.

Ray Haynes, a conservative Republican with ties to the Christian right, won a seven-way primary battle after Republican incumbent Dave Kelley chose to run for the senate. Haynes ran a well-financed general election campaign. He got a $30,500 boost from the conservative Allied Business PAC, and he loaned himself $28,000. Haynes easily defeated his Democratic opponent, Corona building inspector Patsy Hockersmith.

Ray Haynes

PERSONAL: elected 1992; born Aug. 26, 1954, in Merced; home, Murrieta; B.A. California Lutheran University, M.A. and J.D. USC; wife Pamela, two children; Protestant.

CAREER: lawyer; Moreno Valley Planning Commission; founding member and treasurer of Moreno Valley Committee for No New Taxes; free counsel for western Center of Law and Religious Freedom, Riverside Citizens for Responsible Behavior.

COMMITTEES: Agriculture; Education; Water, Parks & Wildlife.

OFFICES: Capitol, (916) 445-1676, FAX (916) 447-4457; district, 29377 Rancho California, 102, Temecula 92591, (909) 699-1113, FAX (909) 694-4457.

TERM LIMIT: 1998

REGISTRATION: 34.9% D, 52.3% R

1992 CAMPAIGN: Haynes – R 58.1% $213,511
Patsy Hockersmith – D 31.4% $21,642
Anne Patrice Wood – P&F 7.1%

RATINGS and **KEY VOTES**: Newly elected

William Hoge (R)
44th Assembly District

The new 44th Assembly District, which includes Pasadena and other communities along the foothills of the San Gabriel Mountains, is Republican territory and was the site in 1992 of one of many clashes between moderate and conservative GOP factions. Ten Republicans ran for the seat, but the major battle was between Pasadena insurance man and civic leader William Hoge, backed by the right, and Barbara Peiper, the choice of Gov. Pete Wilson and other moderates. Hoge topped the field and with a strong GOP registration edge, the Democrats never had a chance to exploit the Republican division.

Hoge thus came to the Legislature with a vow to "rid our personal and business lives of government bureaucracy and regulation."

William Hoge

PERSONAL: elected 1992; born April 2, 1946, in Pasadena; home, Pasadena; attended Pasadena City College; wife Claudette, three children; Protestant.
CAREER: president, Insurance Communicators.

COMMITTEES: Governmental Organization; Labor & Employment; Natural Resources.

OFFICES: Capitol, (916) 445-8211, FAX (916) 323-9420; district, 1276 E. Colorado Blvd., 203, Pasadena 91106, (818) 577-4470, FAX (818) 577-0614.

TERM LIMIT: 1998

REGISTRATION: 44.2% D, 43.1% R

1992 CAMPAIGN: Hoge – R 51.8% $383,448
Jonathan Fuhrman – D 43.9% $13,486

RATINGS and **KEY VOTES**: Newly elected

Kathleen Honeycutt (R)

34th Assembly District

The 34th is the largest and one of the most desolate districts in the Assembly. The district runs up the Nevada border from Riverside County to Mono County. It includes the southeastern edge of Kern County, all of Inyo and most of San Bernardino County, taking in the Victor Valley, where Assemblywoman Kathleen Honeycutt lives. Along with Death Valley and numerous mountain ranges, the district lays claim to several military reservations.

Kathleen Honeycutt

Honeycutt appears well-suited to the conservative district. She received much of her financial support during a heavily contested primary from anti-abortion, anti-tax and pro-gun groups. Her connections to fundamentalist Christians and anti-abortion groups helped her put together a well-organized campaign in a far-flung district that defied conventional campaign strategies. Honeycutt came into the primary with an edge in a field of nine Republican candidates. She won almost 50 percent of the vote. Honcycutt went on in November to easily defeat her Democratic foe, Joe Green.

PERSONAL: elected 1992; born March 21, 1941, in Modesto; home, Hesperia; education, El Camino Community College; husband Theron, three children; Protestant.

CAREER: Partner with her husband in general contracting business 1976-1988; Reagan appointee to San Bernardino County Draft Board, 1981-91; founder of the High Desert Pregnancy and Family Resource Center.

COMMITTEES: Consumer Protection, Governmental Efficiency & New Technologies; Housing & Community Development; Transportation.

OFFICES: Capitol, (916) 445-8102, FAX (916) 323-7467; district, 15888 Main St., 203, Hesperia 92345, (619) 948-4444.

TERM LIMIT: 1998

REGISTRATION: 38.7% D, 46.8% R, 2.6% AIP

1992 CAMPAIGN: Honeycutt – R   64.5% $300,947
                   Joe Green – D   35.5% $1,844

RATINGS and **KEY VOTES**: Newly elected

Paul V. Horcher (R)

60th Assembly District

Republican portions of the otherwise Latino and Democratic San Gabriel Valley southeast of Los Angeles and just north of the Orange County line are folded into

the 60th Assembly District. As created by the state
Supreme Court, the district, which includes such
suburban communities as Whittier and West Covina,
had a Republican registration plurality, which made
it certain that freshman Paul Horcher could win re-
election in 1992.

The seat was held for eight years by Frank Hill,
who moved to the state Senate in 1990 during a round
of musical chairs begun when Bill Campbell left the
Senate. Hill's successor, Horcher, is a lawyer and
former city councilman from suburban Diamond Bar
who moved to the left, including a conversion to
support for state-paid abortions, when he faced an
anti-abortion opponent during his first election.

Paul Horcher

He won that GOP primary election by fewer than 100 votes. In the general
election, Horcher's Democratic opponent, Gary Neely, a Diamond Bar marketing
consultant, tried to pin Horcher with the label of flip-flopper. Two loosely knit
groups of Republicans also opposed Horcher. One campaigned directly for Neely
while the other group asked Republicans to refrain from voting for Horcher because
of his stance on abortion. Neither group proved effective. Horcher outspent Neely
in spades and with a healthy registration margin in the old 52nd District, won the
general election easily.

Horcher had even less trouble winning a second term in 1992, although
reapportionment shaved the Republican voter registration margin slightly. But as
soon as he was sworn in for a second term in December, Horcher found himself in
new political hot water, once again accused of putting career-enhancing expediency
ahead of political principle. Horcher, who had been just another Republican
backbencher during his first term, was plucked from that obscurity by the top
Democrat, Speaker Willie Brown, and named vice chairman of the Assembly Ways
and Means Committee, which wields great power over the state budget and major
legislation. In doing that, Brown ignored the unanimous vote of the Assembly
Republican Caucus, which wanted Dean Andal of Stockton to become Ways and
Means vice chairman.

Brown said he chose Horcher because of his willingness to vote for budgets,
unlike more conservative members such as Andal. In accepting the appointment
Horcher earned bitter enmity from his GOP colleagues. They accused him of
kissing up to Brown rather than standing with the caucus on a partisan squabble.
Horcher refused to resign from Ways and Means and some of his fellow Republicans thought he should be booted from the caucus. Democrats, meanwhile, savored
the split and suggested privately that Horcher might give up his Republican
designation and become an independent, a step that's occurred several times in the
Senate.

PERSONAL: elected 1982; born Feb. 19, 1954, in Whittier; home, Diamond Bar; education, A.A. political science Mt. San Antonio College in Walnut; B.A. political science UCLA; M.A. public administration Pepperdine University, Malibu, J.D. La Verne University; wife Faye, two children; Episcopalian.

CAREER: lawyer; Diamond Bar City Council.

COMMITTEES: Ways & Means (vice chair); Finance & Insurance; Health; Judiciary.

OFFICES: Capitol, (916) 445-7550, FAX (916) 324-6973; district, 325 N. Azusa Ave., West Covina 91791, (818) 967-5299, FAX (818) 967-9159.

TERM LIMIT: 1996

REGISTRATION: 43.6% D, 44.0% R

1992 CAMPAIGN:	Horcher – R	55.7%	$500,952
	Stan Caress – D	36.6%	$3,320
	Robert Lewis – AIP	7.7%	
1990 CAMPAIGN:	Horcher – R	58.9%	$513,681
	Gary Neely – D	41.1%	$35,372

RATINGS:	AFL-CIO	CalPIRG	CLCV	NOW	CofC	CalFarm
	7	32	11	36	89	75

KEY VOTES:

Sales tax hike:	NO	Wealth tax hike:	NO	Strong gay rights:	NO
Parental leave:	NO	Timber compromise:	YES	Execution by injection:	YES
Limited gay rights:	NO	Universal health insur:	NO	1992-93 Budget Act:	YES
Campaign Reform:	NO	Offshore oil ban:	NO	Charter schools:	YES

Phillip L. Isenberg (D)
9th Assembly District

There was a time when Phillip Isenberg, the former mayor of Sacramento, was on the short list of Capitol candidates to succeed Assembly Speaker Willie Brown. But term limits almost certainly cut off that option for Isenberg, who survived a reapportionment that put him and Lloyd Connelly, two veteran Sacramento assemblymen, into a single district. Connelly quit the Assembly and ran for a Sacramento County Superior Court judgeship instead, leaving Isenberg to continue his efforts to carve out a role for himself as a budget bridge-builder at the Capitol. Although he represents a heavily Democratic district, the owlish Isenberg avoids knee-jerk criticism of Republican Gov. Pete Wilson and these days sounds much like a member of the GOP as he discusses the need to scale back government to fit recessionary times.

Phillip Isenberg

Isenberg first won his seat in a 1982 landslide after the district was tailored to his needs by friendly Democrats. His toughest re-election race came in 1988, when his Republican opponent tried to paint him as soft on crime and as too close to liberal Speaker Brown, who has served as something of a mentor to Isenberg. The assemblyman remains a top lieutenant to Brown, who gave him his first job as a lawyer and for whom he once served as chief of staff to the Ways and Means Committee. Isenberg became one of the Democrats' top political strategists, and plays a key role in trying to maintain the Democratic majority in the lower house.

Term limits will force Isenberg to leave the house in 1996, and some believe he will run for the state Senate if and when Leroy Greene steps down. He has steadily moved up in the Democratic hierarchy, becoming chairman of the Judiciary Committee at the start of the 1988 session, a panel with responsibility over such issues as abortion and liability laws.

Isenberg can be charming and witty or arrogant, dogmatic and just plain grumpy. And while other politicians might prefer splashy headlines, Isenberg seems to relish the nuts and bolts of the government process. He is a political insider, knows parliamentary rules and is adept at quietly maneuvering behind the scenes.

While politics are clearly Isenberg's passion, he has made some significant policy contributions as well. In 1989, he pushed through a new law to provide a state-subsidized health insurance program for Californians with pre-existing illnesses who would otherwise be uninsurable. He also played key roles in negotiating compromises on how to spend money from the state's tobacco tax and in the 50-year-old dispute over water diversions from Mono Lake.

No other issue generates more passion in Northern California than water and Isenberg has been in the middle of the continuing war of words between the north and the central and southern parts of the state. Isenberg is considered a major player on water issues, and a maverick one at that. He has argued that less water from the north should go to San Joaquin Valley farms so that more would be available for fast-growing urban areas in Southern California. The position has shaken what has traditionally been a rock-solid alliance between southern and central California interests against the north.

PERSONAL: elected 1982; born Feb. 25, 1939, in Gary Ind.; home, Sacramento; Army 1962-68; B.A. CSU Sacramento; J.D. UC Berkeley; wife Marilyn Araki.

CAREER: lawyer; aide to Assemblyman Willie Brown 1967-68; Ways & Means Committee consultant 1971; Sacramento City Council 1971-75; mayor 1975-82.

COMMITTEES: Judiciary (chair); Health; Revenue & Taxation; Water, Parks & Wildlife; (joint) Courthouse Financing & Construction; Legislative Budget; Legislative Ethics.

OFFICES: Capitol, (916) 445-1611, FAX (916) 327-1788; district, 1215 - 15th St., 102, Sacramento 95814, (916) 324-4676, FAX (916) 322-1239.

TERM LIMIT: 1996
REGISTRATION: 65.8% D, 23.4% R

1992 CAMPAIGN:	Isenberg – D	66.0%	$749,640
	David Reade – R	26.8%	$4,674
	Richard Geiselhart – Green	7.2%	
1990 CAMPAIGN:	Isenberg – D	56%	$393,571
	Tom Griffin – R	38.4%	$8,467

RATINGS:	AFL-CIO	CalPIRG	CLCV	NOW	CofC	CalFarm
	96	100	93	72	22	30

KEY VOTES:

Parent consent abort:	NO	Limit product tort:	YES	Clean Air Act:	YES
Assault gun ban:	YES	Ban AIDS discrim:	YES	Restrict abortion funds:	NO
Sales tax hike:	YES	Wealth tax hike:	YES	Strong gay rights:	YES
Parental leave:	YES	Timber compromise:	NO	Execution by injection:	nv
Limited gay rights:	YES	Universal health insur:	nv	1992-93 Budget Act:	YES
Campaign Reform:	YES	Offshore oil ban:	YES	Charter schools:	YES

J. Ross Johnson (R)

72nd Assembly District

The 72nd Assembly District is in the heart of northern Orange County, covering such communities as Fullerton, Placentia and Yorba Linda. Redistricting slightly altered the lines of the old 64th District, but it remains similar in makeup and, more important, continues to be a Republican stronghold with a 55 percent Republican registration to 33 percent Democratic.

Ross Johnson, the man who has represented the old 64th District for the past decade-plus, is something of an enigma. With a political intelligence that sometimes borders on brilliance, Johnson seemed well-suited to his role as the Assembly's Republican leader. But lurking just beneath the surface of his

Ross Johnson

public personality is an anger that boils up, rendering Johnson virtually incoherent with rage – a trait that leads some Democrats to bait him in public.

During the middle of the tense budget debate in the summer of 1992, Johnson lunged at another GOP member, Charles Quackenbush, who had voted in opposition to Johnson on a highly contentious school-aid bill. The two had to be separated by a sergeant-at-arms before fisticuffs erupted. Earlier that year as the budget debates heated up, Johnson said, referring to his successor as GOP leader, Bill Jones of Fresno: "He's a tower of Jell-O. He's got all the backbone of a chocolate eclair."

Johnson lost the Republican leader's job to Jones in July 1991 after the

Republican Party took a public relations beating during the state budget fight. Gov. Wilson sent caucus members not-so-subtle signals about his displeasure with Johnson and let it be known he thought highly of Jones, who promised to "represent the governor's positions on the floor."

Johnson, an attorney who was active in local civic affairs prior to embarking on a political career, was part of the huge class of Republicans elected to the Assembly in 1978. The group quickly dubbed itself the "Proposition 13 babies" and vowed to wage ideological war on liberals and Democrats. The group asserted itself within months by supporting a coup against the relatively moderate Republican leader of the time, Paul Priolo. That brought Carol Hallett into the leadership position. Johnson helped Pat Nolan, the de facto leader of the Proposition 13 babies, engineer another coup on Hallett's successor, Robert Naylor, in 1984 and wound up as one of Nolan's top lieutenants.

But in November 1988, after Republicans lost several seats to the Democrats and Nolan had become entangled in an FBI investigation of Capitol corruption, Nolan lateraled the leader's position to Johnson. The switch from Nolan to Johnson – which staved off rumblings from moderates in the Republican caucus –had nothing to do with ideology. The new leader was every bit as conservative as the old one.

Johnson has devoted his energies to overhaul of the political system, although his precise motives for that interest, like so many aspects of Johnson's persona, have never been clear. He joined with two other legislators – a Democrat and an independent – to sponsor a campaign finance reform initiative (Proposition 73) in 1988 that imposed limits on contributions and transfers of funds between candidates. Some reformers saw Proposition 73 as a poison pill for a broader reform initiative (Proposition 68) on the same ballot. Since Proposition 73 received more votes, it superseded Proposition 68 in areas of conflict, such as Proposition 73's ban on public financing of campaigns. The measure's provisions outlawing transfers of funds between lawmakers seemed aimed at Speaker Brown's political powers.

Johnson, however, has resented the implication that he had ulterior motives. He has maintained that Proposition 73 was a genuine effort at campaign reform and has fiercely lashed out at Common Cause for suggesting otherwise. Eventually, however, almost all of Proposition 73 was gutted in the courts.

Johnson is a semi-introvert who, aides say, dislikes the political limelight and is interested in political policy-making.

PERSONAL: elected 1978; born Sept. 28, 1939, in Drake, N.D.; home, Brea; Navy 1965-67; education, B.A. CSU Fullerton, J.D. Western State; wife Diane Morris, two children; Protestant.

CAREER: iron worker; lawyer; legislative aide to Assemblyman Jerry Lewis, 1969-1973; Assembly Republican Floor Leader, 1988.

COMMITTEES: Rules (vice chair); Finance & Insurance; Revenue & Taxation; Ways & Means.

OFFICES: Capitol, (916) 445-7448, FAX (916) 324-6870; district, 1501 N. Harbor Blvd., 201, Fullerton 92635, (714) 738-5853, FAX (714) 526-7108.

TERM LIMIT: 1996

REGISTRATION: 32.8% D, 55.0% R

1992 CAMPAIGN:
Johnson – R	61.2%	$402,343
Paul Garza – D	32.4%	$0
Geoffrey Braun – L	6.4%	

1990 CAMPAIGN:
Johnson – R	66%	$535,106
Kevin Gardner – D	34%	$0

RATINGS:
AFL-CIO	CalPIRG	CLCV	NOW	CofC	CalFarm
11	5	5	7	67	65

KEY VOTES:

Parent consent abort:	YES	Limit product tort:	YES	Clean Air Act:	NO
Assault gun ban:	NO	Ban AIDS discrim:	NO	Restrict abortion funds:	YES
Sales tax hike:	NO	Wealth tax hike:	NO	Strong gay rights:	NO
Parental leave:	NO	Timber compromise:	NO	Execution by injection:	YES
Limited gay rights:	NO	Universal health insur:	NO	1992-93 Budget Act:	YES
Campaign Reform:	NO	Offshore oil ban:	NO	Charter schools:	nv

William L. Jones (R)
29th Assembly District

Bill Jones' old 32nd District sprawled over a huge swatch of rural California east of Fresno, including all or parts of four counties. Reapportionment renumbered the district to 29 and reconfigured it to just the eastern portions of Fresno County and the northern part of Tulare County, which didn't change its agricultural orientation one whit. Business, farming and ranching are bywords here, and Republican Jones, a businessman, row-crop farmer and cattle rancher, speaks the language.

Smart but reserved, Jones has carefully built a political career watching out for district interests. He has focused his attention on agriculture, health, work-

Bill Jones

ers' compensation, water, wine production, parks, education and local government. He was among those who helped draft the state's widely copied "workfare" program, where welfare recipients work to receive benefits. He has pushed measures to help reduce prison costs, increase highway funding for rural counties, keep rural hospitals open, recoup welfare overpayments and expand food inspections. He has tangled with Democratic Assemblyman Byron Sher on water pollution issues, generally siding with farm interests that have sought a lenient approach to health standards for water.

Jones was a leader of a relatively moderate faction of GOP members known as the "Magnificent Seven," which was allied with Gov. Pete Wilson in his interparty squabbles with conservatives. In the aftermath of the 1991 budget battles, Jones managed to unseat conservative Ross Johnson to become the caucus leader. But his reign lasted scarcely a year. In late 1992, after his party had lost a seat in elections that had been expected to produce a bumper crop of new Republican legislators, Jones quit and was succeeded in the top GOP job by freshman Jim Brulte.

As both a rank-and-file assemblyman and as GOP leader, Jones has been faulted for being too circumspect, choosing his words carefully and rarely saying anything controversial – or even meaningful. With his time in the Assembly limited to 1996, Jones must now ponder his next political step. He could run for the state Senate seat now held by Senate Republican leader Ken Maddy, whose legislative career will end in 1998 under term limits.

PERSONAL: elected 1982; born Dec. 20, 1949, in Coalinga, Calif.; home, Fresno; education, B.S. CSU Fresno; wife Maurine, two children; Methodist.

 CAREER: chairman of the board of California Data Marketing Inc., a computer service and direct mail firm; family partner in a 3,000-acre ranch and an investments firm.

COMMITTEES: Agriculture; Environmental Safety & Toxic Materials; Water, Ways & Means.

OFFICES: Capitol, (916) 445-2931, FAX (916) 445-3832; district, 2997 W. Shaw, 106, Fresno, 93711, (209) 224-7833, FAX (209) 224-7835.

TERM LIMIT: 1996

REGISTRATION: 44.9% D, 44.5% R

1992 CAMPAIGN:	Jones – R	100%	$1,176,578
1990 CAMPAIGN:	Jones – R	68.8%	$421,830
	Bernie McGoldrick – D	31.2%	$17,844

RATINGS:	AFL-CIO	CalPIRG	CLCV	NOW	CofC	CalFarm
	13	95	0	29	72	60

KEY VOTES:

Parent consent abort:	YES	Limit product tort:	YES	Clean Air Act:	YES
Assault gun ban:	NO	Ban AIDS discrim:	NO	Restrict abortion funds:	YES
Sales tax hike:	YES	Wealth tax hike:	YES	Strong gay rights:	NO
Parental leave:	NO	Timber compromise:	YES	Execution by injection:	YES
Limited gay rights:	NO	Universal health insur:	NO	1992-93 Budget Act:	YES
Campaign Reform:	NO	Offshore oil ban:	NO	Charter schools:	nv

Betty Karnette (D)
54th Assembly District

Gerald Felando was always one of the Capitol's enigmas. A dentist, Felando could be an effective and even sensitive legislator. But on other occasions, he could be as crude as anyone who has ever carried a political title, lashing out at staff members and anyone else who crossed his path. The Capitol's internal intelligence network often carried Felando stories. Felando seemed to mellow after undergoing chemotherapy for cancer in 1989, but with his disease in remission, his old mercurial temperament returned.

Reapportionment split Felando's 51st District and attached each half to other territory, creating two districts in which he could have sought re-election in 1992. He chose the 54th, which included the Long Beach-Wilmington-San Pedro harbor area, Felando's original political base when he was first elected in 1978. And it should have been good for Felando, not only because of his community ties, but because of its Republican voter registration plurality.

Betty Karnette

It was, however, a bad year for Republicans and Felando's career was ended by Democrat Betty Karnette of Long Beach, one of two Democratic wins in two supposedly Republican districts created from portions of Felando's old territory. It was not only a victory for Karnette and the Democrats, but one for the teacher unions in which Karnette had been an activist.

PERSONAL: elected 1992; born Sept. 13, 1931, in Paducah, Ky.; home, Long Beach; education, B.A. and M.A., CSU Long Beach; husband Dick, one child; no stated religious preference.

CAREER: teacher and federal funds coordinator, Los Angeles Unified School District; activist in United Teachers of Los Angeles and California Teacher Association, member of state Democratic Party central committee.

COMMITTEES: Environmental Safety & Toxic Materials; Governmental Organization; Transportation.

OFFICES: Capitol, (916) 445-9234; district, 301 E. Ocean Blvd., 700, Long Beach 90802, (310) 435-5631, FAX (310) 437-3760.

TERM LIMIT: 1998
REGISTRATION: 44.3% D, 42.1% R
1992 CAMPAIGN: Karnette – D   51.9% $212,019
              Gerald Felando (incumbent) – R   43.9% $416,553
RATINGS and **KEY VOTES**: Newly elected

Richard D. Katz (D)

39th Assembly District

Redistricting didn't change the political make-up of this Democratic stronghold in the central San Fernando Valley. Registration is 62 percent Democratic to 27 percent Republican. The moderate San Fernando Valley district includes the largely

Latino and African American neighborhoods of San Fernando and Pacoima, working-class Sepulveda and the seedy Sylmar area. Latino registration in the district is 25 percent, although Latinos make up 62 percent of the population.

Democrat Richard Katz has cruised to lopsided victories in his last four elections. But Katz, seeking to broaden his political horizons, was a candidate and leading contender for mayor of Los Angeles at the time of this writing. The mayoral election, scheduled for April 1993, was set to select a replacement for retiring Mayor Tom Bradley.

Richard Katz

Katz had been eyeing the city's top spot for some time. He hired President Bill Clinton's brilliant and outspoken campaign consultant, James Carville, to run the campaign two months before announcing his candidacy. Katz's chances of winning were enhanced by the decisions of two leading Latinos, county Supervisor Gloria Molina and City Councilman Richard Alatorre, to stay out of the race.

Katz, who was running a graphic arts and printing company when he was elected to the Assembly in 1980, is a pragmatist. He is generally conservative on crime issues, tends to be moderate on fiscal issues and is liberal on social issues such as abortion and the environment. That middle-of-the-road record has allowed him to brush away GOP attempts to exploit his position as one of liberal Assembly Speaker Willie Brown's top lieutenants, a favorite GOP tactic in swing districts.

Katz, in fact, has used his influence and skills to help elect more moderate Democrats. He was an outspoken critic of the Democratic Party's choice of former Gov. Jerry Brown as state chairman.

Aside from Katz's role as political strategist, he also is a key player in the legislative arena. As chairman of the Assembly Transportation Committee, he was a driving force behind the successful effort to get voters to raise the gas tax in 1990 to provide money for the state's highways and mass transit. A few years earlier, at the height of statewide concern about toxic pollutants, Katz pushed a tough law regulating the way toxic waste can be stored and dumped.

He also has seized on issues with which the general public can relate, successfully sponsoring legislation to require gravel trucks to cover their loads with tarps to protect the windshields of cars traveling behind, raising the speed limit to 65 mph on rural highways and making it easier for law enforcement officials to confiscate the assets of drug dealers.

Although generally affable, he is prone to occasional tantrums, and his ambition has caused friction with colleagues. In fact, there was speculation that one reason Assembly Speaker Brown ordered press desks off the sides of the Assembly floor at the start of the 1991-92 session was that a potential opponent for Los Angeles mayor, fellow Democratic Assemblyman Mike Roos, was worried about the time Katz spent talking to reporters.

PERSONAL: elected 1980; born Aug. 16, 1950, in Los Angeles; home, Panorama City; education, B.A. CSU, San Diego; wife Gini Barrett; Jewish.

CAREER: graphic artist and printer.

COMMITTEES: Transportation (chair).

OFFICES: Capitol, (916) 445-1616, FAX (916) 324-6860; district, 9140 Van Nuys Blvd., 109, Panorama City 91402, (818) 894-3671, FAX (818) 894-4672.

TERM LIMIT: 1996

REGISTRATION: 62.0% D, 26.6% R

1992 CAMPAIGN:	Katz – D	69.4%	$708,147
	Nicholas Fitzgerald – R	25.6%	$659
	David George – L	5%	
1990 CAMPAIGN:	Katz – D	68%	$542,221
	Sam Ceravolo – R	32%	$0

RATINGS:	AFL-CIO	CalPIRG	CLCV	NOW	CofC	CalFarm
	87	95	96	100	39	25

KEY VOTES:

Parent consent abort:	NO	Limit product tort:	YES	Clean Air Act:	YES
Assault gun ban:	YES	Ban AIDS discrim:	YES	Restrict abortion funds:	NO
Sales tax hike:	YES	Wealth tax hike:	YES	Strong gay rights:	YES
Parental leave:	YES	Timber compromise:	NO	Execution by injection:	YES
Limited gay rights:	YES	Universal health insur:	YES	1992-93 Budget Act:	YES
Campaign Reform:	YES	Offshore oil ban:	YES	Charter schools:	YES

Johan M. Klehs (D)

18th Assembly District

Democrats don't worry much about the possibility of losing this East Bay blue-collar district, which includes the cities of San Leandro and Hayward, Castro Valley and part of Oakland. It was renumbered from 14 to 18 by the state Supreme Court's reapportionment plan but otherwise changed only slightly.

Johan Klehs, a former aide to Sen. Bill Lockyer, has used his knowledge of the legislative and political system to his advantage. He has risen rather quickly to positions of political power, first as chairman of the Assembly Elections and Reapportionment Committee and now as chairman of the Assembly Revenue and Taxation Committee. In that post, he has attempted to head off efforts to open new loopholes in the state tax code – a refreshing change – but has had only limited success. With the state facing an unprecedented fiscal crisis in 1991, it fell to Klehs to fashion the Assembly Democrats' response to Gov. Pete Wilson's budget revenue proposals.

Klehs, who needn't worry about re-election because of his healthy registration margin, is generally liberal, but at times can be unpredictable. He is an archetypal political animal, the staffer who learned how to push buttons and then used that knowledge for his own benefit.

In recent years, he has proposed many high-profile tax-related bills on a variety of subjects. He teamed with Controller Gray Davis to propose a constitutional amendment to give tax credits to individuals and corporations contributing toward research for an AIDS vaccine. He joined Attorney General John Van de Kamp in proposing that corporate tax loopholes be closed to fund anti-drug programs. He's

Johan Klehs

also proposed letting first-time home buyers use Individual Retirement Accounts to purchase their homes without tax penalties and taking away tax-exempt status from social clubs that discriminate in membership. Count Klehs as another who will be looking for a congressional seat should the opportunity present itself.

PERSONAL: elected 1982; born June 27, 1952, in Alameda; home, Castro Valley; education, B.A. and M.A. CSU Hayward, attended Harvard University's John F. Kennedy School of Government; single; Lutheran.

CAREER: salesman for a direct-mail advertising firm; legislative assistant to Assemblyman Bill Lockyer 1973-1976; San Leandro City Council 1978-1982.

COMMITTEES: Revenue & Taxation (chair); Health; Labor & Employment.

OFFICES: Capitol, 445-8160, FAX (916) 445-0967; district, 2450 Washington Ave., 270, San Leandro 94577, (510) 352-2673, FAX (510) 352-4688.

TERM LIMIT: 1996

REGISTRATION: 60.3% D, 26.3% R

1992 CAMPAIGN:	Klehs – D	65%	$520,379
	Don Grundmann – R	28.1%	$250
	Terry Floyd – L	6.9%	
1990 CAMPAIGN:	Klehs – D	65.8%	$542,134
	Don Grundmann – R	26.6%	$0

RATINGS:	AFL-CIO	CalPIRG	CLCV	NOW	CofC	CalFarm
	98	100	96	86	22	15

KEY VOTES:

Parent consent abort:	NO	Limit product tort:	YES	Clean Air Act:	YES
Assault gun ban:	YES	Ban AIDS discrim:	YES	Restrict abortion funds:	NO
Sales tax hike:	YES	Wealth tax hike:	YES	Strong gay rights:	YES
Parental leave:	YES	Timber compromise:	YES	Execution by injection:	YES
Limited gay rights:	YES	Universal health insur:	YES	1992-93 Budget Act:	YES
Campaign Reform:	YES	Offshore oil ban:	YES	Charter schools:	YES

William J. "Pete" Knight (R)
36th Assembly District

This staunchly Republican district includes the Antelope and Santa Clarita valleys north of Los Angeles. The rapidly growing Palmdale area is included along with a large section of the Angeles National Forest. Most of the newcomers are young, white families who have been forced out of the Los Angeles Basin by high housing costs and burgeoning crime rates in more affordable neighborhoods. The district has a 16 percent Latino population, but only 6.45 percent of them are registered to vote. The combined African American and Asian population is 8 percent.

Pete Knight

William J. "Pete" Knight won the Republican primary by defeating seven other candidates, including Hunt Braly, who was chief of staff to former state Senator Ed Davis. Braly had to move into the district to run for the open seat and he was called a carpetbagger by his opponents, a label that apparently hit a sour note with the voters. Knight, on the other hand, was the first popularly elected mayor of Palmdale and has deep roots in the community. In this safe Republican district, the race was pretty much over when the primary votes were counted. Knight trounced his Democratic opponent, Arnie Rodio of Lancaster, in the general election.

Knight's career in the United State Air Force spanned 32 years. At the time of his retirement, he was a colonel and the vice commander of the Air Force Flight Test Center, Air Force System Command at Edwards Air Force Base. An accomplished aviator, Knight is enshrined at the National Aviation Hall of Fame in Dayton Ohio. He flew the X-15 rocket research aircraft to a record speed of 4,250 mph and received astronaut wings for another flight to an altitude of 280,000 feet. He is past president of the Society of Experimental Test Pilots and is a fellow in the society. Knight has received numerous awards and citations for his endeavors as a pilot, including the Harmon International Aviator's Trophy in 1968 from President Lyndon B. Johnson for his record speed flight and the Octave Chanute Award from the Institute of Aeronautical Sciences.

PERSONAL: elected 1992; born Nov. 18, 1929, in Noblesville, Indiana; home, Palmdale; education, attended Butler and Purdue Universities and the Aviation Cadet Program; wife Gail, seven children; Protestant.

CAREER: retired USAF colonel, vice president in charge of fighter enhancement programs for Eidetics International in Torrence; mayor of Palmdale, 1988-92.

COMMITTEES: Consumer Protection, Government Efficiency & New Technologies; Governmental Organization; Transportation; Health.

OFFICES: Capitol, (916) 445-7698; district, 1529 E. Palmdale Blvd., 308, Palmdale 93550, (805) 947-9664.
   TERM LIMIT: 1998
   REGISTRATION: 35.2% D, 51.5% R, 2.0% AIP
   1992 CAMPAIGN: Knight – R   58.2% $272,924
                 Arnie Rodio – D   33.5% $51,031
                 Ronald Tisbert – L   8.3%
   RATINGS and **KEY VOTES**: Newly elected

David Knowles (R)
4th Assembly District

The new 4th District encompasses the rural counties of Alpine, Amador, Calaveras, El Dorado, Mono
and Placer. The district lost parts of Tuolumne and
Sacramento that had been in what was formerly the
7th District. The changes, however, had little effect
on the outcome of the 1992 election, where Knowles
defeated encyclopedia salesman Mark Norberg with
little trouble.

Back in 1988, Democrat Norman Waters narrowly dodged a political bullet in the November
election when he defeated Knowles, then a mortgage
banker with backing from the religious right. But in
the 1990 rematch, Knowles put cattleman Waters out   **David Knowles**
to pasture. Knowles used every opportunity to link
Waters to Assembly Speaker Willie Brown, who was a major financier of Waters'
campaigns. And while Knowles may have been correct in portraying Waters as
ineffective and beholden to the Democratic leadership, he certainly wasn't the
"liberal" Knowles claimed.

Waters, in that race, portrayed Knowles as a "right-wing nut." And while the
derisive tone of Waters' comment may have been uncalled for, there is no doubt that
Knowles espouses the views of the far right. For example, after a Sacramento
abortion clinic was rammed by an old military vehicle in 1985, Knowles said the act
was "the answer to a prayer." And during the 1990 campaign, Knowles received
substantial financial support from independent groups opposing abortion, against
gun control and backing other conservative causes.

He got off to a stormy start as a freshman legislator, irritating colleagues with his
tendency to speak on many of the bills heard on the floor and repeatedly referring
to "male-to-male anal intercourse" in a committee hearing on a bill that would have
banned discussion of homosexuality in public schools. His most memorable act as
a legislator to date, however, was the floor speech he delivered against a gay rights

bill in which he described gay sexual practices in explicit detail. Even conservative Republicans rebuked him for the graphic language. But Knowles maintained he was simply working to educate his fellow legislators about the dangers of "a radically different lifestyle that has the capability of spreading disease."

Knowles tends to view the world in absolutes, branding those who disagree with him as immoral. During debate on a 1992 child abuse bill sponsored by Assembly-woman Jackie Speier, D-Burlingame, Knowles took the floor and expressed concern that the bill would criminalize acts by parents who beat their children in accordance with the Scriptures. Speier was speechless for a few moments and then declared: "Mr. Knowles, you frighten me."

One of several lawmakers named as assistants by new Republican leader Jim Brulte, Knowles has offered few suggestions on how to deal with the problems facing his district. Instead, he has spoken in the generalities favored by bedrock conservatives, pledging to fight tax increases and crime, wipe out pornography and oppose gun control and abortion-upon-demand.

PERSONAL: elected 1990; born Sept. 5, 1952, Cleveland, Ohio; home, Cameron Park; education, B.A. Oral Roberts University; wife Anne, five children; Protestant.

CAREER: mortgage banker.

COMMITTEES: Education; Natural Resources; Water, Parks & Wildlife.

OFFICES: Capitol, (916) 445-8343, FAX (916) 327-2210; district, 3161 Cameron Park Drive, 214, Cameron Park 95682, (916) 676-5953, FAX (916) 933-5189.

TERM LIMIT: 1996

REGISTRATION: 41.8% D, 45.3% R

1992 CAMPAIGN:

Knowles – R		56.2%	$323,459
Mark Norberg – D		35.3%	$5,713
Gary Hines – L		8.6%	

1990 CAMPAIGN:

Knowles – R		51.4%	$131,409
Norman Waters (incumbent) – D		48.6%	$691,016

RATINGS:

AFL-CIO	CalPIRG	CLCV	NOW	CofC	CalFarm
3	18	02	9	100	85

KEY VOTES:

Sales tax hike:	NO	Wealth tax hike:	NO	Strong gay rights:	NO
Parental leave:	NO	Timber compromise:	NO	Execution by injection:	YES
Limited gay rights:	NO	Universal health insur:	NO	1992-93 Budget Act:	NO
Campaign Reform:	NO	Offshore oil ban:	NO	Charter schools:	YES

Barbara Lee (D)

16th Assembly District

The eastern shore of San Francisco Bay is a region of contrasts: great wealth and great squalor, mind-bending scientific research and mind-destroying drug traffic, industry and social inertia. Oakland lies at the heart of the region, a city that contains all of its contrasts and contradictions. It has a deeply troubled school district that has teetered on financial and political collapse. But with underdog pride it also has witnessed a rebirth of its downtown.

The center of Oakland is also the center of the 16th District, which takes in nearby Alameda and Emeryville. The seat (formerly the 13th District) was occupied for more than a decade by Elihu Harris, who was elected mayor of Oakland in 1990. The district's Democratic registration, about 70 percent, is among the highest in the Assembly. Harris' seat went to Barbara Lee, a former political consultant and aide to Rep. Ron Dellums. Lee had two decades of political experience before running for office. She was a key aide in Rep. Shirley Chisholm's 1972 presidential campaign and a fund-raiser for Dellums and other Democrats over the years. She was active in Jesse Jackson's presidential campaigns. In so doing, Lee has been on a first-name basis with all of the East Bay's most prominent Democratic politicians.

Barbara Lee

Once Harris announced that he was considering running for Oakland mayor, Lee began running for his Assembly seat – 18 months before the primary and well before any other contenders came onto the scene. For all practical purposes, the election was decided in the primary. Lee picked up endorsements from virtually the entire East Bay Democratic legislative delegation and Dellums' progressives. Her most serious primary opponent, Aleta Cannon, an Oakland City Council member, was an ally of Oakland Mayor Lionel Wilson. But Wilson's wing of the Democratic Party took a drubbing in 1990. Wilson fell so far from favor that he did not make it past his re-election primary and Cannon fell with him. Lee's re-election in 1992 was a cakewalk, since reapportionment changed the district only slightly.

As a rookie legislator, Lee weighed in with bills on issues such as abortion. Her AB 1097 made it a misdemeanor to obstruct a health-care facility, such as an abortion clinic. Nor has she been shy on the fund-raising circuit, sending out invitations to a fund-raiser with tea bags attached. Lee appears to be among the brighter – and more ambitious – members of the Assembly Class of '90 and bears watching as her career progresses.

PERSONAL: elected 1990; born July 16, 1946, in El Paso; home, Oakland; education, B.A. Mills College, M.A. UC Berkeley; divorced, two children; Baptist.

CAREER: administrative assistant Rep. Ronald Dellums; owned private consulting business.

COMMITTEES: Health; Public Safety; Rules; Transportation.

OFFICES: Capitol, (916) 445-7442, FAX (916) 327-1941; district, 1440 Broadway, 810, Oakland, 94612, (510) 286-0339, FAX (510) 763-2023.

TERM LIMIT: 1996
REGISTRATION: 69.6% D, 16.2% R

1992 CAMPAIGN:	Lee – D	74.5%	$212,795
	David Anderson – R	20.0%	$4,140
	Emma Wong Mar – P&F	5.5%	
1990 CAMPAIGN:	Lee – D	79.4%	$324,071
	Barbara Thomas – R	20.6%	

RATINGS:

AFL-CIO	CalPIRG	CLCV	NOW	CofC	CalFarm
97	95	100	100	17	20

KEY VOTES:

Sales tax hike:	YES	Wealth tax hike:	YES	Strong gay rights:	YES
Parental leave:	YES	Timber compromise:	nv	Execution by injection:	nv
Limited gay rights:	YES	Universal health insur:	YES	1992-93 Budget Act:	NO
Campaign Reform:	nv	Offshore oil ban:	YES	Charter schools:	YES

Burt M. Margolin (D)
42nd Assembly District

Once there were three solid Democratic districts on the west side of Los Angeles, stretching from downtown Los Angeles to Santa Monica north of Interstate 10. But after the Supreme Court finished its reapportionment plan, there was only one, the 42nd, which encompasses Beverly Hills and the adjacent upscale neighborhoods, such as Westwood. The overwhelmingly Democratic area is the base of operations for the liberal Democratic organization of Reps. Howard Berman and Henry Waxman, which dominates westside politics. Thus it's not surprising that one of its proteges, Burt Margolin, holds the 42nd District seat.

Burt Margolin

Margolin, first elected in 1982, has emerged as a masterful, hard-working and low-key legislative technician with a clear, liberal agenda. He had good training. Margolin was Waxman's chief of staff in Washington and Berman's legislative aide when he was an assemblyman in Sacramento. He is aligned with the "Grizzly Bear" bloc of liberals in the Assembly and is a dependable vote for environmental and consumer protection bills. Margolin moved into his own in 1986, when he engineered the state's bottle and can deposit law. Coaxing reluctant environmentalists and industry lobbyists, Margolin fashioned a complicated compromise that set up the state's recycling container program – and allowed the battling interests to avoid thrashing it out with a costly ballot initiative.

In 1989, Margolin moved on to an even more arcane area of law, workers' compensation. After marathon negotiations that lasted all summer, Margolin worked out a bill that increased benefits to injured workers and trimmed lawyer fees, but that 1989 measure has since been denounced by employers as a backdoor giveaway and hindered efforts by Margolin and others to forge a more comprehensive reform. Another Margolin bill was passed in 1992 but vetoed by Gov. Pete Wilson, who said it was inadequate.

In 1990, Margolin successfully expanded his container recycling law to increase deposits and include wine and liquor bottles. He was unsuccessful, however, in efforts to forge a health-care insurance bill for those not covered by any insurance. He moved bills out of both houses, but by the end of the 1990 session, neither house could come to terms and the issue has been frozen ever since.

Margolin moved from the chairmanship of the Assembly's Insurance Committee in 1993 to head the Health Committee – a victory for medical industry lobbyists, who prefer him to rival Jackie Speier.

PERSONAL: elected 1982; born Sept. 28, 1950, in Chattanooga, Tenn.; home, Los Angeles; education, attended UCLA; wife Laurie Post, one child; Jewish.

CAREER: chief of staff to Rep. Henry A. Waxman 1975-1977 and 1980-1982; legislative consultant to Assemblyman Howard Berman 1978-1979.

COMMITTEES: Health (chair); Finance and Insurance.

OFFICES: Capitol, (916) 445-7440, FAX (916) 445-0119; district, 8425 W. 3rd, 406, Los Angeles 90048, (213) 655-9750, FAX (213) 655-9725.

TERM LIMIT: 1996

REGISTRATION: 59.0% D, 25.3% R

1992 CAMPAIGN:	Margolin – D	67.3%	$311,754
	Robert Davis – R	26.6%	$20,658
1990 CAMPAIGN:	Margolin – D	65.2%	$198,254
	Elizabeth Michael – R	29%	$7,419

RATINGS:	AFL-CIO	CalPIRG	CLCV	NOW	CofC	CalFarm
	98	91	100	93	17	20

KEY VOTES:

Parent consent abort:	NO	Limit product tort:	NO	Clean Air Act:	YES
Assault gun ban:	YES	Ban AIDS discrim:	YES	Restrict abortion funds:	NO
Sales tax hike:	YES	Wealth tax hike:	YES	Strong gay rights:	YES
Parental leave:	YES	Timber compromise:	YES	Execution by injection:	nv
Limited gay rights:	YES	Universal health insur:	YES	1992-93 Budget Act:	YES
Campaign Reform:	YES	Offshore oil ban:	YES	Charter schools:	YES

Diane Martinez (D)
49th Assembly District

The 49th Assembly District encompasses the most racially diverse section of Southern California, a clump of the San Gabriel Valley that includes the cities of Alhambra, Rosemead and Monterey Park. It's an area that has gone from mostly Anglo to a mixture of Latino and Asian in scarcely a generation. The change has sparked numerous ethnic political clashes over such issues as whether business signs should be required to be displayed in English. The 49th is 55 percent Latino and nearly 30 percent Asian.

Diane Martinez

The post-reapportionment election of 1992 demonstrated the culture clash as Democrat Diane Martinez and Republican Sophie Wong vied for the seat being vacated by Xavier Becerra, who was elected to Congress after serving just one term in the Assembly. Martinez, who had been defeated by Becerra in 1990, defeated Wong, thanks largely to the 2-1 Democratic registration majority. Martinez is the daughter of Rep. Marty Martinez and, like her father, enjoys the support of the political organization headed by Reps. Howard Berman and Henry Waxman. Although Berman-Waxman dominates politics on the white, affluent west side of Los Angeles, it dabbles in politics in the African American and Latino sections of the metropolitan area where the elder Martinez was first recruited by the group in 1980 to run for the Assembly seat now held by his daughter.

Diane Martinez, who served on the Garvey School Board before moving to the Assembly, also worked in the telecommunications industry. Few doubt that when her father retires from Congress, she'll be waiting to succeed him.

PERSONAL: elected 1992; born Jan. 14, 1953, in Los Angeles; home, Monterey Park; education, attended East Los Angeles Community College; divorced, one child; Catholic.

CAREER: Pacific Bell and API Security Inc. for 15 years, Garvey School Board member.

COMMITTEES: Consumer Protection, Governmental Efficiency and New Technologies; Education; Local Government.

OFFICES: Capitol (916) 445-7852; district, 320 S. Garfield, 202, Alhambra, 91801, (818) 570-6121, FAX (818) 570-8470.

TERM LIMIT: 1998

REGISTRATION: 60.2% D, 26.4% R

1992 CAMPAIGN:			
Martinez – D	55.5%	$209,825
Sophie Wong – R	40.8%	$158,490

RATINGS and **KEY VOTES**: Newly elected

Juanita McDonald (D)
55th Assembly District

Southwestern Los Angeles County – Long Beach and environs – is generally Republican territory, but there is a considerable pocket of Democrats in the Carson-

Compton area and all of them were packaged into the 55th Assembly District by the state Supreme Court's reapportionment plan. The district wound up with a Democratic registration margin of more than 3-1, reflecting both its working-class ambience and the fact that more than 80 percent of its residents are non-Anglo, with Latinos, over 40 percent, being the largest single ethnic group.

Juanita McDonald

Someday, whenever Latinos become politically active commensurate with their numbers, the 55th District may have a Hispanic representative. But for the time being, it's a battleground for white politicians and 1992 featured one of the state's most bizarre three-way primary battles.

Two of the Capitol's least-loved characters, Democratic Assemblymen Dick Floyd and Dave Elder, both decided that they would lay claim to the 55th after the Supreme Court implemented its reapportionment plan. They felt it contained the best prospects for continued employment by a white Democratic politician in the area. Floyd, whose profane outbursts on the Assembly floor had made him infamous, and Elder, the obvious subject of a very unfavorable "novel" written by his ex-wife, spent the spring months raising money and taking potshots at each other.

But unbeknownst to anyone, it seems, the voters of the 55th decided that they didn't want either Floyd or Elder in Sacramento. When the votes had been counted, the winner of the primary was the third person in the race, previously unheralded Juanita McDonald, a Carson city councilwoman. McDonald received at least some help from motorcyclists who had been angered by Floyd's authorship of a bill requiring them to wear helmets.

Given the voter registration margin, the primary contest was the only one that counted. Republicans didn't even field a candidate for November and thus McDonald joined the swelling ranks of women serving in the Legislature – and one who is likely to remain until term limits force her out in 1998, unless a congressional or state Senate seat beckons.

PERSONAL: elected 1992; born Sept. 7, 1938, in Birmingham, Ala.; home, Carson; education, B.S. University of Redlands, M.A. Los Angeles State University; doctoral applicant University of Southern California; husband Jim, five children; Baptist.

CAREER: teacher, Los Angeles Unified School District; writer and editor of school texts; corporate counselor, Bernard Haldane Associates; councilwoman and mayor, Carson.

COMMITTEES: Governmental Organization (vice chair); Education; Housing & Community Development; Transportation.

OFFICES: Capitol, (916) 445-3134, FAX (916) 322-0655; district, 1 Civic Plaza, 320, Carson 90745 (310) 518-3324, FAX (310) 518-3326.
TERM LIMIT: 1998
REGISTRATION: 68.2% D, 19.9% R
1992 CAMPAIGN: McDonald – D   82.8% $276,035
     Shannon Anderson – L   17.2%
RATINGS and **KEY VOTES**: Newly elected

Gwen A. Moore (D)
47th Assembly District

Court-ordered reapportionment made this district, renumbered from 49 to 47, even more concentrated in terms of non-white ethnicity and Democratic voter registration by slicing off the mostly white beachfront communities such as Marina del Rey. Gwen Moore, who was easily re-elected in 1992 to an eighth term, needn't worry about re-election in a district in which three of every four registered voters are Democrats. The real question is whether Moore, a former deputy probation officer and community college instructor, can find some new venue in which to pursue her political career once term limits end her Assembly tenure in 1996.

Gwen Moore

For several years, Moore has been the Assembly member out front on public utility and cable television issues as chairwoman of the Utilities and Commerce Committee. In that role, she has generally pushed utilities to justify proposed rate increases. And she successfully established a low-cost "lifeline" telephone rate for low-income people. Moore, along with fellow Los Angeles Democrat Maxine Waters, was at the forefront of a movement to get the Legislature to prohibit investments of state pension funds in corporations doing business in South Africa. In 1990, she pushed legislation that would have allowed prosecutors to charge females with statutory rape as well as males, a measure vetoed by Gov. George Deukmejian. She also tried again on a bill that would have required medium and large businesses to give unpaid leave to workers who want to care for sick children or parents, but the measure met the same fate in 1990 that it did in 1987 – a veto from Deukmejian. Nor did it fare any better when Pete Wilson replaced Deukmejian in the governor's office.

In October 1990, federal prosecutors announced that Moore had been cleared of wrongdoing in connection with the U.S. Justice Department's ongoing political corruption probe at the Capitol. Moore had been living under a cloud for more than two years since she was the author of two bills that federal agents pushed through the Legislature that would have benefited two sham companies set up by the FBI to track influence peddling. Her office was one of several raided by the FBI, and one of her former aides was convicted on corruption charges.

With her connections to the political organization of Reps. Howard Berman and Henry Waxman, Moore is being readied to run for Congress when the opportunity arises – perhaps when Rep. Julian Dixon relinquishes his seat. That was supposed to happen in 1992 when Dixon was to have sought a seat on the Los Angeles County Board of Supervisors. Dixon ultimately opted out so Moore continues to wait for another opportunity.

PERSONAL: elected 1978; born Oct. 28, 1940, in Detroit, Mich.; home, Los Angeles; education, B.A. CSU Los Angeles, graduate study at USC, teaching credential UCLA; husband Ron Dobson, one child; Protestant.

CAREER: probation officer; Los Angeles Community College trustee 1975-78.

COMMITTEES: Education; Governmental Organization; Higher Education; Utilities & Commerce (chair).

OFFICES: Capitol, (916) 445-8800; district, 5th Floor, 3683 Crenshaw Blvd., Los Angeles 90016, (213) 292-0605, FAX (213) 736-3099.

TERM LIMIT: 1996

REGISTRATION: 75.0% D, 14.0% R

1992 CAMPAIGN:	Moore – D			80.8%		$211,448
	Jonathan Leonard III – R			14.0%		$1,623
1990 CAMPAIGN:	Moore – D			72.9%		$229,170
	Eric Givens – R			21.9%		$4,130

RATINGS:	AFL-CIO	CalPIRG	CLCV	NOW	CofC	CalFarm
	95	90	96	100	22	30

KEY VOTES:

Parent consent abort:	NO	Limit product tort:	nv	Clean Air Act:	YES
Assault gun ban:	YES	Ban AIDS discrim:	YES	Restrict abortion funds:	NO
Sales tax hike:	YES	Wealth tax hike:	YES	Strong gay rights:	YES
Parental leave:	YES	Timber compromise:	NO	Execution by injection:	nv
Limited gay rights:	YES	Universal health insur:	YES	1992-93 Budget Act:	NO
Campaign Reform:	nv	Offshore oil ban:	YES	Charter schools:	YES

Bill Morrow (R)

73rd Assembly District

This coast-hugging district includes San Juan Capistrano, San Clemente and Laguna Niguel in Orange County and Oceanside, Camp Pendleton and most of Carlsbad in San Diego County. GOP registration is 53 percent and whites outnumber minorities 3-to-1.

Bill Morrow, former chief trial counsel for Camp Pendleton, defeated seven other contenders in the Republican primary in 1992, a contest that caught the interest of Republican legislators in Sacramento. Morrow was supported by Sen. Frank Hill of Whittier and Assemblyman Ross Johnson of Fullerton, while candidate Patricia Bates got a boost from Assemblyman Gil Ferguson of Newport Beach. Gov. Wilson's people put their political clout behind Dana Point Mayor Mike Eggers, but, as in many of the 1992 GOP primaries, Wilson lost his attempt to shore up the moderate contingent within the Assembly Republican Caucus.

Bill Morrow

A conservative with ties to the Christian right, his campaign was aided financially by both Christian and anti-abortion groups. In the general election, Morrow defeated Democrat Lee Walker, a teacher at Saddleback College. Walker ran well, given the Democrats' registration disadvantage, but he was left defenseless by a lack of money.

PERSONAL: elected 1992; born April 19, 1954, in Diamond Bar; home, Oceanside; USMC 1979-1987; education, Mt. San Antonio College, B.A. political science UCLA, J.D. Pepperdine; wife Esther; non-denominational Christian.

CAREER: USMC officer and judge advocate; chief trial counsel Camp Pendleton; legislative aide, California Republican Caucus.

COMMITTEES: Education; Natural Resources; Public Employees Retirement & Social Security.

OFFICES: Capitol, (916) 445-7676, FAX (916) 324-5321; district, 3088 Pio Pico Dr, 101, Carlsbad 92008, (619) 966-4701, FAX (619) 966-4701.

TERM LIMIT: 1998

REGISTRATION: 30.9% D, 53.2% R, 2.0% AIP

1992 CAMPAIGN:			
Morrow – R	54.4%	$315,051
Lee Walker – D	37.5%	$9,168

RATINGS and **KEY VOTES**: Newly elected

Richard L. Mountjoy (R)
59th Assembly District

While the floor of the San Gabriel Valley is a center of Latino population and political power, the residential uplands overlooking the valley are white and Republican. The 59th Assembly District is the heart of the region, with communities such as Monrovia and Arcadia. The district has been represented since 1978 by Richard Mountjoy and he fits his district perfectly: a middle-aged, white Republican businessman who joined the Legislature as one of the self-proclaimed "Proposition 13 babies" and has lost none of his zeal for political infighting in the decade-plus since.

Mountjoy has become the point man for the Republicans in their ceaseless partisan wars with Democrats over reapportionment and legislative procedure. He helped write a 1984 ballot measure aimed at curbing Speaker Willie Brown's powers and was one of the advocates of legislative term limits, approved by voters in 1990. Given that preoccupation, Mountjoy participates only rarely in policy matters and devotes much of his time to plotting strategy.

In 1990, Mountjoy single-handedly campaigned against Proposition 112, the Legislature's ethics reform package. Mountjoy and Ruth Holton, a lobbyist for Common Cause, faced-off on countless radio talk shows on the issue. Mountjoy maintained that while

Richard Mountjoy

the ethical standards were desirable, the measure had a catch: a commission that, he said, almost certainly would give lawmakers a pay raise. He was right. The measure passed, and lawmakers got a raise.

Mountjoy, who approaches politics with unfailing good humor, also has been a leader of the Republican right wing in its battles with GOP moderates led by Gov. Pete Wilson. In the 1990s, workers' compensation reform has become his chief crusade. He introduces many bills, but most are so Draconian they don't go anywhere.

When Mountjoy isn't politicking, he operates a construction company. He also is a former city councilman and mayor of Monrovia and often flies his own plane between Southern California and Sacramento, once surviving a crash-landing at Sacramento's Executive Airport.

PERSONAL: elected 1978; born Jan. 13, 1932, in Monrovia; home, Monrovia; Navy 1951-1955 Korea; wife Earline; three children; Protestant.

CAREER: general contractor; commercial pilot; Monrovia City Council and mayor 1968-1976.

COMMITTEES: Finance & Insurance; Rules; Utilities & Commerce; (joint) Rules.

OFFICES: Capitol, (916) 445-7234, FAX (916) 442-8429; district, 208 N. First Ave., Arcadia 91006, (818) 446-3134, FAX (818) 445-3591.

TERM LIMIT: 1996

REGISTRATION: 39.7% D, 48.3% R

1992 CAMPAIGN:	Mountjoy – R	55.5%	$291,591
	Louise Gelber – D	44.5%	$132,300
1990 CAMPAIGN:	Mountjoy – R	57.9%	$247,724
	Evelyn Fierro – D	38.6%	$101,060

RATINGS:	AFL-CIO	CalPIRG	CLCV	NOW	CofC	CalFarm
	7	9	8	21	94	75

KEY VOTES:

Parent consent abort:	YES	Limit product tort:	YES	Clean Air Act:	NO
Assault gun ban:	NO	Ban AIDS discrim:	NO	Restrict abortion funds:	YES
Sales tax hike:	NO	Wealth tax hike:	NO	Strong gay rights:	NO
Parental leave:	NO	Timber compromise:	NO	Execution by injection:	YES
Limited gay rights:	NO	Universal health insur:	NO	1992-93 Budget Act:	YES
Campaign Reform:	NO	Offshore oil ban:	NO	Charter schools:	YES

Willard H. Murray Jr. (D)
52nd Assembly District

When Republican Paul Zeltner won this largely minority and blue-collar district in 1986 – thanks mostly to a tactical blunder by Assembly Speaker Willie Brown – Brown quickly proclaimed that Zeltner's days as a legislator were numbered. Brown's prediction came true. In 1988, Willard Murray, a former aide to Rep. Mervyn Dymally, edged the first-term lawmaker to reclaim a seat that had traditionally gone to Democrats.

Willard Murray

It didn't take Murray long to get in the middle of controversy. Murray, whose South-Central Los Angeles district includes cities plagued by Uzi-toting gangs, refused to support a measure to restrict semi-automatic military-style assault weapons. In doing so, he was sticking by the National Rifle Association, which had given him a key endorsement against former policeman Zeltner. Ironically, shortly after he was elected, Murray came under fire from the NRA for sending out an endorsement letter without their permission.

Murray was the subject of even controversy before he was elected. During his campaign, he acknowledged that he had never graduated from UCLA despite campaign literature that said he had received a degree in mathematics.

Nevertheless, Murray squeaked by Zeltner in a district that included his home-town of Paramount, Lakewood, Compton, Bellflower and a portion of Long Beach – all areas that were excised from the district as its boundaries were altered and its number changed (from 54 to 52) by the state Supreme Court in its post-1990 census reapportionment. Murray's new district has just a portion of Compton and the remainder is comprised of African American and Latino neighborhoods of the city of Los Angeles. Latinos, in fact, outnumber African Americans now by a 4-3 margin, but the seat is expected to remain politically dominated by African Americans for years to come because of very low levels of voting by Hispanics.

In his first term, Murray concentrated on anti-crime bills, introducing a measure to increase penalties for possession of a machine gun. He proposed improved services for veterans and a program to encourage college students to become teachers. None of his legislation is particularly earthshaking, and he shows all the earmarks of being a permanent backbencher – albeit one who continues to play the outside political game, including proprietorship of a very controversial political slate mailer.

PERSONAL: elected 1988; born Jan. 1, 1931, in Los Angeles; home, Paramount; USAF 1951-1954 (Korea); education, attended CSU Los Angeles; widower, two children; Methodist.

CAREER: engineering; legislative consultant Rep. Mervyn Dymally; chief deputy Los Angeles City Councilman Robert Farrell; executive assistant Los Angeles Mayor Sam Yorty; senior consultant Assembly Democratic Caucus.

COMMITTEES: Local Government; Rules; Utilities & Commerce; Ways & Means.

OFFICES: Capitol, (916) 445-7486, FAX (916) 447-3079; district, 16444 Paramount Blvd., 100, Paramount 90723, (310) 516-4144, FAX (310) 630-0231.

TERM LIMIT: 1996

REGISTRATION: 80.0% D, 11.3% R

1992 CAMPAIGN:	Murray – D	100%	$175,503
1990 CAMPAIGN:	Murray – D	50%	$185,212
	Emily Hart-Holifield – R	41.2%	$22,554
	Arthur Olivier – L	5.9%	

RATINGS:	AFL-CIO	CalPIRG	CLCV	NOW	CofC	CalFarm
	97	86	73	93	22	25

KEY VOTES:

Assault gun ban:	NO	Ban AIDS discrim:	YES	Restrict abortion funds:	NO
Sales tax hike:	YES	Wealth tax hike:	YES	Strong gay rights:	YES
Parental leave:	YES	Timber compromise:	YES	Execution by injection:	YES
Limited gay rights:	YES	Universal health insur:	nv	1992-93 Budget Act:	NO
Campaign Reform:	NO	Offshore oil ban:	NO	Charter schools:	YES

Grace F. Napolitano (D)
58th Assembly District

The 58th Assembly District is another of several created by the state Supreme Court's reapportionment plan to have a decided Latino majority, in this case over 60 percent of the population and nearly 44 percent of voter registration.

The 58th, which encompasses a piece of southeastern Los Angeles County that includes Norwalk, Whittier and Montebello, also was one of several sites where rival Hispanic political factions sought additional clout. But in this case a candidate backed by Los Angeles County Supervisor Gloria Molina lost the primary to a candidate with the official backing of the Assembly Democratic caucus. Grace Napolitano, a Norwalk city councilwoman and mayor, pumped tens of thousands of dollars of her own money into the primary campaign and then had an easy runoff against a little-known and ill-financed Republican.

Grace Napolitano

PERSONAL: elected 1992; born Dec. 4, 1936, in Brownsville, Tex.; home, Norwalk; education, attended Texas Southmost College, Los Angeles Trade Tech and Cerritos College; husband Frank, five children; Catholic.

CAREER: Norwalk city councilwoman and mayor; chair, Los Angeles County Private Industry Council.

COMMITTEES: Housing & Community Development (vice chair); Governmental Organization; Transportation.

OFFICES: Capitol, (916) 445-0965, FAX (916) 327-1203; district, PO Box 408, Norwalk 90650, (310) 406-7322.

TERM LIMIT: 1998

REGISTRATION: 63.8% D, 26.5% R

1992 CAMPAIGN:

Napolitano – D	64.2%	$270,298
Ken Gow – R	28.1%	$0
John McCready – L	7.7%	

RATINGS and **KEY VOTES**: Newly elected

Patrick J. Nolan (R)
43rd Assembly District

Reapportionment changed the number and boundaries but not the proclivities of this Glendale-centered district. After a backroom shuffle in 1992, the district also kept Pat Nolan, its incumbent Republican assemblyman.

Nolan, the acknowledged leader of the "caveman" faction of the Republican caucus, is that rarest of species, a Republican who really likes political rough-and-tumble. Following the court-imposed reapportionment, Nolan faced the possibility of a bitter campaign fight with Democratic Assemblywoman Barbara Friedman, who was left without a district. Had that happened, the subject of the federal anti-corruption investigation looking into Nolan's fund-raising activities would have been a prominent campaign issue.

But fate – or the fine hand of Speaker Willie Brown, an old Nolan ally despite their sharply different ideologies – intervened. One of Brown's lieutenants, Tom Bane, decided suddenly to retire, which allowed Friedman to run in Bane's district.

Nolan faced only token opposition in 1992 and won re-election easily.

One of the "Proposition 13 babies" elected to the Assembly in 1978, Nolan deposed Bob Naylor as Republican leader in 1984. He patterned his leadership after that of his Democratic counterpart by raising vast campaign sums and choosing candidates. Even while bashing Brown as a campaign theme, Nolan reached an accommodation with the speaker that allowed Nolan to pick the committee assignments for Republicans. Nolan reciprocated by protecting Brown from being deposed when the "Gang of Five" Democratic faction sought an alliance with the Republicans.

Pat Nolan

Nolan claimed full credit for the Republican victories in 1986 and predicted that the GOP was on its way toward capturing control of the lower house in time for the post-census reapportionment. Nolan insiders talked of his running for attorney general in 1990.

Then Nolan ran into big troubles. His heavy-handed fund-raising came to the attention of the FBI, which was conducting an undercover investigation of Capitol influence-peddling. Nolan's Capitol office was raided in August 1988 by federal agents armed with search warrants. Nolan had accepted $10,000 in campaign contributions from a sham undercover FBI company that was making the rounds in the Capitol looking to buy help for a bill. The FBI has continued its investigation of Nolan, among others, but years later, federal prosecutors still haven't decided whether he will be prosecuted or cleared. A former Nolan aide has pleaded guilty to federal charges and her sentencing has been delayed while she cooperates with investigators.

When three Republican incumbents – Paul Zeltner, Bill Duplissea and Wayne Grisham – lost in 1988, Nolan saw the writing on the wall and resigned as Assembly Republican leader. He managed to hand the job to a close associate, Ross Johnson of LaHabra. Both were embarrassed when one of their lieutenants, Assemblyman John Lewis, was indicted on forgery charges stemming from the distribution of letters of endorsement for Republican Assembly candidates carrying an unauthorized signature of President Ronald Reagan. There was testimony that both participated in the strategy sessions that led to issuance of the letters. One of the side-effects of the affair was to poison relations between Nolan and the Reagan White House. Lewis eventually had the forgery charge tossed out by an appellate court and never went to trial.

Despite those setbacks, Nolan has not slid very far into the background. He has remained a key strategist for Assembly Republicans. A few short months after he quit as their leader, GOP Assembly members followed Nolan in holding up passage of the budget in 1989 while he fought to redefine the distribution of school money for gifted and disadvantaged programs to get more for the suburbs and less for the inner cities. During the 1990 budget impasse, Nolan circulated a letter pledging not to tamper with Proposition 98's education financing formulas. His actions gave the protection of Proposition 98 a non-partisan patina, and thus backed Gov. George Deukmejian into a corner. Faced with such opposition Deukmejian had no other choice – in large measure because of Nolan – but to bitterly drop his proposal to deeply cut the education budget.

If Nolan can rid himself of the lingering federal investigation, he doubtless will renew his statewide political ambitions. However, Nolan may also be hobbled by his close relationship to the savings and loan industry. A study by Common Cause identified him as one the top legislative recipients of S&L campaign contributions in the last decade, garnering $154,000 in a 10-year period. A Nolan-authored bill in 1982 allowed California-chartered S&Ls to invest 100 percent of their assets in "virtually any type of venture, regardless of the risk," Common Cause said. That bill and a companion measure carried by Bane led to the collapse of several savings and loans in California, including Lincoln Savings, whose demise resulted in the imprisonment of owner Charles Keating.

PERSONAL: elected 1978; born June 16, 1950, in Los Angeles; home, Glendale; education, B.A. and J.D. USC; wife Gail Zajc-MacKenzie, two children; Roman Catholic.

CAREER: lawyer; reserve deputy sheriff, Los Angeles County.

COMMITTEES: Governmental Organization; Higher Education; Rules; Ways & Means (joint) Legislative Budget; Fire, Police, Emergency & Disaster Services.

OFFICES Capitol, (916) 445-8364, FAX 322-4398; district, 143 S. Glendale Ave., 208, Glendale 91205, (818) 240-6330, FAX (213) 620-3028.

TERM LIMIT: 1996

REGISTRATION: 43.3% D, 42.3% R

1992 CAMPAIGN:

Nolan – R	56.2%	$691,980
Elliott Graham – D	37.4%	$1,626
Anthony Bajada – L	6.4%	

1990 CAMPAIGN:

Nolan – R	56.4%	$814,638
Jeanette Mann – D	38%	$62,749

RATINGS:

AFL-CIO	CalPIRG	CLCV	NOW	CofC	CalFarm
11	18	8	21	89	75

KEY VOTES:

Parent consent abort:	YES	Limit product tort:	YES	Clean Air Act:	NO
Assault gun ban:	NO	Ban AIDS discrim:	NO	Restrict abortion funds:	nv
Sales tax hike:	nv	Wealth tax hike:	NO	Strong gay rights:	NO
Parental leave:	NO	Timber compromise:	NO	Execution by injection:	YES
Limited gay rights:	NO	Universal health insur:	NO	1992-93 Budget Act:	YES
Campaign Reform:	NO	Offshore oil ban:	NO	Charter schools:	YES

Jack O'Connell (D)

35th Assembly District

Republicans believe they might be able to win this district – but not until Jack O'Connell moves on. The district stretches from just south of Lompoc in Santa Barbara County to include all of northern Ventura County, including the city of Ventura. O'Connell is a hard-working, quietly effective legislator. He has built a following in his moderate, environmentally conscious district through personal appearances and attention to local issues. A few years earlier, GOP strategists thought they could turn him out of office. Now, they're waiting for state Sen. Gary K. Hart, another popular Democrat from the area, to run for higher office so that O'Connell will run for the Senate and open up the Assembly district.

Jack O'Connell

O'Connell, a longtime resident of the area, served as an aide to former state Sen. Omer Rains of Ventura. He, like Hart, is a former teacher. At the start of the 1991-92 session, O'Connell sponsored one of the high-priority proposals of incoming Gov. Pete Wilson's administration. He proposed a constitutional amendment, ACA 6, which would allow local school bond approval by a simple majority of voters rather than the two-thirds required under provisions of Proposition 13. The measure passed both houses of the legislature in 1992 and will appear on the ballot in June 1994.

Many of O'Connell's bills have focused on education and children's issues. He pushed to extend programs for gifted and developmentally disabled students at a time when they were threatened by partisan politics. He has sought increased penalties on drunken drivers who have children in their cars and for drug dealers who sell near schools. O'Connell drew the ire of gun enthusiasts in 1989, when he voted in favor of a bill to ban most semiautomatic military-style assault weapons. An unsuccessful recall drive was started. He also got involved in the controversial animal-rights issue when he proposed making it a crime to use animals in certain laboratory tests.

O'Connell became speaker pro tem upon the departure of Michael Roos, who resigned from the Assembly early in 1991. The job entails presiding over the daily floor sessions and has been a stepping stone to the speaker's job in the past.

PERSONAL: elected 1982; born Oct. 8, 1951, in Glen Cove, N.Y.; home, Carpinteria; education, B.A. CSU Fullerton, teaching credential CSU Long Beach; wife Doree Caputo, one child; Roman Catholic.

CAREER: high school teacher; aide to Sen. Omer Rains; speaker pro tempore 1991 to present.

COMMITTEES: Education; Finance & Insurance; Ways & Means.
OFFICES: Capitol, (916) 445-8292, FAX (916) 327-3518; district, 228 W. Carrillo St., F, Santa Barbara 93101, (805) 966-3707.
TERM LIMIT: 1996
REGISTRATION: 45.8% D, 37.3% R
1992 CAMPAIGN: O'Connell – D   66.7% $611,879
                              Alan Ebenstein – R   33.3% $59,009
1990 CAMPAIGN: O'Connell – D   66.9% $443,918
                              Connie O'Shaughnessy – R   33.1% $62,845

RATINGS:

AFL-CIO	CalPIRG	CLCV	NOW	CofC	CalFarm
97	100	92	86	28	40

KEY VOTES:

Parent consent abort:	NO	Limit product tort:	YES	Clean Air Act:	YES
Assault gun ban:	YES	Ban AIDS discrim:	YES	Restrict abortion funds:	NO
Sales tax hike:	YES	Wealth tax hike:	YES	Strong gay rights:	YES
Parental leave:	YES	Timber compromise:	NO	Execution by injection:	YES
Limited gay rights:	YES	Universal health insur:	YES	1992-93 Budget Act:	YES
Campaign Reform:	YES	Offshore oil ban:	YES	Charter schools:	YES

J. Stephen Peace (D)
79th Assembly District

San Diego County's 79th Assembly District's southern boundary bumps up against the Mexican border and a section of the district's western boundary includes the shoreline of San Diego Bay, where the once sleepy bedroom communities of National City and Chula Vista awakened in the 1980s. Chula Vista has become home to ritzy bayside hotels, and home developers are paving the mesas above. The problems of this district are those of Mexico, where the First and Third Worlds crash head-on. Illegal aliens and drugs are smuggled across the border at Otay Mesa and elsewhere. Sewage from Tijuana leaks across the border into San Diego and fouls the beaches and horse farms there.

Steve Peace

The Democrat who represents this district, Steve Peace, was once known for two things: He was the producer of the cult film, "Attack of the Killer Tomatoes," and he was Willie Brown's man to see in San Diego. Socially chummy with the speaker, Peace was considered a genius at political strategy – and that may be why the speaker has tolerated Peace so long. Many of Peace's colleagues can't stand him, considering him immature and obnoxious. His floor speeches have sometimes been nothing more than rants. His fabled fight with the Senate's Al Alquist (when witnesses heard Peace call Alquist a "senile old pedophile") earned him the undying hatred of the Senate, but Brown protected him.

Then in 1987, Peace and four of his colleagues turned on Brown, dubbing themselves the "Gang of Five." They pulled parliamentary maneuvers for a year, tying the Assembly up in petty intrigues. They eventually made peace in 1989.

As a legislator, Peace has paid attention to the border issues that so plague his district, working on getting a sewage treatment plant for the area. He has labored for years over a low-level nuclear waste compact with other states (which got him in trouble with Alquist), and he has kept proposed nuclear waste dumps out of Democratic districts.

At the start of the 1991-92 session, the speaker fully restored Peace to his official family. Peace was made chairman of a new Banking, Finance and Bonded Indebtedness Committee. Peace got the "Finance" half of the old Finance and Insurance Committee. Peace's committee has the potential to be one of the most powerful in the Assembly, with wide-ranging authority over bonds, banks, savings and loans and financial legislation. The committee will undoubtedly play a major role in any workers' compensation reform. Peace said in early 1993 that he would move a workers' compensation bill out of his Finance and Insurance Committee by the end of February.

PERSONAL: elected 1982; born March 30, 1953, in San Diego; home, Rancho San Diego; education, B.A. UC San Diego; wife Cheryl, three children; Methodist.

CAREER: partner, Four Square Productions of National City, a film production firm; aide to Assemblymen Wadie Deddeh 1976-1980 and Larry Kapiloff 1980-1981.

COMMITTEES: Finance & Insurance (chair); Environmental Safety & Toxic Materials; Televising the Assembly; Utilities & Commerce.

OFFICES: Capitol, (916) 445-7556, FAX (916) 322-2271; district, 430 Davidson St., B, Chula Vista 92010, (619) 426-1617.

TERM LIMIT: 1996

REGISTRATION: 55.1% D, 30.3% R

1992 CAMPAIGN:

	Peace – D	65.2%	$387,702
	Raul Silva-Martinez – R	27.7%	$51,796

1990 CAMPAIGN:

	Peace – D	57.7%	$214,635
	Kevin Kelly – R	34.9%	$3,193

RATINGS:

AFL-CIO	CalPIRG	CLCV	NOW	CofC	CalFarm
84	86	79	72	28	25

KEY VOTES:

Parent consent abort:	YES	Limit product tort:	YES	Clean Air Act:	nv
Assault gun ban:	NO	Ban AIDS discrim:	YES	Restrict abortion funds:	NO
Sales tax hike:	YES	Wealth tax hike:	YES	Strong gay rights:	YES
Parental leave:	YES	Timber compromise:	YES	Execution by injection:	YES
Limited gay rights:	YES	Universal health insur:	YES	1992-93 Budget Act:	YES
Campaign Reform:	YES	Offshore oil ban:	YES	Charter schools:	YES

Richard G. Polanco (D)

45th Assembly District

Even with reapportionment, Richard Polanco didn't have to worry about winning another term in the Assembly. So he spent most of 1992 dabbling in other districts, representing one of the two major Latino political factions that have emerged in Los Angeles during the last decade.

Polanco is a partner in the alliance that includes state Sen. Art Torres and Los Angeles City Councilman Richard Alatorre. The group is locked in a power struggle with a faction headed by Los Angeles County Supervisor Gloria Molina and Rep. Lucille Roybal-Allard. At stake is the question of who will be in control as Los Angeles' huge Latino population becomes politically active and, someday, dominant.

Richard Polanco

Polanco acts as the Sacramento agent for his group after replacing Alatorre in the Assembly in 1985. His own special election had been one of the many contests between the rival factions.

A onetime aide to Alatorre and several other politicians, Polanco made a big mistake on his very first day in the Assembly. As a member of the Public Safety Committee he voted in favor a bill to authorize a new state prison in East Los Angeles. Heavy community opposition to the prison forced Polanco quickly to reverse course. He became a vocal opponent of the prison, which was to have been built as part of political deal that included construction of another penitentiary in the mostly white desert suburbs of Los Angeles County. Only the desert prison was built.

As a legislator, Polanco has rarely risen above the pedestrian, although in 1990 he won some plaudits in his district for carrying a bill – albeit unsuccessfully – to ban aerial spraying of malathion to combat the Mediterranean fruit fly in urban areas. His major pieces of legislation have been tainted by special-interest sponsorship, such as a tobacco industry-sponsored bill that would have created a law to regulate free promotional distribution of tobacco products statewide. He dropped the bill after health and local government groups argued that the statewide standards would prevent tougher local ordinances.

Given the nature of his district, Polanco probably can remain in office until term limits catch up with him. In the meantime, he will be awaiting an opportunity to move up to the Senate or Congress, or perhaps even the Los Angeles County Board of Supervisors, if it is expanded to seven members from its present five.

PERSONAL: elected 1986 (special election); born March 4, 1951, in Los Angeles; home, Los Angeles; education, attended Universidad Nacional de Mexico and University of Redlands, A.A. East Los Angeles Community College; wife Olivia, three children; Methodist.

CAREER: special assistant Gov. Jerry Brown 1980-1982; chief of staff Assemblyman Richard Alatorre 1983-1985.

COMMITTEES: Agriculture; Health; Rules; Utilities & Commerce; Ways & Means; (joint) Mental Health Research (chair); Rules.

OFFICES: Capitol, (916) 445-7587, FAX (916) 324-4657; district, 110 North Ave., 56, Los Angeles 90042, (213) 255-7111, FAX (213) 620-4411.

TERM LIMIT: 1998

REGISTRATION: 61.9% D, 22.1% R

1992 CAMPAIGN:	Polanco – D	64.6%	$426,039
	Kitty Hedrick – R	26.1%	0
	J. Luis Gomez – P&F	9.3%	
1990 CAMPAIGN:	Polanco – D	78.3%	$362,504
	Dale Olvera – L	21.7%	$0

RATINGS:	AFL-CIO	CalPIRG	CLCV	NOW	CofC	CalFarm
	97	95	96	100	22	20

KEY VOTES:

Parent consent abort:	NO	Limit product tort:	NO	Clean Air Act:	YES
Assault gun ban:	YES	Ban AIDS discrim:	YES	Restrict abortion funds:	NO
Sales tax hike:	YES	Wealth tax hike:	YES	Strong gay rights:	YES
Parental leave:	YES	Timber compromise:	nv	Execution by injection:	YES
Limited gay rights:	YES	Universal health insur:	YES	1992-93 Budget Act:	NO
Campaign Reform:	YES	Offshore oil ban:	YES	Charter schools:	YES

Curtis L. Pringle (R)
68th Assembly District

The city of Anaheim is split among four Assembly districts, the 68th being one of them. This district, which includes parts of Garden Grove, most of Buena Park and western Anaheim, was designed to pack as much of the Orange County Asian population as possible into one district. The district is 17 percent Asian, 23 percent Latino and 58 percent white. Only a handful of African Americans live in this solidly Republican district.

Curt Pringle was elected to the Assembly in 1988 from the 72nd Assembly District and served one term. He was defeated in 1990 by Democrat Tom Umberg of Garden Grove. Pringle's short tenure was

Curtis Pringle

dominated by the controversy surrounding his 1988 win over Democrat Christian F. Thierbach, a Riverside County deputy district attorney. On Election Day, the Orange County Republican Central Committee hired uniformed guards to patrol polling places in heavily Hispanic precincts, and Democrats charged that the guards were posted in an attempt to intimidate Hispanics. When the ballots were counted, Pringle had won by fewer than 800 votes out of more than 93,000 cast. Pringle withstood legal challenges to his election, but he was so distracted that he had no impact as a legislator in Sacramento.

In the 1992 primary, Pringle ran in the new 68th District against two moderate Republican women, who campaigned on Pringle's record, claiming it was an embarrassment to Orange County Republicans. But Pringle prevailed and won with 60 percent of the vote. He went on to easily defeat Democrat Linda Rigney with 57 percent of the vote.

Pringle, who was tapped as a Republican whip by Assembly GOP leader Jim Brulte, will be a dutiful member of the conservative wing of the Assembly Republican caucus.

PERSONAL: elected 1988; born June 27, 1959, in Emmetsburg, Iowa; home, Garden Grove; education, B.A. and M.A. CSU Long Beach; wife Alexis Nease, one child; Methodist.

CAREER: member and chairman of Garden Grove Planning Commission 1986-1988; partner in Pringle's Draperies, a retail and wholesale manufacturing firm in Anaheim.

COMMITTEES: Human Services; Revenue & Taxation; Local Government.

OFFICES: Capitol, (916) 445-8377, FAX (916) 323-5467; 12865 Main St., 100, Garden Grove 92640, (714) 539-7605.

TERM LIMIT: 1998

REGISTRATION: 42.1% D, 45.7% R

1992 CAMPAIGN:	Pringle – R	57.1%	$249,337
	Linda Kay Rigney – D	42.9%	$8,088
1990 CAMPAIGN:	Umberg – D	51.9%	$535,506
	Pringle (incumbent) – R	48.1%	$612,632

RATINGS: Newly elected

KEY VOTES: (votes are from prior Assembly service 1988-90)
Assault gun ban: NO   Ban AIDS discrim: NO   Restrict abortion funds: YES.

Charles W. Quackenbush (R)
24th Assembly District

Reapportionment carved off some of the more conservative pieces of the sole Republican district in the San Jose area and Democrats thought GOP Assemblyman Charles Quackenbush might be vulnerable to a challenge from a well-known local Democrat, James Beall Jr., a 12-year veteran of the San Jose City Council. But voters in the affluent suburbs of Los Altos, Cupertino, Los Gatos, Campbell and Saratoga decided they would stay with the Republican, especially one who echoes their moderate ideologies. Quackenbush was re-elected to a fourth term.

Quackenbush, a tall, youthful-looking former Army captain and high-tech entrepreneur, who is conservative with a bit of an independent streak, wasn't the first choice of the dominant conservative faction of the Assembly Republican caucus when he was elected to office in 1986. In fact, then-Assembly Republican leader Patrick Nolan pumped more than $164,000 into the campaign of an Assembly staffer in an effort to defeat Quackenbush in the GOP primary. But Quackenbush won and then bested Democrat Brent Ventura in the general election. When he arrived in the Assembly, he aligned himself with the moderates in the Republican caucus.

Charles Quackenbush

During his first two terms, Quackenbush wasn't in the forefront of many major legislative issues, save one. His was the key committee vote in support of the landmark bill to outlaw semiautomatic assault weapons. Without his vote, the measure, which ultimately became law, could have died in committee. In exchange for his vote, he got Democrats to outlaw weapons by specifically listing them rather than flatly banning all semiautomatic rifles. Quackenbush also was just one of two Republicans who supported the measure during the Assembly floor vote.

In 1990, Quackenbush tried unsuccessfully to tinker with the state's adoption laws with a bill that would have made it easier for grown adopted children to find their birth parents. The bill was beaten back by adoption organizations, but Quackenbush vowed to try again.

PERSONAL: elected 1986; born April 20, 1954, in Tacoma, Wash.; home, Cupertino; Army 1976-1981; education, B.A. Notre Dame University; wife Chris, two children; Roman Catholic.

CAREER: owner, Q-Tech, an electronics industry employment service, 1979-1989.

COMMITTEES: Governmental Organization; Revenue and Taxation (vice chair); Ways and Means; (joint) Science & Technology.

OFFICES: Capitol, (916) 445-8305, FAX (916) 323-9989; district, 456 El Paseo de Saratoga, San Jose 95130, (408) 446-4114, FAX (408) 379-3976.

TERM LIMIT: 1996

REGISTRATION: 43.7% D, 41.2% R

1992 CAMPAIGN:	Quackenbush – R	49.7%	$483,633
	Jim Beall Jr. – D	43.7%	$356,593
	James Ludemann – L	6.6%	
1990 CAMPAIGN:	Quackenbush – R	59%	$199,841
	Bob Levy – D	34.7%	$20,017

RATINGS:

AFL-CIO	CalPIRG	CLCV	NOW	CofC	CalFarm
12	19	31	36	94	75

KEY VOTES:

Parent consent abort:	YES	Limit product tort:	YES	Clean Air Act:	NO
Assault gun ban:	YES	Ban AIDS discrim:	NO	Restrict abortion funds:	NO
Sales tax hike:	YES	Wealth tax hike:	YES	Strong gay rights:	NO
Parental leave:	NO	Timber compromise:	YES	Execution by injection:	YES
Limited gay rights:	NO	Universal health insur:	NO	1992-93 Budget Act:	YES
Campaign Reform:	NO	Offshore oil ban:	YES	Charter schools:	YES

Richard Rainey (R)

15th Assembly District

This is the only locked-in Republican Assembly district in the liberal San Francisco Bay Area. The district was changed somewhat by reapportionment but retained its solidly GOP bent. It covers the very affluent, white suburbs of central and southern Contra Costa County – Walnut Creek, Orinda and San Ramon. When William Baker, the Republicans' leading figure on the state budget, decided to give up the seat to run for Congress from a newly created district, Democrats didn't even try to bring the 15th into their column. GOP voters outnumber Democrats by a 10-percentage-point margin. And when Contra Costa County's popular sheriff, Richard Rainey, announced that he would run, there wasn't any Republican contest either. Rainey wound up defeating token Democrat Charles Brydon by 17 percentage points.

Richard Rainey

Rainey is considered an ideological moderate and an affable, experienced politician who will fit into the Assembly easily, even though he may not be there very long. He is likely to jump to the state Senate as soon as he gets a chance, which could be 1996, when term limits catch up with Sen. Daniel Boatwright, D-Concord, or earlier if Boatwright is successful in lining up another position, as he reportedly is trying to do. Although Boatwright won re-election easily in 1992, his redrawn district has a decidedly Republican bent and would be perfect for Rainey. In the meantime, Rainey wound up with a plum committee assignment to Public Safety, which handles all criminal legislation.

PERSONAL: elected 1992; born Dec. 5, 1938, in Medford, Ore.; home, Walnut Creek; A.A. Mt. Diablo College, B.A. CSU, Sacramento, M.A. Golden Gate University; wife Sue, seven children; Protestant.

CAREER: police officer city of Compton, two years; Contra Costa County sheriff's office, 29 years, rising from deputy to captain, elected sheriff in 1978 and re-elected three times.

COMMITTEES: Environmental Safety & Toxic Materials; Public Safety; Utilities & Commerce.

TERM LIMIT: 1998

REGISTRATION: 38.1% D, 48.0% R

1992 CAMPAIGN: Rainey – R   58.6% $296,510
                                 Charles Brydon – D   41.4% $22,315

RATINGS and **KEY VOTES**: Newly elected

Bernie Richter (R)
3rd Assembly District

Bernie Richter

Northeastern California farms, mountains and wide-open spaces are the main characteristics of this conservative, rural district that includes the counties of Modoc, Lassen, Plumas, Butte, Sierra, Nevada and Yuba. Richter, an anti-abortion conservative and owner of video and liquor stores, defeated Democrat Lon Hatamiya for the seat after a campaign that focused on such issues as whether Richter was a "porn peddler" because he rented R-rated movies at his video store. Hatamiya also ran ads claiming that Richter let a young boy be propositioned by a man in one of his stores, a charge Richter vigorously denied.

Richter, who during the primary campaign stopped renting Playboy videos and selling non-alcoholic beer (because his opponents suggested he was encouraging children to drink), attributed his victory to voter rejection of the mudslinging. Hatamiya's campaign staff believed racism against their Japanese American candidate was also a factor.

Richter, a one-term Butte County supervisor who made a previous try for the Assembly in 1976, is a former Democrat whose official biography says he "remains a casual dresser" and uses a converted bathroom as his personal office. He told voters he came to Sacramento to eliminate government waste, curb taxes and reform welfare and workers' compensation.

PERSONAL: elected 1992; born Sept. 7, 1931, in Los Angeles; home, Chico; B.A. UCLA 1955; wife Mary La Rae Smith, three children; non-denominational Protestant.

CAREER: Owner, video and liquor-store businesses; U.S. Army Corps of Engineers, 1955-57; founded and operated auto service company, 1958-1966; high school civics teacher, 1967-1975; Butte County supervisor, 1972-76.

COMMITTEES: Environmental Safety & Toxic Materials; Governmental Organization; Higher Education; Natural Resources.

OFFICES: Capitol, (916) 445-7298, FAX (916) 323-3550; district, 2545 Zanella Way, D, Chico 95928, (916) 345-7807, FAX (916) 345-7899.

TERM LIMIT: 1998

REGISTRATION: 43.3% D, 41.8% R, 2% AIP

1992 CAMPAIGN:
Richter – R	51.7%	$594,047
Lon Hatamiya – D	37.7%	$320,333
Vicki Lynn Vallis – L	10.6%	

RATINGS and **KEY VOTES**: Newly elected

Andrea Seastrand (R)
33rd Assembly District

This scenic Central California coastal district includes all of San Luis Obispo and part of Santa Barbara County. It has farm-based communities such as Santa Maria and the sleepy coastal towns of Pismo Beach and Morro Bay. Several state and federal prison facilities lie within the district as does Vandenberg Air Force Base, which has severely cut back its employment.

Andrea Seastrand's husband, Eric, held this seat from 1982 until he died of cancer in 1990. During Eric's years in office and during several prior unsuccessful election tries, Andrea Seastrand was heavily involved in her husband's career while raising the couple's two children. Following her husband's

Andrea Seastrand

death, Andrea easily won election to the seat and was re-elected in 1992 in this heavily conservative district. Assembly Republican leader Jim Brulte named her one of three assistant GOP caucus leaders.

A former teacher, she has taken special interest in youth issues. Like her husband, Seastrand has pledged to continue to support a strongly conservative agenda and remains a staunch supporter of agriculture. Her biography, for example, describes her as "holding dear to family values," conservative jargon for, among other things, opposing abortion. She has spent 25 years working for conservative causes and took leadership roles in Monterey County Republican Party organizations before her election to the Assembly.

In her first months in the Legislature, Seastrand joined six of the most conservative members of the Assembly in sending a letter to Gov. Pete Wilson opposing any tax hike to combat the state's dire budget problems. In 1992, Wilson signed a bill by Seastrand that repealed state bread weight requirements, allowing bakers to sell bread loaves in any size.

PERSONAL: elected 1990; born Aug. 5, 1941, in Chicago; home, San Luis Obispo; education, B.A. DePaul University; widow, two children; Roman Catholic.

CAREER: teacher.

COMMITTEES: Agriculture; Consumer Protection, Governmental Efficiency & Economic Development; Ways and Means.

OFFICES: Capitol, (916) 445-7795, FAX (916) 324-5510; district, 523 Higuera St., San Luis Obisbo 93401, (805) 549-3381.

TERM LIMIT: 1996

REGISTRATION: 38.9% D, 45.2% R, 2.2% AIP

1992 CAMPAIGN:	Seastrand – R	54.6%	$270,148
	John Ashbaugh – D	39.8%	$69,837
1990 CAMPAIGN:	Seastrand – R	64.7%	$183,467
	John Jay Lybarger – D	35.3%	$27,510

RATINGS.	AFL-CIO	CalPIRG	CLCV	NOW	CofC	CalFarm
	0	18	8	21	89	75

KEY VOTES:

Sales tax hike:	NO	Wealth tax hike:	NO	Strong gay rights:	NO
Parental leave:	NO	Timber compromise:	NO	Execution by injection:	YES
Limited gay rights:	NO	Universal health insur:	NO	1992-93 Budget Act:	YES
Campaign Reform:	NO	Offshore oil ban:	YES	Charter schools:	YES

Byron Sher (D)
21st Assembly District

The microchip empire of the Silicon Valley grew up around Stanford University. Thus it may be appropriate that a Stanford professor represents this generally upscale district, which includes Palo Alto, Redwood City and Menlo Park.

Bearded Professor Byron Sher was mayor of Palo Alto for two terms before his election to the Assembly in 1980. He has continued to teach law at Stanford during the fall term, perhaps illustrating that the "full-time" Legislature is not exactly full time.

As chairman of the Assembly Natural Resources Committee, Sher has emerged as one of the Legislature's chief environmentalists. He has pushed for adding rivers to the Scenic Rivers Act, and he

Byron Sher

unsuccessfully tried to pass a three-year moratorium on lumbering old-growth stands along the North Coast. He was out-maneuvered by fellow Democratic Assemblyman Dan Hauser, who inserted killer amendments. Later, the two jointly attempted – unsuccessfully in the ultimate outcome – to enact a compromise timber harvesting law.

Sher's major legislative accomplishment has been in authoring the state's landmark Clean Air Act, which gave new powers and responsibilities to local smog districts and requires localities to begin a phased reduction of smog emissions. Sher took a similar approach in his 1989 legislation revamping the state's garbage management board, a law that is pushing local governments into curbside recycling. The law requires local governments to cut in half the trash sent to dumps by the year 2000. But the measure was a mixed bag in another respect: It established a full-time, lavishly paid board. The $90,852-a-year positions on the Integrated Waste Management Board have proven to be political plums. One of the parting acts of Gov. George Deukmejian was to appoint his chief of staff, Michael Frost, and his finance chief, Jess Huff, to the state garbage board.

In 1990, Sher took on the glass industry – and the Assembly speaker – with a bill beefing up recycling fees on glass manufacturers. The speaker backed a campaign contributor, the Glass Packaging Institute, which had given his campaign $8,000 in the previous two years. But after a public tussle that proved embarrassing, Brown gave in and Sher's AB 1490 was sent to the governor. The higher deposits mandated have since been credited with nearly doubling container recycling in California.

On a local level, Sher fought for years against Deukmejian's vetoes of bills to clean up leaking underground storage tanks, an issue of considerable concern to the Silicon Valley with its many toxic waste sites.

When reapportionment ordered by the state Supreme Court reduced the number of San Francisco Peninsula seats by one, Sher found himself in a backstage tussle with his onetime student, Ted Lempert. Ultimately, Lempert was forced to drop out of the Assembly. Reapportionment also dropped Sher's Democratic registration markedly – to below 50 percent – and Republicans entertained some thought of unseating him. But the effort fizzled and Sher won by a nearly 2-1 margin, defeating former Menlo Park Mayor Jan La Fetra.

Sher has enjoyed cordial relations with Gov. Pete Wilson's administration, and his staff drafted legislation to make a reality Wilson's campaign pledge to create a "California Environmental Protection Agency."

Sher, who is aligned with the Assembly's "Grizzly Bear" faction of liberals, collaborated with his longtime seatmate, Assemblyman Lloyd Connelly, to ferret out and oppose special-interest bills. As the 1993-94 session began, Sher was reappointed to chair the Natural Resources Committee, but he'll be operating without his colleague. Connelly quit the Legislature to become a judge.

PERSONAL: elected 1980; born Feb. 7, 1928, in St. Louis, Mo.; home, Palo Alto; education, B.S. Washington University, St. Louis; J.D. Harvard University; wife Linda, three children; Jewish.

CAREER: law professor, Stanford University; Palo Alto City Council 1965-

1967 and 1973-1980; mayor, 1974-1975 and 1977-1978; commissioner of the San Francisco Bay Conservation and Development Commission 1978-1980.

COMMITTEES: Natural Resources (chair); Consumer Protection, Governmental Efficiency & New Technologies; Finance & Insurance; (joint) Arts; Energy Regulation & the Environment (vice chair); Prison Construction & Operations.

OFFICES: Capitol, (916) 445-7632, FAX (916) 324-6974; district, 785 Castro St., Suite C, Mountain View 94041, (415) 961-6031, FAX (415) 967-6026.

TERM LIMIT: 1996

REGISTRATION: 48.2% D, 35.5% R

1992 CAMPAIGN:	Sher – D	63.2%	$374,008
	Janice La Fetra – R	32.3%	$14,864
1990 CAMPAIGN:	Sher – D	70.9%	$190,630
	Eric Garris – R	29.1%	

RATINGS:

AFL-CIO	CalPIRG	CLCV	NOW	CofC	CalFarm
95	95	100	86	17	25

KEY VOTES:

Parent consent abort:	NO	Limit product tort:	NO	Clean Air Act:	YES
Assault gun ban:	YES	Ban AIDS discrim:	YES	Restrict abortion funds:	NO
Sales tax hike:	YES	Wealth tax hike:	YES	Strong gay rights:	YES
Parental leave:	YES	Timber compromise:	YES	Execution by injection:	nv
Limited gay rights:	YES	Universal health insur:	YES	1992-93 Budget Act:	YES
Campaign Reform:	YES	Offshore oil ban:	YES	Charter schools:	YES

Margaret Snyder (D)

25th Assembly District

The 25th District represents two of the dominant trends of legislative politics in the 1990s – the shift of power away from coastal metropolitan areas into the fast-growing fringe suburbs in interior valleys and the struggle for dominance within the Republican Party between its right-wing and moderate factions.

This new district, centered in Modesto, was one of the reasons Republicans refused to make a reapportionment deal with Democrats and threw the issue to the courts. A shift of seats from the cities to the new suburbs, they believed, would give them a better chance of improving their numbers, perhaps even taking control of the Assembly sometime in the 1990s.

Margaret Snyder

The first stage of the strategy worked brilliantly. The Supreme Court, in creating the 25th and a flock of other new districts, gave the Republicans the chance they had long sought. But the new districts and their attractive registration numbers also generated a renewal of the internecine warfare among Republicans. Conservatives won most of the June primary battles over moderates led by Gov. Pete Wilson, who had feared that right-wing candidates would lose in marginal districts where moderate Republicans could win.

One of those right-wing primary winners was Barbara Keating-Edh, founder of a small pro-business group called Consumer Alert and an anti-abortion crusader. She defeated five male rivals. Democrats, meanwhile, nominated a well-known local school board member, Margaret Snyder, who espoused moderate, pro-choice views. The battle between Snyder and Keating-Edh was one of the major struggles of the 1992 election season and featured sharp personal attacks on both sides. When the dust had settled and the votes had been counted, Democrat Snyder had won by fewer than 5,000 votes – perhaps proving that Wilson and the moderates were right.

PERSONAL: elected 1992; Feb. 25, 1940, in Elizabethton, Tenn.; home, Modesto; paralegal certificate, Humphrey's College; husband Melvin, three children; Protestant

CAREER: Legal secretary and paralegal; elected Modesto school board 1985.

COMMITTEES: Agriculture; Human Services; Judiciary.

OFFICES: Capitol, (916) 445-7906, FAX (916) 445-7344; district, 1101 Standlford Ave., 85, Modesto, 95350, (209) 544-9992, FAX (209) 544-9890.

TERM LIMIT: 1998

REGISTRATION: 48.6% D, 40.6% R

1992 CAMPAIGN: Snyder – D   51.5% $588,196
                              Barbara Keating-Edh – R   48.5% $609,031

RATINGS and **KEY VOTES**: Newly elected

Hilda L. Solis (D)
57th Assembly District

When the state Supreme Court consciously created a number of legislative and congressional districts with Latino population and voter concentrations – required, the justices said, by provisions of the federal Voting Rights Act – it touched off a renewal of the rivalry between two groups of Hispanic politicians. The factions, one headed by Los Angeles County Supervisor Gloria Molina and the other by Los Angeles City Councilman Richard Alatorre and state Sen. Art Torres, chose their candidates to go head-to-head in districts throughout Southern California.

The Alatorre-Torres bloc won most of the contests, but lost one was in the 57th Assembly District, a chunk of the San Gabriel Valley that includes El Monte, Baldwin Park, La Puente and Azusa, previously represented by retiring Assemblywoman Sally Tanner. The Molina group achieved the breakthrough with Hilda Solis, a Rio Hondo college trustee. She bested a field of Democratic candidates in the primary, then had little difficulty overcoming token Republican opposition in November to claim the Assembly seat.

PERSONAL: elected 1992; born Oct. 20, 1957, in Los Angeles; home, La Puente; education, B.A. Cal Poly Pomona, M.A. USC; husband Sam; Catholic.

CAREER: management analyst, U.S. Office of Budget and Management; director of access program, Whittier Union High School District; trustee, Rio Hondo Community College District.

COMMITTEES: Higher Education (vice chair); Environmental Safety & Toxic Materials; Labor & Employment; Utilities & Commerce.

Hilda Solis

OFFICES: Capitol, (916) 445-7610, FAX (916) 327-9696, district, 218 N. Glendora Ave., D, La Puente 91744, (818) 369-3551, FAX (818) 369-2861.

TERM LIMIT: 1998

REGISTRATION: 56.7% D, 31.0% R

1992 CAMPAIGN:	Solis – D	60.9%	$205,467
	Gary Woods – R	34.3%	$3,959

RATINGS and **KEY VOTES**: Newly elected

K. Jacqueline Speier (D)
19th Assembly District

This safely Democratic district takes in the foggy, slightly funky, suburb of Pacifica, but its heart is in the blue-collar suburbs immediately south of San Francisco in San Mateo County, including Daly City, South San Francisco and Milbrae. Older housing tracts dot the hillsides while the flat areas are dominated by industry, Candlestick Park and the Cow Palace.

This district, which retained its number and its general shape after reapportionment, gave California Louis J. Papan, a man noted for his Rambo approach to politics. Papan gave up the seat in 1986 to run for an open state Senate seat and was able to win the Democratic primary by defeating Assembly Speaker

Jacqueline Speier

Willie Brown's hand-picked candidate, Mike Nevin. But neither Papan nor Brown calculated well in 1986. Papan lost the Senate race to independent Quentin Kopp, and an underfinanced San Mateo County supervisor, Jackie Speier, won a close

Democratic primary and then the general election to replace Papan in the Assembly.

Speier was an aide to Rep. Leo Ryan on that ill-fated trip in 1978 to Jonestown, Guyana. Ryan was killed and Speier was shot five times. She lay wounded on an anthill for 22 hours until, near death, she was rescued by the U.S. Air Force. She spent months in a hospital recovering and is still partially paralyzed. She ran unsuccessfully for Ryan's congressional seat.

Speier has turned out to be among the savviest of the newer crop of legislators. She is known as a sharp questioner of administration officials and gained some wider publicity in 1992 by questioning the perks and lifestyle of Gov. Pete Wilson's transportation secretary, Carl Covitz, contributing to his eventual departure from Sacramento.

Speier has waded into health issues with numerous bills. One of her major efforts in 1988 and 1989 was a measure that would have required cholesterol labeling on food products. It ran a heavy gauntlet of lobbyists from the food and agriculture industries before it died in a committee. Many of the bills that she managed to get out of the Legislature did not fare well with Gov. George Deukmejian, who vetoed measures that would have beefed up measles vaccine programs, improved drug abuse and pregnancy programs.

In the 1991-92 session, Speier pushed bills to ban doctors from profiting from lab tests given to their patients or from conducting heart bypass operations without a review board's consent. She also pried open scandals in state regulation of the funeral industry. Speier has been among the Legislature's most vocal protectors of Family Planning and abortion rights.

As she has gained seniority, Speier has also begun to acquire a reputation as a "player" in the Capitol, particularly after the San Francisco Chronicle published a story in July 1990 that reported Speier had lobbied vigorously for state and federal approval of a dump proposed by a political donor who had given her more than $116,000 in campaign contributions. Although the contributions from Browning-Ferris Industries broke no laws and she has maintained that she was working on behalf of San Mateo County, the episode left its tarnish on Speier.

Speier has voted with Speaker Brown in leadership tests, but has shown an independent streak at times in floor votes. She generally allies herself with the Assembly's "Grizzly Bear" liberals. When the chair of the Assembly Health Committee fell vacant after the 1992 elections, Speier and health reform organizations campaigned hard for her to fill the seat, but organized medicine worked just as hard to deny her the influential position. Speaker Brown eventually decided against her, giving the position to Burt Margolin and reappointing Speier as chair of the reconstituted Consumer Protection, Governmental Efficiency and New Technologies Committee instead.

If Speier stays in the Assembly, she has shown herself bright enough – and adept enough – to eventually move into a leadership position, possibly even becoming the Assembly's first woman speaker. However, many insiders have long suspected

Speier has set her sights on Leo Ryan's old congressional seat, which currently is held by Rep. Tom Lantos.

PERSONAL: elected 1986; born May 14, 1950, in San Francisco; home, South San Francisco; education, B.A. UC Davis, J.D. Hastings College of Law; husband, Dr. Steve Sierra, one child; Roman Catholic.

CAREER: lawyer; staff of Rep. Leo Ryan 1969-1978; San Mateo County Board of Supervisors 1981-1986.

COMMITTEES: Consumer Protection, Governmental Efficiency & New Technologies (chair); Finance & Insurance; Health; Judiciary; (joint) Mental Health Research.

OFFICES: Capitol, (916) 445-8020, FAX (916) 445-0511; district, 220 So. Spruce Ave., 101, South San Francisco 94080, (415) 871-4100, FAX (415) 871-4350.

TERM LIMIT: 1996

REGISTRATION: 54.8% D, 30.0% R

1992 CAMPAIGN:	Speier – D	75.1%	$296,613
	Ellyne Berger – R	24.9%	$1,483
1990 CAMPAIGN:	Speier – D	100%	$277,456

RATINGS:	AFL-CIO	CalPIRG	CLCV	NOW	CofC	CalFarm
	98	100	100	72	22	20

KEY VOTES:

Parent consent abort:	NO	Limit product tort:	nv	Clean Air Act:	YES
Assault gun ban:	YES	Ban AIDS discrim:	YES	Restrict abortion funds:	NO
Sales tax hike:	YES	Wealth tax hike:	YES	Strong gay rights:	YES
Parental leave:	YES	Timber compromise:	NO	Execution by injection:	YES
Limited gay rights:	YES	Universal health insur:	YES	1992-93 Budget Act:	NO
Campaign Reform:	YES	Offshore oil ban:	YES	Charter schools:	YES

Stan Statham (R)
2nd Assembly District

There's a little sign outside Assemblyman Stan Statham's Capitol office informing visitors that he represents "the 51st state." That's not quite true, but the new 2nd Assembly District continues to cover a sizable chunk of northeastern California, including Siskiyou, Trinity, Shasta, Tehama, Glenn, Colusa, Sutter and portions of Butte and Yolo counties. As its size implies, the 2nd District is mostly sparsely populated stretches of agricultural fields, rangeland, mountains and timber. Redding is the most prominent city. Small towns are scattered throughout the rest of the territory.

Although the new district has a slight Democratic voter registration edge, it is expected to continue to vote Republican. Statham earned name recognition in the area during a decade as a local television anchorman and won what was then the 1st District seat in 1976 after Democratic Assemblywoman Pauline Davis retired. He has won re-election easily ever since.

Despite his relative seniority among the fast-changing Republican membership of the Assembly, Statham has never achieved much power. That's because he comes from a rural backwater district and because his politics are decidedly more moderate than the prevailing slant in the GOP caucus.

Statham has spent most of his time in the last two years on a crusade to divide California into two or three states. The idea has become the subject of a question on the television game show "Jeopardy" and

Stan Statham

the butt of jokes in Jay Leno's "Tonight Show" monologues. But Statham also saw voters in 27 counties offer their endorsement of the idea in 1992, and he hopes to put a plan before California voters on the 1994 statewide ballot. The fact that Statham would need congressional approval of the idea, however, continues to make it a longshot.

Being a member of the moderate minority within the minority Assembly Republican caucus means that Statham isn't a player on major legislative matters. But his wife, Lovie, has carved out a semicareer of her own as an organizer of political fund-raising events, not only for Statham but other politicians.

In 1993, Statham toyed with running in a vacant senate district, which would have been a logical move for him. But he gave up on the idea after learning that it would cost the nine counties of his Assembly district an estimated $600,000 to hold a special election to replace him. Many of those counties have been teetering on the edge of bankruptcy for years, which is one of the reasons the separate-state drive is so strong in Northern California.

PERSONAL: elected 1976; born April 7, 1939, in Chico; home, Oak Run; Army 1956-1959; education, attended CSU Chico; wife Lovie Plants, two children; no religious affiliation.

CAREER: finance and banking; radio disc jockey; television anchor; news and public affairs director, KHSL-TV Chico, 1964-1975.

COMMITTEES: Televising the Assembly (chair); Health; Finance & Insurance.

OFFICES: Capitol, (916) 445-7266, FAX (916) 448-6040; district, 410 Hemsted Drive, 210, Redding 96002, (916) 223-6300, FAX (916) 223-6737.

TERM LIMIT: 1996

REGISTRATION: 44.3% D, 42.8% R, 2.3% AIP

1992 CAMPAIGN:

Statham – R	64.9%	$265,871
William Brashears – D	35.1%	$7,912

1990 CAMPAIGN: Statham – R   56.5% $271,554
Arlie Caudle – D   42.9% $19,802

RATINGS:

AFL-CIO	CalPIRG	CLCV	NOW	CofC	CalFarm
27	43	13	29	78	45

KEY VOTES:

Parent consent abort:	nv	Limit product tort:	YES	Clean Air Act:	NO
Assault gun ban:	NO	Ban AIDS discrim:	YES	Restrict abortion funds:	nv
Sales tax hike:	NO	Wealth tax hike:	NO	Strong gay rights:	NO
Parental leave:	NO	Timber compromise:	nv	Execution by injection:	YES
Limited gay rights:	NO	Universal health insure:	nv	1992-93 Budget Act:	YES
Campaign Reform:	NO	Offshore oil ban:	NO	Charter schools:	nv

Nao Takasugi (R)
37th Assembly District

This district belonged to conservative Assembly-man Tom McClintock, but McClintock chose to run for Congress in 1992. It was an ill-advised decision for McClintock, as it turned out, because he lost his congressional bid to veteran Democratic Rep. Anthony Beilenson. But McClintock's departure opened up this safe Assembly District in southwest Ventura county. The district includes the farm and port community of Oxnard and Camarillo with its state hospital and youth authority prison, and stretches eastward to the Los Angeles suburb of Thousand Oaks.

Oxnard Mayor Nao Takasugi, a moderate Republican, beat Roz McGrath, a farm manager and teacher, to become the first Asian American in the Legislature

Nao Takasugi

in a dozen years. Takasugi, who was born and raised in Oxnard, is of Japanese descent, and was held in an Arizona internment camp for several months during World War II.

Ventura County Democrats had put great hope in McGrath, a Latina. During the final weekend before the election, Dianne Feinstein traveled to Oxnard to give her a hand and make several campaign appearances with her. But it was too little, too late. McGrath by the final weekend complained that it cost too much to run for the Assembly and she was out of time and out of money.

Takasugi is expected to approach his legislative duties much more pragmatically than McClintock, which may be a relief to Gov. Wilson, who was often the target of McClintock's combative rhetoric.

PERSONAL: elected 1992; born 1922 in Oxnard; home, Oxnard; education, B.S. Temple University; MBA University of Pennsylvania; wife Judy, five children.

CAREER: Owned and operated Asahi Market in Oxnard with wife for 39 years; Oxnard city councilman, 1976-1982; mayor of Oxnard, 1982-1992.

COMMITTEES: Labor & Employment; Local Government; Utilities & Commerce.

OFFICES: Capitol, (916) 445-7827, FAX (916) 324-6869; district 221 E. Dailey Dr., 7, Camarillo 93010, (805) 987-5195, FAX (805) 484-0853.

TERM LIMIT: 1998

REGISTRATION: 40.5% D, 44.3% R

1992 CAMPAIGN:			
Takasugi – R	50.8%	$325,003
Roz McGrath – D	43.4%	$44,203
David Harner – L	5.8%	

RATINGS and **KEY VOTES**: Newly elected

Curtis R. Tucker Jr. (D)
51st Assembly District

This district, encompassing the Inglewood area of Los Angeles, was about 55 percent African American and 20 percent Latino before the state Supreme Court changed its number (from 50) and its boundaries. Its African American population dropped to just over one-third and its Latino population increased to almost a third, which indicates that someday the 51st District seat might be held by a Latino politician. But for the moment, it's considered an African American seat as well as one of the most heavily Democratic districts in the state, with only 20 percent of its voters counted as Republicans.

Curtis Tucker Jr.

For 14 years, the district was represented by Curtis R. Tucker Sr., a former health department worker and Inglewood city councilman. He died in October 1988 of liver cancer, but it was too late to remove his name from the November ballot. Even in death, Tucker Sr. easily defeated his Republican opponent, gaining 72 percent of the vote. That set up a February 1989 special election, and Curtis R. Tucker Jr., a former Pacific Bell manager who was working as an aide to Assemblywoman Gwen Moore, emerged as the easy winner. With backing from Assembly Speaker Willie Brown and utilizing the name identification of his father, Tucker pulled away from a field of four, winning 71 percent of the vote.

Tucker has expressed interest in improving health care, the area in which his father specialized. A proponent of the death penalty, Tucker also listed cracking down on drugs and gang warfare among his priorities. The Assembly hierarchy placed him and Dick Floyd in adjacent seats at the rear of the chambers because both were smokers, but Floyd was defeated in a bid for re-election in 1992. Floyd's loss was Tucker's gain because it opened the chairmanship of the Governmental Organization Committee, whose bland title masks the fact that it is one of the most coveted committee assignments in the Legislature due to its jurisdiction over gambling, horse racing and liquor legislation. Lobbyists for those industries shower members – and especially the committee chairman – with lavish campaign contributions. Speaker Brown gave Tucker that chairmanship in 1993, a reward for his slavish loyalty rather than any demonstrable talent for legislative creativity.

PERSONAL: elected 1989 (special election); born April 6, 1954, in New Orleans; home, Inglewood; education, B.A. CSU Dominguez Hills; wife Dianne, two children; Roman Catholic.

CAREER: consultant to Assemblyman Michael Roos 1983-1988; aide to Assemblywoman Gwen Moore 1988; manager Pacific Bell.

COMMITTEES: Governmental Organization (chair); Labor & Employment; Natural Resources; Public Employees, Retirement & Social Security.

OFFICES: Capitol, (916) 445 7533, FAX (916) 327-3517; district, 1 Manchester Blvd., Box 6500, Inglewood 90306; (310) 412-6400, FAX (310) 412-6354.

TERM LIMIT: 1996

REGISTRATION: 71.1% D, 18.1% R

1992 CAMPAIGN:	Tucker – D	81.9%	$195,358
	Clark Hanley – L	12.3%	
	Xenia Williams – P&F	5.8%	
1990 CAMPAIGN:	Tucker – D	84.7%	$103,300
	Michael Long – P&F	15.3%	

RATINGS:	AFL-CIO	CalPIRG	CLCV	NOW	CofC	CalFarm
	93	77	81	100	17	20

KEY VOTES:

Assault gun ban:	YES	Ban AIDS discrim:	YES	Restrict abortion funds:	NO
Sales tax hike:	YES	Wealth tax hike:	YES	Strong gay rights:	YES
Parental leave:	YES	Timber compromise:	YES	Execution by injection:	nv
Limited gay rights:	YES	Universal health insur:	YES	1992-93 Budget Act:	nv
Campaign Reform:	NO	Offshore oil ban:	YES	Charter schools:	NO

Thomas J. Umberg (D)
69th Assembly District

The 69th Assembly District is entirely in Orange County, the bastion of conservatism in California politics. Yet this district is 65 percent Latino and includes Santa Ana, the Latino neighborhoods of Garden Grove and central Anaheim. But only about a quarter of the Latinos are registered to vote and overall registration in the district – 90,831 – is the lowest in Southern California outside of Los Angeles, and one of the lowest in the state.

For 12 years, the former 72nd District – tailored by Democratic leaders to maximize their chances of holding it – was repre- sented by Democrat Richard Robinson, who left office to seek a congressional seat in 1986. Republican businessman Richard Longshore, who in 1984 had come close to unseating Robinson, won the seat in 1986, but died in 1988. That set the scene for a furious partisan tug-of-war that has not ceased. The current holder of the seat, Tom Umberg, is the third to have it since Robinson. Umberg unseated Curt Pringle, who won re-election to the Assembly from another district in 1992.

Tom Umberg

A former prosecutor with the U.S. attorney's office in Santa Ana, Umberg's 1990 campaign was interrupted when his Army Reserve unit was called up for Operation Desert Shield. Umberg's wife, Robin, a reservist nurse, also was called to active duty during the Persian Gulf crisis and continued to serve during Operation Desert Storm. The resulting publicity was worth more than any campaigning could have produced and Umberg ousted Pringle to retake the seat for the Democrats. In 1992, Umberg successfully ran for re-election in the new 69th District against conservative activist Jo Ellen Allen.

PERSONAL: elected 1990; born Sept. 25, 1955, in Cincinnati; home, Garden Grove; Army 1973-82, reserve; education, B.A. UCLA, J.D. Hastings; wife Robin, three children; Roman Catholic.

CAREER: lawyer; assistant U.S. attorney, Santa Ana; Army Reserve.

COMMITTEES: Environmental Safety & Toxic Materials (chair); Public Safety; Education; Transportation.

OFFICES: Capitol, (916) 445-7333, FAX (916) 327-1783; district, 12822 Garden Grove Blvd., A, Garden Grove 92643, (714) 537-4477.

TERM LIMIT: 1996

REGISTRATION: 53.9% D, 35.8% R

1992 CAMPAIGN:	Umberg – D	60.0%	$929,030
	Jo Ellen Allen – R	34.1%	$383,430
	David Keller – L	5.9%	
1990 CAMPAIGN:	Umberg – D	51.9%	$535,506
	Pringle (incumbent) – R	48.1%	$612,632

RATINGS:	AFL-CIO	CalPIRG	CLCV	NOW	CofC	CalFarm
	88	86	91	86	44	45

KEY VOTES:

Sales tax hike:	NO	Wealth tax hike:	YES	Strong gay rights:	YES
Parental leave:	YES	Timber compromise:	YES	Execution by injection:	YES
Limited gay rights:	YES	Universal health insur:	YES	1992-93 Budget Act:	NO
Campaign Reform:	NO	Offshore oil ban:	YES	Charter schools:	YES

John Vasconcellos (D)

22nd Assembly District

Reapportionment changed the political landscape of the San Francisco Peninsula dramatically, pitting Democrat against Democrat in a tussle for a diminished number of seats. John Vasconcellos, a legislator for a quarter-century and chairman of the very powerful Ways and Means Committee, had the right to choose the best San Jose-area district for himself but decided, instead, the give the safest one, which had a Democratic registration of over 60 percent, to colleague Dominic Cortese. Vasconcellos opted to take his chances in a Republican-leaning district, the 22nd, centered in the suburbs northwest of San Jose, including Sunnyvale and Santa Clara.

John Vasconcellos

Republicans smelled opportunity and a 29-year-old Santa Clara city councilman, Tim Jeffries, ran hard, accusing Vasconcellos of having been captured by the political establishment in Sacramento and losing touch with constituents. Organizations close to Gov. Pete Wilson, most notably the California Correctional Peace Officers Association, dumped money into Jeffries' campaign. Republicans may win the seat someday, after Vasconcellos has been retired by term limits, but in 1992, they strived in vain as Vasconcellos raised big bucks of his own, walked door to door and defeated Jeffries by 15 percentage points.

Thus, Vasconcellos, one of the Capitol's most singular and controversial figures, returned to the Assembly for a 14th term, making him second in seniority only to Speaker Willie Brown. And that means he'll continue to make life miserable for his enemies, real and imagined. Vasconcellos wasn't kidding when he complained that the FBI's undercover corruption investigation of the Capitol was an invasion of "my house." He has spent so much of his adult life in the Legislature that he is body and soul a part of it. And after voters had approved a term limit initiative in November 1990 that also forced deep cuts in legislative staff, a bitter Vasconcellos threatened to quit just months after having been re-elected, saying he didn't "see any point in killing myself for people who apparently don't care if they have decent government or not."

The transformations of John Vasconcellos mirror the social history of California since World War II. He began as an aide to Gov. Pat Brown and was eventually favored with an Assembly seat. He traded his dark suits and crew cut for leather jackets and long hair in the '60s, storming the Capitol's halls with all the anger of the protest era. In the '70s and '80s, Vasconcellos became a convert to the inward-looking human awareness movement.

Some consider Vasconcellos a visionary, others a flake. Whatever he is,

Vasconcellos is nothing if not interesting. He was lampooned by the Doonesbury comic strip for his legislation fathering the state's self-esteem commission. And at the beginning of the 1991-92 legislative session, he sent a letter to colleagues telling them they can begin to solve many of the state's problems if they improve their own self-esteem. He routinely talks not in the language of politics, but in the lingo of encounter groups. The San Jose Mercury News once dubbed him "Mister Touchy Feely."

In the midst of the record budget deadlock in 1990, Vasconcellos carried on a one-way letter-writing campaign with Gov. George Deukmejian, confessing his deepest feelings about the governor's proposals. In one letter, he told Deukmejian he went home crying because he was so depressed about the budget impasse.

Vasconcellos also was one of the few public officials who sought to force the 1990 gubernatorial candidates to answer tough questions about how they would handle the state's impending budget crisis. His efforts met with some success, forcing Republican Pete Wilson and Democrat Dianne Feinstein to grapple at least peripherally with some issues they had sought to avoid.

First and foremost, Vasconcellos is the chairman of the vastly powerful Ways and Means Committee, which rules on the state budget and all proposals to spend money – a position he has used effectively to promote his personal causes, including a long-standing effort to force the University of California to give up some its elitist ways.

Although Vasconcellos embraces raising the self-esteem of citizens in the abstract, his iron-fisted temperamental management of his committee does not do much for the self-esteem of many who come before it or for the committee's staff. Vasconcellos is a difficult boss, and he once threatened to run a reporter over with his car. During floor debates, he has been known to call those who disagree with him "stupid," which even by the Assembly's low standards of decorum goes too far.

Assembly Speaker Willie Brown was said to have tried to ease Vasconcellos out of his Ways and Means post in 1987, but Vasconcellos would not go. Vasconcellos has been one of the "Grizzly Bear" liberals who have been trying to keep the speaker true to his liberal religion. Vasconcellos is one of the rare voices in Capitol life against the influence of special-interest money.

With the Legislature's image increasingly tarnished because of federal investigations and less-than-flattering news coverage, the speaker in 1989 turned to Vasconcellos to chair a special committee on ethics. After months of labor, the committee produced a comprehensive package of institutional reforms. However, Senate President Pro Tem David Roberti upstaged the Assembly version with a proposal of his own, and the speaker allowed it to pass. Vasconcellos was said to be privately furious with Brown for pulling the carpet out from under him.

PERSONAL: elected 1966; born May 11, 1932, in San Jose; home, Santa Clara; Army; education, B.A. and J.D. from University of Santa Clara; single.

CAREER: lawyer; aide to Gov. Pat Brown.

COMMITTEES: Ways & Means (chair); Agriculture; Higher Education; (joint) Legislative Audit; Legislative Budget; Science & Technology.

OFFICES: Capitol, (916) 445-4253, FAX (916) 323-9209; district, 100 Paseo de San Antonio, 106, San Jose 95113, (408) 288-7515, FAX (408) 277-1249.

TERM LIMIT: 1996

REGISTRATION: 48.7% D, 34.1% R

1992 CAMPAIGN:	Vasconcellos – D	54.4%	$723,105
	Tim Jeffries – R	39.4%	$252,119
	Bob Goodwyn – L	6.2%	
1990 CAMPAIGN:	Vasconcellos – D	62.7%	$368,161
	Monica Valladares – R	37.3%	$0

RATINGS:	AFL-CIO	CalPIRG	CLCV	NOW	CofC	CalFarm
	92	86	90	72	11	25

KEY VOTES:

Parent consent abort:	nv	Limit product tort:	nv	Clean Air Act:	YES
Assault gun ban:	YES	Ban AIDS discrim:	YES	Restrict abortion funds:	NO
Sales tax hike:	YES	Wealth tax hike:	YES	Strong gay rights:	YES
Parental leave:	YES	Timber compromise:	YES	Execution by injection:	nv
Limited gay rights:	YES	Universal health insur:	YES	1992-93 Budget Act:	NO
Campaign Reform:	YES	Offshore oil ban:	YES	Charter schools:	YES

Ted Weggeland (R)
64th Assembly District

Registration in this Riverside County district is split almost evenly between Republicans and Democrats, which gives the Republicans a slight advantage at the polls since their numbers tend to vote more faithfully. The district includes all of the cities of Riverside and Norco and half of Corona. It is a mostly white district with a 13 percent Latino registration and a smattering of African Americans and Asians.

Ted Weggeland didn't arrive in Sacramento with a mandate from his constituents. He barely squeezed out a victory after a hard-fought battle with his Democratic opponent, Jane Carney. Weggeland won by 201 votes.

Ted Weggeland

The campaign focused on who could do a better job for the business community. Weggeland, a moderate Republican, comes from a family with strong ties to the area's business community, but his credentials were weakened by his comparative youth and the fact that his professional career has centered on his work as a legislative aide to Rep. Al McCandless. Carney, on the other hand, was a former president of the Riverside Downtown Association and a member of the chamber of commerce board of directors. The campaign turned ugly toward the end, and together the two candidates spent close to $1 million.

When Weggeland arrived in Sacramento, he was named a minority whip by Republican leader Jim Brulte.

Weggeland is involved in the family business, DM Laboratories, a supplier of anti-static topical coatings and of Static Prevention Incorporated, another family-owned business. He is also a principle in EW International, a business venture to provide anti-static consulting, factory audits and static awareness training programs to manufacturing companies in America and the Pacific Rim.

PERSONAL: elected 1992; born Sept. 30, 1963, in Rochester, N.Y.; home, Riverside; education, B.A. UCLA, J.D. Pepperdine University; wife Jennifer; Roman Catholic.

CAREER: businessman, family owned company; governmental relations; congressional aide.

COMMITTEES: Consumer Protection, Governmental Efficiency & New Technologies; Judiciary; Transportation.

OFFICES: Capitol, (916) 445-0854, FAX (916) 323-7179; district 6840 Indiana Ave., 150, Riverside 92506, (909) 369-0366, FAX (909) 369-0366.

TERM LIMIT: 1998

REGISTRATION: 45.0% D, 43.6% R

1992 CAMPAIGN:

Weggeland – R	47.9%	$621,823
Jane Carney – D	46.6%	$417,266
Jane Henson – L	5.6%	

RATINGS and **KEY VOTES**: Newly elected

Paul A. Woodruff (R)
65th Assembly District

This expansive San Bernardino County district includes Redlands, Yucaipa, Big Bear and Twenty-Nine Palms. Nearly two-thirds of the district's voters reside in the fast-growing communities of Riverside County. The area is mostly white and decidedly Republican.

When longtime Assemblyman Bill Leonard decided to run for the state Senate in 1988, he set off a free-for-all. Seven Republicans announced in a district where the GOP nominee is the all-but-certain winner. In the end, Leonard's hand-picked successor, Paul Woodruff, won. Woodruff worked for Leonard as an administrative aide and campaign manager.

Woodruff, who still maintains a campaign consulting business, is a young, baby-faced legislator who spent his first term quietly sitting on the Republican backbenches. Woodruff served as GOP caucus chairman under Bill Jones, who stepped down after the Republicans were embarrassed at the polls in November 1992. At one point during his tenure as caucus chair, Woodruff embarrassed Republican members when he thanked Speaker Willie Brown, in front of cameras and an open microphone, for tolerating the Republican staff's incompetence.

Woodruff won his re-election bid, but he was given a run for his money by a 74-year-old Lyndon LaRouche supporter named Alice Robb, who spent no money and was repudiated by the Riverside County Democratic Party because of her LaRouche connections. Robb garnered 43 percent of the vote in Riverside County, with 48 for Woodruff. But with a strong showing in San Bernardino County, Woodruff won the election 52 percent to 39 percent.

Paul Woodruff

Woodruff's voting record has generally followed the Assembly Republican pack. In early 1993, he introduced a bill that would allow California State University to establish an installment payment plan for student fees.

PERSONAL: elected 1988; born Feb. 13, 1960, in San Bernardino; home, Forest Hills; education, B.A. CSU San Bernardino; single; Protestant.

CAREER: aide, Assemblyman William Leonard 1981-1988.

COMMITTEES: Governmental Organization; Health; Televising the Assembly; Ways & Means.

OFFICES: Capitol, (916) 445-7552, FAX (916) 445-7650; district, 13027 Perris Blvd, 106, Moreno Valley 92553, (909) 242-6588, FAX (909) 242-2078.

TERM LIMIT: 1996

REGISTRATION: 41.6% D, 45.9% R

1992 CAMPAIGN:	Woodruff – R	52.5%	$286,082
	Alice Robb – D	38.7%	$0
	Michael Geller L	8.8%	
1990 CAMPAIGN:	Woodruff – R	56.5%	$298,736
	Raynolds Johnson – D	37.8%	$10,112

RATINGS:	AFL-CIO	CalPIRG	CLCV	NOW	CofC	CalFarm
	9	23	16	21	89	60

KEY VOTES:

Assault gun ban:	NO	Ban AIDS discrim:	NO	Restrict abortion funds:	YES
Sales tax hike:	NO	Wealth tax hike:	NO	Strong gay rights:	NO
Parental leave:	NO	Timber compromise:	YES	Execution by injection:	YES
Limited gay rights:	NO	Universal health insur:	NO	1992-93 Budget Act:	YES
Campaign Reform:	NO	Offshore oil ban:	NO	Charter schools:	YES

7

The Congress — Year of the women

"For too long, the men have messed things up! It's time to give the women an opportunity."
–U.S. Senate candidate Dianne Feinstein, Oct. 9, 1992

In a year of extraordinary political events, one of the standouts of 1992 was the election to the United States Senate of two California women, Dianne Feinstein and Barbara Boxer. California had never had a female senator, and no state had ever had two women serving in the U.S. Senate at the same time. In the same election, California also sent a record seven women to the U.S. House of Representatives — up from three in the previous Congress. All were Democrats. Some would count nine women in the 54 member state delegation in Washington, D.C., as an indication of how little equality women have achieved, but for many more, it was a glorious victory that they hope to replicate again and again in future elections.

The historic dual Senate elections of Feinstein and Boxer were made possible when Sen. Pete Wilson defeated former San Francisco Mayor Feinstein for the governorship in 1990. At the time, Republican Wilson had four years remaining in his Senate term. He was allowed to name his successor and that appointee was required to run for election in 1992 for the right to serve out the last two years of the term. That became known as the "short seat." Wilson's uninspired choice for the job was state Sen. John Seymour of Anaheim, who at the time of his appointment had recently lost a GOP primary race for lieutenant governor.

The six-year seat — or "long seat" — became open in 1992 when Sen. Alan Cranston decided to retire. In a state where U.S. senators are often considered expendable, Cranston served 24 years in the upper house. Only one other elected senator had served longer, Sen. Hiram Johnson (1917-45). Cranston had hoped for a fifth term, but his involvement with Michael Milken, Charles Keating and the savings and loan scandals had caused one of the most productive careers in

California politics to crash and burn. Cranston also had to fight prostate cancer during his last two years in office. He gave up his post as Senate Whip, the No. 2 leadership position among Democrats, and spent the remainder of his term on the periphery of Senate business.

Feinstein had little difficulty defeating Seymour. Marin County's Rep. Boxer emerged from a crowded primary as the Democratic standard bearer and should have had an easy time vanquishing the GOP pick, ultraconservative Bruce Herschensohn. In the final weeks, however, Feinstein had to rescue Boxer's hapless campaign. Boxer won with a half-million votes to spare, but she was held to 47.9 percent.

Following the election, Feinstein and Boxer declared that they would work as a team and "speak with one voice" on California concerns. They promised to be a unifying force in a delegation that has always been fractious. Feinstein began holding bipartisan breakfast meetings for the delegation. Boxer put together a bipartisan task force of Northern and Southern California members to coordinate responses on issues ranging from federal aid to military conversions.

It was during the fall campaign that the two women, who hadn't been friends before, established a genuine rapport as they stumped the state together and then after the election worked at setting up their offices. If their team approach endures, it will be an exception in Congress. Normally, senators and staffs of the same party and state don't work well together since both must appeal to the same general constituencies. That breeds divisive competition and attempts to establish identities apart from each other. Senators of the opposite party, on the other hand, have different constituencies and usually know instantly where they can work together and where they can't. That simplifies things immeasurably. Alan Cranston, for example, practically always had an easier relationship with the four California Republicans who served opposite him than he did with the one Democrat, John Tunney.

In any event, Feinstein had a decided advantage as she began her Senate career. Because she had defeated an appointee, Feinstein was sworn in Nov. 10, 1992, and automatically became first in seniority over an unusually large freshman class of 11 senators. By the time Boxer and the rest took the oath on Jan. 5, Feinstein was California's senior senator, which puts her ahead of the others in terms of all-important committee selections, among other perks. Boxer, at least, had a chance to catch her breath during the interim and will have six years to work up to her next election. But for Feinstein, the campaign never stopped since she must run again in 1994.

The hoopla over California's two women senators tended to divert attention from other changes in the delegation that could have much more profound impact over the long-term. Paramount was the fact that reapportionment gave California seven more House seats in 1992 for a total of 52. Previously, the largest delegations had 45 members and only two states had ever achieved that number: California in the

1980s and New York in the 1930s and 40s. Nearly one House vote in eight is cast by a Californian.

Since California's reapportionment was done by the courts after the 1990 census, the state got a fair remap for a change. It was a far cry from the shamelessly gerrymandered districts drawn by the late Rep. Phil Burton, D-San Francisco, after the 1980 count. After the 1990 elections, the delegation stood at 26 Democrats and 19 Republicans. The GOP claimed the fair reapportionment would give them a majority. But when the 1992 contests were over, the delegation numbered 29 Democrats and 23 Republicans. Democrats picked up five of the seven new seats.

Michigan Rep. Guy Vander Jagt, who chaired the GOP's congressional campaign committee, blamed the poor showing on the Bush campaign. "It was a shame that in California, where we had the most golden opportunities in the gold state, that the presidential campaign, I guess, made a decision to write off California and really didn't do much there in the last five, six weeks of the campaign."

Rep. Vic Fazio, D-West Sacramento, agreed that the national ticket hurt California Republicans. But they also did a lot to hurt themselves, he insisted. "The conservatives are on the ascendancy in the delegation," he said. "They fielded too many candidates who were far to the right of the mainstream of their party. We out-organized them and won some (seats) we didn't expect to." As if to underscore that, immediately after the election California conservatives joined with GOP House members nationwide to oust moderate Rep. Jerry Lewis of Redlands from the chairmanship of the House Republican Conference, the No. 3 position in the caucus.

In what was supposed to be an anti-incumbent year, only two sitting California congressmen lost. First-term Rep. Frank Riggs, R-Windsor, was defeated by Rep. Dan Hamburg, D-Ukiah, and 10-term Rep. Robert Lagomarsino, R-Santa Barbara, was beaten in the primary by Rep. Michael Huffington, R-Santa Barbara.

Seventeen of California's newly elected representatives were freshmen. And 11 were minorities — another record — including Rep. Jay Kim, R-Diamond Bar, the first Korean-American ever elected to Congress. By all accounts, the freshman class was the most accomplished in memory. Among its ranks were two Ph.D's, a gaggle of lawyers, a former college president, some self-made millionaires and a onetime welfare mother who became a successful businesswoman. They brought expertise that was sorely needed.

With retirements, defeats and one resignation, the California delegation lost 137 years of seniority in 1993. Feinstein and Boxer are freshmen senators in a house where seniority plays a critical role in the ability to shape legislation, implement policy and alter the direction of government bureaucracy. Cranston had chaired the Veterans' Affairs Committee. In the House, two senior members of the Appropriations Committee were gone along with the chairmen of the budget and aging committees.

At the same time, however, others were moving up. California Democrats now chair the committees on Armed Services; Science, Space and Technology; Natural

Resources; Public Works and Transportation; and District of Columbia. There also were a number of key subcommittee chairmanships on Appropriations, Ways and Means and subcommittees dealing with energy, foreign affairs, health, housing and education. As the minority party members, Republicans can only hold chairmanships in their own caucus. The highest House committee position they can hold is ranking minority member and California Republicans only had two such posts: Energy and Commerce, and House Administration.

Unity, seldom achieved in the past, will remain difficult for California's representatives to achieve. It's not enough to say that the 54 members are badly divided by differences involving geography and ideology. They're scattered. The delegation has been likened to the cartoon image of a huge dust cloud rolling along the ground with feet and hands sticking out here and there. Members range from the Republican bombasts of Orange and San Diego counties — Robert Dornan, Randy "Duke" Cunningham and Duncan Hunter — to brittle liberals such as Berkeley Democrat Ron Dellums. They often refuse to work together even when obvious interests of the state are at stake. As a result, while Californians quarreled, major federal projects such as the superconducting super collider went to other states.

The two caucus deans, Democrat Don Edwards of San Jose and Republican Carlos Moorhead of Glendale, have toiled for years to bring about some unity. With funding from California business interests, they finally were able to launch the California Institute in 1990. The bipartisan research group, modeled on similar organizations representing Texas and several geographic regions, is to mobilize support for pork-barrel projects and other issues of importance to California.

The institute started by getting delegation members together for social functions — something that had never happened before. Soon they were being asked to sign joint letters. Institute Executive Director Janet Denton said about 80 percent of the delegation can be expected to sign on to any issue. On some issues, every delegation member has participated in a coordinated lobbying effort.

Such was the case when a 1992 bill was being considered to provide money for resettling immigrants. About 60 percent of the assistance grant money goes to California. The state delegation got House approval for $561 million, which was almost double the amount sought by the Bush administration. Denton said she was encouraged by the increased involvement of members with the institute's initiatives.

"Maybe the freshman class can be the glue for the delegation," said incoming Rep. Xavier Becerra, D-Los Angeles. "I've talked to most Republicans and Democrats here and they all feel the same way. We've got a mandate from the public to reform government." But others saw it differently. "I haven't had a very positive experience with bipartisan efforts," said Rep. John Doolittle, R-Rocklin.

University of Southern California political scientist Larry Berg said he saw no reason why there shouldn't be more coalition building. "I'm in an optimistic frame of mind for the first time in so many years that I'm surprised with myself," Berg mused.

BIOGRAPHICAL PROFILES

Following the biographical sketches of the state's two senators and the members of the House of Representatives are election results from the most recent campaigns. To the right of each vote tally is the amount of money raised for those campaigns. The data were compiled from federal disclosure and other records by Jane Mentzinger of the Common Cause office in Washington, D.C.

Ratings are provided by a spectrum of seven ideological and trade groups. A score of 100 indicates the officeholder voted in agreement 100 percent of the time on bills of interest to that organization. Some organizations offer cumulative ratings for all sessions in which the person served. Others rate only a recent session. The organizations are:

ADA — Americans for Democratic Action, Suite 1150, 1625 K St., N.W., Washington, D.C. 20005, (202) 785-5969. Liberal. Issues include civil rights, handgun control, hate-crimes statistics, gay/lesbian discrimination, opposition to the death penalty and defense spending. Based on 1992 votes.

ACU — American Conservative Union, 38 Ivy St., S.E., Washington, D.C. 20003, (202)546-6555. Conservative on foreign policy, defense, social and budget issues. Based on cumulative votes.

AFL-CIO — American Federation of Labor-Congress of Industrial Organizations, Department of Legislation, Room 309, 815-16th St., N.W., Washington, D.C. 20006, (202) 637-5000. The nation's biggest union confederation promotes labor, health, child-care and civil-rights issues. Based on cumulative votes.

LCV — The League of Conservation Voters, Suite 804, 2000 L St., N.W., Washington, D.C. 20036, (202) 785-8683. LCV is a political arm for more than 100 organizations. Issues include global warming, park and stream protection, lead testing, pesticide regulation, timber protection, air and water pollution, wildlife protection, clean energy development and toxic cleanup. Based on votes for 1991.

NCSC — National Council of Senior Citizens, 1331 F St., N.W., Washington, D.C. 20004, (202) 347-8800. The council promotes issues of interest to older people such as Medicare, Social Security, health care, housing, consumer protection and civil rights. Based on cumulative votes.

NTU — National Taxpayers Union, 713 Maryland Ave., N.E., Washington, D.C. 20002, (202) 543-1300. This union of conservatives is devoted to reduced federal spending. Based on 1991 votes.

USCC — United States Chamber of Commerce, 1615 H St., N.W., Washington, D.C. 20062, (202) 659-6000. The nation's largest business trade organization takes a pro-business view of issues involving the budget, taxes, trade, price fixing, defense, energy, environment, civil rights and family leave. Based on cumulative votes.

U.S. SENATE
Dianne Feinstein (D)

Dianne Feinstein heard the shots and smelled the gunpowder. Running down a hallway, she found Harvey Milk, a fellow member of the San Francisco County Board of Supervisors. He was face down in his own blood, dead.

Someone else found Mayor George Moscone's body.

Minutes later, Feinstein was facing television cameras. She spoke each word slowly, trying to drain any emotion from her voice. "Both Mayor Moscone," she began, "and Supervisor Harvey Milk have been shot and killed."

Feinstein's grace on that grim November day in 1978 defined her as no other moment possibly could. What the public did not see on that day was her own personal crisis and the drifting that has punctuated her life.

Dianne Feinstein

Only two hours before the assassinations, Feinstein had told reporters she would not run for re-election. Her husband had recently died. She was tired of the petty City Hall intrigues. Becoming mayor did not seem possible, having run twice and failed. She was through with politics and wanted to do something else.

All that changed with Moscone's death. The crazed gunman was none other than former County Supervisor Dan White, a young political neophyte whom Feinstein had taken under her wing. In the days that followed the shooting, Feinstein, as president of the Board of Supervisors, succeeded Moscone as mayor. She went on to win two terms on her own and to beat a recall attempt. While most politicians attempt to build their careers in carefully orchestrated stages, Feinstein's has been like a ricocheting pinball, bouncing to the next stop.

She was on Walter Mondale's "short list" of possible vice presidential running mates in 1984 but seemed to pursue the opportunity half-heartedly. She considered but rejected running for Congress in a 1987 special election. After leaving the mayor's office in 1988, it took her until early in 1990 to plunge fully into running for governor against Republican Sen. Pete Wilson. The race went down to the wire, but on Election Day Wilson finished ahead by 3 percentage points. That may have been the luckiest of Feinstein's defeats. Not even Wilson realized that he was inheriting a multibillion dollar debt that would paralyze his governorship as the national recession deepened.

Feinstein got another break when Wilson plucked his old pal John Seymour from obscurity and named him to the U.S. Senate seat he had vacated. When Seymour ran for the remaining two years of the term in 1992, Feinstein carved him up like a Christmas turkey and became the first woman ever sworn in as a senator from California.

But then, Feinstein is used to firsts: First woman on the San Francisco Board of Supervisors and first woman chairman. First woman mayor. One of the first politicians to court gay voters and embrace their quest for equality. First woman to make a serious run for governor of California. And now first woman to hold a California seat in the U.S. Senate. Even there, the firsts have continued. First woman on the Senate Judiciary Committee and so forth.

But it hasn't been easy. Feinstein was the eldest of three daughters of Leon and Betty Goldman. Her father was a surgeon and her mother suffered from an undiagnosed brain disorder that manifested itself in fits of rage and alcoholism. After graduating from Stanford University with a less-than-distinguished record, she married Jack Berman, now a San Francisco Superior Court judge, and they had one daughter, Katherine. She was not content, however, to be a homemaker, and they divorced.

At a party, she met neurosurgeon Bertram Feinstein. They married and she began carving out a life in politics. She was well into her career on the board of supervisors when Bertram Feinstein died of cancer. After a year in the mayor's office, investment banker Richard Blum became her third husband in 1979.

The senate race proved easier than anyone expected. Seymour, a onetime mayor of Anaheim and sitting state senator, had just lost a primary race for lieutenant governor when Wilson named him to the Senate. Although a hard-working and productive legislator, it became apparent soon after his elevation to the U.S. Senate that he'd lied about his rags to riches success in the business world. Not only was he not a self-made millionaire, but he had been sued 18 times for fraud when he ran a real estate business. Feinstein was able to pound him for his ties to the savings and loan industry, for blocking the California Desert Protection Act and for spending $1.1 million of tax money on 6 million pieces of junk mail that were sent out under the congressional frank.

At the same time, Seymour was taking heat from the right wing of his own party for a series of flip-flops. A former Catholic, he changed his mind on abortion and also on the death penalty. He began political life as a staunch conservative, but his ideology drifted midstream in tandem with his quest for higher office.

Seymour raised a substantial campaign war chest, but he couldn't match Feinstein there either — especially when all Feinstein had to do was ask Richard Blum for a check. It's hard to say how far Feinstein would have gone in the governor and senate races without the infusions of cash from Blum and contributors he could tap worldwide. But it's interesting to note that she finished the U.S. Senate primary against two statewide officeholders, Lt. Gov. Leo McCarthy and Controller Gray Davis, after raising almost as much money in New York as she did in Southern California. Nonetheless, Blum's involvement also was the source of the biggest headache of her senatorial campaign.

Seymour attempted to capitalize on Feinstein's troubles with the Fair Political Practices Commission, which had sued Feinstein for a record $8.85 million in fines for allegedly committing a raft of campaign law violations when she ran for governor against Wilson. The most serious of the allegations was that she did not disclose that the actual sources of $2.7 million in loans were Bank of America and Sumitomo Bank. Instead, she reported that she was the source of the loans. At the time, Blum owned 2 million shares of BankAmerica Corp. and he sat on the board of directors of Sumitomo. Six weeks after her election, Feinstein settled with the FPPC for $190,000 as part of an agreement that said the "errors or omissions were not intentional in nature." It was the second-largest fine in the history of the watch-dog agency.

Seymour also attacked her for leaving San Francisco in fiscal difficulties and for her coziness with developers (a bizarre charge coming from a Republican Realtor). But none of that seemed to overcome the gender issue that Feinstein raised so successfully. "It's the toughest mountain I've ever had to climb," Seymour would say.

In what was being touted nationally as "The Year of the Woman" in politics, Feinstein and Barbara Boxer, the Democratic candidate to replace Alan Cranston in the other California U.S. Senate seat, made women's issues the centerpiece of their campaigns. The white, good-old-boy, backroom-dealing exclusionary pols were the enemy, and Seymour fit the image perfectly. In a bit of overkill, Feinstein opened her speech at the state Democratic convention in April by saying: "My name is Dianne Feinstein. I am woman" — a play on the 1972 Helen Reddy song.

Since women make up about 57 percent of the state's Democratic voters, their impact was expected to be significant. Feinstein's campaign manager, Kam Kuwata, built a strategy in part around wooing women of all political persuasions who could be counted upon to vote for the more moderate of the two women vying for the senate seats. It worked. On Election Day, Feinstein out-polled Boxer by 680,000 votes. Feinstein's broader appeal was most apparent in Seymour's Orange County. Both Republican senate candidates carried the conservative bastion, but Feinstein ran nearly 50,000 votes ahead of Boxer.

At age 59, Feinstein is older than the norm for first-time senators. But she comes with two big advantages. Because she replaced an appointee, she began her term Nov. 10, 1992 — nearly two full months ahead of the 11 other freshmen. That puts her at the head of her class in seniority for all-important committee assignments.

Of the four new women senators elected in 1992, Feinstein is probably the most moderate and most skillful in practical politics. And she's known as a team player. Those are attributes likely to make her the least threatening to the old boys in the "go-along, get-along" Senate leadership.

Feinstein's first major break in the Senate came when she won seats on both Judiciary and Appropriations. Judiciary was important to her women's constituency since the formerly all-male committee's actions during the Clarence Thomas-Anita Hill hearings became one of the major issues in 1992 Senate races across the county.

But Appropriations was a plum of vital importance to all Californians. The Golden State hasn't had an Appropriations seat since GOP Sen. Thomas Kuchel left the panel in the 1960s. The problem, explained Vic Fazio, a House Appropriations member, is that "we get money in (bills) on the House side, and it goes to the Senate, and we get nothing." Feinstein's tenure there has the potential of becoming the most important gain by the state delegation in the 103rd Congress.

Feinstein, nonetheless, got off to a rocky start when she accepted the free services of a lobbyist for the Recording Industry of America Inc. to organize her Senate office. Feinstein offered a strident defense of her action, saying lobbyist Hilary Rosen was not involved in policy questions. The blatant conflict undoubtedly will come back to haunt her 1994 campaign.

Meanwhile, Feinstein can be expected to pursue her moderately liberal agenda. The long-fought California desert bill that Cranston left behind was the first bill Feinstein introduced and she also seemed destined to be a key player in President Bill Clinton's plans for economic revival. She remained committed to establishing permanent research and investment tax credits plus financing public works improvements. On Judiciary, she is also expected to be active in crime legislation.

PERSONAL: elected 1992; born June 22, 1933, in San Francisco; home, San Francisco; education, B.A. political science, Stanford University 1955; husband Richard Blum; one child, three stepchildren; Jewish.

CAREER: California Women's Board of Terms and Parole, 1960-66; San Francisco Board of Supervisors, 1969-1978; Mayor of San Francisco, 1978-1988.

COMMITTEES: Appropriations; Judiciary.

OFFICES: Suite 331, Hart Building, Washington, D.C. 20510, (202) 224-3841; state, Suite 305, 1700 Montgomery St., San Francisco 94111, (415) 249-4777; Suite 915, 11111 Santa Monica Blvd., Los Angeles 90025, (310) 914-7300; Suite 1030, 705 B St., San Diego 92101, (619) 231-9712.

1992 CAMPAIGN:

Feinstein – D	54.3%	$7,708,664
John Seymour – R	38%	$6,598,426

RATINGS: Newly elected.

Barbara Boxer (D)

Dianne Feinstein won two U.S. Senate seats in 1992 — her own and Barbara Boxer's.

Polls showed Boxer leading Republican Bruce Herschensohn by 22 percentage points shortly after Labor Day. But two weeks away from the Nov. 3 election, ultraconservative Herschensohn was running dead even. In September, Herschensohn began a TV blitz that defined Boxer on his terms: bouncer of 143 checks at the House bank, a big-spending liberal who enjoyed taxpayer-paid limousine rides, a shrill feminist with a poor voting record and nothing better to do than beat up the military while 200,000 defense jobs disappeared in California.

The Boxer campaign allowed the attacks to go largely unanswered while saving TV money for a planned end-of-campaign blitz. When the response finally came, the spots showed Boxer as a strident candidate and failed to shift the focus away from Herschensohn's attacks. In effect they complemented Herschensohn's themes as he continued to speak with perceived clarity about his own plans for addressing pocketbook concerns of the electorate. "She's turned out to be a weak candidate with a very weak campaign," said Sherry Bebitch Jeffe, political analyst from Claremont College.

Barbara Boxer

In rode Feinstein, who was coasting to victory over appointed incumbent John Seymour. Feinstein stumped the state with Boxer in tow, devoting most of her speeches to praise for Boxer. The two had never been close, but only veteran observers would have picked that up while watching them in action. Usually feisty Boxer would stand by smiling while Feinstein would say: "Cagney needs her Lacy. Thelma needs her Louise. And Dianne needs her Barbara in the United States Senate!"

Humbling as that must have been, Boxer seemed to take it in stride. The two appeared to develop a solid relationship and promised to go to Washington as a team working for California's interests. The morning after the election, Boxer would say later, the enormity of victory began to sink in. "It was an extraordinary moment," she said, "to show people that two women could get elected from a state the size of California and that two women could campaign and work together, could set aside their differences without much conversation and just plain do it."

Boxer brought a number of liabilities to her campaign, despite having beaten

U.S. Senators from California
(elected by Legislature prior to 1914)

Seat A			Seat B		
John C. Fremont	D	1849	William M. Gwin	D	1849
John B. Weller	D	1852			
David C. Broderick	D	1857			
Henry P. Haun	D	1859			
Milton S. Latham	D	1860	James A. McDougall	D	1861
John Conness	Un	1863	Cornelius Cole	Un	1865
Eugene Casserly	D	1869			
John S. Hager	D	1873	Aaron A. Sargent	R	1873
Newton Booth	I–R	1875	James T. Farley	D	1879
John F. Miller	R	1881	Leland Stanford	R	1885
A.P. Williams	R	1886			
George Hearst	D	1887			
Charles N. Fenton	R	1893	George C. Perkins	R	1893
Stephen M. White	D	1893			
Thomas R. Bard	R	1899			
Frank P. Flint	R	1905			
John D. Works	R	1911	James D. Phalen	D	1915
Hiram W. Johnson	R	1917	Samuel M. Shortridge	R	1921
William F. Knowland	R	1945	William G. McAdoo	R	1932
Clair Engle	D	1959	Thomas M. Storke	D	1938
Pierre Salinger	D	1964	Sheridan Downey	D	1939
George Murphy	R	1964	Richard Nixon	R	1951
John V. Tunney	D	1971	Thomas Kuchel	R	1952
S.I. Hayakawa	R	1977	Alan Cranston	D	1969
Pete Wilson	R	1983			
John Seymour	R	1991			
Dianne Feinstein	D	1992	BarbaraBoxer	D	1993

Un: Union; I-R: Independent-Republican.

two strong primary opponents — Rep. Mel Levine and Lt. Gov. Leo McCarthy. For many Democrats, Boxer's voting record during five House terms was uncomfortably liberal and characteristic of Marin County, which is to say somewhat apart from reality. Her combative style made it easy to paint her as a strident feminist despite the fact that she has always had a broad political agenda. And there were the bad checks: 143 of them.

First she lied about the checks, and then she tried to make light of the situation ("If you look in my closets, they're messy, too"). Then there was her campaign manager, Rose Kapolczynski, who had snatched defeat from the jaws of victory in 1988 while running Mike Lowry's Senate campaign against Slade Gorton in Washington State. Kapolczynski's focus on scheduling public appearances and detail work rather than honing a positive media image for Boxer made her better suited to running a campaign in Wyoming. As an added negative, the campaign got a reputation for not returning phone calls from reporters and for being condescending with volunteers.

Boxer also was drubbed on her legislative record, or lack thereof, when she shouldn't have been. True, her House record contained no omnibus legislative monument, but that's not because she hadn't worked hard. A measure on government-paid abortions for victims of rape and incest, for example, was vetoed. Boxer's forte has never been in splicing together tedious legislative deals. Her career is distinguished by a mastery at building coalitions that would take issues such as abortion, consumer safety and military accountability to center stage.

In the House, she was elected president of her freshman class and immediately plunged into issues involving ineffective government. She exposed the Air Force purchase of the $7,622 coffee pot and became one of Congress' experts on procurement issues. By her third term, she was on the Armed Services Committee, once one of the most exclusive old-boy clubs of the House. From that perch, she lead the fight for laws requiring more competitive contract bidding, better performance on contracts and protection for whistleblowers.

At the same time, she worked her staff to exhaustion on issues that transcended district interests: AIDS research, transportation, dial-a-porn, consumer protection, offshore oil bans, high-school dropouts, abortion rights and a plethora of other women's issues. In the process, she developed something of a national constituency among women who readily came to her aid when it came time to write checks for her Senate plunge.

But it was a record not taken effectively to voters. Nor did Boxer capitalize until the end of the campaign on Herschensohn being on the unpopular side of practically every major issue from abortion and off-shore drilling to gun control.

In the end, her candidacy also was saved by the Democratic sweep of California and a last-minute smear of Herschensohn, who was accused of frequenting a nude bar and a porn shop. She also benefited from a strong turnout by women voters, the aggressive Democratic voter registration drive and a boost from the six-county Bay

Area, where she won by better than 2-to-1.

The question now is what Boxer will do with the post. Based on past performance, most expect her to assemble a high-profile office with an equally high energy level. She needed no coaxing to carry on Alan Cranston's legacy of fighting for a liberal foreign policy, environmental protection and the rights of the disabled.

Senate leaders showed considerable confidence in Boxer at the start of the 1993 session, when they gave her a seat on the Democratic Steering Committee. The panel hands out committee assignments to members and is an immensely important power base in a chamber where so much happens because of personal friendships and positions within the hierarchy. Boxer also got the assignment she sought on the Banking, Housing and Urban Affairs Committee plus the Environment and Public Works Committee.

Banking especially interested Boxer because its jurisdiction includes financial aid to commerce and industry, housing programs, mass transit and export controls — all important to California business. In addition, it's a premier fund-raising post, as Alan Cranston found during his long Senate tenure. But clearly, it was not lost on Boxer that membership on the committee led to Cranston's role in the savings and loan debacles, and ultimately to his retirement from politics. Public Works is one of the key pork-barrel committees and Boxer has close ties with the chairmen of the House Public Works Committee, Norm Mineta, D-San Jose, and the House Natural Resources Committee, George Miller, D-Martinez.

It was a surprise that she didn't end up on Judiciary, but it appears she deferred to Feinstein. After all, Boxer was among the group of House women who marched to the door of the all-male Judiciary Committee in the fall of 1991 to protest its handling of the Clarence Thomas-Anita Hill hearings. After her election, Judiciary Chairman Sen. Joseph Biden, D-Del., sent Boxer a dozen roses and a note that said: "Welcome to the Judiciary Committee."

It's been a long, but steady climb for the daughter of an uneducated immigrant mother and a father who went to night law school while working days to support his family. Boxer credits her own drive to the model her father provided. She married Stewart Boxer, a labor lawyer, gave up her business career to raise children and then became a "re-entry" woman who worked as a weekly newspaper reporter in Marin County once her two kids were in school. From there, Boxer spent two years as U.S. Rep. John Burton's field representative, which probably gave her invaluable lessons in how to deal with erratic males.

In 1976, she won a seat on the Marin County Board of Supervisors and quickly established herself as a hard worker with a flair for the dramatic. When Burton announced he would step down in 1982 to deal with his chemical dependency problems, Boxer won the seat in a close race but had no trouble holding it after that.

PERSONAL: elected 1992; born Nov. 11, 1940, in Brooklyn, N.Y.; home, Greenbrae; education, B.A. economics, Brooklyn College 1962; husband Stewart, two children; Jewish.

CAREER: stockbroker and financial researcher, 1962-65; reporter for the weekly Pacific Sun, 1972-74; aide to Rep. John Burton, 1974-76; Marin County Supervisor, 1976-82; House of Representatives, 1982-93.

COMMITTEES: Banking, Housing and Urban Affairs; Environment and Public Works; Democratic Steering Committee.

OFFICES: Suite 112 Hart Building, Washington, D.C. 20510, (202) 224-3553; state, Suite 240, 1700 Montgomery St., San Francisco 94111, (415) 403-0100; Suite 545, 2250 E. Imperial Hwy., El Sequndo 90245, (310) 414-5700.

1992 CAMPAIGN: Boxer – D | 47.9% | $10,129,028
                    Bruce Herschensohn – R | 43% | $7,708,664

*RATINGS:	ADA	ACU	AFL/CIO	LCV	NCSC	NTU	USCC
	60	3	95	89	99	32	21

*Based upon votes as member of the House of Representatives.

Congressional Districts

1	HAMBURG, Dan	12	LANTOS, Tom	23	GALLEGLY, Elton
2	HERGER, Wally	13	STARK, Pete	24	BEILENSON, Anthony
3	FAZIO, Vic	14	ESHOO, Anna	25	McKEON, Howard
4	DOOLITTLE, John	15	MINETA, Norman	26	BERMAN, Howard
5	MATSUI, Robert	16	EDWARDS, Don	27	MOORHEAD, Carlos
6	WOOLSEY, Lynn	17	VACANT (Panetta)	28	DREIER, David
7	MILLER, George	18	CONDIT, Gary	29	WAXMAN, Henry
8	PELOSI, Nancy	19	LEHMAN, Richard	30	BECERRA, Xavier
9	DELLUMS, Ronald	20	DOOLEY, Calvin	31	MARTINEZ, Matthew
10	BAKER, William	21	THOMAS, William	32	DIXON, Julian
11	POMBO, Richard	22	HUFFINGTON, Michael	33	ROYBAL-ALLARD, Lucille

34	TORRES, Esteban
35	WATERS, Maxine
36	HARMAN, Jane
37	TUCKER, Walter
38	HORN, Steve
39	ROYCE, Ed
40	LEWIS, Jerry
41	KIM, Jay
42	BROWN, George Jr.
43	CALVERT, Ken
44	McCANDLESS, Al
45	ROHRABACHER, Dana
46	DORNAN, Robert
47	COX, Christopher
48	PACKARD, Ron
49	SCHENK, Lynn
50	FILNER, Bob
51	CUNNINGHAM, Randy
52	HUNTER, Duncan

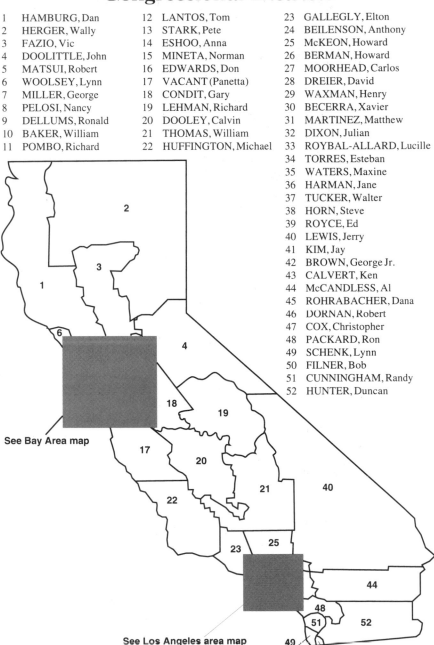

See Bay Area map

See Los Angeles area map

San Francisco Bay Area

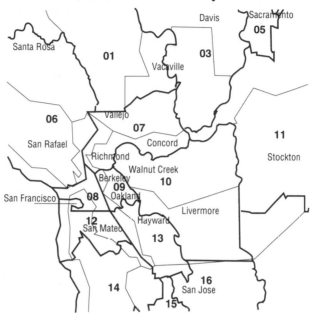

Los Angeles Area

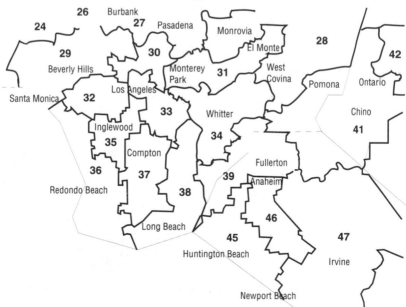

Vacant

17th Congressional District

Former Rep. Leon Panetta had a virtual lock on his increasingly liberal district for 16 years. Then President-elect Clinton tapped him to be budget director. The state delegation lost the chair of the House Budget Committee in the process, but gained an ally with the ear of the president. Campaigns were under way to succeed Panetta as this was written, but the likely new congressman will be Assemblyman Sam Farr, D-Carmel, whose biography appears in the Assembly section.

This is one of the few districts in California where there has been a noticeable shift to the left in the 1970s and '80s. The environmental fights, which always take on increased intensity in coastal areas, are in part responsible for the change as residents have become increasingly concerned about onshore land development and offshore oil drilling. The 17th District takes in some of the most scenic land on the California coast, including Big Sur and Monterey Bay. Preservation of those resources is not a partisan issue. Republican coast dwellers value their views and clean beaches as much as anyone. Another reason for the change is the growth of the University of California, Santa Cruz, at the extreme northern end of the district. The campus is one place that hasn't left the 1960s, and the Santa Cruz City Council is every bit as radical as Berkeley's. Santa Cruz's sharp shift to the political port (it was once a Republican city) neutralizes GOP strongholds in Monterey and San Benito counties, which also are part of the district.

The area is headed for a major economic jolt as Fort Ord closes in 1993 and perhaps as many as 16,000 jobs disappear. That represents a major challenge for the new House member.

REGISTRATION: 52.4% D, 30.6% R

William P. Baker (R)

10th Congressional District

There aren't many Republican enclaves in the east San Francisco Bay Area, but most of them are in the 10th District. Included are the affluent, bedroom areas of Contra Costa and Alameda counties plus the rolling farm country stretching eastward to the San Joaquin County line. Runaway growth over the past 30 years has merged communities such as Walnut Creek, Pleasanton and Livermore into one, highly congested slurb. Housing values and incomes tend to be high, but economic uncertainties also have given jitters to many of those residing within the numerous gated communities.

William P. Baker

William Baker should fit the upscale district to a

T. A former budget analyst with the state Department of Finance, he made tax and money matters his specialty during the 12 years that he represented parts of the area in the Assembly. For both Govs. George Deukmejian and Pete Wilson, he served as point man in virtually all major tax and budget negotiations.

Yet he also established a reputation for acid remarks, and that was nearly his undoing as he ran for this open congressional seat in 1992. His sneering comments about welfare mothers (he called them "breeders"), sexual harassment and abortion advocates were used against him by Democrat Wendell Williams, a Walnut Creek management consultant. Williams came within 10 points of defeating Baker when he challenged the assemblyman's re-election in 1990. This time, both worked overtime digging up dirt on each other in what became one of the nastiest campaigns in the state. And Baker barely squeaked through.

If nothing else, Williams showed how to beat Baker. A better candidate may be able to so in 1994. Much will depend on how well Baker keeps his mouth in check in Congress and the success of the Clinton administration's economic recovery efforts in the next two years. In the meantime, Baker quickly moved into a leadership position in the new Congress. He was elected freshman class representative on the panel that dispenses GOP committee assignments.

PERSONAL: elected 1992; born June 14, 1940, in Oakland; home, Danville; Coast Guard Reserve (six months active duty); education, B.S. San Jose State University, graduate study CSU Long Beach; wife, Joanne Atack; four children; Protestant.

CAREER: businessman; assistant to secretary of the Senate; budget analyst state Department of Finance; Assemblyman, 1980-92.

COMMITTEES: Public Works and Transportation; Science, Space & Technology.

OFFICES: Suite 1724, Longworth Building, Washington, D.C. 20515, (202) 225-1880; district, Suite 103, 1801 N. California Blvd., Walnut Creek 94596, (510) 932-8899.

REGISTRATION: 42.4% D, 43.7% R

1992 CAMPAIGN:	Baker – R	51.9%	$678,050
	Wendell Williams – D	48%	$221,869

RATINGS: Newly elected.

Xavier Becerra (D)
30th Congressional District

Hispanic neighborhoods on three sides of downtown Los Angeles make up the core of this district along with a northeasterly bulge that includes Highland Park and Eagle Rock. Although some parts are increasingly shabby, these are not the poorest of the Hispanic communities. It is an area of rising property values and expectations for many who live there. In the predominately white neighborhoods, there are increasing numbers of Asians.

Among Hispanic officeholders, there is something of a tradition of handing off seats to a relative or an aide. Thirty-year veteran Rep. Ed Roybal tried that when he decided to retire in 1992. His aide, Henry Lozano, was anointed for the post. But when 10 others from various Hispanic factions got into the race, Lozano withdrew in favor of one-term Assemblyman Xavier Becerra, who eventually triumphed.

Becerra, a deputy attorney general and former aide to state Sen. Art Torres, won his Assembly seat in a similar race after it fell vacant when Charles Calderon moved up to the state Senate. Becerra ran an aggressive campaign, using strong grass-roots organizing and direct mail while portraying himself

Xavier Becerra

as a crime fighter. This is the kind of district where Becerra shouldn't have to withstand strong challenges in the future. He has shown promise as a consensus builder and should have the leisure to carve out a strong niche in Congress if he wishes to do so.

PERSONAL: elected 1992; born Jan. 26, 1958, in Sacramento; home, Los Angeles; education, B.A. and J.D. Stanford University; wife, Dr. Carolina Reyes.

CAREER: lawyer; deputy attorney general; aide to Sen. Art Torres.

COMMITTEES: Education and Labor; Judiciary; Science, Space and Technology.

OFFICES: Suite 1017, Longworth Building, Washington, D.C. 20515, (202) 225-6235; district, Suite 200, 2435 Colorado Blvd., Los Angeles 90041, (213) 722-0405.

REGISTRATION: 61.1% D, 23.3% R

| **1992 CAMPAIGN**: | Becerra – D | 58.4% | $332,337 |
| | Morry Waksberg – R | 23.9% | $52,795 |

RATINGS: Newly elected

Anthony C. Beilenson (D)
24th Congressional District

On the south, this district showcases the fabled Malibu Coast between Topanga Canyon and the Los Angeles County line. It laps over the hills into Thousand Oaks and then eastward through Agoura Hills, Woodland Hills, Tarzana, Encino and Van Nuys. Although furs and Rolls Royces abound in the area, most residents are upper middle-class professionals. Lower-income people are disappearing from the hillsides as homes are snapped up by two-income couples with few children.

One might expect a glitzy liberal to represent this area in Congress. But Rep.

Tony Beilenson is one of the more anonymous members of the delegation. He typifies the Jewish professional of the district. He has a solid and conscientious performer whose skills as a legislator are widely respected in the House. He seems nearly devoid of partisanship, which sometimes annoys those who would like to see him use his seat on the Rules Committee to the greater advantage of Democrats. He is an expert on the budget and was responsible for creating the Santa Monica Mountains National Recreation area.

Anthony Beilenson

Beilenson's old district was centered in Beverly Hills and West Hollywood, where he had a testy coexistence with the political organization headed by Reps. Howard Berman and Henry Waxman. But the district was collapsed during reapportionment, forcing Beilenson to move to the San Fernando Valley and a district less friendly for a liberal Democrat.

Conservatives, smelling blood, fielded Assemblyman Tom McClintock, who had been a thorn in the side of Gov. Pete Wilson. But McClintock's extreme views on everything from abortion to gun control didn't ignite a spark in what turned out to be a Democratic year. Beilenson had less trouble than most pundits figured he would.

PERSONAL: elected 1976; born Oct. 26, 1932, in New Rochelle, N.Y.; home, Woodland Hills; education, A.B. Harvard University 1954, L.L.B. 1957; wife, Dolores, three children; Jewish.

CAREER: attorney 1957-59; counsel to Assembly Committee on Finance and Insurance, 1960; counsel to California Compensation and Insurance Fund, 1961-62; Assembly, 1963-66; state Senate, 1966-77.

COMMITTEES: Budget; Rules.

OFFICES: Suite 2465, Rayburn Building, Washington, D.C. 20515, (202) 225-5911; district, Suite 1010, 21031 Ventura Blvd., Woodland Hills 91364, (818) 999-1990; Suite 211, 200 N. Westlake Blvd., Thousand Oaks 91362, (805) 496-4333.

REGISTRATION: 53.4% D, 41.7% R

1992 CAMPAIGN:	Beilenson – D	55.5%	552,071$
	Tom McClintock – R	39.1%	$460,327
1990 CAMPAIGN:	Beilenson – D	62%	$231,386
	Jim Saloman – R	34%	$358,367

RATINGS:	ADA	ACU	AFL/CIO	LCV	NCSC	NTU	USCC
	85	7	74	100	90	63	26

Number of checks bounced at the House bank: 5.

Howard L. Berman (D)
26th Congressional District

This compact district begins at the Ventura Free-way between Van Nuys and Burbank. It runs north-ward in fairly straight lines through North Holly-wood, Panorama City, Pacoima and San Fernando before butting into the Los Angeles City limits. There is a mix of people and an increasing number of apartment houses in the southern end of the district. Hispanic neighborhoods straddle the Golden State Freeway, and there are African American neighbor-hoods in Pacoima.

This could be a good district for a Hispanic candi-date. But Rep. Howard Berman needed a place to run after his old district in the Hollywood Hills was chewed up during reapportionment. Berman shares

Howard Berman

what was once one of the strongest political machines in Southern California with Rep. Henry Waxman. They have legendary fund-raising capability and substantial success at the ballot box. Berman is often the most politically assertive of the two, working hand-in-hand with two ace strategists and campaign managers, Berman's brother, Michael, and Carl D'Agostino. They're often accused of creating puppets and keeping them in power with contributions raised elsewhere. That has been said about Reps. Julian Dixon, Esteban Torres and Matthew Martinez. If that was the intent, it hasn't worked in the cases of Dixon and Torres, who show substantial independence. Martinez, however, doesn't show much of anything.

In the 1992 elections, however, Berman-Waxman backed a series of losers, and pundits have been writing obituaries for the old "westside gang," as they were known. But they still have a powerful base of support that most politicians would rather not challenge.

When Berman was in the Assembly he was a divisive force, fomenting a spiteful revolt against Speaker Leo McCarthy in 1980. Their battle preoccupied the house for a year. Eventually Willie Brown emerged from the fray with Republican backing to win the speakership, beginning his long reign. McCarthy went on to become lieutenant governor and Brown got rid of Berman, a potential rival, by creating a new congressional district for him in Los Angeles. Berman has been more of a team player in Congress, where he is now majority whip-at-large.

As an urban legislator, Berman has been well positioned politically to be a stalwart defender of the United Farm Workers. He has been active on border and immigration issues, anti-apartheid legislation and other civil libertarian matters that play well in his district. But he also has been an astute observer of Mideast politics. He was warning against the consequences of chemical-nuclear capability in Iraq long before the Bush administration figured out that Saddam Hussein could never be a reliable ally. On the Judiciary Committee, he also has been able to assist his show-business constituents with copyright and licensing protections.

PERSONAL: elected, 1982; born, April 15, 1941, in Los Angeles; home, Los Angeles; education, B.A. UCLA 1962, L.L.B. 1965; wife Janis, two children; Jewish.

CAREER: attorney, 1966-72; Assembly 1973-82.

COMMITTEES: Budget, Foreign Affairs, Judiciary, Natural Resources (temporary assignment).

OFFICES: Suite 2201, Rayburn Building, Washington, D.C. 20515, (202) 225-4695; district, Suite 506, 14600 Roscoe Blvd., Panorama City 91402, (818) 891-0543.

REGISTRATION: 60% D, 27.7% R

1992 CAMPAIGN:	Berman – D	61%	$343,552
	Gary Forsch – R	30.1%	$72,928
1990 CAMPAIGN:	Berman – D	61%	$510,538
	Roy Dahlson – R	35%	$83,775

RATINGS:	ADA	ACU	AFL/CIO	LCV	NCSC	NTU	USCC
	85	6	74	92	100	4	26

Number of checks bounced at the House bank: 67.

George E. Brown Jr. (D)
42nd Congressional District

Districts may change, but not Rep. George Brown. One of the House's oldest peaceniks, Brown continues to champion liberal causes despite dramatic gains in his district's Republican registration and non-stop efforts by GOP candidates to unseat him. The cigar-chomping Brown comes from Quaker stock and is both a physicist and nuclear engineer. He was talking about global warming and the virtues of solar energy long before it was fashionable.

In 1991, Brown became chairman of the Science, Space and Technology Committee, where he and Rep. George Miller of Natural Resources have been attempting to refashion national energy policy. In 1987, Brown quit the Intelligence Committee, saying

George Brown Jr.

he couldn't live with the committee's gag rules on topics that are general knowledge elsewhere.

Brown's long career in the House began in 1962. In 1970, he nearly won the Democratic U.S. Senate primary and probably could have dumped GOP Sen.

George Murphy. But that privilege went to neighboring House member John Tunney. Brown sat out for two years and was re-elected, but he returned to the House without those eight years of precious seniority.

He represents a district far different from the one that first sent him to Congress. Monterey Park, where Brown first ran for public office in 1954, is some 20 miles from the district's nearest border. Today, Brown represents the most densely populated area of San Bernardino County — the city of the same name, the industrial towns of Colton, Rialto and Fontana and Rancho Cucamonga. Many of the people living in those smog-choked cities are there for lack of choices. They include many blue collar and older people who can't afford to move to more pleasant environs.

For years, Republicans had been throwing far-right candidates against Brown. In 1992, with a district more Republican than the previous one, they fielded a folk hero of sorts, Dick Rutan. In 1986, the fighter pilot and aeronaut flew a wispy plane called Voyager around the world on one tank of fuel. But Rutan proved to be a better pilot than a political candidate. Brown raised twice as much money as Rutan and in the end, voters decided to keep the Science, Space and Technology chairman, hoping perhaps, that Brown is better positioned to help the district's sagging aerospace economy.

PERSONAL: elected in 1962 and served until 1971, re-elected in 1972; born March 6, 1920, in Holtville, Calif.; home, San Bernardino; education, B.A. UCLA 1946; wife Marta, four children; United Methodist.

CAREER: U.S. Army, 1942-45; Monterey Park City Council, 1954-58, mayor 1955-56; engineer and management consultant, city of Los Angeles, 1946-58; Assembly 1958-62.

COMMITTEES: Agriculture; Science, Space and Technology (chairman).

OFFICES: Suite 2300, Rayburn Building, Washington, D.C. 20515, (202) 225-6161, FAX (202) 225-8671; district, 657 La Cadena Dr., Colton 92324, (714) 825-2472.

REGISTRATION: 53.2% D, 37.2% R

1992 CAMPAIGN:	Brown – D	59.6%	$835,671
	Dick Rutan – R	43.9%	$347,999
1990 CAMPAIGN:	Brown – D	53%	$818,181
	Bob Hammock – R	47%	$538,281

RATINGS:	ADA	ACU	AFL/CIO	LCV	NCSC	NTU	USCC
	95	6	91	85	94	5	22

Number of checks bounced at the House bank: 26

Ken Calvert (R)
43rd Congressional District

The west end of Riverside County, from the grimy cities of Riverside and Corona to the open country around Lake Elsinore, became a new Republican district in 1992 after reapportionment. Yet many of those Republicans were unemployed or worried about losing their jobs at the time. That enabled Democrat and junior high teacher Mark Takano to come within a hair of winning the seat that year. In fact, he did squeak by on Election Day, but when the absentee votes were counted, industrial Realtor Ken Calvert took the seat with just 519 votes.

It is a seat Calvert should be able to hold, providing he works at it. He was slow to launch a serious campaign in 1992 until polls showed he was in trouble. Residents of the area tend to be conservative. Many are young families who bought homes in the area with the hope that one day they could cash in their equity and move closer to their jobs in less smoggy areas of the Los Angeles Basin. The trouble

Ken Calvert

is, many of them spend two to four hours a day commuting. They come home so drained by the experience that they don't get around to participating in community activities such as voting.

Calvert has a long history of party activism, which includes holding top posts in two of Pete Wilson's statewide campaigns and California co-chair of George Bush's 1988 presidential campaign in California. He is expected to be a team player in the conservative faction of the state GOP caucus.

PERSONAL: elected 1992; born June 8, 1953 in Corona; home, Corona; A.A. Chaffey College, B.A. San Diego State University; wife Robin; Protestant.

CAREER: restaurant manager, 1975-79; commercial and industrial Realtor and president of his own firm since 1981.

COMMITTEES: Natural Resources; Science, Space & Technology.

OFFICES: Suite 1523, Longworth Building, Washington, D.C. 20515, (202) 225-1986; district, Suite 200, 3400 Central Ave., Riverside 92506, (909) 784-4300.

REGISTRATION: 42.4% D, 45.7% R

1992 CAMPAIGN:			
Calvert – R		46.7%	$407,821
Mark Takano – D		46.4%	$240,905

RATINGS: Newly elected.

Gary Condit (D)
18th Congressional District

The 18th District includes the richest agricultural region in the San Joaquin Valley and is growing both more Hispanic and more politically diverse as Bay Area workers filter into the valley in search of less expensive housing. Nearly a quarter of the residents now have Spanish surnames.

The district begins at Ripon, in southern San Joaquin County, and takes in all of Stanislaus and Merced counties. It twists around the population centers of Madera

County before ending abruptly on the stark, north-western reaches of Fresno County. Fast-growing Modesto is the population center. The district has been safe turf for conservative Democrats since the 1950s. Newcomers may bring changes, but probably not dramatic ones.

Gary Condit

From this fertile ground came Rep. Tony Coelho, who in just eight years went from freshman to majority whip, the No. 3 Democratic position in the House. But then came revelations about a questionable junk-bond purchase and personal loan. Rather than face a gauntlet such as those that have felled others in high position, Coelho resigned in midterm.

Gary Condit, then an assemblyman from Ceres, easily won the post in a 1989 special election. But it hasn't been easy filling Coelho's shoes. Condit, who has the most conservative voting record of any California Democrat in Congress, never learned to play by the rules. It is not unusual to find him siding with Republicans on a crime, civil rights or budget matters. He has also been an inattentive member of the House Agriculture Committee.

Condit showed a similar disposition during his seven years in the Assembly. Crime and drug bills occupied most of his time, and he was one of the dissident "Gang of Five" who made life unpleasant for Assembly Speaker Willie Brown. In the Congress, he is part of the "Gang of Six," which has similar interests in internal reform and sides with Republicans on efforts to pass a balanced budget amendment.

Such behavior earned him a sharp knuckle-rap from the House leadership in 1991, when he sought a seat on the House Energy and Commerce Committee. House leaders saw no reason to oblige him. In 1992, he shook out his office and staffed it with some seasoned pros. But his voting record was of little help to those who could advance his career. Condit has been relegated to backbencher status, and he is apt to be there for a long time. His district is so safe that he didn't even draw a Republican opponent in 1992.

PERSONAL: special election 1989; born April 21, 1948 in Salina, Okla.; home, Ceres; education, A.A. Modesto College 1970, B.A. Stanislaus State College 1972; wife Carolyn, two children; Baptist.

CAREER: production worker, Riverbank Ammunition Depot, 1972-76; community relations, National Medical Enterprises, 1976-82; Ceres City Council, 1972-74, mayor 1974-76; Stanislaus County Board of Supervisors, 1976-82; Assembly 1982-89.

COMMITTEES: Agriculture; Government Operations.

OFFICES: Suite 1123, Longworth Building, Washington, D.C. 20515, (202) 225-6131, FAX (202) 225-0819; district, 415 West Main St., Merced 95340, (209) 383-4455, 920 13th St., Modesto 95354, (209) 527-1914.

REGISTRATION: 53% D, 36% R 1989

1992 CAMPAIGN:	Condit – D		84.6%	$269,036
1990 CAMPAIGN:	Condit – D		66%	$234,432
	Cliff Burris - R		34%	$23,939

RATINGS:	ADA	ACU	AFL/CIO	LCV	NCSC	NTU	USCC
	55	40	3	38	61	68	40

Number of checks bounced at the House bank: 4.

Christopher Cox (R)
47th Congressional District

Christopher Cox

Beginning at the Anaheim Hills, this Orange County district waddles west through Tustin and east to the San Bernardino County line. It then swings southwesterly through Irvine, the vast undeveloped holdings of the Irvine Co., and Laguna Hills, where mountain lions still roam. The 47th ends with a window on the Pacific Ocean between Newport Beach and Laguna Beach.

From top to bottom, the district is wealthy Republican country and conservative as only Orange County can be. In the 1970s and '80s, the area became almost a second downtown Los Angeles as companies established regional offices and research parks amid acres of parking lots. The University of California, Irvine, was a magnet for some of the growth along with the development rules written to Irvine Co. specifications.

The district's lackluster congressman, Robert Badham, hung it up in 1988. The race to replace him was decided in the GOP primary (general elections are perfunctory exercises here) as 14 conservatives vied for attention and votes. The one who emerged by garnering 31 percent of the vote was one of the most interesting, attorney Chris Cox.

Cox, making his first try for public office, had a solid background. He was a Harvard lecturer with strong links to the corporate world, and he also had been a White House counsel. That impressed district residents, but probably not as much as personal campaign appearances on Cox's behalf by Oliver North, Robert Bork and Arthur Laffer. The GOP delegation saw to it that Cox got good committee assignments. By his third term, Cox was moving steadily up in the House GOP hierarchy and succeeded in getting the Republican caucus to move in the direction of term limits for committee chairmen.

PERSONAL: elected 1988; born Oct. 16, 1952, in St. Paul, Minn.; home, Newport; education, B.A. University of Southern California 1973, M.B.A., J.D. Harvard University 1977; single; Roman Catholic.

CAREER: attorney, 1978-86; lecturer, Harvard Business School, 1982-83; White House counsel, 1986-88.

COMMITTEES: Budget; Government Operations.

OFFICES: Suite 206, Cannon Building, Washington, D.C. 20515, (202) 225-5611, FAX (202) 225-9177; district, Suite 430, 4000 MacArthur Blvd., Newport Beach 92660, (714) 644-4040.

REGISTRATION: 30.2% D, 56.4% R

1992 CAMPAIGN: Cox – R   64.9% $294,332

              John Anwiler – D   30.2% $1,675

1990 CAMPAIGN: Cox – R   67% $688,836

              Eugene Gratz – D   33% $43,277

RATINGS:

ADA	ACU	AFL/CIO	LCV	NCSC	NTU	USCC
5	95	6	23	13	95	85

Number of checks bounced at the House bank: None.

Randy "Duke" Cunningham (R)
51st Congressional District

Mushrooming growth in San Diego County gave the area a new congressional district in 1992. The lines were drawn in a northern and very Republican portion of the county. On the ocean side, it stretches from Carlsbad to Del Mar. Inland are the cities of San Marcos, Escondido, Poway, Miramar and a portion of the city of San Diego. One small finger juts into the Mission Valley and stops just short of La Mesa. Retirees make up the biggest population bloc and not all are well off. Many live in aging trailer courts and anxiously await the arrival of their next Social Security checks. But many more live in stately homes and gated communities where the chief frustrations are infirmities associated with aging. For those who

Randy Cunningham

work, the Navy and service jobs are primary sources of income.

For a while, it appeared that two GOP incumbents would go head to head here. Neither Reps. Randy "Duke" Cunningham of Chula Vista nor Bill Lowery of San Diego were happy with the new shape of their districts. Gov. Pete Wilson, who has never quit tinkering in San Diego County politics, tried to persuade Cunningham to stay in the 49th District. But Cunningham would have none of it.

Then Lowery, who had been considered one of the brightest lights in the state GOP delegation, began taking stock of himself. He had been severely criticized for being the House's No. 1 recipient of savings and loan contributions. And he had also had 300 overdrafts at the House bank. Lowery prudently decided to retire from politics.

Cunningham's election in 1990 was something of a fluke. Bucking the odds in what was then the county's only Democratic district, Cunningham took on incumbent Jim Bates just after the House Ethics Committee found him guilty of harassing two female members of his staff. Cunningham squeaked by with only 1,659 votes to spare.

Cunningham didn't even register to vote until 1988. But he brought a lot of pluses to the race in this Navy county. He was one of the most highly decorated fighter pilots of the Vietnam War and the first American fighter ace in that conflict. He holds the Navy Cross, two Silver Stars, 10 air medals, the Purple Heart and several other decorations. Some of his experiences were depicted in the movie "Top Gun." After the war, he taught fighter pilots at the Navy Fighter Weapons School at Miramar and retired as a commander. But he still found time to work in community drug programs and civic organizations.

Cunningham entered Congress in a blaze of glory, but it didn't take long for his light to dim. He quickly aligned himself with Rep. "B-1 Bob" Dornan and the cracker right of his party. He spent the 1992 campaign hurling McCarthy-like charges at Bill Clinton and was one of the unholy quartet who persuaded President Bush to hint that Clinton might have once been a pawn of the Soviet KGB. This is a safe seat for Cunningham, but he doesn't seem destined to do much with it.

PERSONAL: elected 1990; born Dec. 8, 1941, in Los Angeles; home, Escondido; education, B.A. University of Missouri 1964, M.Ed. 1965; wife Nancy, three children; Christian.

CAREER: coach, Hinsdale (Ill.) High school, 1965-66; U.S. Navy fighter pilot, 1966-87.

COMMITTEES: Armed Services; Education and Labor; Merchant Marine and Fisheries.

OFFICES: Suite 117, Cannon Building, Washington, D.C. 20515, (202) 225-5452, FAX (202) 225-2558; district, Suite 320, 613 W. Valley Pky., Escondido 92025, (619) 737-8438.

REGISTRATION: 30.3% D, 51.4% R

1992 CAMPAIGN:	Cunningham – R	56%	$797,149
	Bea Herbert – D	33.6%	$22,839
1990 CAMPAIGN:	Cunningham – R	46%	$539,721
	Jim Bates – D	45%	$773,364

RATINGS:	ADA	ACU	AFL/CIO	LCV	NCSC	NTU	USCC
	5	95	17	0	20	81	90

Number of checks bounced at the House bank: 1.

Ron Dellums (D)

9th Congressional District

Who could bounce 851 checks at the House bank — more than any other congressman — call disclosure of that fact "an unwarranted intrusion" in his family finances, and then win re-election with 72 percent of the vote? Only Rep. Ron Dellums, thanks to a district that includes Oakland and the "People's Republic" of Berkeley. It is an area of unabashed liberalism, where nearly two of every three people are people of color. Many don't vote and those who do seem prone to excuse Dellums' excesses and inattention to district concerns.

Ron Dellums

Dellums, perhaps the most liberal member of the California delegation, has a polarizing effect on people. Constituents seem to either love him or loathe him. And in a district as safe as this one, Dellums can get away with ignoring detractors. It is a posture that was effective in the quirky arena of the Berkeley City Council, where Dellums spent four years. But it has served him less than well in Congress.

Dellums' gift for oratory gave him unusual visibility when he first went to Congress, but it led to few constructive advances for him or his district. He wouldn't help boost the flow of federal money to the University of California, which is its lifeblood. The district has a seething crime problem, substandard schools and housing, and a shrinking job base. But such parochial concerns seemed to bore Dellums. When his vote is needed on issues important to his constituency, Dellums frequently can't be found. That is why like-minded colleagues tended to regard Dellums as an unreliable ally.

In the 1980s, Dellums developed a protective attitude over the huge Oakland and Alameda military bases. But that feeling didn't extend to Hunter's Point in San Francisco with its predominantly African American community. He helped kill a proposal to home-port the battleship Missouri there.

Perhaps his greatest legislative victory was his work to push Congress to impose sanctions on South Africa. He also learned to work with senior leaders, and in 1990, he had a key role in killing several questionable missile systems as chairman of the Armed Services research and development subcommittee.

Then came the Clinton-Gore victory in 1992 and the opportunity of a lifetime for Dellums. Clinton picked Wisconsin Rep. Les Aspin, chair of the Armed Services Committee, to be secretary of defense. That cleared the way for Dellums to use his seniority to claim the Armed Forces chair.

The reaction in the already beleaguered military-industrial complex resembled the explosion of a fragmentation bomb. A self-proclaimed radical who had been called "a positive menace to the U.S. security posture" by a conservative Washington think tank, would now be molding the annual Pentagon budget. Dellums, as usual, pulled no punches. The man who called the "Star Wars" program "a gross case of theft" and who praised Fidel Castro, began by urging annual defense cuts of 15 percent. By the year 2000, he wants the Pentagon budget to be half its current size with the savings earmarked for the nation's poorest people.

Aspin was supportive, noting that he had worked with Dellums on the committee for a number of years. Dellums had been privy to numerous military secrets but never caused a security breach, Aspin pointed out. The Aspin-Dellums relationship could be one of the most fascinating of the Clinton-Gore era.

PERSONAL: elected 1970; born Nov. 24, 1935, in Oakland; home, Berkeley; education, A.A. Oakland City College 1958, B.A. San Francisco State College 1960, M.S.W. UC Berkeley 1962; wife Leola, three children; Protestant.

CAREER: U.S. Marine Corps, 1954-56; social worker, poverty program administrator and consultant, 1962-70.

COMMITTEES: Armed Services (chairman); District of Columbia.

OFFICES: Suite 2136, Rayburn Building, Washington, D.C. 20515, (202) 225-2661, FAX (202) 225-9817; district, Suite 105, 201 13th St., Oakland 94617, (415) 763-0370.

REGISTRATION: 69% D, 14% R

1992 CAMPAIGN:	Dellums – D	71.9	$749,376
	William Hunter – R	23.5%	$70,444
1990 CAMPAIGN:	Dellums – D	62%	$790,386
	Barbara Galewsky – R	38%	$0

RATINGS:	ADA	ACU	AFL/CIO	LCV	NCSC	NTU	USCC
	95	7	93	92	99	52	16

Number of checks bounced at the House bank: 851.

Julian Dixon (D)
32nd Congressional District

Through the 1980s, Democrats controlled the House of Representatives, but not its Committee on Standards of Official Conduct, better known as the ethics committee. That was the fiefdom of Rep. Julian Dixon, and Dixon is his own man. Though a party loyalist on most issues, Dixon is aggressively non-partisan when it comes to issues of right and wrong. And that is true whether the subject of the investigation is someone as obscure as Rep. Jim Weaver of Oregon (who speculated in commodities with campaign funds) or as powerful as Speaker Jim Wright of Texas (whose tangled financial deals eventually drove him from office and whose investigation gave Dixon his first taste of national notoriety).

No sooner did the committee finish with the Wright investigation than it began its first investigation of a fellow California Democrat, Rep. Jim Bates, who was found guilty by the committee in October 1989 of sexually harassing staff members. Bates was defeated the following year just as Dixon was giving up the chairmanship. Normally, the ethics chairman rotates every six years, but Dixon established such a strong reputation for fairness that colleagues had prevailed upon him to stay on for most of the decade.

Dixon showed the same temperament when chairing the Democratic convention's platform committee in 1984. Dixon, an African American, also won't allow race to color his judgment. As a member of the District of Columbia Committee, he has demanded accountability by the city's African American leadership. He also showed no hesitation to brand Yassir

Julian Dixon

Arafat a terrorist at a time when the Rev. Jesse Jackson was comparing the PLO's struggle to the battle for racial equity in this country. In all things, Dixon is a conciliator and a fact-finder. Those are qualities he has used effectively to defuse antagonisms between Jewish and African American communities in the Los Angeles area.

Dixon's district, the second-most Democratic in the state, lies on the floor of the Los Angeles basin between downtown and the Los Angeles International Airport. It takes in poverty-stricken areas of northern Watts and Culver City, which is the home of many middle-and upper-middle-class African Americans. There are middle-class white and Hispanic portions, too. Lingering tensions from the 1992 riots and increasing street gang warfare threaten the stability of the area. Such conditions are feeding an exodus by those who can afford to move. The future of this area may be determined in large part by the success or failure of the "Rebuild LA" effort mounted by business and civic groups following the riots. As of this writing, however, the outlook is not bright.

PERSONAL: elected, 1978; born Aug. 8, 1934, in Washington, D.C.; home, Culver City; education, B.S. Los Angeles State College 1962, L.L.B. Southwestern University 1967; wife Betty, one child; Episcopalian.

CAREER: U.S. Army, 1957-60; Attorney, 1967-73; Assembly, 1972-78.

COMMITTEES: Appropriations.

OFFICES: Suite 2400, Rayburn Building, Washington, D.C. 20515, (202) 225-7084, FAX (202) 225-4091; district, Suite 208, 5100 West Goldleaf Circle, Los Angeles 90056, (213) 678-5424.

REGISTRATION: 76.1% D, 13.1% R

1992 CAMPAIGN:	Dixon – D	87.2	$55,932
1990 CAMPAIGN:	Dixon – D	73%	$161,900
	George Adams – R	22%	$6,600

RATINGS:

ADA	ACU	AFL/CIO	LCV	NCSC	NTU	USCC
80	4	97	85	97	8	26

Number of checks bounced at the House bank: None.

Calvin Dooley (D)
20th Congressional District

When reapportionment's map-makers were through, this swing district took on a strong Democratic hue. Yet it is a conservative one, populated by growers, oil workers, small-town shopkeepers and a growing number of state prison guards who work in the mammoth human vaults that have sprung up in the central and southern San Joaquin Valley.

Calvin Dooley

The northern end of the district takes in part of the City of Fresno, which is the regional hub of the valley and also the home a large number of state and federal workers. It swings west to include farming and oil field regions of Fresno, Kings and Kern counties, and then sneaks into Bakersfield from the south.

Visalia farmer Cal Dooley upset a Republican incumbent here in 1990 and immediately established himself as a rising star in the Congress. He represents a new generation of wealthy growers who are well educated, politically involved and astute businessmen. He entered Congress as a team player and has quickly impressed the leadership with his savvy. Soon, he was awarded with plum assignments on both the Agriculture and Natural Resources committees. In 1993, he was granted an unusual waiver to serve on a third major committee, Banking Finance and Urban Affairs.

California agribusiness, which has a dwindling number of well-placed friends in Washington, hasn't overlooked Dooley's potential. When Vice President Dan Quayle came to Fresno for a fund-raiser in 1992, wealthy growers asked that none of the proceeds be spent helping Dooley's opponent.

Dooley is an articulate spokesman for homespun values who also brings a social conscience to the Congress. In Tulare County, he was active in civic, education and senior citizen endeavors.

PERSONAL: elected 1990; born Jan. 11, 1954, in Visalia; home, Tulare County; education, B.S. UC Davis 1977, M.S. Stanford University 1987; wife Linda, two children; Protestant.

CAREER: cotton farmer; aide to state Sen. Rose Ann Vuich, 1987-89.

COMMITTEES: Agriculture; Banking, Finance and Urban Affairs; Natural Resources.

OFFICES: Suite 1227, Longworth Building, Washington, D.C. 20515, (202) 225-3341. FAX (202) 225-9308; district, 224 W. Lacey Blvd., Hanford 93230, (800) 464-4294.

REGISTRATION: 60.7% D, 28.9% R.

1992 CAMPAIGN:	Dooley – D	64.8%	$457,588
	Ed Hunt – R	35.1%	$170,927
1990 CAMPAIGN:	Dooley – D	55%	$547,763
	Charles Pashayan – R	45%	$557,949

RATINGS:	ADA	ACU	AFL/CIO	LCV	NCSC	NTU	USCC
	75	10	75	62	90	34	50

Number of checks bounced at the House bank: None.

John Doolittle (R)
4th Congressional District

This district takes in the central Sierra Nevada with the sparsely populated counties of Alpine and Mono on the east slope and the booming foothill communities of the northern Mother Lode on the west. It sneaks into the conservative northeast corner of Sacramento County and contains all of Placer County — Rep. John Doolittle's home base — which is one of the fastest-growing counties in the state.

Since the late 1960s, refugees from smog-belt counties have been streaming into the foothills in search of cleaner air, less congestion and more traditional lifestyles free of crime and drugs. The irony, however, is that the foothills have become the state's

John Doolittle

second-most productive marijuana-growing region and are distinguished by a unique population of mass murderers, renegade bikers, grave robbers and cult worshipers.

Doolittle, who was only 29 years old when first elected to the state senate in 1980, always seems to have tough races. He presides over a tight-lipped and sometimes paranoid staff of ideological warriors directed by John Feliz, an ex-Los Angeles police detective. Doolittle doesn't flinch at being called a moral zealot. But he is sometimes more zealot than moral. He is a strident opponent of abortion, soft judges, pornography, declining social standards, gun control and free-spending liberals. Yet when it comes to his personal ambitions, Doolittle finds it easy to stoop in low places. Each of his campaigns has been marked by mudslinging and gross distortion of his opponent's record, and both Doolittle and Feliz have been fined for campaign violations.

In 1992, Doolittle was in a rematch with Patricia Malberg of Lincoln, who ran much closer than any Democrat should in this conservative district. Nonetheless, it was Malberg's third try for Congress (the first was against retired Rep. Norman Shumway) and her third loss. Democrats will have to scratch hard to find a credible opponent to challenge Doolittle in 1994.

Doolittle's ability to slay opponents was not overlooked when he was in the state Senate. Republicans made him the No. 2 Republican after a leadership shake-up in 1987. Doolittle surprised his Senate critics by working well with the Democratic leadership on the body's administrative chores. Many of those same critics predicted Doolittle would miss the Senate once he took up residence on the back benches of Congress. Doolittle, though, clearly had other plans. Before he was even sworn in, conservatives in the California GOP caucus succeeded in making Doolittle their lead man on reapportionment.

Doolittle was part of the upstarts called the "Gang of Seven" who pressured Minority Leader Bob Michel, R-Ill., to make full disclosure of players in the House banking and post office scandals. Yet while helping lead the campaign against congressional perks, Doolittle became the House's top abuser of mailing privileges. In the first three months of 1992, he sent 1.4 million pieces of junk mail to households in his newly apportioned district. That worked out to 4.4 pieces of mail per home.

Doolittle also formed an extraordinary alliance with Rep. Maxine Waters, D-Los Angeles, and the two drew up a list of new perks they thought they should have. The three-page memo, dated Feb. 21, 1991, was presented to the House Administration Committee only six weeks after they were sworn in. Among the bennies they sought were cars, meals, moving expenses, additional cellular telephones and use of public phones to make campaign fund-raising calls.

When the United States went to war in the Persian Gulf, Doolittle, who used student and religious deferments to stay out of the Vietnam War, joined the Dornans and Dannemeyers in calling war protesters "malcontents" and "scum."

Nonetheless, Doolittle is still considered a comer by the GOP leadership. Doolittle has been named to the National Republican Congressional Committee, which will give him more say in advancing the stature of conservatives in the House.

PERSONAL: elected 1990; born Oct. 30, 1950, in Glendale; home, Rocklin, education, B.A. UC Santa Cruz 1972, J.D. McGeorge School of Law 1978; wife Julia, two children; Mormon.

CAREER: lawyer; aide to Sen. H.L. Richardson; state Senate, 1980-90.

COMMITTEES: Agriculture, Natural Resources.

OFFICES: Suite 1524, Longworth Building, Washington, D.C. 20510, (202) 225-2511, FAX (202) 225-5444; district, Suite 260, 1624 Santa Clara Dr., Roseville, 95661, (916) 786-5560.

REGISTRATION: 42% D, 45% R

1992 CAMPAIGN:			
	Doolittle – R	49.8%	$601,276
	Patricia Malberg – D	45.7%	$390,232

1990 CAMPAIGN: Doolittle – R   51% $529,813
                  Patricia Malberg – D   49% $222,011
Number of checks bounced at the House bank: None.
RATINGS: ADA   ACU   AFL/CIO LCV   NCSC   NTU   USCC
              5   100   9   0   20   88   78

Robert K. Dornan (R)
46th Congressional District

In Orange County, it seems appropriate that a congressional district would have freeways for boundaries. The 46th is one of the most intensely congested areas of Southern California. Rush-hour gridlocks are routine and residents have come to support the idea of building toll roads to separate the rich from the riffraff. The district begins at the Los Angeles County line and trends to the southeast between the Santa Ana and San Diego freeways. It ends just south of the Newport Freeway.

Robert Dornan

The area, as the name suggests, was once covered with orange groves. After World War II, it became a lily-white, conservative bedroom community. Construction of Disneyland in the 1950s made the area a world destination, but few attitudes changed. In the 1950s and '60s, there were more John Birch Society memberships in Orange County than in all other California counties combined. The '70s saw an influx of Vietnamese, a few more Hispanics and the decline of some neighborhoods, especially in the Garden Grove area. Today, there are more Vietnamese in the 46th than any other district in the nation.

The congressman who carries the torch for many of the lingering Bircher attitudes is Robert "B-1 Bob" Dornan, the flamboyant, sometimes profane former fighter pilot who never saw a defense appropriation he didn't like.

Many people underestimate Dornan. They argue that a man who bases his campaigns on shrillness, hate and character assassination can't go too far. Yet he shows remarkable staying power and fund-raising ability. When Democrats couldn't defeat Dornan in an ocean-front Los Angeles County district, the late Phil Burton gerrymandered the district in 1982 so that Dornan couldn't be re-elected. Undaunted, Dornan instead raised $1 million for an unsuccessful U.S. Senate primary race against Pete Wilson. He then moved south, took on five-term Democrat Jerry Patterson in 1984 and won.

The 46th, nominally a Democratic district after the 1982 gerrymandering, was by 1984 the first congressional district in the nation where Vietnamese immigrants made an obvious difference. Dornan is their hero, the American who would restart the war in Vietnam if he could. In subsequent elections, even well-financed campaigns haven't been able to dislodge him.

Dornan introduces legislation, but little of it goes anywhere. Despite his identity with the long struggle to approve the B-1 bomber, others get most of the credit for getting it off the ground. Dornan is one of the most widely traveled members of Congress. Some of the junkets, to his credit, have helped close MIA and POW cases from the war years. He also brags that he has piloted every aircraft in the American defense arsenal plus some from Israel, England and France. And no one disputes that he had the most creative excuse in Congress for bouncing his one check at the House bank. Dornan explained that he wrote the check to buy a materials for a back yard shrine to the Virgin Mary.

Dornan helped influence national policy in 1985 when he became the first die-hard conservative to endorse George Bush for the presidency. Before then, many conservatives had questioned whether Bush was "Republican enough." Dornan seconded Bush's nomination at the Republican National Convention, chaired Veterans for Bush and was co-chairman of Bush's California campaign. Many thought Dornan would get a prominent post in the administration. But the Bush administration never called.

As President Bush's re-election campaign began showing stress in the fall of 1992, Dornan helped organize a "truth squad" of conservatives who would take to the well of the House of Representatives and denounce the Clinton-Gore ticket to the C-SPAN television audience. Bill Clinton's patriotism and, in particular, his draft dodging became the favorite target. Dornan focused on a trip that Clinton made to Moscow in 1969 during a break from his Rhodes Scholar duties at Oxford University. Clinton, Dornan suggested, was actually there to meet with Soviet intelligence agents to plot anti-war demonstrations. He said he was able to "surmise" this from the fact that Clinton was there and that he opposed involvement in Southeast Asia, despite the lack of any shred of evidence to support his conclusion. Such McCarthy-like accusations led the California Journal magazine to "surmise" that Dornan had fallen on his head.

Then, the incredible happened. As the Bush campaign became more desperate, Dornan, fellow Southern California Reps. Randy "Duke" Cunningham and Duncan Hunter, and Rep. Sam Johnson of Texas, had a meeting with Bush in the Oval Office and convinced him to take up this traitor theme. The following night, Bush went on CNN and said Clinton should "level with the American people" about his draft status and his Moscow visit. Bush was still wearing the mud on Election Day.

In 1992, with Dornan's new district even more Democratic, the incumbent was held to just over 50 percent of the vote. Dornan spent some $1.2 million, much of it in the primary, but his runoff opponent raised only $5,000. With a credible opponent, Dornan shouldn't be able to survive another election cycle. But that has been said before. Dornan knows his enemies and raises campaign funds non-stop between elections. As he said on KNBC the night of the 1992 primary: "Every lesbian spear-chucker in this country is hoping I get defeated."

PERSONAL: elected 1976 and served until 1983, re-elected 1984; born April 3, 1933, in New York City; home, Garden Grove; education, attended Loyola University, Los Angeles; wife Sallie, five children; Roman Catholic.

CAREER: U.S. Air Force, 1953-58; broadcaster and TV talk-show host, 1965-73; president, American Space Frontier PAC, 1983-88.

COMMITTEES: Armed Services; (select) Intelligence; Narcotics Abuse and Control.

OFFICES: Suite 2402, Rayburn Building, Washington, D.C. 20515, (202) 225-2965, FAX (202) 225-3694; district, Suite 360, 300 Plaza Alicante, Garden Grove 92642, (714) 971-9292.

REGISTRATION: 47.5% D, 41.2% R

1992 CAMPAIGN:	Dornan – R	50.2%	$1,427,191
	R.J. Banuelos – D	41%	$5,000
1990 CAMPAIGN:	Dornan – R	58%	$1,615,282
	Barbara Jackson – D	42%	$0

RATINGS:	ADA	ACU	AFL/CIO	LCV	NCSC	NTU	USCC
	5	97	9	8	7	93	86

Number of checks bounced at the House bank: 1.

David Dreier (R)
28th Congressional District

This contorted district lies in east-central Los Angeles County where the bilious smog piles up against the San Gabriel Mountains. The eastern leg of the district includes Arcadia, Sierra Madre and Monrovia. It jogs around similar neighborhoods of Azusa and Irwindale, for unexplained reasons, and then thrusts a second leg southward through Covina, West Covina, San Dimas, Walnut and Industry. These suburbs are predominantly white, middle- and upper-middle-class areas peopled by economic conservatives.

David Dreier

Twenty-eight-year-old Rep. David Dreier went to Congress in 1980 from this area not to make laws, but to undo them. He is a strident foe of government regulation in most of its forms. He has worked for a balanced budget, for the transfer of more federal lands and services to private hands and for deregulation of trucking, airlines, pipelines and banking. Some senior Republican colleagues in the delegation find his ideological commitment tedious, but none can argue that he is inconsistent.

Although not obnoxious about it, Dreier is close to the Dornan and Dannemeyer Republicans who demand ideological litmus tests before anyone is given full acceptance within party ranks. On that score, he is in step with a large faction of his party in California and was instrumental in December 1992 in toppling Rep. Jerry Lewis, a moderate, from key leadership posts. Dreier took Lewis' place on the National Republican Congressional Committee and became a recruiter of GOP candidates for congressional races in Western states.

It is hard to say who the most influential Republican in the California delegation is these days, but Dreier comes as close as anyone. He is an articulate speaker and has had phenomenal success as a fund-raiser. When the 1992 election year ended, he was sitting on a $2 million war chest and made it known that he was actively considering a run against U.S. Sen Dianne Feinstein in 1994. But like most California congressmen, he suffers from little name identity outside his own district.

PERSONAL: elected 1980; born July 5, 1952, in Kansas City; home, La Verne; education, B.A. Claremont McKenna College 1975, M.A. 1976; unmarried; Christian Scientist.

CAREER: public relations, Claremont McKenna College, 1975-79; public relations, Industrial Hydrocarbons Corp., 1979-80.

COMMITTEE: Rules; Reorganization of Congress (Joint).

OFFICES: Suite 411, Cannon Building, Washington, D.C. 20515, (202) 225-2305, FAX (202)-225-4745; district, 112 North Second Ave., Covina 91723, (818) 339-9078.

REGISTRATION: 41.4% D, 46.4% R

1992 CAMPAIGN:	Dreier – R	58.4%	$216,577
	Al Wachtel – D	36.6%	$10,682
1990 CAMPAIGN:	Dreier – R	63%	$591,313
	Georgia Webb – D	32%	$29,612

RATINGS:	ADA	ACU	AFL/CIO	LCV	NCSC	NTU	USCC
	0	95	1	31	5	97	92

Number of checks bounced at the House bank: None.

Don Edwards (D)

16th Congressional District

In the early days of the Vietnam War, one of the few voices of opposition in Congress came from an eloquent member from San Jose. Rep. Don Edwards' brand of militant liberalism has shown no sign of waning during three decades in Congress. Edwards, a onetime Republican and FBI agent, is the same forceful spokesman for civil liberties and social justice that he always has been.

The Fair Housing Act of 1980 is a triumph that he wears like a badge on his lapel. But that is just one of many. He was a prime mover behind the Equal Rights Amendment, the Voter Rights Act, the fight to abolish the House Un-American Activities Committee and others. He has been a stalwart against attacks on forced busing and abortion, as well. Yet Edwards also is a fair man who insists on procedural integrity in all he does. That reputation has helped him exert some

leadership over the fractious California delegation, of
which he is the dean. But it is a job that tries even
Edwards' patience. The California delegation isn't
just a house divided. It is a rabbit warren.

In the early '90s, Edwards achieved a decade-old
dream when the California Institute was organized
with the help of corporate funding. The institute is
intended to get the California delegation in a mode
where its members will at least talk to each other
about major issues confronting the state. By 1992, all
delegation members were signing letters on issues of
concern to California. Edwards hopes that will lead
to broader cooperation on issues such as efforts to
place a new 4,000-job federal accounting center in
San Bernardino.

Don Edwards

Edwards makes effective use of his seniority on the Judiciary and Veterans'
Affairs committees to assist his district. And despite the fact that he is pushing 80,
he enjoys good health and shows no sign of slowing down.

As the district's prune orchards and dairy farms have given way to electronics
plants and housing tracts, Edwards' liberal philosophy as been less in vogue. But he
rarely even draws a Republican opponent and is immensely popular among the
Hispanic people who are a large block in his district. His turf takes in central and east
San Jose, Milpitas and all of rapidly developing areas of southern Santa Clara
County. In the north, it is essentially a working-class district. But the commute
south to Morgan Hill and Gilroy runs through orchard and ranching country that is
rapidly being covered with middle- and upper-class subdivisions.

PERSONAL: elected 1962; born Jan. 6, 1915, in San Jose; home, San Jose;
education, B.A. Stanford University 1936, L.L.B. 1938; wife, Edith; Unitarian.

CAREER: FBI agent, 1940-41; U.S. Navy 1941-45; title company executive,
1945-62.

COMMITTEES: Judiciary; Veterans' Affairs.

OFFICES: Suite 2307 Rayburn Building, Washington, D.C. 20515, (202) 225-
3072, FAX (202) 225-9460; district, Suite 100, 1042 West Hedding St., San Jose
95126, (408) 345-1711.

REGISTRATION: 55.4% D, 29% R

1992 CAMPAIGN:	Edwards – D		62%	$229,212
	Ted Bundesen – R		31.9%	$1,563
1990 CAMPAIGN:	Edwards – D		63%	$224,999
	Mark Patrosso – R		36%	$2,702

RATINGS:	ADA	ACU	AFL/CIO	LCV	NCSC	NTU	USCC
	100	5	94	92	98	18	18

Number of checks bounced at the House bank: 13.

Anna Eshoo (D)
14th Congressional District

This district, which had long been the home of liberal Republican congressmen, includes all of southern and central San Mateo County plus the Palo Alto, Sunnyvale and Cupertino portions of Santa Clara County. It includes Stanford University and some of the world's foremost computer-electronics firms and also the wealthy enclaves of Atherton and Portola Valley. The education level in the 14th is one of the highest for any congressional district in the nation. But it also has been hard-hit by downsizing in the electronics industry.

Anna Eshoo

When Rep. Tom Campbell, R-Palo Alto, decided to vacate the seat for what proved to be an unsuccessful U.S. Senate bid, his successor was supposed to be San Mateo County Supervisor Tom Huening. The liberal Huening was so sure of himself that he even called a "summit" conference for all congressmen-elect to be held in Omaha after the election.   But his seatmate on the board of supervisors, Anna Eshoo, had different ideas.

Eshoo came within 5 percentage points of beating Campbell in 1988, when the seat was open. Reapportionment made it more friendly for Democrats and Eshoo received substantial voter-registration help in 1992 from her state and national party. In that "Year of the Woman," she campaigned with U.S. Senate candidates Barbara Boxer and Dianne Feinstein at every opportunity while promoting her environmental record and years of civic involvement in the district.

On Election Day, it was a rout. Eshoo ran well ahead of the Democratic registration and beat Huening by 19 points. Unless she stumbles badly, that should be enough to scare away even well-heeled challengers in '94.

PERSONAL: elected 1992; born Dec. 13, 1942, in New Britain, Conn.; home, Atherton; A.A. Canada College, 1978; divorced; two children; Roman Catholic.

CAREER: San Mateo Board of Supervisors, 1983-92.

COMMITTEES: Merchant Marine and Fisheries; Science, Space and Technology.

OFFICES: Suite 1505, Longworth Building, Washington, D.C. 20515, (202) 225-8104; district, 698 Emerson St., Palo Alto 94301, (415) 323-2984.

REGISTRATION: 47.7% D, 35.3% R

1992 CAMPAIGN:		
Eshoo – D	56.7%	$870,921
Tom Huening – R	39%	$626,029

RATINGS: Newly elected.

Vic Fazio (D)
3rd Congressional District

Reapportionment handed Vic Fazio, the most powerful Californian in the House, his worst nightmare. His new district lost heavily Democratic areas of Solano and Sacramento Counties. From the sleepy villages of the Sacramento River Delta, the new district marches up the floor of the Sacramento Valley from Rio Vista to Red Bluff taking in the most conservative agricultural areas and excluding the liberal outpost of Chico. Although nominally Democratic, this is not friendly turf for a liberal who engineers congressional pay raises and has the most expensive office in the Congress (other than the speaker's), according to a USA Today survey.

Vic Fazio

Add to the equation a 1992 opponent named H.L. Richardson, a bombastic conservative with the gun-lobby vote sewed up. Mix in a desire by the national GOP to keep Fazio tied down at home since he also happens to be chairman of the Democratic Congressional Campaign Committee. And the result was a mud-wrestle of an election that cost Fazio $1.7 million. Richardson spent nearly $800,000 and might have even prevailed had he less baggage to carry from the 22 years that he spent as a do-nothing belligerent in the state Senate.

"Anyone who held this seat would not feel it was a safe seat for them, I don't care what party they were in," Fazio said after the election. "It is just a marginal seat with a number of different constituencies who don't feel comfortable about each other."

For the foreseeable future, chronic unemployment and a weak farm economy are apt to be important forces in the district. Fazio's performance is likely to be seen in terms of the successes or failures of the Clinton administration, which owes California farmers absolutely nothing. At the same time, there are environmental factions in the district who expect Fazio to use his clout to do something about declining fish runs, loss of wetlands and the paving over of rich agricultural lands.

Yet, if anyone is up to the task of keeping those constituents placated, Fazio may be the man. Fazio is frequently called the most skillful legislator in the 52-member California delegation and a likely candidate for House speaker one day. He is vice chairman of the Democratic Caucus, the No. 5 position in the House's Democratic hierarchy and a frequent stepping stone to greater things. He is the first person in the history of the Congress to hold two leadership posts.

The former assemblyman came to Washington well schooled in the workings of legislative bodies. He caught the notice of party leaders by doing many of the thankless chores that others eschew, such as facilitating congressional pay raises and serving on the ethics committee. In 1989, he was instrumental in keeping Congress' free mailing privileges intact despite efforts by then-Sen. Pete Wilson to divert a chunk of newsletter funds elsewhere. He also quickly became known as a consensus builder.

As Fazio's power has increased, he has used it to solidify relationships with other congressmen. One of the keys to his strength is the chairmanship of the legislative subcommittee of Appropriations. That gives him enormous say on which programs get funded. He has a reputation for being the man to see in the delegation when there is a difficult political or legislative problem. At the same time, he is known for diligently working for his district and being a friend of the two huge Air Force bases located there, even though he publicly supports cutbacks in Pentagon spending.

He serves on another Appropriations subcommittee with jurisdiction over energy and water projects. That is an extremely important post for his new district, but it also has made Fazio a key mediator in one of the longest-running, no-win disputes in California — whether to build the Auburn Dam on the American River.

Although Rep. Don Edwards of San Jose is the dean of the California Democrats, Fazio is their unofficial leader. He has had a close working relationship with moderates in the state GOP caucus. This session, with more conservative leadership in the GOP ranks, his consensus-building skills should get a workout.

PERSONAL: elected 1978; born Oct. 11, 1942, in Winchester, Mass; home, West Sacramento; education, B.A. Union College in Schenectady, N.Y., 1965, attended CSU Sacramento; wife Judy; Episcopalian.

CAREER: congressional and legislative staff, 1966-75; co-founder, California Journal magazine; Assembly, 1975-78.

COMMITTEES: Appropriations; (select) Hunger.

OFFICES: Suite 2113, Rayburn Building, Washington, D.C. 20515, (202) 225-0354, FAX (202) 225-5716; district, 722B Main St., Woodland 95695, (916) 666-5521.

REGISTRATION: 49% D, 38% R

1992 CAMPAIGN:	Fazio – D	51.2%	$1,699,004
	H.L. Richardson – R	40.3%	$802,648
1990 CAMPAIGN:	Fazio – D	55%	$845,622
	Mark Baughman – R	39%	$40,439

RATINGS:	ADA	ACU	AFL/CIO	LCV	NCSC	NTU	USCC
	90	6	89	69	90	0	30

Number of checks bounced at the House bank: None.

Robert Filner (D)
50th Congressional District

This new district begins just south of the Mission Valley and takes in most urban areas of the city of San Diego except for the affluent coastal strip. It also runs south through National City, Chula Vista and San Ysidro to the Mexican border. Ethnically, it is one of the most diverse districts in California: 41 percent Hispanic, 29 percent white, 15 percent Asian and 15 percent African American. There are solidly middle-class neighborhoods, but many others that are on the decline. As a rule of thumb, the closer one gets to the border, the higher the unemployment, welfare rates and crime rates.

Robert Filner

The economy is firmly tied to the Navy's immense presence in San Diego, which is a cause for jitters. Border issues involving immigration, health, education, crime and pollution are intense. San Diego is a city in need of its own foreign policy.

A Libertarian in the congressional race pulled 11 percent of the vote in 1992, but it was never a contest for Rep. Robert Filner, who ran comfortably ahead of the Democratic registration. Filner is another of the freshmen congressmen who seems overqualified for the job. As a college student in 1961, Filner joined the freedom rides in the South. He spent several months in jail for integrating a lunch counter in Mississippi.

Later, as a history professor who also has a chemistry degree, Filner got into politics when the San Diego School Board threatened to close his children's school. Soon, he was on the school board and shaking things up with major reforms. He was elected to the City Council after a second try, has been on many boards and commissions and worked for three different members of congress, at one time or another, including the late Sen. Hubert Humphrey.

Filner got good committee assignments for his district, but as time goes by he'll probably be angling for posts on either Armed Services or Education and Labor. Border issues are expected to occupy much of his time and even there he has a track record, having once established a community development corporation to help bring jobs to the barrio near the border.

PERSONAL: elected 1992, born Sept. 4, 1942, in Pittsburgh, Pa.; home, San Diego; B.A. Cornell University 1963, M.A. University of Delaware 1968, Ph.D. Cornell 1972; wife Jane, two children; Jewish.

CAREER: history professor, San Diego State University, 1970-92; assistant to Sen. Hubert Humphrey, D-Minn., 1975; assistant to U.S. Rep. Don Fraser, 1976; assistant to U.S. Rep. Jim Bates, 1984; San Diego School Board, 1979-83; San Diego City Council, 1987-92.

COMMITTEES: Public Works and Transportation; Veterans' Affairs.

OFFICES: Suite 504, Cannon Building, Washington, D.C. 20515, (202) 225-8045; district, 430 Davidson St., Chula Vista 91910, (619) 422-5963.

REGISTRATION: 50.3 D, 34.5 R

1992 CAMPAIGN:	Filner – D	56.6%	$828,230
	Tony Valencia – R	28.9%	$45,306

RATINGS: Newly elected.

Elton Gallegly (R)

23rd Congressional District

Since the late 1960s, white families have been fleeing increasingly seedy sections of the San Fernando Valley. New communities have sprouted up beyond the valley's western hills. Towns such as Simi Valley, which were barely more than crossroads 20 years ago, are now flourishing communities in the 23rd District.

Elton Gallegly

The district takes in all of Ventura County except for some bedroom communities near the Los Angeles County line in the Thousand Oaks area. The Ventura Freeway, which bisects the county, is feeding a boom all along its length. Farms are being gobbled up by speculators who have been trading water rights and building sterile-looking subdivisions. Coastal sections of the county are still favored by retirees, many of whom put in time at the big Naval stations at Oxnard and Pt. Mugu. At Ventura County's southwestern edge, the district jogs into Santa Barbara County just far enough to include the sleepy village of Carpinteria.

One of the newcomers to Ventura County in the '60s was an ambitious young man with a real estate license named Elton Gallegly. In time, the boom made him wealthy, he became mayor of Simi Valley and was elected to Congress.

Reapportionment dumped both Gallegly and Rep. Robert Lagomarsino in the same district. Lagomarsino, who appeared to be the safest of the two Republicans, was cajoled into moving northward, where he was subsequently defeated in the GOP primary by Michael Huffington. With a slight edge in the 23rd's registration, Democrats spent freely on Anita Perez Ferguson's attempt to knock Gallegly off. But Gallegly won handily in a campaign with some nasty racial overtones.

Gallegly seems to fit the district well. He is a family man who is devoted to hard work and traditional values. He was elected to chair his freshman Republican caucus and is identified with anti-drug legislation. In his second term, he won a seat on the coveted Foreign Affairs Committee. Yet he probably is best known for proposing a constitutional amendment that would deny citizenship to children of mothers who are not citizens or legal residents. With immigration issues moving to front-burner status, Gallegly is positioned to frame the conservative stance. And not incidentally, it will help him with some of his Anglo constituencies.

PERSONAL: elected 1986; born March 7, 1944, in Huntington Park, Calif.; home, Simi Valley; education, attended Los Angeles State College; wife Janice, four children; Protestant.

CAREER: real estate firm owner, 1968-86; Simi Valley City Council, 1979-80, mayor 1980-86.

COMMITTEES: Foreign Affairs; Judiciary; Natural Resources.
OFFICES: Suite 2441, Rayburn Building, Washington, D.C. 20515, (202) 225-5811; district, Suite 1800, 300 Esplanade Dr., Oxnard 93030, (805) 485-2300.
REGISTRATION: 43.4% D, 41.7% R

1992 CAMPAIGN:	Gallegly – R	54.2%	$824,251
	Anita Ferguson – D	42.4%	$501,760
1990 CAMPAIGN:	Gallegly – R	58%	$599,454
	Richard Freiman – D	35%	$13,706

RATINGS:	ADA	ACU	AFL/CIO	LCV	NCSC	NTU	USCC
	15	91	11	0	10	85	95

Number of checks bounced at the House bank: 5.

Dan Hamburg (D)
1st Congressional District

California's First Congressional District sweeps down the north coast from the Oregon border and dog-legs into the heart of the wine country northeast of San Francisco Bay. It takes in five complete counties - Del Norte, Humboldt, Mendocino, Lake and Napa plus northeast Sonoma County (excluding Santa Rosa) and the population centers of Solano County.

To the north, it is an area dependent on tourism, lumber, fishing and small farms. That gives way to the lush vineyards, mammoth poultry farms and inflated real estate values of Mendocino, Sonoma and Napa counties. At the southern end, the prison towns of

Dan Hamburg

Vacaville and Fairfield, home of Travis Air Force Base, are rapidly becoming bedroom areas for the Bay Area. The Navy shipyard town of Vallejo also is going through something of a renaissance.

Most of the small towns of the north coast are chronically depressed. Lumbermen are constantly at war with fishermen, although almost no one likes offshore oil development. There is a thriving counterculture that is usually held in check politically by conservative, small-town merchants and a growing number of conservative families who have escaped from the Bay Area into the southern reaches of the district. During the 1970s, the district evolved from Republican-voting to Democratic. State officials say marijuana is the area's largest cash crop — a situation that couldn't exist without some tolerance by the establishment.

One of the surprises of the 1990 election came when upstart Republican Frank Riggs beat Rep. Douglas Bosco. A conservative Democrat, four-termer Bosco had managed to anger most traditional Democratic constituencies with a series of anti-environmental votes, lucrative land speculation deals and a closeness with savings and loan officials. Democrats helped defeat him when 15 percent of the vote went for the spoiler in the race, Peace and Freedom candidate Darlene Comingore.

Riggs squeaked by Bosco with 1,500 votes in the heavily Democratic district and was immediately marked for extinction in 1992. Riggs made practically every mistake an incumbent could make, breaking campaign promises not to take a pay raise and fuming about bounced checks from the House bank before discovering that he, too, was a bouncer. Yet he almost survived in a race against Dan Hamburg of Ukiah.

Hamburg, who had been working as a typesetter, was laid off early in the campaign and got by on unemployment checks for a time. Yet he raised a substantial war chest, mostly through staging concerts throughout the district. Three of them featured Bonnie Raitt, who has a home in Mendocino and has an interest in environmental issues.

Hamburg served one term on the Mendocino County Board of Supervisors in the early '80s. Otherwise, he has had a varied career as a teacher and administrator in alternative schools - including one in China - and director of a '60s-style poverty and community service center in Mendocino and Lake Counties.

Hamburg and his wife, a pianist, put all their personal assets at risk for the campaign. They put forth a strong, grass-roots effort that stressed job creation, education and improving federal services. With polls showing Hamburg trailing two weeks before the election, he fired his campaign consultants and stepped up personal attacks on Riggs. Hamburg pulled it off, but got less than 50 percent of the vote and ran behind the Democratic registration in the district.

PERSONAL: elected, 1992; born Oct. 6, 1948, in St. Louis, Mo.; home, Ukiah; education, B.A. Stanford University 1966, M.A. California Institute for Integral Studies 1992; wife Carrie, four children; Jewish.

CAREER: teacher, school administrator, typesetter; Mendocino County Supervisor, 1980-84; manager, North Coast Opportunities Inc., 1986-89.

COMMITTEES: Public Works; Merchant Marine and Fisheries.

OFFICES: Suite 114, Cannon Building, Washington, D.C. 20515; (202) 225-3311; district, 910A Waugh Ln., Ukiah 95482; (800) 303-2515.

REGISTRATION: 52% D, 33% R

1992 CAMPAIGN:	Hamburg – D	47.6%	$576,271
	Frank Riggs – R	45%	$629,525

RATINGS: Newly elected.

Jane Harman (D)
36th Congressional District

From Venice to San Pedro, this new district is a mixture of funky, upscale and industrial communities on the central coast of Los Angeles and the Palos Verdes Peninsula. In Venice, there are people who make their living wearing sandwich boards while rollerblading on the beach boardwalk. Wealthy industrialists live in areas such as Manhattan Beach and Palos Verdes. El Segundo and Torrance are industrial and refinery towns. If there is any binding element, it is a protective attitude toward the coast and the natural air-conditioning it provides all summer long. Even in the refinery towns, where there are a fair number of Sierra Clubers, there is a loathing of offshore oil drilling.

With party registration almost dead even, Republicans should have taken this seat in the 1992 elections with any one of several well-financed candidates such as former "first daughter" Maureen Reagan or Bill Beverly, son of a popular state senator. But the

Jane Harman

candidate who emerged from the 11-person field was Los Angeles City Councilwoman Joan Milke Flores, perhaps the most conservative of the lot.

Entering the fray from the Democratic side was a cerebral and well-connected lawyer, Jane Harman, who had been a deputy Cabinet secretary in Jimmy Carter's White House. Harman is an economic conservative, but as liberal as Flores is conservative on social issues. Harman made women's issues the cornerstone of her campaign while promising aid for the aerospace industries that are an important element in the district. She raised huge sums of money, mounted a voter-registration drive that improved Democratic numbers by 2 percentage points, and may have even helped Democrats farther down the ticket with an aggressive, well-coordinated campaign.

Harman, who has worked as a Defense Department counsel, accomplished the unheard of as a freshman and won a seat on the Armed Services Committee. Barbara Boxer, the ceiling-breaker on that committee, couldn't get a seat there until her third term. Harman promises to be no less a shrinking violet than Boxer when it comes to demanding accountability from the Pentagon brass.

PERSONAL: elected 1992; born June 28, 1945, in New York City; home, Marina Del Rey; B.A. Smith College (Phi Beta Kappa) 1966, J.D. Harvard 1969; husband Sidney, four children; no religious preference.

CAREER: attorney; chief counsel to U.S. Sen. John Tunney, 1972-73; adjunct professor, Georgetown University, 1974-75; chief counsel U.S. Senate Judiciary subcommittee on constitutional rights, 1975-77; deputy White House Cabinet secretary, 1977-78; Defense Department counsel, 1979; general counsel, Harman Industries, 1980-92.

COMMITTEES: Armed Services; Science, Space and Technology.

OFFICES: Suite 325, Cannon Building, Washington, D.C. 20515; (202) 225-8220; district, Suite 940, 5200 W. Century Blvd.; Los Angeles 90045, (310) 640-3366.

REGISTRATION: 42.4% D, 42.7% R

1992 CAMPAIGN: Harman – D   48.4% $1,528,526

                    Joan Milke Flores – R   42.4% $798,593

RATINGS: Newly elected.

Wally Herger (R)

2nd Congressional District

Wally Herger

The Trinity Alps, the southern Cascade Range, the Northern Sierra Nevada and chunks of the Sacramento Valley floor make up this conservative district in the northeast portion of the state. Its 10 counties are arrayed in something of a horseshoe with Trinity (the only California county carried by Ross Perot in 1992) on one end and Yuba and Nevada Counties on the other. Some of the most remote parts of California are within its boundaries, where there are clear vistas to the giant volcanoes, Mounts Lassen and Shasta.

Tourism, timber and farming are the mainstays of an economy that is healthy on the valley floor and often on the slide in wooded sections. Water is plentiful and residents expect their representatives to keep their liquid gold from being siphoned off to other parts of the state. Mountains and remote villages make it an expensive area in which to campaign, a fact that favors incumbents.

Rep. Wally Herger's home in the agricultural heartland of the valley was shaved off the district when reapportionment drew the boundary line just north of his home in Rio Oso in Sutter County. Herger moved to Marysville and won again handily despite the nominal Democratic majority in the new district.

Even with a safe seat, Herger shows no inclination toward activism. During three terms in the Assembly, he was a conservative backbencher who consistently voted "no" on most measures. In Congress, he has shown the same posture. He initiates a few farm bills but little else.

Environmentalists are becoming more vocal about the management of the 10 national forests in the district, but Herger pays them no mind. He ignores vocal critics among owners of small logging companies, who claim he favors the timber giants at their expense. And fishermen are angry that he has done little to change the operations of federal facilities that have been killing salmon runs on the upper Sacramento River. But Herger's inaction sits well with many constituents, who prize self-reliance and less government. In 1993, Herger won seats on both the Ways and Means and Budget Committees. That annoyed growers in his district, who wanted him to stay on the Agriculture Committee. Nonetheless, Herger has more important assignments if he chooses to make use of them.

PERSONAL: elected 1986; born May 20, 1945, in Yuba City; home, Marysville;, A.A. American River College 1968, attended CSU Sacramento; wife Pamela, eight children; Mormon.

CAREER: rancher and operator of family petroleum gas company, 1969-80; Assembly, 1980-86.

COMMITTEES: Budget; Ways and Means.

OFFICES: Suite 2433, Rayburn Building, Washington, D.C. 20515, (202) 225-3076, FAX (202) 225-1609; district, Suite 104, 55 Independence Cir., Chico 95926, (916) 893-8363; Suite 410, 2400 Washington Ave., Redding 96001, (916) 246-5172.

REGISTRATION: 44% D, 42% R

1992 CAMPAIGN:

Herger – R		65.1%	$476,059
Elliot Freedman - D		27.9%	$4,948

1990 CAMPAIGN:

Herger – R		63%	$616,075
Erwin Rush – D		31%	$6,118

RATINGS:

ADA	ACU	AFL/CIO	LCV	NCSC	NTU	USCC
5	98	18	6	8	94	92

Number of checks bounced at the House bank: None.

Steve Horn (R)
38th Congressional District

From Long Beach, this district runs northward through the refinery and aerospace towns of Signal Hill, Lakewood, Bellflower, Paramount and Downey. Some of California's most severe job losses have occurred here, and more are scheduled in 1996, when the Long Beach Naval Station is to close. Even if California's economy recovers during 1992-93, it is unlikely that conditions will be markedly improved here for much of the decade.

Rep. Glenn Anderson represented much of this district for 24 years. When Anderson decided to retire in 1992, there was an attempt to hand the seat to his stepson, Evan Anderson Braude, a liberal Long Beach city councilman. Given the Democratic edge, that

Steve Horn

should have happened. But Steve Horn had other plans and defied the Democratic sweep that year to become the only Republican candidate to take what should have been a safe congressional district for Democrats.

Horn is one of the few people ever elected to Congress who could argue that he is overqualified for the job. A professor and former college president with federal government experience dating back to the Eisenhower administration, Horn ran as a scholar with a 7,000-volume home library on the Congress. Two of the titles were written by him and a third was co-authored. They cover congressional ethics, budgeting and organization.

Horn had been a Washington insider, a Congressional insider and had been a member of a host of high-level boards and commissions. But he ran as an outsider against "career politician" Braude. He refused to take PAC money, but still raised more money than his opponent. It didn't hurt that he had spent 18 years as president of California State University, Long Beach, while holding high-profile positions in civic and commerce organizations.

Braude tried to make much of the fact that Horn was bounced out of his job as Long Beach State president by a faction that accused him of arrogance in dealing with people and poor financial management. But voters seemed more inclined to believe that he was a victim of an old guard faculty faction that feared his reforms. Horn ran 11 points ahead of the GOP registration.

Horn, an outspoken and forceful progressive, joins a state delegation where archconservatives are firmly in control. It is going to be interesting to watch the interaction.

PERSONAL: elected 1992; born May 31, 1931, in San Juan Bautista, Calif.; home, Long Beach; A.B., Ph.D. Stanford; M.P.A. Harvard; wife Nini, two children; Protestant.

CAREER: Army Reserve, 1954-62; aide to U.S. Dept. of Labor secretary, 1958-60; legislative aide, U.S. Sen. Thomas Kuchel, 1960-66; Brookings Institution fellow, 1966-69; dean of graduate studies and research, American University, 1969-70; president, CSU Long Beach, 1970-88, trustee professor political science, CSU Long Beach, 1988-92.

COMMITTEES: Government Operations; Public Works and Transportation.

OFFICES: Suite 1023, Longworth Building, Washington, D.C. 20515, 202-225-6676; district, Suite 160, 4010 Watson Plaza Dr., Lakewood 90712, (310) 425-1336.

REGISTRATION: 49.7% D, 37.9% R

1992 CAMPAIGN: Horn – R   48.6% $428,538

Evan Anderson Braude – D 43.4% $505,865

RATINGS: Newly elected.

Michael Huffington (R)

22nd Congressional District

Money may not buy happiness, but it can buy a seat in Congress. Michael Huffington proved that in 1992 by spending $5.4 million - mostly his own money - in what turned out to be the most expensive House race the nation has ever seen. Until then, the record was $2.6 million spent in 1986 by then-Rep. Jack Kemp in a New York District.

Just how rich is Huffington? Rich enough, he will tell you: "Over a certain amount, it becomes meaningless. I'm in that category. I have no financial needs that cannot be met."

Huffington, who moved to California from Texas in 1991, is chairman of Crest Films, a full-service company known for documentary and adventure films. But his fortune rests on a merchant bank Huffington founded in the 1970s plus his father's Houston oil and gas business (Roy M. Huffington Inc.) which was sold to Taiwan interests in 1990. At the end of the Reagan administration, Huffington was named deputy assistant secretary of defense for negotiations policy with responsibility for arms-control talks.

Michael Huffington

Add to that long-standing status as a major donor to Republican causes, and Huffington's candidacy normally would have had a tumultuous welcome from the GOP. Trouble was, the seat already had been claimed by an 18-year incumbent, Rep. Robert Lagomarsino. Reapportionment had dumped both Lagomarsino and Rep. Elton Gallegly into the same district. With Gallegly considered the more vulnerable of the two Republicans, Lagomarsino heeded the advice of Gov. Pete Wilson and others and gave up his base in Ventura County. The new 22nd District included Santa Barbara County, which Lagomarsino already represented, plus San Luis Obispo County, which was new.

Santa Barbara has long been considered one of the jewels of the coastal counties and an ideal retirement locale. Yet there are plenty of working folks, too, and a number of them lost their jobs when the Reagan administration mothballed much of Vandenberg Air Force Base. Tourism, a pillar of the economy in the district, also has suffered in the recession.

A number of people, from Vice President Dan Quayle on down, tried to talk Huffington out of the race. But he wouldn't be swayed. He vanquished Lagomarsino in the primary (the only California race where an incumbent was defeated) after spending $3.5 million, and then put up another $1.9 million to defeat Santa Barbara Supervisor Gloria Ochoa in the runoff.

With that behind him, one wonders if Huffington has his eye on another trophy. He is well positioned to be Ross Perot's next running mate.

PERSONAL: Elected 1992; born Sept. 4, 1947, in Dallas, Tex.; home, Santa Barbara; B.S. and B.A Stanford; M.B.A Harvard; wife Arianna, two children; Episcopalian.

CAREER: banker, venture capitalist, 1974-present; deputy assistant secretary of defense, 1986-88; film studio owner, 1990-present.

COMMITTEES: Banking, Finance & Urban Affairs; Small Business.

OFFICES: Suite 113, Cannon Building, Washington, D.C. 20515, (202) 225-3601; district, Suite D, 1819 State St., Santa Barbara 93101, (805) 682-6600; Suite A, 1016 Palm St., San Luis Obispo 93401, (805) 542-0426.

REGISTRATION: 41% D, 41.9% R

1992 CAMPAIGN:
Huffington – R	52.5%	$5,387,379
Gloria Ochoa – D	34.9%	$652,172

RATINGS: Newly elected.

Duncan Hunter (R)
52nd Congressional District

The 45th District stretches across most of the bottom of California in an area that has seen momentous change in recent decades and is apt to see much more. On the western end, it begins at La Mesa, Santee and El Cajon. The district skirts most of the rest of San Diego's suburbs, crosses the rock piles of eastern San Diego County and includes all of Imperial County.

Duncan Hunter

The San Diego suburbs are comfortably Republican. Imperial County is becoming solidly Hispanic, but the white grower class still controls the political scene. Immigration pressures, however, are eroding the white dominance everywhere. Imperial County also has far and away the highest unemployment rate in California — more than 30 percent during much of 1992. A wide range of border issues fester in this district: immigration, pollution, drug trafficking and educational and social services for new arrivals. It is going to be difficult for a mere mortal congressman to juggle the issues here in future years with the disparity between haves and have-nots, the racial conflicts and the inconsistent national policies on border issues.

Rep. Duncan Hunter upset a nine-term incumbent in 1980 and went to Congress as a new breed of Republican — an economic conservative but one with compassion and commitment to help those willing to help themselves. He was a combat officer in Vietnam, went to night law school and began his practice in an old barber shop in San Diego's barrio. Hunter annoyed some congressional colleagues by stepping over them to get what he wanted. But his talents were recognized by party leaders. He was given the chair of the Republican Research Committee, charged with developing GOP strategies for emerging issues. Hunter has used the committee to focus on minority recruitment for the party. He also led the charge to put the military into the forefront of drug interdiction efforts.

By 1992, however, things were starting to unravel for Hunter. He had to sell his Coronado home and move a few miles into his reconstituted district. Then came the revelation that he was one of the House check bouncers and Hunter was caught lying about his level of involvement. His numbers kept jumping upward until the total reached 399 - third highest in the California delegation and one of the worst in Congress. Then the conservative National Taxpayers Union revealed that Hunter had spent $1.5 million of the taxpayers' money to send newsletters to constituents. That made him the third worst junk mailer in the House.

About that time, Hunter joined Rep. "B-1 Bob" Dornan and became one of the shrillest Bill Clinton baiters in the House. He will always be remembered as one of those who persuaded President George Bush to suggest that Clinton might have been working with the Soviet KGB on Vietnam War protests. And then he drew an opponent named Janet Gastil, who came at him with a frenzied campaign. In the end, however, Gastil couldn't overcome the registration edge in the district nor could she match Hunter's fund-raising ability. Nonetheless, Hunter will be wearing those scars into 1994.

PERSONAL: elected 1980; born May 31, 1948, in Riverside, Calif.; home, El Cajon; B.S.L. Western State University 1976, J.D. 1976; wife Lynne, two children; Baptist.

CAREER: U.S. Army, 1969-71; attorney, 1976-80.

COMMITTEES: Armed Services; (select) Hunger.

OFFICES: Suite 133, Cannon Building, Washington, D.C. 20515, (202) 225-5672, FAX 202-225-0235; district, 366 South Pierce St., El Cajon 92020, (619) 579-3001; Suite G, 1101 Airport Road, Imperial 92251, (619) 353-5420.

REGISTRATION: 38.6% D, 45.6% R

1992 CAMPAIGN:	Hunter – R	52.8%	$519,631
	Janet Gastil – D	41.2%	$143,752
1990 CAMPAIGN:	Hunter – R	73%	$368,560
	Joe Shea – D	27%	$0

RATINGS:	ADA	ACU	AFL/CIO	LCV	NCSC	NTU	USCC
	15	93	21	6	11	92	85

Number of checks bounced at the House bank: 399.

Jay Kim (R)
41st Congressional District

The smog capital of California is found in the eastern Los Angeles Basin, where Los Angeles, Orange, Riverside and San Bernardino Counties come together. From the south, the 41st district begins in outer neighborhoods of Anaheim. It jogs to the east as far as the city of Industry, to the west to Ontario and sends a finger northward through Upland. The Whittier Hills separate Yorba Linda from Pomona, Chino, Montclair and Ontario, which tend to run together in one undistinguished blob.

Much of this area was once orange groves and dairy farms. Long ago, most of them gave way to commercial strips and boxy subdivisions. Many of the residents were forced into the district by the high price of housing in Los Angeles and Orange

Counties. Many who can afford it are leaving to escape the smog and congestion, but the recession has slowed the exodus.

With the sour economy in the minds of many, Reagan Democrats in the area returned to their party in 1992. Democratic candidates did very well here for the first time in years. But not well enough to keep Jay Kim from becoming the first Korean-American ever elected to Congress. Kim's toughest race was in the Republican primary, where he beat former Assemblyman Chuck Bader and former White House aide Jim Lacy. The runoff proved to be a cake walk against a defense analyst named Bob Baker. Kim raised more than $700,000 for his campaign. He

Jay Kim

made a personal loan of $150,000, but much of the rest came from individual contributors.

Kim, the mayor of Diamond Bar, came to the United States in 1961 and later founded Jaykim Engineering, a planning and construction firm that has built everything from sewers to prisons. Once elected, he put the company up for sale, saying civil engineering firms have many government customers and he wanted to avoid anything that looked like a conflict of interest.

Kim is a pro-abortion, social moderate and economic conservative. His experience in business and tax matters should serve him well in Congress.

PERSONAL: elected 1992; born March 27, 1939, in Seoul, Korea; home, Diamond Bar; B.S., M.S. University of Southern California, M.A. CSU, Los Angeles; wife June, three children; Methodist.

CAREER. South Korean Army, 1959-61; civil engineer and company president, 1976-92; Diamond Bar councilman 1990-91 and mayor 1991-92.

COMMITTEES: Public Works & Transportation; Small Business.

OFFICES: Suite 502, Cannon Building, Washington, D.C. 20515, (202) 225-3201; district, Suite 160A, 1131 W. 6th St., Ontario 91762, (714) 988-1055.

REGISTRATION: 39.6% D, 48.7% R

1992 CAMPAIGN:			
Kim – R		59.6%	$690,539
Bob Baker – D		34.4%	$1,200

RATINGS: Newly elected.

Tom Lantos (D)
12th Congressional District

Reapportionment shifted this district northward into the southwest corner of San Francisco, where there is a rapidly growing Asian population. From the city limits, it extends claw-like into northern San Mateo County. On the ocean side, the district runs as far south as Half Moon Bay. On the San Francisco Bay side, it goes to

Redwood City. At the northern end are the boxy, working-class homes of Daly City and San Bruno plus Colma, the graveyard for more than a million San Franciscans. South of the airport, the suburbs become ritzier and more wooded. But congestion is every-where — on the freeways, the streets and even the bicycle paths.

Tom Lantos

Residents tend to be pro-environment, well-edu-cated and not particularly burdened by a social con-science. But the district's lack in social conscience didn't rub off on Rep. Tom Lantos, who, as a youth, fought the Nazis in the Hungarian underground. Lantos works tirelessly for social and economic re-form, and for betterment of the oppressed peoples of the world. Unlike most congressmen, he'll wade into a state issue such as the fight to restore the Cal-OSHA worker safety program.

In 1989-90, Lantos was Congress' point man on the Housing and Urban Development agency scandals. His intense questioning of HUD officials kept the pot stirring for months and gave him enviable visibility on nightly news programs. He has shown the same zeal in going after the fast-food industry for child labor law violations. Yet he has demonstrated considerable independence in Congress, often tending to vote his conscience rather than the party line. Lantos' devotion to the cause of Israeli security may have allowed him to be blind-sided as Congress was debating whether to enter the Persian Gulf War. As co-chair of the Congressional Human Rights Caucus, Lantos held hearings featuring a teenager identified only as Nayirah. She offered what allegedly was an eyewitness account of Iraqi atrocities in Kuwait, including the unplugging of babies in hospital incubators and tossing them on the floor.

Months later, it became public that the tearful Nayirah was actually the daughter of the Kuwaiti ambassador to the United States. Her testimony - which was never substantiated - was arranged by the Hill & Knowlton public relations firm and Lantos knew it at the time.

None of that, however, seemed to hurt Lantos politically. The former economics professor came from behind in 1980 to unseat a Republican who had served less than a year. Once in office, he immediately amassed a large campaign war chest and has had no serious opposition since.

PERSONAL: elected 1980; born Feb. 1, 1928, in Budapest, Hungary; home, Burlingame; education, B.A. University of Washington 1949, M.A. 1950, Ph.D UC Berkeley 1953; wife Annette, two children; Jewish.

CAREER: Economics professor and administrator for San Francisco State University and the California State University system, 1950-80; part-time bank economist and television commentator.

COMMITTEES: Foreign Affairs; Government Operations; (select) Aging.

OFFICES: Suite 2182, Rayburn Building, Washington, D.C. 20515, (202) 225-3531, FAX (202) 225-3127; district, Suite 820, 400 El Camino Real, San Mateo 94402, (415) 342-0300.

REGISTRATION: 55.5% D, 28% R.

1992 CAMPAIGN:	Lantos – D	68.8%	$466,948
	Jim Tomlin – R	23.3%	$5,554
1990 CAMPAIGN:	Lantos – D	66%	$788,298
	Bill Quraishi – R	28%	$97,638

| **RATINGS**: | ADA | ACU | AFL/CIO | LCV | NCSC | NTU | USCC |
| | 95 | 7 | 95 | 85 | 96 | 12 | 25 |

Number of checks bounced at the House bank: None.

Richard H. Lehman (D)
19th Congressional District

The 1992 congressional race here was what reapportionment was supposed to be all about. A complacent, five-term incumbent came within 1,130 votes of being knocked off by a novice who had never run for anything but the presidency of the college fraternity. If incumbent Rick Lehman thinks he can coast for another two years, he is sure to be history after the 1994 election.

Richard Lehman

Lehman had an exceedingly safe mountain, farm and blue-collar district that the late Rep. Phil Burton carefully crafted in 1981 to take in areas with 58 percent Democratic voter registration. But when court-ordered reapportionment was in place in 1992, Democratic registration dropped to 47 percent. Fifty percent of the district was new to Lehman, and he no longer represented his home base of Sanger.

The district takes in Mariposa and most of Madera counties, and eastern portions of Fresno and Tulare counties. It carefully corkscrews around practically all urbanized areas on the San Joaquin Valley floor, except for the city of Madera and part of the city of Fresno. It takes in rural and foothills communities, plus the great national parks: Yosemite and Sequoia-Kings Canyon. Lehman had a history of keeping agricultural and environmental factions of the district happy, but the new district also contains many small-town merchants and newly arrived retirees with a decidedly conservative bent.

Lehman had to outspend 28-year-old businessman Tal Cloud by better than 5-to-1 to keep the seat in a race as nasty as any seen in California in years. At one point, Cloud used a TV spot showing Lehman swilling food at a banquet and then making a goofy face. Yet a number of things broke Lehman's way. He was able to show that Cloud's paper company had failed to pay $72,000 in state payroll taxes. When then-Vice President Dan Quayle came to Fresno for a fund-raiser, farmers leaned on the organizers to keep the proceeds away from both Cloud and the GOP candidate opposing Democratic Rep. Cal Dooley in an adjoining district.

Lehman seemed to have a great deal of trouble explaining his coziness with the savings and loan industry, and why he was so ineffective in heading off legislation to redefine Central Valley Project water rights so that urban areas could get more water at the expense of farms. In the end, he was probably saved by the 6 percent of the vote that went to a Peace and Freedom candidate who didn't even campaign and a Christian Coalition candidate from Fresno who siphoned off 885 write-in votes.

Lehman is a onetime legislative aide who won a seat in the Assembly at age 28. He went to Congress at age 34 and, once there, quickly established himself as a friend of both mountain wilderness and agribusiness. He has worked for education, consumers rights and drug rehabilitation programs. Those issues, however, may be muted in the current term as he tries to mend fences at home in advance of the 1994 race.

PERSONAL: elected 1982; born July 20, 1948, in Sanger Calif.; home, North Fork; education, A.A. Fresno City College 1968, attended CSU Fresno, B.A. UC Santa Cruz 1986.

CAREER: California National Guard, 1970-76; legislative aide 1970-76; Assembly, 1976-82.

COMMITTEES: Energy and Commerce; Natural Resources.

OFFICES: Suite 1226 Longworth Building, Washington, D.C. 20515, (202) 225-4540. FAX (202) 225-4562; district, Suite 105, 2377 W. Shaw Ave., Fresno 93721, (209) 248-0800.

REGISTRATION: 47% D, 42% R

1992 CAMPAIGN:	Lehman – D	46.9%	$858,082
	Tal Cloud – R	46.4	$152,637
1990 CAMPAIGN:	Lehman – D	100%	$302,473

RATINGS:	ADA	ACU	AFL/CIO	LCV	NCSC	NTU	USCC
	60	5	83	54	95	27	25

Number of checks bounced at the House bank: 10.

Jerry Lewis (R)
40th Congressional District

In an extremely short period of time by congressional standards, Rep. Jerry Lewis became the No. 3 Republican in the House and had a shot at being minority leader one day. But his downward slide was even faster. As conservatives gained the upper hand in first the California Republican delegation and then the House GOP caucus, the moderate Lewis was stripped of his power. The final blow came at the beginning of the 1992 session when Rep. Richard Armey of Texas replaced Lewis as chair of the Republican Conference. The vote was 88-84 with his own California Republicans giving Armey his margin of victory.

All Lewis has left is a key position on the Appropriations Committee. But that is not much inducement to stay in a House, where he is an outcast. The former assemblyman has flirted with statewide races before, but his fall from grace hasn't left him with much of a launching pad.

When he was unofficial head of the state GOP delegation, Lewis and his Democratic counterpart,

Jerry Lewis

Vic Fazio, were one of the best bipartisan teams in Congress. Lewis even played a role in stopping the Reagan administration from weakening the Clean Air Act, a law that is extremely important in smog-burdened portions of his district. But none of that set well with the growing conservative faction in the caucus, who considered him disloyal. When their numbers increased after the 1990 elections, conservatives bounced Lewis as the California representative on the Committee on Committees. Rep. Ron Packard took his place and now has the job of deciding which committee assignments California Republicans get.

Most of Lewis' constituents are packed into the southwest corner of his district around Redlands and Loma Linda. But he represents a vast area stretching from the San Bernardino suburbs all across the Mojave Desert to the Arizona line. And he also represents Inyo County, the sparsely populated desert region on the southeastern edge of the Sierra Nevada. Some of the desert areas, however, are growing very fast — particularly around Victorville. Retirees are a growing force in the 40th as are young families who have been forced eastward by housing prices in Los Angeles and Orange counties.

Defense cutbacks are having a severe impact in the district. The Northrop Corp. alone laid off 1,500 people and both Norton and George Air Force Bases are closing. For once, there is a bipartisan effort to bring a proposed Defense Department accounting center to Norton, which would provide 4,000 badly needed jobs. But California is competing with a dozen other states.

PERSONAL: elected, 1978; born Oct. 21, 1934, in Seattle; home, Redlands; education, B.A. UCLA 1956; wife Arlene, seven children; Presbyterian.

CAREER: insurance agent and manager, 1959-78; field representative to Rep. Jerry Pettis, 1968; San Bernardino School Board, 1965-68; Assembly, 1968-78.

COMMITTEE: Appropriations.

OFFICES: Suite 2312, Rayburn Building, Washington, D.C. 20515, (202) 225-

5861, FAX (202) 225-6498; district, Suite 104, 1826 Orange Tree Lane., Redlands 92373, (714) 862-6030.

REGISTRATION: 38% D, 52% R

1992 CAMPAIGN:	Lewis – R	63.1%	$399,709
	Donald Rusk – D	31.1%	$19,832
1990 CAMPAIGN:	Lewis – R	60%	$452,381
	Barry Norton – D	33%	$0

RATINGS:	ADA	ACU	AFL/CIO	LCV	NCSC	NTU	USCC
	10	85	15	8	19	65	80

Number of checks bounced at the House bank: None.

Matthew G. Martinez (D)
31st Congressional District

This district begins in the East Los Angeles barrio and follows the San Gabriel Valley through Alhambra, Monterey Park, El Monte, Irwindale and Azusa. The district becomes more affluent the further north one travels. Neighborhoods are heavily Hispanic but there are growing numbers of Koreans, Chinese and other Asians who own many of the retail businesses along the crowded thoroughfares. Anglos still dominate neighborhoods in the northern tip of the district.

Matthew Martinez

On paper, this should be fairly safe Democratic turf. But it hasn't always turned out that way. Many of the upwardly mobile Hispanics and Asians appear to have left their Democratic roots in poorer neighborhoods. They're ticket-splitters and often favor candidates who promise less government intervention in their lives.

And then there is their congressman, Matthew Martinez, who seems to have trouble relating to the constituency. He has had a series of difficult primaries and runoffs. In 1992, he had to fight off three primary challengers, but took 62.5 percent of the vote in the runoff. For Martinez, that was a landslide.

Some claim Martinez is simply a creation of Reps. Howard Berman and never would have gained public office without the help of Berman and Rep. Henry Waxman and their organization's cash and campaign moxie. Berman plucked Martinez from obscurity to run against an incumbent assemblyman, Jack Fenton, during a nasty Assembly leadership battle in 1980, and then boosted him into Congress just two years later.

Whatever his political origins, Martinez has been a less-than-impressive political figure. A California Magazine survey rated him the dimmest bulb in the delegation and one of the five worst representatives overall, someone who makes little impact even on his own district.

PERSONAL: elected 1982; born Feb. 14, 1929, in Walsenburg, Colo.; home, Monterey Park; education, attended Los Angeles Trade Technical School; divorced; Roman Catholic.

CAREER: U.S. Marine Corps, 1947-50; upholstery shop owner, 1957-82; Monterey Park City Council, 1974-76; mayor, 1976-80; Assembly, 1980-82.

COMMITTEES: Education and Labor; Foreign Affairs.

OFFICES: Suite 2231, Rayburn Building, Washington, D.C. 20515, (202) 225-5464, FAX (202) 225-5467; district, Suite 214, 320 S. Garfield Ave., Alhambra 91801, (213) 722-7731.

REGISTRATION: 58.6% D, 28% R

1992 CAMPAIGN:	Martinez – D	62.5%	$115,848
	Reuben Franco – R	37.4%	$193,847
1990 CAMPAIGN:	Martinez – D	59%	$209,495
	Reuben Franco – R	36%	$72,572

RATINGS:	ADA	ACU	AFL/CIO	LCV	NCSC	NTU	USCC
	95	7	98	62	97	11	24

Number of checks bounced at the House bank: 19.

Robert T. Matsui (D)

5th Congressional District

Robert Matsui

The 5th District includes Sacramento and south suburbs as far as Elk Grove. With the state Capitol and some 41,000 state workers, the area is more strongly identified with government than any other part of California. But the government influence doesn't stop with the state. There are nearly 25,000 more federal paychecks from military installations or regional offices in or adjacent to the district. Such a strong civil service presence normally means friendly turf for a Democrat and Rep. Robert Matsui represents the district ably. It was a tribute to Matsui's strength that he could advocate shutting down Mather Air Force Base (5,600 jobs) as a federal cost-cutting move and no one even mentioned the word "recall."

Reapportionment was especially kind to Matsui, drawing a denser district and taking away conservative suburbs. Life could be exceedingly easy for Matsui, but that is not his nature. He is considered one of the brighter lights in the congressional delegation and is known for working long hours. In 1991, he was named treasurer of the National Democratic Party, where he played an important, but scarcely visible role in the Clinton-Gore victory the following year.

In 1993, the tax-fraud indictment of a senior House member gave Robert Matsui the chairmanship of the Ways and Means subcommittee on human resources. That gives him control over welfare, Social Security, child care and unemployment legislation, all high-visibility areas in the Clinton-Gore era.

Many of the reforms pushed through that subcommittee in recent years were felled by George Bush vetoes. Among Matsui's first tasks was to bring legislation such as the Family Preservation Act back to life. But Matsui also has been stridently critical of House Speaker Tom Foley, D-Wash. If that keeps up, Foley may send a harpoon Matsui's way.

Matsui and his wife, Doris, are one of Washington's power couples. She also worked in the Clinton-Gore campaign and was a member of Clinton's transition board. She then became deputy director of public liaison in the White House, the No. 2 position in the office that courts groups outside Washington to support the president's agenda. As soon as Doris' appointment was announced, the Matsuis accepted an invitation from ARCO to host a $5,000 reception in their honor. Neither Matsui seemed bothered by the obvious conflict.

As an infant, Robert Matsui was sent to a Japanese-American internment camp during World War II. In Congress, reparations for victims of the relocation became one of his causes. His legislative interests are quite diversified, however, ranging from foster care and job training to medical care for the elderly. On Ways and Means, he has had an important role in shaping tax reform. His congressional posture has been similar to the one he established on the Sacramento City Council: a quiet and effective consensus builder.

Those are not attributes that transfer well to a statewide campaign. Matsui has tried to put a campaign together for a U.S. Senate seat from time to time, but, like most members in the vast California House delegation, he is virtually invisible outside his district.

PERSONAL: elected in 1978; born Sept. 17, 1941, in Sacramento; home, Sacramento; education, A.B. UC Berkeley 1963, J.D. Hastings College of Law 1966; wife Doris, one child; United Methodist.

CAREER: attorney, 1967-78; Sacramento city councilman, 1971-78.

COMMITTEES: Budget; Ways and Means.

OFFICES: Suite 2311, Rayburn Building, Washington, D.C. 20515, (202) 225-7163, FAX (202) 225-0566; district, Suite 8058, 650 Capitol Mall, Sacramento 95814, (916) 551-2846.

REGISTRATION: 59% D, 30% R

1992 CAMPAIGN: Matsui – D   68.6% $1,215,753
                  Robert Dinsmore – D   25.4% $20,083

1990 CAMPAIGN: Matsui – D   60% $1,207,843
                  Lowell Landowski – R   34% $4,545

RATINGS:

ADA	ACU	AFL/CIO	LCV	NCSC	NTU	USCC
80	5	88	77	90	23	26

Number of checks bounced at the House bank: 25.

Alfred A. McCandless (R)
44th Congressional District

This fastest-growing district in California begins at the city of Riverside's eastern suburbs runs all the way across Riverside County's high desert to the Arizona border. Once beyond Moreno Valley, Sun City and Hemet, the towns are clustered along Interstate 10 as it bisects the county. At the western end, there are the trailer towns loaded with retirees and young families in the sterile Moreno Valley subdivisions. Further east are the lavish desert communities of Palm Springs and Palm Desert. From there, it is on to Indio and the rich farmlands of the Coachella Valley, then across the scorching desert to Blythe.

Alfred McCandless

The Palm Springs area is home to movie stars and retired captains of industry, plus former President Jerry Ford and former Vice President Spiro Agnew. But there are many less-well-off retirees living in condos and fading trailers. The service-sector is dominated by Hispanics, many of whom travel some distance to their low-paying jobs.

Their congressman is a desert native, Rep. Al McCandless, who was once a General Motors dealer in Indio. McCandless is one of the most conservative members of the delegation. Outside his district, he is probably best known for the video privacy bill he authored after a keyhole reporter got hold of Judge Robert Bork's rental list during his unsuccessful Supreme Court confirmation bid. McCandless has shown interest in legislation benefiting handicapped people but devotes most of his time to mustering "no" votes on any bill with an appropriation.

McCandless got a scare in 1990 when actor Ralph Waite (TV's Papa Walton) of Rancho Mirage became the Democratic nominee. In 1992, it was a little-known county employee from Perris who got a respectable vote despite spending less than $10,000. If a strong contender turns out for the 1994 race, McCandless might decide it is a good time to retire.

PERSONAL: elected 1982; born July 23, 1927, in Brawley, Calif.; home, La Quinta; B.A. UCLA 1951; wife Gail, five children; Protestant.

CAREER: U.S. Marine Corps, 1945-46 and 1950-52; auto dealer, 1953-75; Riverside County supervisor, 1970-82.

COMMITTEES: Banking, Finance and Urban Affairs; Government Operations.

OFFICES: Suite 2422, Rayburn Building, Washington, D.C. 20515, (202) 225-5330; district, Suite 155, 22590 Cactus Ave., Moreno Valley 92553, (909) 656-1444; Suite 112, 73-710 Fred Waring Dr., Palm Desert 92260, (619) 340-2900.

REGISTRATION: 44.5% D, 43.8% R

1992 CAMPAIGN:	McCandless – R	54.2%	$251,337
	Georgia Smith – D	40.1%	$5,748
1990 CAMPAIGN:	McCandless – R	50%	$551,786
	Ralph Waite – D	45%	$6

RATINGS:	ADA	ACU	AFL/CIO	LCV	NCSC	NTU	USCC
	10	90	3	11	8	87	89

Number of checks bounced at the House bank: None.

Howard McKeon (R)

25th Congressional District

This new district doesn't look like most of Los Angeles, but the canyons and flinty hills are rapidly urbanizing in the same haphazard way that the rest of the megalopolis has. It begins in the northern San Fernando Valley and takes in all of the mountain and high desert area of northern Los Angeles County. Rampant crime and the search for affordable housing have pushed young families into stucco cliff-like dwellings in the Santa Clarita Valley, where the state's biggest incorporation occurred in 1987. Those seeking a bit more space and willing to commute even farther are rapidly filling up the Antelope Valley.

Hispanics dominate in the shabby neighborhoods of the upper San Fernando Valley. But the rest of the communities are predominately Anglo and conservative. The safe Republican numbers brought out a gaggle of GOP contenders in the primary, including former Rep. John Rousselot, Assemblyman Phil Wyman and County Assessor John Lynch. But the voters chose Santa Clarita's first and only mayor, Howard "Buck" McKeon, whose family owns a 50-store chain of western wear shops. Unless he does something unseemly, McKeon should be safe here.

PERSONAL: elected 1992; born Sept. 9, 1939, in Los Angeles; home, Santa Clarita; B.S. Brigham Young University; wife Patricia, six children; Mormon.

CAREER: businessman, banker; school board 1978-86; Santa Clarita mayor, 1987-91.

COMMITTEES: Education & Labor; Public Works & Transportation.

OFFICES: Suite 307, Cannon Building, Washington, D.C. 20515, (202) 225-1956; district, Suite 410, 23929 W. Valencia Blvd., Santa Clarita 91355, (805) 254-2111; Suite D, 1008 W. Avenue M-4, Palmdale 93551, (805) 948-7833.

REGISTRATION: 38.5% D, 48.7% R

1990 CAMPAIGN:	McKeon – R	51.9%	$432,190
	James Gilmartin – D	33%	$109,398

RATINGS: Newly elected.

George Miller (D)
7th Congressional District

The 7th District begins in the backwaters of San Francisco Bay and stretches inland along both sides of Carquinez Straight as far as Pittsburg. The grubbiest of the industrial towns in the district is Richmond, which also is more than 50 percent African American. To the east lie a series of roughneck refinery and factory towns — Pinole, Hercules, Rodeo and Martinez. North of the waterway, the district takes in Vallejo, Benicia, Cordelia and Suisun City. To the south, it dips into the affluent suburb of Concord.

There are fewer youngish families in the district. Those who can are fleeing blighted areas and mostly childless couples have begun rehabilitating homes in the industrial areas. The trend in the district is toward

George Miller

more older and conservative voters, but it continues to be a Democratic bastion and a good fit for Rep. George Miller.

Cold shivers went through California's agriculture community in January 1990, when Miller took over the Interior Committee, which he renamed Natural Resources. Miller, one of the most committed environmentalists in the House, had been battling for years with agribusiness over water giveaways and wasteful irrigation practices. Miller immediately set out to overhaul the farmer-friendly Central Valley Project. His plan called for recasting the CVP governing rules to allow diversion of more water for urban use, enhancing water quality, and restoration of wetlands. The effort sputtered for a while, but by the time the heat was rising in the 1992 campaigns, Miller had everything in place.

With strong backing from environmental and urban interests, Miller cut a deal with Sacramento Valley rice growers to mute their opposition and help save their congressman, Vic Fazio. Then he hitched his reform package to a huge public works pork-barrel bill with goodies for both Republican and Democratic representatives from Western states. While California farm interests fumed, Gov. Pete Wilson made a last-minute flight to Nashville, where President George Bush was campaigning, to argue for a veto. But Bush had enough problems without worrying about farmers in a state he couldn't carry anyway. He signed the measure on the Friday before the Nov. 3 election. Not only could Miller savor the passage of his long-sought reforms, but he had sullied agriculture, Wilson and the failing campaign of Sen. John Seymour in the process. How sweet it was.

During his long House tenure, Miller has gained a reputation for tirades and occasional oafish behavior. That is probably why he failed to show up on the Clinton-Gore list of possible candidates for interior secretary. But he also knows practically every civic and labor leader in the district by first name and works tirelessly on behalf of middle-class social and economic concerns. It is a grass-roots approach that he learned from his father, a longtime state senator. With Democrats in the White House, Miller can be expected to play an ever-larger role in both conservation and energy policy. He is also part of the Democratic leadership as a majority whip-at-large.

PERSONAL: elected 1974; born May 17, 1945, in Richmond; home, Martinez; education, A.A. Diablo Valley College 1966, B.A. San Francisco State College 1968, J.D. UC Davis 1972; wife Cynthia, two children; Roman Catholic.

CAREER: legislative aide, 1969-74; attorney, 1972-74.

COMMITTEES: Education and Labor; Natural Resources (chairman).

OFFICES: Suite 2205, Rayburn Building, Washington, D.C. 20515, (202) 225-2095; district, Suite 14, 367 Civic Dr., Pleasant Hill 94523, (415) 687-3260; Suite 280, 3220 Blume Dr., Richmond 94806, (415) 222-4212.

REGISTRATION: 62% D, 24% R

1992 CAMPAIGN:	Miller – D	70.3%	$515,589
	David Scholl – R	25.1%	$60,748
1990 CAMPAIGN:	Miller – D	61%	$469,400
	Roger Payton – R	39%	$47,918

| **RATINGS**: | ADA | ACU | AFL/CIO | LCV | NCSC | NTU | USCC |
| | 85 | 28 | 90 | 85 | 96 | 55 | 23 |

Number of checks bounced at the House bank: 99.

Norman Y. Mineta (D)
15th Congressional District

The 15th District includes a piece of San Jose, which surpassed San Francisco to become the third-largest city in California in 1989, plus the suburbs of Campbell, Santa Clara, Los Gatos and Saratoga. Then it swings westward taking in the sparsely populated northern part of Santa Cruz County.

Most of the growth in this area has been in the affluent suburbs, but skyrocketing housing values in the San Jose area are changing the economic mix of this region. At the same time, the region's computer electronics industries have been downsizing, putting many well-paid people out of work. Few of the lower-paid workers who have been able to escape layoffs in those industries can afford to live near their jobs.

Norman Mineta

Increasingly, the area is peopled with affluent, often childless, couples while those with families commute long distances from the East Bay.

In the Santa Cruz portion of the district, there are still scars from the Loma Prieta earthquake in 1989. That acted to depress housing values in the wooded hills separating the Silicon Valley from the coast, and also encouraged those who could afford it to move elsewhere. The San Andreas Fault slices almost through the middle of the district.

Despite a slight conservative trend among district voters, Rep. Norm Mineta consistently runs ahead of the Democratic registration in the district. The popular former San Jose mayor seems fully recovered from a heart attack in 1986. In 1993, he took over the long-coveted job of chairman of the Public Works and Transportation Committee, one of the primo pork committees in Congress. Mineta made a stab at winning the chairmanship in 1990, succeeding in dumping longtime colleague Glenn Anderson, D-San Pedro, as chair, but failing to beat Rep. Robert Roe, D-N.J., for the post. Roe retired after just one term, opening the way for Mineta.

For some years, Mineta's seniority on the committee had made him the Californian to see for airport development money and other aviation issues. Now as chairman, he'll be in a position to direct public works spending nationwide and is likely to play an important role in President Clinton's plans to rebuild the nation's transportation infrastructure. The position also is apt to feed Mineta's appetite for junkets, which has been voracious over the years. When Clinton was forming his Cabinet, he considered Mineta for transportation secretary. The job wasn't offered, but Public Works chairman is a more powerful position in any event. Mineta also is deputy whip in the Democratic caucus.

Like Rep. Robert Matsui, Mineta spent part of his youth in a Japanese detention camp during World War II. He has led the fight to redress those wrongs. In another arena, however, he has been in the forefront of efforts to open up Japanese markets to Silicon Valley products. He has also pressured the Japanese to end whaling and protect arctic wildlife.

PERSONAL: elected 1974; born Nov. 12, 1931, in San Jose; home, San Jose; education, B.S. UC Berkeley 1953; wife May, two children; United Methodist.

CAREER: U.S. Army 1953-56; insurance agency owner, 1956-74; San Jose City Council, 1967-71; San Jose mayor, 1971-74.

COMMITTEES: Public Works and Transportation (chairman).

OFFICES: Suite 2221, Rayburn Building, Washington, D.C. 20515, (202) 225-2631; district, Suite 310, 1245 South Winchester Blvd., San Jose 95128, (408) 984-6045.

REGISTRATION: 46.2% D, 38% R 1988

1992 CAMPAIGN:	Mineta – D	63.5%	$980,940
	Robert Wick – R	31.2%	$49,760
1990 CAMPAIGN:	Mineta – D	58%	$666,915
	David Smith – R	35%	$670

RATINGS:	ADA	ACU	AFL/CIO	LCV	NCSC	NTU	USCC
	100	4	90	85	91	15	26

Number of checks bounced at the House bank: 3.

Carlos Moorhead (R)
27th Congressional District

Most of this district is in the San Gabriel Mountains, where the population is made up chiefly of snakes, jack rabbits and coyotes. Most of the remainder runs along with the southern base of the range with its dense suburbs of Burbank, Glendale, Pasadena, South Pasadena and San Marino. Pasadena and San Marino are the most affluent suburbs in the Los Angeles smog belt and tend to be mostly white and Republican. The populations of Burbank and Glendale are more diverse but tend to be moderate-to-conservative as one travels from west to east. South Pasadena is largely middle-class Hispanic.

Carlos Moorhead

During reapportionment, this district lost strongly Republican areas north of the San Gabriels and picked up more Democrats in Burbank and South Pasadena. But the affable congressman from the area, Carlos Moorhead, apparently failed to notice until late in the campaign that his district had gone from solidly Republican to nominally so. He got the surprise of his 22-year career on Election Day in 1992, when an opponent who spent a little more than $100,000 held him under 50 percent. Moorhead will be 72 years old in 1994 and can probably expect another rugged campaign.

Moorhead is the dean of the Republican delegation. But he doesn't try to assert his leadership very often, perhaps because he knows it would be a waste of time. GOP members have a history of independence and some seem to regard the solidly Republican Moorhead as not ideological enough to suit their tastes.

Moorhead busies himself with legislation in a variety of important areas — but none that attract much attention — such as patent and copyright law, energy conservation, natural gas deregulation and operations of the border patrol. Almost alone, he has battled with Pacific Northwest congressmen to give California a fair share of the federal low-cost power generated in that region. He is the ranking minority member on Energy and Commerce, and No. 2 minority member on Judiciary, making him the single most powerful representative in the state GOP delegation. He is also known for faithful constituent service.

PERSONAL: elected 1972; born May 6, 1922, in Long Beach; home, Glendale; education, B.A. UCLA 1943, J.D. USC 1949; wife Valery, five children; Presbyterian.

CAREER: U.S. Army, 1942-45 (retired Army Reserve lieutenant general); attorney, 1949-72; Assembly, 1967-72.

COMMITTEES: Energy and Commerce (ranking minority member); Judiciary.

OFFICES: Suite 2346, Rayburn Building, Washington, D.C. 20515, (202) 225-4176, FAX (202) 226-1279; district, 420 North Brand Blvd., Glendale 91203, (818) 247-8445; 301 East Colorado Blvd., Pasadena 91101, (818) 792-6168.

REGISTRATION: 42.9% D, 43.9% R

1992 CAMPAIGN:	Moorhead – R	49.7%	$629,896
	Douglas Kahn – D	39.4%	$119,003
1990 CAMPAIGN:	Moorhead – R	59%	$444,157
	David Bayer – D	35%	$40,872

RATINGS:	ADA	ACU	AFL/CIO	LCV	NCSC	NTU	USCC
	5	95	7	15	7	96	90

Number of checks bounced at the House bank: None.

Ronald C. Packard (R)
48th Congressional District

This huge district sprawls through northern San Diego County, laps into Riverside County as far as Temecula, and also includes southern Orange County areas as far north as Laguna Niguel and Mission Viejo. The Camp Pendleton Marine Corps Base sprawls though the center. To the north and south are the wealthy coastal towns of San Juan Capistrano, San Clemente and Oceanside. Inland are pleasant retirement communities and some shabby trailer courts inhabited by GI families and civilian defense workers.

Ronald Packard

The climate is one of the most ideal in the United States. Waspy retirees dominate most communities and crowd the golf courses. Spouses of Marines and a few Hispanics are available for the service-sector jobs. Politically, attitudes are in step with hard-core Orange County Republicans to the north. Yet San Clemente homeowners weren't so Republican that they welcomed having the Western White House in their midst during Richard Nixon's presidency. There were many complaints that property values were being hurt. Residents have high educational levels and intense interests in property and private enterprise. Most can afford insurance and that liberates them from government health plans.

Their congressman, however, is anything but a right-wing ideologue. Rep. Ron Packard, a dentist, is a conservative but practical man with a commitment to assisting local government. Roll Call, the Capital Hill newspaper, called him one of the most obscure members of Congress in 1992. Yet he has taken on thorny problems such as Indian water rights and negotiated a settlement that pleased all sides. He also has made a mark in aircraft safety legislation. In 1991, Packard became the California representative on the GOP's Committee on Committees, which decides assignments for members. That makes him one of the most powerful members of the delegation.

When first elected, Packard was only the fourth person in American history to win a congressional seat through a write-in campaign. In the 1982 primary, with 18 contenders running for an open seat, he was second by 92 votes to a local businessman. Packard triumphed in November. Since then he has had easy races.

PERSONAL: elected 1982; born Jan. 19, 1931, in Meridian, Idaho; home, Oceanside; education, attended Brigham Young University and Portland State University, D.M.D. University of Oregon 1957; wife Jean, seven children; Mormon.

CAREER: U.S. Navy 1957-59; dentist, 1957-82; trustee, Carlsbad Unified School District, 1962-74; Carlsbad City Council 1976-78, mayor 1978-82.

COMMITTEE: Appropriations.

OFFICES: Suite 2162, Rayburn Building, Washington, D.C. 20515, (202) 225-3906, FAX (202) 225-0134; district, Suite 205, 221 E. Vista Way, Vista 92084, (619) 631-1364; Suite 204, 629 Camino de los Mares, San Clemente 92672, (714) 496-2343.

REGISTRATION: 30.2% D, 56.4% R

1992 CAMPAIGN:	Packard – R	61.1%	$315,870
	Michael Farber – D	29.2%	$64,212
1990 CAMPAIGN:	Packard – R	86%	$167,017

RATINGS:	ADA	ACU	AFL/CIO	LCV	NCSC	NTU	USCC
	0	91	7	0	9	92	90

Nancy Pelosi (D)
8th Congressional District

All of San Francisco except for the areas south of Golden Gate Park lies within this district, an activist Democratic enclave as strong as any in the nation. From the Golden Gate to Candlestick Park, it is the San Francisco that most tourists come to see. Yet it also is an area of enormous social complexity. It abounds with ethnic and neighborhood factions that can be counted upon to pursue their issues stridently.

Longtime party activist Nancy Pelosi won a special election in 1987 over gay Supervisor Harry Britt. But there was no lingering bitterness. Pelosi had many gay supporters and also was an acceptable choice for Roman Catholic, society, environmental and labor factions. Pelosi came to Congress a wealthy

Nancy Pelosi

housewife who long ago paid her dues licking envelopes and walking precincts in Democratic campaigns. Her father, a congressman from 1939-47, and a brother were mayors of Baltimore. Pelosi had been state Democratic Party chairwoman, a member of the Democratic National Committee and chaired the Democratic National Convention in 1984.

In 1992, she was an early Clinton supporter and chaired the national convention's platform committee. From her seat on the Appropriations Committee, she is expected to be a strong player in pushing the Clinton-Gore agenda in Congress. At the same time, she is the senior of the seven women in California's House delegation. As Northern California Democratic whip and a member of the executive board of the Democratic Study Group, she is in a position to be a mentor for those women.

Pelosi also occupies a unique position in both the California delegation and Congress because of her closeness to California's two new senators. Before the 1992 campaign, Dianne Feinstein and Barbara Boxer weren't friends. But Pelosi was a friend of both. Probably no one in Congress has more influence with the two senators. The three tend to see themselves as a team.

Pelosi has a bright career ahead of her in Washington. But she has other options. San Francisco Mayor Frank Jordan finishes his first term in 1995. If Pelosi chooses to run for mayor, she could be the one to beat.

PERSONAL: elected 1987; born March 26, 1940, in Baltimore; home, San Francisco; education, B.A, Trinity College, Washington, D.C., 1962, husband Paul, five children; Roman Catholic.

CAREER: public relations executive, 1984-86.

COMMITTEES: Appropriations; Standards of Official Conduct.

OFFICES: Suite 240, Cannon Building, Washington, D.C. 20515, (202) 225-4965; district, Suite 13407, 450 Golden Gate Ave., San Francisco 94102, (415) 556-4862.

REGISTRATION. 64% D, 16% R

1992 CAMPAIGN:	Pelosi – D			82.5%		$257,374
	Mark Wolin – R			11%		$30,511
1990 CAMPAIGN:	Pelosi – D			77%		$462,664
	Alan Nichols – R			23%		$153,947

RATINGS:	ADA	ACU	AFL/CIO	LCV	NCSC	NTU	USCC
	90	1	95	92	100	9	17

Number of checks bounced at the House bank: 28.

Richard Pombo (R)
11th Congressional District

This new district takes in farm areas of Sacramento County and all but a southern piece of San Joaquin County. Included on the northern end are Rancho Cordova and a piece of Carmichael. Except for a few affluent enclaves such as Gold River and Rancho Murieta, the district is largely blue collar and middle- to lower-middle class. It contains sleepy Delta towns, some of Sacramento's ever-expanding suburbs, and the grimy Stockton Area with its unemployment rate stuck solidly in double digits.

Rep. Richard Pombo, a fourth-generation rancher and small businessman, comes from Tracy, where he sat on the City Council for just two years prior to winning his congressional seat. It is hardly fair to say that Pombo won the election. Patti Garamendi lost it.

Even though Democrats in the 11th District tend to be conservative, a Republican of the John Doolittle mold shouldn't be able to win here. But the Democratic nominee, wife of state Insurance Commissioner John Garamendi, who once represented the area in the state Senate, proved to be the poorest of candidates. Since 1990, Patti Garamendi has been

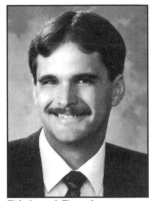

Richard Pombo

defeated in races for both the state Senate and Assembly. She angered law enforcement by being an apologist for musician Ice T, writer of the song "Cop Killer." Her apparent lust for office - any office - was easy for Pombo to exploit along with the fact that she seemed to raise campaign money everywhere but in the district.

Garamendi raised $300,000 more than Pombo, but he was helped by lower-than-average turnout in San Joaquin County and a Libertarian candidate who sucked up nearly 7 percent of the vote. The GOP leadership saw to it that Pombo got good committee assignments for his district. But in 1994, Democrats are likely to make Pombo their No. 1 congressional target if they can field a strong candidate.

PERSONAL: Elected 1992; born Jan. 8, 1961, in Tracy; home, Tracy; attended California State Polytechnic University, Pomona; wife, Annette; one child; Roman Catholic.

CAREER: rancher and small businessman; Tracy City Council, 1990-92.

COMMITTEES: Agriculture; Natural Resources.

OFFICES: Suite 1519, Longworth Building, Washington, D.C. 20515, (202) 225-1947; district, 2321 W. March Ln., Stockton 95207, (209) 951-3091.

REGISTRATION: 51.6% D, 38% R

| **1992 CAMPAIGN**: | Pombo – R | 47.6% | $512,793 |
| | Patti Garamendi – D | 45.6% | $805,447 |

RATINGS: Newly elected.

Dana Rohrabacher (R)
45th Congressional District

Orange County's "Gold Coast" from Seal Beach to Newport Beach is the most conspicuous feature of this very Republican district. From the coastal yacht basins, the district reaches past the stately homes in Huntington Beach and Costa Mesa to the affluent inland communities of Fountain Valley and Westminister. It then runs north as far as Stanton. The naturally air-conditioned area has a diverse job base. There are many upper-middle-class and wealthy people, only some of whom were inconvenienced by the recession.

The laissez-faire congressman is Rep. Dana Rohrabacher, onetime editorial writer for the conservative Orange County Register and speech writer for former President Ronald Reagan.

Few freshmen attract national attention, but Rohrabacher succeeded in spades during his first term in 1989-90. He emerged as Sen. Jesse Helms' chief House ally to prohibit National Endowment for the Arts grants from going to projects they considered to be obscene or sacrilegious. Arts supporters prom-

Dana Rohrabacher

ised a national effort to try and unseat Rohrabacher in 1990, but that fizzled. Rohrabacher has said he will spend no more than 10 years in Congress. So, it looks as if the arts crowd will have to put up with him for three more terms.

Rohrabacher has been dogged by claims that he was a heavy drug user in younger days. But that hasn't stopped him from winning increased stature among conservatives in the state caucus. He has worked for restrictions on immigration and the proposed balanced budget amendment. In 1992, he spent large amounts of money against a minor-league candidate, but only won 54 percent of the vote. In a closer race, he could have trouble with a committed bloc of Libertarian voters in the district.

PERSONAL: elected 1988; born June 21, 1947, in Corona, Calif.; home, Lomita; B.A. CSU Long Beach 1969; M.A. USC 1971; unmarried; Baptist.

CAREER: journalist, 1970-80; speech writer for President Reagan, 1981-88.

COMMITTEES: District of Columbia; Foreign Affairs; Science, Space and Technology.

OFFICES: Suite 1027, Longworth Building, Washington, D.C. 20515, (202) 225-2415, FAX (202) 225-0145; district, Suite 304, 16162 Beach Blvd., Huntington Beach 92647, (714) 847-2433.

REGISTRATION: 34.7% D, 51.3% R

1992 CAMPAIGN:	Rohrabacher – R	54.5%	$308,047
	Patricia McCabe – D	38.9%	$29,975
1990 CAMPAIGN:	Rohrabacher – R	59%	$423,924
	Guy Kimbrough – D	37%	$29,555

RATINGS:	ADA	ACU	AFL/CIO	LCV	NCSC	NTU	USCC
	20	97	11	15	20	97	88

Number of checks bounced at the House bank: 8.

Lucille Roybal-Allard (D)

33rd Congressional District

There are 95,448 registered voters — the lowest of any California congressional district — in this new district, which is 83 percent Latino. There is a pocket of Asians living near downtown Los Angeles. From there, the district runs east and south through East Los Angeles and the cities of Huntington Park, Bell Gardens, Commerce, Maywood, Vernon and South Gate. Unemployment and crime rates are high; education levels are low. Day and night, trucks rumble down grimy streets carrying wares to and from industrial areas that intrude on blighted neighborhoods. The South-Central Los Angeles riots of 1992 spilled into this area, and there are still burned-out buildings from the days of rage following the acquittal of Rodney

Lucille Roybal-Allard

King's assailants. The new congresswoman from this dreary center of the Los Angeles Basin is Lucille Roybal-Allard, a former United Way planner and the daughter of a legendary figure in East Los Angeles politics, Rep. Edward Roybal.

In a 1987 special election to fill the seat vacated by Assemblywoman Gloria Molina when she was elected to the Los Angeles City Council, Roybal-Allard came out of nowhere to overwhelm a crowded field. In the Assembly, she was a liberal, though a quiet one. She often sided with an informal group of Democrats known as the "Grizzly Bears," who shared strategy and information on bills. Much of her time was devoted to district chores. In her new congressional district, her work is cut out for her.

PERSONAL: elected 1992; born June 12, 1941, in Boyle Heights; home, Los Angeles; education, B.A. CSU Los Angeles; husband Edward T. Allard III, two children and two step-children; Roman Catholic.

CAREER: planning associate; past executive director, National Association of Hispanic Certified Public Accountants; past assistant director, Alcoholism Council of East Los Angeles; Assembly, 1987-92.

COMMITTEES: Banking, Finance and Urban Affairs; Natural Resources; Small Business.

OFFICES: Suite 1717, Longworth Building, Washington, D.C. 20515, (202) 225-1766; district, Suite 11860, 255 E. Temple St., Los Angeles 90012, (213) 894-4870.

REGISTRATION: 66.9% D; 22.1% R

1992 CAMPAIGN:

Roybal-Allard – D	63%	$253,173
Robert Guzman – R	30.3%	$160,459

RATINGS: Newly elected.

Edward R. Royce (R)

39th Congressional District

This district straddles the Los Angeles-Orange County line from Los Alamitos to La Habra Heights and then swings eastward into the GOP bastions of Fullerton and Placentia. Democrats and a growing number of Hispanics and Koreans are clustered around the southern end of the district. White Republicans people the center and northern reaches, and Vietnamese are a growing factor throughout the area. The Clinton-Gore ticket did surprisingly well in this area in 1992. Fullerton was even the spot Clinton chose for his last California campaign stop. That was a reflection, no doubt, of the job losses in the area and general dissatisfaction with Republican handling of the economy.

Edward Royce

The somewhat reconfigured district had sent William Dannemeyer to Congress by comfortable margins. But Dannemeyer left the seat for a divisive and unsuccessful run in the GOP primary against U.S. Sen. John Seymour. That cleared the way for one of the most undistinguished members of the state Senate, Ed Royce, to move up to Congress. Royce, once an accountant for a cement company who cut his political teeth in Young Americans for Freedom, had been marking time in the Senate since 1982. He seldom spoke except to vote "no" and carried light legislative loads. One of his accomplishments was a 1987 bill sponsored by Mothers Against Drunk Driving requiring automatic revocation of a driver's license of anyone who refuses to take a roadside sobriety test.

Royce skirted the edges of a few low-grade controversies. Democrats accused him in the 1988 election of circumventing federal campaign laws to give $5,000 from his campaign fund to Republican Rep. Wally Herger of Yuba City. Herger gave the money back, and the Federal Election Commission — not untypically — dropped the matter.

Royce raised $500,000 for his congressional race and easily beat an underfunded Fullerton city councilwoman. This should be a safe seat for him, but it seems likely that few Californians outside the district will ever hear of Royce again.

PERSONAL: elected 1992; born Oct. 12, 1951, in Los Angeles; home, Fullerton; education, B.A. CSU, Fullerton; wife, Marie Porter; no children; Roman Catholic.

CAREER: corporate tax manager and controller; state Senate 1982-92.

COMMITTEES: Foreign Affairs; Science, Space & Technology.

OFFICES: Suite 1404, Longworth Building, Washington, D.C., 20515, (202) 225-4111; district, Suite 300, 305 N. Harbor Blvd., Fullerton 92632, (714) 992-8081.

REGISTRATION: 39.4% D, 48.7% R

1992 CAMPAIGN: Royce – R   57.3% $514,904

　　　　　　　　Molly McClanahan – D   38.2% $89,577

RATINGS: Newly elected.

Lynn Schenk (D)
49th Congressional District

One of the crown jewels of the California Coast lies in the 49th District from Del Mar to the Mexican border. This land of millionaires and Navy bases has some of the most photogenic communities in the nation: Torrey Pines, La Jolla, Mission Beach, Point Loma and Coronado. There is an eastward bulge up the Mission Valley that stops just short of La Mesa. On the southern end, the district narrows as it runs along the Silver Strand and then juts eastward just far enough to include all of Imperial Beach.

Lynn Schenk

This district is solid Republican country and prob-ably would still have a GOP congressman if three incumbents hadn't decided to move out and run elsewhere (Bill Lowery, Randy Cunningham and Duncan Hunter). That set up a divisive Republican primary won by businesswoman Judy Jarvis. She faced Port Commissioner Lynn Schenk in the runoff and Jarvis may still be wondering what it was that hit her on Election Day. Schenk ran an incredible 12 points ahead of the Democratic registration for the most impressive win by any of the 17 newcomers in the state delegation.

But then again, Schenk is no party hack. She is the daughter of immigrants who worked as a tailor and a manicurist and went to law school. She has been a utility lawyer, White House fellow for Vice Presidents Nelson Rockefeller and Walter Mondale, and a Cabinet officer for Gov. Jerry Brown, among other accomplish-ments. She toiled for years in Democratic races, which gave her many chits to call in when fund-raising. And she had been out front on women's issues for years, founding job training and children-at-risk projects, plus a women's bank. By Election Day, she had raised over $1 million, compared to $363,000 for Jarvis.

Schenk put together an aggressive congressional office and will need it as she deals with a district being hit by military downsizing and beset by festering border problems.

PERSONAL: elected 1992; born Jan. 5, 1955, in New York City; home San Diego; B.A. University of California, Los Angeles, J.D. University of San Diego; attended London School of Economics; husband, C. Hugh Friedman; Jewish.

CAREER: deputy state attorney general; attorney, San Diego Gas & Electric; White House fellow, 1976-77; banker; state secretary of business, transportation and housing 1980-83; San Diego Unified Port District commissioner, 1990-92.

COMMITTEES: Energy and Commerce; Merchant Marine and Fisheries.

OFFICES: Suite 315, Cannon Building, Washington, D.C. 20515, (202) 225-2040; district, Suite 200, 3900 5th Ave., San Diego 92103, (619) 291-1430.

REGISTRATION: 39.1 D, 42.8 R

1992 CAMPAIGN: Schenk – D   51.1% $1,085,199
                    Judy Jarvis – R   42.6% $363,335

RATINGS: Newly elected.

Fortney H. "Pete" Stark (D)
13th Congressional District

From South Oakland, the 13th District runs south-easterly along San Francisco Bay taking in all the scruffy suburbs between Oakland and San Jose. Alameda, San Leandro, San Lorenzo, Hayward, Fremont and Milpitas were originally working-class communities. But as Bay Area housing prices have soared, all those fading, stucco bungalows have become increasingly desirable to more affluent residents.

That could be an unpleasant change for a liberal such as Rep. Pete Stark. Yet his growing seniority and clout in tax and health matters provide a solid platform from which to assist the district. Stark is high in seniority on the powerful Ways and Means

Pete Stark

Committee. One day he may chair it. That has made him a key player in tax reform and a factor in almost any California issue that includes a money component.

Stark also is used to swimming against the tide and winning. During the Vietnam War era, he started his own bank in Walnut Creek and pulled in deposits throughout the Bay Area by using peace symbols on his checks. By age 31, he had founded his second bank and was well on his way to multimillionaire status. With such personal wealth and banking skills, it was something of a marvel that he managed to bounce 64 checks at the House bank. While that was going on, he compiled the dubious record of sixth-highest congressional spender on junk mail sent to constituents. The National Taxpayers' Union estimated that his mailings cost taxpayers $93,765 in 1991-92.

In 1986, the political arm of the American Medical Association spent some $200,000 to bankroll an opponent, but Stark crushed him, garnering 70 percent of the vote. Stark continues to be a consistent "no" vote on issues that pit the AMA against consumers. He has since become chair of the Ways and Means health subcommittee in charge of Medi-Care.

In 1993, Stark took over chairmanship of the District of Columbia Committee. The committee does little to boost Stark's stature in his district and requires a great deal of time. Nonetheless, he has always been a diligent member of the panel.

PERSONAL: elected 1972; born Nov. 11, 1931, in Milwaukee, Wis.; home, Fremont; education, B.S. Massachusetts Institute of Technology 1953, M.B.A. UC Berkeley 1960; wife Carolyn, four children; Unitarian.

CAREER: U.S. Air Force, 1955-57; founder and president of a bank and a savings and loan institution, 1961-72.

COMMITTEES: District of Columbia (chairman); Ways and Means; (select) Narcotics Abuse and Control; Joint Economic Committee.

OFFICES: Suite 239, Cannon Building, Washington, D.C. 20515, (202) 225-5065; district, Suite 500, 22320 Foothill Blvd., Hayward, 94541, (415) 635-1092.

REGISTRATION: 58% D, 27% R

1992 CAMPAIGN:	Stark – D	60.2%	$539,560
	Verne Teyler – R	31.6%	$37,305
1990 CAMPAIGN:	Stark – D	59%	$525,271
	Victor Romero – R	41%	$206,798

RATINGS:	ADA	ACU	AFL/CIO	LCV	NCSC	NTU	USCC
	95	6	90	100	95	51	19

Number of checks bounced at the House bank: 64.

William M. Thomas (R)
21st Congressional District

The outline of the 21st District doesn't resemble anything tangible since it was pieced together out of what was left over when the San Joaquin Valley was reapportioned. Nonetheless, its boundaries make some sense. It includes the mountain and foothill areas on both sides of the southern end of the valley. Here and there, it intrudes on the valley floor to take in much of Bakersfield and the small towns running north as far as Visalia. The economy is based on oil and agriculture, and is bedrock conservative.

The longtime congressman from the area, William Thomas, was once a rising force in Republican politics. He was vice chair of the National Republican Congressional Committee, California representative

William Thomas

on the GOP policy body that makes House committee assignments and was considered an expert on reapportionment. He seemed to know what buttons to push to get recalcitrant Republicans aboard Reagan administration bills. And the former community college instructor has done a lot to bring young people into the party, using campaign funds to conduct talent searches for people to fill minor posts and holding weekend retreats for college students.

GOP infighting, however, has greatly diminished his role over the years. First he was smacked by moderates in the delegation, who bounced him off the panel that dispenses committee assignments. Then conservatives came after him with a one-two punch. Rep. David Dreier of Claremont replaced him on the National Republican Congressional Committee and Rep. John Doolittle of Rocklin took over as the state GOP point-man on reapportionment. More recently, House GOP Whip Newt Gingrich was behind an attempt to remove Thomas as ranking Republican on the House Administration Committee.

Back home, his tinkering in state party and Kern County politics has distanced him from some of his oldest allies: former Assemblyman Joe Shell of Bakersfield and state Senate Minority Leader Ken Maddy of Fresno. "The Thomas faction and its leader believe if you're not with us 1,000 percent, you're against us," said former Assemblyman Phil Wyman, R-Tehachapi. "It's the kind of mentality you expect from a warlord." But Thomas contends that his adversaries "don't want to broaden the base of the party." Too many of the party's current leaders, he says, have developed comfortable niches in the GOP hierarchy and don't want to risk them by sharing power with others.

Despite his setbacks, Thomas is an important minority party player on fiscal matters in the House, having secured seats on both the Budget and the Ways and Means committees. He has supported increasing the retirement age for Social Security and was chief Republican sponsor of a bill to require uniform poll-closing hours so that early results from Eastern states don't influence the national outcome.

PERSONAL: elected 1978; born Dec. 6, 1941, in Wallace, Idaho; home, Bakersfield; education, A.A. Santa Ana College 1959, B.A. San Francisco State University 1963, M.A. 1965; wife Sharon, two children; Baptist.

CAREER: instructor, Bakersfield Community College, 1965-74; California assemblyman, 1974-78.

COMMITTEES: House Administration; Ways and Means.

OFFICES: Suite 2209, Rayburn Building, Washington, D.C. 20515, (202) 225-2915, FAX (202) 225-8798; district, Suite 220, 4100 Truxton Ave., Bakersfield 93309, (805) 327-3611; 319 W. Murray St., Visalia 93291, (209) 627-6549.

REGISTRATION: 41.6% D, 46.4% R

1992 CAMPAIGN:	Thomas – R	65.2%	$586,000
	Deborah Volmer – D	34.7	$23,260
1990 CAMPAIGN:	Thomas – R	59%	$430,525
	Michael Thomas – D	36%	$695

RATINGS:	ADA	ACU	AFL/CIO	LCV	NCSC	NTU	USCC
	15	77	13	15	9	75	92

Number of checks bounced at the House bank: 119.

Esteban E. Torres (D)
34th Congressional District

It seems appropriate that a large chunk of the district that sent Richard Nixon to Congress nearly a half-century ago is now represented by a Latino. From Montebello to La Puente and from Whittier to Santa Fe Springs, this area was almost exclusively white suburbs in Nixon's time. Citrus was still a major industry and voters were died-in-the-wool Republicans.

Esteban Torres

Today, the 34th is one of the most diverse middle-class districts in California. Hispanics are the largest single ethnic group followed by whites, Asians, African Americans and Pacific Islanders. Many of the residents work in aerospace, manufacturing, retailing, refinery and government jobs, and two-income families are common. Defense cutbacks have hit hard in the area. A growing number of Koreans are taking over the retail shops that clutter the main streets. Most voters are traditionally Democratic, but conservative and committed to family values.

Their congressman, Esteban Torres, shares those family concerns and is strongly anti-abortion. But on most other matters, he is stridently liberal. His preoccupation with the welfare of Third World countries and encouraging large social programs from Washington doesn't play particularly well in this district. That helps explain why he has had well-financed challengers from time to time.

Torres helps compensate for his more-liberal-than-the-district views by campaigning almost nonstop. He is constantly in the district, attending community gatherings, visiting nursing homes and assisting Democratic hopefuls at other levels. One of his causes has been the seriously polluted water table in the San Gabriel Valley. The issue has given him a lot of visibility, but meaningful cleanup is probably impossible. Torres' staff is considered one of the better in the delegation. And he also has another ace in his hand: the fund-raising support of the Berman-Waxman machine.

Like many of the residents, Torres got where he is by working hard and overcoming racial barriers. He went from assembly-line worker to union official, to poverty programs and then on to posts where he could promote his concerns in President Jimmy Carter's administration. He remains committed to government as a force in improving social interaction in society. The district seems to be moving away from him ideologically, but not quickly enough to threaten his tenure. And as more people lose their jobs, Torres' views become more popular.

PERSONAL: elected 1982; born Jan. 30, 1930, in Miami, Ariz.; home, La Puente; education, A.A. East Los Angeles Community College 1959, B.A. CSU

Los Angeles 1963, graduate work at the University of Maryland and American University; wife Arcy, five children; no religious affiliation.

CAREER: U.S. Army, 1949-53; assembly-line worker, Chrysler Corp., 1953-63; United Auto Workers representative, 1963-68; director, East Los Angeles Community Union, 1968-74; UAW representative, 1974-77; ambassador to UNESCO, 1977-79; special assistant to President Jimmy Carter, 1979-81; president, International Enterprise and Development Corp, 1981-82.

COMMITTEE: Appropriations.

OFFICES: Suite 1740, Longworth Building, Washington, D.C. 20515, (202) 225-5256, FAX (202) 225-9711; district, Suite 101, 8819 Whittier Blvd., Pico Rivera 90660, (213) 695-0702, (818) 961-3978.

REGISTRATION: 61.6% D, 28.2% R

1992 CAMPAIGN:	Torres – D	61.2%	$203,790
	Jay Hernandez – R	34%	$119,177
1990 CAMPAIGN:	Torres – D	61%	$241,635
	John Eastman – R	39%	$75,581

RATINGS:	ADA	ACU	AFL/CIO	LCV	NCSC	NTU	USCC
	85	2	98	92	97	12	24

Number of checks bounced at the House bank: None.

Walter R. Tucker (D)
37th Congressional District

Walter Tucker

This district begins in South-Central Los Angeles and runs south through Lynnwood, Compton, Carson and parts of Long Beach and Signal Hill. To the north are the bleak neighborhoods that were part of the riot corridor following the acquittal of the police officers charged in the Rodney King beating. The farther south one goes, the more middle-class the communities become. But they are still predominately blue-collar areas where many people have lost jobs in the aerospace industry. Latinos outnumber African Americans in the district and the most affluent families usually have two wage-earners. Crime, jobs, health care and the general quality of life are important issues among those who vote. The district, however, has one of the lowest rates of turnout in the state.

Rep. Mervyn Dymally tried to hand off this district to his daughter when he ended his lackluster career here in 1992. But she lost in the primary to Compton Mayor Walter Tucker, who had no Republican opponent in November. Tucker, whose father also was mayor of Compton, could have pursued a career in more pleasant surroundings. But the criminal attorney, former teacher and minister, returned to his home and worked diligently to make a difference in a high-crime community where unemployment exceeded 20 percent through all of 1992.

Tucker went to Washington from a safe district and as a young man by congressional standards. If he chooses to stay in Congress, he'll have a unique opportunity to work for social change.

PERSONAL: elected 1992; born May 28, 1957, in Compton; home, Compton; attended Princeton University, B.A. University of Southern California, J.D. Georgetown University; wife Robin, two children; non-denominational Protestant.

CAREER: teacher, 1984-86; attorney, 1986-present; minister, Bread of Life Christian Center; mayor of Compton, 1991-92.

COMMITTEES: Public Works and Transportation; Small Business.

OFFICES: Suite 419, Cannon Building, Washington, D.C. 20515, (202) 225-7924; district, 145 W. Compton Blvd., Compton 90220, (310) 763-5850.

REGISTRATION: 76.8% D, 13.3% R

1992 CAMPAIGN: Tucker – D   85.7% $225,817

RATINGS: Newly Elected.

Maxine Waters (D)
35th Congressional District

This district slid somewhat southward after reapportionment, removing a large chunk of Watts, the center of the infamous riots of the mid-1960s and again in 1992. Neighborhoods in Inglewood, Hawthorne and Gardena were added, but it continues to be California's most heavily Democratic district. Times may change, but there is a constancy to the issues here — poverty, crime, drugs, lack of community facilities, poor schools, substandard housing and a police force that shows little sensitivity to the problems.

One newer element is street gangs. The area was mostly African American when Watts was burning nearly a quarter century ago. Now, African Ameri-

Maxine Waters

cans and Latinos are about evenly matched, and the two cultures collide nightly in vicious gang warfare. The conflict is not all racial, however. It is often black against black or brown against brown in battles where crack cocaine figures prominently as the cause — or at least as a co-conspirator. There had been a growing influx of Korean shopkeepers. But the violence directed against them during the 1992 riots has caused an exodus.

This tough area has spawned an equally tough congresswoman, Maxine Waters. She is a brassy bundle of energy who approaches most issues with a firmly closed mind. Facts don't interest her, only preconceived notions. Around the state Capitol, where she spent 14 years in the Assembly, Waters was known as "Mama Doc" for her absolutist approach to politics. Always strident, sometimes yelling, "She has a tongue that could open a wall safe," a colleague said. When Dan Lungren was trying unsuccessfully to win confirmation as state treasurer, Waters openly baited other minorities who testified in his behalf. But with Speaker Willie Brown as her mentor, Waters could get away with almost anything.

No one has ever accused Waters of shirking work, however. She grew up in poverty and began her career as a Head Start teacher and civic organizer in Watts. She was an aide to Los Angeles City Councilman David Cunningham before winning her Assembly seat in 1976. Thanks to Brown, Waters held key committee appointments that gave her the clout to wage war for "my constituency," as she calls it: the poor, the non-white and women. She had a fair number of successes. But there doubtless would have been many more if it had not been for her caustically combative style. Republicans tended to vote against almost any Waters bill simply because she was the author.

Along the way, Waters established herself as a player in national politics, one of an inner circle of advisers to Jesse Jackson and his 1984 and '88 campaigns for the presidency. She was instrumental in persuading Willie Brown to become Jackson's national campaign chairman in 1988. In 1992, she again stumped for a Jackson candidacy well into the primary season and long after it was clear Jackson had no chance of winning the Democratic nomination.

But then came the verdict in the Rodney King trial and Los Angeles again exploded in flames. Waters emerged as the African American leader most frequently quoted by the news media. That didn't escape the notice of the Clinton campaign, which was attempting to sow alliances with other African American opinion leaders after having sidelined Jackson. Mickey Kantor, Clinton's national campaign chairman, recruited Waters for the largely symbolic position of campaign co-chair along with Los Angeles County Supervisor Gloria Molina.

It must have given Bill Clinton and Al Gore pause when Waters began calling President Bush a "racist" and said just after their nomination: "I hope the ticket gets elected, but this is the last time I will support an all-white anything." Nonetheless, she spent the fall working tirelessly for the ticket. They owe her. As the Clinton-Gore era opened, Waters was positioned not only to push for White House support for her legislative agenda, but to demand the federal aid that Bush promised for South Los Angeles but never delivered.

PERSONAL: elected 1990; born Aug. 15, 1938, in St. Louis, Mo.; home, Los Angeles; education, B.A. CSU Los Angeles; husband Sidney Williams, three children.

CAREER: Head Start teacher; chief deputy to Los Angeles City Councilman David Cunningham, 1973-76; partner in a public relations firm; assemblywoman, 1976-90.

COMMITTEES: Banking, Finance and Urban Affairs; Veterans' Affairs.

OFFICES: Suite 1207, Longworth Building, Washington, D.C. 20515. (202) 225-2201, FAX (202) 225-7854; district, 4509 S. Broadway, Los Angeles 90037, (213) 233-0733.

REGISTRATION: 79.9% D, 11.1% R

1992 CAMPAIGN:	Waters – D	82.5%	$182,045
	Nate Truman – R	14%	$6,918
1990 CAMPAIGN:	Waters – D	80%	$740,793
	Bill De Witt – R	18%	$0

RATINGS:	ADA	ACU	AFL/CIO	LCV	NCSC	NTU	USCC
	95	0	100	77	100	59	11

Number of checks bounced at the House bank: 5.

Henry A. Waxman (D)
29th Congressional District

Mention Los Angeles to most Americans and they begin picturing the palm-draped mansions of Beverly Hills, svelte bodies strolling Rodeo Drive and intrigues by Hollywood movie titans. It is all here in the 29th District, which stretches along the southern flank of the Hollywood Hills from Santa Monica's beaches to Interstate 5. Since World War II, this ever-spreading center of the entertainment industry has been solidly Jewish and liberal. At the southern and seedier end of the district, an area where the Hollywood technicians and extras once lived, the residents are increasingly Hispanic and Korean. These minorities, however, tend to vote in small numbers. There also are an increasing number of gays, especially in West Hollywood, and they do vote.

Henry Waxman

Rep. Henry Waxman, one of the sharpest intellects in Congress, has drawn on the extreme wealth of the district to build one of the most important power bases in the Democratic Party with Rep. Howard Berman. The Berman-Waxman organization raises vast sums of money and conducts hardball political campaigns, often with extensive use of direct mail.

Most of the day-to-day operations are run by Berman's brother, Michael, and Carl D'Agostino, who own a campaign management firm known as BAD Campaigns. But the congressmen are instrumental in recruiting promising candidates and in seeing to it that their campaigns get infusions of money and workers. Their interests don't stop with Congress. Their hands reach deeply into local and national politics as well. Gary Hart's presidential campaign was one of their causes until he crashed and burned.

The "westside gang," as they are known, backed a series of losers in the 1992 campaigns and also made some important blunders such as getting out their primary slate mailer late. But they remain a potent force by dint of their access to money, if nothing else.

Waxman has bucked the House seniority system to grab key subcommittees, where he advances his interests in health, clean air and geriatrics issues. Probably no Democrat has more influence on health issues. During the Reagan and Bush administrations, he was the Democrats' first line of defense against weakening health and air programs. He was also a leader on abortion rights and funding for AIDS research.

Waxman's seat is secure, which apparently is why he can bounce 434 checks at the House bank (second highest in the delegation) and then say his financial affairs are "a private matter." Waxman has never been known for humility, but he does carry heavy legislative loads. He is on the verge of moving into the top leadership of the House. If the right openings occur, it shouldn't take much to propel him further.

PERSONAL: elected 1974; born Sept. 12, 1939, in Los Angeles; home, Los Angeles; education, B.A. UCLA 1961, J.D. 1964; wife Janet, two children; Jewish.

CAREER: attorney, 1965-68; Assembly, 1968-74.

COMMITTEES: Energy and Commerce; Government Operations; (select) Aging.

OFFICES: Suite 2408, Rayburn Building, Washington, D.C. 20515, (202) 225-3976, FAX (202) 225-4099; district, Suite 400, 8425 West Third St., Los Angeles 90048, (213) 651-1040.

REGISTRATION: 57.6% D, 27.8% R

1992 CAMPAIGN:	Waxman – D	61.3%	$361,280
	Mark Robbins – R	25.7%	$142,692
1990 CAMPAIGN:	Waxman – D	69%	$500,847
	John Cowles – R	25%	$1,835

RATINGS:	ADA	ACU	AFL/CIO	LCV	NCSC	NTU	USCC
	95	6	88	92	99	11	22

Number of checks bounced at the House bank: 434.

Lynn Woolsey (D)
6th Congressional District

Some of the great mortgages of the Western world are nestled among the fir and redwood trees of Marin County, which makes up half of the 6th District electorate. The remainder live in all but the northeast corner of Sonoma County, where the population ranges from affluent urbanites and vintners to retirees with modest means, poverty stricken farm workers and a thriving counterculture. Some of the latter who have been there since the '60s are sitting on extraordinarily valuable real estate.

Although the liberal San Francisco portion of the district was lost to reapportionment, the district that spawned Sen. Barbara Boxer should be safe haven for a liberal Democrat. Its residents are informed people who turn out to vote. Marin is still the trendsetter, a bastion of yuppie attitudes long before the term was coined. Voters tend to be environmentally aware, demanding of public services and economically conservative.

Lynn Woolsey

When Boxer decided to move on, however, her heir apparent appeared to be Assemblyman Bill Filante of Greenbrae, a hard-working and almost-liberal Republican who had been bucking the Democratic registration in the district for 14 years. But shortly after the primary, Filante had surgery for brain cancer and was forced to turn his campaign over to surrogates. Until Election Day, Filante's representatives continued to insist he would recover. He died within six weeks.

That left the field clear for an obscure Petaluma councilwoman named Lynn Woolsey, who raised a huge war chest and campaigned tirelessly as though she were the underdog. Woolsey subsequently became the first former welfare mom to be elected to Congress.

Woolsey landed on welfare after a 1968 divorce that left her with children ages 1, 2 and 5. She got a job as a secretary, but couldn't earn enough to support the family. She has called that period "the hell years of my life," as she struggled unsuccessfully to get child support from her deadbeat ex-husband. Woolsey eventually remarried, earned a night college degree, built up a successful personnel business and spent two terms on the Petaluma City Council.

As one might expect, her priorities in Congress include assisting welfare recipients to move into productive employment and making deadbeat dads accountable. She has also been a booster of tax incentives for business expansion, spending for education and for using the peace dividend to finance national health care. From the Committee on Education and Labor, she'll be well-positioned to work in those areas.

PERSONAL: Elected 1992; born Nov. 3, 1937, in Seattle; home, Petaluma; B.A University of San Francisco, 1980; separated, four children; Presbyterian.

CAREER: office worker and personnel manager, 1969-80; owner of personnel business, 1980-92; lecturer, College of Marin and Dominican College; Petaluma City Council, 1984-92.

COMMITTEES: Education and Labor; Government Operations.

OFFICES: Suite 439, Cannon Building, Washington, D.C. 20510, (202) 224-3121; district, Suite 205, 1301 Redwood Way, Petaluma 94954, (707) 795-1462; Suite 140, 1050 Northgate Dr., San Rafael 94903, (415) 507-9554.

REGISTRATION: 54.8% D, 30.4 R

| **1992 CAMPAIGN**: | Woolsey – D | 65.2% | $515,460 |
| | William Filante – R | 33.6% | $410,461 |

RATINGS: Newly elected.

8

Lobbyists–a vital link in the process

When infamous lobbyist Artie Samish appeared on the cover of Collier's magazine in 1949, posed with a ventriloquist's dummy on his knee, he etched an image into the political consciousness of California: lobbyists as puppeteers standing in the shadows pulling strings while legislators danced vacuously on the public stage. Reality is much more complicated and far less sinister. Lobbyists are neither good nor evil. They have become, however, a linchpin in the legislative process, and their importance will grow even more in the coming years as voter-mandated legislative term limits take effect.

Lobbyists are a critical link between lawmakers and industries, professional associations, consumer advocates and other combatants in California politics. They carry the intricate information about the details of an industry or the desires of a professional group to the people who make the laws. The lion's share of the bills introduced in the Legislature are proposed, and at least sketched-out, by lobbyists. They also help devise legislative strategies, manage bills, work with staff members, produce grass-roots pressure and, often, manage the media.

Legislative advocates, as they prefer to call themselves, are the professionals in the multilayered, arcane world of California politics. They deal in a bewildering system that has more twists and turns and hidden hallways than the Capitol. It is an environment in which the unguided can easily end up running down a corridor that goes nowhere.

Influential lobbyists are successful for a host of reasons. Chief among them is the ability of their clients to make campaign contributions – or "participate in the political process," as it is euphemistically called in the trade. But that is only one tool, and few advocates remain effective using money alone. The vast majority trade heavily on their knowledge of the Legislature and the causes they represent, their political acumen, the grass-roots connections of their clients and, perhaps most important, their individual relationships with elected officials and staff.

One of most profound changes in the "third house," as the lobbying corps is called, is the shift to the full-service lobbying company. There are fewer and fewer major one- or two-person operations that rely on their good will in the Capitol and their overall knowledge of the political system. Instead, as in Washington, D.C., a cadre of firms have sprouted with specialists, in-house attorneys, public relations experts – all of which look and run like law firms. In fact, to explain their role, lobbyists most often compare themselves with lawyers. They say they are advocates, plain and simple. They are hired to win today and again tomorrow and to protect their clients just as lawyers do whatever is possible to protect theirs. California's massive growth has created even more demand for advocates. As the booms continue in population, business and government, as society grows more complex, as every interest in the state becomes more and more interwoven with government, the demand for lobbyists has increased.

In 1977, the secretary of state's office registered 538 lobbyists and 761 clients who had hired them. In 1992, there were 925 lobbyists and 1,615 clients. Ironically, the passage of anti-government, anti-tax Proposition 13 in 1978 helped fuel that growth by centralizing the financing of schools and local governments in Sacramento. Interests with a stake in those finances muscled up by hiring more lobbyists in the capital. The best measure of growth is the amount of money spent lobbying the Legislature. According to the Fair Political Practices Commission, $40 million was spent on lobbying during the 1975-76 session of the Legislature. In just the first half of the 1991-92 session, more than $106.3 million was spent by trade associations, corporations, utilities, public interest groups and others.

A GROWTH INDUSTRY

Lobbyists say privately that one major reason for the increased demand is that everybody else is getting a lobbyist these days. Interests entering the legislative field feel like soldiers without rifles if they are not armed with a good lobbyist.

But it is not just an arms race in dealing with the Legislature that has sparked the explosion. Industries and interests are coming to realize that all levels of government, including state agencies and commissions, require expert representation. The state's gigantic bureaucracy can be even more unfathomable than the Legislature. A growing number of lobbyists are former state officials who have learned the pathways and players in key state agencies. And they are finding themselves in demand from a variety of interests with huge stakes in the decisions dealt out by the regulators. The state Departments of Food and Agriculture and Health Services, for example, played key roles in defining and administering Proposition 65, the 1986 Safe Drinking Water Act. That law has had a multimillion-dollar impact on scores of businesses. As a result, chemical, pesticide, agricultural and other California companies with a stake have lobbyists working those agencies.

The labyrinthine legislative process and the ever-increasing demands on law-makers' time and attention make it nearly impossible for someone outside of the inner political circles to have much of an impact on the workings of the Legislature. Given the lobbyists' essential role, it would seem the door is open for them to play puppet-masters in the way Artie Samish once did. But that is not the case. In fact, the same system that makes lobbyists so vital prevents any one advocate or interest from asserting control. There are so many interests and so much pressure from every quarter, that it is virtually impossible for one lobbyist, or even a handful, to indiscriminately muscle bills through.

It takes a monumental effort to push any measure burdened with controversy through the Capitol. The bill must survive at least two committees and a floor vote in each house, possibly a conference committee and other floor votes, and then it must win the governor's signature. Those are seven chances, at a minimum, to kill a bill. Passing it means winning at every step. And it is easy for many lobbyists, especially those representing single-issue interests, to throw enough doubt into lawmakers' minds to get them to vote "no" or at least to be absent so there are not enough votes to pass a bill. For legislators, there is always less political damage in sticking with the status quo. In fact, much of what lobbyists do is defensive. They spend much more energy trying to kill bills that might hurt their clients than breaking new ground or pushing proposals.

ALL SHAPES, SIZES AND SKILLS

So, with all those lobbyists wandering the halls of the Capitol, the teeming atmosphere of California politics looks at first glance as if it might fit the image of the marketplace of ideas and interests envisioned by the framers of American democracy. But only at first glance. The Capitol is not a place where decision-makers blend those ideas and choose simply on merit. And if any one set of players is responsible for influencing the decision-making process, it would be the lobbyists.

For one reason, lobbyists, like anyone else, come in a variety of levels of skill, influence and experience. The better ones often win regardless of the merits of their case because victories in the Capitol are based on politics, not virtue. Each different species of lobbyist brings its own weapons and weaknesses. These include:

• **Public-interest lobbyists**: Often called "white-hat lobbyists," these are the people who work for consumer groups, good-government organizations, environmentalists or any of those people who aim to represent the public at large. These lobbyists, for the most part, are the weakest in the Capitol. Their best weapon is public sentiment. Because of that, they are about the only lobbyists consistently willing to talk with reporters and to make their issues public. They often resort to calling press conferences to announce their positions or unhappiness, hoping it will generate enough public reaction to influence the votes of legislators. But with only meager financial resources they have little to offer lawmakers other than public approval. As often as not, they are fighting against moneyed interests, and unless the issue is something that will ignite the public – and there are few of those since most Californians pay scant attention to the Legislature – public-interest lobbyists spend much of their time working on damage control rather than passing legislation.

• **Association lobbyists**: These are the advocates who work for one specific organization, such as the California Association of Realtors. Some of these organizations have tremendous resources, a large grass-roots network and fat campaign war chests to dole out. And depending on their causes they, too, sometimes feel comfortable using the press and public sentiment to help push their issues. But they also have some disadvantages. Since their legislative goals have to be agreed upon by the association's directors and membership, they often have less flexibility to adjust in midstream. In addition, they spend a good deal of their time organizing their association, and trying to keep internal politics out of state politics.

• **Contract lobbyists**: These are the hired guns, the quintessence of what the public envisions as the lobbying corps. And for the major contract lobbyists and the powerful lobbying firms handling large client loads, that image generally fits. These individuals often have been around the Capitol for years, know the game from every angle and have enough of a client list, campaign war chest, history in politics, stored up favors and political acumen to make lawmakers listen. But contract lobbyists come in many sizes and shapes. Some work for public-interest groups, which forces them to operate like those "white-hat lobbyists." Others represent cities or semipublic entities and can distribute few campaign contributions. Still others work for smaller, less powerful companies or industries and have never gathered enough clout to make the inner circles.

• **Company lobbyists**: Some of the larger companies have their own in-house advocates. They are some of the real inside players in the Capitol, with the resources and money to be influential. And like many contract lobbyists – and legislators – they often are most comfortable functioning out of the glare of public scrutiny. Since they work for only one client, they generally have the flexibility to compromise and roll with the inevitable political punches. But because they only represent one company, no matter how powerful, they usually need to work within coalitions or at least try to eliminate opposition from companies within their industry. If they cannot, they can find themselves with minimal influence.

THE IMPORTANCE OF MONEY

For lobbyists, success goes to those who understand best the nature of influence. They understand timing, organization and the value of information. They have built relationships with legislators, consultants, even a key secretary or two. And, for the big-time lobbyists, they understand the connection between politics and money.

It is an axiom of modern political life, especially in a state such as California, that a politician without money is not a politician for long. In these days of computer-aided, television-oriented, high-tech campaigns, no candidate without a healthy chunk of cash can hope to win. And no group is more aware of that than the lobbyists. They have found themselves squarely in the middle of the campaign financing free-for-all.

Lobbyists have become the middlemen between clients requesting favors and politicians seeking campaign contributions. But take lobbyists out of the picture and the interests that contribute and the legislators who raise money would still find ways to connect. In fact, many lobbyists portray themselves as victims of a system that requires nearly constant fund-raising. That view is in vivid contrast to the widely held image of lobbyists padding the halls of the Capitol hoping to corrupt legislators with bundles of bills in their briefcases.

Victims or not, those with money still win their share of Capitol battles. And the need for cash is a fact of life lobbyists frequently have to sell to clients. Without money, the lobbyists lose access to legislators.

The actual impact of campaign contributions on the drafting of laws can be small since many other lobbyists and interests are also buying access. Generally, money plays the deciding role only in turf fights that do not affect a legislator's district or do not become an issue in the media, such as when banks and savings and loans battle over state regulations.

While the influence of money is not necessarily direct, it is thorough. For starters, the big-money interests can afford to hire the best lobbyists, who in turn use that money to conduct public relations campaigns, to organize in the districts of targeted legislators and to hire enough staff to make sure nothing is missed.

In addition, the skills of those top lobbyists often include the judicious deployment of the client's campaign contributions. Many lobbyists make sure a client's money goes to legislators in a position to help that client, but they also funnel some of that money to lawmakers who have been consistent friends. That in turn adds clout to the lobbyist's own status independent of his or her clients.

When a lawmaker is approached by a top lobbyist such as Clayton Jackson, that legislator is not simply thinking about the one employer whose cause Jackson may be advocating, but about Jackson's long list of clients, which in his case includes insurance, finance and high-tech companies whose combined campaign contributions total more than $2 million annually. Legislators have too little time to see all the people who want to argue their cases. And when push comes to shove and there are two lobbyists waiting in the office lobby, the one who will get in is always the one who has consistently contributed to campaigns.

ALL RELATIONSHIPS ARE PERSONAL

In fact, the investment of campaign money earns more than simple access because, as in any business, when two people have dealt with and grown to trust each other over the years, a relationship develops. That brings up another primary rule of California politics: Everything that happens in the Capitol comes down to basic human relationships, rather than institutional ones. Lobbyists and legislators hold nothing more precious than their relationships with each other. If a lawmaker likes you and trusts you, he will listen. If a lobbyist thinks of you as a friend, he will make sure you receive timely information and equally useful campaign contributions.

In the storm that is Capitol politics, both legislators and lobbyists are grateful for any safe harbor. For veteran lawmakers and influential lobbyists, those symbiotic relationships often grow into genuine friendships. And those friendships, creations of convenience though they may be, can have as much influence on California's laws as any other aspect of the state's politics.

The most notable advantage of a lobbyist's friendship with a legislator is the member's willingness to listen to a friend argue for or against a bill. That becomes even more significant during the end-of-session tempests, when hundreds of bills can be dispatched in a few hours. That is when bills are being revised, members are under the gun and a lobbyist doesn't have time to document arguments about a set of amendments. Members are left with no choice but to ask the lobbyist if the changes are acceptable to his or her clients. If they trust each other, the lobbyist can look the legislator in the eye and tell him the truth – with neither feeling nervous.

A study done for former Assembly Speaker Jesse Unruh during the mid-1970s asked legislators what they thought was the most corrupting influence in politics. The answer that came back the most often was "friendship." One legislator said, "I never voted for a bad bill, but I voted for a lot of bad authors."

THE INVASION OF EX-MEMBERS

Former lawmakers are a rapidly growing class of lobbyists that begin with ready-made friendships in the Capitol. These people have worked together, seen each other almost every day, experienced the same pressures and developed the same interests. They have an emotional bond like university alumni. Approximately two-dozen former legislators lobby either full- or part-time. Others are not registered, either because they do not lobby enough to qualify as official lobbyists or because their contacts and connections are less direct.

The list of some of the more prominent or active among the former legislators includes former Sens. John Briggs, Clair Burgener, Dennis Carpenter, John Foran, Bob Wilson and George Zenovich; and former Assembly members Gordon Duffy, Jean Duffy, Joe Gonsalves, John Knox, Frank Murphy Jr., Robert Naylor, Paul Priolo and John P. Quimby. Former Sen. William Campbell also belongs on the list. As president of the California Manufacturers Association, he is not registered to lobby. But Campbell spends a great deal of his time maintaining old Capitol ties, getting the word out on what would be good for the CMA and showing up on the legislative floors – just coincidentally, he insists – about the time a vote is due on a critical CMA issue.

In addition, former legislative or administration staff members turn their expertise and inside relationships into influential lobbying jobs, often focusing on the committees and subject areas in which they had been involved. There are dozens of lobbyists who are ex-legislative staff members, but the largest group is probably the legion of former aides to Assembly Speaker Willie Brown, which includes Bill Rutland, Kathleen Snodgrass, Jackson Gualco, John Mockler and Kent Stoddard.

Former administration officials, of course, find themselves in great demand to lobby the agencies in which they once worked. No major Wilson aides had defected to the lobbying corps by early 1993, but the third house is full of former Deukmejian administrators, including Michael Franchetti, Deukmejian's first finance director; David Swoap, once a health and welfare secretary; David Ackerman, a former deputy business, transportation and housing undersecretary; Rodney Blonien, a former corrections undersecretary; and Randy Ward, who headed the state Department of Conservation. Former Deukmejian chief of staff Steven Merksamer also must be included in that list, although he is not a registered lobbyist. Merksamer's law/lobbying firm – Nielsen, Merksamer, Hodgson, Parrinello & Mueller – represents some of America's largest companies and is one of the most influential firms on the state scene. Another person who exerts great personal influence is Kirk West, a business, transportation and housing secretary under Deukmejian who currently heads the California Chamber of Commerce. There also are top lobbyists who were state officials in earlier administrations, including Richard B. Spohn, former Gov. Jerry Brown's director of the state Department of Consumer Affairs; and George Steffes, an aide to then-Gov. Ronald Reagan in the early 1970s.

A study in 1986 by political scientists Jerry Briscoe and Charles Bell, then at the University of the Pacific and the University of California, Davis, respectively, found 36 percent of the registered lobbyists had served in government. This steady stream from the Capitol to the third house for years inspired "anti-revolving door" bills from lawmakers or public-interest groups such as Common Cause. Those proposals would have prohibited state officials and lawmakers from lobbying their former houses or agencies for a year or two after leaving state service, but most of them were brushed aside by the people who had the most to lose, the legislators themselves.

In 1990, however, constituents and good-government groups were putting pressure on lawmakers to clean up their ethics. Under the cloud of an FBI investigation, and worried about looming ethics and term-limit initiatives, the lawmakers passed their own half-hearted ethics reform bill and put it before voters as Proposition 112. The measure, which limited lawmakers' outside income in exchange for creating the independent Citizens Compensation Commission to set salaries, included anti-revolving door provisions that prohibited former lawmakers or top-level administrators from lobbying their old colleagues for one year after leaving office.

Proposition 112 was approved by voters in June 1990, and those locks on the revolving doors were to go into effect Jan. 1, 1991. But then-Gov. Deukmejian, ever-watchful for the interests of his friends, forced the effective date to be changed to Jan. 7 – the day after he left office – which made his entire staff exempt.

The fact that former lawmakers and staffers are in demand as lobbyists underscores the changes in the third house in recent years. One of the biggest changes may be the nature of the relationships between lawmakers and lobbyists, which today are most often based on shared interests and friendships. Sometimes families of lawmakers and lobbyists play together on weekends or holidays. That is a far cry from the days of duck hunting or drunken revelry in the 1930s, '40s and '50s, when Artie Samish said he supplied his legislative friends with "a baked potato, a girl or money."

While Samish, who was imprisoned for tax-evasion in 1956, was probably the most extreme case in California, many lobbyists used a few good meals or a round of drinks to create a bridge to lawmakers. With that bridge, they could then argue the merits of their cases. Those bridges were built on an old-fashioned, good-old-boy network. Some of the more well-known lobbyists ran up tabs of $1,500-a-month wining and dining legislators. And, not infrequently, lawmakers signed a lobbyist's name to a restaurant or bar tab even when the lobbyist was not there.

There also were regular, institutionalized social affairs paid for by a number of lobbyists and open to all lawmakers and many key members of their staffs. The most spectacular of those was the "Moose Milk," a lavish lunch and open bar held Thursdays in the former El Mirador Hotel across from the Capitol. There also was the lunch at the Derby Club on Tuesdays and the "Clam and Corral" at the Senator Hotel on Wednesdays. The purpose was nothing more than good times, good will and, of course, access.

THE OLD-BOY NETWORK BREAKS DOWN

Those days began to change in 1966, when Californians made their Legislature full time. That meant career politicians and full-time staff. No longer were lobbyists the only people who understood the state's industries and the fine points in bills. Lawmakers and their larger staffs had more time and more information of their own. And with the professionalization of the Legislature, lawmakers began to develop both areas of expertise and fiefdoms to protect. Specialists, usually committee chairmen, emerged in banking, insurance, health and dozens of others fields. For lobbyists that had two implications.

First, it meant that lobbyists had to have better, more specific information. A simple "trust me on this one" became less convincing. Lobbyists had to learn the fine points of the industries and clients they represented. And second, with power spread through the committee chairmen and their staffs, it became increasingly difficult for just a few lobbyists to handle major legislation. So lobbyists, too, became specialists. Not only did they concentrate on specific subjects, but different lobbyists became valuable to clients because of their relationships with specific lawmakers.

The biggest step in the transformation of the lobbying corps from the days of camaraderie to a law firm-like atmosphere was Proposition 9, the Political Reform Act passed in 1974. That initiative required detailed disclosure, and it limited the gifts and meals lobbyists could buy legislators to $10 a month. With that act, the Moose Milk and the free meals disappeared, eventually to be replaced by a more businesslike lobbying industry. In fact, that measure inspired a group of longtime lobbyists to form the Institute of Governmental Advocates, an association to lobby for lobbyists. The institute filed a successful lawsuit to set aside portions of the measure.

With the increasing difficulty of establishing social relationships with lawmakers, the growing complexity of society and the heightened representation of interests in recent years, many people predict the slow extinction of the one-person lobbying operation. In its place has emerged the multiservice firm with a number of lobbyists, lawyers and public-relations specialists. Some small lobbying operations have merged, others have joined with political consulting or public relations companies and still others have grown out of law firms. Whatever their origin, lobbying firms with big staffs, big client lists and big campaign war chests are coming to dominate the political landscape.

That also has changed the outside view of lobbyists. Potential clients are wooed not by connections and understanding of the system, as the old, one-person operations used to do. Instead, the big firms advertise themselves as people with the wherewithal to handle every aspect of the legislative and political battle.

There has been a change in the relationship with lawmakers as well. Because lobbyists with large client lists have less and less time to deal with their clients, they have less ability to impress upon their employers the reality of politics. Lobbyists often need to spend much of their time convincing clients to ask for tiny changes that take place over several sessions rather than to expect major revisions in the law. But as their firms grow, they simply lose the ability to convince their clients to go slow. That means lobbyists bring more and more unfiltered demands to lawmakers, making it harder for legislators to reconcile requests from different interests. The result: legislative stalemate, or lobbylock, as it is called around the Capitol.

THE ERA OF LIMITS

Passage of Proposition 140 in 1990 put in motion a radically new dynamic in the legislator-lobbyist relationship. The so-called term limits measure by retiring Los Angeles County Supervisor Pete Schabarum imposed the following:

• Constitutional officers, like the governor, are limited to two terms of four years each, or eight years. The initiative did not mention the newest constitutional officer, the insurance commissioner, thus that position has no term limit.

• State senators elected in 1990 (the even-numbered seats) are limited to two terms of four years each, or eight years. State senators who were not up for election in 1990 get one more term if they were re-elected in 1992. That anomaly in the initiative creates a paradox: State Sen. William Leonard, R-Big Bear, first elected to the Senate in 1988, must leave by 1996. However, Sen. Ralph Dills, R-Garden

Grove, first elected to the Legislature in 1938 and re-elected to the Senate in 1990, is not required to leave until 1998.

• Assembly members, who face election every two years, are limited to three terms in office, or six years. All of those elected in 1990 will be gone at the end of 1996.

• The Legislature's retirement system was eliminated.

• The Legislature's operating budget was cut by 38 percent.

• All limits were imposed for life, thus legislators and constitutional officers cannot sit out a term before running for their former offices. They can, however, seek a new office. Legislators wasted no time in seeking new career opportunities after the 1990 and 1992 elections. Some of the most knowledgeable and adept members were the first to go.

Meeting the new budget restrictions required a massive reduction in personnel, which created critical vacancies on key committee staffs. Their departure also contributed to one of the rockiest – and most unproductive – starts for a legislative session in modern times.

The loss of vast amounts of institutional memory and expertise had the immediate effect of strengthening the hand of lobbyists. As the term limits take effect, lobbyists and a dwindling number of staff members will be the only true experts in the Capitol. Opportunities for manipulation, special-interest dealing, bill drafting errors and just plain mischief will abound in coming years. The interaction between an increasing number of novice legislators and old-pro lobbyists is potentially the most important story in Sacramento during the 1990s.

9

California's movers and shakers

To the larger public, politics is an activity of politicians, the men and women who offer themselves for public office. But behind the candidates exists a complex network of professionals and amateurs who design, finance and manage the campaigns that voters see. These are the movers and shakers of politics, who have at least as much influence as the out-front candidates for office. Their motives range from ideological conviction to greed, and, if anything, their role is increasing as campaigns become more expensive and sophisticated.

California's power brokers are especially obscure because of the state's unique political system, features of which include weak party structures, non-partisan local governments and a multitude of locally based political organizations. Other major states such as Illinois and New York have more formalized political power structures. During Richard Daley's heyday as mayor of Chicago, for instance, no one doubted that he was the boss, not only in his city, but of the entire Illinois Democratic Party. Those who aspired to office, whether it was the clerkship of the smallest court or the president of the United States, had to clear through Daley or his minions.

Behind-the-scenes political power in California is wielded more indirectly. And in a state of media and money politics, rather than street-level organizations, those with access to money form the elite, a fact that becomes ever-more important as California's clout in national politics expands. The Los Angeles area has evolved into a source of national political money at least as important as the concrete canyons of New York and continues to gain strength as new campaign finance laws make direct contributions more difficult.

California has also developed a cadre of professional campaign organizers—"consultants," as they prefer to be called—who have pioneered in the sophisticated

414

techniques of mass political communications: television, computer-directed mail and, most recently, prerecorded video tapes that combine the impact of television with the selectivity of mail.

THE HOLLYWOOD BRANCH

Every four years, a little ritual takes place. Those who aspire to the White House begin booking flights to Los Angeles International Airport, not to present themselves to voters, but to schmooz with a handful of men and women who reside within a few miles of one another on the west side of Los Angeles. Most of those who make the pilgrimage to Los Angeles are Democrats because most of the west side's political financiers are Democrats, connected to the huge, Los Angeles-based entertainment industry. But not a few of them are Republicans. Prior to the 1988 presidential primary season, Republican Bob Dole raised more money out of Hollywood than did Democrat Michael Dukakis.

Hollywood types tend to be passionate about their causes and free with money, which is exactly what politicians want. It's been estimated that the Los Angeles region accounts for a fifth of all the money spent on presidential primaries.

"There's an increasingly mutual attraction between political people and entertainment people," says Stanley Scheinbaum, an economist and political activist. "The politicians like the glitz and the entertainment people like the power." But Scheinbaum and others have qualms about the growing influence of entertainers— most of whom are naive—on politics through these in-and-out fund-raising visits.

"I don't think it's healthy," he says. "Basically, a few rich people get that opportunity (to meet the politicians), and I don't think the influence of these kind of people should be any greater than of those folks in the ghettos and barrios."

Television producer Linda Bloodworth-Thomason sees the same thing in a different way. "There's a definite connection between entertainment and politics," she told one interviewer in 1992, "and the line is definitely getting more blurred. But I don't think that's a bad thing."

Bloodworth-Thomason was in a position to make that observation because she and her husband, Harry, may have been the most important two people in the rise of Bill Clinton from the relative obscurity of governing Arkansas to victory in the 1992 presidential sweepstakes.

The Thomasons, Arkansans themselves and creators of such shows as "Designing Women" and "Evening Shade," have been friends with Clinton for more than a quarter-century and first applied their media magic to Clinton after a long, boring keynote address to the 1988 Democratic national convention had made him a national laughingstock. The Thomasons arranged for Clinton to appear on the Johnny Carson show shortly thereafter to make light of his gaffe and that went a long way toward dissipating the political fallout.

As Clinton launched his 1992 campaign, the Hollywood power couple was glued to his side, introducing him into the glittery world of entertainment politics, raising money, producing his national convention video biography, overseeing his inaugural ceremonies and acquiring an $8 million beach house near Santa Barbara for Clinton to use as his vacation getaway.

Another television producer acquired political clout in 1992 despite having no direct connections with Clinton. Diane English, producer of "Murphy Brown" and other shows, was thrust into prominence when then-Vice President Dan Quayle cited "Murphy Brown" as an example of Hollywood's trashing of family values because the lead character had a child out of wedlock.

Mickey Kantor, a Los Angeles attorney with strong connections in both the entertainment and political worlds, converted his personal friendship with Clinton into the chairmanship of the Arkansan's campaign and seemed ticketed to play a major role in the formation of the Clinton administration until he was shunted aside in a power struggle with other advisers after the election. He had to settle for being Clinton's trade representative. Kantor is one of the country's most prominent political attorneys, along with partners Charles Manatt, a former national Democratic chairman, and John Tunney, a former U.S. senator. Kantor had been identified with former Gov. Jerry Brown's many campaigns until latching onto Clinton after serving with Hillary Clinton on the board of a charitable organization.

Among Democrats, two organized groups have emerged in recent years. One is the Hollywood Women's Political Committee, founded in 1984 by singer/actress Barbra Streisand. The committee specializes in star-studded fund-raising extravaganzas on behalf of liberal candidates and causes. Streisand, for instance, staged a big fund-raiser for California Sen. Alan Cranston at her Malibu ranch in 1986 and repackaged the entertainment as a television special, thus magnifying its financial impact.

The second and newer organization is the Show Coalition, known as ShowCo, founded in 1988 by younger Hollywood figures, most of whom had been identified with Gary Hart's abortive presidential bid. ShowCo has not yet become a major fund-raising source but acts as an intermediary between politicians and entertainers, staging seminars and other non-financial events.

Sometimes the relationships between politicians and entertainers can backfire. State Sen. Tom Hayden, the former radical and former husband of actress Jane Fonda, took a group of "brat pack" actors to the 1988 Democratic convention in Atlanta for an immersion in politics. Among the young stars was Rob Lowe. Months later, it was revealed that Lowe had made explicit videotapes of sexual escapades with local girls during the convention.

Streisand and actor Robert Redford (who starred together in the semipolitical movie "The Way We Were") are the prototypical Hollywood liberals, willing to devote time and money to their candidates and causes. While Streisand prefers to work directly for candidates, Redford takes a loftier, issue-oriented approach through a foundation that he has endowed. But they are not alone. Others who share their ideological commitment include Morgan Fairchild, who was especially close to Cranston before his career self-destructed; Sally Field; Cher; Gregory Peck; Ally Sheedy; Ed Begley Jr.; Bette Midler; Goldie Hawn; Chevy Chase; and Bruce Willis.

Jerry Brown developed particularly tight ties to the Hollywood Democrats during his eight years as governor and as a perennial candidate for president and U.S. senator. He was singer Linda Ronstadt's self-proclaimed "boyfriend" for a time, dated other Hollywood figures and made Lucy's El Adobe Cafe, a hangout for actors, his unofficial Los Angeles headquarters. Actors such as Warren Beatty and Jane Fonda and singers such as Ronstadt and Helen Reddy raised tons of money for Brown's non-stop campaigns, and director Francis Ford Coppola produced an ill-fated live television program in Wisconsin during Brown's second unsuccessful campaign for the presidency in 1980. Gary Hart was the Hollywood liberals' clear favorite for president in 1984 and again in 1988 until he was forced to withdraw.

Ronald Reagan personified the blurry line that separates politics and show business, and during his political career solidified the ties that bind many in Hollywood to the GOP. The most outwardly political of the Hollywood conservatives these days is Charlton Heston, who makes commercials for Republican candidates and has often been mentioned as a potential candidate himself–so often that he's developed a stock rejoinder: "I'd rather play a senator than be one."

Comedian Bob Hope is a mainstay of Republican fund-raising events and, not surprisingly, most of the other Hollywood conservatives are of the older generation, such as Frank Sinatra, Fred MacMurray, James Stewart and Robert Young. But some newer and younger stars also side with the GOP, such as Sylvester Stallone, Tony Danza, Chuck Norris, Jaclyn Smith and strongman-turned-actor Arnold Schwarzenegger, who's married to Kennedy clanswoman Maria Shriver.

Hollywood politics, however, involve more than the men and women whose names are found on theater marquees and record labels. The business side of show business is also heavily involved in politics in terms of both personal conviction and financial betterment. The most prominent of the Hollywood tycoons who dabble in politics is Lew Wasserman, head of the huge MCA entertainment conglomerate (which was sold to Japanese investors in 1990) and he plays both sides of the partisan fence. Wasserman is a Democrat but had particularly close ties to Reagan from the latter's days as an MCA client and star of MCA-produced television programs. Republican Gov. Pete Wilson also established a close relationship with Wasserman during his U.S. Senate career, blocking aid to any would-be political rival. The entertainment industry, like any other, has business in Washington and Sacramento, mostly involving tax treatment on movie and television deals. Wilson, for instance, endeared himself to the showbiz tycoons by protecting their interests during the writing of federal tax reform laws.

Movie mogul Jerry Weintraub is another Hollywood businessman who dabbles in politics. He served on Republican George Bush's finance team in 1988, although he's best known as a Democratic campaign contributor. Producer Norman Lear has made liberal causes his second career and Frank Wells, head of the Walt Disney entertainment empire, toyed with the idea of making a bid for a U.S. Senate seat from California in 1992.

Hollywood's political activists were deeply involved in 1990 elections as they were recruited by proponents and opponents of ballot measures to both raise money and appear in television commercials. The Legislature's Democratic leaders recruited Jack Lemmon to make a series of TV ads–widely criticized as misleading–opposing measures to overhaul legislative redistricting processes and later persuaded Angela Lansbury, James Garner and others to pitch against legislative term limits. The first campaign worked but the second failed. (A state senator at one point publicly suggested that Garner run for governor–a suggestion ridiculed at the time but in hindsight one that might have worked better than the losing campaigns waged by more conventional Democratic politicians in 1990.) The environmentalists in Hollywood, meanwhile, went all out for "Big Green," a major environmental protection measure that was rejected by voters, and "Forests Forever," another rejected measure that would have imposed severe logging restrictions.

Abortion rights, gay rights and AIDS research also are high on priority lists of Hollywood liberals and when Colorado voters repealed laws making gays a protected minority group in 1992, Streisand and others called for an entertainment world boycott of the state–which forced some actors and musicians to give up their customary skiing holidays in Aspen and Vail.

Much of the Hollywood hierarchy is Jewish and politicians who want its support must adhere to a strongly pro-Israeli line. That's why Jerry Brown, Alan Cranston, Pete Wilson, Ronald Reagan and any other California politician who aspires to the political big time in Washington can be counted in Israel's corner. By contrast, when Rep. Pete McCloskey ran for the Senate in 1982 as a critic of Israel, he bombed in Hollywood and Republican Rep. Ed Zschau suffered a similar treatment when he ran against Cranston in 1986.

ELSEWHERE IN THE SOUTHLAND

Not everybody who writes a fat check to a politician in California is an entertainment industry figure. As a prosperous and fast-growing state, California has produced more than its share of wealthy people who give to candidates from both parties or–perhaps more important–can ask others to contribute as peers rather than political beggars.

Southern California aerospace executives tilt toward the Republicans with their promises of greater military spending. When, for instance, George Bush made a quick, money-raising trip to Southern California in 1988 while seeking the Republican presidential nomination, he stopped at the TRW aerospace plant in Redondo Beach, then headed for private fund-raising events at the Bel Air home of real estate tycoon Howard Ruby and the Rancho Mirage estate of publisher Walter Annenberg. But when the Pentagon began to cut spending late in the Bush administration, much of the aerospace industry support dissipated.

Donald Bren, head of the big Irvine Co. land development firm in Orange County, has emerged in recent years as a Republican financial power, supplanting such older kingmakers as auto dealer Holmes Tuttle, who was part of the group that persuaded Ronald Reagan to run for governor in 1966. (Most of those prominent early Reagan backers have since died.) Pete Wilson's win of the governorship in 1990 may have made Bren the most influential of the new kingmakers. He and Wilson served in the Marine Corps together and Larry Thomas, Wilson's (and George Deukmejian's) one-time press secretary, serves as Bren's chief media spokesman. The Irvine Co. connection to Wilson was underscored when Wilson chose John Seymour, a state senator from Orange County with strong ties to the Irvine Co., as his successor in the U.S. Senate (Seymour was unseated by Dianne Feinstein in 1992).

Financier David Murdock is another Southern California business mogul with strong Republican connections, as is Lodwrick Cook, chairman of Atlantic Richfield Co. Philip Hawley, chairman of the Carter-Hawley-Hale department store chain, was once a major Republican player, but with his company's shaky financial situation in recent years, his political star was virtually extinguished.

Potent new players on the scene are a group of conservative businesspeople with ties to the religious right and the California Gunowners PAC. Their Capitol Commonwealth Group and related organizations pumped $1.5 million into various campaigns and PACs in 1992. More than half of that amount came from billionaire Howard Ahmanson Jr., whose father founded Home Savings and Loan. "We're a funny combination of the moral majority and libertarianism," Ahmanson's wife, Roberta, has said. Major beneficiaries of their largess were conservative Assembly candidates who ran opposite Gov. Wilson's more moderate slate.

Capitol Commonwealth members gave much of their money through another committee they formed, Allied Business Political Action Committee, and other organizations like the California Pro-Life Council and Family PAC. A frequent partner in giving is Robert Hurtt Jr., president of Container Supply Co. in Orange County. In 1992, Hurtt and his wife, Esther, gave more than $521,000 to candidates and political organizations. Other partners are Roland and Lila Hinz of Mission Hills, who gave $124,625, and Edward Atsinger III of Camarillo, who donated $83,625. Hinz, a Democrat, owns Daisy/Hi-Torque Publications, which publishes Dirt Bike magazine. Atsinger owns a chain of Christian-format radio stations.

The Southern California business types who lean toward the Democratic side include Richard O'Neill, heir to vast land holdings in Orange County who has been known to devote weekends to precinct-walking and once served as state Democratic chairman. Michael Milken, the junk bond whiz kid who served a stretch in federal prison, was closely identified with several Democratic political figures, including Cranston and former Rep. Tony Coelho. Coelho, in fact, was forced to resign from Congress after revelations that he had acquired a bond through Milken under suspicious circumstances.

One of the towering figures of Southern California political financing defied easy categorization. The late Armand Hammer, oilman, philanthropist and private diplomat, was an adviser to and fund-raiser for countless California politicians of both parties.

San Diego, which tries to insulate itself from Los Angeles, has developed its own power-broker infrastructure. Newspaper publisher Helen Copley is a powerhouse, as is Joan Kroc, who inherited the McDonald's hamburger empire and a baseball team from her late husband, Ray. Banker and deal-maker Richard Silberman was a big political player–even serving for a time in Jerry Brown's administration in Sacramento–and was married to a San Diego County supervisor, Susan Golding. But Silberman was indicted in 1989 on drug-money laundering charges and later convicted, thus ending his political career as well as his civic and business standing, although Golding, after divorcing the imprisoned Silberman, was elected San Diego mayor in 1992.

Fast-food moguls represent a particular subspecies of political financiers in California. In addition to the Krocs, Silberman once headed the Jack-in-the-Box hamburger chain in partnership with Robert Peterson, whose wife, Maureen O'Connor, was Golding's predecessor as mayor. And Carl's Jr. chain founder Carl Karcher is a patron of Republican and right-wing causes in Orange County.

MOVERS AND SHAKERS OF THE NORTH

Northern California's power brokers tend to operate more quietly than their counterparts in Los Angeles and Hollywood. Among Republicans, no one is quieter or more influential than David Packard, a co-founder of the Hewlett-Packard computer firm and perhaps California's richest man, with a personal fortune exceeding $2 billion (Bren also vies for this unofficial title.) Packard tends to support moderate to liberal Republicans; he was instrumental in helping Tom Campbell unseat a conservative Republican incumbent, Rep. Ernest Konnyu, in 1988 in his home district on the San Francisco Peninsula, and in Campbell's unsuccessful U.S. Senate bid in 1992.

Packard is the grand old man of Silicon Valley, the center of California's computer industry. As computer entrepreneurs have matured in business terms, they also have become civic and political leaders. One, Ed Zschau, won a seat in Congress and came within a few thousand votes of unseating Sen. Alan Cranston in 1986. He has since returned to business but indicates that if his private career allows, he may seek another statewide office in 1994, possibly lieutenant governor.

To date, the computer moguls have wielded influence mostly at the local level, helping San Jose and the rest of Silicon Valley develop an infrastructure to match their population and economic growth. But some, such as Packard, have moved beyond. His influence extends from the state Coastal Commission to the White House, and he quietly prodded Gov. George Deukmejian to do something about California's traffic problems.

A number of the most prominent Silicon Valley executives deserted the Republican Party in 1992 and endorsed Clinton, thanks to his promises of a tougher line on trade with high-tech competitors overseas and to the Pentagon cutbacks, which hit the industry hard. High-tech industry leaders such as Apple Computer chairman John Sculley and Hewlett-Packard president John Young were promised, in effect, key roles in shaping Clinton's economic policies.

Two other Northern California tycoons whose influence extends well beyond the state are the Bechtels, Stephen Sr. and Stephen Jr., who run San Francisco-based Bechtel Corp., a worldwide construction and engineering firm. At one time, it seemed as if half the Reagan administration in Washington consisted of ex-Bechtel executives, such as Secretary of Defense Caspar Weinberger and Secretary of State George Schultz.

Among Northern California Democratic financiers, none ranks higher than San Francisco real estate investor Walter Shorenstein. He labors tirelessly on behalf of the party's coffers and is courted just as tirelessly by presidential hopefuls. In 1989, however, Shorenstein declared independence after ex-Gov. Jerry Brown became state party chairman. Shorenstein and Bruce Lee, a high-ranking United Auto Workers official, established a "soft-money" drive to aid Democratic presidential nominee Michael Dukakis in California in 1988 and decided to continue the separate organizational fund despite entreaties from Brown that they fold their operation into his party apparatus. Shorenstein's light dimmed after a former employee lodged sexual harassment charges against him.

Another San Franciscan who has wielded a big stick in Democratic financial circles is attorney Duane Garrett, although his standing fell in 1988 after he attached himself to Bruce Babbitt's ill-fated voyage into presidential waters. He suffered another setback in 1990 when ex-San Francisco Mayor Dianne Feinstein lost the governorship, a campaign in which Feinstein's husband, investment counselor Richard Blum, emerged as a willing political financier, at least when his wife was involved. And among San Francisco insiders, Henry Berman, a "consultant" to the Seagram's liquor empire, carries much clout for his political fund-raising ability. He has been especially close to Assembly Speaker Willie Brown but also aided Feinstein's 1990 campaign.

Shorenstein, Garrett and Berman are valued not so much for their personal wealth, which is fairly modest in the case of the latter two, but for their organizational ability. They can pull together a substantial amount of political money simply by making a few phone calls or placing their names on invitations.

Gordon Getty, who may be California's second- or third-wealthiest man, is a different kind of political financier. Getty, a San Francisco resident, is an heir to the Getty oil fortune but devotes much of his time to private endeavors, especially composing classical music. Wife Ann Getty is a political junkie who lends her husband's name and her energies to political enterprises and was particularly active in ex-Gov. Brown's campaigns.

The East Bay—Oakland, Alameda County and Contra Costa County—has developed its own coterie of political pooh-bahs. Jack Brooks, a part-owner of the Raiders football team, carries a lot of weight among Democrats, and developers Joe Callahan, Ron Cowan and Ken Hoffman play major roles at the local levels. Ken Behring, a developer and owner of the Seattle Seahawks football team, has developed a reputation for political dealing at the local level with influence that stretches into the state Legislature.

Sacramento, another fast-growing area, has seen its developers become political heavyweights, and not just at the local level. The Northern California and Republican equivalent of the Manatt-Tunney law firm in Southern California is to be found in Sacramento headed by, among others, Steve Merksamer, a one-time top aide to Deukmejian. Merksamer and his colleagues at the firm represent top-drawer corporate clients in political affairs while Merksamer functions as a Republican insider. He played a seminal role in persuading Pete Wilson to give up his Senate seat for a successful run at the governorship.

Two of Sacramento's developers, Angelo Tsakopoulous and Phil Angelides, were big-money contributors and fund-raisers for fellow Greek-Americans Michael Dukakis and Art Agnos (mayor of San Francisco) in 1988, and Angelides, a former Capitol aide, is considering a run for statewide office himself in 1994 (if he doesn't take a position in the Clinton administration) after performing brilliantly as Jerry Brown's successor as the state Democratic Party chairman.

They exemplify another trend in political financing in California: the creation of groups that help people of similar ethnic backgrounds pursue their political careers. Frozen out of traditional sources of Republican campaign money, for instance, George Deukmejian tapped the state's large and wealthy Armenian-American community. Los Angeles lawyer Karl Samuelian organized the effort, and with Deukmejian's victory, he became a major power in Republican politics. Similar organization efforts have aided Asian politicians such as Los Angeles City Councilman Michael Woo and Sacramento Rep. Robert Matsui, while Los Angeles' large Jewish community has been a major source of campaign money for both parties, and not just for Jewish candidates.

Hispanics and African Americans have yet to develop similarly powerful ethnic fund-raising networks, although African American entertainers have helped such political figures as Los Angeles Mayor Tom Bradley. The most important African American political financier in the state has been Sam Williams, a Los Angeles attorney who is close to Bradley.

DOWN ON THE FARM

In California's major agricultural valleys the financial and political powers are, not surprisingly, connected to agribusiness. The state's wealthiest agribusinessmen—and two of the most influential—are Modesto's Gallo wine-making brothers, Ernest and Julio. The secretive brothers have personal wealth estimated at nearly $1 billion and are powerful political figures. They played major roles in organizing and financing the successful campaign in 1990 against a ballot measure that would have sharply increased taxes on liquor.

Further south, amid the cotton fields of the lower San Joaquin Valley, the powers are the Boswells and the Salyers, two agribusiness families whose holdings sweep across the now-dry expanse of Tulare Lake. The Boswells—the largest privately owned farming operation in the world with interests in other states and in Australia—and the Salyers play political hardball with campaign funds and high-priced lobbyists to protect their interests in Sacramento and Washington, D.C. And their major interests lie in protecting and enhancing the public water supplies vital to their farming operations.

Norma Foster Maddy has double-barreled political clout. She's not only the heiress to the Foster Farms chicken empire, but she's married to state Sen. Ken Maddy, the Republican leader of the Senate. Maddy's partner in the horse racing business is John Harris, head of Harris Farms. The wine-making families of the Napa and nearby valleys are major powers in local politics and the scion of one family, Don Sebastiani, briefly served in the state Legislature.

LABOR'S LOST LOVE

At last count, about 2 million California workers belonged to labor unions, a number that's holding steady even as labor's overall share of the expanding work force has slipped under 20 percent. Despite that decline, California labor leaders remain powerful political figures, able to turn out bodies and distribute money at levels that are decisive in many political conflicts. A prime example occurred in 1987, when a big labor turnout helped Democrat Cecil Green capture a Los Angeles County state Senate seat that seemed destined to go Republican. Labor fired up its troops on an issue dear to workers' hearts: Republican Deukmejian's unilateral closure of the state's occupational safety and health inspection agency. Later, labor obtained voter approval of a ballot measure reinstating the agency and won approval of a major increase in California's minimum wage. So, while labor's ranks may have thinned, they can still be potent.

The leading labor figure in California is Jack Henning, an old-school orator and organizer who serves as secretary-treasurer of the California Labor Federation (the AFL-CIO umbrella organization) and is largely a one-man band. Henning walks the hallways of the Capitol personally to lobby legislation affecting labor's interests and battles privately and publicly with employers and politicians who don't follow his bidding. A major overhaul of the state's system of compensating injured workers in 1989 was Henning's major accomplishment of the decade and, some believe, the high note on which he will retire. But if Henning is ready to step down, labor doesn't have anyone positioned to step into his shoes. Bill Robertson, the AFL-CIO's man in Los Angeles, is a secondary labor power, as is United Auto Workers official Bruce Lee, who joined with Walter Shorenstein in a fund-raising campaign independent of the state Democratic Party when Jerry Brown was the state party chairman.

Cesar Chavez was an enigmatic and influential figure of the 1970s as head of the United Farm Workers Union, but in recent years, with a hostile Republican administration in Sacramento, his clout and that of the United Farm Workers Union has dropped like a stone.

Labor's major gains in recent years have been among public employees, and the leaders of their unions have seen their visibility and power increase, especially since they are free with campaign funds. Ed Foglia, who headed the California Teachers Association, is one of labor's new power figures. His stock rose when the CTA won voter approval in 1988 of a major overhaul of school financing. Alice Huffman, the CTA's Sacramento-based political director, is a major player in insider Capitol politics.

The large California State Employees' Association is also a major source of campaign money, but it rotates its presidency often, which prevents any one person from becoming a figure of independent stature. The California Correctional Peace Officers Association, which represents prison guards, and the California Association of Highway Patrolmen also have expanded their clout in recent years. The prison guards committed upward of a million dollars to Pete Wilson's 1990 campaign for governor and quickly gained most-favored-union status when Wilson went head-to-head with other unions over pay cuts and reductions in school aid.

ORGANIZATIONS OF OTHER COLORS

The public employee unions exemplify another trend in California political financing: the increasing clout of large organizations with direct financial interests in political decision-making.

In the halls of government in Sacramento, big business doesn't loom very large, although Kirk West, a veteran Republican staffer who heads the California Chamber of Commerce, and William Campbell, a former state senator who now runs the California Manufacturers Association, do have clout. The groups that really count—because they annually distribute hundreds of thousands of dollars to political campaigns—are the associations of professionals, such as the California Trial Lawyers Association, the California Medical Association and the California Nurses Association. They approach fund-raising as a cost of doing business and operate their distribution operations in close consultation with their lobbyists, who daily walk the halls of the Capitol seeking to pass and kill legislation that impacts people they represent. But that workaday attitude toward political financing also is accompanied by relative anonymity. The men and women who operate these and other associations aren't political kingmakers in the usual sense of the word, although they wield considerable political power. They are narrowly focused on their issues and disinterested in the larger political picture.

THE INITIATIVE ENTREPRENEURS

Before California voters started taking a decidedly negative view of ballot propositions in 1990, the state's most powerful political agenda-setters may have been those who were most adept at writing, financing and organizing campaigns for the increasingly numerous ballot measures.

The prototypical initiative entrepreneurs were Howard Jarvis and Paul Gann, two old men (both have since died) who sponsored Proposition 13 in 1978. The financial and political impact of Proposition 13 made Jarvis and Gann, especially the former, into high-profile political figures and thus into political powerhouses in the media-heavy atmosphere of the 1980s. They were besieged with requests to lend their names to additional ballot measures and to endorse candidates for office and they did both. Gann even became a candidate himself for the U.S. Senate in 1980, losing to Alan Cranston.

In the mid-1980s, a new crop of initiative designers arose, this time on the left side of the political ledger. Initially, the most spectacularly successful was Harvey Rosenfield, a young consumer advocate and Ralph Nader disciple who founded "Voter Revolt." He put together a successful auto insurance reform initiative in 1988, winning in the face of a $60 million-plus opposition campaign financed by the insurance industry.

Rosenfield, whose penchant for publicity has been likened to that of Jarvis, immediately launched a second initiative campaign for the 1990 ballot, aimed at modifying Proposition 13 to remove its benefits from business property. And he, too, played political kingmaker by endorsing a candidate for the state insurance commissioner's position. But his candidate, Conway Collis, lost badly and none of Rosenfield's other initiatives made it to the ballot. Rosenfield's organization, meanwhile, experienced severe money problems and he was forced to pare staff and close offices, desperately seeking some new issue that could put him back on top.

In Sacramento, meanwhile, an informal coalition of environmentalists has established its own ongoing initiative factory and already has several wins under its belt. Gerald Meral, mild-mannered administrator of the Planning and Conservation League, operates as the consortium's coordinator, and he and his colleagues have devised a unique system of promoting their measures. Groups are invited to join the consortium and supply a quota of cash or signatures to entitle them to direct a share of the proceeds. The system was used on a park bond issue and a cigarette tax measure in 1988, and was then used for a big rail-bond issue and a liquor tax measure for 1990. The first effort won, but the second lost.

Tom Hayden, as an assemblyman and former antiwar radical, was a force behind the anti-toxics initiative, Proposition 65, in 1986 and the so-called "Big Green" environmental protection measure in 1990. Big Green ran afoul of the anti-initiative mood of voters.

Republicans, too, have used the initiative as a tool of partisan and ideological warfare. Ross Johnson, a conservative Republican leader in the Assembly, has been especially active. He co-sponsored a campaign finance reform measure, Proposition 73, approved by voters in 1988 and backed one of the unsuccessful reapportionment initiatives in 1990. But beyond Johnson, the right-wing side of the initiative business is moribund after the deaths of Jarvis and Gann.

MERCENARIES OF THE POLITICAL WARS

Standing just behind the candidates and the front men for the initiative campaigns are legions of professionals to whom the explosion of political activity in California is a lucrative growth industry, so much so that pros who used to practice out of Washington and New York are shifting their operations to California. Professional signature-gathering firms, fund-raisers, media consultants, pollsters, campaign strategists, accountants and even attorneys who specialize in writing, attacking and defending ballot propositions reaped tens of millions of dollars in the 1980s as the mercenaries of the initiative wars. The most obviously profitable of those campaigns was the $100 million battle over five insurance initiatives in 1988.

The consultants, however, aren't just paid soldiers in California's political wars. Whether they are helping candidates or fighting over ballot measures, they also have become major players in determining who runs or what proposal is put before voters. They, too, shape the political agenda. Some specialize in Democratic or liberal candidates and causes, while others work exclusively for Republicans and the conservative side. And a few plow the middle, working for whoever has the most money or the best chance of winning.

Although professional campaign strategists theoretically stand in the background while the candidate is out front, sometimes their importance is reversed. When Clint Reilly announced in 1989 that he was giving up his management of Dianne Feinstein's campaign for governor, it was a political event of the first magnitude since Reilly, a credentialed professional, had been one of the ex-San Francisco mayor's most valuable assets. Reilly's departure lowered Feinstein's political stock and forced her to engage in a damage-control operation.

Dozens of campaign management firms operate in California but only a relative handful command statewide attention. Reilly, who operates under the name of Clinton Reilly Campaigns, is based in San Francisco. Reilly managed Feinstein's mayoralty campaigns and has advised Bill Honig, who was elected as state superintendent of public instruction in 1982. Reilly also has done a number of local campaigns, including Gary Condit's 1989 victory in a special congressional election in the San Joaquin Valley. But he earned his biggest fee, more than $10 million, as the major strategist for the insurance industry in the 1988 ballot battle. And he kept the money despite the industry's wipeout at the polls. Abrasive and opinionated, Reilly is a controversial figure who feuded publicly for years with Assembly Speaker Willie Brown.

A rising star among the Democratic-oriented consultants is Richie Ross, who was Willie Brown's chief political adviser until striking out on his own after Brown lost some Assembly races in 1986. Ross, headquartered in Sacramento, had two statewide victories in 1988: Proposition 98, a school financing measure, and Proposition 97, a labor-backed proposal to restore the state worker safety program that had been canceled by Gov. Deukmejian. He also managed Art Agnos' come-from-behind campaign for mayor of San Francisco in 1987 and was tapped by Agnos to run the campaign for a new baseball stadium in 1989. Ross suffered a big setback in 1990, however, when his candidate for governor, John Van de Kamp, blew an early lead and lost the Democratic nomination to Dianne Feinstein. And he also saw the baseball stadium drive and Agnos' own campaign for re-election go down.

The man who engineered Ross' San Francisco setbacks from the other side was Jack Davis. The two consultants have a personal feud as well as a professional rivalry and in recent years Davis has been getting the better of it. His greatest triumph was managing Frank Jordan's come-from-behind ouster of Agnos in 1991.

The most prominent Democratic campaign management firm in Southern California is BAD Campaigns, operated by Michael Berman, brother of Rep. Howard Berman, and Carl D'Agostino, a former aide to Ken Cory when Cory was state controller. BAD, based in Beverly Hills, specializes in candidates endorsed by the political organization headed by Reps. Howard Berman and Henry Waxman. The Berman-Waxman organization dominates politics on Los Angeles' west side and dabbles in campaigns throughout Southern California. BAD also advised Gray Davis, the westside Democrat elected as state controller in 1980.

Things went badly for BAD in 1992. Reapportionment wiped out the strong-holds of many of the Berman-Waxman organization's figures and BAD's two candidates for the U.S. Senate, Rep. Mel Levine and Controller Davis, lost badly in the June primary. State Sen. Herschel Rosenthal, meanwhile, lost to Tom Hayden in a hard-fought race in Beverly Hills.

Los Angeles-based Cerrell Associates functions mostly as a public relations company, but it also handles some Democratic campaigns. Firm owner Joe Cerrell has national influence in Democratic politics.

A newcomer to the upper ranks of Democratic consultants is the Sacramento firm headed by David Townsend, a former legislative staffer. Townsend broke into the ranks of statewide campaign consultants in 1988, when his firm managed—unsuccessfully—the campaign against a statewide ballot measure to raise the cigarette tax. Townsend is beefing up to go after other statewide candidates and issues and also is adding public relations to his array of services for corporate and political clients.

REPUBLICAN RANKS SWELLING

There seem to be more professional Republican campaign management firms than Democratic ones, perhaps because the Republicans, as the minority party, lack the campaign-staff-in-place on the legislative payroll. While legislative staffers regularly take leaves from state service to go into the field to manage Democratic campaigns for the Legislature, Republicans usually call upon professionals.

For years, the GOP professional field was dominated by Stu Spencer and Bill Roberts. But with the latter's death and the former's semiretirement, a new flock of GOP-oriented consultants has arisen. The hottest of them was Otto Bos, a former San Diego newspaper reporter who became then-Mayor Pete Wilson's press secretary and then segued into statewide politics when Wilson ran for the U.S. Senate in 1982. Bos ran Wilson's second-term campaign in 1988 and went into business for himself with Wilson, the Republican candidate for governor in 1990, as his chief client. Bos, however, died a few months after Wilson became governor, leaving his erstwhile partners, such as George Gorton, on their own. Gorton ran Wilson's welfare and budget reform initiative in 1992, but it lost badly. He is expected to be deeply involved in Wilson's re-election campaign in 1994.

Until a few years ago, the splashiest Republican consulting firm was based in Sacramento and operated by two young former legislative staffers, Sal Russo and Doug Watts. They made a name for themselves as managers of Ken Maddy's spectacular, if failed, bid for the governorship in 1978, then hit the big time as operators of George Deukmejian's narrow victory for governor in 1982. They also managed the successful campaign against the Peripheral Canal in 1982 and even moved briefly into official positions in the new administration.

Russo and Watts added Ed Rollins, the former Reagan White House political director, to their firm and did much of the media work for Ronald Reagan's presidential re-election campaign in 1984. But after that spectacular rise, the firm fell on hard times and eventually broke up. Watts is now a New York-based political consultant while Russo has remained in Sacramento and has a new firm, Russo, Marsh and Associates. Russo was briefly involved with Ross Perot's presidential campaign, because ex-partner Rollins was Perot's co-chairman for a few weeks.

Another GOP campaign consultant with a string of strikeouts is Los Angeles-based Ronald Smith, who specializes in moderate to liberal Republican candidates. Smith came close with then-Rep. Ed Zschau's campaign for the U.S. Senate in 1986 and has had to settle for wins at the local level, including Tom Campbell's congressional campaign in 1988 on the San Francisco Peninsula. He tried again in 1990, but suffered another loss when state Sen. Marian Bergeson failed to win the lieutenant governorship. He also managed Campbell's unsuccessful bid for the U.S. Senate in 1992.

Another consultant who concentrates on moderate GOP candidates is Joe Shumate of San Francisco. He's confined himself to local campaigns, and scored a noteworthy win in 1988 when a pro-choice Republican, Tricia Hunter, won a hard-fought special election for the state Assembly in San Diego County. But Shumate suffered a big-time loss when he directed legislative campaigns on behalf of Gov. Wilson in 1992 and saw most of his candidates defeated—thanks to Democratic organizational work and a divisive split among Republicans over ideology.

The Dolphin Group of Los Angeles has tried to move into the big time, but so far has settled for pieces of larger campaigns and a few local efforts on its own. Allan Hoffenblum of Los Angeles eschews statewide campaigns in favor of handling many Republican legislative and congressional candidates and has maintained a high batting average. Gary Huckaby and Carlos Rodriguez, partners in a Sacramento firm, are trying to emulate Hoffenblum's approach with some success, as are Wayne Johnson and Ray McNally, who also operate their own firms in Sacramento.

Ken Khachigian was a speech writer for Reagan and Deukmejian and now hires out as a media and strategy specialist. He directed the Senate campaign of Los Angeles television commentator Bruce Herschensohn in 1992 and won plaudits for overcoming long odds and bringing Herschensohn close to a victory over Democrat Barbara Boxer after defeating Campbell in the primary.

While most California campaign consultants have partisan identification, some purposely avoid such labeling and concentrate, instead, on the increasingly lucrative ballot measure field. The granddaddy of these operations is Woodward & McDowell of Burlingame, known for its high-budget campaigns for and against major propositions for a generation. It was W&M, for instance, that persuaded Californians to adopt a state lottery in 1984, working with money from a major lottery supply firm.

The campaign firm, operated by Richard Woodward and Jack McDowell, hit a wall in 1988. It lost a campaign to change the Gann spending limit in June and then had a mixed result on auto insurance initiatives in the fall. It successfully battled insurance industry-sponsored measures, but was unable to secure passage of its own insurance proposition, sponsored mostly by trial lawyers. The firm staged a major comeback in 1990 when it managed the campaign against the year's highest profile ballot measure, a sweeping environmental initiative dubbed "Big Green" and scored again in 1992 by running the successful campaign against a major business tax measure, Proposition 167.

TESTING THE PUBLIC MOOD

The most basic tool of contemporary politics and political journalism is the public opinion poll and California abounds with takers of the public pulse.

The best known of California's public opinion pollsters is Mervin Field of San Francisco, whose California Poll has been a staple of newspapers and television broadcasts for decades. Field's California Poll has itself become a major factor in handicapping politicians by determining how much attention from the media and respect from potential contributors a candidate can command. But Field doesn't offer his services to individual politicians or campaigns.

When political strategists want to know what California voters are thinking to help tailor their campaigns, they must turn to the private political pollsters, some based in California and others elsewhere but offering their services in the state. Like consultants, pollsters tend to be identified with one party or the other and some have long-standing relationships with consultants. Sacramento's Jim Moore, for instance, is known best for his efforts on behalf of candidates and causes managed by Richie Ross.

As with consultants, there seem to be more pollsters working the Republican side of the street than the Democratic. Besides Moore, the most heavily used Democratic-oriented polling firm is Fairbank, Bregman and Maullin of San Francisco. Partner Richard Maullin first achieved prominence as a strategist in the 1970s for Gov. Jerry Brown and served for years in Brown's administration before moving to private consulting. Among the firm's clients have been Cranston and Los Angeles Mayor Tom Bradley.

There are three major Republican polling firms that handle all of the major GOP candidates. They are Arthur J. Finkelstein & Associates of Irvington, N.Y., whose California clients include state Sen. Ed Davis; Tarrance & Associates of Houston, who has handled polling for, among others, Gov. Deukmejian; and The Wirthlin Group of McLean, Va., a Republican White House favorite that has done work in California for Ed Zschau and former Lt. Gov. Mike Curb.

10

County government–at the crossroads

On June 2, 1992, Californians went to the polls in 31 of the state's 58 counties and cast advisory ballots on whether to secede from California. The secessionists won in 27 counties.

"We are deadly serious. . . . I will predict that there will be more than one California by the year 2000," said Assemblyman Stan Statham, R-Oak Run, the self-appointed leader of the breakaway movement. Statham's personal preference is to spilt California into three states "since San Francisco does not want to be in the same state with Los Angeles, and rural counties don't want to be in the same state with either San Francisco or Los Angeles."

That should have been a message to Gov. Pete Wilson and legislators that there is profound unhappiness among voters in wide stretches of California. Voters were telling the Sacramento power brokers that they are sick of being taken for granted, fed up with being ordered to provide certain programs without the money to pay for them and disgusted with legislative gridlock in Sacramento while their natural resources are being plundered and human services suffer.

But instead of being a wake-up call, the vote was ignored and the state budget was enacted three months later with some $1.3 billion in new reductions for counties, cities and special districts such as fire protection and parks. Practically all the votes for secession came from rural and agricultural counties with a combined population of less than 15 percent of California's total. So, most legislators could care less. Like at least eight previous efforts to split California, this one, too, seems doomed to fail. But that hasn't stopped Statham. He aims to put the plan before voters statewide in 1994.

The lack of county clout in Sacramento stems from the fact that there is nothing logical about the organization of California's counties. They come from a system of government suited to the 18th century, and each wave of growth in California has made that system less relevant.

Colonial Americans went back to what they knew when they set up local government. They borrowed the concept of counties from Great Britain – where those territories were administered by a count – an idea eventually adopted by every American state, except Alaska.

They also borrowed the dual nature of counties, which are at once independent local units and vassals to a larger central government. It is this dual nature that lies at the heart of the crisis in county government in California today, a problem so severe that some critics say counties should be abolished. That is not likely to happen, but as the 21st century draws near, California counties need fundamental changes to function in a world very different from the 19th century, post-gold rush era in which most were created.

Nineteenth century politics and economics dictated the boundaries. The small, elongated counties of the old gold-mining region along the Sierra foothills, for example, were drawn to keep every miner within a day's horseback ride from a county seat where he could file claims. Southern California in those days was an unpopulated desert, and there was no reason to divide it.

As California's population grew in the late 19th century, local boosterism and political differences created the impetus for breaking up big counties. Mariposa County, for instance, once contained most of Southern California, the lower San Joaquin Valley and the Central Coast. More than a dozen counties have been carved out of that vast territory. One is San Bernardino, still the nation's largest – and bigger than a half-dozen states.

San Francisco County once contained not only the city of San Francisco but what is now San Mateo County. When San Francisco combined its city and county governments, a group of crooked politicians lopped off San Mateo, via their friends in the Legislature, to keep control over a friendly environment. Cattle ranchers and farmers south of Los Angeles seceded to create Orange County, fearing domination by the municipal colossus then slowly forming.

The last county broke away just after World War I, when Imperial County was carved out of the arid eastern reaches of San Diego County. Since then, the number has been fixed at 58, even though the state's population has increased many times over. The counties range in population from the more than 8 million people of Los Angeles County to the 1,100 spread around Alpine County. More than half of the state residents live in seven counties in Southern California. In size, there is the 49-square mile, city-county combination of San Francisco on one end and the 20,000-square-mile San Bernardino at the other.

Today almost every large local government is trying to create new regional planning mechanisms to deal with such knotty issues as transportation and air pollution, issues that spill easily across county boundaries. These regional governments represent one possible direction for counties. As some see it, counties should cede their land-use planning and other large-scale functions to regional entities and evolve into mere subagencies of the state. Others would have counties merge at least administratively with the cities within their boundaries so local governments could cooperate rather than compete on local planning and growth.

Either way, counties have a pack of problems to fix. From the earliest days of the state, counties have had inherent conflicts with their dual roles. On the one hand, counties are purely units of local government, providing police, fire, transportation, judicial and other services to the people living outside incorporated cities. On the other hand, counties do as they are ordered by the state, which includes running welfare and health-care systems.

Into the counties' treasuries come property taxes, sales taxes on transactions outside of cities and money handed down from state and federal governments and other sources. In theory, the state is supposed to pay for what it requires counties to do. In practice, state aid rarely comes close.

The system worked as long as local revenues grew and remained flexible. Originally, county supervisors could adjust property tax rates to cover whatever was needed. But the system stopped working in 1978. As state aid stagnated during the 1970s and property values soared, property tax bills went through the roof. Angry homeowners trooped to the polls to pass Proposition 13, which staggered county governments like a blow to the head.

Proposition 13 cut and then clamped a lid on property taxes. For counties, that meant a loss of billions of dollars yearly, and a plunge into financial peril. The state stepped in – sort of – to help the counties. But that aid continued to dwindle as demands grew.

When Proposition 13 passed, the state was sitting on nearly $4 billion in reserves, built up because of the tax on inflated property values around California and because of the tight-fisted policies of then-Gov. Jerry Brown. The state started draining off that reserve to help local governments, particularly counties, in the post-Proposition 13 era. But in the early 1980s, recession and inflation hit at just about the time the reserve ran out.

George Deukmejian inherited the mess when he was sworn in as governor in 1983. Backed by a Legislature with tax-cut fever, Deukmejian preferred to tighten state belts rather than increase government's revenue, which forced more money management onto the counties.

THE THREAT OF BANKRUPTCY

Rural counties have felt the pinch the hardest, since local government revenues rely on local property values and retail activity. The resource-based economies – timber, minerals, ranching and farming – of a broad swath of California, ranging from Siskiyou and Modoc counties on the state's northern border to Imperial County in the extreme south, have fallen on hard times. The young have fled to cities as local jobs disappeared, causing the populations to stagnate in numbers and to advance in age. Tourism and recreation businesses have eased the economic crises in some areas, but those are even more seasonal and erratic than the traditional industries. With high unemployment (20 percent or more in some counties), demands of health and welfare services have gone up as revenues have become scarce. Local services such as sheriff's patrols and road maintenance have declined, but the state mandates continue to drain off budget resources. As a result, supervisors have become increasingly militant in their dealings with lawmakers in Sacramento.

20 fastest growing counties in California

County	Population on 4/1/80	Population on 4/1/90	Percent difference
Riverside	663,199	1,170,413	76.48
San Bernardino	895,016	1,418,580	58.48
Amador	19.314	30,039	55.53
Calaveras	20,710	31,998	54.51
Nevada	51,645	78,510	52.02
Placer	117,247	172,796	47.38
El Dorado	85,812	125,995	46.83
San Benito	25,005	36,697	46.76
Solano	235,203	340,421	44.75
Tuolumne	33,928	48,456	42.82
San L. Obispo	155,435	217,162	39.71
Madera	63,116	88,090	39.57
Stanislaus	265,900	370,522	39.35
Lake	36,366	50,631	39.23
San Joaquin	347,342	480,628	38.37
Kings	73,738	101,469	37.61
Kern	403,089	543,477	34.83
San Diego	1,861,846	2,498,016	34.17
Sacramento	783,381	1,041,219	32.91
Merced	134,538	178,403	32.58

Source: Bureau of the Census, 1991

Tehama County supervisors became national celebrities when they declared a revolt against state mandates. In Lassen County, the supervisors talked about being annexed by Nevada. Nearby Shasta County also received a flurry of publicity when it shut down its public libraries. Humboldt County supervisors allowed paved roads to revert to gravel.

In 1988, Gov. Deukmejian and the Legislature threw the counties a bone when the state assumed from counties some costs of running the court system, but that just relieved a few immediate cash-flow crises and did little to slow what some county supervisors saw as an impending disaster.

Butte County was saved from becoming the first U.S. county to file for bankruptcy with state bailouts in 1989, 1990 and 1991. Other rural counties, including Yolo, Del Norte and Trinity, are almost in the same shape as Butte and, according to a study commissioned by the County Supervisors Association of California, possibly two dozen others are slipping into trouble. By 1992, unpaid furloughs of whole county staffs had become popular. Usually, it was a few days without pay here and there. But Sonoma County shutdown during Christmas week of that year and reduced all paychecks accordingly.

Some cities, mostly free of the big-ticket health, welfare and educational responsibilities, actually found themselves in better shape after Proposition 13. Besides having major sources of revenue that are independent of the property tax, many cities have evolved into entrepreneurs of sorts, doing everything from encouraging development within their boundaries to running mini-prisons for the state.

Before Proposition 13, property owners were required to pay separate property taxes to their county governments and to cities, if they were inside an incorporated area. That discouraged incorporation of county areas outside established cities. But the 1978 tax initiative ended that. And the loss of property tax revenue shifted local government attention to the sales tax. Under California law, a chunk of sales tax is returned to the local government in which the sale occurred. If a mall is inside a city, the city's coffers get the sales tax, not the county's. Suddenly cities were drawing new boundaries to include shopping centers, auto dealerships and other high-volume retail areas. More than 35 new cities have been formed since Proposition 13, most of them in suburbs and some containing huge populations.

County officials, who once encouraged the creation of new cities to relieve themselves of the cost of police and other services, found they were losing more and more tax revenue as cities gobbled up sales-tax-producing businesses and development. And that fight over sales taxes to replace the lost property taxes has driven counties into bitter rivalries with each other and with city governments. The scramble for taxable development has become so intense that in some counties, land-use decisions are based almost entirely on competition for revenue rather than good planning.

As California expands by more than 5 million people a decade, growth fights will become even more dominant. Both large-scale policies and individual projects will face intense scrutiny, and the old cozy friendships between supervisors and developers will be strained.

San Diego County is dealing with the growth fight by requiring major development to occur only within a city, negating much of the land-use power that has translated into political power in many counties. The city of San Diego has become the de facto regional decision-maker for the county.

A different direction for county evolution may be found in the San Francisco model. Even though city-county consolidation plans failed at the polls in Sacramento County in 1974 and 1990, local officials there are looking at ways to combine some offices, including the planning departments, as a way of discouraging incorporation efforts that could siphon off sales taxes.

Alameda County

Area: 825.4 sq. mi.; Population: (1990) 1,279,182, (1980) 1,105,379; Registration: (1992) D-61.6% R-22.7%; Unemployment: (Oct. 1992) 6.4%; County supervisors: Edward Campbell, Keith Carson, Mary King, Don Perata, Gail Steele; 1221 Oak St., Room 536, Oakland 94612; (415) 272-6347.

Writer Gertrude Stein once said of Oakland, Alameda County's principal city, "There's no there there." She didn't mean it that way, but the phrase has come to stand as a declaration that Oakland and, by extension, Alameda County, lacks character.

What Alameda County, on the eastern shore of San Francisco Bay, really lacks is a spotlight. It exists in the shadow of San Francisco, its big-city cousin across the bay, despite the best efforts of community boosters to establish a separate image.

Were it not in that shadow, Alameda County clearly would be one of California's most notable areas. It contains a piece of almost every social group in the state – from the funky, 1960ish ambiance of Berkeley, home of the University of California's first and most important campus, to the wealth of Piedmont, the industrial communities of Fremont and San Leandro and the problem-plagued city of Oakland.

Every time Oakland seems ready to take a step away from its difficulties, a new crisis pushes it back. On Oct. 17, 1989, it was the Loma Prieta earthquake, which made a shambles of the poorest sections of the city. A major road artery, an 18-block section of the Interstate 880 freeway, collapsed, killing 43 people. That the scars have been slow to heal is a gross understatement. Two years later, almost to the day, another disaster hit. A grass fire in the affluent Oakland Hills smoldered into a firestorm that has been called the worst urban conflagration in modern history. By the time it was over, 25 people had died, 150 were injured and 2,536 homes were destroyed. Damage estimates topped $1.3 billion.

On the first anniversary of the fire, only 51 homes had been rebuilt as survivors struggled with endless red tape and insurance companies slow to pay. A newspaper survey also found that only two out of 10 survivors believe the city is better prepared to fight another inferno. City officials were still arguing about whether they should standardize fire plugs so that emergency vehicles from outside the city could hook up.

Those were some of the same city officials who always find money to subsidize pro ball teams, but can't seem to plan a viable redevelopment project or bail out a nearly bankrupt school system. The political establishment, in one of the rare major cities dominated by African Americans, has been fragmented and ineffective, especially in dealing with vicious crime and drug problems.

For years, the political leader of Oakland was Lionel Wilson, a former judge. The mayor from 1976 to 1990, Wilson ran out of steam in the primary election of 1990. Former Democratic Assemblyman Elihu Harris beat Councilman Wilson Riles Jr. in the runoff. Harris has yet to prove that he can make a difference.

Meanwhile, the southern and eastern reaches of Alameda County seem a world away. They are part of the California Sun Belt, the fast-growing suburbs dotted with business and commercial centers. Communities such as Livermore and Pleasanton are exploding with people and jobs, and the Association of Bay Area Governments, the regional planning agency, has projected that 70 percent of Alameda County's job growth between 1985 and 2005 will be in the southern and eastern parts. Alameda's diversity produces political tension that is both geographic – urban Oakland and Berkeley vs. the suburbs – and social. The fast-growing suburbs are gaining political clout that may move the county's politics to the right.

At the polls, Alameda County, thanks to Oakland and Berkeley, is as consistently left-of-center as nearby San Francisco, giving Democratic candidates for statewide office a substantial Bay Area base. Democrats outnumber Republicans by 2.5 to 1, which gives the county all-Democrat legislative and congressional delegations. And those Democratic lawmakers are on the left side of the spectrum, even within their own party.

The politics of Berkeley – known to detractors as "Berserkeley" – are so far to the left that conventional liberals are, in relative terms, the local right-wing. Berkeley established a national trend for left-of-center cities, most of them college towns, to involve themselves in issues of international politics. Gus Newport, Berkeley's mayor for much of the 1980s, was a globe-trotting apostle for the left-wing.

But while Berkeley's politics evolved out of the University of California and the "free speech," civil rights and anti-war movements of the 1960s, the politics of the campus itself are more moderate now. Student government, in fact, has strong conservative factions and the fraternity and sorority systems are stronger than ever, leading to a rather odd twist of the traditional town vs. gown tensions.

University officials want to expand the campus and its support facilities, especially student housing, but city officials resist. The standoff has meant an annual scramble for housing and another of the Bay Area's miserable traffic scenes. UC officials even found it necessary to move their statewide administrative offices out of Berkeley altogether.

But the future of Alameda County and the region hinges more on economic trends than local politics. The Port of Oakland is a highly sophisticated doorway for commerce between California and the Pacific Rim nations. Those rapidly growing suburbs of the southern and eastern county include many high-tech plants, an extension of the Silicon Valley across the bay. The Association of Bay Area Governments projects a growth of Alameda County jobs from about a half-million in 1980 to nearly 800,000 by 2005. That boom would far exceed population growth and make Alameda County a destination for commuters, many from the even-newer suburbs in the San Joaquin Valley to the east.

Yet as the suburbs become ever more congested, increasing numbers of residents are saying enough is enough. Slow-growth mayors have been elected in Livermore and Pleasanton. City councils have increasing numbers of slow-growth members. It will be interesting to watch where those new leaders take the area.

Alpine County

Area: 726.6 sq. mi.; Population: (1990) 1,113, (1980) 1,097; Registration: (1992) D-38.3% R-42.3%; Unemployment: (Oct. 1992) 13.9%; County supervisors: Pierre Blumm, Cameron Cralk, Donald Jardine, Eric Jung, Claudia Ann Wade; P.O. Box 158, Markleeville 96120; (916) 694-2281.

A brochure from the county's Chamber of Commerce advises visitors to "Get lost in Alpine County." It would not be hard.

This is California's smallest county in population, a tiny reminder of California's 19th century beginnings south of Lake Tahoe. There certainly is no boom here. Alpine grew by only 16 people for the entire decade of the 1980s and actually lost about 80 people in the last two years. Of the remaining 1,000-or-so people, 23 percent claim Indian ancestry.

Not that local residents mind the isolation. Most live there because they enjoy solitude, which is a good thing, since winter snows close all but a few roads. Mining was the county's original reason for being, but ranching and later tourism – especially skiing – have become its economic mainstays.

Like the rest of California's mountain regions, Alpine is politically conservative.

Amador County

Area: 601.3 sq. mi.; Population: (1990) 30,309, (1980) 19,314; Registration: (1992) D-46.9% R-41.3%; Unemployment: (Oct. 1992) 8.8%; County supervisors:

Edward Bamert, John Begovich, Stephanie D'Agostini, Timothy Davenport, Louis Boltano; 108 Court St., Jackson 95642; (209) 223-6470.

Like other counties in the "Mother Lode" east of Sacramento, Amador is experiencing the joys and pains of growth. Swollen by commuters and retirees, Amador is the state's third-fastest-growing county and the most rapidly developing of the foothill areas. In the 1980s, population boomed by more than 55 percent.

But the numbers are deceiving. The census counts the inmates at the new Mule Creek State Prison near Ione, and they represent more than a third of the growth. But there are still many newcomers who bring money into the county, as do the tens of thousands of tourists who flock to its gold-rush-era towns on weekends.

There is some friction, as might be expected, between the old-timers and the steady stream of "flatlanders." The new settlers often bring higher incomes or big-city equity that pumps up local real estate prices beyond the reach of some longtime residents.

The county was once conservatively Democratic, but the newcomers have moved it to the right – a fact most keenly felt by former Assemblyman Norm Waters, a conservative Democrat who survived by a whisker in 1988 and then lost in 1990 in a rematch with Republican David Knowles.

Butte County

Area: 1,664.8 sq. mi.; Population: (1990) 182,120, (1980) 143,851; Registration: (1992) D-44.3% R-41%; Unemployment: (Oct. 1992) 10.7%; County supervisors: Jane Dolan, Mary Ann Houx, Bob Meyer, Edward McLaughlin, Gordon Thomas; 25 County Center Drive, Oroville 95966; (916) 538-7224.

Just say "Butte County" and watch any county official in California cringe. Butte has become the watchword for the financial woes that counties continue to face. In 1989, then again in 1990, Butte County came within days of becoming the first county in the United States to file for bankruptcy. It was saved by the state with a $2.8 million bailout in 1989 and another $11 million in 1990, still leaving the county more than $3 million in the hole.

According to reports from the state legislative analyst and the California Counties Foundation, many of the reasons for Butte's troubles went beyond the control of county supervisors. The county has been plagued by slow growth in property values, made worse because supervisors, when they had the discretion before Proposition 13, had always been reluctant to hike property tax rates. The county has lost tax revenue to city incorporations and annexations, continues to attract people in need of health and welfare services, and maintenance costs continue to escalate on everything from roads and buildings to sheriffs' patrol cars, some of which have rolled up more than 300,000 miles.

Voters, meanwhile, have rejected every tax hike put before them. In 1990, they turned down four tax increases or bond measures, leaving county libraries closed, animal control services abandoned, the jails overcrowded and county firefighters on the brink of being disbanded.

Butte County is in the middle of the vast, largely rural area north and east of Sacramento with neither rich natural resources nor the attributes attractive to home buyers. While growing at the average rate for California counties, about 25 percent, most of the region has missed the statewide economic boom, partly because it was bypassed by Interstate 5, the main north-south highway through California, leaving it a little too inaccessible for major developers. Cheap housing, though much of it is substandard, has made the area especially attractive to welfare recipients who have fled high-cost and high-crime areas.

The fastest growing area is not Oroville, the county seat, but Chico, home to the only branch of the state college system in the region and an attractive town of 35,000 with tree-lined streets, 19th-century Victorian homes and a park where Errol Flynn and Olivia de Havilland filmed "The Adventures of Robin Hood."

The presence of California State University, Chico, gives the community a lively political and cultural life. In the early 1980s, adherents of Tom Hayden's economic democracy movement won control of the city government. But they were ousted a few years later by a right-wing countermovement. Of the left's brief hegemony, only Jane Dolan, Chico's liberal county supervisor, remains.

The bulwarks of the local economy are the university, an agricultural industry dominated by orchard crops and some tourism, much of it attracted by the state-owned Oroville Reservoir. But the university's Center for Economic Development and Planning is trying to foster an interest in wider economic development throughout the 12-county region centered in Butte.

The center sees the agricultural and other resource-based elements of the local economy continuing to lag and predicts the area, with its comfortable rural life and relatively low living costs, is primed for development. But if that growth spurt does come, it will be years away.

Butte is a conservative area, Chico and the university notwithstanding, with about an equal number of Republicans and Democrats. But it votes very Republican.

Calaveras County

Area: 1,036.4 sq. mi.; Population: (1990) 31,998, (1980) 20,710; Registration: (1992) D-44.6% R-43.1%; Unemployment: (Oct. 1992) 13.2%; County supervisors: Richard Gordon, Michael McRay, Michael Dell'Orto, Thomas Taylor,

Thomas Tyron; 891 Mountain Road, San Andreas 95249; (209) 754-6370.

The most famous thing about Calaveras County is a fictional frog-jumping contest that became real. Writer Mark Twain described it in a whimsical tale about life during the gold rush. Now, the town of Angels Camp runs a real version each spring.

Hordes of tourists attracted to the frog-jumping contest are a big piece of the changing local economy, which has moved away from agriculture and mining. That change is illustrated by the precarious future of an asbestos mine, the nation's largest, which provides 5 percent of all county jobs. The impact of the retirees and the growing tourism can be seen on Sundays, when Highway 49, which cuts through the county, slows to a crawl.

The population, as in other counties in the Sierra foothills, is growing far faster than most of California. It was up by more than 54 percent. But in sheer numbers, its growth does not approach the boom that is hitting foothill counties closer to Sacramento. As the county grows it continues a slow shift to the right politically. Democrats are close to becoming a minority.

Colusa County

Area: 1,155.8 sq. mi.; Population: (1990) 16,275, (1980) 12,791; Registration: (1992) D-46.1%-R-43.3%; Unemployment: (Oct. 1992) 16.3%; County supervisors: W.D. Mills, Kay Nordyke, Patricia Scofield, William Waite, David Womble; 546 Jay St., Colusa 95932; (916) 458 2101.

Colusa County gets a lot of visitors. Of course, few of them know it. Interstate 5, California's main north-south artery, bisects the county about an hour's drive north of Sacramento. But it bypasses the county seat, Colusa, and at 65 mph, Williams, a town of 2,000, is not much to notice.

There are a few highway-related businesses in Williams, but the county's chief economic underpinning is agriculture. In 1988, Williams annexed more than 2,000 acres of farmland – more than three times the size of the city then – in hopes of attracting high-tech industry or at least food processors or canneries, but so far the move has had little impact on the area's economy. The Employment Development Department estimates that farming provides nearly half of the county's direct employment. The chief crop is rice, which is subject both to the availability of water and the vagaries of international markets. And, as would be expected of rural counties in California, supervisors have been struggling every year to pass a leaner and leaner budget.

Colusa is too far from Sacramento, the closest urban area, to be much of a target for suburban home buyers, and the area has neither the mountains nor the lakes and rivers that have made other rural regions havens for retirees. The population is growing about as fast as California as a whole, but there seem to be few indications that Colusa's basic character will change soon.

Contra Costa County

Area: 797.9 sq. mi.; Population: (1990) 803,732, (1980) 656,331; Registration: (1992) D-50.8% R-35.4%; Unemployment: (Oct. 1992) 6.9%; County supervisors: Gayle Bishop, Sunne McPeak, Tom Powers, Jeffrey Smith, Thomas Torlakson; 651 Pine St., 11th floor, Martinez 94553; (415) 646-2371.

A generation ago, Contra Costa County was a typical Northern California bedroom suburb. The county's lush hills and valleys were a refuge for commuters who spent their days working in Oakland or San Francisco and were affluent enough to live in the well-kept country atmosphere in communities such as Walnut Creek, Moraga, Orinda and Lafayette.

But in recent years, Contra Costa has exploded with jobs in places such as San Ramon's Bishop Ranch. New complexes along highly congested Interstate 680 have become destinations for less affluent commuters, who have moved even further east in search of affordable housing in the new bedroom communities of the San Joaquin Valley.

Between 1985 and 1990, Contra Costa's employment increased by more than 20 percent. Acres and acres of development along I-680 have spawned a new phrase, "Contra Costapolis," and sparked a no-growth backlash among residents fed up with hours-long traffic jams. As in so many growing areas, local politics of the 1980s became defined by that single issue, and politicians caught being too cozy with developers felt the lash of angry voters. The issue came to a head in 1985, when anti-growth candidates won a series of local elections and slow-growth ballot measures were adopted.

In many ways, the county is a microcosm of California. Along the outer reaches of San Francisco Bay, communities such as Martinez, Pittsburg and Antioch remain blue-collar bastions filled with oil refineries and other industrial facilities. But even those areas are sprouting suburban housing developments. Richmond, on the east shore of San Francisco Bay, has a large and Democratic-voting African American population, and many of the urban problems to match. It is a high-crime area with a school system in bankruptcy. The more affluent eastern suburbs, as would be expected, supply legions of Republican voters, leaving the county's voter registration relatively close to California's as a whole.

Also like the rest of the state, Contra Costa is fighting the battle of the dwindling budget. It has continually delayed a new jail, among other county responsibilities. Supervisors have been shopping around for years, trying to find a place to put the county's garbage or industrial sludge, and have even tried to pay other, more impoverished, counties to take it.

Contra Costa's most dominant political figure is not a politician, but Dean Lesher, the outspoken octogenarian who publishes the Contra Costa Times newspaper. Lesher battles ceaselessly against anti-growthers and for the establishment of a state college campus in the county, known locally as "Dean Lesher U."

Del Norte County

Area: 1,003 sq. mi.; Population: (1990) 23,460, (1980) 18,217; Registration: (1990) D-46.5% R-35.8%; Unemployment: (Oct. 1992) 14.8%; County supervisors: Robert Bark, Mark Mellett, Clarke Moore, Jack Reese, Glenn Smedley; 450 H St., Crescent City 95531; (707) 464-7204.

Del Norte County is about as far north as you can go and still be in California. For generations, the local economy was based on cutting trees and catching fish. Both industries fell on hard times during the 1970s and '80s, and local boosters pushed hard to add a third element: keeping bad guys behind bars. That "dream" was supposed to be realized when the state opened Pelican Bay State Prison in the late 1980s, where the worst of California's inmates live in extreme isolation.

Del Norte found itself in a rare surge of commercial investment as the prison took shape near the Oregon border north of Crescent City, and the $32 million annual payroll pumped new life into the economy. Suddenly, one of the state's most chronically depressed areas was beginning the look like one of its more prosperous. But the prison brought new problems. So far, commercial investment has lagged behind projections, the state didn't provide all the promised services, many of the jobs went to people from outside the county and welfare rolls have increased as families of prisoners moved into the area.

El Dorado County

Area: 1,804.8 sq. mi.; Population: (1990) 125,995, (1980) 85,812; Registration: (1990) D-41.6% R-45.2%; Unemployment: (Oct. 1992) 7.5%; County supervisors: William Sam Bradley, William Center, J. Mark Nielsen, Ray Nutting, John Upton; 330 Fair Lane, Placerville 95667; (916) 626-2464.

The names of the county and its county seat, Placerville, reveal their origins as one of the centers of the 19th-century gold rush. In the late 20th century, El Dorado County is at the center of another land rush.

Retirees and commuters are packing into El Dorado County, seeking cleaner air,

friendlier communities and more reasonable living
costs. But their sheer numbers threaten to destroy
those qualities. As one recent arrival put it in a
newspaper interview: "Everywhere I look, I'm
threatened."

Between 1980 and 1990, the county's population
surged by almost 47 percent as developers converted
pastures into "ranchettes" and rolling hills into subdivisions. Population growth is highest in the communities closest to Sacramento, such as Cameron
Park and El Dorado Hills, and water shortages have
become common.

As it grows, El Dorado is turning to the right politically. In 1990, Republicans
moved ahead of Democrats in registration for the first time.

Fresno County

*Area: 5,998.3 sq. mi.; Population: (1990) 667,490,
(1980) 587,329; Registration: (1992) D-52.6% R-
37.1%; Unemployment: (Oct. 1992) 16.1%; County
supervisors: A. Vernon Conrad, Sharon Levy, Deran
Koligan, Stan Oken, Doug Vagim; 2281 Tulare St.,
Room 300, Fresno 93721; (209) 488-3531.*

Fresno County is the middle of California geographically, culturally and politically. Its major city,
Fresno, is big enough – over 300,000 – to have some
big-city advantages and ills. But it remains, at heart,
an overgrown farm town. Its image was captured perfectly by a satirical television
movie "Fresno," in which things of little consequence had great consequence there.

The county's location, equidistant from Los Angeles and San Francisco, and its
relatively low labor and land costs, have sparked flurries of non-agricultural
industrial development, but the city and the region remain dependent upon agriculture. It was in Fresno County that the term "agribusiness" was coined, and large-
scale, scientific agriculture remains the heart of both its economy and its culture.
Crops as varied as cotton and grapes abound in the fertile flatlands of the nation's
most productive agricultural county.

As the unofficial capital of the San Joaquin Valley, Fresno also has developed
educational, medical and governmental facilities to serve the region. Despite that,
the county continues to be one of the most depressed areas of the state. A United
Way study completed in 1992 found that more than 15 percent of Fresno County's
households earn less than $10,000 a year. The county's per capita income of
$11,807 was nearly $4,000 below the state average.

The city of Fresno also became the crime capital of the Central Valley. A rate of 124 crimes per 1,000 people was second worst among California's metropolitan areas. Only Oakland's was higher.

More than a third of Fresno County's population is Hispanic (35.5 percent), but, as in other areas of the state, they have not developed into a strong political force. Instead, voters in Fresno County and the San Joaquin Valley mirror statewide political trends. They are nominally Democratic but lean toward the conservative, often willing to elect Republicans.

That puts the valley into the swing position when it comes to close statewide races and explains why candidates for state and national offices spend disproportionately large amounts of scarce campaign time around Fresno's isolated media market. One would expect all that attention to boost voter turnout, but not so. In 1990, Fresno County was second to last in voter turnout among California's 58 counties. In 1992, the county moved up just one notch to finish ahead of two other valley counties: Stanislaus and San Joaquin.

The exception to the conservative tilt is the more liberal city of Fresno, due largely to its blue-collar and farm-worker residents. George McGovern, Walter Mondale, Michael Dukakis and Bill Clinton all won in the city itself, but did miserably in the rest of the county.

But centrism is still the dominant political credo of Fresno County. Local government is the spawning ground for most legislators and congressmen, who tend toward the pragmatic. Chief among them is state Sen. Ken Maddy, the Senate's Republican leader and a one-time gubernatorial possibility who is married to the heiress of the Foster Farms chicken empire - the perfect combination of politics and agribusiness.

Glenn County

Area: 1,319 sq. mi.; Population: (1990) 24,798, (1980) 21,350; Registration: (1992) D-44.9% R-43%; Unemployment: (Oct. 1992) 13.8%; County supervisors: Marilyn Baker, Ken Burbank, Keith Hansen, Charles Harris, Dick Mudd; P.O. Box 391, Willows 95988; (916) 934-3834.

The 19th-century courthouse in Willows is a symbol for all of Glenn County: quiet, tradition bound, slow to change. Interstate 5, the state's main north-south freeway, bisects Willows and the county, but has had small impact. There are a few highway-related businesses, but otherwise the city and the county remain what they have been for generations – agricultural communities whose economies are tied to the value of farm products. Farming and government account for half of Glenn's employment.

Jim Mann, a dairy farmer turned county supervisor, is trying to change that. Mann works for a regional economic development center in nearby Chico and is trying to offset chronically high unemployment by promoting the area as a site for light industry, stressing the low cost of living and the easy freeway access. But so far, there have been no big takers, and the voters dumped Mann from office in 1992.

Like the rest of the region, Glenn County is struggling with its budget and is politically conservative.

Humboldt County

Area: 3,599.5 sq. mi.; Population: (1990) 119,118, (1980) 108,525; Registration: (1992) D-53.2% R-30.4%; Unemployment: (Oct. 1992) 9.8%; County supervisors: Stan Dixon, Julie Fulkerson, Bonnie Neely, Anna Sparks; 825 Fifth St., Eureka 95501; (707) 445-7509.

Eureka (population 25,000) is the political, economic and cultural center of California's beautiful north coast. The region was settled by loggers, who felled giant redwoods and cut them into timbers to shore up gold mines in the mid-19th century. Cutting and processing timber, and catching and processing fish, have been Humboldt County's economic mainstays for generations, even after a substantial, if seasonal, tourist trade developed after World War II.

Both of those resource-based industries have fallen on hard times in recent years, however, and many of the area's young men and women moved away looking for more dependable jobs. As they left they were replaced in the 1960s and '70s by urban refugees, universally dubbed "hippies," and an economic and political transformation of the area began. In the 1980s, the urban refugees had sold homes in Los Angeles or the San Francisco Bay Area, and were a bit more conservative, but only a bit.

Marijuana is a substantial cash crop. Environmentalism is a powerful movement. And the politics of the area, once conservative, have moved leftward, with liberal Democrats replacing Republicans in legislative seats. There are still major political battles between the pro-lumber businesses and the environmentalists. But most often, the latter win.

Imperial County

Area: 4,597.4 sq. mi.; Population: (1990) 109,303, (1980) 92,110; Registration: (1992) D-53.5% R-34.6%; Unemployment: (Oct. 1992) 30.4%; County supervisors: Bill Cole, Robert Bradford Lucky, Sam Sharp, Dean Shore, Wayne Van De Graaff; 940 W. Main St., El Centro 92243; (619) 339-4220.

If farmers in this region couldn't grow three crops a year at times, it is doubtful that many people would live in the Imperial Valley. Much of the valley, which occupies California's southeastern corner, lies below sea level and is covered with sand. Summer temperatures can reach more than 120 degrees in the sparse shade of the almost treeless landscape.

Imperial was the last California county to be created, carved off San Diego County just after World War I. There is a lively trade in both goods and human bodies over the Mexican border south of El Centro, and Imperial County has California's highest concentration of Hispanic residents, nearly 66 percent in the 1990 census.

That fact is accompanied by a harsh reality: Imperial also has the state's highest unemployment rate and is chronically near the top in terms of poverty. In 1992, nearly one worker in three was looking for a job. The county also is chronically on the financial edge as it tries to pay for health and welfare services.

Local boosters hope that a fledgling winter vacation industry – a kind of poor man's Palm Springs – will brighten the local economy. But the only good economic news in recent years has been the decision to build two new prisons in the county.

Inyo County

Area: 10,097.9 sq. mi.; Population: (1990) 18,281, (1980) 17,895; Registration: (1992) D-39.8% R-48.5%; Unemployment: (Oct. 1992) 10.4%; County supervisors: Warren Allsup, Julie Bear, Sam Dean, Robert Gracey, Paul Payne; P.O. Drawer N, Independence 93526; (619) 878-2411.

There is only one word to describe Inyo County. empty. That is only in terms of people, however. Inyo, wedged onto the eastern slope of the Sierra, next to Nevada, contains some of the state's most spectacular, if starkest, natural scenery plus an active volcanic field.

Inyo is California's second largest county in size, but it has the second slowest growth rate. The population grew by a whopping 386 people during the 1980s.

The federal government owns more than 85 percent of the land. Extraction of minerals from Inyo's arid mountains, ranching and tourism are the county's chief economic activities; hating Los Angeles – which locked up the area's water in backroom maneuvers a half-century ago and which supplies hordes of summer and weekend visitors – seems to be the chief local pastime. Mining has been on the wane in recent years as has agriculture – thanks to water exports to Los Angeles. Local leaders have been looking for something – perhaps a prison – to replace the lost employment.

Politically, Inyo's voters give Republican candidates big majorities.

Kern County

Area: 8,170.3 sq. mi.; Population: (1990) 543,477, (1980) 403,089; Registration: (1992) D-44.3% R-44.2%; Unemployment: (Oct. 1992) 16.9%; County supervisors: Roy Asburn, Ben Austin, Pauline Larwood, Ken Peterson, Mary Shell; 1415 Truxton Ave., Bakersfield 93301; (800) 322-0722.

If California is a small scale model of the United States, then Kern County is its Oklahoma. There are oil wells, farms and country music recording studios. And many of the county's inhabitants trace their ancestry to the waves of migrants from Oklahoma, Texas and Arkansas before, during and after World War II.

When the oil and farming industries are down, Kern County is down. When they are up, the county rolls in money. There have been efforts to diversify the county's economy, taking advantage of its location 100 miles north of the Los Angeles megalopolis. The chief new industry is state prisons, but for the foreseeable future, farming and oil will rule.

True to its cultural roots, Kern County is very conservative politically. It elects Republicans to its legislative and congressional seats and gives GOP candidates at the top of the ticket big margins. But it could give them even more if people were inclined. In the 1990 elections, Kern had the lowest voter turnout in the state and the 1992 numbers were only slightly better. As elsewhere, the county's large Hispanic minority (28 percent) is politically impotent.

Kings County

Area: 1,435.6 sq. mi.; Population: (1990) 101,469, (1980) 73,738; Registration: (1992) D-51.1% R-36.8%; Unemployment: (Oct. 1992) 14.8%; County supervisors: Joe Bezerra, Jim Edwards, Joe Hammond Jr., Nick Kinney, Ron Stockton; Government Center, Hanford 93230; (209) 582-3211.

Kings County, sliced from a corner of neighboring Tulare County in the late 19th century, has achieved a remarkable economic diversity to accompany its large-scale agricultural base.

Starting in the early 1960s, the county lured such non-agricultural projects as a tire factory, the Lemoore Naval Air Station and a carpet mill. In recent years, the state has built two large prisons in the small farming towns of Avenal and Corcoran. The county seat, Hanford, has even developed a mild tourism industry centered on the town square, its old-fashioned ice cream parlor and 19th-century buildings redeveloped into shops. There's also a small Chinatown.

That non-farm development has given it a more stable economy than many other San Joaquin Valley counties and also has fueled a relatively fast population growth. Its 37 percent increase from 1980 to 1990 is unusually big for an area in the middle of the farm belt.

Politically, Kings mirrors the valley: conservative-voting on most issues, but willing to elect Democrats who do not tilt too far to the left.

Lake County

Area: 1,326.5 sq. mi.; Population: (1990) 50,631, (1980) 36,366; Registration: (1992) D-52.8% R-34.7%; Unemployment: (Oct. 1992) 14.4%; County supervisors: Gary Lambert, Karan Mackey, Bill Merrymen, Helen Whitney, Walter Wilcox; 255 N. Forbes St., Lakeport 95453; (707) 263-2367.

Lake County's name says it all. The county's major asset, scenically and economically, is Clear Lake, California's largest natural body of fresh water. Dotted along the lake are dozens of small communities that subsist on summer tourism, fishermen and retirees.

There are so many retirees settling in Lake County, a three-hour drive from San Francisco, that the median age of residents is about 15 years higher than the state's average. The retirees tend to be of the working-class variety, so the local politics remain pro-Democrat. The county's economy has other elements, such as ranching and geothermal power development, but retirees' pension checks are becoming steadily more important. At the same time, retirees have also produced a steady increase in the demand for county services, while property values have been virtually flat. Lake County is another on the long, long list of counties that had to cut services and trim jobs to balance its budget.

The Clear Lake basin is a favorite hunting ground for archaeologists as it has been inhabited for centuries. One stone tool fragment from the area has been dated to 10,000 years.

Lassen County

Area: 4,690.3 sq. mi.; Population: (1990) 27,598, (1980) 21,661; Registration: (1992) D-48.% R-37.3%; Unemployment: (Oct. 1992) 8.9%; County supervisors: James Chapman, Gary Lemke, Jean Loubet, Lyle Lough, Claude Neeley; 707 Nevada St., Susanville 96130; (916) 257-8311.

The biggest employer in Lassen County, on the northern Nevada border, is the California Department of Corrections. Beyond the prison at Susanville,

Lassen is mostly timber and ranch country, with a steady summer and fall tourist trade. It shares Lassen National Volcanic Park with three other counties, but the active volcano that gave the county its name, Mt. Lassen, is actually in Shasta County.

Many – perhaps most – of Lassen's residents are happy the county has missed out on the industrialization and population growth hitting much of California. Indeed, when the state decided to expand its prison and add more jobs, it was opposed by local residents, who would prefer to leave things as they are: quiet and peaceful. But the expansion is going forward anyway.

Lassen's population is growing at about the average California rate, and many of the newcomers are retired ex-urbanites who traded in the equity on their homes for the quiet of the country. Financially and politically, the county is like the rest of northeastern California: the county's budget is in miserable shape, the community college is precarious financially, and the people are conservative with a don't-tread-on-me attitude toward government and taxes.

Los Angeles County

Area: 4,079.3 sq. mi.; Population: (1990) 8,863,164, (1980) 7,477,517; Registration: (1992) D-55.1% R-32.3%; Unemployment: (Oct. 1992) 9.5%; County supervisors: Michael Antonovich, Yvonne Brathwaite Burke, Deane Dana, Ed Edelman, Gloria Molina; 500 W. Temple St., Los Angeles 90012; (213) 974-1411.

For the second time in a generation, South-Central Los Angeles exploded in flames on April 29, 1992. Frenzied mobs were unleashed by the acquittal of four Los Angeles policemen who were charged in the beating of motorist Rodney King. The rioters murdered, burned and looted, and then went home to watch themselves on stolen television sets. When the acrid smoke began to clear, 53 people were dead, 1,100 buildings were destroyed and the damage total exceeded $850 million. America's worst civil discord in this century had once again revealed a county splintered by race and class, paralyzed by dysfunctional government, and policed by forces woefully unequal to the task. Even the much-vaunted California National Guard came off looking like the Keystone Kops.

If then-74-year-old Mayor Tom Bradley had any hopes of running for a sixth term in 1993, they were an early casualty of the rioting. Police Chief Daryl Gates, who began to display bizarre personal behavior, was soon forced into retirement as was the Guard chief, Maj. Gen. Robert Thrasher.

To be sure, there were promises of new beginnings. From pulpits and entertainment figures came appeals for unity and a new compact based upon mutual respect. From the White House and corporate board rooms came promises of massive aid.

Peter Ueberroth, everyone's favorite Mr. Fixit, was recruited to lead a new organization called Rebuild LA.

As time passed, it became apparent that the promised gush of aid would be only a trickle. Resolutions were passed in Washington and Sacramento, but little money was attached to them. Some businesses made notable contributions, but most did not. Six months after the riots, 40 percent of the 789 businesses damaged or looted were no longer operating. Crime, poverty, unemployment and random acts of viciousness were more widespread than ever before. Compton Councilwoman Patricia Moore would say: "It's becoming more difficult each day to persuade stable citizens to stay here. It's like our leadership has given up on urban America. It's expected to fail. It's expected to have problems. So people have written it off."

This in a county that contains more than 30 percent of California's people and which wields cultural, economic and political influence of global scope. Just a few blocks from the shattered neighborhoods of Compton and Watts, people seemed warier than before. But the pace of life continued as it has for decades.

Los Angeles, both the city and the county, has huge enclaves of Hispanics, African Americans, Koreans, Armenians, Chinese, Japanese, Vietnamese and other ethnic groups. Each plays its own role in shaping the society that evolved from a dusty outpost of the Spanish colonial empire. They participate in an economy that is as diverse as the state, ranging from heavy manufacturing to Pacific Rim trade, high-tech manufacturing, entertainment, tourism and sweatshop factories.

Other communities may throb, but the city of Los Angeles and the dozens of other towns that comprise Los Angeles County hum with the 24-hour-a-day freeway traffic that is the county's most pervasive feature. What is considered rush-hour traffic anywhere else can be found in Los Angeles at almost any time: hundreds of thousands of vehicles in a slowly oozing stream, most of them transporting no more than the driver. This has given Los Angeles one of the nation's worst smog problems and has produced new government attempts to deal with it, including the establishment of a regional body – the South Coast Air Quality Management District – with vast new powers to influence the way people live, work, commute and even barbecue their food. But any solution to the smog problem, if there is one, is years away. Meanwhile, the freeways become more clogged.

It is a problem made worse by the inexorable shift of population out of the city's center and into the suburbs on the edge of the San Fernando Valley and the Mojave Desert. People seeking affordable homes pay instead with ever-longer commutes, even though job growth is spreading into the suburbs.

The influx of immigrants, most from Asia or Latin America, added more than 1.4 million to Los Angeles County's population in the last decade. That growth is more than twice as much as any other county, although in percentage terms it is a bit under the statewide average. The slower-than-average population growth, coupled with the tendency of Hispanic and Asian immigrants not to vote, means an erosion of Los Angeles County's overall political clout. But the county is still a giant.

County politics tend to split rather evenly down party lines. It is slightly more Democratic in registration than the state as a whole, but many Democrats tend to support Republicans for top offices. The strongly pro-Republican tilt in the remainder of Southern California more than offsets the Democratic edge in Los Angeles and gives the region a very dependable GOP flavor in races for U.S. senator, governor and president.

Within Los Angeles County, politics tend to run to extremes. Some of the state's most conservative and most liberal officeholders can be found in its legislative and congressional delegations. The central and western portions of the county – downtown Los Angeles, heavily African American South-Central Los Angeles, Hispanic East Los Angeles and the wealthy Beverly Hills, Santa Monica and Westwood areas on the west side – are strongly Democratic. State Senate President Pro Tem David Roberti, ex-radical Tom Hayden, now a state senator, and Reps. Howard Berman and Henry Waxman, who head a powerful political organization, are among the Democrats from the west side. But Long Beach – ex-Gov. George Deukmejian's home – and the Anglo suburbs on the fringes of the county vote Republican, while the San Fernando Valley is a toss-up, Democratic in the southern part, Republican in the north.

A third of the county's population is Hispanic and 10 percent is Asian; both groups are beginning to put people in strategic offices. The county Board of Supervisors, for instance, was composed of five Anglo men until recently, despite the fact that Anglos are less than half of the county's population. Now there are three white men and two women – one African American, one Hispanic.

Those five positions are among the most powerful in the nation. Each supervisor has nearly 2 million constituents, a huge personal staff and a vote on a $9 billion budget. Without an elected head of county government, the supervisors wield vast authority over land-use, transportation, health care and other matters.

The county's split political personality is revealed in the makeup of the board, three Democrats and two Republicans. Republican Deane Dana represents a coastal district and the other Republican, Mike Antonovich, has a chunk of the suburbs. The three Democrats are Ed Edelman, who represents the largely Jewish west side; Yvonne Brathwaite Burke, a former congresswoman, who represents overwhelmingly African American South-Central Los Angeles; and Gloria Molina, a former legislator and Los Angeles city councilwoman, whose district includes Boyle Heights, East Los Angeles and part of the San Gabriel Valley.

Molina's ascendency to the board from the Los Angeles City Council in early 1991 marked one of the most dramatic political shifts in the county during this century. Republicans had controlled the board through the 1980s, but the U.S. Justice Department filed suit in 1985, claiming the board's GOP majority had reapportioned the county in a way that would deny Hispanic representation. The board fought the suit unsuccessfully, eventually spending nearly $10 million of the taxpayers' money on legal fees.

That forced new boundaries and a special election to replace retiring Supervisor Peter Schabarum. Molina, a farm worker's daughter who rose from grass-roots politics, beat state Sen. Art Torres to become the first Hispanic elected to the board since the 1870s.

It has been a different story on the 15-member City Council. When the Justice Department began raising questions in the mid-'80s, the council acted quickly and redrew district lines to create two seats for Hispanics. With more than a third of the city's population, Hispanics could claim at least five of the 15 council seats. The 1993 elections could bring substantial changes.

It was the onset of World War II that propelled Los Angeles into the industrial age. As factories, warehouses, docks and other facilities were quickly built to serve the war, its population doubled and redoubled as defense workers poured in. The San Fernando Valley and other one-time ranch lands were turned into housing tracts. The naturally arid region had assured itself of a dependable water supply, thanks to some not altogether savory dealings by local landowners.

Los Angeles' boom did not slow after the war. Factories that had turned out bombers began making airliners. The automobile, a necessity in such a sprawling city, sparked the development of the freeway. The state's first freeway, connecting downtown Los Angeles with Pasadena, the traditional home of moneyed families, is still carrying cars.

With so many new people coming to town, with so much money to be made and with so little sense of civic identity, Los Angeles was ripe for corruption. The 1974 movie "Chinatown" accurately captured the ambiance of Los Angeles in the 1940s. Police, city officials and newspapers were corrupt. Los Angeles was a civic joke, its downtown area a seedy slum, its once-extensive trolley system ripped out by money-grubbing bus and oil companies, its development governed by which subdivider was most willing to grease the right palms.

Slowly, Los Angeles developed a sense of civic pride that extended beyond the latest land deal. Slowly, the city's notorious Police Department was cleaned up by William Parker, a reformist chief. The Los Angeles Times, once considered the nation's worst large newspaper, came under the control of Otis Chandler, a member of the family that had owned it for generations, and the new publisher turned the Times into an institution with international stature. Los Angeles developed a culture to match its fast-growing population: art museums, a symphony, charities and other amenities helped the nouveau riche – including those from the movie industry – acquire a social respectability.

While the city's upper crust began developing a social sense, the city itself continued to change. As the immigrants moved in and multiplied, the Anglos moved out to the San Fernando Valley and other suburbs, many of which are still within the city limits. The 1990 census found Los Angeles, with Anglos in the minority, to be one of the nation's most ethnically diverse cities.

But for decades, Los Angeles' politics, like the city itself, was a whites-only business. Mayors – honest or crooked – were all men who professed a conservative ideology, and none showed more than token ability to project an image beyond the city. Race relations, like much of the Los Angeles lifestyle, were conducted at long distance. If anything, the 1965 riots in the Watts section of Los Angeles widened the gulf between Anglos and non-Anglos. It was a more violent replay of the "Zoot-suit riots," which had pitted Hispanics against white servicemen during World War II.

All of that seemingly changed in 1973, when Tom Bradley, an African American and one-time Los Angeles police lieutenant, won the mayorship. Bradley projected hope to minorities and pro-development moderation to the white business and political establishment. And he has survived, winning re-election four times, by continuing to walk that tightrope.

Bradley's chief mayoral accomplishment – made in close collaboration with the business community – has been the revitalization of the city's downtown. Oil companies, banks and other major corporations dumped money into the Bunker Hill project to give the downtown a skyline, even though the lower reaches of the area remain a slum. Beyond that, Bradley has delivered a city government that is reasonably efficient, reasonably honest and reasonably inclusive, especially when compared to many of the nation's other big cities.

Yet Bradley, who twice ran unsuccessfully for governor, saw much of that progress slipping away during his last term. He must carry the responsibility for more than 400 gang-related murders a year and the inability of the police department to deal with both that and the explosion of drug-induced crime. Smog is worsening, traffic congestion grows exponentially and polls indicate that most Los Angeles residents think their quality of life has deteriorated. One survey found half of those polled had considered moving.

Development has re-emerged as a top political issue among the majority of those who turn out to vote. Environmental protection is a popular cause on the west side and in the San Fernando Valley, occasionally taking on a tone of racial exclusivity.

Despite the enormity of the city's problems, there was no shortage of people willing to fill Bradley's huge shoes. Among those on the campaign trail in early 1993 were Assemblyman Richard Katz, D-Sepulveda; Councilmen Michael Woo, Nate Holden and Joel Wachs; Julian Nava, a former school board president and U.S. ambassador to Mexico; County Transportation Commissioner Nick Patsaouras; former Deputy Mayor Tom Houston; and millionaire businessman Richard Riordan.

The question, however, was whether any of them would possess the commitment, imagination and resources to make a difference in the burned-out neighborhoods of South-Central Los Angeles. Absent that, it seems inevitable that the flames will erupt again.

Madera County

Area: 2,147.1 sq. mi.; Population: (1990) 88,090, (1980) 63,116; Registration: (1992) D 50.6% R-39.4%; Unemployment: (Oct. 1992) 16%; County supervisors:

Harry Baker Jr., Alfred Ginsburg, Rick Jensen, Jess Lopez, Gail McIntyre; 209 W. Yosemite Ave., Madera 93637; (209) 675-7700.

Madera County is farm country, and far enough removed from the state's urban centers to avoid, at least for a while, the dubious benefits of suburbanization. Its population is growing, up 39 percent between 1980 and 1990, and much of it is in foothill areas popular with retirees. A steady stream of tourists passes through the county on its way to Yosemite National Park, a portion of which lies in the county, and many other recreational sites, such as Millerton and Bass lakes.

The city of Madera and surrounding communities have had a modest amount of industrialization, most of it spilling over from the Fresno area to the south. But agriculture – especially grapes and dairy products – remains the economic linchpin, accounting for a third of the region's employment.

Despite the strong Democratic registration edge typical of San Joaquin Valley counties, Madera votes conservatively, and its growing Hispanic population of 34.5 percent remains largely powerless.

Marin County

Area: 588 sq. mi.; Population: (1990) 230,096, (1980) 222,592; Registration: (1992) D-52.2% R-30.7%; Unemployment (Oct. 1992) 5.3%; County supervisors: Brady Bevis, Harold Brown, Gary Giacomini, Annette Rose, Bob Roumiguiere; Civic Center, Room 315, San Rafael 94903; (415) 499-7331.

They make jokes about Marin. They write books, movies and songs about Marin. It even shows up occasionally in comic strips. It's that kind of place. The Golden Gate Bridge lands on its southern tip, whales and great white sharks pass close to its spectacular coastline, and mountains and woods rise in all corners of the county.

It also is one of those places on which California's reputation – deserved or not – is built. The county is a combination of bohemianism, bourgeoisie, activism, money, exclusivity and liberal social attitudes, overlaid with an almost religious sense of environmental protection.

As the San Francisco Bay Area suburbs boomed in the early 1970s, Marin County fought to hold the line on growth, long before such movements became popular elsewhere. And Marin residents have pretty much succeeded. Between

1980 and 1990, for example, its population grew only 3.3 percent, less than a seventh of the statewide rate and by far the slowest of any urban county.

But the success of the growth-control movement has had side effects: an incredible rise in housing costs, which has driven out the non-affluent (the median income is over 50 percent higher than neighboring Sonoma County) and major traffic problems. The traffic comes from both a boom in commuters driving northward toward Sonoma and south toward San Francisco, and from the sharp increase of jobs in Marin itself, which brings workers into the county.

Still, much of Marin remains dedicated to keeping its natural attributes relatively undisturbed. One coastal community even refuses to have signs directing traffic to itself, so intense is the desire for isolation.

A major showdown on the growth issue occurred in 1989, when voters decided the fate of a large proposed residential and office development on the site of the former Hamilton Air Force Base. Despite the shortage and high cost of housing and support from such prominent Democrats as Lt. Gov. Leo McCarthy, the project was rejected. A corollary situation involves occasional rumblings out of Sacramento about closing San Quentin Prison and selling its exquisite site for development. Marin County residents would rather keep the prison.

Politically, Marin was once steadfastly Republican but has been moving left as environmentalism has become a more potent political force. The only Republican officeholders who survive now are those who embrace that cause.

Mariposa County

Area: 1,460.5 sq. mi.; Population: (1990) 14,302, (1980) 11,108; Registration: (1992) D-42.8% R-41.6%; Unemployment: (Oct. 1992) 7%; County supervisors: Arthur Baggett, Doug Baimain, Eric Erickson, Garry Parker, Gertrude Taber; P.O. Box 784, Mariposa 95338: (209) 966-3222.

Once, in the mid-19th century, Mariposa County covered a huge swath of California, including most of the San Joaquin Valley and Southern California. But year after year, the county's boundaries were whittled down to form new counties, eventually spawning 11 in all. What's left are 1,460.5 square miles of scenic territory that include the most famous and most visited portions of Yosemite National Park.

Each year, hundreds of thousands of people visit Mariposa County's rolling foothills, quaint gold-rush era towns and craggy mountains. And each year, a few more decide to stay, which is why the county's population grew by almost 30 percent between 1980 and 1990. The county's population has nearly tripled since 1960. Many of the newcomers are retirees, who bring conservative attitudes that are turning the county into a Republican bastion.

The state projects that Mariposa's population will continue to grow rapidly, reaching 20,000 by the turn of the century as the demand for recreational opportunities continues to expand.

Mendocino County

Area: 3,510.7 sq. mi.; Population: (1990) 80,345, (1980) 66,738; Registration: (1992) D-54.3% R-29.3%; Unemployment: (Oct. 1992) 11.9%; County supervisors: Norman DeVall, James Eddie, Liz Henry, Frank McMichael, Seiji Sugawara; Courthouse, Room 113, Ukiah 95482; (707) 463-4221.

Mendocino County, like the rest of Northern California's rugged, spectacular coast, was once timber country. Cutting and processing the trees of the densely forested areas of the county remain a huge part of the economy, but within the last generation a revolution hit the county.

A wave of urban emigres flooded the area in the 1960s and '70s, creating a new economy rooted in tourism, crafts and, although illegal, the cultivation of marijuana. The extremely quaint little coastal towns such as Elk and Mendocino (the setting for Cabot Cove, Me., in the "Murder She Wrote" TV series) acquired rafts of bed-and-breakfast inns and trendy restaurants to serve weekenders from the Bay Area. And in the late 1980s, the southern part of the county started turning into suburbs as Bay Area commuters pressed ever-outward, searching for affordable housing. Politically, the change moved Mendocino County leftward, with liberal Democrats replacing conservative Democrats in elected offices.

The county's budget, however, suffers many of the same problems facing other rural counties. In fact, supervisors went so far as to take out a mortgage on their courthouse to help balance the 1990-91 budget.

Merced County

Area: 2,007.7 sq. mi.; Population: (1990) 178,403, (1980) 134,558; Registration: (1992) D-53.1% R-34.7%; Unemployment: (Oct. 1992) 15.7%; County supervisors: Michael Bogna Jr., Ann Klinger, Jerald O'Banion, Dean Peterson; 2222 M St., Merced 95340; (209) 385-7366.

Merced County advertises itself as the gateway to Yosemite National Park, but its future appears to be tied less to the mountainous eastern end of the county than to its western flatlands, which are on the verge of a suburban explosion.

The mind may boggle at the prospect, but Los Banos, a quiet and fairly isolated farm town on the west side of the San Joaquin Valley, is laying plans to become part of the San Francisco Bay megalopolis as rising housing costs drive commuters further from the central cities. In this case, the upgrading of Highway 152 to a full freeway will give commuters a straight drive from little Los Banos into the packed Santa Clara Valley south of San Jose. Even without such suburbanization, Merced County's population is up more than 32 percent between 1980 and 1990, thanks, in part to the influx of Southeast Asians who now account for eight percent of the residents. And its politics, which had been conservative Democrat, seem to be edging rightward with the growth.

Merced is considered as well-managed a county as any in the state, according to the California Counties Foundation. But as in many other counties, budget writers have been tightening belts yearly and soon may have no room left.

Modoc County

Area: 4,340.4 sq. mi.; Population: (1990) 9,678, (1980) 8,610; Registration: (1992) D-44.3% R-43.4%; Unemployment: (Oct. 1992) 12%; County supervisors: Edgar Carver, Joe Earl Colt, Nancy Huffman, Ron McIntyre, John Schreiber; P.O. Box 131, Alturas 96101; (916) 233-3939.

A form letter that Modoc County employment officials send to would-be job seekers says it all. The weather can be extreme, the economy is seasonal and "Modoc County (has) virtually no growth," the letter bluntly tells those who think that the isolated, rugged and beautiful county would be a paradise.

Yet the people living in California's upper right-hand corner like it just the way it is: remote, iconoclastic and sometimes 30 degrees below zero in winter. The chief lament is that the lack of jobs forces young people to seek work in cities hundreds of miles away.

Timber and cattle are mainstays of the economy, although government – local, state and federal – is the largest employer. Increasingly, summer homes are being built by urbanites seeking isolation. There are so many summer residents, in fact, that something of a political schism has developed between them and the year-round people. Apart from that, the politics are solidly conservative.

Since 1912, Modoc had been California's bellwether in presidential elections - voting for the winner every time. That ended in 1992 when Modoc residents went for George Bush. Locals attributed that to a growing influx of retirees who've brought their conservative values with them.

Mono County

Area: 3,103 sq. mi.; Population: (1990) 9,956 (1980) 8,577; Registration: (1992) D-35.4% R-44.9%; Unemployment: (Oct. 1992) 17.6%; County supervisors: Tim Alpers, Michael Jarvis, Andrea Lawrence, Dan Paranick, William Reid; P.O. Box 715, Bridgeport 93517; (619) 932-7911.

The dominant feature of Mono County – and one focal point of its politics – is Mono Lake and the striking geologic features nearby. The lake has shrunk markedly in the last half-century, a constant reminder that the county's fate is largely in the hands of Los Angeles.

Through a series of subterfuges, Los Angeles gained control over water supplies on the eastern slope of the Sierra and pipes much of that southward. Local residents are caught in the political and legal battle over whether the diversions should continue uninterrupted or whether more water should be allowed to flow into Mono Lake and thus save the scenic and ecological wonder from shrinking further. It's been a long and expensive matter, but court decisions are headed in the direction of lake preservation.

Mono Lake also symbolizes the tourism industry that has gradually replaced ranching and mining as the chief source of jobs. Contributing to that economic evolution is Mammoth Lakes, a world-class skiing area. Mammoth Lakes became Mono's only incorporated city during the 1980s. It is now the economic center of the county and is large enough to dictate political policy to the rest of the residents.

But also in the '80s, Mammoth Lakes was found to be sitting atop an active volcano. At one point, it became so restive that a state of emergency was declared. Tourism and housing values took an immediate plunge, and Mammoth politicians responded with demands that state and federal geologists suppress all future negative news of that sort. Time has brought a little more enlightenment to the political leadership, but not much.

Monterey County

Area: 3,324.1 sq. mi.; Population: (1990) 355,660 (1980) 290,444; Registration: (1992) D-49.2% R-34.4%; Unemployment: (Oct. 1992) 10.8%; County supervisors: Marc Del Piero, Sam Karas, Thomas Perkins, Barbara Shipnuck, Karin Strasser Kauffman; P.O. Box 1728, Salinas 92902; (408) 424-8611.

Even in a state blessed with great natural beauty, Monterey County is something special. Its abundant attractions – rugged coastline, windblown woods, quaint towns and nearly perfect weather – have become the focal point of county politics. Bluntly put, those who have already captured a piece of Monterey for themselves are increasingly active in protecting it against outsiders. Almost any development project, from a hotel to a highway, sparks controversy. Politics in Monterey, Carmel and other Monterey Peninsula communities revolve around that tension.

The mayorship of Monterey and the balance of power on the City Council shifted out of the hands of pro-development forces in the early 1980s after Monterey underwent a surge of hotel construction, including erection of a downtown hotel dubbed "Sheraton General" for its hospital-like appearance.

At the same time, however, the peninsula's economy is almost entirely dependent upon the tourist industry. The result is non-stop political churning over the future of the area, a two-hour drive south from San Francisco. The battle of Monterey achieved national publicity in 1986 when actor Clint Eastwood was elected mayor of Carmel for two years on a pro-development platform.

Outside of the Peninsula, most of Monterey County is agricultural. While the county's two major population centers, Monterey and Salinas, are only a few miles apart, economically and socially they are two different worlds. Salinas and other inland communities rely on the price of the vegetables they produce, but they also are beginning to feel suburbs creeping in as commuters spill farther and farther out of the San Jose area to the north.

The politics of Salinas and environs are being altered by the new suburbs and also by the slowly emerging strength of Hispanics. Although more than a third of the population in many communities, Hispanics have been politically powerless. But key court decisions have opened avenues of political activity at the local level, especially in Salinas, which shifted to a district form of city voting after a court decision ordered districts formed in nearby Watsonville.

The economic and social contrasts found within the county are mirrored in its politics – liberal-environmentalist along the coast and conservative inland. Overall voting patterns are similar to those of the state, but they are not stable. Suburban development pulls the county toward the Republicans while Hispanic political activity pushes toward the Democrats.

The 1990s will see the closing of one of Monterey County's economic mainstays – the Army's rambling compound at Ft. Ord. Local business and government are apt to be devastated in the short term. The eventual use of the property will say much about future directions of the region.

Napa County

Area: 796.9 sq. mi.; Population: (1990) 110,765, (1980) 99,199; Registration: (1992) D-50.7% R-36.7%; Unemployment: (Oct. 1992) 8.8%; County supervisors: Paul Battisti, Vincent Ferriole, Fred Negri, Mike Rippey, Mel Varrelman; 1195 Third St., Napa 94559; (707) 253-4386.

Not too many years ago, the Napa Valley was a little-known corner of California. That seems like a fairy tale these days. As wine-drinking evolved into something akin to a secular religion in the 1970s and '80s, the Napa Valley became a mecca. Napa County's once quiet agricultural valley, an hour's drive northeast from San Francisco, evolved with astonishing speed into a tourist draw. Wineries sprouted like mushrooms and the valley acquired bushels of inns, hotels, restaurants and other tourist-oriented facilities.

In the early 1980s, there began a backlash among residents tired of weekend traffic jams and jacked-up prices. While rising home prices, controls on new development and a lack of local jobs all have kept population growth minimal, the battles over tourist-oriented development remain intense. One publicized statewide is a squabble over a "wine train" that runs through the valley.

Nevada County

Area: 992.2 sq. mi.; Population: (1990) 78,510, (1980) 51,645; Registration: (1992) D-37.5% R-46.5%; Unemployment: (Oct. 1992) 8.6%; County supervisors: Karen Knecht, Melody Lane, Bill Schultz, Dave Tobiassen, Jim Weir; 950 Maidu Ave., Nevada City 95959; (916) 265-1480.

Nevada County, with the highest percentage of white residents in the state (93.9 percent), is typical of the fast growing Sierra foothill region. Between 1980 and 1990, it recorded a whopping 52 percent population growth, the fifth-largest rate in the state, as increasing numbers of retirees, Sacramento commuters and urban escapees settled there.

The county has developed a home-grown electronics industry and a burgeoning retail trade market, supplemented in some corners by marijuana cultivation. The Nevada City-Grass Valley area has become a regional commercial, medical and cultural center, and there is a thriving arts community in North San Juan. The combination of foothill and mountain beauty and mild climate continues to draw both visitors and those looking for new roots. And the major question facing the county is whether to impose stricter curbs on development.

Nevada County, like other foothill communities, has been moving to the right politically. Despite that, Supervisor Jim Weir switched his registration from Democrat to Green Party last year. Republicans outnumber Democrats and voters have that "leave-me-alone" philosophy that dominates the region.

Orange County

Area: 785.1 sq. mi.; Population: (1990) 2,410,556, (1980) 1,932,921; Registration: (1992) D-34.5% R-52.3%; Unemployment: (Oct. 1992) 6.6%; County supervisors: Thomas Riley, Don Roth, Roger Stanton, Gaddi Vasquez, Harriett Wieder; 10 Civic Center, Santa Ana 92701; (714) 834-3100.

No piece of California typifies the state's development rush more than Orange County, a patch of coastline and rolling hills immediately south of Los Angeles. Prior to World War II, Orange County was cattle ranges (controlled by big, Spanish-land-grant ranchers such as the Irvines and the O'Neills), vegetable fields and citrus orchards. After the war, and especially after 1955, the county exploded with houses and suburbs. It achieved national and international attention for two very different attributes: it is the home of Disneyland and is a major hotbed of right-wing politics.

As the British Broadcasting Corp. said in a 1976 documentary on Orange County: "This is the culmination of the American dream." That dream was a home in the suburbs, two cars and maybe a ski boat, and a barbecue in the back yard. Orange County reproduced it hundreds of thousands of times in one generation.

When Walt Disney opened his amusement park in 1955, Anaheim was a city of 35,000. Over the next 30 years, along with the growth of motels, fast-food outlets and restaurants, Anaheim's population increased ninefold, matching what was happening in Orange County as a whole, which became the state's second-most populous county.

But the county continues to exist in the shadow of much-larger, infinitely-more-glamorous Los Angeles to the north. Even its professional sports teams, the Los Angeles Rams football team and the California Angels baseball team, don't take their names from the county. And Orange County is the largest urban area in the country without its own network television service.

Although no one city dominates Orange County, Irvine and nearby Costa Mesa are the urban centers. The region's dazzling performing arts center is in Costa Mesa, and the county's growing airport, named for the late actor and county resident John Wayne, lies just outside that city. Together with the development of the UC Irvine campus and the community of Irvine, the two cities have created a cultural locus that had been lacking during the county's go-go phase of growth.

This area, sprawled on both sides of Interstate 405, epitomizes the change that occurred in the 1970s. While new suburbs sprouted further east in Riverside County, slowing the population growth in Orange County, the region became a center for the development of California's post-industrial economy rooted in trade, services and high-tech fabrication. Only downtown Los Angeles rivals the area's concentration of office space. UC Irvine has become a center for biotech research and development and the county has more than 700 high-tech companies.

The evolution of the Irvine-centered commercial and cultural complex also reflects the shift of emphasis from the older cities of Santa Ana and Anaheim in the north to the central and southern parts of the county. The older communities, meanwhile, have found themselves with large and growing Hispanic and Southeast Asian communities. The Hispanics have not become a political force, but Vietnamese Americans were a key factor in U.S. Rep. Robert "B-1 Bob" Dornan's election to Congress in 1984.

As Orange County developed into an employment center, the commute patterns also changed, eventually producing traffic congestion of titanic proportions. No one makes plans, no one gives directions, no one shops without considering traffic. Besides the local drivers, the county's mostly older freeways handle thousands and thousands of cars from suburbs in Riverside and elsewhere – suburbs created in response to the skyrocketing home prices in Orange County. Traffic, in turn, has fueled a local anti-growth movement that has drawn support from both conservatives and liberals. And it has convinced people of the need for toll roads.

As home prices went up, population growth slowed further. In the early 1980s, the county was growing slower than the state as a whole and by the mid-1980s, San Diego supplanted Orange as the state's second-most populous county. Growth in the county's southern portion in the late 1980s pushed Orange County's growth rate up to just about the state average of 25 percent for the decade.

Even though Democrats achieved a short-lived plurality of voter registration in the mid-1970s, politics always have been conservative and sometimes wacko conservative. Arguably, no other county could have produced two congressmen as nutty as Dornan and William Dannemeyer. Yet Orange County also bore the brunt of the collapse of the aerospace industry in the early 1990s. GOP registration slipped by 3.3 percentage points in 1992, most of that going to the independent column.

Under the direction of county chairman Howard Adler, the Democrats made serious inroads in the 1992 elections. Orange was the only major California county that the Bush presidential campaign carried in 1992, but Bush won by only 106,000 votes - which is less than a third of his 1988 plurality. Bush took 43 percent of the vote compared to 32 percent for Bill Clinton and 24 percent for Ross Perot. Obviously, the Perot candidacy hurt Bush much more than it hurt Clinton.

More telling was the U.S. Senate race that pitted Dianne Feinstein against the GOP's John Seymour, a former Anaheim mayor whom Orange County residents had elected to the state Senate on three occasions. Feinstein lost Orange to Seymour by 92,000 votes, but Seymour needed at least a 200,000-vote margin to make up for projected losses elsewhere in the state.

Placer County

Area: 1,506.5 sq. mi.; Population: (1990) 172,796, (1980) 117,247; Registra-

tion: (1992) D-40.8% R-46.3%; Unemployment: (Oct. 1992) 8.4%; County supervisors: Rex Broomfield, Alex Ferreira, Ron Lichau, Phil Ozenick, Kirk Uhler; 175 Fulweiler Ave., Auburn 95603; (916) 823-4641.

Fast-growing Placer County represents three distinct pieces of the variegated California landscape.

The western portion, centered in and around Roseville, has evolved into a booming residential and industrial suburb of Sacramento County, with an expanding connection to the Silicon Valley computer complex. The middle part of the county around Auburn, the quaint, gold rush era foothill county seat, is growing rapidly too, with commuters, retirees and urban expatriates. And the eastern part of the county is high-mountain country that includes the northern shore of Lake Tahoe, which also is feeling development pressure.

The common denominator – and a major reason for the county's growth – is Interstate 80, the major east-west highway that connects San Francisco and Sacramento with the rest of the continent. The county's population grew by nearly 50 percent in the 1980s, and it will continue to expand at that rapid clip.

Growth is moving the area's politics ever rightward, but oddly, has not generated a consensus on construction of the Auburn Dam on the American River. Auburn is the last major dam site in the lower 48 states that has a chance of being built. Incredibly, the controversy over whether to build it has been raging since 1947.

Plumas County

Area: 2,618.4 sq. mi.; Population: (1990) 19,739, (1980) 17,340; Registration: (1992) D-47.8% R-38.4%; Unemployment: (Oct. 1992) 10.6%; County supervisors: Phil Bresciani, Bill Coates, Fran Roudebuch, Robert Meacher, Paul Simpson; P.O. Box 207, Quincy 95971; (916) 283-0280.

Plumas County folks often feel more cultural and economic affinity with Nevada than with expansive, fast-changing California. Reno, 80 miles to the southeast, is the nearest big town, and much of the county's economic activity crosses the state border.

Seventy percent of the county's land is owned by the federal government, mostly by the Forest Service. The troubled lumber industry is the mainstay of the economy, which gets a little supplement from tourism. It shares with other rural counties a chronically high unemployment rate and major budget problems. Plumas' population is growing at about half the rate of the rest of the state, and most of those newcomers are retirees and others seeking quiet refuge in the area's heavily forested lands. County politics are predictably conservative, although there has been a years-long battle for control of the Board of Supervisors that has included charges of election-rigging.

Riverside County

Area: 7,243 sq. mi.; Population: (1990) 1,170,413, (1980) 663,199; Registration: (1992) D-43% R-45.1%; Unemployment: (Oct. 1992) 14.4%; County supervisors: Bob Buster, Kay Ceniceros, Melba Dunlap, Patricia Larson, A. Norton Younglove; 4080 Lemon St., Riverside 92501; (714) 787-2010.

Riverside County is Southern California's newest boom area and the state's fastest growing county by far. Until the recession slowed the pace in 1992, Riverside and neighboring San Bernardino Counties were developing at a breakneck rate reminiscent of the San Fernando Valley and Orange County development after World War II. The cause of the growth is the same: young families searching for affordable suburban homes.

While median home prices soared to the quarter-million-dollar mark in Los Angeles and Orange counties, developers subdivided large tracts of arid Riverside County and sold houses for less than half that amount. Newly minted Riverside residents are willing to commute as long as two hours each way to job centers closer to the coast.

The county, which began the 1980s with 663,199 people, exploded by 76 percent by 1990. Impacts of that dizzying growth have been many, ranging from suddenly crowded freeways to worsening smog problems. Untold acres of orange groves – which had been the county's chief economic support until the real estate boom – were uprooted to make room for the new subdivisions and that, in turn, sparked an anti-growth backlash in the mid-1980s.

While growth issues remain the focus of the county's major political battles, the suburban-style expansion has moved Riverside sharply to the right in the same way growth affected Orange County after World War II. Not too many years ago, Riverside was solidly Democratic, but by 1988 Republicans had pulled ahead in registration and the remaining Democratic officeholders faced perilous times.

Riverside County's growing conservatism is getting a shove from Palm Springs, the high-desert community where retired captains of industry live. Given its new large and conservative population, Riverside should have benefited from the post-1990 census reapportionment, which should have meant more opportunities for Republicans. But the problem for the GOP was that the newcomers were unwilling to add a trip to the polls to a day already burdened by long commutes. And with a recession breathing down their necks, those young conservatives who did vote deserted the GOP in droves in 1992 and gave the county to Bill Clinton. Democrat Rep. George Brown again astounded the pundits and won a 16th term while GOP candidate Ken Calvert won by a whisker in a new congressional district. The state of the economy in 1994 could dictate whether 1992 was an aberration or the beginning of a new political trend in Riverside County.

Sacramento County

Area: 1,015.3 sq. mi.; Population: (1990) 1,041,219, (1980) 783,381; Registration: (1992) D-52.8% R-35.6%; Unemployment: (Oct. 1992) 7.7%; County supervisors: Illa Collin, Grantland Johnson, Toby Johnson, Muriel Johnson, Dave Cox; 700 H St., Suite 2450, Sacramento 95814; (916) 440-5451.

For decades, the Sacramento area slept while other urban areas boomed. It was known as a terminally dull government community, filled with civil servants who labored not only for the state but for dozens of federal offices as well.

More than 40 percent of the Sacramento County's work force collects public paychecks, and the metropolitan area, which includes most of the county as well as chunks of neighboring counties, seems to be nothing but a collection of endless suburban tracts and shopping centers – including California's first shopping center, which was built shortly after World War II.

In the late 1970s, however, the Sacramento region began to awaken. Soaring Bay Area housing costs and clogged roads began pushing development outward, and Sacramento, with its cheaper housing and relatively easy lifestyle, became an attractive spot for employers looking to relocate. Today, government continues to be the economic backbone of the area, but the hottest growth is in the private sector. The downsizing of state government and closure of two major military facilities (Mather Air Force Base and Sacramento Army Depot) will hasten the erosion of the Sacramento-area's public employment base.

Downtown Sacramento began sprouting skyscrapers in the 80s, fertile fields were converted to high-tech job centers and dozens of subdivisions sprang up. By 1989, Sacramento had been featured on the cover of a national news magazine as one of the country's best places to live. It had become the fastest growing region in the state and one of the nation's fastest growing metropolitan areas.

But there have been down sides to Sacramento's heady growth, such as crime, traffic congestion and worsening air quality. And the area is beset by perhaps the worst mish-mash of governmental authority in the state. The city of Sacramento is only a fifth of the metropolitan area, and the county has the highest proportion of unincorporated, urbanized land of any county in the state. Attempts at city-county consolidation failed in 1974 and again in 1990. That left the city and county to squabble over development, sales taxes and political influence. Although the supervisors represent much more of the county, it is the City Council that reaps most of the publicity, for better or more often worse.

Sacramento is the largest city in the state with a part-time council. Two-term Mayor Anne Rudin stepped down in 1992, to be replaced by councilman and government professor Joe Serna, whose political mentor in the late '60s was then-state Sen. Mervyn Dymally. Serna's election, along with the addition of two more conservatives to the board of supervisors signaled a strengthening of developer dominance of governing boards which Rudin fought so hard to minimize.

As with most government enclaves, Sacramento County has been dependably Democratic. But with suburbanization and private-sector job development, that, too, is changing. Democrats still dominate in the city, but the fast-growing suburbs are increasingly represented by candidates from the Christian right. In 1992, the conservative Christians financed campaigns to seize several park boards and make inroads in school board elections. Their leaders promised to go after more elective slots at every level.

San Benito County

Area: 1,397.1 sq. mi.; Population: (1990) 36,697, (1980) 25,005; Registration: (1992) D-49.2% R-36.6%; Unemployment: (Oct. 1992) 18.3%; County supervisors: Rita Bowling, Curtis Graves, Mike Graves, Ruth Kesler, Richard Scagliotti; 440 Fifth St., Hollister 95023; (408) 637-4641.

San Benito County lies in a little recess of public consciousness, overshadowed by its larger and/or more glamorous neighbors, Santa Clara and Monterey counties. But that may be changing.

As the extended Bay Area continues to march southward, San Benito is growing at a healthy rate and seems poised for a boom. From 1980 to 1990, the county population swelled by 46 percent, and as Highway 152, the major east-west route through the county, is converted into a full freeway, more commuter-oriented development appears certain.

The question is whether this growth will overwhelm the slow-paced, rural lifestyle that has been San Benito's hallmark. Another question is whether the county's very large Hispanic population (second highest in the state with 46 percent) will assume political power in keeping with its numbers or continue to play a secondary role.

San Bernardino County

Area: 20,164 sq. mi.; Population: (1990) 1,418,380, (1980) 895,016; Registration: (1992) D-44.9% R-43.6%; Unemployment: (Oct. 1992) 9.9%; County super-

visors: Jerry Eaves, Jon Mikels, Barbara Crum Riordan, Marsha Turoci, Larry Walker, 385 N. Arrowhead Ave., San Bernardino 92415; (714) 387-4811.

San Bernardino County – or San Berdoo, as it is almost universally called – is huge. The county covers more land than any other in the United States, and its 20,000-plus square miles constitute more than an eighth of California. But most of those square miles are unpopulated desert, and more than three-fourths of them are owned by the federal government.

Politically, culturally and economically, most of what counts in San Bernardino lies in the western portion nearest Los Angeles, and that's a sore point with residents in the rest of the county. There was a failed effort in 1988 to split San Bernardino County and create a new county in the desert called Mojave.

The western slab of San Berdoo, along with neighboring Riverside County, is what boosters call the "Inland Empire," and that fanciful name is taking on new weight as commuters in search of affordable homes convert the once-grimy industrial towns of western San Bernardino County, such as Rialto and Fontana, into bedroom communities. San Bernardino was second only to Riverside County in population growth, expanding by about 58 percent between 1980 and 1990.

Along with the growth have come all the usual problems: environmental damage, smog, and social dislocation. There is some growth in jobs in the area, especially around Ontario International Airport, but the job-people mix is a continuing headache for local leaders.

The heavy industries that had been San Bernardino's economic foundation, typified by the now-cold steel works at Fontana, have given way to shopping centers, freight handling and other post-industrial economic activities. Dairy farmers around Chino, who used to supply much of the Los Angeles area's milk, are finding that the scent of cows is not compatible with the dreams of new suburbanites.

On the plus side, the growth in land values has given San Bernardino one of the healthiest county budgets in the state.

Politically, San Berdoo has historically been blue-collar Democrat, tending to vote conservatively: Republican at the top of the ticket and Democrat for local and state offices. But the suburbs brought partisan change. In 1988, Democrats dropped below Republicans in registration, and local Democratic officeholders are feeling the pinch while Republicans see a bright future.

San Diego County

Area: 4,280.6 sq. mi.; Population: (1990) 2,498,016, (1980) 1,861,846; Registration: (1992) D-37.4% R-45.4%; Unemployment: (Oct. 1992) 7.8%; County

supervisors: Brian Bilbray, Diane Jacob, John MacDonald, Pam Slater, Leon Williams; 1600 Pacific Highway, San Diego 92101; (619) 531-5198.

San Diego is the California of popular legend: sunny days, sparkling beaches, sail-bedecked harbors, red-tiled roofs, palm trees and laid-back people everywhere. A lot of folks want a piece of that legend, which makes San Diego County a popular destination for everyone from young professionals to retirees.

In a state of diverse geography, San Diego might have the most variation in one county. Within a few miles, there are ocean beaches, rolling hills, sometime-snowy mountains and stark desert. That diversity means people looking for just about any environment have wandered in. In fact, it has become the second-most populous county in the state. By 2010, nearly 1 in 10 Californians will be a San Diegan.

But the rocketing growth in San Diego over the past generation, more than doubling in population since 1960, also raises the question: If everyone comes for the San Diego lifestyle, will there be any of that lifestyle left? For many, the answer is No. That's why growth and its control have become the overriding political issue in the county.

Two recent events crystallized San Diego's uncertainty about its future and its collective fear about becoming another Los Angeles. Voters rejected a couple of growth restriction ballot measures in 1988, but when San Diego Gas and Electric Co. proposed to merge with Los Angeles-based Southern California Edison, there was a fear bordering on panic among residents and politicians of both parties.

San Diego also has a tense relationship with its neighbor to the south – Tijuana. The contrast between Tijuana, with its 1.5 million mostly poor residents, and San Diego could not be more striking. It is where the Third World bumps into the First World. And like matter meeting anti-matter, the collision is often explosive. Drugs and illegal aliens steadily flow across the border, and Mexican and American border police have exchanged gunfire, mistaking each other for bandits. A routine sight every evening are the campfires of Mexican nationals lining up along the border to dash into San Diego after dark.

San Diego is also downhill from Tijuana, which means Mexican sewage pollutes San Diego beaches. The problem has become so severe that San Diegans are pressuring Gov. Pete Wilson, a former San Diego mayor, to declare a state of emergency. More than any area of the state, San Diego is one city that needs a foreign policy.

For most of the 20th century, San Diego had been known mostly as a Navy town and as a center for aircraft production. But in the mid-1960s, San Diego County began diversifying economically and its population started to grow. With growth controls in the city of San Diego, the fastest-growing part of the county is the north. The San Diego Association of Governments estimates that between 1980 and 2000, central San Diego County will grow by only 12 percent while outlying suburbs will more than double in population.

Politically, San Diego always has been a paradox. A tolerant attitude toward lifestyles and a strong blue-collar manufacturing base have not prevented San Diego from being largely Republican territory. But local GOP leaders, including Wilson, tend to be from the moderate wing of the party. In addition, a core of Democratic activists keeps the party fairly well represented in legislative seats.

Recent mayors such as Wilson, Roger Hedgecock and Maureen O'Connor (a Democrat) all fit that centrist mold. The current mayor, former County Supervisor Susan Golding, is a pro-growth Republican who bucked several trends when she narrowly defeated UC Irvine professor Peter Navarro in 1992. It was an exceedingly nasty race and the most expensive local election in San Diego history. Some $1.5 million was spent by the two sides.

At the same time, Bill Clinton was beating George Bush in a county that hadn't voted for a Democratic president since Franklin Roosevelt's last election in 1944. Gov. Wilson spent substantial time in the county during the last week of the election trying to salvage Republican seats, but he had little to show for it. Democrats took two congressional seats and increased their numbers in the Assembly. State Sen. Lucy Killea, a Democrat turned independent, also beat off a lethargic challenge from retired GOP state Sen. Jim Ellis.

Part of the Republican problem had to do with voter turnout. For reasons that perplex the pundits, San Diego County has had low turnouts in the past decade. That was true even when hometown candidate Pete Wilson was locked in a tight race for governor in 1990. Unless Wilson can arouse more interest among San Diego moderates and conservatives in 1994, San Diego County could be his Waterloo.

San Francisco County

Area: 49 sq. mi.; Population: (1990) 731,700, (1980) 678,974; Registration: (1992) D-63% R-17.1%; Unemployment: (Oct. 1992) 7%; Mayor: Frank Jordan; City/county supervisors: Roberta Achtenberg, Angela Alioto, Sue Bierman, Annemarie Conroy, Terence Hallinan, Tom Hsieh, Barbara Kaufman, Willie Kennedy, Bill Maher, Carol Migden, Kevin Shelley; 400 Van Ness Ave., San Francisco 94102; (415) 554-5184; Incorporated: 1850.

In a sophisticated city like San Francisco, nothing succeeds like a sophisticated scam. At least that's the way many saw it when Mayor Frank Jordan called a news conference in mid-1992 to announce that he had reorganized his entire administration to focus on one issue: keeping the Giants baseball team in San Francisco. The "crisis" had been created when Giants owner Bob Lurie, having had yet another new stadium proposal voted down by San Franciscans, announced that he had found a new home for the team. St. Petersburg, Fla., had an empty stadium and backers willing to pay $115 million for the Giants.

Many would argue that San Francisco, California's only consolidated city-county, had many problems far more pressing than whether a bunch of sweaty guys retired to Florida. After all, Jordan had promised to do something about the filthy streets and 6,000-to-10,000 homeless people camping out in city parks and plazas. But the mayor had been in office nearly six months and there was no juggernaut being assembled to take on those problems. In addition, the city had an AIDS epidemic, a failing school system, had curtailed library hours and other services, and was facing civil service layoffs to solve a $200 million budget deficit.

In recent years, San Francisco has lost its maritime trade to more modern ports such as nearby Oakland. Its industrial base, including the famous fishing industry, has shrunk. It has lost its position as the West's financial capital to much-hated Los Angeles. It continues to lose office jobs to suburban centers in Contra Costa and San Mateo counties. It is losing middle-class whites to the suburbs and gentrification has driven many African Americans out as well. The economic slide has weakened and scattered the organized labor strength, which once made San Francisco the most heavily unionized city west of Chicago. And after the 1989 Loma Prieta earthquake, San Francisco had even lost some of its allure for tourists and conventioneers. The danger of those trends is that San Francisco will become a caricature of itself, a place where only the wealthy and the poor live, a city dependent on the fickle tourist trade that increasingly attends matinees in the city's theaters since at night many of the dark and filthy streets are littered with undesirables.

Those concerns were being voiced at the time of the Giants' announcement, but few could hear them. The sports boosters were marching forward with the news media braying for all to clear the way. The Giants were the lead in most news broadcasts; the San Francisco Chronicle and the San Francisco Examiner often draped three or four Giants stories daily across their front pages. The slant of the coverage was called "unconscionable" by the newspaper's own reporters. "I was forced to draw the conclusion that the Chronicle's corporate and monetary interests were influencing its Giants' coverage – the type of conflict of interest story that interests us every day," said political reporter Susan Yoachum. "Shame on us!"

There was the mayor, mobilizing the city's millionaires to bail out a team that draws most of its support from outside the city. When it was all over, the Giants stayed, Lurie was still be biggest shareholder and a team that Lurie paid $8 million for in 1976 now had a new combination of owners who had ponied up $100 million. As the city abolished the jobs of health workers and librarians, the price of the Giants' lease of Candlestick Park was cut from $750,000 a year to $1. The Giants would keep all scoreboard advertising and parking-lot profits while the city paid for most utilities and field maintenance. In all, it was estimated that the deal would cost the city $3.1 million a year.

Oh, well, San Franciscans seemed to say. Politicians come and go. And some day the Giants may, too. But in the meantime, it is still a dazzling city with cosmopolitan attitudes found in few places in the West. It has become, in effect, the capital of Asian California. And the gay rights movement is just the latest manifestation of San Francisco's well-known tolerance for unconventional lifestyles, a tradition that is rooted in the city's founding as a port of entry for gold-rush fortune seekers and has continued through decades of boom and bust, crooked mayors, quakes and fires.

San Francisco is a city of intense politics resembling those of New York or Chicago more than Los Angeles or San Diego. Every San Franciscan, or so it can seem, belongs to some political pressure group. These range from lifestyle-and ethnic-oriented groups to neighborhood and environmental associations. And they exist to oppose – strenuously – anything envisioned as a threat to their value systems. Republicans are an endangered species in a city that a couple of generations ago was a GOP stronghold, so most of the political plotting pits Democrat against Democrat.

Political generalizations are dangerous amid such diversity, but there is a broad issue at the core of the city's recent political history: development. Although San Francisco's population is stable and much of its employment base has fled, there is continuing pressure to develop hotels and other tourist-related and retail facilities. San Francisco's business community bases its hopes on the city's continued attractiveness to out-of-towners, either shoppers from the suburbs or tourists and conventioneers. But development, in the minds of many, threatens the "real San Francisco," however that may be defined.

City politics swerve back and forth as first one group then the other dominates. That's why San Francisco has freeways that stop in midair, dropping streams of cars onto city streets at the most inopportune places, and why every proposal for change creates a volcanic reaction. The pro-development mayorship of Joseph Alioto was followed by the liberal reign of George Moscone. But Moscone was shot and killed in his office, bringing in another pro-development mayor, Dianne Feinstein. When Feinstein's second full term ended in 1987, it was time for another great debate over the future of San Francisco.

The winner against pro-development candidate John Molinari was one of the city's two assemblymen, Art Agnos. Agnos galvanized groups united by their distaste for business as usual: gays, environmental activists, ethnic minorities and others. But Agnos' administration spent much of its efforts handling crises, most of them caused by events far beyond Agnos' control. At the end of four years, he had antagonized most of the factions that he had so skillfully brought together. Former police chief Jordan took out Agnos by 4 percentage points at the polls.

Jordan's Giants "victory" not withstanding, it was a rocky first year for the mayor. Bad appointments, turnover among his top staff and no clearly defined agenda were just some of his most obvious problems. On top of that, Jordan was urging people to volunteer to staff libraries and clean graffiti off public structures at the same time that he and his bride, Wells Fargo attorney Wendy Paskin, were busy acquiring a $745,000 home in Pacific Heights. If such missteps continue, Jordan is likely to have plenty of opponents next time around. One could be Leo McCarthy, one of San Francisco's most enduring political figures. He has served as a supervisor, a state assemblyman (he was Willie Brown's predecessor as speaker) and, since 1983, as California's lieutenant governor.

The longer-term questions about San Francisco center on its diversity. The old power structure based on the late Rep. Phil Burton's political machine seems to be breaking down. But no single political group is rising to replace it. Instead, dozens of interest groups battle constantly among themselves for power and influence at City Hall, and the alliances are as solid as the fog that flows in and out of the Golden Gate.

San Francisco is the nation's most ethnically mixed city, and the most noticeable element of that diversity are the Asians, who have moved beyond Chinatown and Japantown to become an important economic factor in virtually every neighborhood. Asians are the city's latent political powerhouse, but, at least to date, they do not vote in great numbers and they lack a charismatic leader.

African Americans are declining in number as soaring housing costs drive them out of the city, but they continue to enjoy political power disproportionate to their number. Hispanics from a dozen nations continue to settle in San Francisco, but, as in other California cities, they have yet to solidify into a political bloc.

Beyond ethnic lines, San Francisco's people are spread across a rainbow of ideologies and lifestyles. The most visible are lesbians and gays, whose political leadership has been decimated by AIDS. Gays are demanding more power to accompany their rising economic clout, and the city is likely to produce the state's first openly gay state legislator. There is even a residue of conservatism to be found in middle-class neighborhoods, personified by state Sen. Quentin Kopp, a Democrat-turned-independent.

The city, meanwhile, continues to grow less like a mini-New York, dominated by banks and big business, and to resemble more a collection of identifiable communities with employment concentrated in smaller businesses. A 1988 study by Bank of America concluded that San Francisco's future depends on the expansion of small business, and it is in those neighborhood-based businesses that much of the city's economic vitality and political activism is found. Gays have been especially successful in translating neighborhood businesses into economic and political clout. Asians seem to be following that model as well, but African Americans and Hispanics have not moved into those channels.

San Franciscans scarcely acknowledged the 1989 event that was front-page news elsewhere. The state Department of Finance, in its periodic updating of population data, calculated that San Jose, 50 miles to the south, had passed San Francisco to become the state's third most populous city behind Los Angeles and San Diego. So what, San Franciscans shrugged. They have the cable cars, the hills, the tall buildings, the banks, the bay, the opera, the theater, the Giants, the 49ers and the tourist business. San Jose just had people, they seemed to say, and not very interesting people at that.

San Joaquin County

Area: 1,436.2 sq. mi.; Population: (1990) 480,628, (1980) 347,342; Registration: (1992) D-52.8% R-37.3%; Unemployment: (Oct. 1992) 14.9%; County supervisors: George Barber, Robert Cabral, Ed Simas, William Sousa, Douglass Wilhoit; 222 E. Weber St., Stockton 95202; (209) 944-3113.

It wasn't too many years ago that in California's vast Central Valley, San Joaquin County was farm country. But the crop thriving in many of those fields these days is housing for San Francisco Bay Area refugees. San Joaquin County's population is up more than 38 percent since 1980, and it is a change most noticeable in the once-quiet farm towns such as Tracy and Manteca in the county's southern and western corners.

The change is less dramatic in San Joaquin County's biggest city, Stockton, but even that town is changing from an agricultural center with a few non-farm industries into a regional retail and service hub that includes two colleges, most notably the University of the Pacific.

San Joaquin voters mirror those in the Central Valley in registering Democrat but often voting conservatively. Stockton, however, with its ethnic diversity and industrial base, is a dependable Democratic area. Yet despite hot races for Congress and the Assembly in 1992, San Joaquin had the lowest rate of voter turnout in the state - 63.6 percent. That helps explain why both races went narrowly Republican.

San Luis Obispo County

Area: 3,326.2 sq. mi.; Population: (1990) 217,162, (1980) 155,435; Registration: (1992) D-39% R-44.5%; Unemployment: (Oct. 1992) 7%; County supervisors: David Blakely, Ruth Brackett, Evelyn Delany, Laurence Laurent, Harry Ovitt; County Government Center, San Luis Obispo 93408; (805) 549-5450.

Midway between San Francisco and Los Angeles, blessed with a beautiful blend of coastline, beaches, mountains and near-perfect weather, San

Luis Obispo, both city and county, represents another version of California heaven. The county's soaring population is up by about 40 percent since 1980.

Folks fleeing the pains of urban life have cashed in their inflated home equities and headed either north or south along Highway 101. But, as in so many other places around the state, the newcomers are pumping up local housing costs and threatening to damage the qualities that make "SLO-town," as local college students call it, so pleasant.

For the time being, San Luis Obispo County seems to be weathering the assault, mostly because it has a well-balanced economy rooted in agriculture, tourism and the civil service payrolls of a state university, a state prison and a state hospital.

Politically, despite the presence of the college and so many public employees, San Luis Obispo is Republican and unlikely to change.

San Mateo County

Area: 530.8 sq. mi.; Population: (1990) 649,623, (1980) 587,329; Registration: (1992) D-52.5% R-32%; Unemployment: (Oct, 1992) 5.3%; County supervisors: Ruben Barrales, Mary Griffin, Tom Huening, Mike Nevin; 401 Marshall St., Redwood City 94063; (415) 363-4000.

San Mateo County, the swath of the San Francisco Peninsula directly south of San Francisco itself, isn't very large, but it contains all the enormous social and economic extremes of California.

Portions of the hilly county such as Hillsborough and Atherton are as wealthy as California gets. The business executives and professionals – many with prime offices in San Francisco – who live in those communities of gently winding, tree-shaded streets earn an average of more than $100,000 a year.

Northern San Mateo County, nearest to San Francisco and containing San Francisco International Airport, is blue collar and middle class, with incomes a third of those found in the wealthier areas. Along the coast there is everything from middle-class suburbs to the ramshackle houses of the 1960s and '70s runaways. And at the southern edge of the county along the bay there is East Palo Alto, a mostly African American community where people struggle to survive against drugs, crime and poverty.

San Mateo is typical of California's closer-in suburban areas: there is scant population growth (just 10 percent between 1980 and 1990), soaring home prices and expansive employment growth, mostly in white-collar and service jobs. As a recipient of commuters as well as a supplier, the county suffers changing and confusing traffic problems.

The Association of Bay Area Governments estimates that between 1985 and 2005, San Mateo will employ 90,000 more people, with the majority of jobs in finance, insurance and real estate accounting. Hard evidence of that trend includes the new office complexes along the Bayshore Freeway or in Foster City, which was created 30 years ago on San Francisco Bay landfill.

San Mateo has the political diversity to match its social differences. The blue-collar and poorer areas are rock-solid Democratic, while the affluent middle of the county tends to be Republican, albeit of the moderate, pro-environment, libertarian-lifestyle variety personified by ex-Rep. Pete McCloskey, one of the area's best known political figures.

Santa Barbara County

Area: 2,744.7 sq. mi.; Population: (1990) 369,608, (1980) 298,694; Registration: (1992) D-42.5% R-40.2%; Unemployment: (Oct. 1992) 8.1%; County supervisors: William Chamberlain, Tom Rogers, Naomi Schultz, Tim Staffel, Michael Stoker; 105 E. Acapamu St., Santa Barbara 93101; (805) 681-4200.

Santa Barbarans live in dread of a perpetually voracious animal – Los Angeles. Santa Barbarans fear that the pulsating powerhouse to the south will swallow up their pleasant lifestyle and convert their region into just another suburb.

"Quality-of-life," however defined, is the dominant political and social issue of the area. To some, it means a never-ending anger at the presence of oil-drilling platforms off the coast, with the latent danger of another serious spill. That's why "GOO," standing for "Get Oil Out," adorns the bumpers of many local cars. And to others, it means resisting new subdivisions in the hills or more hotels along the waterfront.

Santa Barbara County is growing, though at a slower rate than the state average. Local activists have managed to block most major development and the payback for that has been soaring real estate prices that preclude all but the affluent. The resultant somewhat exclusive social atmosphere is reinforced by the trendy shops in Santa Barbara's ranch-style downtown business district.

Outside of the city, Santa Barbara is self-consciously rural. Ex-President Ronald Reagan's ranch typifies life in the hills and horse country above the coast, and there are several small communities that serve these affluent rustics. There also is Vandenberg Air Force Base space center on the northern edge of the county, near Santa Maria, from which many satellite-carrying rockets are launched.

Politically, Santa Barbara County has a near tie between Democrats and Republicans, although Democrats recaptured the registration lead in 1992. That translates into something of a split political personality. Santa Barbara tends to vote Republican at the top of the ticket, but both state legislators from the area are liberal Democrats who have withstood Republican challenges.

Santa Clara County

Area: 1,315.9 sq. mi.; Population: (1990) 1,497,577, (1980) 1,295,071; Registration: (1992) D-49.1% R-34.8%; Unemployment: (Oct. 1992) 6.9%; County supervisors: Rod Diridon, Ron Gonzales, Michael Honda, Zoe Lofgren, Dianne McKenna; 70 W. Hedding St., 10th floor, San Jose 95110; (408) 299-2323.

Santa Clara County is one of the engines that drives the economy of the San Francisco Bay Area, and its fuel is the computer-electronics industry. Between 1980 and 1985, nearly half of all new jobs in the nine-county region were created in Santa Clara County, and most were connected to "Silicon Valley," which used to be a geographic term but now is a generic description for the electronic industries found in and around Santa Clara County.

The Association of Bay Area Governments estimates that between 1985 and 2005, Santa Clara will add nearly 400,000 new jobs, more than half of them in manufacturing and wholesale trade. While the high-tech companies have had their peaks and valleys, the direction over the long term has been consistently upward. But economic success has had its price, including toxic contamination of groundwater from chemicals used in the high-tech plants.

San Jose, the county's largest city, is a nationwide joke on how not to deal with growth. Homes, shopping centers and business complexes sprang up everywhere with little thought to transportation or other infrastructure. San Jose and other Santa Clara County cities competed, rather than cooperated, and developers played political leaders against each other. For years the downtown looked like a victim of aerial bombing as stores fled for suburban shopping centers.

But in recent years, led by former Mayor Tom McEnery, the city has been reborn. San Jose has completed the first phase of a trolley system; begun a downtown redevelopment project that includes a convention center, a Fairmont hotel and a high-tech museum; improved its airport; and started planning for a major sports complex.

San Jose still has a long way to go. Its school system filed for bankruptcy protection in the mid-1980s. Like other big cities, it has smog, poverty, drug and crime problems. Mayor Susan Hammer, a liberal Democrat like McEnery, continues to push in the aggressive direction set by her predecessor. While Santa Clara, the fourth most populous county in the state, is still growing, high home prices (the median is about $250,000) and traffic jams worse than anywhere in the state except Orange County have removed much of the bloom from the rose.

A partial saving grace has been that Santa Clara's business and political leaders saw the king-size traffic headache relatively early and moved to deal with it. In 1985, Santa Clara was the first county to enact a local sales tax increase to pay for transportation improvements, a step that other congested areas continue to struggle with. The added sales tax was approved by voters because local industry put its financial muscle behind the campaign, and the victory marked the maturation of the high-tech industry and its executives into a civic force. Some executives – David Packard most prominently – have become compelling political and civic figures, and the industry is providing the financial and political muscle for San Jose's redevelopment.

Santa Clara's transportation and other infrastructure improvements also are made easier because Santa Clara representatives virtually control the state budget process. A San Jose senator, Alfred Alquist, chairs the Senate's budget committee, and the Assembly's committee is chaired by San Jose Assemblyman John Vasconcellos.

Despite the county's effort, however, the mismatch of job development and population will continue to cause strains. The county budget is feeling the strain of growth and social change. It assumes one of the largest social welfare budgets of all California counties, partly because of the growing number of Asian immigrants and other poor people. The county coffers have been saved in the past by high property values, but property values are almost flat and damage from the 1989 Loma Prieta earthquake is still another budget drain.

Besides San Jose, which recently surpassed San Francisco to become the state's third-largest city, there are other communities of importance. Palo Alto, on the county's northern edge, is the home of Stanford University. It was the presence of Stanford that initially gave rise to the high-tech industry.

Along Highway 101 south of San Jose, the one-time farm towns of Morgan Hill and Gilroy (which bills itself as the garlic capital of the world) are growing rapidly as they fill up with spillover from Silicon Valley. Fields and orchards are turning into subdivisions and industrial parks.

With its population and economic clout, Santa Clara County has become an area of great political importance. Generally, it has been faithfully Democratic, a reflection of its working-class history. But as home prices soar and affluent people steadily move in, Santa Clara's politics seem to be edging toward the center.

Santa Cruz County

Area: 439.6 sq. mi.; Population: (1990) 229,734, (1980) 188,141; Registration: (1992) D-55.1% R-26.3%; Unemployment: (Oct. 1992) 8.1%; County supervisors: Janet Beautz, Ray Belgard, Fred Keeley, Gary Patton, Walt Symons; 701 Ocean St., Santa Cruz 95060; (408) 425-2201.

Three decades ago, Santa Cruz was a quiet, conservative, seaside community. But the opening of the unconventional University of California campus in

1965, the coming of the hippie era and Santa Cruz's scenic beauty have turned the region – particularly the city of Santa Cruz – into one of the bohemian capitals of California.

The county's politics have turned sharply to the left and become hostile to new development – especially after Santa Cruz began attracting commuters from the nearby Silicon Valley. Into the foreseeable future, the development wars will be a huge element of local politics.

Santa Cruz has had some new dilemmas recently. Its liberal attitudes, lush mountains and pleasant weather have attracted a large number of homeless people and just plain wanderers, placing another burden on an already strained county budget and creating more arguments about whether to be harsh or helpful. The county's budget was almost pushed over the brink by the 1989 Loma Prieta earthquake, which destroyed bridges, roads and buildings, including the Pacific Garden Mall in downtown Santa Cruz. Although the county has used a number of revenue hikes recently permitted by the state, its budget remains in woeful shape and many downtown businesses have not returned.

Local politics are intense. The Santa Cruz City Council is sometimes even quirkier than Berkeley's. The Board of Supervisors is usually split between shrill liberals and bombastic conservatives. It can be quite a show.

Shasta County

Area: 3,850.2 sq. mi.; Population: (1990) 147,036, (1980) 115,715; Registration: (1992) D-43.1% R-43.8%; Unemployment: (Oct. 1992) 11.4%; County supervisors: Patricia Clarke, Irwin Fust, Maurice Johannessen, Francie Sullivan, Molly Wilson, 1500 Court St., Room 207, Redding 96001; (916) 225-5556.

After Butte and Yolo Counties, Shasta may be next on the list of counties in horrible fiscal shape. It already has taken some drastic steps. The public library system was closed in 1988, and voters defeated two tax hikes that would have reopened some or all of the branches. In 1987, the county's general hospital was shut down, bankrupted, according to a County Supervisors Association of California study, by slow or inadequate state reimbursement for services to its patients, a vast majority of whom were indigent.

The county has been helped – a bit – by recent climbs in property values and by tight money management, but its budget remains on the critical list. The property value increase has come from strong growth, particularly in Redding, the county's only city of any size. The area's hot summers and mild winters, the beauty of nearby mountains and Lake Shasta, and great outdoor recreation are drawing "urban-equity refugees," the empty-nesters and retirees seeking less hectic lifestyles.

Shasta County's population has been expanding faster than average, although unemployment remains high. Major employers in the county continue to be resource-oriented manufacturing, principally lumber and mineral products, but those businesses are slowly shrinking. Local boosters hope to attract one of the three new University of California campuses now in the planning stages. Politically, Shasta is conservative and becoming more so.

Sierra County

Area: 958.6 sq. mi.; Population: (1990) 3,318, (1980) 3,073; Registration: (1992) D-46%, R-38.3%; Unemployment: (Oct. 1992) 8.6%; County supervisors: Donald Bowling, Lenny Gallegos, Nevada Lewis, Jerry McCaffrey, Donald McIntosh; P.O. Drawer D, Downieville 95936; (916) 289-3295.

Sierra County, the second least populous California county, has a chronically high unemployment rate that is usually more than double the state average. But local politics do not hinge on such mundane matters as economic growth and population change. Few though they may be, Sierra County's residents fight old-fashioned political turf battles mixed in with sometimes wild moves and countermoves.

The division is mostly geographic, the eastern side of the county against the west. Sierrans fight over such things as whether the county seat should remain in Downieville, in the west, or be moved to Loyalton, in the east. At one point, a male county supervisor was sued for sexual discrimination by a female supervisor. All of that makes the twice-monthly board meetings the best show in the county.

When not fighting with each other, Sierrans usually vote conservatively, although there's a vociferous liberal/environmental contingent.

Siskiyou County

Area: 6,318.3 sq. mi.; Population: (1990) 43,531, (1980) 39,732; Registration: (1992) D-49.3% R-36.8%; Unemployment: (Oct. 1992) 12.8%; County supervisors: Clancy Dutra, Gary Giardino, George Thackeray, Ivan Young, Roger Zwanziger; P.O. Box 338, Yreka 96097; (916) 842-8081.

A half-century ago, there was a semi-serious political drive mounted in the northernmost California counties and the southernmost Oregon counties to break away and create a new state, called "Jefferson." Residents of the area felt they were at once being dominated and ignored by far distant urban centers. Secessionist fever cooled, but there remains a residual feeling – one very evident in scenic and sparsely populated Siskiyou County – of colonial status. Siskiyou residents are among those enthusiastically supporting the latest movement to divide California.

The fate of Siskiyou's timber industry, which accounts for at least one of every 10 jobs, is dependent on the outcome of battles in Sacramento or Washington, D.C., over preservation or use of federally owned timber in the county. There's an equally emotional battle over proposals for a major ski resort on Mount Shasta, the volcano that is Siskiyou's most dominant landmark.

Siskiyou County does have one part of its make-up that is unusual for a rural California county: an African American population that grew out of workers imported from the South by lumber mills. In 1986, Charles Byrd became California's only elected African American sheriff.

Solano County

Area: 872.2 sq. mi.; Population: (1990) 340,421, (1980) 235,203; Registration: (1992) D-55.6 R-31%; Unemployment: (Oct. 1992) 8.7%; County supervisors: Sam Caddle, Barbara Condylis, William Carroll, Ed Schlenker, Skip Thompson; 580 W. Texas St., Fairfield 94533; (707) 429-6218.

Solano County used to be a predictable part of California. Vallejo was an industrial city, the site of a major Navy shipyard and water-oriented industries. Fairfield was the county seat but otherwise a farm town on the edge of the Central Valley. Benicia was a sleepy little bit of history, the site of a former military arsenal and, briefly, a 19th-century California capital. And Vacaville was another farm town that also had a state prison. But relentless growth has changed Solano County in ways no one would have imagined a few years ago.

Vallejo has become a tourist center with the relocation of Marine World-Africa USA on a former golf course. Industry – most prominently a big Anheuser-Busch brewery – has come to Fairfield. And throughout Solano County, the sounds of hammers and saws at work have become part of the background noise as field after field has been transformed into subdivisions and shopping malls. Solano's population shot up by more than 44 percent between 1980 and 1990, and there is no sign that it will slow.

Solano County is being loaded from two directions. While the western portion is transformed into a suburb of the Bay Area, the eastern side, including the once-sleepy farm town of Dixon, falls within the orbit of fast-growing Sacramento. The county's location between the two major Northern California urban complexes also makes it attractive to industrial developers. The Association of Bay Area Governments predicts that Solano will add 58,000 jobs and about 150,000 residents between 1985 and 2005. Not unexpectedly, the county is experiencing growing pains: traffic jams, overburdened water and sewage treatment facilities, and other services. The county's budget is feeling the strain as most of the revenue benefits from growth are going into the coffers of its incorporated cities, while the county continues to foot the bill for more and more services.

As would be expected, growth also has fueled a backlash among residents worried that their rural lifestyles are being destroyed. The county has been Democratic territory – especially blue-collar Vallejo. But with suburbanization comes a noticeable shift to the right, with Republicans looking for future gains.

Sonoma County

Area: 1,597.6 sq. mi.; Population: (1990) 388,222, (1980) 299,681; Registration: (1992) D-56% R-33.9%; Unemployment: (Oct. 1992) 6.8%; County supervisors: Michael Cale, Ernest Carpenter, Nick Esposti, James Haberson, Tim Smith; 575 Administration Drive, Santa Rosa 95403; (707) 527-2241.

In 1986, the Sonoma County Planning Department told county supervisors that the county was growing so fast that it already had as many people as had been predicted by the turn of the century. And there is no end in sight.

When Marin County virtually shut down development in the 1970s, pressure shifted directly to the north, rapidly changing Petaluma – the one-time "chicken capital of the world" – and Santa Rosa, the county seat, into big suburbs. Those cities are changing even more as Santa Rosa develops a significant employment base of its own and becomes a destination point for commuters from housing developments even further up Highway 101, the main north-south artery.

The Association of Bay Area Governments notes that Sonoma County's population tripled between 1950 and 1980, with half of that growth coming in the last decade. It is expected to increase by another 44 percent between 1985 and 2005.

Jobs are growing more slowly, so Sonoma is expected to continue in its role as a bedroom community, at least until after the turn of the century. But as in so many other areas, the qualities that have made Sonoma County so attractive – the rural lifestyle, the soft natural beauty – are threatened by the immensity of the growth. The political leadership has been slow to deal with growth problems. Santa Rosa's sewage problems, which contributed to severe pollution of the scenic Russian River, have been a major embarrassment. And the county was so broke at the end of 1992 that all county offices shutdown for Christmas week.

Meanwhile, an anti-growth backlash has developed, with environmentalists and chicken farmers forming unusual political alliances to fight the conversion of agricultural land into houses and shopping centers. Petaluma was the site of an early development battle when local officials, trying to curtail the damage to the agricultural community in the 1970s, passed a law limiting housing development to 500 units a year. The ensuing lawsuit reached the U.S. Supreme Court, which ruled in Petaluma's favor and thus validated local growth-control laws. A poll of residents listed traffic as the most important issue, followed by education and development.

Politically, Sonoma County has a split personality. The western portion, home to a large gay community and environmental activism, is Democratic and liberal, while the rapidly suburbanizing eastern portion is conservative and Republican. For years, politicians have divided the county more or less along north-south Highway 101 while drawing congressional and legislative districts. Republicans represent the wine country in the eastern portion of the county, while Democrats win in the west.

Stanislaus County

Area: 1,521.2 sq. mi.; Population: (1990) 370,522, (1980) 265,900; Registration: (1992) D-53.4% R-36.1%; Unemployment: (Oct. 1992) 16.4%; County supervisors: Nick Blom, Paul Caruso, Tom Mayfield, Pat Paul, Raymond Clark Simon; 1100 H St., Modesto 95354; (209) 525-6414.

Nowhere in California are the changes that come with suburbanization more starkly evident than in Stanislaus County. For decades, this San Joaquin Valley county was purely agricultural, home of some of the nation's best-known farm products, such as Gallo wine and Foster Farms chicken. But its relative proximity to the San Francisco Bay Area meant it was destined to explode with houses and shopping centers as commuters, especially young ones without big paychecks, searched for affordable homes. Stanislaus' population swelled by over 39 percent between 1980 and 1990.

As the character of the area changes, so do its politics, away from agriculture and toward issues more identifiable with suburban life, some of which conflict with farming. Stanislaus and its major city, Modesto, sit in the middle of a long-term fight over how suburban the region will become.

A decade ago, Modesto put a damper on runaway expansion by requiring that sewer truck expansion proposals be placed on the ballot. But in 1992, a countywide initiative to put a 20-year moratorium on development of farm land was buried at the polls after heavy spending by developers.

Sutter County

Area: 607 sq. mi.; Population: (1990) 64,415, (1980) 52,246; Registration: (1992) D-38.8% R-49.2%; Unemployment: (Oct. 1992) 16.8%; County supervisors: Dick Akin, Joan Bechtel, Joseph Benatar, Casey Kroon, Pete Licari; 463

Second St., Yuba City 95991; (916) 741-7106.

Yuba City and its sister city just across the river, Marysville, found themselves in the national spotlight in 1986 when Rand McNally listed the area as the worst place to live in the United States. The ranking was based on a mish-mash of statistics better suited to large cities than to relatively rural towns. The area was dragged down by such things as its lack of rapid transit and cultural amenities, as well as one very legitimate factor: its high unemployment rate. Unemployment is a sticky problem in agricultural Sutter County, but the region may be on the verge of an economic boom.

Highway 99, which links Yuba City-Marysville with Sacramento, 40 miles away, will be a four-lane freeway within a few years, and there are indications that the population boom in the Sacramento area will zoom up that freeway. A county-commissioned study predicts the first area to become suburbanized will likely be the southern reaches of the county, which will be a shorter commute from downtown Sacramento than the crowded areas of eastern Sacramento County. In anticipation, developers have been quietly acquiring tracts of farmland for years.

Politically, Sutter County is very conservative, with a Republican registration majority, and is likely to remain so.

Tehama County

Area: 2,976 sq. mi.; Population: (1990) 49,620, (1980) 38,888; Registration: (1992) D-48.1% R-38.4%; Unemployment: (Oct. 1992) 13%; County supervisors: Floyd Hicks, Jo Ann Landingham, Shirley Marelli, Barbara McIver, Kathleen Rowen; P.O. Box 250, Red Bluff 96080; (916) 527-4655.

A 1988 article in a California magazine described them as "The Revolutionary Junta of Tehama County." Time magazine told the same story, albeit more briefly, in an article entitled "Going Broke in California." Tehama County supervisors put themselves in the spotlight when they threatened to shut down county government because Proposition 13 and a stingy state government had left them without enough money to take care of legal mandates. They backed down and the state took over partial funding of trial courts.

Tehama County subsists on agriculture – mostly cattle – and timber production, but much of the potential commercial activity is siphoned away by the larger and more vigorous communities of Redding and Chico, both outside the county. That leaves Tehama County with relatively low sales-tax revenues and a woeful budget that hinges on help from the state.

Tehama County sits in the middle of the upper Central Valley with few landmarks of note and attracts relatively few tourists or retirees. Its most notable feature may be that Red Bluff, its chief city, sometimes makes the weather charts as the hottest place in the state.

Trinity County

Area: 4,844.9 sq. mi.; Population: (1990) 13,063, (1980) 11,858; Registration: (1992) D-47.1% R-37%; Unemployment: (Oct. 1992) 13.3%; County supervisors: Norman Burgess, Robert Huddleston, Matthew Leffler, Stan Plowman, Arnold Whitridge; P.O. Drawer 1258, Weaverville 96093; (916) 623-1217.

Nothing is more pervasive in Trinity County than a sense of disconnection to late 20th-century California. Perhaps that helps explain why it was the only California county carried by Ross Perot in 1992.

Weaverville, the county seat and only town of consequence, still contains 19th-century storefronts built during the gold rush. And much of the county's population is scattered in homesteads and tiny communities with names like Peanut, Hayfork and Burnt Ranch. Most of Trinity County's residents are happy in their isolation. They cut timber, raise cattle, and occasionally pan for gold – or grow marijuana – to support themselves and wish the rest of the world would leave them alone.

As legend has it, Weaverville was the inspiration for the fictional kingdom of Shangri-la, and there is something mystical about the Trinity Alps, the magnificent and sometimes impenetrable range of mountains dominating much of the county. It is unlikely Trinity will share in any of the changes sweeping the state since it is a long and difficult drive from any population center.

Like other rural counties, the budget coffers are getting pretty bare. Voters turned down a 1988 sales-tax hike and state bailout measures have not helped much. For example, a plan to let the counties keep traffic fines has mattered little in a county without a single stoplight.

Tulare County

Area: 4,844.9 sq. mi.; Population: (1990) 311,921, (1980) 245,738; Registration: (1992) D-46.8% R-41.4%; Unemployment: (Oct. 1992) 17.9%; County supervisors: Charles Harness, Jim Maples, Bill Maze, Melton Richmond, Bill Sanders; 2800 W. Burrel, Visalia 93291; (209) 733-6271.

Although in the middle of San Joaquin Valley, Tulare County is not just another valley farming community. The county and its principal city, Visalia, have worked for economic diversification with uncommon vigor, and it has paid off with dozens of industrial facilities.

Tulare County's location in the middle of the valley and its nearness to recreation spots in the Sierra has helped economic development. So has an almost entrepreneurial approach to government. But despite the new industry and accompanying services, unemployment still runs at twice the state average, a reflection of the seasonal nature of agriculture, the top industry. In addition, the demand on the county for health and welfare services is far outgrowing the new revenue as the growth also brings more poor people to the area. The county is one of six in the state that spends more than half of its budget on those services.

Politically, Tulare is moderately conservative, voting for Democrats only when they avoid the liberal label.

Tuolumne County

Area: 2,292.7 sq. mi.; Population: (1990) 48,456, (1980) 33,928; Registration: (1990) D-48.6% R-39.9%; Unemployment: (Oct. 1992) 9.9%; County supervisors: Kathleen Campana, Bill Holman, Ken Marks, Larry Rotelli, Norman Tergeson; 2 S. Green St., Sonora 95370; (209) 533-5521.

Tuolumne County was born in the California gold rush and 130 years later finds itself in the midst of a new one. A huge new gold mine, working the spoils of generations of mining operations in the area, opened in 1986 and gave the county a much-needed steady payroll.

But overall, an even bigger rush is being made to develop the areas around some of Tuolumne's scenic wonders. Its population is growing fast – almost 43 percent between 1980 and 1990 – and most of that growth comes from retirees and other people escaping cities. Drawn by the county's mild climate, slow pace and recreational opportunities, the newcomers are fueling the economy with pensions and the investment of equity from the sale of urban homes. The construction of homes and new retail services have become new foundations of the economy.

Growth is taking its toll on county services, too. As crime increased with population, Tuolumne County poured funds into a money-wasting hodgepodge of four courtrooms spread among four buildings. Still awaiting funds are a solid waste problem, an aging county hospital, road improvements and new fire equipment in a county ravaged by major forest fires in recent years.

Politically, Tuolumne County is conservative and likely to become more so as it grows.

Ventura County

Area: 1,863.6 sq. mi.; Population: (1990), 669,016, (1980) 529,174; Registration: (1992) D-41.1% R-43.8%; Unemployment: (Oct. 1992) 9.3%; County supervisors: Maggie Erickson Kildee, John Flynn, Vicky Howard, Susan Lacey, Maria Vanderkolk; 800 S. Victoria Ave., Ventura 93009; (805) 654-2929.

Not too many years ago, Ventura was considered a rural county. Its dominant industries were oil, cattle, citrus and other agriculture. The pace of life was slow. Los Angeles was a long hour's drive away.

But in an astonishingly short time, Ventura County has been overrun by the ever-expanding Southern California megalopolis. As freeway routes were punched through the coastal hills from the San Fernando Valley and into the cities of Oxnard, Santa Paula and Ventura, developers began turning agricultural tracts into subdivisions, shopping centers, office complexes and industrial parks.

One area of the county has been dubbed "Gallium Gulch," a takeoff on Silicon Valley, because it has become a center for developing gallium arsenide into a commercial product. The new technology has drawn some of the largest names in American industry. Meanwhile, as the farm economy continues to stumble along, more and more farmers sell their land to developers.

Ventura County also has begun to exploit its coastal resources, seeking some of the recreational and vacation activity that the rest of Southern California has long enjoyed. The city of Ventura, long accustomed to having tourists pass through en route to Santa Barbara to the north, is now developing marinas, hotels and other facilities of its own. It also is starting to make a big deal out of its historic roots as a mission town (the official name of the city is San Buenaventura, after the local mission).

As Ventura County evolves economically, it is changing socially. The agricultural and blue-collar workers now face soaring home prices. And the county is feeling all the other common growing pains, including heavy traffic, especially on Highway 101, the major route connecting it with Los Angeles.

The change may be especially evident in Oxnard, a one-time farm town with a large Hispanic population. Its proximity to the Pacific and to freeways leading to the San Fernando Valley and Los Angeles is converting Oxnard into a somewhat expensive, white-collar bedroom town. The county has long managed one of the state's most stable budgets, but even Ventura may soon be feeling the money crunch hitting most other counties, according to a 1990 report from the California Counties Foundation.

County politics also are becoming more conservative. It has a Republican voter majority, and Democratic candidates are finding that an ever-steeper hill to climb.

Yolo County

Area: 1,034 sq. mi.; Population: (1990) 141,092, (1980) 113,374; Registration: (1992) D-55.7% R-29.7%; Unemployment: (Oct. 1992) 8.8%; County supervisors: George DeMars, Betsy Marchard, Michael McGowan, Frank Sieferman, Helen Thomson; 625 Court St., Woodland 95695; (916) 666-8195.

Many observers expected Yolo County to be the state's first to declare bankruptcy, and only continual belt-tightening has kept it from fiscal disaster. It has huge health and welfare expenses, a low tax base, and it lost a big chunk of revenue when West Sacramento incorporated. In 1990, even the county hospital had to be closed.

West Sacramento, just across the river from downtown Sacramento, had been ignored by the bigger city's boom and had an image of a low-income, seedy, quasi-red-light district. It is counting on a huge, upscale marina-commercial-residential project along the Sacramento River to upgrade its image and its fortunes.

West Sacramento is one end of the vividly contrasting county. Away to the west and north are rolling hills, farms and a few sparse towns that seem to belong to a different time. In between are two very different cities: Woodland, the conservative county seat that is a farm town on the verge of becoming a suburb and distribution center, and Davis – or the People's Republic of Davis, as its detractors call it.

Davis is the university town, with political activism that extends down to the street-light level and a city council that, at times, is as quirky as Berkeley's. Councilwoman Julie Partansky has argued passionately of late that the crossing guard at the Davis Farmers' Market should be dressed as a vegetable. Davis has been trying to resist developer pressure to become yet another Sacramento bedroom, but even that progressive city is slowly failing.

Yuba County

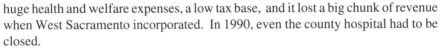

Area: 639.1 sq. mi.; Population: (1990) 58,228, (1980) 49,733; Registration: (1992) D-46.6% R-39.6%; Unemployment: (Oct. 1992) 15.9%; County supervisors: Brent Hastey, Michelle Mathews, John Mistier, Jay Palmquist, Joan Saunders; 215 Fifth St., Marysville, 95901; (916) 741-6461.

Yuba County is next door to Sutter County. The county seats, Yuba's Marysville and Sutter's Yuba City, are just one river apart. But the two counties are developing along different lines.

Much of Sutter lies next to Sacramento County. It is likely to become more and more suburban. But most of Yuba County lies well to the north of Sacramento County and it is likely to remain rural for the foreseeable future.

Marysville may be destined for semisuburban status as the highways connecting it and Yuba City to both Sacramento and the burgeoning high-tech industrial areas in nearby Placer County are widened into freeways.

In addition, the area can count on a steady payroll from Beale Air Force Base, which not only escaped the recent round of base closures but is growing as units shift from other bases, particularly Mather Air Force Base in Sacramento County.

Yuba County has a large enclave of Sikhs, a number of whom have become wealthy farmers. That has made for some interesting educational issues in the county, but the Sikhs tend to maintain a closed society and have not become a political force. Democrats have a registration edge, but residents tend to vote conservatively.

11

Press vs. politicians–never-ending war

An aide to Assembly Speaker Willie Brown once put out a 15-page guide with detailed advice for legislators on how to deal with the news media. On the cover was a cartoon with a farmer, sitting on a tractor, telling a reporter that the two of them are in the same business.

"We are?" the reporter asks.

"This here's a manure spreader," the farmer responds.

That about sums up the mutual feelings of California's politicians and the people who cover them for print and broadcast media around the state. Pretty much, each thinks the other is spreading manure.

It has become an axiom in American politics that a certain tension and wariness exists in the dealings between reporters and politicians. That is certainly the case in California. Gone are the days when the Capitol press corps and the state's political media were part of the inside establishment. Gone are the times when most reporters and politicians ate and drank together, and neither group judged the other too harshly.

What has emerged instead is constant sparring and occasional slugging between politicians and news people, two groups who need each other and, frankly, hate it.

Their relationship, which has been evolving for decades, has rapidly changed in recent years. Nowhere has that been more evident than in campaign coverage. Where reporters were once satisfied to cover the candidate's speeches and the campaign strategies, suddenly there are stories examining the veracity of TV ads, in-depth issue coverage (even if candidates have not brought those issues up) and attention to economic conflicts and voters' anger. In return, some campaigns have manipulated coverage, particularly TV coverage, as never before and have peppered reporters with constant complaints of bias.

490

Which is not to say that politicos and the political media don't agree on some campaign coverage. For instance, they both get caught up in insider-obsessed, horse-race-crazy, what's-the-latest-poll thinking, much to the boredom of the public.

But coverage of the Capitol has evolved beyond campaign stories. Probably the first big wave of change hit with the creation of a full-time, professional Legislature in the mid-1960s. Then, in the wake of the Vietnam War and Watergate, a whole new generation of more serious, more critical reporters came to journalism. Despite occasional chumminess between some reporters and politicians today, the press continues to move toward harder reporting about campaign spending, conflicts of interest and ethical problems, not to mention a continuing FBI investigation that began after prosecutors read newspaper accounts of Capitol influence peddling. All of which adds to the battles between reporters and politicians.

Politicians have an almost single-minded concern about their image, as might be expected of people whose careers depend upon public approval. To project any image, they need the media. But often the publicity they get is not what they wanted, especially when reporters, striving for the journalistic Grail of objectivity, feel compelled to throw in other views and counterarguments.

Many legislators and others in the Capitol have lists of complaints about the media. They say both privately and publicly that stories about FBI investigations, campaign contributions and political shenanigans stain the Legislature with a few broad strokes, obscuring the hard work and good intentions of many lawmakers. Reporters don't buy that argument. If anything, they feel their stories often make legislators look too statesmanlike. They say most stories deal with the substance and progress of bills and budgets, and that too few reports cover the wheeling and dealing that goes into most legislation or the enormous influence that powerful interests exert in the Capitol.

No better example of the different views can be found than in the media's on-going battle with Willie Brown. In early 1991, Brown said in a series of interviews that opponents and the press had created a completely inaccurate image of him. He insisted that voters had not heard that he really is a consummate political negotiator, an achiever of big public policy steps and an "extraordinarily sensitive human being." He said reporters have been too happy to carry stories criticizing him as well as the Legislature. Reporters rolled their eyes at Brown's comments. Most Capitol news people feel they fall far short of revealing all the ways Brown manipulates the legislative process for purely political ends. But despite their distaste, most went back and dutifully reported Brown's complaints, substantive or not, and then tried to find critics to give their stories balance.

INHERENT DIFFERENCES

But the differences between political reporters and the people they cover run much deeper than simply the nature of the stories.

Reporters see it as their job to be, in a sense, the loyal opposition, always asking critical questions, always making elected representatives justify why they should remain in office. When politicians try to tell only part of a story, reporters feel it is their obligation to bring the other side to the public.

Such independence does not sit well with some career politicians. Loyalty is everything to them. Reporters, instead, try to be loyal to their stories. The politicians do not easily accept the idea that reporters or editors can function without grinding personal or political axes. Instead, they assume, as they would of anyone who causes problems, that news people oppose them for ideological or political reasons. Some politicians are left feeling betrayed when they joke with reporters, talk about movies or restaurants or their children's baby teeth, and then find a critical story the next day. Their frustration is deepened by their inability to control news people. Everyone else in the system is willing to negotiate or compromise, except the media. Politicians know they need the press, but it is the one major piece of the political picture outside their grasp.

Reporters, for their part, often feel they are being manipulated too much. If a politician understands the news media's universally accepted rules of engagement — for example, that every side gets to have a say, that the opinions of major figures such as the governor or the Assembly speaker usually are newsworthy, that reporters cannot simply say somebody is lying or distorting information — they can color the reporting of events.

It is just such manipulation that has given rise to "spin doctors." While still less prevalent in Sacramento than in Washington D.C., political consultants, knowing that reporters are always hungry for quotes, have created a new art form of interpreting events — attempting to put "spin" on them — to make their candidates look good.

Efforts to control media coverage have heightened the tension between the media and politicians. During the two-month-long budget stalemate in 1992, news people were constantly complaining that they were being dragged into a multisided public relations campaign, rather than a policy fight. The worst incident was an attempt by Gov. Pete Wilson to address a statewide TV audience. His staff promised stations up and down California that his speech would be non-political, focusing instead on the mechanics of issuing state IOUs. Many stations gave Wilson what he wanted: free, live coverage. Wilson then went out and blasted the Democrats in the Legislature, leaving some TV news directors swearing that they would never again give Wilson live air time for anything but his official State of the State speech or his funeral.

The other major media-control tactic being honed by politicians everywhere is press bashing. The idea is to discredit the message by blaming the messenger. In 1992, it was the Republicans who used this the most, largely because President George Bush was doing dismally in statewide polls. Republican leaders, trying to keep up fund-raising enthusiasm and to prevent other Republican candidates from being swamped by re-energized Democrats, complained bitterly that the media were overplaying the story whenever they reported that polls showed Bush far behind or that the economy was not showing signs of recovery. To an extent the tactic worked. In an attempt to "balance" their stories, reporters included those complaints.

A HARDER EDGE TO COVERAGE

It is hard to assess the impact that complaints of bias have on the public's perception of a story, but it is clear they have done little to cool the media's intense scrutiny of the Legislature and political campaigns. While only the major papers devote large chunks of news space and resources on long, investigative pieces on the Legislature and other Capitol stories, almost every one of the two-dozen papers and news services that cover the Capitol has added a harder edge to its coverage in recent years and given more attention to ethics and political reform.

At the same time, many of the newspapers, including the Orange County Register, the Riverside Press Enterprise and the Los Angeles Daily News, are focusing on issues that affect their circulation areas and leaving broad, statewide topics to the wire services and papers such as the Los Angeles Times and the Sacramento Bee, which offer their own news services. In part, this emphasis on legislators and issues particular to a circulation area comes in response to newspaper marketing surveys that show readers are more concerned with local issues and events and have limited interest in state politics.

The situation is much different in the world of television news, which has all but abandoned state Capitol coverage. During the 1960s and 1970s, most large stations in San Francisco, Los Angeles and San Diego maintained Sacramento bureaus, lured by the glamour of Govs. Ronald Reagan and Jerry Brown and by a desire to emulate the networks in covering hard news. The San Diego stations were the first to pull out, leaving more than a decade ago, and the last Los Angeles station left in 1983. KRON-TV in San Francisco, the last out-of-town holdout, closed its Capitol bureau in 1988.

Television news has not entirely given up on political coverage. The Sacramento stations still cover the Capitol — although less and less — and most major stations spend a good deal of resources covering statewide races and important ballot measures. But a University of Southern California study found stations outside Sacramento averaged barely one minute per news hour of coverage of the Legislature during a period of intense activity during the 1988 session.

Television is shying away from politics for a number of reasons, and money is at the top of the list. At one time television stations made money almost faster than they could count it, and the local news operations were their biggest earners. But now television stations face competition from cable networks, superstations and video recorders, as well as from talk and game shows on competing stations. In response, station managers are listening more and more to their consultants, who produce surveys that say viewers hate politics. In addition, as smaller profits have lessened resources, expensive out-of-town bureaus have become expendable. Thus, with the exception of the major news stories such as budget stalemates, state politics are covered almost exclusively by short mentions of legislative action or reports about a local visit by a politician.

NEW FORMS OF TV COVERAGE

There have been a few developments running counter to that trend. One has been the growth of Northern California News Satellite, which sells Capitol coverage to about two dozen stations. But much of that coverage is often used as brief stories rather than the more in-depth reports that bureaus might have supplied, and the ready pictures with a sound bite can be a too-easy substitute for real reporting.

The other change was the start of live broadcasts of legislative proceedings and the development the California Channel, the cable service channel modeled after C-SPAN, which covers Congress.

Speaker Brown was the force behind the $2 million-plus effort to begin televising the Legislature. First the Assembly and then the Senate bought robotic cameras, a full control room and the rest of the equipment needed to cover floor sessions and selected committees and to produce interviews with members to be sent to hometown stations.

The Legislature gives its live picture to the California Channel, which packages it and sells a daytime broadcast to California cable systems. The California Channel plans eventually to carry news conferences and programs with commentary and analysis of state politics. In addition, commercial stations who patch into the legislative feeds or buy the California Channel can use the broadcasts on their news shows. The consensus among those involved with the live TV so far has been that the California Channel's impact on the Legislature as been about the same as was C-SPAN's effect on Congress: Lawmakers dress up a little more, try to slim down and occasionally remember they are on camera.

Opening the Assembly for live television caused another fight between Brown and the press corps. Saying he was trying to improve decorum in his house, the speaker banished reporters from the edges of the Assembly floor, where they had roamed for years, chatting with members and filling in their stories without formal press conferences. Reporters were given desks off the floor in the back of the chamber with the staff. The Capitol press corps was livid, as were a number of Assembly members who liked having reporters nearby — the easier to get their names in the news.

Brown's corralling of reporters and the interest in televising the Legislature were signs that California politicians have become media savvy, or at least media conscious. This is most visible in those campaigns where candidates and consultants have mastered the "bite of the day" technique of presenting splashy, often vague statements designed to boost their images rather than explain campaign issues.

Campaign consultants also have become more adept at whispering in reporters' ears, attempting to plant story ideas that help their candidate or hurt their opponent, or to put spin on everything involved in the campaign, from polling to money-raising to issues.

At the same time, reporters are trying to do more than carry campaign statements to their readers and viewers. Most major papers are trying to examine candidates more carefully, over a longer period and on more issues than ever before. They are looking not only at voting records but consistency, ethics, financial holdings, spouses' activities and, occasionally, their private lives.

That, too, has contributed to the increased wariness, even on the often long campaign trail. Where once reporters and candidates would relax after a campaign swing with dinner or drinks, both groups now keep their distance. And where once consultants would answer questions about their polling or money-raising honestly, now every utterance has the best face painted on it. So, candidates are careful with what they say, and reporters believe only half of what they hear.

Still, media coverage is crucial to the success of political campaigns, especially statewide contests. There are thousands of miles to cover and dramatically varied constituencies to persuade. In fact, just about the only effective way to reach the state's 15 million registered voters is through television. Candidates and initiative sponsors are eager to get on the local news, especially in Southern California, and local news stations are eager to cover big-name candidates and major ballot campaigns. Television news, despite all but abandoning the dull and gray day-to-day political coverage in the off season, is still interested in the horse race and name-calling of lively campaigns.

Politicians and political consultants are thrilled by this turn. Local TV news reaches many more people than do newspaper stories, and because it is the magic of television, it has more impact. In addition, campaigns can occasionally get messages out without a balancing point of view by playing to TV's fascination with live technology. A live interview or live coverage of an event can give viewers a much less filtered theme or message than even a 15-second sound bite.

Outside of campaigns, consultants and politicians are working harder than ever to attract and control press coverage. While they want their names in the news, they ask a lot more from their publicity than just spelling their name correctly. One device to gain favorable coverage is the age-old media stunt. Recent examples include an ambulance delivering petitions to the Capitol from people supporting money for emergency rooms, and a group of about 1,000 hospital administrators lined up like a marching band spelling out H-E-L-P to ask for aid to hospital budgets. Another of the more common moves is the press conference to announce the introduction of a bill. That gives one or more legislators a chance to be identified with a newsworthy issue. Sometimes a serious effort to move the bill follows, but just as often the bills are abandoned, having served their purpose by letting the lawmakers take a tough stand without angering any of the interests opposed to the measure.

Another ploy is the ever-popular "spontaneous" statement during a legislative debate. It sounds like an heartfelt line coming from that lawmaker's deep well of conviction. As often as not, these are suggested by aides, practiced beforehand and timed to fit a TV sound bite.

PROFESSIONAL MEDIA MANAGERS

The increased sophistication in the interplay with the media has moved politicians to seek professional help in hunting for press coverage. Even legislators who are rarely quoted in hometown media are employing aides whose sole responsibility is to deal with the press or sometimes to chase down reporters to get their boss's name in the paper. But on-staff press aides are only so effective. In greater and greater number, even unspectacular legislators who are not running for higher office — at least for now — are hiring the services of a growing number of political public relations firms. These firms also are being used by special interests pushing or resisting particular bills in the Capitol. In fact, it is not uncommon to have every side represented by PR people.

One big job for these firms is to put their clients, either politicians or special interests with a stake in legislation, in touch with the media. The major firms that engage in political PR around Sacramento — among them the PBN Company; Stoorza, Ziegaus and Metzger; and Townsend, Hermocillo, Raimundo and Usher — all employ people who either were members of the Capitol press corps at one time or who dealt with the press at length in legislative offices. They know what reporters are interested in and how to get their client's views into a story. And they realize that competition for reporters' time and interest is intense, so they can help their clients by making it easier and faster for reporters to get information.

Many PR people also try to call attention to their clients by putting them in touch with newspeople through casual breakfasts or lunches or even backyard barbecues. No immediate stories are expected, but it makes the reporters and politicians feel more comfortable with each other and, as often as not, the politicians may find their names appearing in stories a little more readily. In effect, this new breed of political PR consultant is a lobbyist of the media, working in conjunction with those who lobby officeholders.

The attention being focused on California's political press is beginning to be matched by the media's own introspection. Some newspapers have taken long, and critical, looks at campaign and political coverage, and almost all have wondered in print and in private whether political reporting could be improved. In addition, the press corps had an internal debate over the role of journalists in fighting for access to information when a few legislators introduced bills to reduce access to public records. Although all the proposals died, they created some bitter divisions between people who believe reporters should actively lobby lawmakers to keep information public and those who argue that journalists have a responsibility to their readers and viewers, and that by lobbying for anything, journalists compromise themselves. Capitol reporters also have wrestled with mixed success over the ethics of outside income — such as speeches to trade associations and free-lance writing for professional or industry publications — or possible conflicts of interest created by the jobs held by spouses.

Newspapers and news services

ASSOCIATED PRESS

Sacramento bureau: 925 L St., Suite 320, Sacramento 95814; (916) 448-9555, FAX (916) 446-2756.

David Morris, correspondent; Doug Willis, news editor and political writer; reporters: Steve Geissinger, Kathleen Grubb, Jennifer Kerr, John Howard, Steve Lawrence; photographers Slava J. "Sal" Veder and Rich Pedroncelll.

The Associated Press is a news cooperative with approximately 100 member newspapers and 400 broadcasters in California who receive AP reports. The Sacramento office is an all-purpose news bureau covering breaking stories from Fairfield east to the Nevada border and from Stockton north to the Oregon border. Roughly two-thirds of the bureau's time is spent reporting on California politics and state government.

Morris moved to Sacramento as the bureau chief in December 1991. For the previous six years, he was a political writer in the Harrisburg, Pa. bureau of the AP. Before that, he worked for three Pennsylvania dailies.

Willis has been in AP's Sacramento bureau since 1969 and directed the bureau from 1974 to 1991.

The AP staff is a veteran one: Geissinger moved to the bureau in 1984 from the Salinas Californian; Grubb joined AP in 1987 from the Vacaville Reporter; Howard joined the bureau in 1980 from AP's San Francisco office; Kerr joined AP in 1973 and has been in Sacramento since 1978; Lawrence came to Sacramento in 1973 from AP's Los Angeles office; Veder has been with AP since 1961 and is in his second stint in Sacramento. He won the Pulitzer Prize in 1974 for his photograph of a Vietnam POW's reunion with his family. Pedroncelli, a former Sacramento Union photographer and longtime AP stringer, joined the staff in 1990.

BAKERSFIELD CALIFORNIAN

Capitol bureau: 925 L St., Suite 1190, Sacramento 95814; (916) 324-4585.
The position was vacant in early 1993.

CAPITOL NEWS SERVICE

1713 J St., Suite 202, Sacramento 95814; (916) 445-6336, FAX (916) 443-5871.
David Kline, editor; Randall Thompson, reporter.
A small, independent news service serving small dailies and weeklies. The news

service was founded in 1939 and was taken over by Fred Kline, a veteran newsman, in 1971. David Kline, no relation to Fred, took over the service in 1992.

CHICO ENTERPRISE-RECORD
Capitol bureau: 530 P St., No. 31, Sacramento 95814; (916) 444-6747.

Mike Gardner, reporter. The opening of this bureau in 1990 was prompted by the paper's need to report on attempts to obtain state aid for fiscally strapped Butte County. Gardner, who has been with the paper since 1986, concentrates on stories of interest to Chico-area readers.

CONTRA COSTA TIMES/LESHER NEWSPAPERS
Capitol bureau: 925 L St., Suite 348, Sacramento 95814; (916) 441-2101, FAX (916) 441-6001.

Virgil Meibert, bureau chief. The bureau covers local legislators, the effect of state government decisions on local communities and regional issues for six Lesher newspapers in the San Francisco Bay Area: the Contra Costa Times, Antioch Daily Ledger, Pittsburg Post-Dispatch, San Ramon Valley Times, Valley Times in Pleasanton and West County Times covering the Richmond-Pinole area. Prior to becoming Lesher's Sacramento bureau chief in 1988, Meibert spent 24 years with the Oakland Tribune, the last 14 years as its Sacramento bureau chief.

COPLEY NEWS SERVICE
Capitol bureau: 925 L St., Suite 1190, Sacramento 95814; (916) 445-2934, FAX (916) 443-1912.

Robert P. Studer, bureau chief; James P. Sweeney, political writer. The bureau covers stories of particular interest to a group of Copley newspapers in the Los Angeles area: the Torrance Daily Breeze, the San Pedro News and the Santa Monica Evening Outlook. It occasionally helps another Copley newspaper, the recently merged San Diego Union Tribune, which also has a Sacramento bureau. In addition, the Copley bureau serves roughly 100 California clients, including daily and weekly newspapers and broadcasters who subscribe to the Copley News Service.

Studer, who also writes analyses on statewide issues, has been with the Copley chain for more than 50 years and has been Sacramento bureau chief since 1974. Sweeney joined the bureau in 1985 from the Torrance Daily Breeze, where he had been an assistant city editor.

DAILY RECORDER
1115 H St., Sacramento 95814; (916) 444-2355, FAX (916) 444-3358.
Steve Towns, editor.

This Sacramento-based legal-profession newspaper is one of several owned by the Daily Journal Corp. of Los Angeles. It concentrates on news of interest to the legal community, lobbyists and Capitol staffers.

GANNETT NEWS SERVICE

Capitol bureau: 925 L St., Suite 110, Sacramento 95814; (916) 446-1036, FAX (916) 446-7326.

Jake Henshaw, bureau chief; Ray Sotero, reporter.

The bureau covers stories of local and statewide interest to the chain's California newspapers: the Marin Independent Journal, the Palm Springs Desert Sun, the Salinas Californian, the San Bernardino Sun, the Stockton Record and the Visalia Times-Delta. The bureau also occasionally covers stories for the Reno Gazette Journal and USA Today.

Henshaw came to Sacramento in 1987 from the GNS Washington bureau, where he had worked since 1978. He became bureau chief in Sacramento in 1990. Sotero moved to GNS in 1990 from The Sacramento Bee's Capitol Bureau, where he had covered issues for the Fresno Bee and Modesto Bee since 1988. He was one of the original co-authors of the California Political Almanac.

LOS ANGELES DAILY JOURNAL

Capitol bureau: 925 L St., Suite 325, Sacramento 95814; (916) 445-8063, FAX (916) 444-3358.

Thomas L. Dresslar, bureau chief; Hallye Jordan, reporter.

The bureau covers news of interest to the legal community ranging from the death penalty to probate law. In addition to the Daily Journal, the bureau's work appears in the San Francisco Banner Journal and other Daily Journal Corp. publications.

Dresslar came to the bureau from the Daily Recorder in Sacramento in 1987. Jordan joined the bureau in 1987 from the Orange County Register.

LOS ANGELES DAILY NEWS

Capitol bureau: 925 L St., Suite 335, Sacramento 95814; (916) 446-6723, FAX (916) 448-7381.

Sandy Harrison, bureau chief.

Los Angeles office: Rick Orlov, political writer, (213) 485-3720.

The bureau's primary focus is on state government, political news of interest to its San Fernando Valley readers and major statewide stories.

Harrison joined the bureau in 1989 and had covered local government for the Daily News.

Orlov covers City Hall and state and local politics from the Los Angeles office. He has been with the paper since 1977 and previously worked for Copley News Service.

LOS ANGELES TIMES

Capitol bureau: 1125 L St., Suite 200, Sacramento 95814; (916) 445-8860, FAX (916) 322-2422.

Armando Acuna, bureau chief; George Skelton, columnist; staff writers: Eric Bailey (Orange County edition), Virginia Ellis, Ralph Frammolino (San Fernando Valley edition), Jerry Gillam, Mark Gladstone (suburban editions), John Hurst, Carl Ingram, Paul Jacobs, Max Vanzi (news editor), Daniel Weintraub, Don Woutat (business).

Los Angeles office: Cathleen Decker, (213) 237-4652, and Bill Stall, (213) 237-4550, political writers.

The Los Angeles Times Sacramento bureau primarily takes a statewide approach to its coverage of Capitol issues. It does in-depth political analyses, personality profiles and investigative stories involving the state bureaucracy as well as daily coverage of the Legislature, the governor and other state agencies. The Times also provides stories of local and regional interest to its primary audience of Los Angeles area readers. Three reporters within the bureau focus on news of local interest to Times editions in Orange County, the San Fernando Valley and Los Angeles area zones. Times stories also appear in newspapers that subscribe to the Times-Mirror wire service.

Acuna became bureau chief in January 1993. He joined the Times in 1985 and last served as city editor of the now defunct San Diego edition. Before moving to the Times, he worked for 12 years for the San Jose Mercury News, the last year of which was spent in Sacramento as a Capitol correspondent.

Skelton, a former Capitol correspondent for UPI who moved to the Times in 1974, was bureau chief prior to shifting to his columnist role in 1992. He has also worked as Times politics editor in Los Angeles and as White House correspondent.

The Times bureau includes Bailey, who joined the office in December 1992 and has been with the Times since 1983; Ellis, who came to Sacramento in 1988 from the Dallas Times Herald, where she was chief of its Capitol bureau in Austin; Frammolino, who moved to Sacramento in 1989 from the Times' San Diego edition; Gillam, a longtime officer in the Capitol Correspondents Association and a member of the bureau since 1961; Gladstone, who joined the bureau in 1984 and has been with the Times since 1981; Hurst, who has been with the Times since 1976 and who was a former state reporter for the paper; Jacobs, who has been with the Times since 1978 and who moved to Sacramento in 1983; Ingram, a former UPI Capitol correspondent who joined the Times in 1978; Vanzi, who moved to the bureau in 1990 from the Times main office, where he had worked since 1984 as an assistant city editor; Weintraub, who arrived in 1987 after four years in other Times assignments; and Woutat, a Times employee since 1981 who joined the Sacramento staff in early 1993 to cover business issues.

Decker and Stall are based in Los Angeles and cover statewide and national political stories. Decker joined the Times in 1978 after having worked as a Times intern. She had been primarily covering local and national politics since 1985 before being designated a political writer in 1990. Stall, a veteran Times writer, was an editorial writer for the Times when he returned to political writing in 1990.

OAKLAND TRIBUNE

Capitol bureau: 925 L St., Suite 385, Sacramento 95814; (916) 447-9302, FAX (916) 447-9308.

Sam Delson, bureau chief. The bureau focuses on issues of interest to the East Bay. Delson moved to the Tribune's Capitol bureau in January 1993 shortly after the paper was purchased by the Alameda Newspaper Group. He has worked for the group for eight years, first as a political writer and then as city editor at the Alameda Times-Star. The ANG also owns the Argus in Fremont, Daily Review in Hayward and the Tri-Valley Herald in Pleasanton.

ORANGE COUNTY REGISTER

Capitol bureau: 925 L St., Suite 305, Sacramento 95814; (916) 445-9841, FAX (916) 441-6496.

Marc S. Lifsher, correspondent.

Santa Ana office: Dennis Foley, political editor, (714) 953-4915.

The bureau's main mission is to cover political and government stories of statewide and local interest for the rapidly growing Orange County daily. Lifsher joined the bureau in 1983 from the Dallas Times Herald.

RIVERSIDE PRESS-ENTERPRISE

Capitol bureau: 925 L St., Suite 312, Sacramento 95814; (916) 445-9973, FAX (916) 442-7842.

Dan Smith, bureau chief.

Riverside: Joan Radovich, political writer, (909) 782-7567.

The bureau's main charge is to cover Riverside County legislators and issues of local interest as well as major breaking political and government stories.

Smith became the Press-Enterprise's Capitol correspondent in 1988. He has worked for the paper since 1984 and had previously covered local politics and government.

Radovich, the paper's former City Hall reporter, became its political writer in 1989.

SACRAMENTO BEE / McCLATCHY NEWSPAPERS

Capitol bureau: 925 L St., Suite 1404, Sacramento 95814; (916) 321-1199, FAX 444-7838.

William Endicott, bureau chief; Amy Chance, deputy bureau chief; Dan Walters, columnist; staff writers: Stephen Green, Rick Kushman, Jon Matthews, Katherine Zimmerman McKenna, Pamela Podger (Fresno Bee coverage), James Richardson, Herbert A. Sample, Kathie Smith (Modesto Bee coverage).

McClatchy Newspapers: John Jacobs, political editor, P.O. Box 15779, Sacramento 95852; (916) 321-1914.

Fresno Bee: Jim Boren, political writer, (209) 441-6307.

The Sacramento Bee's Capitol bureau primarily takes a statewide view in its coverage of issues and politics. It regularly offers political analyses, features and daily coverage of state government and political issues. In addition, bureau members work on in-depth special projects ranging from investigative reports on the Legislature and state government to examination of emerging political trends. In election years, bureau reporters cover both state and national campaigns. The impact of The Bee's political, legislative and state government coverage has increased in recent years with the growth of the McClatchy News Service. About 60 California newspapers subscribe to MNS, with many using stories covered by The Bee's Capitol bureau.

Bureau Chief Endicott took over The Bee's Capitol bureau in 1985, coming to the paper from the Los Angeles Times, where he had worked for 17 years in various positions, including San Francisco bureau chief, political writer and the last two years as the Times' Capitol bureau chief.

Chance became deputy bureau chief in 1991. She has been in the Capitol Bureau since 1986, primarily covering the governor and writing about statewide political campaigns and issues. She joined The Bee in 1984, coming to Sacramento from the Fort Worth Star Telegram to cover Sacramento City Hall.

Walters' column appears six days a week in The Bee and is distributed statewide by McClatchy News Service. He joined the paper as a political columnist in 1984 after 11 years with the Sacramento Union, the last nine in its Capitol bureau.

John Jacobs became the political editor of McClatchy Newspapers in February 1993 following the retirement of Martin Smith, who had filled the role since 1977. Jacobs had been the San Francisco Examiner's chief political writer since 1987, and he had joined that paper in 1978. As McClatchy's political editor, Jacobs writes a political column three times a week and is a member of The Sacramento Bee's editorial board.

The Bee's Capitol staff includes: Green, who moved to The Bee in 1978 from the Seattle Post-Intelligencer and to the Capitol bureau in 1985; Kushman, a former Sacramento Union reporter and television assignment editor who joined the bureau in 1987; Matthews, who joined the bureau in 1986 from the Anchorage Daily News; McKenna, a former Capitol correspondent for the Oakland Tribune who joined The Bee in 1993; Podger, who moved to Sacramento to cover the Capitol for the Fresno Bee in 1992 after spending a year in the Fresno newsroom; Richardson, who became the Riverside Press Enterprise Capitol bureau chief in 1985 and moved to The Bee in 1988 (He will be on leave for most of 1993 on an Alicia Patterson Foundation fellowship to write a book about Assembly Speaker Willie Brown); Sample, a former Los Angeles Times reporter who joined the bureau in 1986, left to join the Dallas Times Herald as its Capitol bureau chief in Austin in 1991 and returned to The Bee when the paper folded the following year; and Smith, who had worked at The Modesto Bee since 1978 before joining the Capitol bureau as the Modesto correspondent in 1991.

Boren covers politics for the Fresno Bee. He joined the paper in 1972 and has been the political writer since 1980.

SACRAMENTO UNION
301 Capitol Mall, Sacramento 95812; (916) 440-0547, FAX (916) 440-0524.
J.P. Tremblay, reporter.

The Union no longer has a separate Capitol bureau but instead covers Capitol and political news primarily of local interest to Sacramento area readers out of its main office. The Union generally relies on wire stories for its major breaking news reports on state government and political issues.

Tremblay has covered politics and the Capitol for the Union since 1990. He previously worked in the Union's editorial department, where he had been a copy editor, since 1989.

SAN DIEGO UNION TRIBUNE
Sacramento bureau: 925 L St., Suite 1190, Sacramento 95814; (916) 448-2066, FAX (916) 444-6375.

Ed Mendel, bureau chief; Dana Wilkie, staff writer.

San Diego office: Gerald Braun, (619) 293-1230; John Marelius, (619) 293-1231, reporters.

This Copley newspaper's Sacramento bureau splits its time covering stories of local interest, including the San Diego area's 11-member legislative delegation, and statewide political and government stories. The two writers also regularly contribute stories that are distributed by the Copley News Service.

Mendel, a former Sacramento Union reporter, worked as editor of the now-defunct Golden State Report prior to joining the San Diego paper in 1990. He became bureau chief in 1991. Wilkie has been with the paper since 1987 and in the Capitol bureau since September 1991.

Braun and Marelius cover statewide political issues and are based in the main office in San Diego.

SAN FRANCISCO CHRONICLE
Sacramento bureau: 1121 L St., Suite 408, Sacramento 95814; (916) 445-5658, FAX (916) 447-7082.

Vlae Kershner, bureau chief; Rob Gunnison, Greg Lucas, Ann Bancroft, staff writers.

San Francisco office: Jerry Roberts, political editor, (415) 777-7124; Susan Yoachum, political writer, (415) 777-7123.

The Sacramento bureau's primary emphasis is on statewide government and political news. Chronicle Capitol bureau stories also move over the New York Times wire and are picked up by other subscribing California newspapers.

Kershner, who joined the bureau in 1989, was economics editor for the Chronicle prior to becoming bureau chief in 1990. Gunnison moved to the Chronicle in 1985 from United Press International's Sacramento bureau, where he had worked for 11 years. Lucas joined the bureau in 1988 from the Los Angeles Daily Journal's Sacramento staff. Bancroft is in her second stint in the Chronicle's Capitol bureau.

Roberts, a longtime Chronicle staffer, has been the paper's political editor since 1987. He and Yoachum, a former San Jose Mercury-News reporter who joined the Chronicle in 1990, do much of the local, state and national political reporting from the home office in San Francisco.

SAN FRANCISCO EXAMINER

Sacramento bureau: 925 L St., Suite 320A, Sacramento 95814; (916) 445-4310, FAX (916) 448-7820.

Steven A. Capps, bureau chief; Tupper Hull, reporter.

This Hearst paper's Sacramento bureau covers major statewide stories and stories of interest to San Francisco Bay Area readers.

Capps joined the bureau in 1980 after spending three years with United Press International in San Francisco and Los Angeles. Hull joined the bureau in late 1989 after serving as the Los Angeles Herald Examiner's Sacramento bureau chief since 1985.

SAN FRANCISCO RECORDER

Sacramento bureau: 1127 11th St., Suite 605, Sacramento 95814; (916) 448-2935.

Bill Ainsworth, reporter.

This paper covers state government, politics and lobbying from a legal perspective. Ainsworth, a former Sacramento Union reporter, opened the bureau in 1990.

SAN JOSE MERCURY-NEWS

Sacramento bureau: 925 L St., Suite 345, Sacramento 95814; (916) 441-4601, FAX (916) 441-4657.

Gary Webb, Tom Farragher and Mitchel Benson, staff writers.

San Jose office: Phil Trounstine, political editor, (408) 920-5657.

The Sacramento bureau relies on wire services to cover the bulk of daily Capitol stories and concentrates more on off-agenda and investigative stories of statewide and local interest. Stories also move over the Knight-Ridder wire and are picked up by other newspapers.

Webb came to Sacramento in 1989 from the Cleveland Plain Dealer, where he had been an investigative reporter in the statehouse bureau in Columbus. Farragher, who has been with the Mercury News since 1987, was the City Hall reporter in San Jose when he moved to Sacramento in late 1990. Benson, who has been with the paper for five years and formerly covered environmental issues, joined the bureau in 1991.

Trounstine is responsible for national, statewide and local political coverage from the home office. He joined the paper in 1978 from the Indianapolis Star and has been political editor since 1986.

UNITED PRESS INTERNATIONAL
Sacramento bureau: 1127 11th St., Suite 830, Sacramento 95814; (916) 445-7755.

Clark McKinley, news editor, Ted Appel, reporter.

UPI's bureau is responsible for covering breaking news in the northeastern quadrant of California, although the bureau's emphasis is on government news.

McKinley has been with UPI for 20 years and in Sacramento since 1978. Appel transferred to Sacramento from UPI's Los Angeles bureau in 1989.

Magazines

CALIFORNIA JOURNAL
1714 Capitol Ave., Sacramento 95814; (916) 444-2840, FAX (916) 444-2339.

Tom Hoeber, publisher; Richard Zeiger, editor; A.G. Block, managing editor.

The California Journal, founded by a group of Capitol staffers as a non-profit institution, celebrated its 20th anniversary in 1989. The monthly magazine, which relies primarily on free-lance writers, takes an analytical view of California politics and government. It has a circulation of about 19,000. The California Journal also publishes various books about California government and politics. It became a for-profit organization in 1986 with Tom Hoeber, one of the founders, as publisher.

Zeiger took over as the magazine's editor in 1984. Prior to that, he had been with the Riverside Press-Enterprise for 16 years, the last seven as its Sacramento bureau chief. Block was a free-lance writer when he joined the magazine in 1983.

Newsletters

CALIFORNIA EYE / THE POLITICAL ANIMAL
1052 W. Sixth St., Suite 600, Los Angeles, 90017; (213) 481-3809, FAX (213) 482-0717.

Bill Homer, editor; Joe Scott, editor emeritus.

In January 1993, Homer, a former syndicated columnist, took over these two biweekly political newsletters started by Scott. The California Eye, begun in 1980, is aimed at analyzing and forecasting trends in state politics, while The Political Animal, started in 1973, takes a nationwide approach with some California news included.

CALIFORNIA POLITICAL WEEK
P.O. Box 1468, Beverly Hills 90213; (310) 659-0205.

Dick Rosengarten, editor and publisher.

This newsletter takes a look at trends in politics and local government throughout the state. It was established in 1979. Rosengarten is a former print and broadcast journalist who has also worked in public relations and as a campaign manager.

EDUCATION BEAT

926 J St., Room 1218, Sacramento 95814; (916) 446-3956, FAX (916) 446-3956.

Larry Lynch, editor and co-publisher; Bud Lembke, co-publisher.

Lynch, the former Capitol bureau chief for the Long Beach Press-Telegram, became editor in November 1991 of this newsletter, which looks at educational trends. He also is a partner with Bud Lembke in the Political Pulse.

POLITICAL PULSE

926 J St., Room 1218, Sacramento 95814; (916) 446-2048; FAX (916) 446-5302.

Bud Lembke, editor and co-publisher; Larry Lynch, co-publisher.

This newsletter, which looks at political news, trends and personalities, was started in 1985 by Lembke.

Lembke was a Los Angeles Times reporter for 21 years and a former press secretary to Senate President Pro Tem David Roberti. Lynch, Sacramento correspondent for the Long Beach Press-Telegram until the bureau was closed, became a co-owner of the newsletter in September 1992.

NEW WEST NOTES

P.O. Box 221364, Sacramento 95822; (916) 395-0709.

Bill Bradley, editor and publisher.

Formerly called the Larkspur Report, this monthly newsletter aims to give a California perspective to political and economic affairs through Bradley's analysis. Bradley was a senior consultant to former U.S. Sen. Gary Hart in his presidential bids. He also writes columns for the Sacramento News and Review and California Business Magazine.

Radio

CALIFORNIA ELECTION REPORT / AP RADIO

926 J St., Suite 1014, Sacramento 95814; (916) 446-2234.

Steve Scott, correspondent.

Scott has covered the Capitol for various radio stations since 1986.

KCBS-San Francisco

Capitol bureau: 2404 Hurley Way, 4, Sacramento 95825; (916) 445-7372, FAX (916) 443-5159.

Jim Hamblin, correspondent.

Hamblin covers the Legislature and government stories as well as other breaking news for this San Francisco-based news radio station. Hamblin has covered state government and politics for 20 years and has been based in Sacramento since 1987.

KXPR/FM

3416 American River Drive, Suite B, Sacramento 95864; (916) 485-5977, FAX (916) 487-3348.

Mike Montgomery, reporter.

This member station of the National Public Radio network is one of the few that regularly covers the state Capitol and government. Montgomery has been covering political and Capitol stories since December 1983.

Television

Los Angeles

KABC-TV

4151 Prospect Ave., Los Angeles 90027; (213) 668-2880.

Mark Coogan, John North, Linda Breakstone, correspondents.

Coogan, Breakstone and North cover major local and state political stories and collaborate on events such as conventions or elections.

Coogan, who started at KABC in 1976, spent 1979 and 1980 as the southern Africa bureau chief for ABC News, then came back to KABC as a political reporter in 1980. North, who started covering California politics in 1979 for KABC, also spent some time at the network until he came back to KABC in 1982. Breakstone, a former political writer for the old Los Angeles Herald Examiner, joined the station in 1990.

Sacramento

KCRA-TV

3 Television Circle, Sacramento 95814; (916) 444-7316, FAX (916) 441-4050.

For many years, this local station had a top-notch political reporter in Steve Swatt, who left to join a political consulting firm in 1992. No one has been named to take over the Capitol beat.

KOVR-TV

2713 KOVR Drive, West Sacramento 95605; (916) 374-1313, FAX (916) 374-1304.

Jack Kavanagh, reporter.

This ABC-affiliate covers the Capitol as news stories occur. Kavanagh, a veteran KOVR reporter, took over the Capitol beat in 1990.

KTXL-TV

4655 Fruitridge Rd., Sacramento 95820; (916) 454-4548, FAX (916) 739-0559.
Lonnie Wong, Debra Steele reporters.

Wong has been covering the Capitol and state government for radio and television since 1973. He has been with KTXL, an independent station that covers politics on a spot-news basis, since 1980. Steele also covers some political stories for the station. She moved to Sacramento in January 1993 from KSBW in Salinas.

KXTV

400 Broadway, Sacramento 95818; (916) 321-3300, FAX (916) 447-6107.
Deborah Pacyna, Capitol correspondent; Tom Marshall, "The Insider."

Pacyna has covered state politics and government for this CBS-affiliate since 1984 and also covers national politics during election years. She came to the station from WPXI-TV in Pittsburgh, Pa. Marshall, a veteran of more than 10 years with the station, does a special report called "The Insider," investigating tips on questionable activity in state government.

NORTHERN CALIFORNIA NEWS SATELLITE

1121 L St., Suite 109, Sacramento 95814; (916) 446-7890, FAX (916)446-7893.
Steve Mallory, president; Bill Branch, news editor/reporter.

NCNS is a video wire service that covers the Capitol, state government and other major breaking news for subscribing television stations stretching from San Diego to Medford, Ore. It offers voice-overs, live interviews, election coverage as well as daily reports, all transmitted by satellite. In addition, its facilities are often used by out-of-town stations that travel to Sacramento to cover news. NCNS made its first news transmission in July 1987 and has filled a void created by the closure of all out-of-town television news bureaus.

This is Mallory's second stint in Sacramento. He served as KNBC's Sacramento bureau chief for three years before moving to Beirut as an NBC correspondent in 1978. Subsequent assignments for NBC took him to London, Moscow and Tokyo before he returned to set up his company. Branch has been with the service since mid-1991 after working with the local-ABC affiliate for 20 years.

San Francisco

KGO-TV

900 Front St.; San Francisco 94111; (415) 954-7936.
Lisa Stark, correspondent.

This ABC-affiliate formerly had a bureau in Sacramento but has been covering the Capitol and other statewide stories out of the main office. Stark is a general assignment reporter who does the bulk of the station's political reporting. She came to the station in 1984 from Portland, Ore., where she also did political reporting.

KRON-TV

1001 Van Ness Ave., San Francisco 94109; (415) 441-4444.

Rollin Post, political correspondent.

Post covers state and local politics and offers political analysis for this NBC-affiliate. Post has been with the station since 1989 and has covered politics for San Francisco area stations since 1965. KRON had the distinction for several years of being the only station outside Sacramento to maintain a full-time Capitol bureau, but it closed its Sacramento operation in 1988.

Index

510

California Political Almanac staff

Amy Chance is deputy bureau chief of The Sacramento Bee's state Capitol bureau. She joined The Bee in 1984 as a city government reporter and moved to the Capitol bureau two years later. Formerly a reporter for the Fort Worth Star-Telegram, Chance now covers California's governor and other state politicians. Born in Wilmington, Del., she is a graduate of San Diego State University. She began her career as an intern at the Los Angeles Times in San Diego County.

Stephen Green has worked for The Sacramento Bee since 1978 as both a writer and editor. Since 1985, he's covered state government and politics from the Capitol bureau. Previously, he worked for the Portland (Ore.) Journal, the Seattle Post-Intelligencer, the Associated Press in Philadelphia and the National Observer in Washington, D.C. The Spokane native holds bachelor's and master's degrees in journalism from the University of Oregon and was a Fellow at the Washington Journalism Center in Washington, D.C.

John L. Hughes worked for three years as The Sacramento Bee's Capitol bureau news editor before taking his current position as the paper's letters editor. Born in Champaign, Ill., and raised in Los Angeles, he served in the Navy during the Vietnam War. He attended Los Angeles Valley College and the University of Southern California. He worked for newspapers in Burbank and Lodi, Calif., before coming to The Bee in 1980.

James Richardson, a native of Berkeley, was graduated from UCLA and has studied government at Cambridge University, England. He has been covering the state Capitol since 1985, first as correspondent for the Riverside Press-Enterprise and then with The Sacramento Bee. Previously, he was a local political reporter for The San Diego Union. Richardson is on leave from The Bee as an Alicia Patterson Fellow and is working on a biography of Willie Brown.

Lori Korleski Richardson is a graphics editor at The Sacramento Bee. Prior to joining the paper in 1987, the University of Houston graduate and Houston native worked as an assistant news editor at The Orange County (Calif.) Register. She also has worked at the Dallas Morning News, the St. Petersburg (Fla.) Times, The Beaumont (Texas) Enterprise, and The Dallas Times Herald.

Rick Rodriguez is an assistant managing editor at The Sacramento Bee and also writes a weekly column. For four years, he was deputy chief of The Bee's Capitol bureau after serving a stint as an editorial writer. He joined the Capitol bureau as a reporter in 1982. He has worked for The Fresno Bee and his hometown paper, the Salinas Californian. He is a graduate of Stanford University.

Kathie Smith joined The Sacramento Bee Capitol bureau as The Modesto Bee correspondent in 1991, after 13 years in Modesto as an editor and reporter. Previously, she worked as a reporter, city editor and managing editor of her hometown newspaper, the LaPorte (Ind.) Herald-Argus. She attended Purdue University and Modesto Junior College and was a member of the 1985-86 class of the Journalists in Residence fellowship program at the University of Michigan at Ann Arbor.

Dan Walters has been a journalist for 32 years, half of which have been spent covering the Capitol, first for the Sacramento Union and since 1984 for the Sacramento Bee. He writes the only daily newspaper column about California politics, which appears in some 50 papers, and is the author of The New California: Facing the 21st Century, now in its second printing.